Educational Psychology

Constructing Learning

SECOND EDITION

To each other, as authors, colleagues
and, most importantly, friends.

Educational Psychology

Constructing Learning

SECOND EDITION

Dennis M. McInerney
Valentina McInerney

Prentice Hall

SYDNEY ▪ NEW YORK ▪ TORONTO ▪ MEXICO ▪ NEW DELHI
LONDON ▪ TOKYO ▪ SINGAPORE ▪ RIO DE JANEIRO

Acquisitions Editor: Mark Burgess
Production Editor: Elizabeth Thomas
Copy editor: Jo Rudd
Cover and text design: Ramsay Macfarlane
Typeset by The Type Group, Wollongong, NSW

Printed in Singapore by Kyodo Printing Co. Ltd.

3 4 5 02 01 00 99

ISBN 0 7248 0399 8

National Library of Australia
Cataloguing-in-Publication Data

McInerney, D. M. (Dennis M.)
Educational psychology: constructing learning.

2nd ed.
Bibliography.
Includes index.
ISBN 0 7248 0399 8.

1. Educational psychology. I. McInerney, V. II. Title.

370.15

PRENTICE HALL

An imprint of Pearson Education

Brief Contents

Contents

PART 2: MANAGING EFFECTIVE LEARNING

Introduction

Welcome to the second edition of *Educational Psychology: Constructing Learning*. We are delighted to have been asked by Prentice Hall to revise our text for its second edition. This has given us the opportunity to listen closely to the text's users, and to incorporate their many useful suggestions into the revision. We have also been able to ensure the currency and accuracy of the material covered so that it is, we believe, the best available for preparing educators for the 21st century.

Content The second edition has been thoroughly reorganised and updated. While maintaining its strong contemporary focus on constructivism, cross-cultural and multicultural issues, technology and learning, cooperative and self-regulated learning, and alternative means of evaluation and assessment, we have added substantial sections on play, adolescent development and alienation, Sternberg's triarchic theory of intelligence, metacognition and social development. Over 200 new references are cited in this edition.

Thematic sections The text is divided into three main sections: stimulating effective learning, managing effective learning, and understanding developmental needs of children and effective teaching and learning.

Chapter contents and overview Each chapter has a listing that acquaints you with its organisation and content. A variety of headings, subheadings and icons will help you find your way through the text. We have also included a brief overview which sets the scene for the material to be covered.

New features of the second edition

A number of new features have been included which we hope will make the book a valuable learning and teaching resource.

Teaching Competence boxes These present the basic teaching competencies for beginning teaching drawn from the National Competency Framework for Beginning Teaching produced by the Australian Teaching Council. Throughout we illustrate how material covered in the text addresses these competencies and provides the reader with suggestions on how to demonstrate these competencies through the relevant indicators.

Learning-Centred Psychological Principles These boxes present key psychological principles drawn from research that should guide effective teaching and learning. Through the text we elaborate on, and provide applied examples of, these principles.

Action station We often learn most effectively when theory is put into practice. Included throughout each chapter is a number of interesting practical exercises to challenge you. In many cases they provide the opportunity to investigate, first hand, the use of theory in practice.

Question point Each chapter has a range of questions distributed through the text to stimulate further study or group discussion.

Teacher's case book Selected case studies, drawn from the National Competency Framework for Beginning Teaching and produced by the Australian Teaching Council, provide a bird's eye view of teacher/student interaction in real educational settings. An associated case study activity provides an opportunity to explore teachers' common knowledge and theory.

What would you do? Additional case studies, also drawn from the National Competency Framework for Beginning Teaching, present an opportunity to test your solutions to real problem situations against the solutions of actual teachers. Again, this provides a great opportunity to put theory into practice.

Essentials of ... Throughout the text we have summarised the essential practical implications of key topics from both teacher and student perspectives. These 'essentials of' tables not only serve as a practical guide for classroom practices, but help to clarify the relevance and importance of theory.

Recommended reading At the end of each chapter we suggest a range of articles and texts that will further develop your understanding of the topics discussed.

Photo captions The photographs have been chosen to stimulate thought and discussion on the topics illustrated. Many photographs have question-focused captions for you to consider.

Marginal text We have included in the margins a glossary of major terms and brief summary text on key concepts dealt with.

Instructor's Manual To facilitate the use of our text we have written an Instructor's Manual which draws together the instructional features of the text and gives guidelines on the use of these.

Acknowledgments

Many people have supported us in the preparation of the second edition. In particular, we wish to thank those who reviewed individual chapters in the first edition to suggest where improvements could be made. We sincerely thank Ray Debus, Sue Dockett, Bob Perry, Bill Rogers, Ken Sinclair, Ian Smith, Bob Tremayne, Richard Walker and Helen Woodward. We also thank our anonymous reviewers.

Our special thanks go to John Wiley for his wonderful cartoons, which enliven the text, and to Lee-Anne Bethel, whose excellent illustrations help to clarify points discussed. Thank you also to those who provided materials such as photographs and textual material. Credits are given for these contributions in the appropriate part of the text.

Two individuals at Prentice Hall deserve special thanks: Mark Burgess and Elizabeth Thomas for their determination to turn our manuscript into a quality production. We would also like to sincerely thank Jo Rudd for her outstanding copy editing of this edition.

Finally, our thanks go to all our colleagues who encouraged and supported us in our work, and to our two children who mostly tolerated and often encouraged us in the long hours we spent revising the text.

Dennis and Valentina McInerney

PART 1

Stimulating effective learning

CHAPTER 1

Effective teaching and learning

OVERVIEW

When he was a child, one of the authors wanted to be a teacher. He spent endless hours playing at school, and particularly enjoyed yelling at imaginary kids and belting them with a strap if they misbehaved (which says a lot about the models of teaching he was exposed to!). Other careers, such as fireman or engine driver, did not appeal at all. The female author always wanted to be a doctor, but was subtly pressured by her immigrant parents into choosing teaching as a career—'Medicine is not a career for a woman; it's better for you to be a teacher, you can always be available for your children and husband'—the words still echo in her ears. Well, here we are today many years later, teachers. Through all those long years we have found teaching exhilarating and exhausting, rewarding and disappointing, but never, never dull.

We often think about our careers and wonder why we decided to become teachers and whether we made the right decision. Certainly, in the first case, the author's socialisation as the son of a schoolteacher, with a sister already a schoolteacher, seems to have circumscribed the choices available. Indeed, he can't remember ever questioning that this would be the best job. In the second case, the author's decision was very much limited by parental expectations of what 'a good girl should do'. She still harbours some disappointment that she did not go into medicine.

In this chapter we introduce you to the role of educational psychology in understanding this fascinating profession. In particular, we introduce the guiding frameworks for this book: the Learner-centred Psychological Principles developed by the American Psychological Association, and the National Competency Framework for Beginning Teaching developed by the Australian Teaching Council. Throughout the text we refer to these as they relate to the material covered. Our final framework, constructivist approaches to learning and teaching, is outlined briefly and some key terms introduced.

Effective teachers teach for student learning. In this chapter we give a broad overview of some characteristics of effective teachers that will prepare you to consider many of the topics covered in the text.

EFFECTIVE TEACHING AND LEARNING—PERSPECTIVES FROM EDUCATIONAL PSYCHOLOGY

What makes an effective teacher? What makes an effective learner? And what role does educational psychology play in helping teachers and learners to be effective? These are the central themes of the text. In a sense, we set out to tell the story of teaching and learning as interconnected processes guided by three basic frameworks: the Learner-centred Psychological Principles developed by the American Psychological Association, the National Competency Framework for Beginning Teachers developed by the Australian Teaching Council, and constructivist views of the learning process.

Learner-centred Psychological Principles

The scientific study of psychology in education has provided vital information on the learner and the learning process (see, for example, Wittrock 1992). The Learner-centred Psychological Principles apply to all learners and provide a very useful framework for understanding effective learning and its relationship to effective teaching. These principles refer to cognitive and metacognitive factors, motivational and affective factors, developmental and social factors and, lastly, to individual differences. Throughout the text we include excerpts from these psychological principles and relate them to the material covered.

'Oh! Why thank you Brutus. An early Christmas Present. And here I was thinking of you as a murderous thug.'

National Competency Framework for Beginning Teaching

The second framework for developing our story about effective teaching and learning is drawn from the National Competency Framework for Beginning Teaching (Australian Teaching Council 1996). There are five areas of competency that we address throughout the text:

- ☐ Using and developing professional knowledge and values
- ☐ Communicating, interacting and working with students and others
- ☐ Planning and managing the teaching and learning process
- ☐ Monitoring and assessing student progress and learning outcomes
- ☐ Reflecting, evaluating and planning for continuous improvement as a teacher

Each of these areas of competency is elaborated through a series of criteria referred to throughout the text.

In the sections that follow we explore some of these principles of effective teaching and learning, and set the scene for their further elaboration.

CONSTRUCTIVIST VIEWS OF LEARNING

The third framework for developing our story, **constructivism**, is drawn from cognitive psychology. Cognitive psychology, in general, and learning theories derived from cognitive psychology, in particular, have become very important in helping to explain effective learning and its relationship to effective teaching. Implicit in these cognitive views of learning is the notion that effective learning occurs when individuals **construct** their own understandings. In other words, there is an emphasis in cognitive theories on the active role of the learner in building personal meaning and in making sense of information (Poplin 1988).

Personal constructivism/ radical constructivism: focus on intrapersonal dimensions of learning

There are many varieties of constructivism (Moshman 1982; Phillips 1995). Some constructivist approaches concentrate attention on the cognitive contents of the minds of individual learners, such as the individual's existing understandings and knowledge, attitudes, motivational level and interests, and how this is extended through the learners' personal interactions with physical events in their daily lives. These approaches are often labelled **personal constructivism** (or, at times, radical or endogenous constructivism) (see Driver et al. 1994; Hendry 1996; Moshman 1982; von Glasersfeld 1995; see also Pressley 1995). These approaches explicitly emphasise the intrapersonal dimensions of learning and, in particular, believe that knowledge is not transmitted directly from one knower to another, but is actively built up by the learner through child-determined exploration and discovery rather than direct teaching. Hence, classrooms reflecting this perspective would prepare well-designed practical activities that challenge learners' prior conceptions, encouraging learners to reorganise their personal theories. We examine this in some detail in our discussion of Piaget (Chapter 2), information processing (Chapter 4) and Bruner and Ausubel (Chapter 5).

Other constructivist approaches, labelled **social constructivism** (Driver et al. 1994) (sometimes called exogenous; see Moshman 1982; see also Pressley 1995), focus on the growth of 'public' subject matter of individuals in social domains and in particular in relationship to families, peer groups and schools which orient children to interpret and make sense of their world of experiences. This process of knowledge construction comes about as learners become encultured into the knowledge and symbols of their society. This view moves away from the position that children learn best when they self-discover to a position that advocates collaborative enquiry through which individuals appropriate information in terms of their own understanding of, and involvement in, the activity. In cases where children are having difficulty, or are being challenged to extend their understanding, teachers and others provide the prompts, scaffolding and guidance needed. This form of social constructivism emphasises the importance of continuing interaction between the child and its social environment to facilitate meaningful learning (Greeno 1997; Anderson, Reder & Simon 1997). We examine this approach in our discussion of Vygotsky (Chapter 2), social cognitive theory (Chapter 6) and **cognitive apprenticeships** and **reciprocal teaching** (Chapter 5).

The essential element in the constructivist view of learning is that there is an active involvement of the learner, and a shift in focus from what the teacher may do through explicit teaching to influence learning, to what the learner does as an active agent in the learning process. None of these views of constructivism necessarily entails specific teaching practices but, rather, each provides a general orienting framework within which to address teaching issues and to develop instructional approaches (Cobb 1994).

We should also note that the constructivist maxim that students construct their own knowledge can be taken to imply that students can construct their *own* ways of knowing in even the most teacher-directed instructional situations (see Cobb 1994). For this reason we also deal with alternative views of effective

- **Personal constructivism**—Focus on the individual's internal mental state and transformations of understanding that occur within the individual
- **Social constructivism**—Focus on the construction of knowledge in a social context, with the individual making personal meaning from socially shared perceptions

teaching derived from non-cognitive theories of learning. Through this we hope to establish a bridge that spans the supposed dichotomy between instructional approaches overtly based on student construction of knowledge and those instructional approaches based on transmission of knowledge.

We return to these classifications when considering a number of features of effective teaching and learning throughout the text.

ACTION STATION

Graham Hendry (1996) lists seven constructivist principles and their classroom applications. Consider these in the light of the discussion below of what makes an effective teacher. Refer to them again as we describe the many faces of constructivism throughout this text. Do they all apply to each approach? Would you add other principles? Would you delete some principles?

Principle 1 Knowledge exists only in the minds of people. In the classroom, knowledge exists in the minds of students and the teacher, not on the blackboard, in books, on floppy disks, in teacher or student talk or in the activities that teachers and students devise.

Principle 2 The meanings or interpretations that people give to things depend on their knowledge. Teachers and students give meaning to instructional materials according to their existing knowledge and may, therefore, generate different meanings for the same materials and experiences.

Principle 3 Knowledge is constructed from within the person in interrelation with the world. Teachers or teaching methods *per se* do not change students' ideas; rather, change or construction occurs from within, through students' interrelation with the world of which teachers are a part. Students do not simply absorb transmitted knowledge.

Principle 4 Knowledge can never be certain. There are no absolutely right or wrong answers or ideas, only ones that are more or less useful and sustainable. Thus, all knowledge can be reconstructed and should be continually open to re-examination.

Principle 5 Common knowledge derives from a common brain and body which are part of the same universe. Children share the same brain processes and body characteristics and inhabit the same world, and can construct common knowledge through their discussion of solutions to the same problems. Despite the individual nature of the construction of knowledge, this knowledge construction is based upon common biological processes (such as perception) across humans. This knowledge will reflect the biological and experiential maturity of the individuals.

Principle 6 Knowledge is constructed through perception and action. In particular, learning is facilitated by active involvement in problem solving and conflict resolution.

Principle 7 Construction of knowledge requires energy and time. Individuals are most motivated to construct knowledge in non-threatening, supportive and challenging learning environments. The construction of knowledge is promoted by encouraging students to discuss, explain and evaluate their thoughts within a social context.

Question point: *Explore your implicit theories of teaching and learning. How might these have evolved? Is teaching an art or a science?*

BOX 1.1 TEACHING COMPETENCE

The teacher plans purposeful programs to achieve specific student learning outcomes

Indicators

The teacher:

- relates learning programs to educational goals and objectives;
- establishes clear purposes for learning programs in terms of agreed student learning outcomes;
- selects and sequences learning activities to achieve planned student outcomes;
- takes account of students' goals and prior learning;
- relates assessment processes and strategies to learning objectives, content and tasks.

Case studies illustrating National Competency Framework for Beginning Teaching, National Project on the Quality of Teaching and Learning, Australian Teaching Council, 1996, Element 3.1, p.46. Commonwealth of Australia copyright, reproduced by permission.

ACTION STATION

Consider the following questions (Conners, Nettle & Placing 1990).

1. Describe the kind of teacher you would like to be.

2. Describe two significant incidents/experiences in your life that you consider have influenced your view of teaching.
3. When you think about yourself teaching, what subjects or activities would you most like to teach?
4. Are there any subjects or activities that you would not like to teach?

Question point: Discuss these issues in a group of four or five students and then make a full class report.

WHAT MAKES AN EFFECTIVE TEACHER?

In the following sections we look at some of the features that characterise effective teaching. Several years ago, a national magazine published a feature article entitled 'What makes a great teacher?' (Boag, *Bulletin*, 18 July 1989; see also Kutnick & Jules 1993). It was derived from a survey of educational 'experts' and listed 15 attributes of 'great' teachers:

1. Enthuse students.
2. Treat students as individuals.
3. Know the subject.
4. Be loving and warm.
5. Teach for learning.
6. Empathise with students.
7. Relate to parents and the wider community.
8. Be firm, fair and flexible.
9. Be organised.
10. Prepare students for life.
11. Manage the classroom.
12. Have high self-esteem.
13. Have a sense of humour.
14. Be a total person with a full life outside school.
15. Take risks.

Not surprisingly, many of these attributes are the same as those that researchers have identified as characteristics of effective teachers (Berliner & Tikunoff 1976). Research that identifies **effective teaching** is really talking about 'particular teaching procedures and behaviours that are related to positive student learning outcomes and student attitudes to learning' in particular classrooms (Mason & Levi 1992). An important consideration to keep in mind is that what constitutes effective practice in one classroom or school setting may not do so in another. The reasons for this include differences in students (ability, background, prior knowledge and interests), parental commitment to education, and school climate (collaboration between teaching peers, and agreement on approaches to instruction, classroom management and curriculum development).

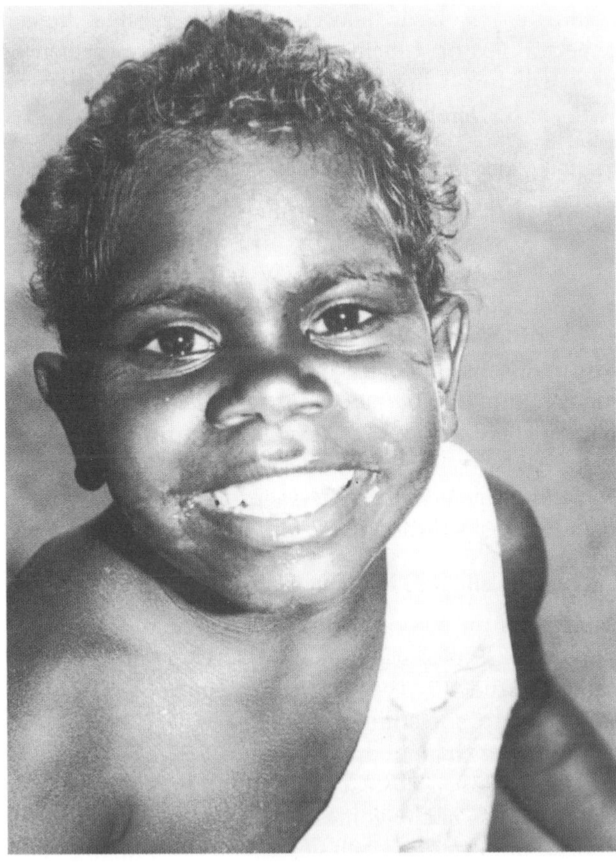

To see the joy in our students' eyes is one of the greatest satisfactions of teaching. Photo: WA Education News

What, then, are the characteristics that make teachers effective?

Effective teachers teach for learning

In saying that effective teachers teach for student learning, we are assuming that you actually perceive your role in this way; that is, that you have a sense of **self-efficacy** as a teacher. According to Dunkin (1990a, 1990b, 1991), teacher self-efficacy refers to your perceived **personal power** to influence student learning (outcome expectations) as well as the **confidence** that you have the teaching competence actually to make a difference (efficacy expectations). Brophy and Evertson (1976) found that there was a marked difference between how effective and ineffective teachers described their roles. Ineffective teachers saw teaching as a dull job in which they did not take personal responsibility for student learning: they did not feel that they made a difference and believed that 'problems' such as poor behaviour and low ability were insoluble. On the other hand, effective teachers saw themselves as having control over problems that

Teacher self-efficacy

Positive attitude: helping students to learn

could be resolved. Successful teachers had higher expectations for students and saw themselves primarily as instructors whose task it was to help them learn (Gibson & Dembo 1984).

Planning learning experiences

Lesson beginnings

Effective teachers plan learning experiences within which individually and socially constructed learning can occur (Wragg 1995). Before any learning can take place, the **attention** and **interest** of the students must be gained. This is evident in the lessons of novice or student teachers, or those who cannot be bothered to put mental effort into planning the most effective ways of introducing their material. Not surprisingly, these teachers find that classroom management becomes a problem with students going off tasks through lack of interest and motivation.

Introducing effective learning experiences

A **focus** for the session is vital. This can take the form of a sensory experience related to the content to be covered; students may be asked to hear, look at, feel, smell or taste something.

Another technique is to use an **advance organiser** (Ausubel 1968, 1978; Corkhill 1992) which places the new material in the context of what students already know. For example, when describing the human body's circulation system an interesting advance organiser might sound something like this:

The human body's circulation system is like the sanitary system of a city. In both, there is a pumping station, pipelines of various sizes to carry clean water, a filtration mechanism to clean dirty water, an exchange terminal and a method of disposing wastes.

Adapted from Eggen and Kauchak 1988

The term **anticipatory set** (Hunter 1982, 1991) focuses student attention and reminds them of what they already know that is relevant to the topic to be covered. For example, when beginning a lesson on mass, volume and capacity, the teacher might focus with:

What have you noticed about the level of the water when you get into a full bath and then get out again? Is it any different if someone else gets in as well?

Sometimes a **review** is appropriate as an introduction to the lesson. Knowledge is constructed cumulatively, not just swallowed in separate whole chunks. Therefore, students need to have the connections with concepts and ideas covered in earlier lessons made for them through brief revision. For example:

This week we have been learning about mammals. Let's think for a moment about what we have found so far. Jot down, or discuss with your neighbour first, three of the general characteristics that distinguish mammals from other groups of creatures such as reptiles. (Discussion and sharing of knowledge takes place for the next few minutes.) Today's lesson will look at a special subgroup of Australian mammals which are called marsupials and which have a unique set of characteristics that distinguish them from other mammals. How many of you have seen a kangaroo? Well, a kangaroo is a marsupial. Can anyone think of anything different about a kangaroo from a dog, which is also a mammal? Jamie? ... Good—kangaroos have pouches in which they carry their young. Anything else? ... Phuong?

Developing learning experiences

There are many different ways of presenting learning experiences that reflect constructivist as well as other approaches to teaching and learning: **direct teacher instruction** (reception learning), **guided discovery** (induction), **group discussion, cooperative group learning, peer** or **cross-age tutoring, individualised self-instruction** via computer or resource package (sometimes referred to as **programmed instruction**) and a host of others. Effective teachers vary the **mode of presentation** according to the material and the students' skills and experience. Younger children, for example, may not benefit greatly from group discussions and will flounder in ignorance trying to 'discover' principles that the teacher could more effectively communicate in a direct way. Nevertheless, the often quoted argument that children don't know how to cooperate and therefore can't learn through cooperative groups should not be the excuse for avoiding this form of presentation. Rather, the teacher needs to teach the skills required to work collaboratively and to explore opportunities where children can practise them frequently (such as working with a partner to present an oral book report; designing a poster in a trio; interviewing a partner about their eating habits or daily routine in a 'Who am I?' topic) before being thrown into a cooperative group to complete a project.

Keeping students actively involved during their learning

Active involvement For effective learning to occur, students need to be actively involved. Such involvement may be through **manipulating materials** to explore 'what happens if ...?'; pondering over **higher cognitive-level questions** which challenge their thinking and force them to apply, analyse, synthesise or evaluate what they have learned ('Why do you think...?'

'What would happen if...?' 'How might we do this differently?'); encouraging them to **find applications or examples** of newly learned concepts; **brainstorming** solutions to problems; **practising problems** to ensure retention and transfer of new material.

Providing effective feedback Good and Brophy (1991; see also Crooks 1988; Kulik & Kulik 1988) point out the importance of providing students with immediate feedback on their learning, while it is emerging, to keep them on task (and thereby also preventing students from practising mistakes for too long). Effective feedback should specify exactly what is correct or incorrect about a student's work. Feedback should also give students corrective information about what they need to do to rectify problems (Crooks 1988). Most importantly, it should be communicated positively (Elawar & Corno 1985), not as one third-grade teacher was heard to remark: 'Haven't you put anything down on paper yet? For goodness sake, you will never be a good writer the way you're going!'.

Feedback should be immediate and corrective, and expressed positively

Far more conducive to improvement in both effort and product would be a comment such as: 'I can see that you are having trouble thinking of ideas for what to write. Just jot down any single words that come to mind and then have a look in your book for some pictures that might help your imagination. When you have done that, come out to show me and we'll see how they can be put together into a story. I know you'll be surprised with what you come up with.'

Opportunity should also be given to children to self-evaluate and to implement alternative learning strategies as they see appropriate.

Ending learning experiences

'Well, that's it. The end. Thank you for your attention —you can go back to your seats now.'

This was the closure of a measurement lesson with a small group of eight children conducted by a beginning teacher trainee during a practice teaching session. It is not an uncommon conclusion to many (otherwise well-planned) lessons we have observed over the years. Student teachers often ask, 'What do you do at the end of the lesson?'. The answer is to 'pull the lesson together' by reviewing with the students what has been learnt, **summarising** the content of the lesson and arriving at a conclusion. It is akin to writing an essay: tell them what you are going to say (effective teachers tell their students what the lesson will be about and how and for what purpose they will be involved in the learning activities); say it (they then direct students through these activities ensuring maximum student involvement in a variety of forms); and then, remind them about the main message (finally, the content of the lesson is reviewed and a summary given or requested from the students: 'What did you learn today about ...?'). (See also Cole & Chan 1987; Turney et al. 1985b.) Remember, there may well be a difference between individual 'knowing' and collective, socially negotiated 'knowledge' as transmitted through language.

For the student teacher above, the advice would be to conclude with something like:

Today you have been estimating and measuring the length, width and perimeter of a range of large and small areas. I would like everyone in both groups to write down which measuring tools you found most useful for the particular areas that you had to measure, and why they were the most suitable. (Students do so.) All right, let's hear what each group found and then we'll see what conclusions we come up with.

Additionally, students themselves should be asked to **reflect** on and summarise what they have learnt from the experience, and to suggest what they may further need to do to extend their understanding.

EFFECTIVE TEACHING AND TEACHING SKILLS

Naturally, in order to design and facilitate effective learning experiences, teachers need to have appropriate skills. These are detailed in Table 1.1 on p.12. These are also skills that beginning teachers have some anxiety over when they start teaching (Reynolds 1992; Sinclair & Nicholl 1981; Veenman 1984).

Knowledge skills

Effective teachers are **knowledgeable**, though not necessarily expert, about the material to be learnt. More importantly, they must be able to communicate this knowledge to the students or demonstrate how to access it in a way that shows its utility or place in the world outside school. This knowledge will not translate into student learning unless students see that it has a purpose and is related to their world of understanding. Above all, good teachers show that education is about learning to live and to learn. The effective teacher is a professional who keeps up to date with developments in education, and models that learning is a lifelong process.

Knowledge—possessed by teacher and able to be accessed by student

Management skills

The effective teacher is **organised**. From general curriculum documents, programs of lessons (for a

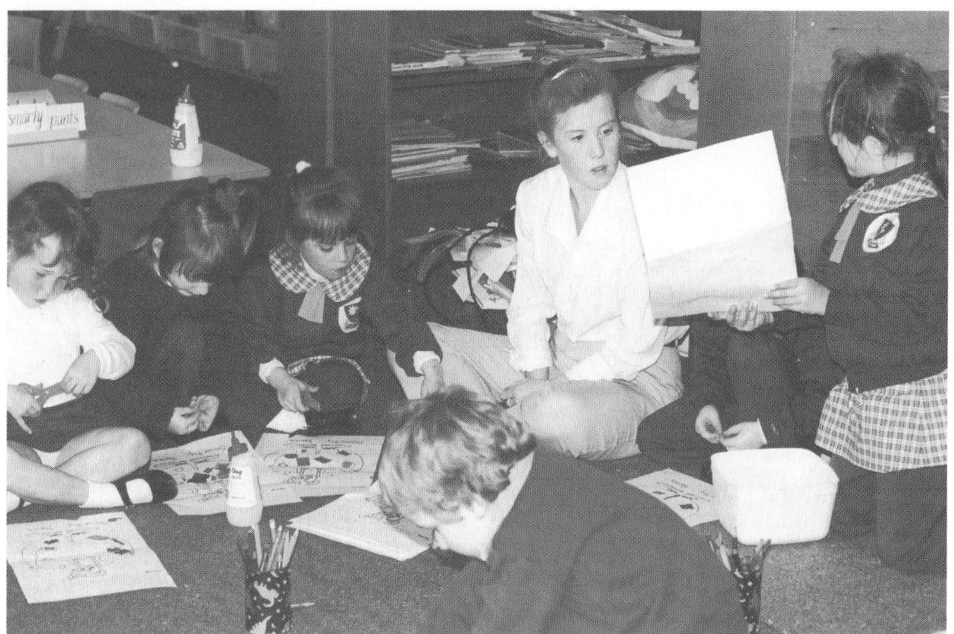

Increasingly teachers are seen as facilitators of learning rather than 'authority figures'. Photo: authors

week, term or year) must be designed that are appropriate to the age and abilities of the students. In addition to content, the effective teacher plans for the strategies that will be most effective in helping students learn this material. As discussed in Chapter 10 (on classroom management), this teacher organises the physical layout of the classroom, the supplies, and the rules and procedures at the start of the year. These rules and procedures are taught to students in the first weeks of school, and routines are developed to make classroom interactions more efficient. Routines maintain the activity flow in the classroom by defining appropriate behaviours for a variety of classroom activities—whether whole-class, small groups, peer tutoring or individual work (Anderson 1986). Students know, for example, what to do when they want the teacher's help, need to leave the room, have to form groups for cooperative teamwork, or forget to complete or to bring their homework to school.

Effective management requires careful organisation

Questioning skills

Questioning takes a central role in the instructional process and the use of questions should not be a 'hit or miss' exercise. The issues teachers should consider in planning for effective questioning episodes include: how much emphasis should be placed on lower and higher cognitive questions; whether to use a recitation or discussion participant structure; how to frame questions clearly; how much wait-time to allow before eliciting a response; whether to elicit an individual or group response; how to react to students' answers; and how to adjust their questioning strategy to a particular instructional context (Gall & Artero-Boname 1995). And you thought questioning was the easy aspect of teaching!

Good and Brophy (1990; see also Gall & Artero-Boname 1995) point out that effective teachers carefully plan **sequences of questions** for achieving particular objectives. For instance, if the objective of a lesson is for students to analyse Hamlet's relationship with his mother, initial questions might focus on knowledge, followed later by increasingly higher-order questions that would help the students to integrate the 'facts' and draw conclusions. In other words, the effective teacher does not ask questions haphazardly; there is a logic to the content and type of questions used in an instructional sequence which is closely related to the teacher's objectives, or the expected learning outcomes for the students.

Plan sequences of questions

The quality of the questions themselves (i.e. their clarity and relevance) is very important to their effective use. It is obvious that poor questions are those that are vague, ambiguous, lengthy, rhetorical, 'closed' (lead to yes/no answers), use complex language, or encourage guessing.

What, then, are 'good' questions? Effective questions are **clear and brief**, and **identify** the aspects to which the students are expected to respond (see Barry & King 1993; Cole & Chan 1987; Groisser 1964; Turney et al. 1985a). For example, 'What do you notice about spiders?' does not give direction to students as to the information required. A better question would be 'What is the body structure of a spider?' or 'What is the shape of a spider's web?'

Clarity

Effective questions have a **purpose**. As described earlier, questions should be sequenced in accordance with the instructional objectives. They should also be brief. A series of questions that progress a step at a time is preferable to one long one in which the focus is lost. 'What were some of the different cultural groups that have come to

Purpose and brevity

Australia and their reasons for settling here?' is far less effective than the following sequence: 'Name the European groups that migrated to Australia in the first hundred years after settlement. Why did each group come out?' followed by 'Groups from the Middle East and Asia have come to Australia for different reasons in the past 20 years. Which groups are these? Why did each group leave their homeland?'

How does good questioning facilitate effective learning?
Photo: Authors

Higher cognitive-level questions also stimulate student interest and provide opportunities for clarifying their ideas. In this regard, an effective teacher understands that students need to learn how to answer such questions and supports the development of this skill. Students can be given time to jot down some ideas in answer to the question and then share these with a peer before answering out loud. Not only do they need to develop the skills for thinking out loud, but students need **time** in which to do so.

Stimulate student interest

Research has shown how very important it is for teachers to wait after they have asked a question of the whole class and then again after nominating one student to answer (Tobin 1987). This 'wait-time' should be no less than three seconds and has been shown to increase the amount and quality of student discussion considerably, as well as facilitating higher cognitive-level learning by providing teachers and students with additional time to think (Swift & Gooding 1983; Tobin 1987; Turney et al. 1985a, 1985b). Teachers typically tend to wait no longer than half a second before they rephrase their own question, or worse still, answer it themselves (Swift & Gooding 1983). Teachers taught to monitor their wait-time by using an electronic (red light 'stop', green light after three seconds 'go') device reduced their disciplinary comments dramatically, while the amount of relevant discussion by students, the proportion of students engaged in discussion, and the cognitive level of their answers were considerably raised. However, there may be little to be gained in providing students and teachers with additional time to think if recall of factual information is required. If simple recall or rote learning is the intended goal of the questioning, it may be better to use a shorter wait-time and move the activity along at a brisk pace (Tobin 1987).

Wait-time

Research on questioning has shown that both higher and lower cognitive-level questions can lead to effective learning (Gall 1984). However, much of the evidence is quite conflicting. What does emerge is that higher-level questions (i.e. those that require comprehension, application, analysis, synthesis or evaluation) are not necessarily better than lower-level (factual or knowledge) questions. Students in the primary grades, those with low ability, and those from lower socioeconomic backgrounds benefit from questions that allow for a high proportion of correct answers, especially when learning basic skills. These are the lower cognitive-level questions that ask for recall of knowledge, questions where there is only one right answer (Stallings & Kaskowitz 1975). Students with average to high ability, on the other hand, learn effectively from difficult questions at both lower and higher cognitive levels, especially when critical feedback is given by the teacher. Examples of effective higher-level questions are: 'Do you have any other ideas ...?' 'Why did you come up with that conclusion?' How could you find out ...?' 'What would you do if ...?' Why do you think this happens?'

To this point we have emphasised the teacher's role in questioning. Research also demonstrates that **reciprocal peer questioning** and teaching students to ask questions of themselves in a guided way facilitates student learning. We consider both these aspects of questioning later in the text. Table 1.1 summarises the essential teaching skills for effective learning.

Consider the case study 'How do I know they know?' on the value of using questions to stimulate learning and monitor student's understanding.

TABLE 1.1

ESSENTIAL TEACHING SKILLS FOR EFFECTIVE LEARNING

For teachers

- Demonstrating appropriate knowledge.
- Utilising appropriate management skills.
- Implementing effective questioning techniques.
- Setting appropriate instructional objectives.
- Teaching for learning outcomes.
- Using motivational strategies.
- Monitoring and evaluating student learning.
- Communicating enthusiasm, warmth and humour.

Setting appropriate instructional objectives

Effective teachers plan their instruction around general and specific objectives so that there is a clear purpose to the content and activities that comprise the teacher's daily classroom interactions (see also Chapter 13). Bloom, Madaus and Hastings (1981) remind us, also, that statements of instructional objectives are specific descriptions of what each student should be able to do, produce or possess as a personal attribute (values, attitudes and feelings) after the instruction. The focus on instructional objectives dates back to the important work of Robert Mager (1973, 1990a, 1990b) which drew attention to the need for teachers to:

- ☐ specify the student behaviour or learning outcome that should result from the learning experience, and the level at which the performance would be considered acceptable;
- ☐ describe the conditions under which the behaviour should occur and which would allow the teacher to be able to assess whether the standard had been met;
- ☐ determine the minimal level considered acceptable.

Similar to the guidelines offered by Mager, but presented as a very simple mnemonic, is the following ABCD format for writing objectives suggested by Armstrong and Savage (1983). Keep in mind:

A. the *audience* (i.e. each student) for whom the objectives are written;

B. the *behaviour* that will indicate that learning has occurred;

TEACHER'S CASE BOOK

HOW DO I KNOW THEY KNOW?

Ben, Sam and Rachel have just presented a movement piece they have devised, based on some music they have chosen. It is quite abstract, well controlled and focused. They've used a variety of elements such as locomotion, levels, force and speed, stillness and so on.

At the end of drama lessons and at the conclusion of some specific activities, Mrs Hinley and her students sit and discuss elements of their work. Discussion is an important element of their work: it gives individual students the opportunity to articulate their ideas, thoughts and opinions and it gives Mrs Hinley a chance to 'see inside their heads'—'What have they gained? What experiences have they benefited from? Was this activity worthwhile? Why? what makes it so? How will I develop this, alter, redirect it to enhance the students' learning?'

Mrs Hinley now turns to the movement group. 'You were obviously engrossed in the performance today, Toby ... What was it about this group's work that appealed to you?' The answer to this prompting question was the focus for further questions and discussion with both the audience and the performers. Mrs Hinley considers and shapes her questions carefully. They are focused open questons which allow her to monitor the learning process that occurred. Students are asked to articulate their own learning process (e.g. How did you arrive at the decision to start your movement piece in that particular way? The use of simple props was effective, how did that evolve?).

The students' reflection not only confirms for Mrs Hinley what they are learning, but also gives her an opportunity to plan, revise and develop her teaching.

Case studies illustrating National Competency Framework for Beginning Teaching, National Project on the Quality of Teaching and Learning, Australian Teaching Council, 1996, p. 40. Commonwealth of Australia copyright, reproduced by permission.

C. the *conditions* under which the behaviour should occur;

D. the *degree* of competency required.

An example may best illustrate the way in which objectives would be written using this format:

A. The *audience* are Muhammed, Paloma, Matthew and Jennifer (first-grade children who are grouped for the purpose of remedial work in basic language skills). Muhammed and Paloma come from non-English-speaking home backgrounds; Matthew has a mild intellectual disability; and Jennifer is an Aboriginal child who has recently moved from a remote country school where access to a wide range of books was not available at home or at school.

B. The *behaviour* is the ability to recognise and distinguish between the various vowel sounds, and to pronounce them correctly while reading.
C. The *conditions* are in the class reader *Wombat Stew* by Marcia Vaughan (1984; Ashton Scholastic: Gosford, NSW).
D. The *degree* of competency required eight out of ten vowels sounded out and pronounced correctly as part of the word (80%).

Written as it might appear in a teaching program, this objective would read:

Muhammed, Paloma, Matthew and Jennifer will be able to recognise, distinguish between, and pronounce correctly 80% of the vowel sounds they meet when reading *Wombat Stew*.

Most recently, Norman Gronlund (1991) has argued that objectives should first be stated *generally*, using words such as 'know', 'understand', 'apply' and 'interpret'. Thus, for example, in a science course, some general objectives might be:

- ☐ Know correct laboratory procedures.
- ☐ Understand scientific facts and concepts.
- ☐ Apply scientific facts and concepts to new situations.
- ☐ Interpret data in scientific reports.

Gronlund recommends that, for effective planning of instruction, these general objectives should then be broken down into specific objectives which are, in effect, sample behaviours that demonstrate that students have achieved the general objective. For instance, in the science example above, 'Know correct laboratory procedures' would be described by such sample behaviours as choosing appropriate equipment for a procedure, assembling and operating equipment correctly, following safety rules, and cleaning and replacing equipment in the proper way.

Teaching for learning outcomes

Effective teachers communicate clear instructional objectives as anticipated learning outcomes to students so that their learning is goal-directed. These teachers also introduce new material by relating it to key concepts that the students already have (advance organiser) which enables them to see a connection between previous learning and the new material. Both the advance organisers and stated learning outcomes provide students with a **learning set**. They understand the purpose of the activity to which their attention has been drawn, and appreciate the anticipated academic benefits.

It will be evident by now that effective teachers are clear in their own minds about what they want students to learn. They are organised and they plan. They will have diagnosed the individual learning needs of their students as well as having programmed the curriculum requirements stipulated by government bodies for their particular whole class group and teaching discipline (in secondary school).

These needs and curriculum requirements will have been used as the basis for determining the learning outcomes for that class of children, and will be expressed as specific outcome statements (for individual children and for groups with common needs) that describe what the students will be able to do at the completion of the learning tasks.

It is all very well to say that effective teachers write objectives for student learning, but how do they actually decide what these should be? We discuss sources of educational objectives and task analysis in Chapter 13. You are advised to refer to this material. The selection of tasks and associated activities is paramount in achieving effective learning outcomes. Effective teachers work hard to ensure that their approaches are appropriate, interesting, well organised, and varied as the need arises.

Using motivational strategies

Effective teachers implement specific strategies to enhance class and individual motivation. We discuss a range of these in Chapter 9, in some detail. At this point we wish to highlight some of the key strategies based on the work of Ames and Ames (1991), namely reducing social comparison, stimulating student involvement in learning, focusing on effort, promoting personal beliefs in competence and increasing chances of student success. Table 1.2 presents these key strategies.

TABLE 1.2

ESSENTIALS OF EFFECTIVE STRATEGIES TO ENCOURAGE MOTIVATION

For teachers

Reduce social comparison by:

- avoiding social comparison and external and public evaluation;
- emphasising achievement in terms of personal best rather than comparative norms reflected through grades and marks;
- using a range of measurement, evaluation and reporting schemes;
- using evaluation that relates to the 'real' world of the student.

Stimulate student involvement in learning by:

- using variety in your teaching methods (including group work, peer tutoring, games and simulations);
- allowing students choice and control over their learning related to method, pace and content;
- situating learning in relevant 'real life' contexts.

Focus on effort by:

- emphasising personal effort as the means for improvement;
- helping students see that mistakes are part of learning;
- setting realistic expectations on 'reasonable effort';
- helping students establish realistic goals.

Promote beliefs in competence by:

- helping children develop metacognitive and self-regulatory skills;
- communicating positive expectations;
- making plans with students for improvement.

Increase chances for success by:

- modelling learning approaches and motivation in the classroom;
- teaching learning skills and strategies;
- individualising instruction;
- using cooperative and peer learning situations.

(based on Ames & Ames 1991)

Question point: Discuss how an effective teacher may reduce social comparison, increase student involvement in learning, focus on student effort and promote student belief in their competence.

Monitoring and evaluating learning

Effective teachers monitor student progress both throughout the learning activity and at its conclusion (see Chapter 13). They do this through questioning, observation of work samples, tests and quizzes, collection of homework assignments, and projects. An important additional means of evaluation is that performed by the student. Self-evaluation is considered a vital skill in a rapidly changing society where the emphasis is on being autonomous and independent as a learner (Boud 1985; Falchikov & Boud 1989; Hall 1992; Woodward 1993). Perhaps more important than learning a whole pile of facts, which are readily available in a multitude of forms (e.g. computer databases), is the opportunity for students to learn how to determine where strengths lie in their work and how to remedy weaknesses. Teach your students how to reflect upon their learning, evaluate their own work and that of others (sensitively). Another effective strategy to foster the development of self-evaluation is to have students maintain a folder of all work that is submitted for assessment as a means of providing them with a concrete basis for self-evaluation. It is easy, then, to sit with students periodically and go through their folders to evaluate the extent to which progress has been made. Asking them, 'Is this your best work?' or 'What have you learnt?' can be placed in the context of their own personal best, not that of the class norm. (See, for example, Paulson, Paulson & Meyer 1991; Wolf 1989.) Students can be trained in the use of such metacognitive strategies as planning, monitoring and evaluating, which help them to control their own learning (see Chapter 4).

Communicating enthusiasm, warmth and humour

As an effective teacher you need to communicate genuine enthusiasm about what you are doing in the classroom, as well as be able to motivate your students. Enthusiasm is expressed in observable ways such as varied tones of voice, lively eyes that make frequent eye contact with students, use of gestures, and an energetic manner while moving around the room. Enthusiastic teachers show the emotions of surprise, joy and excitement in facial expressions and in voice.

No doubt, we have all experienced a teacher who droned on monotonously when explaining something (without humour or colourful examples), and who tended to stand or sit in one place throughout a lesson looking at one small group of students only. This

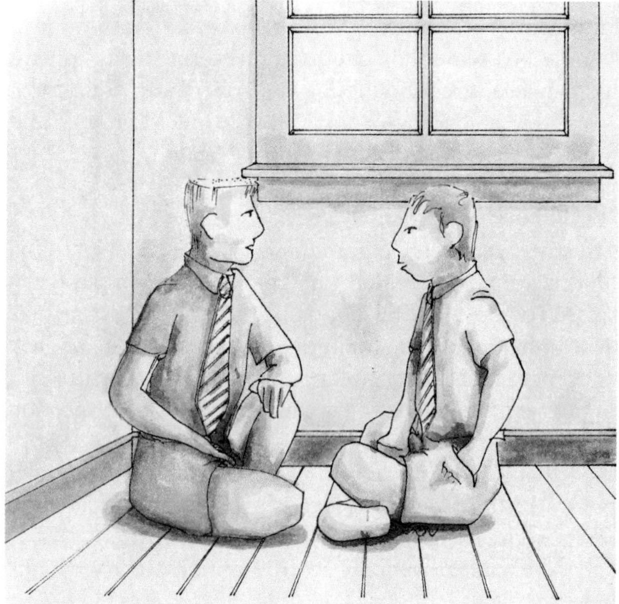

'Just say that your dog chewed it up ... I'm sure she's never heard that one before.'

teacher's classroom was a boring place and we didn't really look forward to being there, nor did we learn very much. Not surprisingly, research has shown that both student attitude and achievement are positively affected by teacher enthusiasm (Larkins et al. 1985; Rosenshine 1971). The attitudes that you model to your students will play a large part in determining their level of interest and enthusiasm. If you communicate lack of interest in the material—'Sorry, but I have to teach this topic. It's in the curriculum'—students are obviously not likely to be enthused either.

Training in enthusiasm-showing behaviours

Can one be trained to be enthusiastic? You may be saying at this point that your personality is not naturally enthusiastic; that you are a shy person. Larkins et al. (1985) showed that teachers can be trained successfully in 'enthusiasm-showing behaviours' (dynamic voice and manner; teaching techniques that create suspense and build interest) with the result that students rate their teachers and the teaching more favourably. Students may not necessarily gain higher scores on achievement tests, but the classroom learning climate is improved as a result of positive student attitudes. One qualification is needed here: keep the enthusiasm to a moderate level—excessive teacher enthusiasm may create discipline problems in the primary school grades where children need clear and consistent guidelines for appropriate behaviour (McKinney et al. 1983).

Extrinsic motivation: surface learning

Enthusiasm has a lot of bearing on what psychologists talk of as motivation (see Chapter 9). Children will go to school because they are pressured to by parents and school authorities, at least until a certain age, but such **extrinsic motivation** will encourage only superficial learning or, as Biggs (1991; Biggs & Moore 1993) calls it, a 'surface approach to learning' wherein the student focuses on gaining rewards or avoiding failure (for fear of punishment or loss of rewards). **Intrinsic motivation** is that in which students find the learning tasks genuinely interesting and relevant. The teacher's enthusiastic attitude and energy encourage a learning climate in which such interesting and personally meaningful tasks can flourish. The result is 'deep learning' (Biggs 1991) and a sense of purpose in classroom activities.

Intrinsic motivation: deep learning

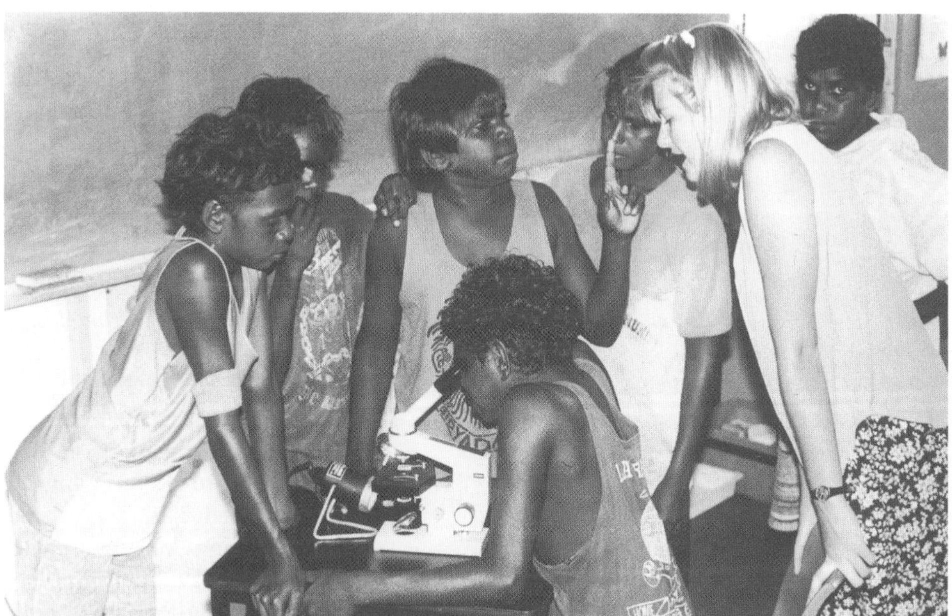

Good rapport is essential if we are to teach culturally different children effectively.
Photo: Mark F. Pearce

Warmth and humour

As with enthusiasm, warmth and humour are personal-style characteristics rather than teaching behaviours and are difficult, therefore, to define objectively. Nonetheless, research has shown that students whose teachers use humour (such as anecdotes and examples) retain more of the material they have been taught than those whose teachers use no humour (Kaplan & Pascoe 1977). Student attention and interest are improved through the use of humour, although the effects on effective learning are not as clear (Powell & Anderson 1985). As with enthusiasm, the use of humour can be learned, and is clearly related to positive student attitudes and classroom climate—important conditions for effective learning to take place. Take care, however, that humour is appropriate and in good taste (no jokes about cultural groups, for example) or your credibility will be lowered and the atmosphere soured. Excessively used, humour will reduce your ability to maintain classroom control.

What about warmth? It goes without saying that, for effective teachers, teaching is more than just a job that involves imparting information to students; these teachers care about children and genuinely like being with them. As would be expected, research in this area suggests that, in terms of influencing achievement, a friendly climate is preferable to one that is negative and critical. However, extreme friendliness such as the over-frequent use of praise is counterproductive. Rather, a more businesslike, or neutral, emotional climate is strongly correlated with increases in student learning, especially for primary aged children from middle and upper class backgrounds (Brophy & Good 1986; Kutnick & Jules 1993; Soar 1966; Soar & Soar 1979).

Question point: *Are positive teacher attitudes and enthusiasm more important at some grade levels than others? Why? Are they more important in some curriculum areas than others? Why?*

a

ACTION STATION

What makes an effective teacher? The answer isn't simple. Techniques and approaches that work well with one class and particular children may be quite ineffective with other classes and other children. Teacher personality and school dynamics (such as SES, cultural background, grade levels), among other factors, all influence how effective particular teachers are with particular students. There are, of course, some general principles that apply (such as being well organised and showing a personal interest in the children) but, in practice, effective teaching is a product of a very complex set of variables. A good place to start in understanding what makes effective teaching is to ask practitioners and children what they think. Therefore, while practice teaching:

1. *Discuss* with your supervising teachers what they think makes teaching effective and relate this to the material covered in your text.
2. *Discuss* with two or three students in your class what makes an effective teacher. You may need to phrase the question appropriately (e.g. What does a teacher do to help you learn? When do you enjoy learning? How do you know that you have learnt something?).
3. *Record* your findings and relate them to what the teacher and text suggest are important elements of effective teaching.

Consult your tutor/lecturer for advice on how to conduct these interviews so that you are sensitive to the classroom teacher and students concerned.

Teaching is a dynamic career. Making your lessons relevant to students from diverse backgrounds is a great challenge.
Photo: authors

THE CRAFT AND ART OF TEACHING

As we have indicated, effective teaching involves the use of a complex set of skills to evoke effective learning—skills such as lesson design and implementation, assessment and evaluation, questioning and motivating. However, effective teaching is not simply the ability to apply techniques and skills, but also involves the art of being reflective—thoughtful and inventive—about teaching. Peterson (1988, pp. 5–6) highlighted the importance of this for both the teacher and the student:

The thoughtful professional is engaged continuously in the process of learning. Not only is the thoughtful professional teacher engaged in 'learning to learn' and in 'higher-order learning' but she or he also inspires and facilitates this kind of higher-order learning in students. Second, the above image of the thoughtful professional defines the teacher in terms of the kind and quality of decisionmaking, thinking, and judgment in which the teacher engages, not just in terms of his or her behavioural competencies. Thus, teachers' thoughts, cognitions, judgment, thinking, and learning processes become important dimensions in studying the teacher and teaching and in determining what constitutes 'effective teaching'. Finally, the above image of the teacher suggests that teachers' thoughts, knowledge, judgments, and decisions will have a profound effect on the way teachers teach as well as on the way students learn and achieve in their classrooms. Thus, students' thoughts and cognitions are important determinants of students' achievement in the classroom.

Stages of development: novice to expert teacher

A number of theorists have attempted to describe the 'stages' of professional development as a teacher from novice to expert (Ingvarson & Greenway 1984). A knowledge of 'stages' may give you a framework for analysing your own professional development.

Three models that have been developed are those of Fuller (Fuller 1969; Fuller & Brown 1975), Berliner (1986, 1988) and Reynolds (1992). In the Fuller model there are four stages. In the first, preteaching stage, individuals tend to identify realistically with pupils, but unrealistically with teachers. They really don't understand the dynamics of teaching. In the second stage they are most concerned with survival and, in particular, class control, content mastery and personal adequacy as a teacher. In the third stage, teachers are concerned with the limitations and frustrations of teaching situations, while in the last stage, they become concerned with pupil needs (social, academic and emotional) and their ability to relate to the pupils as individuals. The model is seen as hierarchical and focuses attention on the evolution of the teacher from egocentric to pupil-centred concerns.

In Berliner's model, teachers move from the stage of novice, where the beginning teacher is consciously learning the tasks of teaching and developing strategies, through to the proficient and expert teacher, where intuition and knowledge guide classroom performance. In these latter stages, teachers operate on 'automatic pilot' without consciously being aware of what they are doing or why. Indeed, when asked to explain or reflect on their performance, expert teachers are likely to have trouble describing the processes engaged in.

Reynolds (1992), in distinguishing between competent, experienced and beginning teachers, discusses the differences on three levels. First, experienced teachers comprehend, critique and adapt content, materials and teaching methods more effectively, and prepare plans, materials and physical space more appropriately. Reynolds terms these **preactive tasks**. Second, experienced teachers are more competent at implementing and adjusting plans during the instructional period, and at organising and monitoring students, time and materials during instruction, and evaluating the students' learning. This is referred to as skill with the **interactive tasks** of teaching. Last, on **postactive tasks**, experienced teachers reflect on their own activities and student responses in order to improve teaching, continue professional development and interact with colleagues more effectively than beginning teachers.

Preactive tasks

Interactive tasks

Postactive tasks

Referring to these three models, the beginning teacher may appreciate that teaching is pre-eminently perceived as a developmental career. No beginning teacher is expected to have an expert's control of the teaching process. Nevertheless, beginning teachers can be quite competent in their own right and indeed, in many cases, can facilitate learning among children more effectively than some veterans.

Consider the following case study of a beginning teacher, and discuss her development in terms of issues covered in this chapter.

TEACHER'S CASE BOOK

CAN I FULFIL THE EXPECTATIONS OF ME AS A TEACHER?

Miss Fraser can remember how totally inadequate she felt on her first day of teaching. She wasn't sure how she was going to cope. She was feeling unsure about what was expected of her in the school as a beginning teacher. She felt that everyone had high expectations of her as a person and as a teacher.

Planning was a major problem: it ate up massive chunks of her time because she felt she was under scrutiny. Her first planning meeting with a senior staff member was absolutely terrifying, not because of the senior member of staff, who was really supportive, but because Miss Fraser still wasn't sure of the expectations.

Miss Fraser desperately wanted approval and this she received. Until that happened she was experiencing a great deal of doubt in her ability as a teacher. That feedback was incredibly important. It was a turning point in her first term of teaching. After that initial planning meeting, she felt greater confidence in herself as a teacher and was much more relaxed and really able to enjoy what she was doing.

Miss Fraser felt underprepared leaving uni and realised the importance of drawing on the experience and resources of more experienced teachers within the school. She needed the security of a set curriculum to follow, so that she knew she was on the right track. As the year passed and Miss Fraser has grown in confidence, she feels the need for this less and less and is a great deal more flexible and adaptable than she felt she could be at the start of the year.

The amount of planning she is doing now has been reduced a great deal. She used to write down everything and stick to it at all costs but now she feels more able to justify what she does, why she's doing it and for which children. With the help and support she has received from senior staff she now feels comfortable and confident about her planning and is able to concentrate on her teaching and the children's learning.

Case study illustrating National Competency Framework for Beginning Teaching, National Project on the Quality of Teaching and Learning, Australian Teaching Council, 1996, p.31–32. Commonwealth of Australia copyright, reproduced by permission.

***Question point:** Discuss the characteristics of two or three of the best teachers that you have come into contact with. Analyse their characteristics in terms of the points covered in this chapter.*

ACTION STATION

Interview two teachers, one who has been teaching more than ten years, and one who has begun teaching relatively recently (up to five years), about their teaching concerns. Pool your information with the rest of your class. Are there any patterns characterising the responses? Are there differences between the older and newer teachers' concerns?

BOX 1.2 TEACHING COMPETENCE

The teacher critically reflects on his/her own practice and develops professional skills and capacity to improve the quality of teaching and learning

Indicators

The teacher:

- evaluates teaching and learning programs;
- keeps a record of selected experiences/incidents;
- reflects on successes and areas for improvement in teaching;
- monitors the outcomes of teaching and learning;
- involves colleagues in planning to improve teaching and learning;
- acts to extend his or her repertoire of skills and capacities;
- participates in voluntary activities such as those provided by professonal associations and teacher unions;
- undertakes further training, development and professional reading.

Case studies illustrating National Competency Framework for Beginning Teaching, National Project on the Quality of Teaching and Learning, Australian Teaching Council, 1996, Elements, 5.1 and 5.4, p.61 and 64. Commonwealth of Australia copyright, reproduced by permission.

Question point: The teacher of tomorrow will no longer be the knowledgeable classroom authority on everything but rather a flexible improviser and team player. What is your opinion?

You—the reflective teacher

Throughout this book, we hope that you not only learn about the way in which children construct their understanding of the world around them as motivated thinkers and learners, but also that you take the time to reflect upon yourself, as a learner and thinker. Increasingly, teaching is being looked upon, not as the end point of some training course, but rather as a lifelong process which includes continual learning, critical reflection and growth. With a deeper understanding of your own learning, you will be in a better position to assist students to learn (e.g. see Clark 1988; Floden & Klinzing 1990; Henderson 1992; Hewitson, McWilliam & Burke 1991; Koop & Koop 1990; Lampert & Clark 1990; Laskey & Hallinan 1990; Peacock & Yaxley 1990; Peterson 1988).

Your reflections will call into play your background experiences as a learner (both as a child and now as a university student, in both formal and informal settings), the ideas and theories presented to you by others, and the constant flow of information and judgments from classroom experiences and other sources. Many of these will be considered in this text, and through our coverage we hope to help you construct increasingly valid and accurate personal theories of teaching and learning.

Recommended reading

Anderson, L. W. (ed.) (1989) *The Effective Teacher. Study Guide and Readings*. New York: McGraw-Hill.

Biggs, J. B. (1991) (ed.) *Teaching for Learning. The View from Cognitive Psychology*. Hawthorn, Vic. ACER.

Brookhart, S. M. & Freeman, D. J. (1992) Characteristics of entering teacher candidates. *Review of Educational Research*, 62, 37–60.

Cobb, P. (1994) Constructivism in mathematics and science education. *Educational Researcher*, 23, 4.

Cobb, P. (1994) Where is the mind? Constructivist and sociocultural perspectives on mathematical development. *Educational Researcher*, 23, 13–20.

Hendry, G.D. (1996) Constructivism and educational practice. *Australian Journal of Education*, 40, 19–45.

Nuthall, G. & Alton-Lee, A. (1990) Research on teaching and learning: Thirty years of change. *The Elementary School Journal*, 90, 547–70.

Phillips, D.C. (1995) The good, the bad, and the ugly. The many faces of constructivism. *Educational Researcher*, 24, 5–12.

Porter, A. C. & Brophy, J. (1988) Synthesis of research on good teaching: Insights from the work of the Institute for Research on Teaching. *Educational Leadership*, 45, 74–85.

Reynolds, A. (1992) What is competent beginning teaching? A review of the literature. *Review of Educational Research*, 62, 1–35.

Von Glaserfeld, E. (1995) *Radical Constructivism: A Way of Knowing and Learning*. London: Falmer Press.

Wragg, E. C. (1995) Lesson structure. In L. W. Anderson (ed.), *International Encyclopedia of Teaching and Teacher Education*, 2nd edn. New York: Pergamon: 207–11.

CHAPTER 2

Developmental perspectives on cognition and effective learning

OVERVIEW

Our three-year-old daughter, Laura, was staring mesmerised at a bug flying around our living room light when she spontaneously said, 'It's clever to fly. I wish I could fly, but I can't.' On another occasion, while watching her father hack away at the jungle we call a back yard, Laura asked, 'Are we at the bottom of the sky?' As a much more grown-up eight-year-old she amazed her father with: 'Can I ask you a question that has been bothering me for a long time?' I was unprepared for the question: 'Why am I here? What's the purpose of me being born?'

Young children are forever learning about the world around them. Concepts such as number, time, weight, measurement, space and existence are the everyday subjects being mastered by children through their world of experiences. As children grow older they develop more mature cognitive processes which enable them to adapt increasingly efficiently to the world around them.

In this chapter we consider two important, and contrasting, views on this cognitive development, those of Jean Piaget and Lev Vygotsky. Each believes that learning is an intentional process of constructing meaning from experience, but the means by which this knowledge construction occurs is considered differently. Three questions are raised in this chapter:

1. What is the best way to characterise children's intellectual functioning at various key points in their growth?
2. What is the best way to characterise the process by which children progress from one of these points to the next?
3. How can the developmental process be optimised?

Our first focus is on Piaget's theory of intellectual development. The first concept dealt with is structuralism which relates to Piaget's notion that cognitive growth occurs through a series of stages: sensorimotor, preoperational, concrete-operational and formal, each characterised by qualitatively different cognitive structures. The second concept discussed is personal constructivism which relates to Piaget's notion that individuals construct their own meanings through the interacting processes of assimilation, adaptation, accommodation and equilibrium, and the extension of schema, or ways of thinking.

Piaget's theory is quite complex, so we have selected elements that we believe have applied significance for educators. We discuss the current status of Piaget's theory and indicate that there is presently a de-emphasis on the structuralist components and an emphasis on the constructivist components. Important cross-cultural implications of Piaget's theory are also highlighted.

Our second focus examines Vygotskian theory, which presents a contrast to Piagetian theory. While Vygotsky emphasises the active role played by the learner in constructing meaning, he focuses on the role of social factors within the external environment. In particular, his theory of social constructivism stresses the interplay between a supportive learning environment, represented by parents, teachers and peers, and the individual's internal manipulation of information to facilitate meaningful learning. Key elements of Vygotsky's theory, such as the zone of proximal development, holistic education and mediated learning through social interaction, are considered.

Contrasts are drawn between Piaget and Vygotsky regarding the nature and function of discovery in learning, the role of social interaction in learning and the relationship between language and learning.

LEARNER-CENTRED PSYCHOLOGICAL PRINCIPLE 1

The learning of complex subject matter is most effective when it is an intentional process of constructing meaning from information and experience.

Students have a natural inclination to learn and pursue personally relevant goals. They are capable of assuming personal responsibility for learning—monitoring, checking for understanding, and becoming active, self-directed learners—in an environment that takes past learning into account, ties new learning to personal goals, and actively engages individuals in their own learning process. In meaningful life situations, even very young children naturally engage in self-directed learning activities to pursue personal goals. During the learning process, individuals create and construct their own meanings and interpretations, often in interaction with others, on the basis of previously existing understandings and beliefs.

Reprinted with permission APA Task Force on Psychology in Education (1993, January), p.6.

PIAGET'S THEORY OF COGNITIVE DEVELOPMENT

Structuralism and constructivism

The theory of psychologist Jean Piaget (1896–1980) has had a profound impact on the way that teachers and other professionals think about cognitive development and learning. His theory has dual and complementary perspectives which may be termed **structuralism** and **constructivism** (Cellerier 1987; Inhelder & de Caprona 1987). First, Piaget postulated that intellectual development occurs through a series of stages characterised by qualitatively discrete cognitive structures (what we call structuralism). Second, Piaget argued that children construct their own understanding through interaction with their environment—that is, through their actions on objects in the world (what we call constructivism). In effect, Piaget viewed the child as a young scientist, constructing ever more powerful theories of the world, as a result of applying a set of logical structures in increasing generality and power (Case 1992). While the structuralist aspects of his theory are having less impact on educational practice today, the constructivist aspects are strongly influencing current practice.

Assimilation and accommodation

Piaget's theory is complex. Our description of the structuralist elements highlights some important aspects, but is also simplified. (More detailed treatments may be found in Forman 1980; Ginsburg & Opper 1988; Wadsworth 1989.) As a biologist, Piaget was impressed with the way in which all species systematise and organise their processes into coherent biological systems and are able to **adapt**, as necessary, to the environment through processes such as **assimilation** and **accommodation**. He brought his eye as a biologist to the task of explaining the development of cognitive processes in children, and introduced a conceptualisation (which sometimes intimidates the uninitiated) derived from the language of biology. Piaget compared the process by which children construct understanding of their world to that used by natural organisms adapting to changes in their environment. He maintained that the growth of intelligence is regulated by the same processes that determine the growth of morphology and changes in the physiology of all living systems (Forman 1980).

Biological model of cognitive development

While working with the Binet Laboratory, Piaget was given the task of standardising a French version of a number of English reasoning tests. However, Piaget noted that there was a regularity in the way children *misanswered* questions, and decided that it was far more important to discover how each child reasoned out an answer, especially when the answer was wrong, than it was to establish norms for correct answers (Forman 1980; Ginsburg & Opper 1988). Furthermore, he became interested in how children learn to correct certain errors in their thinking. Through close examination of his own three children, Piaget plotted the course of cognitive development, much of it relating to the children's answers to questions about their environment. He noted how the structure of these answers changed over a period of years.

Piaget believed that infants have relatively few functioning cognitive systems (e.g. reflexes and some rudimentary thought processes) for handling the world of experiences, but great potential to develop increasingly complex means of internally organising their own cognitive structure in interaction with the external world. The infant is believed to be an active agent whose mind reconstructs and reinterprets the environment to make it fit in with its own existing mental framework (Flavell 1985). These ways of dealing with experiences Piaget termed **schemes**, and the schemes are organised as cognitive structure. As novel experiences occur, such as learning to drink juice rather than milk from a teat, for example, the child adapts by relating this new experience to familiar ones (i.e. juice is different, yet similar to milk). This process is called **assimilation**. At times, however, the novel experience requires a more radical adaptation on the part of the child to cope with something quite new; for example, when the child learns to drink from a cup rather than from a teat. This process is called **accommodation**. This, in effect, leads to the development of a new scheme for drinking into which various new drinking vessels can be assimilated. The period of adjustment is called a period of **cognitive conflict** and successful adaptation leads to what is termed **equilibrium**, that is, a state of psychological and biological peace. The tension that exists between the demands of accommodation and assimilation, when the child adapts to or learns about novel situations, is the power that impels the child to develop new understandings and a new equilibrium (Flavell 1985; McNally 1977). No doubt, you too can think of ways in which you still learn about the world by these mutual processes of assimilation and accommodation.

Schemes
Organisation
Assimilation
Adaptation
Accommodation
Equilibration

For Piaget, therefore, cognitive development involves an interaction between assimilating new facts to old knowledge and accommodating old knowledge to new facts and the maintenance of structural equilibration (Halford 1989). Furthermore, as children mature, they develop a series of operations or thought processes that become increasingly able to handle inferential thinking. While the young infant is limited to thinking about problems and experiences in concrete terms (termed **figurative knowledge**), the adolescent is capable of thinking about problems using more sophisticated operational schemes (**operative knowledge**).

Operations: figurative knowledge, operative knowledge

Operations and their groupings are the main object of Piaget's developmental approach to concept formation. On the basis of his many experimental observations and clinical interviews with children of all ages, Piaget postulated that there are four main stages in cognitive development through which the vast majority of children pass.

PIAGET'S STAGES OF INTELLECTUAL DEVELOPMENT

The four main stages of cognitive development in children, and their approximate age span are:

1. sensorimotor stage (birth to 2 years)
2. preoperational stage (2–7 years)
3. concrete-operational stage (7–12 years)
4. formal-operational (12 to adult)

Piaget believed that in each of these stages there is a characteristic way in which children think about the world and solve problems. We must warn here that these age limits are only guidelines and there are many inconsistencies. At each stage, children develop increasingly sophisticated mental processes, leading to the acquisition of fully logical cognitive operations. While later researchers have confirmed the sequence of stages as Piaget described them, there is sufficient evidence to show that Piaget underestimated the degree of competence and organisation of very young children's thinking.

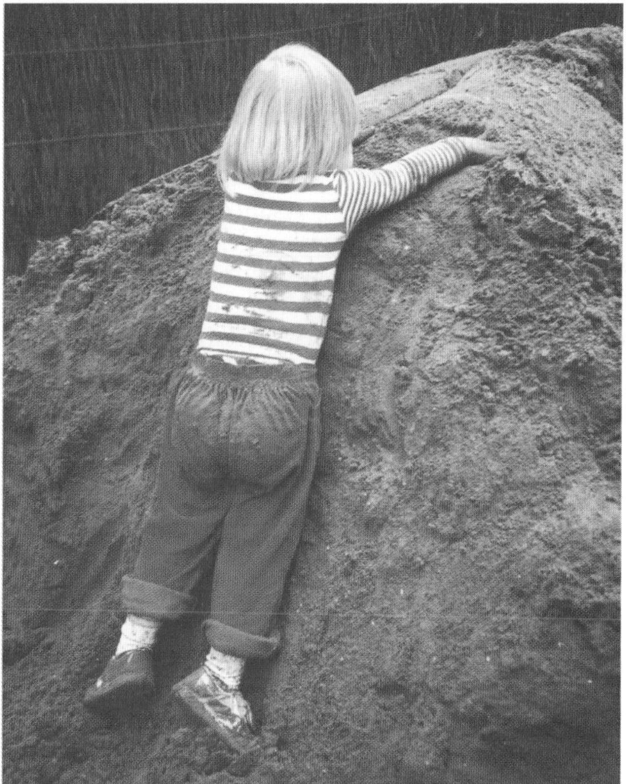

Concrete experiences are essential for young children.
Photo: authors

Sensorimotor stage

Piaget believed that during the first two years of life children learn about the world primarily through motor activity. By gradually reorganising their sensorimotor actions, infants construct a basic understanding of their environment (Bidell & Fischer 1992). Through grasping, sucking, looking, throwing, and generally moving themselves and objects about, children begin to recognise an identity separate from their surrounding world and learn about the permanence of objects and certain regularities in the physical world. They develop an elementary understanding of causality, shape and size constancy. By two years of age, children can solve most sensorimotor problems; for example, they can obtain desired objects, use objects in combination, and mentally 'invent' means that will permit them to do the things they want. In Piagetian terms, children by two years of age have acquired a much larger and more sophisticated set of cognitive schemes than at birth as a result of sensorimotor interaction with the environment and, in particular, the ongoing processes of assimilation and accommodation which enable children to handle the world more effectively.

Representational thinking, which is the basis for anticipating actions mentally, is the outcome of sensorimotor constructions (Bidell & Fischer 1992). By gradually reorganising their sensorimotor actions, infants construct a basic understanding of the permanence of objects in space and a rudimentary ability to represent people and objects not immediately present.

Representational thinking: basis for anticipating actions mentally.

Preoperational stage

During the preoperational period, between about two and seven years, children begin to know things not only through their physical actions but symbolically as well. Naturally, with the acquisition of language there is a great leap forward in the ability of children to reason about the world around them and to solve problems. Symbolic games (such as talking on the toy telephone, or pretending to be imaginary characters) serve an important role in the development of children's intellectual abilities.

Nevertheless, according to Piaget, children at this stage do not use logical operations to solve problems or interpret experiences in the physical world, hence the term preoperational. Preoperations are internalised actions that have not yet been integrated into complete systems and as such are not yet true operations.

In a number of his books (Piaget 1954, 1971, 1974; see also Elkind 1974) Piaget describes some features of young children's mental characteristics that give rise to their 'cute' expressions and behaviours. For example, young children have a tendency to project their anger or fear impulses onto inanimate objects. Having hurt herself by running into a chair, or slipping down some stairs, our daughter Laura was often heard saying 'Naughty chair!' or 'Silly stairs'. Such attribution of lifelike qualities to inanimate objects has been termed **physiognomic perception**. We are not convinced that it disappears as individuals grow older. The author has been heard to mutter 'Blasted hammer!' after hitting his finger, and it is amazing how many students kick and swear at the computer for 'bombs' which may be directly attributable to their own inadequacies.

Physiognomic perception: attributing lifelike qualities to inanimate objects

Young children also show a strong tendency to regard events that happen together as having caused one another, for example, children often think that raising the blind brings out the sun, or that rain comes to stop them going out to play. This type of thinking is labelled **phenomenalistic causality**. Adults often inadvertently reinforce the development of this form of thinking when, for example, they say 'The sun has gone to sleep so it is time for bed'. Another aspect of preoperational thinking is the young child's ready belief in magic and ritual which is tied in with phenomenalistic causality. For young children it is perfectly reasonable that magic things can happen. As children grow older and gain a stronger grasp of causality they begin to debunk magic—or at least try to understand the underlying processes involved in it.

Phenomenalistic causality: regarding things happening together as causally related

As with physiognomic perception, this characteristic does not disappear entirely as the child gets older, and accounts for the superstition we observe in older children and adults. For example, do you have any preparation rituals for exams? We know students who get particularly unsettled if they don't have their favourite pen for an exam or are prevented from sitting in a favourite position.

Young children also invest words and language with a power far beyond that allowed by the arbitrariness of language. This characteristic is termed **nominal realism**. For example, names of things are often sacrosanct and the quality of the object (e.g. heat or light) is thought to reside intrinsically in the name of the object, such as sun or moon. Because of this, very young children won't rename objects. Furthermore, words are very powerful. A child hates to be called stupid, because being called stupid may make one stupid.

Nominal realism: the power of words

The development of children's cognitive abilities is reflected in the growth of their powers of perception, language, reasoning and problem-solving abilities. Children's perception becomes increasingly freed from the limits of the physical appearance of objects and takes into account a range of aspects of objects, integrating this information into a more holistic understanding. Because attention becomes less centred on perceptual clues, and children are able to reorganise and integrate information coming from a range of sources, they become more flexible thinkers.

Development of powers of perception, language, reasoning and problem solving

Let us look closely at the function of perception as a vital force behind the nurturance of accurate concept development, which enables children to detect and interpret relevant environmental information.

Our daughter, Laura, was looking at the sky when she spotted a plane. 'There's a little plane,' she exclaimed. We explained to her that it was actually a jumbo jet, but a long way away. The idea that an object is the same size whether it is far away or close, and that shapes are constant no matter from what perspective they are viewed, develops with time. Many early preschool and kindergarten activities, such as stacking objects, labelling positions, looking at things from different angles and so on, are designed to develop perceptual concepts such as 'big' and 'small', 'close' and 'far'. Understanding **spatial relationships** is especially important for a child's accurate interpretation of the environment. So concepts such as left and right, short and long, near and far, are developed through appropriate experiences.

Developing spatial relationships

Classifying objects into sets

Classifying objects into sets appears to be very difficult for young children. They also experience difficulties in understanding the relationship that exists between subclasses and classes. For example, if we present children with four red plastic flowers and two blue plastic flowers and ask them to tell us whether there are more red or more blue plastic flowers, they answer the question easily. However, there is confusion between wholes and parts if we ask them whether there are more red or more plastic flowers. Often children will answer that there are more red flowers. As children grow older they classify classes and subclasses effectively.

Preschool children frequently seem to make quantity judgments on the basis of perception alone; they appear to be unable to make accurate quantity discriminations logically, independent of misleading perceptual cues. Children will fight over the larger glass of cordial because it appears larger, or the other is only half-full (despite the fact that this glass is twice the size of the other glass). Maybe a residue of this way of thinking remains with adults. If we want our mother to think she is being fed a lot when she visits we put the food on a relatively small plate. If she complains that we give her

Perception and judgments of quantity

too much to eat we put the same amount of food on a large plate. Advertisers also make use of this technique with their deceptive packaging of material so that it looks as if buyers are getting more than they actually are. As clever shoppers we all know that we must take careful notice of the perceptual cues given to us by packaging, and discount much of the visual information. Because of the power of visual cues, and the fact that there is quite a subjective element in interpreting them (e.g. when a man wears a slightly shrunken shirt everyone asks whether he is putting on weight; when he wears an oversize shirt everyone comments on how thin he looks), concepts such as larger, smaller, less, few, some and many are frequently bewildering for young children. As they grow older, however, they become quite adept at using these concepts in many different ways and contexts.

There is usually a significant gap between preschoolers' counting abilities and their ability to understand conceptually what is being counted. Abstract concepts of measurement, simple addition and fractional amounts develop with time. When mathematical processes are couched in real examples, such as dividing lollies among children, preschoolers show a surprising command of counting principles. Gelman (cited in Flavell 1985) distinguishes between young children's number abstraction and their numerical reasoning principles. Prominent among the number abstraction abilities is the preschooler's developing command of five **counting principles**:

1. Assign one and only one number name to each and every item to be counted (one–one principle).
2. When counting, always recite the numbers in the same order (stable order principle).
3. The final number uttered at the end of a counting sequence denotes the total number of items counted (combinatorial principle).
4. Any sort of entity may be counted (abstraction principle).
5. It does not matter in what order you enumerate the objects (order–irrelevance principle).

One of the numerical reasoning principles that children acquire is the number conservation rule—that merely spreading out a set of objects does not change the number of objects in the set.

Time concepts: past, present and future

Children in the early years of preschool and school also have an undeveloped sense of time. They ask many time-related questions such as 'Is it morning now?', 'When will it be tomorrow?', 'Is it Wednesday or Saturday?' and so on, indicating an interest in time. By four years old, many children measure out their week in days at preschool, days with grandma, days with mum and dad, and weekends, and have a developing sense of time. Young children also have a limited grasp of the past and the future. However, as they get older, they have a growing interest in the concepts of past and future and a growing control of the elements of time. Obviously, concepts of history and the future develop slowly, which has implications for the introduction of historical and other time-related studies into the school curricula. An interesting discussion of the development of time, space and number concepts is also found in Siegler (1991) where some alternative findings and explanations are given.

Water play helps children develop quantity concepts. What other play activities may be helpful in developing shape, size and class concepts? Photo: authors

Importance of language to cognitive development While Piaget emphasised the limited nature of young children's cognitive abilities relative to older children and adults, we would rather draw your attention to the astounding growth that takes place from birth through the early school years in children's concepts of space, number, time and quantity. Furthermore, children acquire increasing ability to solve problems in a systematic way by using processes of discrimination and coordination of concepts and generalisations and, most importantly, by beginning to work through problems in their heads rather than with physical objects. Language is central to this development, and children's growing command of language is at once a part of, and a sign of, the development of mental capacities. For many theorists, language enables the developing child to explore the world of thoughts, and acts as a mediating process for the analysis of information received through the senses.

How do we distinguish preoperational thinking from later levels? The usual method for distinguishing preoperational thinking from later levels is by 'testing' children on a number of problems that require logical thought and on the operations discussed earlier in the chapter (Cowan 1978; Ginsburg & Opper 1988; Wadsworth 1989). Basically, preoperational children are unable to conserve and make deductive inferences. The following 'tests' illustrate characteristic elements in the preoperational child's thinking. After observing one of two equal lumps of clay being squashed, the preoperational child will typically suggest that one lump will have more or less clay than the other in terms of the physical appearance of the two lumps. After witnessing one of two jars of water of equal quantity being poured into a third jar of different size, the child will typically suggest that the amount of water in the new jar (usually a flat, shallow container) contains less than the water in the other full jar. If confronted with two equal pencils next to each other on a table, with one point protruding past the end of the other pencil, the child will typically argue that one or other of the pencils is longer; when asked to count two equal rows of coins, one spread out more than the other, the child will typically say that one row has more coins than the other despite having 'accurately' counted the two rows, and, indeed, even having seen the two rows of coins lined up equally. (See the figure on the next page for an outline of some Piagetian tests.)

Tests of conservation

In each of these cases the preoperational child appears to be illustrating a preoccupation with the visual perception. This is called **centration** when only one feature of the problem is attended to. Furthermore, the child does not appear to attend to the **transformation** from one state to another; for example, not understanding that, in pouring the water from one container to another, the quantity of water hasn't been altered, although the final state may appear different. A simple demonstration of this is to ask a child to draw the successive points through which a vertical pencil will move to assume the horizontal position: the preoperational child cannot effectively do this. Piaget believes these experiments demonstrate the child's inability to **reverse thinking**, that is, to mentally reverse the operation witnessed to realise that there has been no change in substance, only appearance. Compounding this limited ability of preoperational children to perceive several dimensions of a problem at once is the child's **egocentricity**, whereby children are blithely unaware that anyone would hold a perspective different from their own. It is worth noting here that such 'egocentrism' is meant in relation to cognition and does not imply that the young child is selfish or ungenerous.

Centration: preoccupation with visual perception

Transformation: attending to changes in states

Reverse thinking: mentally reversing operations

Egocentricity: assuming others experience the world as we do

According to Piaget the characteristics of preoperational thought described above function as obstacles to logical thinking in an adult sense, and derive from limitations in the ability to understand conservation. **Conservation** is the conceptualisation that the amount or quantity of particular matter stays the same regardless of any changes in shape or position of the matter. Researchers have been particularly interested in when children acquire the capacity to conserve, and whether this is consistent across a number of domains such as number, area and volume. There does appear to be a sequence, with the conservation of number, substance, area, weight and volume being achieved in that order.

Conservation: characteristics of an object remain the same despite changes in appearance

ACTION STATION

This activity is designed to give you some insight into a young child's conception of the world.

Select three children of four, five and six years old. Give the following instructions to each child separately:

'We are going to play a game. I am going to ask some questions and I'd like you to tell me what you think. What do you think it means to be alive? Is a cat alive? Why? Tell me something else that's alive. How do you know it's alive (or not alive)?'

Repeat this, substituting for 'cat' each object on the list below. Show the child the first five objects if possible. Record verbatim the answers given by the children. Summarise the reasons given by each child for each object. Are there any common patterns? Any distinct differences? What conclusions can you draw about young children's thinking?

stone	chipped	tree	fire
pencil	cup	sun	dog
broken	bike	wind	grass
button	river	car	bug
watch	clouds	bird	flower

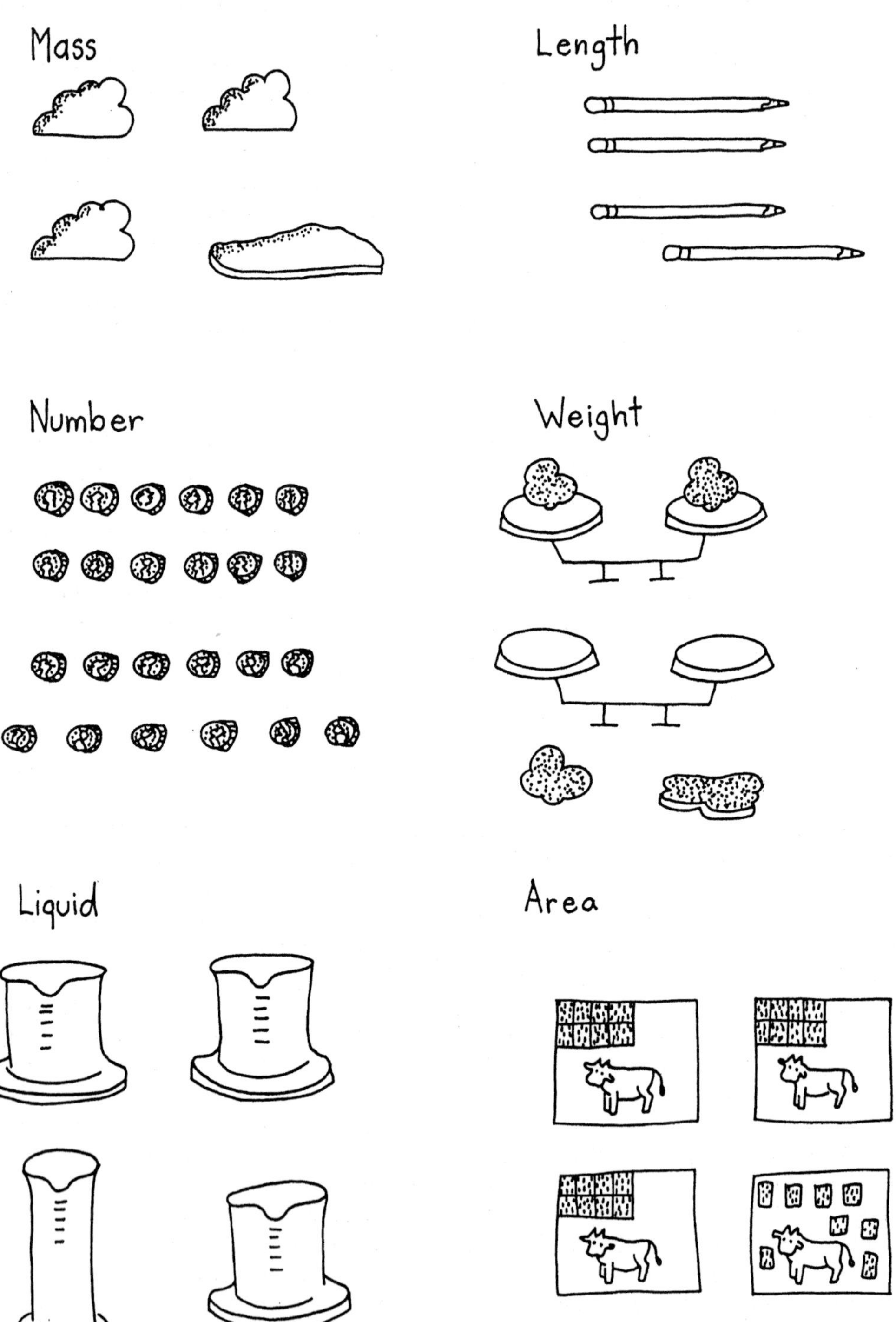
Piagetian Conservation Tasks
Mass
Length
Number
Weight
Liquid
Area

Concrete-operational stage

While preoperational children's thinking appears to be characterised by centring on one perceptual aspect of a stimulus, concrete-operational children seem to take into account all salient features of the stimulus, and thought becomes decentred. In contrast to the preoperational child, the concrete-operational child can attend to successive stages in the transformation of an object from one state to another, and mentally reverse the operations that produce an outcome. One good example of the ability to reverse thought is shown by an experiment with three different coloured balls and a non-transparent tube. The balls are put into the tube in the order red, blue, green, and the child is asked to indicate the order in which they will come out the other side. The child predicts correctly red, blue, green. On the next test the balls are added in the same order, but the tube is rotated through 180°. Again the child is asked to predict the order in which the balls will come out. A preoperational child predicts the order red, blue, green, while a concrete child predicts the right order, green, blue, red. Why?

For Piaget the clearest indication that children have reached the concrete level of reasoning is the presence of conservation. When asked whether the two lumps of clay mentioned earlier are the same or different, concrete-operational children will quickly respond 'the same'. When asked why, children might answer with a range of logical reasons: **invariance, compensation** or **reversibility**. For example, they might answer 'You didn't add anything or take anything away, you simply changed the shape' (invariant quantity) or 'While the pancake is thinner than the ball it is also wider' (compensation) or 'See, I can roll it back up into a ball again' (reversibility). In fact, older children become irritated when you ask them the reason for their answer—'It's so obvious!' they say. Preoperational characteristics of children's thinking disappear as they acquire a firm grasp of physical causality.

Aspects of conservation: invariance, compensation and reversibility

Among other logical operations achieved during the period of concrete operations is the ability to organise the elements of a series in either ascending or descending order of size, called **seriation,** and the ability to construct classes and subclasses of objects, called **classification**.

Seriation: organising elements by size
classification: constructing classes of objects

It is obvious, therefore, that concrete-operational children are capable of using a variety of logical operations to reason about the world, and to solve problems; however, these operations are restricted to concrete experiences. In other words, the content of the operations are real, not hypothetical, objects or situations.

PLAY AND COGNITIVE DEVELOPMENT

Before looking at play from a Piagetian perspective, we need to define what is meant by **play**. For behaviour to be defined as 'play', a number of qualities need to be evident in combination. The behaviour will:

- be intrinsically motivated, that is, spontaneous and self-initiated;
- be relatively free from externally imposed rules; if there are rules, they are imposed by the players, not by adults;
- be carried out as if the activity were 'for real'; by the use of pretence, children are demonstrating the ability to distinguish reality from fantasy;
- focus on the process of playing, rather than on any product produced;
- be dominated by the players;
- require the players to be actively (mentally or physically) involved.

(Dockett & Lambert 1996; Rogers & Sawyers 1988)

In relation to cognitive development, Piaget described three types of play: practice play, symbolic play and games with rules. The first of these, **practice play**, relates to the sensorimotor stage of development after about six months of age, and describes the intentional repetition of particular actions and use of objects by infants in their exploration of their immediate world of physical objects. For instance, anyone who has had the opportunity to observe an infant over a period of time would notice the rapid transition from initially random movements such as arm waving, which might have caused a toy suspended over head to swing, to progressively more deliberate efforts to recreate this interesting experience.

Practice play: use of objects to explore the world

Symbolic play begins to emerge as the infant's ability to use mental representations of objects and events develops, especially the ability to imitate, both while the model is present and at a later time. Piaget describes an example of deferred imitation when his daughter of about 16 months exhibited a temper tantrum in her playpen one afternoon, identical in vocalisations and mannerisms to that performed in front of her by a child the same age on the previous day. Symbolic play—which includes pretending, fantasy and sociodramatic play (when two or more children are involved in playing imaginary roles together)—is characteristic of preoperational children and begins at two or three years, continuing until about six or seven years.

Symbolic play: using mental representation of objects to imitate the real world

At the end of the preoperational stage, children begin to show less interest in games of pretence, and engage frequently in **games with prescribed rules** such as hide-and-seek, hand clapping, marbles or board games. This development follows the shift from preoperational to concrete-operational thinking or an extension of constructive and sensorimotor activities with the added element of externally defined rules (Smilansky 1990). Constructive play emerges out of sensorimotor activities when the child has begun to form symbolic representations of experiences and objects: What appears, therefore, as 'playing with blocks' will be represented mentally by the child in constructive play as 'building a house'.

Games with rules

How do children construct knowledge through play? Children's play is full of physical and social activity, conversation and pictures, both real and imaginary. These are the essential elements through which they construct their cognitive, social and emotional worlds. The role of the carer–educator requires a recognition that it is through play, rather than structured activities in which children receive information about the world and directives on how to behave, that young children learn. Good teachers provide rich opportunities for play with plentiful resources, and time without adult interruption unless there is need to refocus because of potentially disruptive behaviour (Jones & Reynolds 1992).

What is the role of the adult in children's play? During practice play, exploration of the self, others and the immediate world is what absorbs the young child. For the adult–carer to support this exploration, an environment with a wide range of sensorimotor experiences and modelling of oral language is necessary, along with protection from the physical danger that exploration can bring.

At the stage of symbolic play, the sensitive teacher understands that children come to 'know' by doing; personal experiences and spontaneous actions teach them about the world and about others. The important role for the teacher here is to provide the **tools and symbols** for repre-

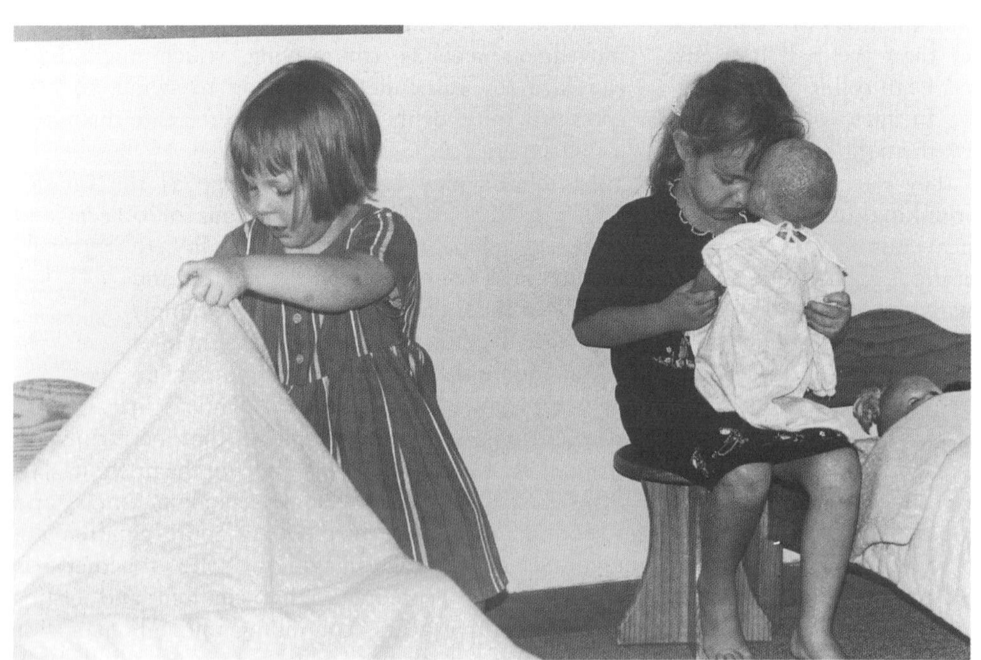

How does make-believe play help children learn about their world? Photos: authors

senting personal reconstructions of experience: models of language (spoken and written) to describe experiences and a range of media for building, making objects and creating images. Thus, the preoperational child has available pencils, crayons and markers with which to 'write' shopping lists and signs; play dough (wet sand or even mud!) for creating objects or just for experimenting with; construction materials such as wood or paper scraps and glue, blocks or toys such as Lego, and tools; and costumes for dramatic play with character enactment.

Play provides tools and symbols for representing personal reconstructions of experience

In the concrete-operational stage, where the child is now in formal schooling, the teacher's role is to provide opportunities for the integration of play skills developed in the previous stage into tasks required in the primary school. For example, as children learn to use written symbols to record their stories, they should be encouraged to talk out loud and draw as well (Jones & Reynolds 1992). 'Writing evolves as children discover that people draw not only things, but speech' (Dyson 1989, p.7). Teacher-designed concrete experiences should provide intellectual challenges for children to discover important concepts while they 'play'. These should be balanced with self-chosen, spontaneous activities in which children can investigate and think critically about their own discoveries. From a Piagetian perspective, such activities allow for the assimilation of new concepts, or the experience of cognitive conflict through which accommodation to existing understanding may occur, bringing about a sense of cognitive equilibrium.

As they begin to focus on games with rules during this stage, children of primary school age also need to learn how to use problem-solving skills independently in conflict situations. This should be done through teacher modelling of thinking processes, language and behaviour.

Problem-solving skills and play

The role of information technology as a tool for symbolic representation and exploration, and for the development of higher-order mental processes through play should not be overlooked. With computers today, it is possible to play alone, play cooperatively with others, or play with a virtual community in interactions distributed between children at separate locations, and the technology. We look further at the role of information technology in cognitive development and play in Chapter 7.

Role of technology in play

What is the role of the social context in cognitive development through play? Not only does there need to be a stimulating environment in which children can investigate and resolve cognitive conflict, but also the encouragement, guidance and active involvement of older children and adults in scaffolding children's pretend play has been shown to be very important (Haight & Miller 1993). For example, Farver and Wimbarti (1995) have shown that older Indonesian children, who often participate in pretend play with their young siblings more than mothers, act as guides and 'expert partners' (Smolucha 1992) in stimulating make-believe play by challenging the thinking of their younger siblings and suggesting ideas for making the play more elaborate.

ACTION STATION

Consider the preoperational and concrete-operational stages of early and middle childhood as described by Piaget and brainstorm ways in which the teacher can act to foster cognitive development through play. Observe a group of children at play and note the opportunities for teacher interaction that would not interrupt the play process but might scaffold learning in the Vygotskian sense.

***Question point:** Many schools and curricula reflect a Piagetian approach to programming and teaching in which learning experiences are presented at what are deemed developmentally appropriate times. Consider the strengths of this approach. What are some potential weaknesses?*

Formal-operations stage

During the period of formal operations there emerges the ability to think abstractly and in a scientific way. The formal-operational individual possesses a unified logical system with which to explore systematically abstract relations independent of content, and hypothetical situations. Formal thought refers to the ability individuals have to set up and test hypotheses, think propositionally, and to take into account all possible combinations or aspects of a problem without reference to physical reality. As with the earlier stages, a number of 'tests' have been constructed to illustrate the presence of formal thinking in adolescents and adults.

To test whether children are able to use formal-operational logic—that is, whether they can set up, test and confirm or deny hypotheses—they are given problems where they must handle several variables at the same time. A common problem is the colourless liquid problem, in which children are presented with five bottles of colourless liquid and must decide which combination of three liquids produces a yellow colour. Concrete-operational children will simply

Tests of formal thinking

try various pairs of liquids, or combine all five liquids to no avail, and eventually give up. Formal-operational children establish a systematic procedure for testing the liquids in various combinations in order to arrive at the solution. They can also verbalise the logic they used to solve the problem.

Combinatorial logic

Propositional thinking

With propositional thinking, formal-operational children can work through statements of an argument in their mind. For example, the formal-operational child uses deductive logic to answer the following syllogism:

All Bs are As
All Cs are Bs
Then all As are______.

Or, given the syllogism:

Bob is fairer than John
John is darker than Bruce
Then Bruce is——than Bob?

Students will say that, from the information given, Bruce could be lighter or darker than Bob, showing that they have reasoned correctly. These types of syllogism appear to be beyond concrete-operational children.

Proportional reasoning: applying ratio to solve problems

Formal-operational children are able to apply the concept of ratio and proportion to solve problems. A common problem consists of giving children two cards on which stick figures are drawn, one being two-thirds the height of the other. These stick figures are constructed so that they measure four and six paper clips high respectively. The child is then asked to measure both the stick figures with eight connected paper clips, and to record the heights in paper clips. The paper clips are then replaced with smaller paper clips and the child is asked to measure only the large stick figure with the small paper clips. The child is then asked to decide how high the small stick figure is in small paper clips without measuring directly. In other words the child has to apply proportional reasoning to solve the problem. Maybe you would like to try this problem yourself?

Hypothetical reasoning: reasoning based on assumptions

We know that topics for debates are often based on hypothetical situations. For example, an intriguing debate could be had on the topic: 'That this world would be better if water was pink'. Concrete-operational children would have difficulty mounting a logical argument that followed from the premise that water could be pink, as water is colourless in reality. Adolescents in the formal-operational stage can abstract the structure of the argument from its content and argue hypothetically. While debates in the primary school are related to the real world, debates in the secondary school can be related to purely hypothetical issues. A popular television show, 'Hypotheticals', illustrates some adults' capacity to reason hypothetically. It also illustrates the *incapacity* of some adults to reason hypothetically!

Studies indicate that simply arriving at the age appropriate to formal thinking does not ensure that an individual will practise formal thought (Renner et al. 1976). It appears that two things are necessary: level of cognitive maturity and domain-specific opportunities to practise formal thinking. If individuals are not confronted with the necessity to reason formally (that is, if concrete modes of thinking appear more adaptable) then formal thought will not be used. Indeed, most people probably go through most of their days reasoning at a concrete or preoperational level. Furthermore, even

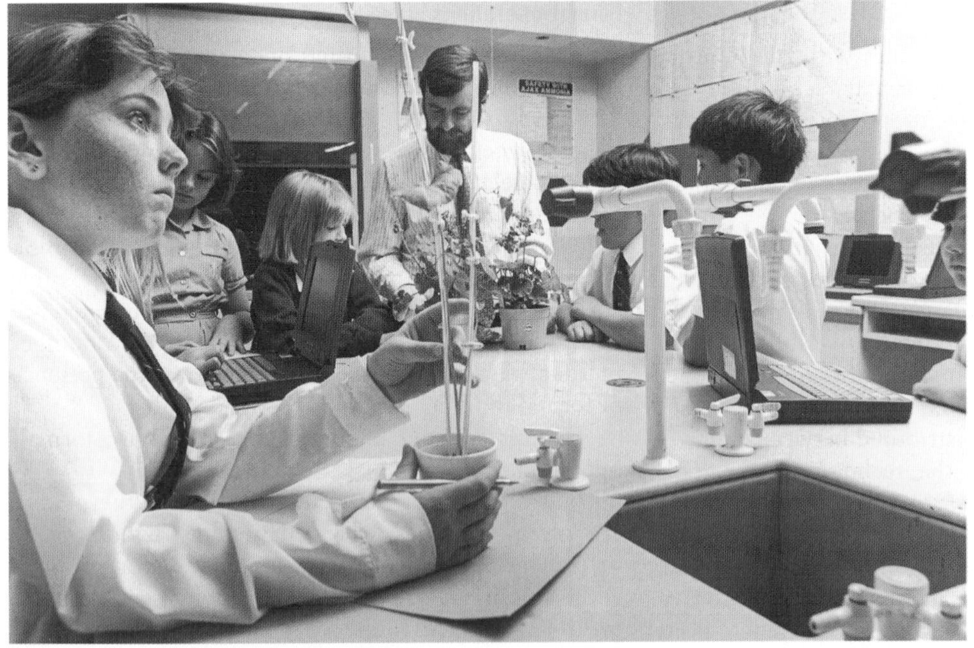

During the stage of formal operations, children can solve problems through logical operations. Photo: McKenzie & Associates P/L

when individuals are quite adept at formal thinking it is often domain-specific. For example, while the author can hypothesise and manipulate data related to psychology, he depends on concrete (and perhaps, more often than not, sensorimotor) reasoning when he is working out carpentry problems. Conversely, most carpenters can work out solutions to tricky and involved building problems symbolically. Consequently, we cannot presume as teachers that all adolescent children think formally. The theory holds that, while they have the capacity, relevant experiences may be necessary to 'stimulate' its use.

Question point: *Science teaching should promote formal thought, but it cannot do so if concrete-operational thinkers are asked to interact with science on a purely verbal level and their teachers teach them as though they think formally. Concrete-operational learners must interact with science at the concrete level, they cannot do otherwise (see Cowan 1978, p. 278).*

What are the implications for science and maths programs in secondary schools?

The underlying logical structure, which is at the base of logical thinking, is what Piaget calls the structure of 'groupings'. The child's ability to group is the requisite for conservational thought and for reasoning out problems of classification, seriation, number and space. The six conditions of grouping which form a logico-mathematical scheme are:

Structure of groupings

1. *Composition*: Any two units can be combined to produce a new unit.
2. *Reversibility*: Two units combined may be separated again.
3. *Associativity*: The same results may be obtained by combining units in different ways.
4. *Identity*: Combining an element with its inverse annuls it.
5. *Tautology*: A classification or relation that is repeated is not changed.
6. *Iteration*: A number combined with itself gives a new number.

While these groupings appear somewhat abstruse, they can be explained simply with examples. Any two numbers **combined** together must give a third number, e.g. 3 + 5 = 8. We can **reverse** this operation, e.g. 8 – 3 = 5. We can achieve the same result by different number **associations**, e.g. (2 + 1) + (3 + 2) = (6 + 2). If we take an **identity** from itself we end up with 0; or, all animals less all animals equals no animals. If we *repeat* a classification, a relation or a proposition, it is unchanged, such as all men plus all men = all men (**tautology**). If we combine a number with itself the result is a new number (**iteration**) (see Case 1985b; McNally 1977). Each of these logical processes gradually develops through the stages described above.

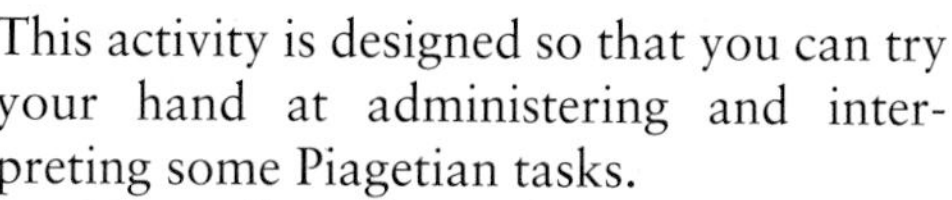

ACTION STATION

This activity is designed so that you can try your hand at administering and interpreting some Piagetian tasks.

You will need two balls of modelling clay or play dough, each about the size of a golf ball. Administer the conservation of substance task individually to four children between the ages of four and ten. There are three forms in which the task is given: ball vs sausage, ball vs two smaller balls and ball vs pancake.

1. Show the child two equal-sized balls of clay and say: 'In this game we will play with clay. This will be your clay, and this will be mine. Do you have just as much clay as I do?'

   If necessary, adjust the amounts of clay in the two balls until the child agrees that he has just as much clay as you have. Then say to the child: 'I am going to roll my clay into a sausage.' Roll your clay into a sausage. Then ask: 'Now, do you still have just as much clay as I have, or do you have more, or do I have more?'

   After the child responds, say: 'Tell me why?' Record the child's responses.
2. Begin with the same sequence of questions as above. Then divide your ball into two pieces out of which you form two smaller balls. Ask the same sequence of questions as above and record the responses.
3. Begin with the same sequence of questions as above. Then divide your ball into two pieces, one of which you flatten into a pancake. Ask the same sequence of questions as above and record the responses.

You might like to try administering the conservation of liquids test as well.

Using your data, consider the concept of conservation and the arguments children use to justify their responses.

IMPLICATIONS OF PIAGET'S STRUCTURALIST THEORY FOR THE CLASSROOM

Developmentally appropriate education

In the following sections we describe some implications of Piagetian theory for the classroom. Piaget emphasises that children should be **actively engaged** in the content to be learnt. There should be an optimal match between the developmental stage of the child and the logical properties of the material to be learnt. This approach has been labelled developmentally appropriate practice in education (see Dockett 1996).

To assist with this, Piaget and his followers have written books on how primary and secondary school students learn number concepts, concepts of time, movement and speed, geometry, chance and probability, logic and causality (Forman 1980). Many of the materials used to teach maths and science at school have been based on Piagetian theory. Indeed, a number of curricula and teaching materials used in our schools have been based on Piaget's stage theory, and indicate the sequence in which material should be taught, and the experiences the children should have to maximise their learning. In some cases, Piagetian theory is also used to justify why some experiences are considered unsuitable for young children.

Social interaction and cognitive development

Interaction with peers through group work and discussion in the classroom, while a necessary part of socialisation, is also of considerable importance in liberating children from their egocentrism in order to facilitate cognitive growth. Children's exposure to different points of view forces them to defend, justify, modify, concede or relinquish their position, all of which actions oblige them to modify thoughts, that is, to accommodate and assimilate. With peer interaction the mismatch between those operating at slightly higher and lower levels is likely to be optimal, to challenge each individual to progress their understanding. This is one of the reasons why group work and excited busy noise is so important in today's classrooms.

First-hand experience with the 'real world'

Teachers should give children first-hand experiences with the natural world in order to help them form concepts of living and non-living, of identity and causality. Let them interact with each other, encourage them to talk and think about their experiences in order to stimulate the growth of logical thinking and the development of language to express their thoughts. Creative play in the classroom should also be encouraged, because play, according to Piaget, is an assimilation of reality into the self.

Spiral curriculum and curriculum integration

Important aspects of the curriculum should be revisited at different stages and the child required to think and act at different levels of thought and action. This can be achieved by posing questions at a range of levels to stimulate disequilibrium.

Presenting material at higher developmental levels

From a Piagetian perspective there is considerable merit in developing themes in which a number of different content areas are combined and integrated. Teachers should thus try to identify structural similarities in different content areas. In the 'old days' this was called doing an integrated project. For example, a thematic approach to 'shapes' could encompass shape in a musical composition, in a poem or story, in mathematical and geometric constructs, in a painting, in social relationships such as 'the shape of my family', and in the natural world.

Cohesion of knowledge

Cooperative interaction and concrete experience are essential elements in children's construction of learning. Photo: McKenzie & Associates P/L.

Motivation and discipline

There is no place in Piaget's theory for competition,

grades and places in class relative to others. Rather, motivation is derived from 'real' interest, that is, when the challenge is neither too easy nor too difficult for an individual's current cognitive structures. Moderately novel learning tasks are considered to be very motivational. Furthermore, the self-selection of learning activities is more likely to provide for genuine interest and progress at the child's own rate. Mundane rote learning of facts is hardly likely to provide the motivation to challenge thought.

Discipline problems typically emerge in the stage of late concrete operations/early formal operations and reflect the child's developing peer orientation and ability to analyse and criticise adult control. Teachers could provide means for debate, small group discussion and social interaction, and opportunities for children to determine for themselves the class rules. In particular, the opportunity for adolescents to engage in shared reflections on issues of personal concern recognises their new cognitive egocentrism in which they focus on what they imagine others are thinking of them, and how they might 'change the world'.

Acceleration of stage development

In general, Piaget was not impressed with the notion of trying to accelerate the development of children through the cognitive stages nor, in particular, accelerating their mastery of conservation. Some acceleration may be possible if procedures involve setting up a disequilibrium in children between their cognitive level and the new concept, thus forcing them to 'accommodate'. However, research on acceleration indicates that it is probably not worth the effort as children regress when the supporting educational structures are absent. Furthermore, the gains in levels of reasoning are not substantial relative to those of non-'trained' peers.

Acceleration is most likely to occur when children are already on the verge of acquiring the concept being taught. Research also shows that certain kinds of training in conservation are more effective than others. Field (1981) showed that three- and four-year-olds who were given verbal rules to explain why objects did not appear the same when they really were, were most likely to conserve when they used the identity rule rather than the reversibility or compensation rules. Children who 'mentally' returned the material to its original state or appearance (reversibility rule) or made allowances for different dimensions (compensation rule) conserved better than children who didn't add anything or take anything away (identity rule). Furthermore, the four-year-olds benefited more from the training than the three-year-olds, suggesting that children benefit most when intellectual structures are well enough developed to handle the principle of conservation.

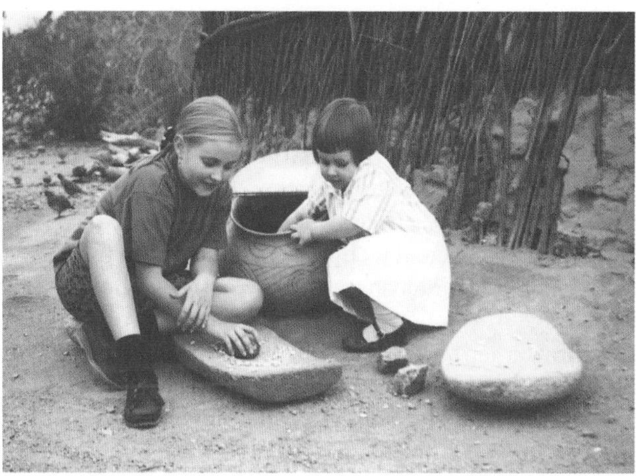

You can see why first-hand experience with the real world helps construct knowledge. Photo: authors.

Table 2.1 lists the essentials for education of a Piagetian structuralist perspective.

TABLE 2.1

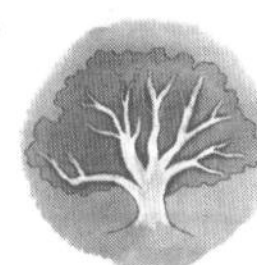

ESSENTIALS OF A PIAGETIAN STRUCTURALIST PERSPECTIVE FOR EDUCATION

For teachers

- an awareness of the stage characteristics of the students' thought processes;
- an awareness that children of a particular age are not necessarily functioning at a particular cognitive level; e.g. reaching adolescence or adulthood does not guarantee the ability to perform formal operations;
- avoidance of efforts to 'push' a child to the next higher stage;
- individualisation of learning experiences so that each student is working at a level that presents an optimal mismatch between what the student knows and the new knowledge to be acquired. Moderate novelty will foster motivation (disequilibrium);
- provision of concrete experiences necessary for the development of concepts prior to their use in language;
- individualised evaluation of students with the goal of improving their personal performance;
- using materials that encourage creative thought and avoiding those that discourage it.

(based on Webb 1980, pp. 96–7)

Summary

For Piaget, intellectual development occurs progressively as the growing child moves through a series of stages—characterised by qualitatively different cognitive processes

—and is confronted with new experiences that must be related to the existing mental schemes of the child. Through the processes of assimilation and accommodation, the child either incorporates new experiences into existing schemes, or constructs or alters schemes to make them more useful. As the child develops, these intellectual schemes become more sophisticated, so that by the formal stage the child is capable of the full range of logical operations characteristic of adult thought. At each stage of development the child is confronted with situations that cannot be easily resolved by resorting to existing schemes, and so conflict occurs, causing disequilibrium. The child, for example, may be faced with a conservation-like problem such as being given a certain size glass to drink from that appears to hold less than other children's glasses. The child may complain that she hasn't been given as much as the others. The parent explains otherwise, the other children at the table argue otherwise, and demonstrations of the equality of quantities are given. Such cognitive conflict! While the child may not initially understand the equivalence, a repetition of this and similar situations over a period of time 'causes' the child to adapt and develop schemes for discounting perceptual cues along only one dimension, while taking into account a number of salient cues. Through this process the ability to conserve is developed, and in each resolution of conflict, with the development of more adequate cognitive schemes, equilibrium is achieved. The resolution of cognitive conflict drives cognitive growth.

PIAGET AND PERSONAL CONSTRUCTIVISM

A major aspect of Piagetian theory is his belief that children construct their own tools for understanding and discovering the world (Bidell & Fischer 1992; Carey 1987; Inhelder & de Caprona 1987; Sigel & Cocking 1977). Piaget's constructivism is based on three interrelated conceptions:

1. the relation between **action** and **thought**;
2. the construction of cognitive **structure**;
3. the role of **self-regulation** or, more abstractly, equilibration in the development of thought.

(Chapman 1988, cited in Bidell & Fischer 1992)

Piaget's basic position was that our knowledge is primarily constructed from our own actions in the process of regulating our interactions with the world. By actively coordinating actions from different situations or contexts, an individual stores or internalises actions that can be reused as representations to anticipate action in other contexts. Representation in the form of internalised action provides our most fundamental knowledge about how the world works because it tells us what we can *do* with the world (Bidell & Fischer 1992).

It is significant that Piaget emphasises that actions should not be limited to the concrete, rather, that they should be developed and schematised into **mental operations**. This is achieved by encouraging the child to rely on progressively less direct support from externals—for example, moving from the physical through to pictorial representations, then to cognitive anticipations and retrospections of operations not actually being performed at that moment.

Piaget's theory has been a great catalyst for the development of educational curricula, methods and evaluation techniques within our classrooms (Gallagher & Easley 1978). Rather than applying Piaget's structuralist perspective literally to education, as some curriculum developers have done, DeVries (1978) believes that two more general, philosophical approaches to education emerge from Piaget's constructivism. First, the emphasis shifts from trying to foster directly the characteristics of a future stage of development to maximising children's opportunities to create and coordinate the many relationships of which they are currently capable. Second, there is an emphasis on providing children with opportunities to construct meaning out of the experiences presented. Learning is essentially considered a constructive process. Ultimately, elements of Piaget's theory, such as the types of experience presented to children, the nature of active learning and the importance of interest, autonomy and peer interaction, are related to this important notion that children construct their learning from this world of experience.

Table 2.2 summarises the essentials for education of a Piagetian personal constructivist perspective.

TABLE 2.2

ESSENTIALS OF A PIAGETIAN PERSONAL CONSTRUCTIVIST PERSPECTIVE FOR EDUCATION

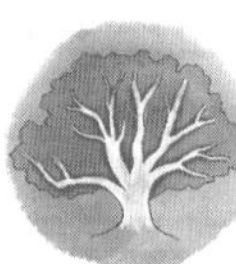

For teachers

- a belief that learning is an active restructuring of thought rather than an increase in content, and that reconstruction (recall) will reflect the particular schema of the learner;
- an appreciation that, as each person constructs learning in terms of his or her own schemes, no two people will derive the same meaning or benefit from a given experience;
- a high regard for self-regulated learning;

- an awareness and judicious use of cognitive conflict to promote the consolidation of concepts;
- provision of activities that provoke thought about change and the relative nature of any 'fact', rather than activities that teach the child to see discrete, static stimuli or absolute facts;
- provision of a wide variety of experiences to maximise cognitive development;
- use of wrong answers in helping students to analyse their thinking in order to retain the correct elements and revise misconceptions;
- use of social interaction to promote increases in both interest and comprehension in learning;
- commitment to spending many hours observing children.

For students

- active physical and mental involvement;
- manipulating concrete objects directly and ideas indirectly;
- posing questions and seeking their own answers;
- reconciling what is found at one time with what is found at another;
- comparing findings with those of other children.

(based on Forman 1980)

CURRENT STATUS OF PIAGET'S THEORY

Piaget's theory has attracted voluminous research, some of which has been conducted by followers intent on providing a wider research base for the theory than Piaget's original limited clinical method, while others have conducted research to test elements of the theory (Halford 1989). In particular, research has addressed the following questions: Are the stages that Piaget described really universal? Do they cut across domains of knowledge? Do the various cognitive abilities associated with the stages emerge at the ages that Piaget predicted? Are the developmental stages he described invariant across individuals and cultures? (Bidell & Fischer 1992; Rogoff & Chavajay 1995). Probably most research has been conducted in the area of conservation and, in particular, whether the acquisition of conservation is invariant across groups, and whether it can be accelerated through various educational programs (Brainerd 1978; Modgil & Modgil 1976, 1982).

Problems with Piaget's theory

Among the problems noted with Piaget's theory are the following:

- ☐ the local success of many short-term training studies on Piagetian tasks; that is, successes that exerted an impact on one class of task without affecting any other task that was supposed to be 'structurally related';
- ☐ the apparent 'unevenness' of children's intellectual development when measured across different tasks, contexts or domains;
- ☐ individual differences in the order of task acquisition, which gave rise to low correlations among tasks that were supposedly dependent on the same underlying structure (Case 1992).

In addition to these difficulties, some researchers think the theory lacks explicitness, neglects individual differences, and fails to consider affect or perception as factors influencing intellectual development.

Unfortunately, the research in this area is too voluminous, convoluted and equivocal in its findings to deal with in detail here. Suffice to say that for every experimental design constructed to demonstrate the 'fallibility of the theoretical framework' other experimental designs have been constructed that support the general tenets of the theory (see Bidell & Fischer 1992; Halford 1989).

Criticisms of the Piagetian tests

The Piagetian tests have also been subjected to considerable critical review with many researchers considering the form of the tests (particularly the language used, relevance of the questions to background experiences, and the requirement that children justify their 'correct' answers in the 'correct' way) inadequate (e.g. Rogoff & Chavajay 1995).

Michael Siegal (1991) has written a particularly interesting critique of the language framework used in the test of conservation and argues that younger children's apparent inability to conserve and decentre can be explained in terms of a clash between the conversational worlds of adults and children. In particular, Siegal believes that the framework for the Piagetian questions breaks conversational rules that children implicitly hold. While these conventions may be broken for specific purpose in adult speech, young children, in general, abide by them. Specifically, Siegal believes that problems arise because Piagetian experimenters pose questions where the answer is obvious or repeat questions when an answer has already been given. Young children may not recognise that the purpose underlying these departures from conversational rules is to establish their understanding of concepts. Instead, they may assume that, for example, repeated questioning (characteristic of the Piagetian test) implies an invitation to switch the second time around because the first answer was incorrect. For example, in the conservation of liquids test, children who answer that the two flasks of water are equal may switch their answers after one flask has been poured into a different container, despite believing the volumes are still the same. They may do this because they want to please the experimenter and give the answer they think is expected. Siegal believes that, when given the appropriate verbal cues that take into account the relative immaturity of their language skills, young children disclose what they know. An impressive research base supports his belief.

Developmentally appropriate education revisited

As parents we are pretty sure that classical Piagetian theory underestimates young children's reasoning capacity. We have no doubt that our daughter Laura, at three, had notions of causality and a conception of time, was able to classify elementary groupings, and was often able to take the perspective of others, showing great concern and understanding of feelings, and modifying her attitudes and behaviour accordingly. This discrepancy between what classic Piagetian theory tells us should be the case and what we observe may be because we have an exceptionally bright child (all parents think their children are exceptionally bright!), or it might be that the original Piagetian methodology did not allow the full capacities of children to be explored. More advanced research techniques (such as video camera and audio recorder) are now available for observing infants and children and for determining what they can or cannot do (Flavell 1985). In general, research using alternative methodologies and new techniques establishes that Piaget underestimated the cognitive capacity of children (e.g. Gelman & Baillargeon 1983; Halford 1989; Siegler 1991). Such discrepancies between the theory and what we now know children are really capable of calls into question the usefulness of what has been termed 'developmentally appropriate practice in education' (see Dockett 1996), reflected in many curricula and teaching materials. Maybe developmentally appropriate education sells students short in terms of what they could actually learn. What do you think?

a

ACTION STATION

Design a range of activities for children in organised settings in which they can reflect on their own thinking in a range of situations, and on that of others. Plan some role-taking situations for children to participate in.

ACTION STATION

a

Obtain a copy of an infants, primary and lower secondary curriculum in mathematics (or science). Compare the programmed activities with the supposed conceptual abilities of children at these levels. If possible, obtain a copy of a teacher's program for these classes and analyse its consistency with current thought on the conceptual abilities of children.

Neo-Piagetian theories

As a reaction to the perceived limitations in Piaget's theory there have been basically two developments. First, there has been a reformulation of the model by a number of theorists to address the limitations, while preserving those features of the model that appear to have withstood the rigours of contemporary debate and experimentation. These approaches are generally termed neo-Piagetian (Biggs & Collis 1982; Case 1985a, b; Demetriou 1987; Halford 1982; Pascuale-Leone 1969). Neo-Piagetian theories make an important contribution to our understanding of children's intellectual development. However, as they are many and complex, it is beyond the scope of this book to describe them. Readers are referred to Case (1985), Demetriou (1987) Flavell (1985), and Halford (1993).

A second development has occurred within the Piagetian camp where Piagetians now re-emphasise components of the theory that deal with **constructivism** rather than the part that deals with **structuralism** (Bidell & Fischer 1992; Carey 1987; Inhelder & de Caprona 1987; Sigel & Cocking 1977). Structuralism and constructivism are discussed earlier in this chapter.

CROSS-CULTURAL PERSPECTIVES ON PIAGET'S THEORY

Piaget's theory has also attracted considerable attention from cross-cultural psychologists keen to demonstrate the applicability or otherwise of the theory to non-Western cultural groups such as the Australian Aboriginal and the New Zealand Maori (Dasen & Heron 1981; Irvine & Berry 1988; Keats & Keats 1988).

As we have seen, much of Piaget's theory of cognitive development is based on the organising principles of perception, and the processes of adaptation and assimilation. There is abundant evidence from cross-cultural and anthropological research that the manner in which individuals perceive, structure, interpret and relate to their world is very much a function of what the physical and social environment has influenced (Deregowski 1980; Pick 1980) (indeed,

Piaget, as a biologist, would have accepted this notion of variability). Hence, there is an innate danger in setting up rules or stages of cognitive development on the basis of information drawn from one cultural group and applying the derived principles to other cultural groups. The power of perception in modifying individuals' methods of relating to the world is well captured in this story taken from Feuerstein (1991):

I remember working with children who came to Israel directly from Yemen on the operation of 'Flying Carpet'. There was no illiteracy in that group and a great desire to read. Since they did not have enough books, it was not uncommon that 15–20 students shared the same book and read it simultaneously, looking at the page from different angles. They even had to learn how to read upside down. I remember one Israeli mother, who adopted a Yemenite child, and came to me for advice because she suspected that the child was not normal: 'he reads from the other side!' She thought that something was wrong with his perception! *(pp. 23–4)*

Piaget's theoretical framework and methodology spawned a vast amount of research in cross-cultural contexts (Irvine & Berry 1988). In the early research there was little questioning of the relevance of the constructs or the methodology (the clinical interview and Piagetian tasks) with the major cross-cultural concession being in the use of interpreters. Early research reported by Dasen and Heron (1981), for example, suggested that in a number of cultural groups, including the Australian Aboriginal, up to 50% of their mature adult population were unable to conserve quantity, weight or volume, as measured by standard Piagetian tests. One could argue that such findings call into question the universal nature of cognitive development as proposed by Piaget. On the other hand, it could be said that they may reflect limitations in the methodology: for example, the limited number of tests used which may not have been adequate to demonstrate the existence or otherwise of conservation and formal thinking; the subjects may not have been familiar with the materials of the test; and inadequate or incomplete communication between tester and testee. In other words, the interpretation of the answers and their significance, particularly when expressed through a translator, may not have been recognised as demonstrating conservation when in fact, with further elaboration or probing, or a change in the content of the tasks, conservation may have been clearly demonstrated (Irvine & Berry 1988; Pick 1980).

A number of other studies indicated a 'lag' in the development of conservation for members of some cultures in comparison to others (Dasen 1974; Goldschmid et al. 1973; Heron & Dowel 1973; de Lemos 1969). However, some researchers believe that this 'lag' can be explained in terms of level of education and familiarity with the tasks (Pick 1980). It is generally accepted today that the requirements of a culturally different environment, such as that of the Aboriginal or Maori, lead to different types of spatial orientation. Hence, tests devised to assess conservation must take this into account.

More recent criticism of this earlier research has led to a growing trend among educators and researchers to reject the notion of inherent intellectual inferiority among culturally different groups and to accept the universality of cognitive functioning. In other words, all groups are perceived equally capable of the diverse ways of thinking and processing information that characterise learning in a modern environment, and no group is inherently inferior. Whatever differences there may be reflect experience and opportunity. Educators develop programs on the basis of this belief. We deal extensively with this issue in Chapter 12.

Universality of cognitive functioning

THEORIES OF MIND

As noted in our earlier discussion of constructivism (Chapter 1), children learn through making sense of their world of experiences. Young children explain their world through what might be termed naive physical, biological and psychological 'theories' (see Dockett 1994, 1995a, 1996; Wellman & Gelman 1992). In other words, children make sense of physical events (e.g. the sun rising), biological events (e.g. growing) and psychological events (e.g. interactions with others), in non-scientific ways, but in ways that prepare them to understand with greater sophistication physical, biological and psychological experiences as they develop and are exposed to more complex explanations. Theories of mind relates to children's ability to impute mental states to oneself and others and involves appreciating the distinction between these mental states and external reality, as well as understanding the causal relationships that exist between the two (Davis & Pratt 1995). Recent research has explored 'theories of mind' as a means of defining more precisely what children are capable of understanding and learning. In particular, this approach seeks to examine how children use mental representation to interpret and reflect upon their physical, biological and psychological world. In general, the results of this work indicate that children are more capable of sophisticated thinking than was

Theory of mind: a person's model of how the mind works

earlier thought. This suggests that educators should do two things: encourage children's reflection on their thinking and that of others and challenge the notion of developmentally appropriate practice in educational settings.

LEARNER-CENTRED PSYCHOLOGICAL PRINCIPLE 2

The successful learner, over time and with support and instructional guidance, can create meaningful coherent representations of knowledge.

Learners generate integrated, commonsense representations and explanations for even poorly understood or communicated facts, concepts, principles or theories. Learning processes operate holistically in the sense that internally consistent understandings emerge that may or may not be valid from an objective, externally oriented perspective. As learners negotiate understandings with others and internalize values and meaning within a discipline, however, they can refine their conceptions by fillings gaps, resolving inconsistencies and revising prior conceptions.

Reprinted with permission APA Task Force on Psychology in Education (1993, January), p. 6.

VYGOTSKY AND SOCIAL CONSTRUCTIVISM

Piaget made a very important contribution to our understanding of the way in which children develop. However, Piagetian theory left many issues still to be addressed, in particular the sociocultural aspect of learning and the role of human mediators in children's learning (see Kozulin & Presseisen 1995). Lev Vygotsky (1896–1934) was a contemporary of Piaget. For Vygotsky, the learning process was not a solitary exploration by a child of the environment, as suggested by Piaget's personal constructivist theory, but rather a process of appropriation by the child of culturally relevant behaviour (Kozulin & Presseisen 1995).

Cultural-historical theory

A central theme in Vygotsky's social constructivist theory (also referred to as **cultural-historical theory**) is that cognitive development can be understood as the transformation of basic, biologically determined processes into higher psychological functions. According to the theory, children are born with a wide range of perceptual, attentional and memory capacities which are substantially transformed in the context of socialisation and education, particularly through the use of cultural inventions such as tools, social structures and language, to constitute the higher psychological functions or the unique forms of human cognition (Diaz et al. 1990; Vygotsky 1978). In a sense, children are wrapped around by their culture (represented by these tools, social structures and language) and this directs the form and extent that cognitive development takes. On one level we have the continuing evolution of the cultural group through the collective activity of its members, and on the other we have the development of the individual as part of this collective. Individuals are therefore both part of, and the product of, this collective culture.

Tools of learning

Learning is thus a process through which we become one with the collective through carrying out personal activity in collaboration with other people (e.g. Davydov 1995). As the tools, inventions and language of one culture may be significantly different from those of another culture, education must place learning within the appropriate social and cultural contexts.

For Vygotsky, therefore, cognitive development is not so much the unfolding of mental schemas within the individual so much as the unfolding of cognitive understandings of social beings within social contexts. In a sense we become part of the community and the community becomes part of us in the sharing of knowledge. Throughout this text we emphasise this cultural/social dimension of learning and teaching.

The zone of proximal development

For Vygotsky who focused on the importance of sociocultural dimensions and language as important characteristics of formal schooling and learning (Moll 1990), the social system in which children develop is crucial to their learning. Parents, teachers and peers interact with the child and mediate learning through socially organised instruction. Vygotsky believed that the task of teaching children is particularly complex because, in order to be effective, teachers need to know each individual student very well, be familiar with the social dynamics of each child's social setting, and have a good understanding of their own teaching skills so that these may be used effectively to facilitate the learning of students.

Mediated learning: Learning through socially organised instruction

One of the major elements of Vygotsky's theory, derived from this belief that learning occurs in social contexts, is his notion of a **zone of proximal development**. This is typically thought of as each person's range of potential for learning, where that learning is culturally shaped by the social environment in which it takes place (Smagorinsky 1995). For Vygotsky, teaching is only good when it 'awakens and rouses to life those functions which are in a stage of maturing, which lie in the zone of proximal development' (quoted in Gallimore & Tharp 1990, p. 200). Vygotsky defines the zone of proximal development as the distance between the actual developmental level of a child as determined by independent problem solving, and the level of potential development as determined through problem solving under adult guidance or in collaboration with more capable peers (Vygotsky 1978). Learners ultimately appropriate and internalise the knowledge transacted through assisted performance so that it becomes their own. A teacher's task is to place learning within this zone.

Zone of proximal development: the stage at which a child's skills can be developed with the assistance of others

To place learning in the zone of proximal development an appropriate level of difficulty needs to be established. This level, assumed to be at the proximal level, must be challenging, but not too difficult. The educator then needs to provide for assisted performance. This is referred to as **scaffolded instruction**. The adult provides guided practice to the child with a clear sense of the goal or outcome of the child's performance. As with scaffolding around a building, it is gradually removed so that the child can perform the task independently.

Appropriate level of difficulty

Scaffolded instruction: providing guidance

If the learning experience has been carefully structured and situated within the child's zone of proximal development, the child should be able to perform the task independently. To assess the success of the learning experience, therefore, the educator should evaluate the independent performance of the child on the task.

Evaluate performance

Three key principles underline the effective use of the zone of proximal development to facilitate the cognitive development of children: education must be **holistic**; it must be situated in a social context that mediates the learning; and it must allow for change and development in the child. For learning to be holistic, the unit of study should be the most meaningful unit, rather than the smallest or simplest. For Vygotsky, the division of potentially meaningful material into small skills and subskills to facilitate learning is actually counterproductive, as its essential meaningfulness is lost. The 'whole language' approach to teaching reading, which emphasises that reading comprehension and written expression must be developed through functional, relevant and meaningful uses of language rather than through the discrete learning of subskills (such as phonic decoding), illustrates this idea.

Principles underlining the effective use of the zone of proximal development: ZPD and holistic education

The importance of **social interaction** between adults and children, and, in particular, the role played by adults in guiding and **mediating learning** for children is paramount for Vygotsky. Central to this interaction is instruction that develops in children an increasing mastery of the language of learning and instruction so that they acquire conscious awareness and voluntary control of knowledge (Moll 1990). An example of a teaching method based on this principle is the reciprocal teaching approach developed by Brown and Palincsar (1989) and considered later in this book. Vygotsky also suggests that formal learning (such as that characterised by learning scientific information) and everyday learning (such as that characterised by learning in the home) are interconnected and interdependent. Vygotsky believed that it is through the use of everyday concepts that children make sense of the definitions and explanations of scientific concepts (or schooled concepts). However, everyday concepts are also shaped and moulded by

ZPD and mediating learning

Vygotsky stresses the importance of adult – or peer – mediation in children's cognitive development. How might these older tutors be helping the young learners? Photo: Leo Kiriloff

exposure to scientific concepts and, because of this, children become more aware, and in control, of their everyday worlds (Moll 1990). Hence, an effective relationship must exist between the everyday world and the 'schooled world' for learning to be significant, effective and of practical value.

To facilitate the development of learning embedded in the everyday world, teachers, students and peers must interact, share ideas and experiences, solve problems and be interdependent. This interdependence in social contexts is central to a Vygotskian analysis of instruction (Moll 1990).

The teacher must also be aware that what children are able to do with assistance and collaboration today, they will be able to do independently tomorrow (Vygotsky 1978). Consequently, learning needs to be structured so that there is an expanding zone challenging children to move forward. An interesting implication of Vygotsky's approach, which stands in contrast to some of the implications that may be drawn from Piaget's theory, is that children should be challenged to be engaged in activities that appear to be beyond their current level of development. Children can often complete activities with the collaboration of teachers and peers that they could not complete on their own. In time, with this assistance and verbal mediation, the needed skills are gradually internalised and the children learn to perform them independently.

ZPD and change and development in children

Teaching and the zone of proximal development

Tharp and Gallimore (1988) give the following definition of teaching based upon Vygotskian ideas: 'Teaching consists of assisting performance through the Zone of Proximal Development. Teaching can be said to occur when assistance is offered at points in the ZPD at which performance requires assistance.' According to Gallimore and Tharp (1990) there are four stages in the zone of proximal development that a child goes through:

1. In the first stage the performance is assisted by more capable others such as parents, teachers and peers.
2. In the second stage there is less dependence on external assistance and the performance begins to become internalised. The children help themselves by using self-directed speech. In other words, children (and adults, too) talk to themselves about what they are doing and so begin to assume responsibility for self-guidance and self-regulation of the learning.
3. In the third stage the performance is developed, automated and fossilised. At this time assistance from others and self-directed speech is unnecessary and, indeed, may be irritating. Task performance is smooth and integrated, internalised and automated.
4. Finally, Gallimore and Tharp (1990) talk of a fourth stage, where 'deautomatisation' of performance leads the individual to re-enter the zone of proximal development. For example, at times even well-learned responses are 'forgotten', or become 'rusty'. At these times the individual re-enters the ZPD and consciously talks through the matter internally or seeks external assistance. To this extent there is a continual movement in and out of the ZPD, what Gallimore and Tharp term 'recursion'.

Recursion: moving in and out of the ZPD

As the nature of the assistance to be given by teachers (and parents and peers) to support cognitive growth was not spelt out by Vygotsky, contemporary authors have described a range of strategies that fit within a Vygotskian perspective. Gallimore and Tharp (1990) discuss modelling, contingency management, feedback, questioning and cognitive structuring from a Vygotskian perspective. Tudge (1990) discusses the usefulness of peer collaboration, and Diaz, Neal and Amaya-Williams (1990) self-regulated learning. All these teaching approaches are covered elsewhere in the text.

Table 2.3 lists the essentials for education of a Vygotskian social constructivist perspective.

TABLE 2.3

ESSENTIALS OF A VYGOTSKIAN SOCIAL CONSTRUCTIVIST PERSPECTIVE FOR EDUCATION

For teachers

- a belief that education is to develop students' personality;
- a belief that education is to facilitate the development of the creative potential of students;
- a belief that effective learning requires the active involvement of the learner;
- a belief that teachers direct and guide the individual activity of the students but they do not dictate or force their own will on them. Authentic teaching and learning come through a collaboration by adults with students;
- a belief that the most valuable methods for students' teaching and learning correspond to their developmental and individual characteristics, and therefore these methods cannot be uniform;
- a belief that schools should provide the tools that learners need to internalise the ways of thinking

central to participation in the cultural world around them.

(Adapted from Davydov 1995, p.13, and Smagorinsky 1995)

a

ACTION STATION

This activity is designed so that you may appreciate the influence that parents have in stimulating their children in a variety of ways that are important to the children's perceptual and cognitive development.

Locate a mother or father with a young infant (birth to three years). Observe the interaction between the parent and child in one or more play situations. Particularly note visual, auditory and tactile stimulation. Compile a detailed record of the interaction observed and relate your observations to principles of cognitive development discussed in this chapter.

a

ACTION STATION

Much can be learnt from closely observing an infant's interaction with the physical world. Locate an infant up to two years of age. Over an extended period, observe the child's interaction with his or her environment. Make detailed notes on the child's activities. What learning do you think is taking place? Discuss your observations from the perspective of Vygotsky's *zone of proximal development.*

TEACHER'S CASE BOOK

LEARNING CENTRES

Every Thursday Anna sets up a number of learning centres for the children in her composite 1/2 class. These change regularly. For example, a mathematical centre catered for the interests and abilities of Troy, a gifted child who loves to be challenged. The children had been working on a space topic. Using a calculator, Troy was able to estimate the distance between planets. This task, involving very high numbers and vast differences, absorbed and extended Troy.

Tim likes to tinker with things, so Anna set up a centre where children could discover how things work. It included a broken sewing machine, a typewriter and an old bar heater. Tim made himself a skateboard from the heater!

Hilly is a Down's syndrome child who loves art. Anna planned for classical music to accompany the fingerpaint.

Others prefer to use blocks. 'A lot of the younger children are into game making at the moment, so they'll do that,' reports Anna. 'The learning centres can give the children a chance to consolidate something. For example, Katy might sometimes go to her handwriting and sit there and practise for a while. It also gives the chance to children who want to, to extend themselves.' Anna finds it works well.

Case studies illustrating National Competency Framework for Beginning Teaching, National Project on the Quality of Teaching and Learning, Australian Teaching Council, 1996, p. 24. Commonwealth of Australia copyright, reproduced by permission.

Case study activity

Consider the usefulness of such learning centres from both the Piagetian and Vygotskian perspective. Why do you think they work well?

VYGOTSKY AND PIAGET—A COMPARISON

From a Piagetian perspective, direct teacher involvement with a learner may actually inhibit a child's understanding if instruction gets in the way of the child's own exploration (Newman et al., quoted in Smagorinsky 1995, p.197). This contrasts with Vygotsky's notions of scaffolding and guided discovery, and his belief in the importance of continuing interaction between the child and its environment to facilitate the child's understanding of the world about him.

Guidance and assisted discovery

Piaget suggests that developmental maturity must exist in order for children to benefit from particular learning experiences, and focuses on the importance of unstructured experiences and self-initiated discovery for children's cognitive development. Vygotsky emphasises the need for guidance and assisted discovery to lead development (Blanck 1990; Tharp & Gallimore 1988). Teachers need to design instruction that lies within the range of possibilities represented by the child's real level of development and the child's potential for development (the zone of proximal development) (Blanck 1990).

Higher mental processes

In contrast to Piagetian theory, which holds that 'higher' mental processes are characterised by formal and specific operations, Vygotskian theory holds that there are no specific operations that characterise higher mental processes but that these are shaped by the sociocultural situation in which an individual is located. Indeed, mental processes from a Vygotskian perspective are both **elastic** and **unbounded.** In other words, cognitive growth is elastic in that it may take many different directions preparing the individual for survival within its sociocultural context. We take up this idea when we discuss the cultural dimensions of learning later in the book. Second, cognitive growth is unbounded because learning occurs in the zone of proximal development and this, for any individual, is continually in a state of evolution.

Language and learning

Vygotsky (1962, 1978) emphasises language as a major means by which cognitive development occurs. Piaget, in contrast, believes that cognitive development occurs independently of language development, and facilitates the acquisition of language. Indeed, Piaget and Vygotsky interpret children's early self-talk (i.e. talk not directed to others) in quite different ways. For Piaget it illustrates children's cognitive egocentrism which they grow out of with the acquisition of more mature schemas of social behaviour and social speech. Vygotsky, on the other hand, interprets this self-talk as **private speech** which reflects a developmental phase between that of purely social speech and that of inner speech, or thought. Initially, children are subjected to public speech which guides their behaviour (e.g. the instructions given to them by their parents to perform particular behaviour). As children develop they become more able to use their own speech (rather than the speech of others) to guide their behaviour and solve problems. This speech is used publicly, but not socially. They instruct themselves about what they should do. In its initial stages these instructions are aloud. As the child develops, this speech becomes increasingly quieter, and subvocalised, until eventually it is internalised and silent. At this stage the child is using thought to control actions. For Vygotsky, language remains important throughout life for the higher mental processes such as planning, evaluating, remembering and reasoning (Berndt 1992). Indeed, adults are often heard to use private speech to help structure cognitive activity when they are trying to solve complex problems. The reason for this, according to Vygotsky, is that language is a sequential way of representing the holistic experience of thought (Vygotsky 1987).

Private speech

There are, nevertheless, many similarities in the implications for learning of Vygotsky's and Piaget's theories. Both emphasise the importance of active involvement by children in learning, and the *process* of learning rather than the *product*. They both emphasise the importance of *peer interaction*, grounding learning experiences in the *real world of experiences* for children, and the need for the adult (parent or teacher) to take account of *individual differences* when structuring learning experiences for children.

TEACHER'S CASE BOOK

WEIGHTS AND PULLEYS

When I looked at last year's lesson plan on pulleys in the Year 8 physics unit it revived vivid memories of a multitude of tangled ropes and pulleys which kept slipping off the ropes. The students kept pulling over the retort stands so that the weights and pulleys went crashing to the floor.

This year I decided that I would just demonstrate the pulley systems which were set up by the laboratory technician rather than have the students construct their own. Also, this would leave half the lesson to review the work covered so far. I was not entirely happy with this method but I could not think of a better alternative.

We had just finished investigating the pulleys when Sarah raised her hand.

'Yes, Sarah?'

'I think there is crane at the chapel site with a pulley,' she said.

At present, a chapel is being built at the front of the school. Another student remarked that she thought she had seen pulleys on the weight machines in the school gymnasium. I thought for a moment. We could review our work tomorrow. I made a spontaneous decision to dispense with the lesson plan. 'Well,' I said. 'Why don't we all go down to the chapel site?'

When we arrived there was a crane and also a hoist which was used to lift the sandstone blocks to the top of the walls. The workman at the site agreed to operate the hoist so that the students could see the pulley system in action. Then we went to the gymnasium. The students had a great time using the weight machines and rowing machines. They competed to see who could lift the heaviest weight. When I asked, I found that several students were able to explain how the pulley systems worked on the different machines.

After all my careful lesson planning, I realised that these students already understood what I was trying to teach them. Next year I plan to book the gymnasium and let students work out for themselves how pulleys work.

Case studies illustrating National Competency Framework for Beginning Teaching, National Project on the Quality of Teaching and Learning, Australian Teaching Council, 1996, p.50. Commonwealth of Australia copyright, reproduced by permission.

Case study activity

Analyse this case study from both a Piagetian and Vygotskian perspective. What does it say about effective teaching and learning?

Discuss your analyses with other students.

Recommended reading

Case, R. (1992) Neo-Piagetian theories of child development. In R. J. Sternberg & C. A. Berg (eds), *Intellectual Development*. New York: Cambridge University Press.

Davydov, V. (1995) The influence of L. S. Vygotsky on education theory, research, and practice (trans. by S. T. Kerr). *Educational Researcher*, 24, 12–21.

Dockett, S. (1995a) Young children's play and language as clues to their developing theories of mind. *Journal for Australian Research in Early Childhood Education*, 2, 61–72.

Dockett, S. (1995b) 'I tend to be dead and you make me alive': Developing Understandings through Sociodramatic Play. Watson, ACT: Australian Early Childhood Association.

Dockett, S. (1996) Children as theorists. In M. Fleer (ed.), DAPcentrism: Challenging Developmentally Appropriate Practice. Watson, ACT: Australian Early Childhood Association.

Halford, G. S. (1989) Reflections on 25 years of Piagetian cognitive developmental psychology, 1963–1988. *Human Development*, 32, 325–57.

Halford, G. S. (1993) Children's understanding: The development of mental models. London: Lawrence Erlbaum.

Jones, E. & Reynolds, G. (1992) *The Play's the Thing*. New York: Teachers College Press.

Kozulin, A. & Presseisen, B. Z. (1995) Mediated learning experience and psychological tools: Vygotsky's and Feuerstein's perspectives in a study of student learning. *Educational Psychologist*, 30, 67–75.

Moll, L. C. (1990) *Vygotsky and Education*. Cambridge: Cambridge University Press.

Moyles, J. R. (ed.) (1995) *The Excellence of Play*. Buckingham: Open University Press.

Siegal, M. (1991) *Knowing Children: Experiments in Conversation and Cognition*. Hillsdale: Lawrence Erlbaum.

Smagorinsky, P. (1995) The social construction of data: Methodological problems of investigating learning in the zone of proximal development. *Review of Educational Research*, 65, 191–212.

Vygotsky, L. S. (1987) *Thinking and Speech* (ed. & trans. by N. Minick). New York: Plenum.

CHAPTER 3

Alternative perspectives on cognition, intelligence and effective learning

OVERVIEW

In Piagetian theory a child's capacity to reason at various levels is believed to be biologically controlled, and the development of increasing cognitive abilities reflects natural development in an interactive environment. Hence, children reasoning at a lower level are not less intelligent than others, but at a different stage of development. While Piaget would agree that there are individual differences in mental capacity, his theory emphasises the need to develop each individual's capacity through appropriate experiences, rather than merely categorising the bright and less bright.

Vygotsky's view emphasises the social dimension of learning and the zone of proximal development. Hence, Vygotsky's focus moves beyond what the child currently knows to what is possible, and to the processes most relevant to stimulate this growth. Furthermore, because of the very strong social and cultural component of Vygotskyian thought, what is considered 'intelligent' behaviour is more broadly viewed than simply being good at school and having a lot of 'knowledge'.

In this chapter we look at other alternative views on intelligence and cognition. In particular, we focus on views that consider intellectual functioning as an interaction between the individual and his or her environment rather than an innate quality. We highlight theories that describe intelligence as multifaceted, and defined by such qualities as flexibility of thought, efficient working memory, adaptability, creative productivity, insight skills, social skills, and effective use of domain knowledge. In this approach, one's culture and specific contexts are considered to be important determinants of intelligent behaviour as individuals interact with the external world.

We also discuss psychometric views of intelligence. Intelligence testing is dealt with in some detail and we introduce the notions of mental age, intelligence quotient and individual and group tests of intelligence. Limitations of the psychometric approach to intelligence testing are also described, especially problems emanating from cultural differences.

In each case we draw out the relevance of the approach to understanding effective learning.

GARDNER'S MULTIPLE INTELLIGENCES

Individuals differ from one another in their ability to understand complex ideas, to adapt effectively to the environment, to learn from experience, to engage in various forms of reasoning, to overcome obstacles by taking thought. Although these individual differences can be substantial, they are never entirely consistent: A given person's intellectual performance will vary on different occasions, in different domains, as judged by different criteria. Concepts of 'intelligence' are attempts to clarify and organize this complex set of phenomena.

Neisser et al. 1996

Howard Gardner believes that all definitions of intelligence are shaped by the time, place, and culture in which they evolve (Kornhaber, Krechevsky & Gardner 1990). The developmental theories of both Piaget and Vygotsky, discussed in Chapter 2, certainly bear the imprint of their historico-cultural times. Three factors appear to influence what is considered to be important in the cognitive development of individuals:

1. the domains of knowledge necessary for survival of the culture, such as farming, literacy or the arts;
2. the values embedded in the culture, such as respect for elders, scholarly traditions or pragmatic leanings;
3. the educational system that instructs and nurtures individuals' various competencies. (Kornhaber, Krechevsky & Gardner 1990).

From this you can see that the cognitive skills needed to survive in a farming or herding society may be quite different from those required for survival in a technological society. Furthermore, conceptions of what is intelligent behaviour may also vary accordingly. For example, in an agrarian subsistence society, intelligent behaviour may be related to the production of food and skill in interpersonal relations to maintain the community's social ties. In a non-agrarian modern society, it might be related to technological expertise and independence. Increasingly, in modern societies, intelligent behaviour has become identified with successful performance at school, in mathematics and language in particular. For Gardner this is a very limited perspective on intelligence.

Gardner claims that the capacity of individuals to acquire and advance knowledge reflects the priorities and opportunities that society presents in a cultural domain. In this framework, intelligence is seen as a flexible, culturally dependent construct and as such it reflects a social constructivist perspective (Kornhaber, Krechevsky & Gardner 1990).

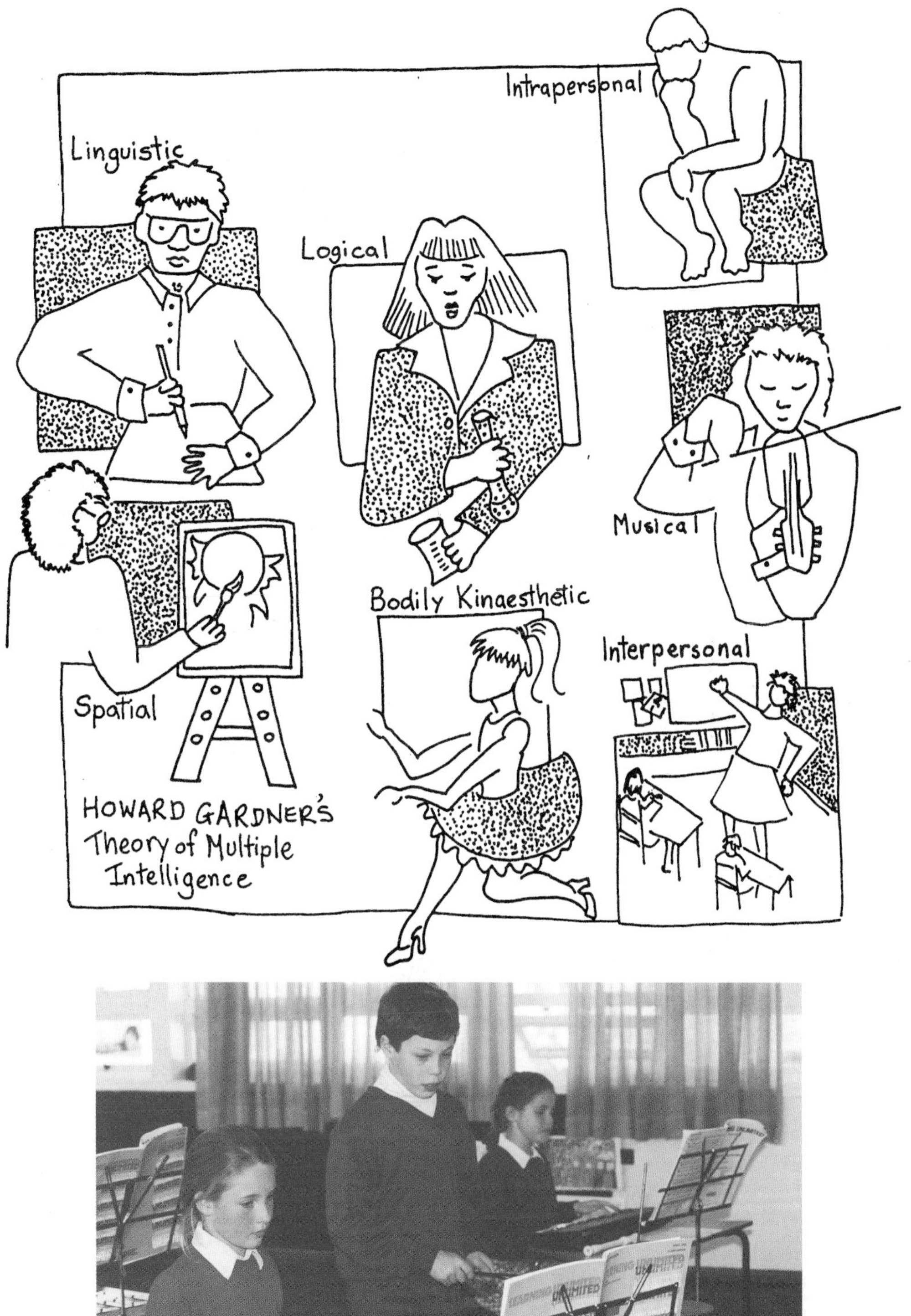

Music should play an important role in any school curriculum.
Photo: authors

Gardner (1983; Gardner & Hatch 1989) proposes a theory of multiple intelligences—specifically, seven intelligences—(although Gardner insists that this is a tentative list and others could be included). The seven intelligences are logical-mathematical, linguistic, musical, spatial, bodily kinaesthetic, interpersonal and intrapersonal. Each is characterised by core components such as sensitivity to the sounds, rhythms and meanings of words (linguistic) and capacities to discern and respond appropriately to the moods, temperaments, motivations and desires of other people (interpersonal). Although few occupations rely entirely on a single intelligence, an individual with a highly developed intelligence in one of these areas may become a composer (musical), a dancer (bodily kinaesthetic) or a therapist (interpersonal). Other occupations might require a blend of intelligences. Gardner and Hatch give the example of a surgeon who needs both the acuity of spatial intelligence to guide the scalpel and the dexterity of the bodily kinaesthetic intelligence to handle it.

Gardner's theory of multiple intelligences

Developmental patterns in multiple intelligences

According to Gardner, each intelligence has a developmental pattern that is relatively independent of the others. For example, linguistic intelligence is acquired by most individuals with little tutoring relatively early in life, whereas speed and extent of musical intelligence development vary widely from person to person. It is also important to note that the relative strengths of the seven intelligences vary within and among individuals (see Kornhaber, Krechevsky & Gardner 1990) and are believed to be biologically determined (Gardner 1993). The development of these intelligences depends on the interaction of children with adults, and the great majority of what is learned after the age of two is socially constructed.

The educational implications of Gardner's multiple intelligences

At the very least, Gardner's view challenges our notion of what is intelligent behaviour. In particular, he challenges the emphasis placed in schools on the development of verbal and mathematical abilities of children to the exclusion of a broader range of intelligent behaviours. Furthermore, this approach to viewing intelligent behaviour and its development suggests a range of educational and assessment practices to encourage effective learning.

Social context is a powerful influence on the development of multiple intelligences

- ☐ First, because of the importance of the **social framework** in which intelligent behaviour develops, educational practices such as **mentoring** and **apprenticeships**, where expert members of society are involved in tutoring individuals, are strongly endorsed. In particular, such teaching approaches, together with the **cooperative involvement of parents** and others in the surrounding community, are seen to strengthen the cognitive outcomes of the community's schoolchildren (see Kornhaber, Krechevsky & Gardner 1990).
- ☐ Second, in order for learning to be meaningful, material to be learnt should be presented in **authentic environments** rather than in decontextualised settings.
- ☐ Third, to encourage children to develop competence in the various intelligences, an **interdisciplinary curriculum** should be developed, and equal time should be given to each area of development.
- ☐ Four, education should be firmly **grounded in the institutions and practices of society**, such as art and science museums, gymnasiums, factories, technology institutions and so on.

In essence, Gardner's theory makes clear that intelligence in its many facets reflects potentials that must be fostered in the environment. They will not develop fully without stimulation, encouragement and extensive practice.

Assessment of learning across the multiple intelligences should integrate curriculum and assessment and be flexible to allow individuals to demonstrate their various competencies in authentic settings which relate directly to the specific task being measured. Assessments should be intrinsically interesting, and tests for specific intelligences should be appropriate to that intelligence. Hence assessments such as work samples, child observations and portfolios are encouraged.

Table 3.1 shows the essentials of a multiple intelligence perspective.

TABLE 3.1

ESSENTIALS OF A MULTIPLE INTELLIGENCE PERSPECTIVE FOR EDUCATION

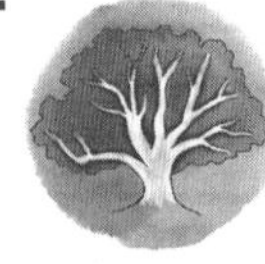

For teachers

- Present material to be learnt in authentic environments.
- Encourage all children to develop competencies across all intelligences.
- Utilise mentoring and apprenticeships with experts in the area of development.
- Develop an interdisciplinary curriculum to facilitate the interconnections between the intelligences.

- Encourage the cooperation of parents and community in students' education.
- Ground education in the cultural institutions and practices of the society.

Implications for assessment

- Integrate curriculum and assessment.
- Be flexible in assessment practices to allow individuals to demonstrate their various competencies.
- Develop authentic assessments.
- Develop alternative assessments such as portfolios and work samples.
- Develop intrinsically interesting assessments.
- Set fair assessments that don't depend on other competencies as intermediaries.

Some schools have designed their curriculum around the notion of multiple intelligences, whereby children are given the opportunity to discover their areas of strength and to develop the full range of intelligences (Vialle 1991, 1993). We believe that consideration of a broader range of talents within schools will give an opportunity for many children to excel who had previously been considered unexceptional, or even at risk for school failure. What do you think?

TEACHER'S CASE BOOK

MULTIPLE INTELLIGENCES AND SCHOOL SETTINGS

Cook Primary School, ACT, is a suburban, traditional, single-classroom school with a high degree of community involvement in policy *and* decision making. There is a wide range of socio-economic backgrounds and about 10% are NESB students.

Multiple intelligence theory is seen at Cook Primary to be an ideal framework to ensure good teaching and therefore improved outcomes for students. At Cook an agreed aim was to develop each child to reach her or his greatest potential and this theory made provision to catch those children who might slip through the net.

Each classroom teacher was asked to analyse a 'typical week' from their daily planner and to total the time or the number of occasions each week they had devoted to each of the seven MI areas. This was a private analysis; however, teachers were pleased to share with other staff members their 'learnings' and omissions. They were asked to address any imbalances and report to future weekly staff meetings.

Each classroom and support teacher was asked to rank every child they taught in the seven MI areas. There were three rankings—'white' meant highly developed, 'pink' was showing some glimmer and 'red' meant the teacher did not know, or the child showed a deficit in that area. Numerical rankings were avoided to reduce the temptation to average out a score. Teachers noted that there were some children about whom they knew little other than in the linguistic and logical-mathematical areas. Other teachers noted that they knew very little about a lot of children in a particular MI area. They resolved to address this.

When it was believed that there was sufficient understanding, a pilot project was set up: the children were put into homogeneous groups, junior and senior, and each of seven teachers elected to be an expert in one of the seven areas. Their task was to come to a real 'understanding' of their area and to locate resources in the school and the wider community that could be used to develop their area of intelligence. Each teacher had to prepare a bank of exercises related to their area and lead the groups through them. The set of experiences was offered seven times to the homogeneous groups who rotated through each teacher one morning a week for seven weeks. Teachers were asked to report at each weekly meeting about their findings. This provided professional development for other teachers who would eventually incorporate that perspective into their daily practice.

After the children had rotated through the seven groups they were asked to assess themselves. Grade 3 and above were given a paper medallion entitled 'I am 100% intelligent' and they had to construct a pie chart of seven segments to total the sum of their intelligence. They were also asked to write, draw/talk about themselves and their strengths in each area. This was a positive and affirming exercise, not a defect-detecting exercise. Teachers filled out a rating sheet on each child three times a year, the object of which was to ensure the teacher viewed each child from various frames of mind.

Case study provided by Judy Perry, Principal, Cook Primary School, ACT

Case study activity

How might a multiple intelligence approach be applied to other schools? Could such a system be applied within one classroom? How would you go about this?

STERNBERG'S TRIARCHIC THEORY OF INTELLIGENCE

Sternberg's triarchic theory of intelligence: componential, experiential, contextual

Gardner's view has given us much food for thought about intellectual functioning and has sensitised educators to the need to stimulate students' cognitive development over a range of skill areas. But is expertise (or lack of it) in one or more of these seven areas necessarily a reflection of intelligence (or its lack)? For example, one can be tone deaf, physically clumsy and socially inept, yet still function effectively as a human being. What are the essential intellectual capacities that are needed for individuals to manage everyday life? Sternberg (1985, 1986) addresses this question by considering intelligence as a kind of mental self-management consisting of three basic elements: **componential intelligence** (also referred to as analytic intelligence), **experiential intelligence** (also known as creative intelligence) and **contextual intelligence** (or practical intelligence). As these three intelligences govern intelligent behaviour, the theory has been called a **triarchic theory**.

1. *Componential intelligence.* Each of the three intelligences refers to different aspects of intelligent behaviour. At the heart of Sternberg's theory are components such as higher-order executive processes

involved in planning, monitoring and decision making in task performance (labelled **metacomponents**); **performance components**, used in the execution of the task, and **knowledge-acquisition components** that are used in gaining new knowledge. These elements comprise **componential intelligence** which relates to an individual's capacity to acquire knowledge, think and plan, monitor his or her own cognitive processes and act in accordance with these.

2. *Experiential intelligence*. Experiential intelligence refers to how an individual uses experience, insight and creativity to solve new problems, and how quickly these novel solutions can be turned into routine processes to solve later related problems. This latter characteristic is labelled **automaticity**.
3. *Contextual intelligence*. Contextual intelligence refers to how individuals adapt to contexts to make the most positive use of them. Adaptations may consist of selecting environments in which one can function optimally, shaping or changing the environment to suit one's purpose better, or moving out of one environment to another that is more compatible.

The three intelligences could be summarised in this way:

- ☐ *componential intelligence* ability to acquire knowledge, think and plan, monitor cognitive processes and determine what is to be done;
- ☐ *experiential intelligence* ability to formulate new ideas to solve problems;
- ☐ *contextual intelligence* ability to adapt to contexts to optimise opportunities.

See Table 3.2 for a list of the essentials of a triarchic intelligence perspective.

TABLE 3.2

ESSENTIALS OF A TRIARCHIC INTELLIGENCE PERSPECTIVE FOR EDUCATION

For teachers

- Model reflective processes during learning activities.
- Have students keep a reflective learning diary.
- Teach metacognitive strategies.
- Encourage use of problem-solving strategies.
- Provide varied contexts for problem-solving skills learned in relation to one domain to transfer to others.
- Teach students to use brainstorming as a tool for generating ideas.
- Incorporate cooperative learning activities that involve group investigation.
- Use debates to develop creative solutions to problems.
- Use role play and sociodramatic play with young children.
- Provide opportunities for students to work in a variety of environments and contexts.
- Encourage and model adaptable behaviour.

ACTION STATION

Teachers often make their own *ad hoc* assessments of intelligence. This activity is designed to explore the kinds of student behaviour a teacher uses to estimate a student's intelligence.

Ask a sample of teachers what kinds of behaviour they use to gain an estimate of a student's intelligence. Put these behaviours on a list. Ask several other teachers to rank them on a five-point scale (5 = very important, 1 = unimportant) in terms of how much these factors influence their judgment of a child's intelligence.

Then ask each teacher to think of one pupil they consider very bright and one who is slow. Have each teacher go through your list and indicate those behaviours in which the chosen students deviate markedly, positively or negatively, from the norm. Do not let the teachers see their previous ranking of importance.

If the teachers are consistent, behaviour scaled 4 or 5 should be marked by + or –. If this is the case, then the teachers are consistent in their observations. If not, ask the teachers what other kinds of student behaviours they use in their assessments.

What elements of Sternberg's triarchic intelligence theory can you find here? Photo: NSW Board of Studies

GUILFORD'S STRUCTURE OF THE INTELLECT

A number of older theories also considered intelligence multifaceted. In order to explain the obvious differences in performance of individuals across a number of cognitive areas, Thurstone (1938) construed intelligence as consisting of a number of factors which he called **primary mental abilities**. These are: verbal meaning, number facility, inductive reasoning, perceptual speed, spatial relations, memory and verbal fluency. Many tests are based on these conceptualisations of discrete mental abilities. Probably the most extreme case of regarding intelligence as multifaceted is Guilford's structure of the intellect model (1967). Guilford proposed that performance on any cognitive task can best be understood by analysing the task into the kind of mental operations to be performed, the type of content or test material on which the mental operation is performed, and the resulting product of performing a particular operation on a particular type of content. Guilford considers five possible kinds of operation, four types of content and six products. These are listed below:

Operations	*Content*	*Products*
1. cognition	1. figural	1. units
2. memory	2. symbolic	2. classes
3. divergent thinking	3. semantic	3. relations
4. convergent thinking	4. behavioural	4. systems
5. evaluation		5. transformations
		6. implications

Each of these facets can potentially interact, resulting in a particular demonstration of intelligence. In fact, there are exactly 120 factors comprising the structure of intelligence in this model (5 operations by 4 contents by 6 products). Recently, changes have been made to the model increasing the number of factors to 150, with the figural stimulus content being replaced by auditory and visual stimulus contents (Gardner & Clark 1992; Lohman 1989). The research evidence supporting the model is weak and it has declined in influence over the past few years (Lohman 1989). Nevertheless, the structure of the model suggests some interesting implications for educational use, and we will consider one of these in our later discussion of creativity.

ACTION STATION

For a given intelligent behaviour (e.g. writing an assignment, designing and producing an article of clothing, managing a meeting), illustrate which facets of intelligence may be called into operation. Illustrate how individual variations in expertise may reflect differential abilities on specific facets of intelligence.

You should remember that each of the above approaches is theoretical; there isn't a cube in our brain with each of Guilford's factors embedded in it, or a bank of primary mental abilities. Nor do Gardner's 'intelligences' exist as tangible, measurable entities. What these theories set out to do—some from a psychometric perspective, others from a more qualitative perspective—is explain variation in intellectual performance both within an individual and across individuals. They are convenient ways of labelling a phenomenon and as such they make a valuable contribution to our understanding of human characteristics.

Question point: *How would you define intelligence and measure it?*

Question point: *What do you think would be Piaget's attitude to intelligence testing? What do you think would be the attitude of Vygotsky?*

ACTION STATION

This activity is designed to highlight the difficulty of defining intelligence and measuring the construct. In a group, discuss the concept of intelligence and decide on a definition of intelligence that reflects group consensus. Design a series of items or activities to measure your conception of intelligence. Administer your test to another group while completing the other group's test. Discuss your findings.

PSYCHOMETRICS AND COGNITION

As we have seen above, theorists such as Gardner argue that there are several relatively autonomous human intellectual competencies, which he calls human intelligences, or frames of the mind. These 'multiple intelligences' are relatively independent of one another, and are fashioned and combined in a multiplicity of adaptive ways by individuals and cultures to produce intelligent behaviour. His theory stems from his beliefs that it is nonsense to reduce the notion of intelligence to a homogeneous mental construct. Furthermore, Gardner believes that historical and contemporary conceptualisations of intelligence measured by simplistic tests fail to pay sufficient attention to intelligence and problem solving as it is displayed in the real world characterised by social and cultural diversity. In effect, Gardner is criticising the psychometric approach to intelligence definition and measurement. We now direct our attention to this view of intelligence.

The psychometric approach to cognitive development and its measurement has, in fact, inspired the most research and is the most widely used in practical settings. It seeks to define and quantify dimensions of intelligence, primarily through the collection of data on individual differences and through the construction of reliable and valid mental tests (Gardner & Clark 1992). The questions that are a focus of the psychometric approach are:

- ☐ How can cognitive development be quantified?
- ☐ How can such measurements be used to predict later intellectual performance?
- ☐ How can the intelligence of individual children be meaningfully compared?
- ☐ What factors make up intelligence, and do these factors change with age?

(Siegler & Richards 1982)

Mental age

The pychometric approach to intelligence, and the concept 'mental age' in particular, stems from the work of Alfred Binet and Theophile Simon in France early this century, when they were given the task of devising a means of measuring children's ability to succeed at school. One of Binet's basic assumptions, which became the basis of many tests, was that people are thought of as normal if they can do the things people of their age normally do, retarded if performance corresponds with the performance of people who are younger, and accelerated if the performance exceeds that of people in the subject's own age group. This led to the concept of **mental age**—that is, that we can take a measure of a person's intellectual development in much the same way that we can assess chronological or physical age. Mental age is based on the number of intelligence test items an individual answers correctly relative to the number of items an average individual at various ages answers correctly. Thus, if a six-year-old child has a mental age of seven, he is performing as well as the average child whose actual chronological age is seven. Later, William Stern, a German psychologist, conceived of the intelligence quotient, which is the ratio of mental age to chronological age multiplied by 100:

$$\text{intelligence quotient} = \frac{\text{mental age}}{\text{chronological age}} \text{ X } 100$$

It can be seen that, if a child has an IQ of 100, his or her performance is average for a child of his or her age. As the IQ rises above 100, the child is considered increasingly superior to other children at that age and, as it drops below 100, the child is doing relatively less well than his or her peers. An adjustment was later made to convert the units to standard scores so that IQs across various age groups were comparable in meaning.

IQ scores are often poorly understood by parents, children and teachers alike. A joke goes that one parent, on hearing of his child's IQ score, was absolutely delighted. It was the first time that his child had scored 100 out of 100!

Assumptions underlying the Binet intelligence test

Three general assumptions underlie Binet's approach to assessing intelligence:

1. General intelligence is a trait that develops with age;
2. Performance in the form of skills is assessing an underlying capacity to learn;
3. What has been learnt is a measure of what could be learnt in the future.

The intention in the Binet-Simon test was to measure general intelligence at work by sampling various types of mental activities such as comprehension, vocabulary knowledge, logical reasoning through analogies, knowledge of opposites, similarities and differences, ability to complete verbal and pictorial compositions, identifying absurdities, drawing designs and memory for meaningful material and for digits. The test was individually administered and consisted of a series of questions and activities chosen because they were representative of levels of knowledge and abilities at particular ages. The Binet-Simon test became known as the Stanford-Binet after it was revised a number of times at Stanford University. The latest revision was completed in 1986 (Thorndike, Hagen & Sattler 1986). The Binet-Simon test was the forerunner of a whole range of individual tests designed to measure intelligence. Unfortunately, because of this, the notion of intelligence and intelligent behaviour became identified with those individual attributes that appear most obviously related to academic achievement, are readily able to be measured, and are able to distinguish between children's ability to learn effectively in the school setting.

Wechsler intelligence tests

David Wechsler, a psychologist at Bellevue Hospital in New York, worked with children and adults afflicted with various forms of mental illness. He was impressed by the fact that many mentally ill people perform very well on standard intelligence tests, which measure academic ability, but are relatively incompetent in everyday problem solving and social interaction. Considering tests such as the Binet test inadequate because they are verbally and academically biased,

Wechsler set about constructing a test that took more account of intellectual potential in relation to experience, motivation and personality factors. This was based on the rationale that emotional factors may heighten attention, persistence and adaptability, or they may impair ability to mobilise intellectual resources. While the Wechsler scales were initially intended to assess the intellectual skills of older adolescents and adults, there have been two downward extensions of the original scale (the Wechsler Adult Intelligence Scale: WAIS); these are the Wechsler Intelligence Scale for Children (WISC-R, the revised edition) and the Wechsler Preschool and Primary Scale (WPPSI-R, the revised edition). The tests are produced by and available from Psychological Corporation (Gardner & Clark 1992).

The Wechsler tests have considerable clinical value. They also show up patterns presented by certain psychotic groups and some patterns of brain damage. These tests have been used in Australia and New Zealand with small changes to a few items.

Tests similar to those in the various Wechsler intelligence scales. These questions are examples of six verbal subtests.

1. *General information*: These questions relate to a range of information—for example, 'How many hands do you have?' and 'How many cents make up a dollar?'
2. *Comprehension*: These questions test practical information and the ability to evaluate past experience—for example, 'What do you do when you cut your foot?' and 'Why do we keep money in the bank?'
3. *Mathematics*: These questions test arithmetic reasoning—for example, place eight blocks in a row before the subject and ask them to 'count these blocks with your finger', 'If 14 apples weigh 4 kg, how much do 21 weigh?'
4. *Similarities*: These questions ask in what way certain objects or concepts are similar; measures abstract thinking—for example, 'What is the relation between a piano and a violin?'
5. *Vocabulary*: These questions test word knowledge—for example, 'What is the meaning of knife, table, ... dilatory?'
6. *Digit span*: These questions test attention and rote memory by presenting a series of digits auditorily which the individual has to repeat either forward or backwards.

There is also a performance scale that consists of a variety of manipulative tasks which require the individual to complete patterns, arrange pictures, assemble objects and relate numbers to marks.

Group tests of intelligence

Individual intelligence tests such as the Stanford-Binet and the Wechsler tests are time-consuming, expensive and require expert administration and analysis. Because of this they are most often used in clinical situations. Group tests of intelligence, often called **pen and paper tests**, were developed to make testing speedy and cheap, while retaining accuracy and predictive validity. One of the initial reasons for the development of group tests was to select men for the United States Army during World War I. These army tests were used to select individuals for various levels of army training, or to exclude them altogether if they were considered unsuitable for any training (Aiken 1979). After the appearance of these initial group tests there was an explosion in the development of pen and paper tests. Among common group tests used in Australia and New Zealand are the ACER Junior A Test, ACER Intermediate Test A and ACER Intermediate D, ACER Advanced Test B40 and ACER Advanced Test N, ACER Test of Reasoning Abilities, the Otis Higher Test and the Slosson Intelligence Test. The norming base for the ACER tests is Australian. However, the format and style of the tests, and the psychometric techniques of item construction and validation are strongly influenced by overseas models, in particular, the work of the Educational Testing Service (ETS) in the United States (Keats & Keats 1988).

Pen and paper tests

These group tests of intelligence have been used extensively in the past to **stream** children into different levels of schooling, with the purpose of providing special opportunities for the very bright, as well as for those with intellectual deficits.

Group tests used for academic streaming

Over the past ten years there has been a movement away from using group tests for streaming purposes towards individual assessment for the purpose of integrating children with intellectual disability into the mainstream classes (Doherty 1982). To a certain extent this movement against mass tests has been the product of lobbying by immigrant and minority communities concerned that the language component in general ability tests may militate against the fair assessment of the children of migrant and non-English-speaking-background origins. The Australian Teachers Federation, together with various teachers' groups, has also been influential in the partial demise of group tests. These groups are concerned with the possibility of inherent biases in the tests. In particular, it is thought that children from advantaged socioeconomic and racial groups would be better prepared to answer the questions because of their greater access to information (Keats & Keats 1988).

Question point: *Do you think it is more useful to consider intelligence quantitatively or qualitatively?*

THE LIMITATIONS OF INTELLIGENCE TESTS

What the original Binet-Simon intelligence test (and other tests following in its footsteps) measured was *actual acquired learning*, which was then used as an index to what might be expected from individuals in the future. As such, these tests have always correlated very highly with each other and with academic performance at school, and have been reliable guides as to what individuals might achieve at school if, and this is important, schools emphasise as their primary goal an individual's acquisition of knowledge in the form of facts and figures, and the development of particular reasoning skills.

Alternative notions of intelligence

However, as you can probably see, the psychometric notion of what constitutes intelligence is limited to what the test developers define as intelligent behaviour. It excludes other very valuable forms of expressing intelligent behaviour through creativity, social skills and excellence in physical performance (refer to the earlier section on multiple intelligences). Furthermore, it takes little account of children who have had atypical or different experiences, poorly preparing them to achieve in such tests. Gross examples of this, of course, are the application of such tests to non-English-speaking background children, children from cultural backgrounds other than the one in which the test is located, or children who have not received appropriate, or extended, schooling (Rogoff & Chavajay 1995). The ACER tests used in Australia and New Zealand have included children from immigrant families in the samples used to derive the test norms, and so it is reasonable that these tests be used in circumstances where the children are quite familiar with the language and have been in Australia or New Zealand for more than four years (Keats & Keats 1988).

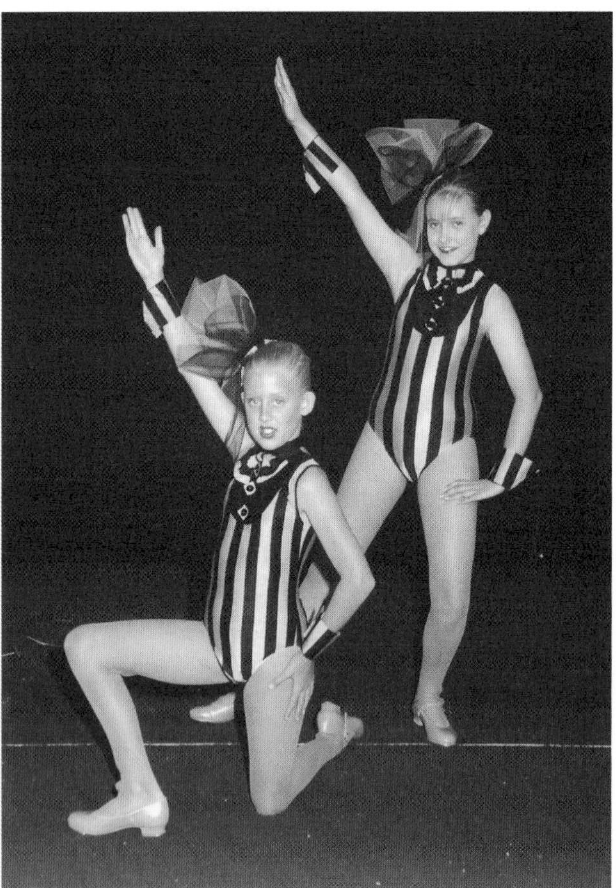

Many talents illustrate intelligence. Why have schools defined intelligence only in terms of academic work?

Personality characteristics

Personality characteristics are not well accounted for in group tests, so that a score may well reflect a person's concern with diligence or neatness, rather than attention to speed to get as many questions right as possible (many tests have speed of completion as an important criterion of performance). A number of Australian studies (Goodnow 1976, 1990; Kearins 1988; Klich 1988; Munnings 1980; also Pick 1980) suggest that more attention needs to be paid to what is regarded as good performance and the 'right' way to approach cognitive tasks, particularly in cross-cultural assessment. For example, the author, as a youngster, sat for the grade 5 intelligence tests that were common in the past. In her early days at school, as a non-English speaker, she was taught skills of diligence and attention to detail, so much so that her performance at school was excellent. Her teacher therefore was puzzled why she had performed so poorly in an intelligence test. On being asked by the teacher how she had gone about the task of completing the test, she related that she took her time to make sure every answer was correct, wrote very neatly and erased any untidy work. Consequently, she did not complete the test. She resat the test with the instructions to move as quickly through the items as possible, not to worry about neatness and so on. Her score was markedly better. But how many children get such individual attention when completing group tests?

TABLE 3.3

LIMITATIONS OF VERBAL INTELLIGENCE TESTS

1. Measure academic (school) learning only.
2. Do not measure creativity, social skills or excellence in physical performance.

3. Biased against those from different backgrounds in relation to school performance (e.g. language, experiential background).
4. Measure speed but not necessarily diligence and attention to detail.

Examples of group tests of intelligence

Group tests of intelligence are often designed to measure individuals' general intelligence as revealed by their performance on verbal and numerical questions. Items are generally arranged in ascending order of difficulty and may include analogies, classifications, synonyms, number and letter series, and questions involving arithmetical and verbal reasoning. These tests are usually timed. Typically these tests say:

This is a test to see how well you can think. It contains questions of different kinds. Some examples and practice questions will be given to show you how to answer the questions.

This is then followed by instructions which might say:

Try each questions as you come to it but if you find any question too hard, leave it out and come back later if you have time. Do not spend too much time on any one question. Try to get as many right as possible.

Questions are then asked similar to the following:

1. Foot is to man as claw is to (?)
   1. dog 2. horse 3. lion 4. cat 5. bird ( )
2. Book is to library as animal is to (?)
   1. beach 2. boat 3. house 4. zoo ( )
3. What is the next number in this series (?)
   2, 4, 6, 8, 10 ( )
4. What is the next number in this series (?)
   1, 5, 2, 5, 3, 5, 4, 5 ( )
5. What group of letters comes next in this series (?)
   AA, BB, CC, DD ( )
6. What group of letters come next in this series (?)
   AC, BD, CE, DF ( )
7. Four of the following words are alike—what is the other word?
   1. coat 2. shirt 3. singlet 4. sweater 5. socks ( )
8. Four of the following words are alike. What is the other word?
   1. laugh 2. giggle 3. chuckle 4. smirk 5. cry ( )
9. Large means:
   1. cold 2. big 3. short 4. funny 5. small ( )

Non-verbal intelligence tests

To alleviate the potential bias inherent in verbal tests, a number of non-verbal tests have been designed which measure intelligence through activities such as pattern completion (Raven Progressive Matrices), pictures and diagrams (ACER Junior Non-verbal Test; Jenkins Intermediate Non-verbal Test, Peabody Picture Vocabulary Test—PPVT, Tests of General Ability TOGA) and drawing (Goodenough-Harris Drawing Test). Test writers have also given their attention to developing culture-fair tests, with the Raven Progressive Matrices and the Culture Fair Intelligence Test as examples of these. Details on these tests, and others, may be found in Aiken 1979.

Non-verbal tests use pattern completion, pictures, diagrams and free drawings

Variables influencing measured IQ scores

Some of the variables that may influence measured IQ scores are presented in Tables 3.4 and 3.5. As you can see, they are quite extensive.

TABLE 3.4

TEST VARIABLES INFLUENCING MEASURED INTELLIGENCE

1. The actual test administered

Different tests measure different attributes—verbal, motor, perceptual, abstract reasoning and so on. Intelligence tests seldom tap interpersonal skills, athletic abilities, creativity and a variety of other desirable human attributes.

2. Cultural differences

There may be cultural and social factors operating that influence a person's performance on IQ tests.

3. Inappropriate norms

Norms for tests quickly become dated and unreliable. Tests are not frequently updated.

4. Test-taking experience

Competence in taking tests comes with training and practice. Trying to guess the expected answer is a trap for the inexperienced test-taker.

TABLE 3.5

MOTIVATIONAL VARIABLES INFLUENCING MEASURED INTELLIGENCE

1. *Parental pressure* (you must do well to get into the selective high school).
2. *Positive or negative school experiences* (this is a 'daggy' school and I'll show them what I think by not bothering about the test).
3. *Peer affiliations* (it's not good to be seen doing too well at school).
4. *Rapport with teachers and testers* (I'll try my hardest for my teacher because I like her).
5. *The educational policy of the school* (some schools emphasise competition, grading, ability grouping, promotion).
6. *Personality of the child* (test of general anxiety, impulsiveness, persistence, conformity).
7. *Health* (I've got a headache and it's a hot day so I won't bother).

Examples of non-verbal tests

Non-verbal tests of intelligence often consist of pattern completion exercises. They may begin with a statement such as:

> This test consists of a series of patterns in which the bottom right square has been left blank. Complete the pattern by drawing in the design you think should be there. These tests may be timed or untimed. Usually there is a cut-off point where the test is terminated if the individual fails to answer correctly a sequence of pattern completions. Try your hand at the following.

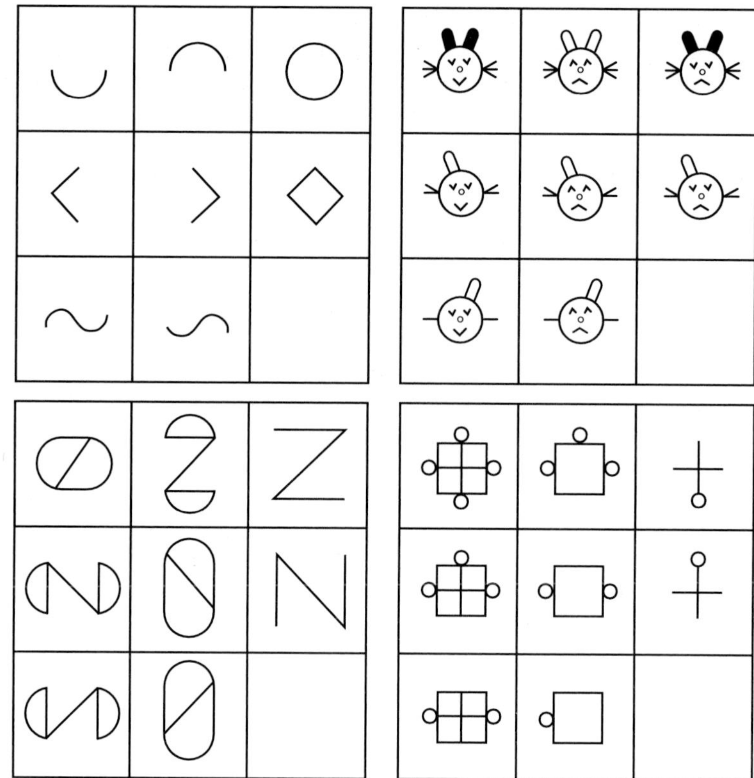

An IQ score, therefore, may not so much record an individual's intellectual capacity as the combined effect of all the factors operating on the child at the time of the testing, and the extent to which individuals are consciously acquainted with the rules and procedures of test-taking (this is particularly important if the test is being given to groups not used to taking such tests, such as traditional Aboriginal, Maori and Islander groups). In the long term, any marked changes in an individual's physical or emotional environment, such as moving from the country to the city, losing a parent through death or divorce, and periods of ill health may result in a change in intellectual performance. IQ scores, to be of much use, should be continually updated, and results from a range of tests should be taken into account.

Because of these variables it is dangerous to assume that a child with a high IQ will necessarily perform well, while a child with a low IQ will perform poorly. IQ scores should be used as a *guide only*. Teachers should consider primarily the individual's ability as demonstrated in class, rather than what the IQ score leads them to expect.

PRACTICAL USE OF INTELLIGENCE TESTS

The practical use of intelligence tests and IQ scores depends on their validity, reliability and stability. Technical issues of validity and reliability in test construction are considered in Chapter 13. IQ scores, in general, appear valid and predict fairly accurately a child's performance in *academic work*, but they do not predict performance in non-academic areas. The normal distribution of IQ scores is represented in the figure below.

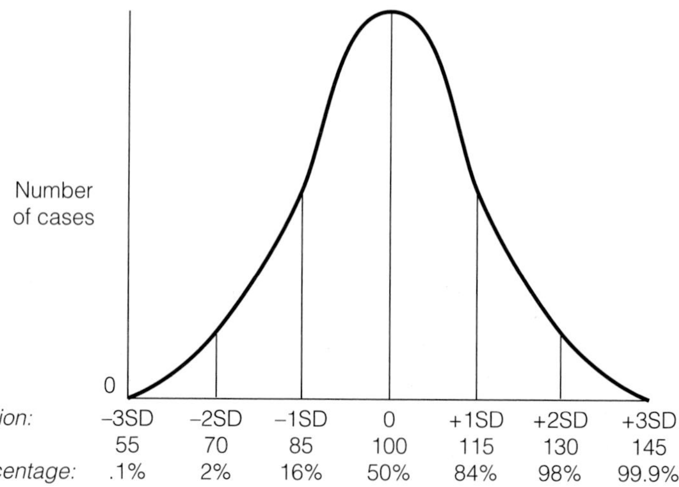

Intelligence test scores are also fairly stable as children grow older—the average change in IQ score between the ages of 12 and 17 is about 7.1 IQ points, with a variation of up to 18 points for some individuals (see Neisser et al. 1996). It is important to note here that, while IQ scores remain stable, this does not indicate that the performance of individuals is the same over this time. Individuals gain in knowledge, reasoning skills and vocabulary. However, what does not change is the individual's score relative to others of the same age.

It is also important that IQ scores are reliable for individuals if they are to have any value in terms of the programs that teachers develop for students on the basis of their scores. In fact, IQ scores can be subject to a variation of up to 20 points on successive testings as they can be influenced by many non-intellectual factors at the time of testing. We should look therefore at individual scores within a broad range of scores. Furthermore, it is important to note that the boundaries of what is normal intellectual capacity are very wide, and encompass most children in our schools. Hence there is little justification for streaming on the basis of intelligence scores (except perhaps for the extremely talented, and the uneducable).

Question point: Research shows that intelligence tests predict school performance fairly well, and also predict scores on school achievement tests that are designed to measure knowledge of the curriculum. However, academic performance is not explained by intelligence alone. Successful school learning depends on many personal characteristics other than intelligence. List a number of personal characteristics that might affect school learning. What other factors might also influence school learning and achievement?

Psychometric view of intelligence and developmental change

Piaget and Vygotsky attempted to explain developmental changes in intellectual functioning. While psychometric theories of intelligence were developed mainly with adolescents and adults in mind, there are ways in which these theories can accommodate developmental change. For example:

- ☐ Changes in the number of dimensions characterising intelligent thought. As children grow older, the number of psychometric dimensions that can be meaningfully measured increases. In other words, there appears to be an increasing differentiation in mental functioning.
- ☐ Changes in the relevance or weights of dimensions with age. As children grow older, dimensions measured by tests become more or less important in discriminating between individuals. For example, infants may be most distinguished by perceptual-motor factors and older children by verbal-symbol manipulation factors.

Other elements of psychometric analysis that indicate developmental change are beyond the scope of this text but may be followed up in Sternberg and Powell (1983).

Are we becoming more intelligent?

An intriguing aspect of the measurement of intelligence by psychometric tests is that, across successive generations, intelligence levels appear to be increasing by about 3 IQ points per decade, despite the fact that tests are renormed periodically to adjust for increasing test sophistication (Flynn 1996; see also Neisser 1996). What is particularly interesting is that the gains appear greatest on tests that were designed to be free of cultural bias such as the Raven Progressive Matrices. A further interesting aspect of this phenomenon is the lack of relationship between increasing levels of intelligence as measured by intelligence tests and actual school or academic performance which has not, in general, improved.

What are the explanations for increasing intellectual performance? Three explanations have been given to account for this effect. The first of these relates to the increased complexity of most people's daily lives through exposure to much more information. The many forms of mass media and technology, extended and more sophisticated schooling, and the array of new and ever changing experiences to which people are exposed may have produced corresponding changes in complexity of mind, and in certain psychometric abilities.

Exposure to mass media

A second explanation attributes gains to improvements in nutrition. Most people are aware that children, on average, are growing taller and larger as a result of dietary changes (this is particularly noticeable in certain Asian countries such as Japan). Perhaps brain size is also increasing and affecting intellectual functioning.

Improved diet

Lastly, some argue that intelligence as such has not risen but, rather, one aspect of thinking is improving, that of abstract problem solving. This improvement in abstract thinking may be the result of greater exposure of individuals to opportunities to use abstract thought in their everyday lives. As abstract thinking is a major component of IQ testing it is plausible that people will increasingly perform better on this dimension of thinking.

Abstract problem solving

Children are growing taller, larger and hungrier today. Is this contributing to their increased intelligence?
Photo: authors

Question point: *These are interesting hypotheses explaining increases in measured intelligence. What do you think of each?*

ACTION STATION

Consider a range of intelligence tests (such as the Stanford-Binet, ACER tests, WPPSI, Goodenough-Harris Draw-a-Person, and Progressive Matrices). Consider the tests critically in the context of the theory of psychometric testing of intelligence. Indicate clearly:

1. the nature of each test;
2. the underlying constructs each test is attempting to measure;
3. the strengths of each test;
4. the weaknesses of each test;

Discuss your conclusions within a group.

HEREDITY AND ENVIRONMENT

The topic of heredity and environment and their relative impacts on physical and psychological development is vast and complex, and beyond the scope of this text (see Papalia & Olds 1989; Turner & Helms 1991). However, we wish to highlight a number of points for you to consider in the context of this chapter and later chapters on individual development.

Development: heredity versus environment

It is clear that all genetically programmed effects on the development of an individual are potentially modifiable by the environment (even those that are hard to observe and may be biochemical in nature). It is also clear that all environmental effects on the development of physical and psychological characteristics involve genetic structures. The essence of the heredity and environment issue lies in the relative importance of each of these to human development, and how environmental factors (and interpersonal and cultural factors especially) may facilitate the development of genetic potential, inhibit its development, or compensate for the inadequate inherited potential of an individual. Two extreme positions are possible. On one hand, it is argued that individual potential is very malleable and, provided the environment is healthy and stimulating, individuals may develop many different physical and psychological skills and talents, irrespective of supposed limitations from their genetic inheritance. This is referred to as the **environmentalist** position. On the other hand, it is argued that individual development reflects genetic potential and that no amount of environmental engineering can alter the course of development of the individual. This is referred to as the **hereditarian** position. If we hold the position that the behaviours of the young, whether physical, emotional, social or intellectual, are the result of maturation alone then all we need to do is let the children grow by themselves.

Heredity: genetically programmed development

Environment: genetically programmed development is influenced by external forces

In many areas of human development the hereditarian position appears to have considerable strength. It is virtually impossible to change environmentally the development of height, eye and hair colour, and the acquisition of various motor skills such as toilet training and walking (although, of course, an impoverished environment or ill health may retard natural growth). However, when we consider the vast array of behaviour that characterises human beings, it becomes problematic to argue that genetic potential alone is the primary cause of development. In accounting for intelligence, personality characteristics, creativity, physical skills, interpersonal skills and so on, we are confronted with the strong probability that the development of such skills is highly influenced by the environment.

Educators generally aspire to the view that both environment and hereditary potential are important in their interaction on the development of individuals. This interrelationship explains the marked variations in the patterns of development of different children. If human development was due to maturation alone, as in some animal species, there would be no such thing as individuality.

Streaming and ability grouping

Streaming and ability grouping is an example of a hereditarian view of education

Both the environmentalist perspective and the hereditarian perspective have, at various times, influenced educational practice. When educationalists believe that the development of children reflects genetic potential, there is an emphasis on testing for potential and streaming children accordingly, so that individual development is maximised (within the constraints set by that genetic potential). Consequently, educational environments based on such a belief stream children into classes of different abilities and talents, and restrict activities to those thought most appropriate for the children within a particular ability grouping. Special schools are established to cater for the very talented and the physically, mentally or socially disabled children. The emphasis in such settings is on the individual development of the child in the context of assessed potential to benefit from particular educational programs.

Mainstreaming and integration

Mainstreaming and integration is an example of the environmentalist perspective on education

When educationalists believe that the environment is particularly powerful in shaping human development, there is an emphasis on having children experience a range of environments to maximise individual development. Educational environments based on this belief have parallel classrooms, and children with assessed developmental or learning difficulties are mainstreamed so that they may benefit from the enriched environment of the regular classroom (see Chapter 11). Progression and exposure to a variety of enrichment or special programs is in terms of presumed ability of individuals to benefit from such programs.

When we were growing up we were seldom exposed to children whose development differed greatly from ours. As children it was quite a shock for us to see learning-disabled and physically disabled children. Many educators of the time felt that, as such children appeared to have very limited capacity to develop, or to learn to speak, read or write, there was little point in giving them an education. As a consequence many children were restricted to their family home and attendance at special schools with very limited social and educational programs.

Many years later, as academics, we were visiting friends in England who had a Down's syndrome son. Rather than allow the child's potential for development to wither both parents spent endless time with Alun, enriching his world and stimulating his interest and motivation to learn. Over the years, Alun learnt to speak, read and write. He learnt how to look after himself, use public transport, and the skills of a trade. He now lives in a special community that provides some independence, has a girlfriend and holds down a job. Apart from improved medical treatment, what made the difference was that Alun was stimulated and allowed to grow.

Today in Australia and New Zealand there is an emphasis on mainstreaming (dealt with in greater detail later in the text). We would draw your attention to one key theme of ours—that all children have potential and it is our duty and privilege as educators and parents to facilitate their development through attention to their needs and support in providing a stimulating learning environment. There is no predetermined ceiling on intellectual development. The intellectual capacity of children is not a fixed quantity with which we have to work, but a variable that can be modified and enhanced by social policy, good educational practices and plentiful resources (see Neisser et al. 1996).

Question point: Analyse Alun's case history above in terms of the theoretical perspectives covered in this chapter—namely, Gardner, Sternberg and the psychometric perspective.

Recommended reading

Gardner, H. (1993) *Multiple Intelligences: The Theory in Practice. A Reader.* New York: Basic Books.

Gardner, M. K. & Clark, E. (1992) The psychometric perspective on intellectual development in childhood and adolescence. In R. J. Sternberg & C. A. Berg (eds), *Intellectual Development.* New York: Cambridge University Press.

Keats, D.M., E Keats, J. A. (1988) Human assessment in Australia. In S. H. Irvine, J. W. Berry (eds.) *Human Abilities in Cultural Context.* Cambridge: Cambridge University Press.

Kornhaber, M., Krechevsky, M. & Gardner, H. (1990) Engaging intelligence. *Educational Psychologist*, 25, 177–199.

Neisser, U. et al. (1996) Intelligence: Knowns and unknowns. American Psychologist, 51, 77–101.

Rogoff, B. & Chavajay, P. (1995) What's become of research on the cultural basis of cognitive development? *American Psychologist*, 50, 859–77.

Sternberg, R. (1985) *Beyond IQ: A Triarchic Theory of Human Intelligence*. New York: Cambridge University Press.

Sternberg, R. (1986) *Intelligence Applied: Understanding and Increasing Your Own Intellectual Skills*. New York: Harcourt Brace Jovanovich.

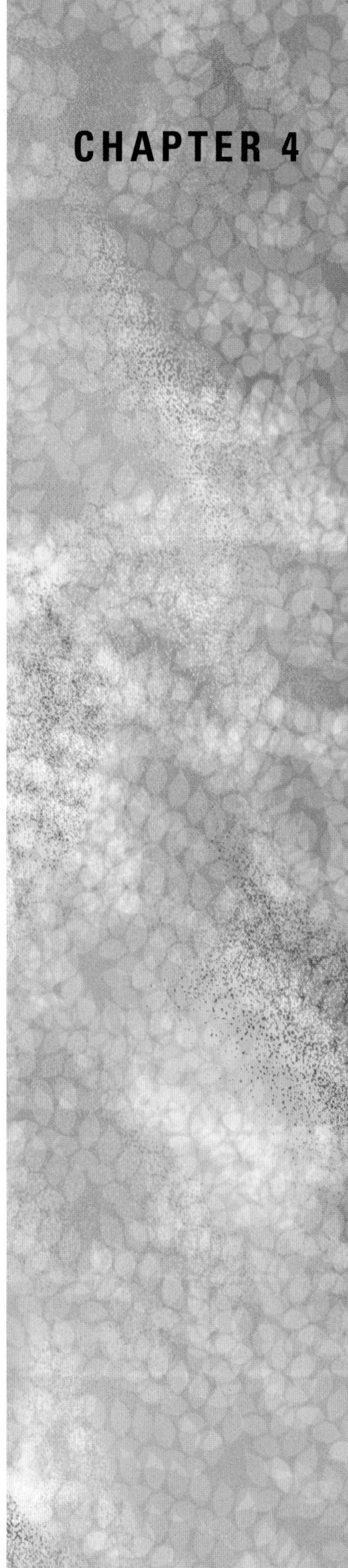

Information processing and effective learning

OVERVIEW

In this chapter we focus on information processing as a model for explaining human learning. We explore in detail the computer as an analogy for the learning process by examining the way in which information is attended to, encoded, processed, stored and retrieved.

Results of information processing research apply in three areas of learning. First, information processing suggests that there are limits to the amount of information that learners can attend to and process effectively. If we overload our processing system, the working memory is unable to cope with the demands and processing becomes inefficient. In this chapter we present many ideas on how long and complex, or new and potentially difficult information can be restructured so that mental demand is reduced. Such facilitation can be accomplished by emphasising procedures and activities that are directed towards schema acquisition (i.e. combining elements of information into fewer elements) and automation (i.e. skills for retrieval from long-term memory with less demand on the working memory). Techniques such as chunking, mnemonics and coding schemes (such as networks and concept maps) should be used in the classroom to overcome cognitive overload. We also discuss the serial position effect and how it might be overcome by verbal markers, advance organisers and variation in presentation so that student performance may be enhanced.

The second finding from information-processing research that has specific implications for facilitating learning relates to the need for the learner to be actively engaged in processing the information in order to transfer it from the working memory to the long-term memory. We refer to this as learning for retention. We discuss methods such as whole and part learning, repetition and drill, and distributed practice as effective techniques to be used. Simple techniques such as elaboration, review, rehearsal and summarising may also be used to facilitate retention after the material has been processed.

The third implication from information-processing research for learning is that learnt material should be encoded in such a way as to facilitate recall. Meaningful material is learnt more easily, retained more effectively and recalled more efficiently than non-meaningful material. We discuss methods for enhancing meaningful learning.

LEARNER-CENTRED PSYCHOLOGICAL PRINCIPLE 3

The successful learner can link new information with existing knowledge in meaningful ways.

Given that the backgrounds and experiences of individual learners can differ dramatically, and given that the mind works to link information meaningfully and holistically, learners interpret and organize information in ways that are uniquely meaningful to them. A goal in formal education is to have all learners create shared understandings and conceptions regarding fundamental knowledge and skills that define and lead to valued learning outcomes. In these situations, teachers can assist learners in acquiring and integrating knowledge (e.g. by creating opportunities for discussion and dialogue and interaction among learners and between learners and adults; by teaching them strategies for constructing meaning, organizing content, accessing prior knowledge, relating new knowledge to general themes or principles, storing or practicing what they have learned, and visualizing future uses for the knowledge).

Reprinted with permission, APA Task Force on Psychology in Education (1993, January), p. 6.

BOX 4.1 TEACHING COMPETENCE

The teacher engages the student actively in developing knowledge

Indicators

The teacher:

- makes explicit connections between content and students' prior learning, contexts and interests;
- presents content with confidence;
- encourages students to acquire and organise knowledge and to convey it to others appropriately.

Case studies illustrating National Competency Framework for Beginning Teaching, National Project on the Quality of Teaching and Learning, Australian Teaching Council, 1996, Element 3.8, p.53. Commonwealth of Australia copyright, reproduced by permission.

INFORMATION PROCESSING AND CONSTRUCTIVISM

Information processing

Currently, information processing is probably the leading conceptual framework for the study of cognitive development and learning (Kail & Bisanz 1992; Kantowitz & Roediger 1980; Lohman 1989; Siegler 1991; Wessells 1982; Winne 1995a). In the emphasis on the cognitive mechanisms by which information is processed—that is, the active role of the learner, and the importance of personally meaningful elaborations—it is a **constructivist**

WHAT WOULD YOU DO?

HE'LL SPEAK TO HIS BRAIN

Andrew was a very slow writer. He constantly stared into space and was easily distracted and yet didn't admit he had a problem. Miss O'Brien believed that a lot of Andrew's behaviour was linked to being afraid of getting it 'wrong' and she had her suspicions that pressure came from home. She developed a strong relationship with Andrew and he eventually admitted to her that he had a problem with his writing.

One day when Miss O'Brien was working with Andrew, she asked him why he couldn't write what was in his head. He said, 'When I get up to five things in my head they burst like a bubble—it's like trying to pick up a bubble, when you touch it, it bursts.' It was a real insight into Andrew. He had just shown her how able he was at using and controlling language to capture his thoughts and feelings. He had identified his short-term memory problems. After that Andrew really unburdened himself, saying that he was anxious that Mum and Dad might realise he had a problem and that he believed himself that he couldn't write. Together Miss O'Brien and Andrew devised three ways to help.

What three ways would you suggest? See p.87 for the teacher's solution.

Case studies illustrating National Competency Framework for Beginning Teaching, National Project on the Quality of Teaching and Learning, Australian Teaching Council, 1996, p. 10. Commonwealth of Australia copyright, reproduced by permission.

approach to learning. In the emphasis on the way in which teachers can manipulate and teach cognitive strategies to facilitate student learning, while de-emphasising the idiosyncratic personal characteristics of the learner, such as interest and motivation, and interpersonal dimensions such as peer interaction, educational practices based on this model are most accurately classified as representing a form of **information-processing constructivism** (see Winne 1995a).

The information-processing approach has challenged some of the fundamental premises of the Piagetian approach, particularly in regard to the mechanics of processing information by younger and older people (Flavell 1985). Information-processing theories had their origins in cybernetics, game theory, communication theory and information theory, and reached their full fruition with the development of computer hardware and computer programs. In their conception, the mind is a processing system in which knowledge is represented in the form of symbols, and processing is fundamentally symbol manipulation according to a set of rules. A variety of frameworks are used to characterise cognition and cognitive processing. These take the form of:

1. A computer language with a precisely defined syntax and set of procedures;
2. Graphic models (such as flow designs and decision trees) that represent the temporal course of processing information and embody particular assumptions or theories as to the organisation of knowledge in memory;
3. Higher-order concepts such as plans, scripts, schemata and frames that embody larger units of cognitive organisation.

Researchers use the information-processing model of learning and memory to study how individuals learn, remember and use the verbal and mathematical symbol systems necessary for communication. It is very important for teachers to understand how information is **encoded, processed, stored** and **retrieved,** because it is their job to help students acquire the facts, concepts, principles and skills important in our culture.

How has information-processing theory been derived from computer models?

Basically, information-processing psychologists seek to explain the relations between observable stimuli (input) and observable responses (output) by describing activities that intervene between input and output.

Computer analogy

According to Kail and Bisanz (1992) a complete model of cognition for a certain task should incorporate the specific mechanisms for all cognitive activities that underlie performance, including perceptual mechanisms for encoding information, processes for manipulating and storing information, processes for selecting and retrieving stored information, and processes that decide among alternative actions. Also important in a complete model would be specification of the ways in which information is organised, sequenced and represented internally. The computer is, therefore, an appropriate model to illustrate the integrated components of the information-processing model, through which a parallel is drawn between the functional components of the computer and psychological structures (Beilin 1987; Flavell 1985; Kail & Bisanz 1992; Lohman 1989). Flavell states that in this approach the human mind is conceived of as a complex cognitive system analogous in some ways to a digital computer. Like a computer, the system manipulates or processes information coming in from the environment or already stored within the system. It processes the information in a variety of ways: encoding, recoding or decoding it; comparing or combining it with other information; storing it in memory or retrieving it from memory; bringing it into or out of focal attention or conscious awareness, and so on.

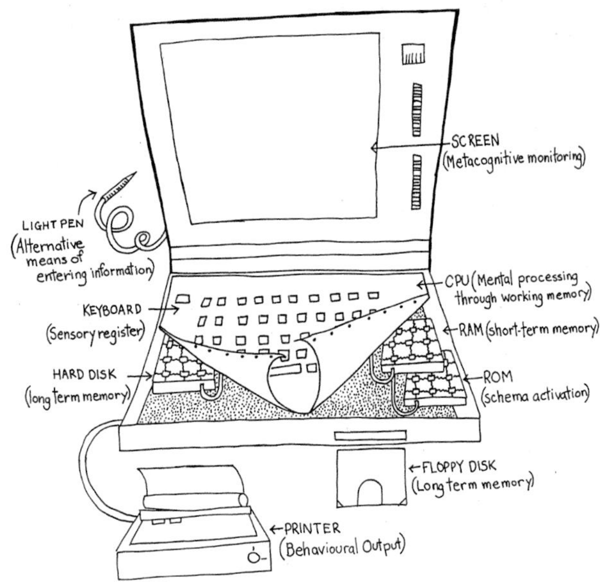

Computer simulation and artificial intelligence

Computer simulation is also used by some information-processing psychologists to model their view of how human information processing occurs. In artificial intelligence research a match is sought between computer performance based upon artificial intelligence models and human performance to evaluate the effectiveness with which elements of the artificial intelligence program captured elements of human information processing. If the match is high, researchers argue that they have captured in a physical model what they theorised was occurring with human mental processing (Kail & Bisanz 1992).

Input of information

Each of the components of a computer has a specific function to perform, and if any one component is faulty the computer will be functioning less than optimally. Indeed, if a major fault is present in any component the computer will not be able to function at all. We once had a keyboard for our personal computer that had been given such a hard time over the years that the letter 'e' literally dropped off. You hav* no id*a how oft*n you us* th* l*tt*r wh*n you ar* typing. Imagine what would happen if you also lost the letter 'a'. C*n you im*gin* how difficult th* t*sk of typing would b*com*? Of course if we lost three or more letters the keyboard and computer would be virtually useless.

Processing information

The ability of a computer to manipulate and process the input depends on the quality of the computer software program and the processing size of the central processing unit (CPU). The CPU for most microcomputers enables users to analyse large data sets with complex statistical methods, to use electronic mail, and to word process with only several dozen basic instructions.

Storing information

In order to retain a permanent record of our work on the computer we need to save the file. Lots of us have had disastrous experiences such as a sudden electrical surge, a clumsy foot dislodging the power cord, the wrong cut-and-paste procedure, or a system fault, only to see our hard work lost before we could make a permanent copy. Some of us have had the unlucky experience of safely storing our work on a hard or floppy disk, only to forget the name of the file under which the material was stored. Of course, the material is useless unless it can be retrieved in some form. This information may be stored in a variety of forms (e.g. hard disk; floppy disk) and the quantity that can be stored depends on the capacity of the disks.

Retrieving information

Finally, having successfully processed the material and stored it, we then need to be able to retrieve the file for printing. We once had the experience of being able to call up a file on screen, only to be given the message that no file existed when we put in a command for that particular file to be printed. On other occasions we were told that the software package couldn't read the file and so we couldn't access the information we had so laboriously stored earlier. No doubt you have had a similar experience!

The components of the human information-processing system

Forming perceptions As you can see, the computer is an integrated system, and if any one component is malfunctioning or inefficient, the system will be less effective. Well, you might ask, what has this to do with human thinking and learning? The computer analogy is actually quite a neat model of one view of what happens conceptually when a person learns. In the figure on the next page the computer components are shown paralleled with the components of the information-processing model. Each of the components of the human system on the right of the diagram are also integrated, and must function effectively for the system as a whole to be effective.

Sensory receptors, working memory, and long-term memory We describe each of these components briefly and then address the information-processing model in more detail. The **sensory receptors** (such as our eyes, ears, touch, smell and taste) are the senses through which we perceive stimuli. Depending on an individual's orientation, particular stimuli are selected for attention. The **working memory** is that part of the

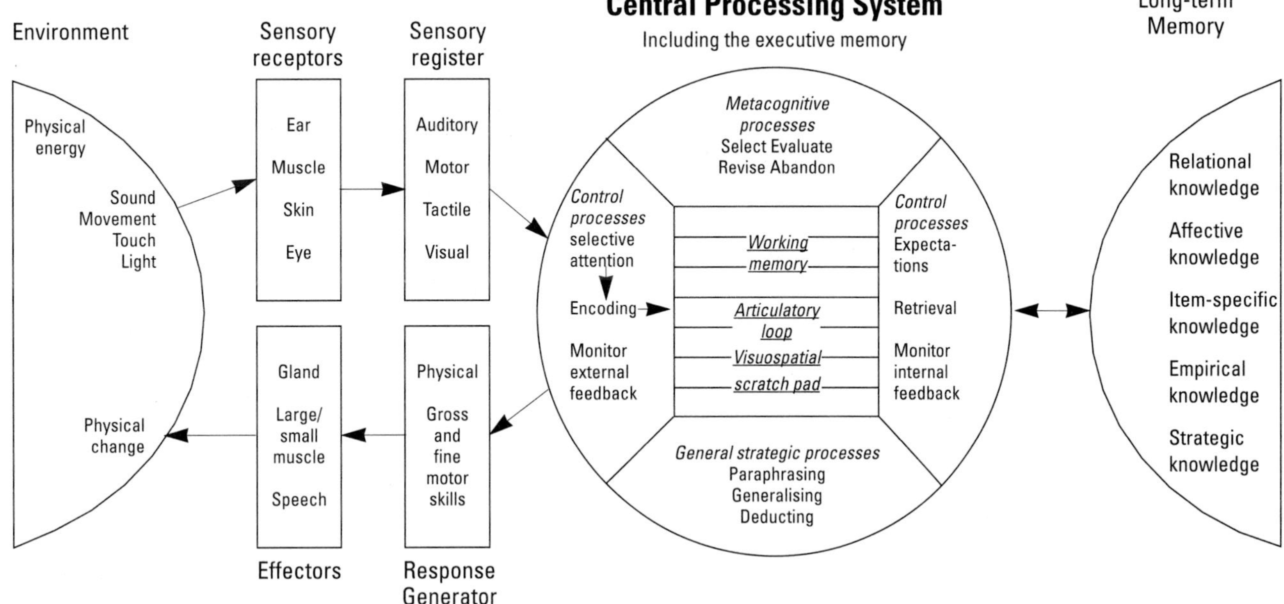

Reprinted with permission G. J. Marchant, 1985.

person's mind that processes information, first in the short-term memory (which has limited capacity for registering the sensory input for processing by the working memory), and then through conscious and active rehearsal which manipulates the information. Only limited chunks of information can be worked on, and the information can only be stored for a brief period. In a sense, the working memory is the 'workpad' or 'jotter' of the mind (Kumar 1971; Taylor 1980), the place where the construction process occurs—that is, the place where incoming information makes contact with prior knowledge and the interaction between the two produces an interpretation of the incoming information (Royer 1986). As such, the working memory functions very much like the RAM (Random Access Memory) in a computer system. **Long-term memory** is the repository of stored information (Royer 1986) and is very much like the floppy disk or a hard disk. The long-term memory is a permanent store of information, and appears to be unlimited in capacity (unlike computer storage systems). Unfortunately, most of us use only a limited amount of our capacity, and a lot of what is stored is irretrievable. At the end of processing, action is performed by the person's muscle systems on instruction from the working memory which calls up information from the long-term memory for enacting behaviour (akin to making a computer printout).

When we consider each of these components in turn we will see how the information-processing model is very useful in helping teachers analyse tasks presented to students so that they are most easily perceived with attention, actively memorised, effectively stored and retrieved for future action.

Sensory input: the importance of effectively functioning sensory organs

For sensory input to be effective, the senses must be fully operational. Just as a faulty keyboard will prevent the effective input of information to the computer, the child who cannot see or hear properly, or is poorly oriented to attend to appropriate stimuli will not be in a position to input information effectively into the working memory. Where sensory problems are evident, the teacher needs to take remedial action. This action may be as simple as moving children who cannot see or hear properly to the front of the room, or more intrusive interventions such as the use of hearing aids and eyeglasses. With the mainstreaming of special needs students into regular classrooms, it is even more critical for teachers to pay attention to how well individual students can perceive and receive the sensory stimulation of the classroom (refer to Chapter 11). Very often, however, poor attention (or poorly focused attention) is the root cause of faulty input, and so the teacher must always be aware of the need to orient students to attend to appropriate stimuli. Means of doing this are covered in a number of other places in the text.

Importance of attention to sensory input

Obviously we must make salient features of the stimuli prominent so that children can attend to the correct cues. Here we introduce two further terms, **figure** and **ground.** When interpreting information in the environment we are continually distinguishing main figures from the background in order to perceive patterns accurately. When figure and ground are ambiguous, or not easily distinguishable, problems in interpretation occur (see the figure below).

There are implications here for reading, mathematics and other subjects. In reading, for example, if students focus on the white page as the figure and the black marks as background they will have great difficulty reading. Examine Figure (c) below. Focus on the black. What do you see? Focus on the white. What do you see? It might help you to draw a line across the top and bottom of the diagram. When we do this, the pattern becomes instantly meaningful as we have been able to distinguish figure and ground effectively. Visual illusions such as this are informative about fundamental perceptual processes involved in learning (Gordon & Earle 1992; Wenderoth 1992). Figure and ground can also be thought of as auditory concepts. For most students their teacher's lectures and questions are the main figures of their attention, and background noise stays in the background. If a student perceives the buzz of fluorescent lights, the hum of the heater of air conditioner, or the shuffling of feet and papers as the figure, and the teacher's voice as background, learning will suffer.

Question point: Constructivists believe that cognitive processes like perception and memory involve interpretation. Do you agree? In what ways are interpretative processes involved in perception and memory?

Perception

We cannot presume that what we, as teachers, perceive is what children also perceive, or that it is grounded in the same experiences. Merely because someone familiar with the topic (a teacher or expert) may see an organising structure with many interrelationships among the various parts (or other stimuli) does not mean that the novice learner can make sense out of them (Shuell 1990). The case study opposite illustrates the point very well.

Mismatch between teacher and student perception

Research by Tasker (1981) presents a good example of the mismatch that may exist between teachers' perceptions and students' perceptions, leading to significant learning problems. Of central interest to Tasker is the finding from a number of Australian and New Zealand studies that secondary (and, indeed, university) students tend to retain their intuitive understanding of science concepts despite significant exposure to scientific models (Osborne 1980; Osborne & Gilbert 1980). In his explanation of this, Tasker highlights the gap that exists between the teacher's perception of the learning episode and that of the students. Lessons are perceived by students as isolated events, while to the teacher they are parts of a related series of experiences. Tasker comments:

Intuitive understanding and the learning of science

This narrow focus of some pupils is of significance for teachers who draw heavily on previous classroom experiences when setting the scene for a task at hand. Links which a teacher perceives as strong and obvious, especially if they relate to the scientific ideas taught in previous lessons rather than to what pupils did or what happened, may be far from obvious to pupils whose concern is with what they will have to do today. Another aspect of this problem is that as teachers we often refer to these past experiences in terms of our own perceptions and unfortunately ... these perceptions are often not those of our pupils. (p. 34)

There can also be a mismatch between the perceived purpose of the task for the teacher and student, with pupils constructing the purpose of the task to be either following the set instructions or getting the right answer. Students' perceptions of the nature of a task may not include those critical features that teachers assume they are aware of. Furthermore, the knowledge structures that teachers assume students use while investigating science concepts, for example, may not be the ones actually used by students, usually because students lack the assumed prerequisite knowledge, or are unable to grasp the mental set required. As if this were not enough, at the output level the students' perceptions relating to the significance of the task

(a) What do you see in this picture?

(b) Compare these those three drawings. One is ambiguous? Why?

(c) Focus on the black, what do you see? Focus on the white, what do you see?

TEACHER'S CASE BOOK

BUTTER MENTHOLS OR FRUIT TINGLES?

'I'd like you to think about blood. Try to remember what we've discussed so far. Can anyone tell me what blood is made of? Put your hands up, remember, don't call out. What is blood made of?' Mrs Fraser waited 10–15 seconds until over half the class had their hands up and then asked Frank, who answered, 'It's got cells ... and liquid?'

'Yes, Frank, that's right. Cells and liquid. Today I want to talk to you about the cells, specifically one type of cell. Who can tell me the name of the most common type of blood cell? Wait, Jenny, just put your hand up. Think carefully, what is the most common blood cell?' Again Mrs Fraser waited until there were plenty of hands up before selecting a student.

'White cells...?' was Gina's response.

'No, Gina, there are white cells, but they're not the most common type. Can someone else tell me what is the most common blood cell?' Mrs Fraser chose another student.

'Yes, Brendan?'

'Red blood cells ... I think ... they're called.'

'Thanks, Brendan, yes they're red blood cells and they're called erythrocytes. I'll write it on the board for you—they're called erythrocytes or red blood cells.

'There are millions of erythrocytes in even a small drop of blood, but it's the shape of the red blood cell that I want you to take note of. They're round ... and they're flat ... can anyone remember? It's a bit like a butter menthol or you say it's a bit like a doughnut. Not so much a doughnut, more a butter menthol. You know what I mean by a butter menthol? They're round, and they dip in the middle on either side, but it's not like a lifesaver where the hole goes right the way through, it's just got a dip in it. Now that's significant for all sorts of reasons but I'm not going into that. Let's say this diagram here on the blackboard represents a red blood cell ...'

Jamie's hand was up. When Mrs Fraser asked for his comment, he upset this idea: 'But butter menthols aren't shaped like that, they're square. They come in square packets.'

The realisation hit Mrs Fraser. Someone had changed the shape of her butter menthols! Mrs Fraser's mental image was of a round lolly but the students were seeing a square butter menthol and wondering how on earth that could be like a round, red blood cell. Mrs Fraser stopped and with the class worked out a better analogy, one they were all happy with. The students and Mrs Fraser came to the conclusion that, to use her words, 'Fruit tingles were a better example of red blood cells because they're more the right shape—they're solid but with a concave on both sides.'

Case studies illustrating National Competency Framework for Beginning Teaching, National Project on the Quality of Teaching and Learning, Australian Teaching Council, 1996, p.38. Commonwealth of Australia copyright, reproduced by permission.

outcomes achieved may not be those the teacher assumes are perceived!

How does information get into long-term memory and how is it retrieved?

Encoding, retention and retrieval

The next three elements of the model are best looked at in terms of two key questions: How do we get information from the working memory into the long-term memory? And, perhaps more importantly, how do we retrieve the information for use? To answer these questions we consider means by which the individual gathers and represents information—a process we call **encoding**; the means by which material is retained—**retention**; and the means by which we get information when it is needed, in other words the **retrieval** system used. In the old days it seemed a lot simpler; all we learnt about was how people remembered and why they forgot!

Just as the CPU on a computer processes a large amount of information with a combination of relatively few basic instructions, information-processing psychologists assume that the number of fundamental processes underlying human cognition is relatively small and attempt to identify these. They also seek to discover how higher-order intellectual functions are formed from more elementary cognitive processes. In the following sections we outline some of the elements considered important for effective encoding of new information (see also Siegler 1991).

Why is some information easier to process?

Meaningfulness and effective processing

A friend regularly drives an hour to work on a major highway, mostly by farms and fields. On several occasions he feared he had missed his turning because he saw a building or sign that he had never noticed before. This fear subsided when a check of the watch informed him that he could not possibly be too far off track, or when he saw a familiar landmark. Experiences like this inform us that simple repetition of information or an event may not lead to effective processing. Probably the most important aspect of the material being presented is its **meaningfulness.**

Meaningful material is encoded and stored more efficiently than non-meaningful material. But what do we mean by meaningful material? Remember the computer analogy? All computers require a software program of some kind in order to recognise material being fed into the computer. With the Macintosh, a friendly smiling face greets you when it accepts a disk that can be read by its system program. On the other hand, if you put in a disk that is unfamiliar to the system, you get a frown! In other words, the computer has an existing framework for recognising and incorporating commands. In information-processing terms, your short-term memory operates as a system that processes new information more readily when it is related to information already held in the long-term memory. So, in effect, meaningful material really means material that can be related to already existing schemes of knowledge. The new material is recognised in terms of prior knowledge and concepts already understood. When adults are given a mental task to perform in an area in which they have little knowledge, they often process the information less efficiently than children who have knowledge in that area (Flavell 1985).

Consider the following lines of text. Try to memorise each one in turn and note the number of trials taken.

He clasps the crag with crooked hands
Close to the sun in lonely lands
Ringed with the azure world he stands.

Puisque sept péches de nos yeux
Ferment la barriére des cieux, Reverend Pére,
Je vous jure de les abhorren en tout point.

Hap ock laba tch
Crtch mit fer tch laf
Mag tenkt pate bork fizt tchnt.

Which of the three passages was the easiest to learn? As fluent speakers of English the first passage is most meaningful to us because the language is familiar and it is patterned in a logical way. Indeed, it might become even easier if you are told before memorising the lines that they are taken from a short poem by Tennyson called *The Eagle*. If we were French-speaking we would probably find the second passage easier to learn, and if we were Martian, the third! For us, however, the third passage is very difficult because it is neither familiar nor patterned, and therefore gives us fewest associations to help understand and remember it.

Compare the first quotation above, from *The Eagle*, with the following:

Clasps he hands the crooked crag with
Lands to sun in close the lonely
The stands with world azure he ringed.

Makes it harder, doesn't it? The words are familiar, but they are not patterned in a familiar way. We should not presume that material that is inherently meaningful to us as teachers is meaningful to the students. We conduct a little experiment when lecturing on the topic of meaningfulness, using the following three lines of words.

1. *sleck ploge sengs bligo lange prack reldi roeda celnt talma*
2. *xtspi ltspi axpti lxtvo ntvmq stvaz ztvso tsvnp tlpsa mptst*
3. *hcnul tsaot sknis riahc elbat efink repap orcim etalp noops*

We introduce the task by saying that we have three lists containing ten five-letter combinations and we want to ascertain how quickly, and by what means, students learn the lists. We uncover the first row and ask students to memorise it from left to right for two minutes and then recall as many words as possible. We then present the second list and ask them to repeat the procedure. We then present the third list, giving them the same two minutes, and a recall time. We then ask the student to rate the lists in terms of difficulty.
Why don't you do the task before we tell you how the students rate the lists?

Nine minutes later. In most cases the students rank the second list as the hardest (there is no accounting for the students who regularly rank one of the other lists as harder!). In about two-thirds of the cases the first list is ranked the easiest, and the third list that of middle difficulty. (How did you rank them?) We then discuss why the second list is the hardest and the means students use to try to simplify the encoding. Usually students refer to the non-meaningful nature of the material, its length and complexity, the fact that it is hard to chunk syllables without vowels, and so on. Indeed, some of the techniques used to remember the material are quite ingenious—the similarity of the material to car number plates, and the use of rhythm and rhyme. When questioned about the first list, many students indicate that they find it relatively easy because they can make the nonsense words into real words; for example, 'sleck' is like slack, and 'seng' like sang. When asked why they found the third list harder, the usual comment is that the words are less like real words and so techniques such as imagery, and rhythm and rhyme don't work so well.

We then turn our attention to the one-third of students who ranked this list the easiest and ask why? Of course, it's because the third list consists of *real words* spelt backwards, and what's more, they are all words relating to the kitchen. So for those who crack the code, the list is meaningful, and items on the list are able to be chunked around kitchen items. In fact, some students make up a story containing the words, and then simply retell the story to recall the words later. Has the penny dropped for you?

Two important issues arise from this example. First, it is not always obvious to the learner that material is meaningful. Often we, as teachers, need to indicate to students the patterns that exist in the material that will make it easier for them to relate it to their existing schemes. For example, if we had told the groups before starting that one of the lists contained words spelt backwards, the task would have become immeasurably easier.

Learning set: learning expectations

Second, at times we can be given a **learning set** that creates the wrong expectations so that we end up making a task harder than it really needs to be. In this case, most students were led to believe that the three lists consisted of nonsense syllables and looked no further for meaningful patterns. Often we generate expectations for children that work will be difficult, or that a particular procedure must be used to solve a problem. There are studies showing that when students have been led to believe that only a long and rather tedious approach will solve particular maths problems they become blind to the simpler solutions that could be applied in particular instances.

Demonstrate meaningful patterns

In the structure of our lessons, and the sequence of presentation of material, we can set up many wrong expectations and cause children greater difficulty in encoding the material presented than is necessary. The converse is also true. The demonstration of meaningful patterns to children to facilitate learning is of fundamental importance in the teaching of reading, mathematics and science.

One final note on the experiment described above. Even after pointing out the patterns that exist in the third list, some students remain convinced that list one is the easiest. Why? Because they cannot read right to left, and find the task of reverse reading cognitively very difficult. What would you do in cases like this?

THE IMPORTANCE OF PRIOR KNOWLEDGE TO EFFECTIVE LEARNING

Activating prior knowledge

The importance of material being meaningful and relevant to the learner is not new, and indeed is the cornerstone of all cognitive approaches to learning (see Alexander, Kulikowich & Jetton 1994; Bruner 1961, 1966, 1974; Ausubel 1963, 1977). The most powerful and positive learning outcomes occur in those contexts where students' knowledge and interests are well matched to the nature of the learning task (Alexander et al. 1994). The activation of prior knowledge about a topic before presenting new material is, therefore, very important. This can be student-induced or teacher-facilitated. Furthermore, when students are asked to participate in learning tasks for which they are ill prepared and which they perceive as irrelevant to their personal goals or aspirations, effective learning is made very difficult. How many times have you been asked to learn material that you perceive as irrelevant, or too difficult given your present level of understanding or expertise?

Can the activation of prior knowledge cause learning problems?

Students' informal knowledge and learning

At times we wish to teach children new material (such as some scientific laws or processes) that conflicts with their pre-established intuitive understandings. In this case, the new material is non-meaningful in terms of the children's pre-existing schema. This informal knowledge that children bring to the learning situation can hinder effective learning and can be quite resistant to change. There are two points we wish to make here. First, teachers should make a conscious effort to find out what students' informal knowledge is before teaching new concepts. Second, where this informal knowledge is likely to conflict with teaching, attempts need to be made to have the children alter their misconceptions so that an adequate knowledge base is developed. Doing this is not easy, and involves helping the children see the limitations in their understandings and convincing them of the merits of the alternative (see Chinn & Brewer 1993; Prawat 1989).

Incongruent knowledge

At times the students' knowledge base is not inaccurate but nevertheless interferes with the retention of new information because it is incongruent. Lipson (1983) reports a study in which grade 4, grade 5 and grade 6 students, who were enrolled in either Catholic or Hebrew parochial schools, were given three passages to read and recall. One passage was culturally neutral (dealing with Japan), the second was about a bar mitzvah, and the third about first communion. As was expected, there was a greater exact recall and greater recall of correct inferences with material that was congruent with the children's religious background. In contrast to this there were more distortions in recall of the incongruent passages. In particular, the students tended to distort the information presented in the incongruent text to make it consistent with their own knowledge of religious ceremonies. To handle this kind of situation, teachers need to help students to identify information that is inconsistent with their prior beliefs and then to teach them to process such information so that they remember the accurate text rather than a version distorted by incompatible prior knowledge (Pressley et al. 1989).

LEARNER-CENTRED PSYCHOLOGICAL PRINCIPLE 4

The successful learner can create and use a repertoire of thinking and reasoning strategies to achieve complex learning goals.

Learners generate integrated, commonsense representations and explanations for even poorly understood or communicated facts, concepts, principles or theories. Learning processes operate holistically in the sense that internally consistent understandings emerge that may or may not be valid from an objective, externally oriented perspective. As learners negotiate understandings with others and internalize values and meanings within a discipline, however, they can refine their conceptions by filling gaps, resolving inconsistencies and revising prior conceptions.

Reprinted with permission, APA Task Force on Psychology in Education (1993, January), p. 6.

STRATEGIES TO HELP LEARNING

Chunking

Chunking long and complex material into more meaningful units

Even potentially meaningful material is, at times, difficult to encode because of its complexity, length or mode of presentation. A simple demonstration will illustrate this. Have a look at the following letters:

EVLEWTSIEMITEHT

Such a combination of letters is particularly hard to encode. However, the following arrangement is easier,

THETIMEISTWELVE

particularly when it is broken into these units:

THE TIME IS TWELVE

In the last example it is easy to encode the material and remember it because there are fewer units to learn and they are now more meaningful. One of us remembers teaching a year 5 class about long division. I began with one method, and was very happy that everyone in the class appeared to have 'cottoned on'. I thought, 'Great, now I will explain another approach.' I was pleased when it seemed as if a fair number of the class had also followed this second approach. I then launched into the third, different explanation. I was devastated at the end when I found that no one was able to follow what I was talking about, and had also forgotten or confused the first two approaches. Many teachers attempt to teach students too much at one time. We can only absorb so much. After a certain amount of information has been presented it may be a waste of time presenting more because people just cannot absorb more. The time would be better used consolidating the information already encoded. Learning tasks that are too long or too complex for the learner not only fail to teach the extra facts presented but also interfere with earlier material that could easily have been learnt.

Story-grammar training

Two strategies that have been found useful for facilitating encoding of textual material are story-grammar training and question-generation strategies. Story-grammar training consists of teaching students to ask themselves five questions as they read stories:

1. Who is the main character?
2. When and where did the story take place?
3. What did the main characters do?
4. How did the story end?
5. How did the main character feel?

In posing and answering these questions while reading, children are more actively involved in mentally processing the elements of the story so that encoding, retention and recall are facilitated (Pressley et al. 1989).

Self-questioning

Question generation

With question generation students are taught how to generate integrative questions concerning text that capture large units of meaning. This facilitates encoding because readers become more active and, in particular, monitor their own reading, so that problems in their comprehension become more apparent. As part of the training in one study (Davey & McBride 1986), students were instructed specifically about the need for integrative questions, were taught to evaluate whether their questions covered important information, whether their questions were integrative, and whether they could answer the questions. Students were given practice in developing these types of question and received feedback from the teacher.

SQ3R and PQ4R

One way of using questions is to turn text headings into questions and then to read the text material with answering the question in mind. Reading to answer a question was a prominent feature in the SQ3R (Survey, Question, Read, Recite, Review) approach (Robinson 1961) and the PQ4R (Preview, Question, Read, Reflect, Recite, Review) variation (Thomas & Robinson 1972). With the PQ4R, the reader *previews* the material to be read, generates questions from the headings, *reads* the material for the main ideas and supporting details, *reflects* on connections between the new information and what was previously known, *recites* the answers to the questions, and *reviews* what is known and still left unanswered. Try it for yourself while you are reading this chapter.

Summarisation

A final strategy that could be mentioned here is the use of **summarisation**. The active generation of summaries has been found to facilitate the comprehension and retention of textual learned material (Wittrock & Alesandrini 1990). There are many techniques suggested for using summaries (Pressley et al. 1989; Snowman 1986) that are too extensive to develop in this text. No doubt you are familiar with some of them (e.g. marginal notes, underlining topic sentences, highlighting key ideas). Many of these techniques are quite structured and methodical. For students to use them successfully they need to be actively taught the strategies. However, the usefulness of summarisation training for children younger than about ten years of age is not conclusive. One technique (Berkowitz 1986) will be elaborated upon.

Berkowitz taught grade 6 students to construct maps of passages. The title of the passage was written in the centre of a plain sheet of paper, and students were instructed to survey the passage for four to six main ideas, which were to be written in their own words and arranged in a circle around the title. Students were then asked to find two to four important details in the passage that were associated with each of the main ideas. These were summarised briefly and written under the main idea. To make the presentation more visually graphic, boxes were drawn around each main idea and its supporting details. Students were then taught to use this graphic summary to self-test until they could recite the main ideas in order together with their supporting details. Overall recall of the passages was improved by the use of this graphic summarising technique.

LEARNING NON-MEANINGFUL MATERIAL

Not all material to be learnt is inherently meaningful—for example, lists of dates, telephone numbers, the names of a class, algebraic formulae, spelling words, periodic tables (perhaps even multiplication tables?). To the degree that the material to be learnt is not meaningful, it puts an extra burden on the processing unit to encode the material. There are a number of strategies such as chunking mental imagery and mnemonic imagery that will improve the encoding, and retention, of this type of material as we have indicated earlier. These same techniques are also useful for remembering meaningful material that is long and complex.

Chunking

Our short-term memory is limited in the number of units of information we can process at one time. This is usually estimated to be between three and seven, depending on age, although some people appear to be able to process more. The units are *chunks* rather than number of physical units. A letter, a number, a word or a familiar phrase can function as a single chunk because each is a single unit of meaning. Thus it is as easy to remember a set of three unrelated words with nine letters (e.g. hit, red, toe) as it is to remember three unrelated letters (e.g. q, f, r) (Miller 1956; Siegler 1991). Chunking is a mental strategy by which we break long and complex series into smaller chunks to facilitate learning and recall. Have a look at the following words:

TSNUKEBIERHCSZRUK
KURZSCHREIBEKUNST

You would probably find the second word easier to encode as you can chunk it into *kurz schrei bekunst* (especially if you have any knowledge of German). Long spelling words, long stanzas of poetry and telephone numbers can all be chunked and, as chunks, become easier to encode.

In these instances, teachers need to present the material in a way that facilitates the chunking.

Using mental imagery

Representational images

There are two different types of image that can be constructed to assist with retention and recall of verbal material. The first, called representational images, exactly represent the content of the prose to be learnt. For example, 'The dog barked when the cat ran near him' can be directly represented, as we can form an image of each element in the prose that will facilitate recall. There is consistent research evidence that active construction of representational images, that is, creating visual images of what one is reading or hearing, facilitates children's learning of text (at least from the age when children begin to process concrete stories).

Mnemonic images

Sometimes it is more difficult to imagine elements of prose and at this time proxies may be used to stand for elements to be remembered. These proxies are called **mnemonic images** (Pressley et al. 1989). Mnemonic imagery is useful when we are trying to learn information about totally unfamiliar concepts such as the accomplishment of unfamiliar people or information about unknown countries. It seems especially useful when there are many previously unknown concepts that must be acquired in a relatively short time. There are simple mnemonic devices, such as rhymes, acrostics and acronyms, and more complicated forms such as the keyword method.

We use mnemonics when we deliberately impose some sort of order on the material we want to learn. For example, if we want to remember the definitions of *sine*, *cosine* and *tangent*, and especially which is opposite or adjacent to the hypotenuse, we may use the mnemonic SOHCAHTOA:

Sine Opposite Hypotenuse
Cosine Adjacent Hypotenuse
Tangent Opposite Adjacent Angle

Acrostics and acronyms

We are all familiar with rhymes such as 'Thirty days has September, April, June and November', and 'All Good Boys Deserve Fruit', which help us remember lists of items. Again the principle is to reduce the amount that has to be encoded into a form that is easily retrievable later (this is a crucial point). Red, Orange, Yellow, Green, Blue, Indigo and Violet becomes reduced to three units ROY G. BIV. In this latter case an **acrostic** is used to help encode the information. An acrostic is a sentence made up of words that begin with the first letter of each item to be learned. Even simple acronyms, where only the first letters are used, are useful as shorthand for remembering long names. Be careful, however—we know one librarian who can rattle off thousands of library acronyms, but when asked what they stand for hasn't got the foggiest! Acronyms tend to acquire a life of their own (and breed as well).

Keyword mnemonics

With the keyword method, a word is keyed to the prose so that it triggers off a rich set of associations that recall the prose (Carney, Levin & Morrison 1988; Levin 1985). Levin, Shriberg and Berry (1983) report on a study in which some students were given the keyword 'frost' to stand for a story about a fictitious town of Fostoria which was noted for abundant natural resources, advances in technology, wealth and growing population. The students were then shown a picture in which the attributes of the town were covered with frost. At a later time, when presented with the name Fostoria, students were able to recall the frost and what it covered. Children who were not exposed to the keyword mnemonic recalled fewer of the town's attributes. In this case, it was important to select a mnemonic that related to the name of the town.

Peg-type mnemonics

Other strategies that students find useful are **peg-type mnemonics** where particular concepts to be remembered are located in some space (such as a living room) and identified with common objects (e.g. in the living room). This is called a **loci** peg-type mnemonic and has been used for centuries. Greek and Roman orators advised their students to remember the points in a speech they were to make by forming images of the points and locating them at successive places along a familiar path. When they were to give the speech, they could retrieve the points they wished to make by mentally walking down the path and 'looking' to see images of the different points (Kantowitz & Roediger 1980). Imagine you have a 15-item shopping list consisting of the following: milk, eggs, flour, peas, carrots, bread, washing powder, detergent, meat, toilet paper, tissues, fly spray, cheese, ice cream and can of sardines. To employ the loci method as a mnemonic you would locate these items in various parts of your house and then mentally take a walk through your house when at the shop. Each item should be more easily recalled by association with a particular room.

Pegword mnemonics

A **pegword mnemonic** associates an item with a rhyme such as in one-bun, two-shoe, three-tree and so on. With a shopping list each item would be associated with the rhyming pair so that the recall of the pair should trigger off the image of the required item. For example, the carton of eggs may be imagined as sitting on a bun, a milk carton stuffed into a shoe, peas hanging off a tree and so on. At the cue 'tree', you should remember the incongruous image of peas hanging from the tree. Another device, the **link method**, simply constructs an overall image in which the items to be remembered form component and interacting parts. You could visualise each of the items on the shopping list interacting in some way, such as a milk carton balancing on an egg surrounded by flour, and so on. Alternatively, you could construct a sculpture of your shopping list, as shown on the next page. While walking through the shop you simply have to remember your sculpture and the items should also be recalled. Of course, a shopping list would be easier, but, sometimes, we are not able to carry a written record of what is to be remembered, such as a role in a play, or points for an examination. In such cases, mnemonics are invaluable. Certainly, some great feats of memory are the result of well-applied mnemonics (see Lorayne & Lucas 1974; Wollen Weber & Lowry 1972; Yates 1966).

Why do mnemonics work? The usefulness of a variety of mnemonic devices is currently being researched, but the general results indicate that the use of well-constructed mnemonic devices in encoding enhances

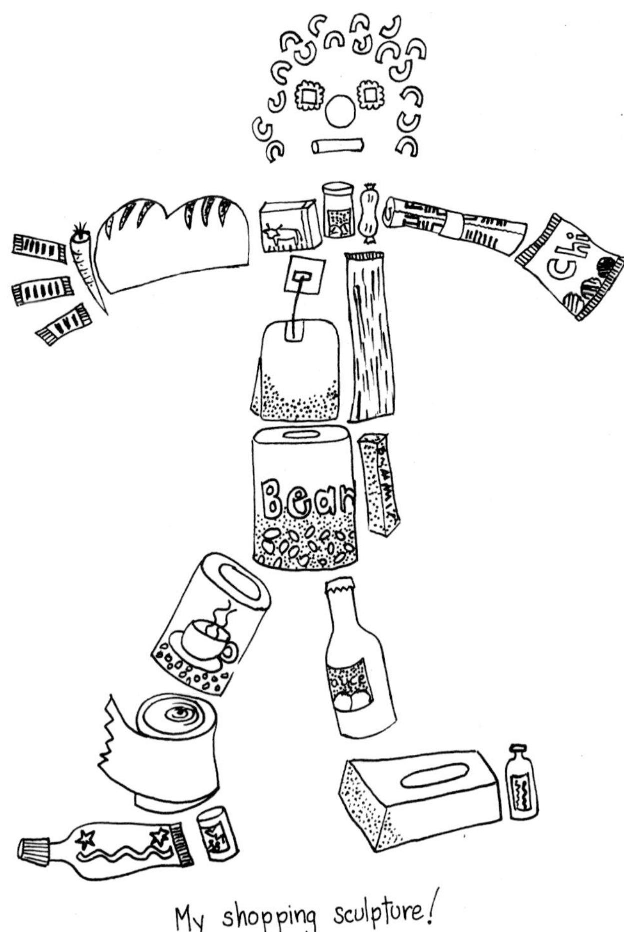

Mnemonic devices: the link method

TEACHER'S CASE BOOK

GREEN FOR UP BOWS

Rebecca is a year 4 student who has been learning the violin for two years. She practises regularly but has problems getting her bow direction right.

Over the last few weeks she had played 'Musette' with any old bowing, usually a different direction each time. Janette, her teacher, had colour-coded the bows on the music in her book and made a teaching tape for her practice, all to no avail. Each week she came back performing it incorrectly. In desperation, Janette rewrote the song on large staff lines and coloured the notes in green and pink highlighter—green for up bows and pink for down bows. During the lesson she went over and over the tricky bowing, and the colour coding seemed to work.

When Rebecca arrived for the next lesson she had a secretive little smile on her face.

Rebecca: You are going to be surprised today.
Janette: Oh, good. Why?
Rebecca: Because my bows are right this week. Shall I play 'Musette'?
Janette: Yes, please. Go ahead.

With a furtive glance to see Janette's reaction, Rebecca played with almost perfect bowing.

Case studies illustrating National Competency Framework for Beginning Teaching, National Project on the Quality of Teaching and Learning, Australian Teaching Council, 1996, p.17. Commonwealth of Australia copyright, reproduced by permission.

Case study activity
Why did the colour coding help?

retrieval (Snowman 1986). It appears that many people use these skills spontaneously (Carney et al. 1988). Indeed, the spontaneous use of mnemonics is so pervasive that it is difficult to set up a controlled experiment to test the effect of subjects' use of trained mnemonic devices because members of the control group (those not trained in the use of the particular mnemonic) also engage in constructing spontaneous mnemonics to cope with the learning task—hence the differences between controls and experimental subjects are minimised!

Mnemonics seem to assist with encoding because they provide meaning through associations with more familiar, meaningful information. Forming images of the material to be learnt greatly aids later recall. Mnemonics also assist the learner to organise unrelated and often abstract material. Importantly, they associate the material to be learnt with retrieval cues—for example, with the peg method we have only to remember one bun and the incongruous image will be triggered. Mnemonics should be easy to learn, interesting and fun, and as such they should enhance the motivation of students to learn. Indeed, some of the strongest evidence favouring the teaching of mnemonic imagery skills is that students appear to be impressed by how effective these strategies are when they use them and tend to incorporate them into their learning styles (see Pressley et al. 1989).

Hidden dangers in using mnemonics

However, strategies such as the ones described above have some hidden dangers. For example, we may become quite inflexible in our recall, or if an element of the mnemonic is missing we may not be able to retrieve the rest. Most of us have to recite the little poem on the months of the year to remember the number of days in each. When flexibility of recall is important the encoding should not be tied too tightly to a rigid mnemonic, and of course the most useful devices of encoding are those that are inherently meaningful in themselves.

How does coding and classifying help learning?

For many cognitive psychologists it is the linkages and relationships seen between pieces of information that are the hallmark of understanding and effective learning (Prawat 1989). The adequacy of the organisational structure connecting elements of the knowledge to be retained determines the accessibility or availability of the information at a later time. Some quite elaborate coding systems have been devised to assist students see the connectedness of information and to facilitate the encoding and retention of quite difficult material. Coding is particularly useful for structuring both meaningful and non-meaningful material so that it is more easily learnt and recalled later. Often all one has to do is to remember the structure and the elements will also be remembered. Imagine that you have to remember the following list and the characteristics of the elements comprising the list:

platinum	silver	gold
aluminium	copper	lead
bronze	steel	brass
sapphire	emerald	ruby
limestone	granite	slate

Quite a job! However, if we organise the material into a **coding frame**, or **classification table** as it is sometimes called, starting with the general and working to the specific in a hierarchical form, the task is simplified.

The organisation of this material into a form of hierarchical tree makes it more meaningful, and therefore encoding, retention and retrieval should be enhanced (see Bower et al. 1969; Anderson 1990).

MINERALS				
METALS			STONES	
RARE	COMMON	ALLOYS	PRECIOUS	MASONRY
platinum	aluminium	bronze	sapphire	limestone
silver	copper	steel	emerald	granite
gold	lead	brass	ruby	slate

Concept mapping Concept mapping (Novak 1981; Pines & Leith 1981), a more elaborate form of coding, is a useful strategy for teaching students about concepts. Concept mapping allows the student to combine elements into meaningful statements or propositions. This linking helps students to see the relationships between concepts and build on their conceptual framework.

A **concept map** is a two-dimensional diagram representing the conceptual structure of subject matter. To construct a concept map, we first identify the concepts and principles to be taught. Then the content elements are arranged in a hierarchical order from general to detailed, top to bottom. Finally, a line is drawn between each two related elements to show the linkage (Van Patten, Chao & Reigeluth 1986). For example, students are asked to identify the relevant concepts in a section of their textbook. A good way to begin is to pass out small paper rectangles and have students write all the key concepts that appear in the study material on these rectangles. The students are then asked to organise these concepts into a hierarchy, with the most general, most inclusive concepts at the top and the more specific concepts in two or more 'levels' below this. After a concept hierarchy is built, the students use narrower paper rectangles to write the relevant proposition to 'link' the concepts. A sample concept map constructed by a student in a year 7 science class is in the diagrams opposite. You can see from this example how the concepts 'plants' and 'energy' are linked by the word 'need' to form the proposition 'plants need energy'.

In some instances teachers find it useful to have students develop a prediction map which helps integrate their understanding. A prediction map is presented opposite. What do you think of it?

Often students are asked to discuss their concept maps in class. This helps them to assess what they know and to clarify their understanding of concepts. Concept mapping, once learned, becomes a very valuable evaluation tool. Research carried out by Joseph Novak (1981) has identified three criteria of effective concept maps:

1. Does the map show a good hierarchy? There is no best hierarchy but consider whether the concepts and propositions shown represent an acceptable order in terms of moving from a more general, more inclusive concept to a less general, less inclusive concept as related to the particular study material.
2. Are the propositions shown valid and 'correct'? Are all concepts 'connected' into propositions?
3. Are there cross-linkages between segments of the map?

Networking Another form of concept mapping is networking. Networking requires students to identify the important concepts or ideas in the text and to describe the interrelationships among these ideas in the form of a network diagram using nodes and links. Dansereau (1985) asserts that students' application of this networking technique will result in their improved comprehension and retention of the material since the network diagram provides a visual, spatial organisation of the information and helps the student see an overall picture of the material. A teacher-made network can be

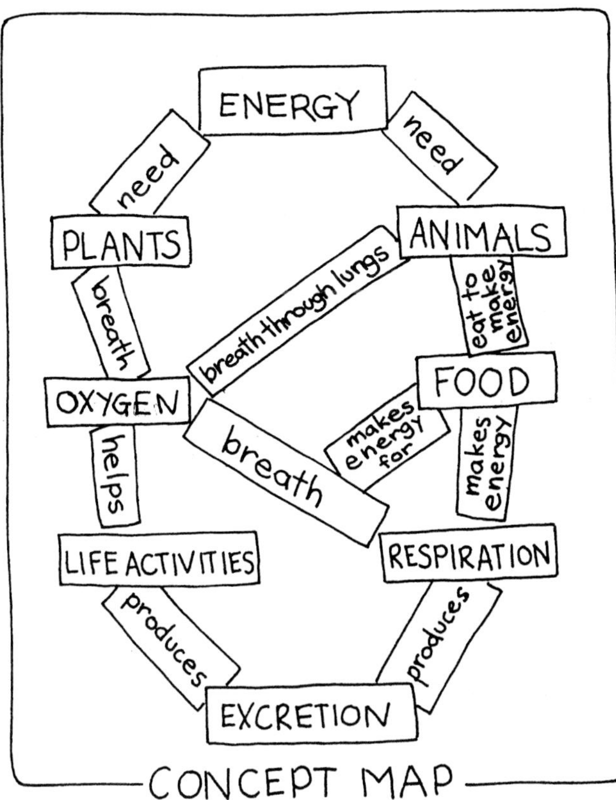

Map showing concepts and linking propositions

used as an advance organiser (Ausubel 1963, 1978) and incomplete or inaccurate networks completed by students can be used by the teacher to assess their level of comprehension and any misconceptions they might have.

Making good use of networking and concept maps is not without difficulties (Van Patten et al. 1986). First, students have to be trained for hours before they can use the techniques proficiently. Second, many types of relationships (conceptual, propositional, procedural, cause–effect, factual) are present simultaneously and

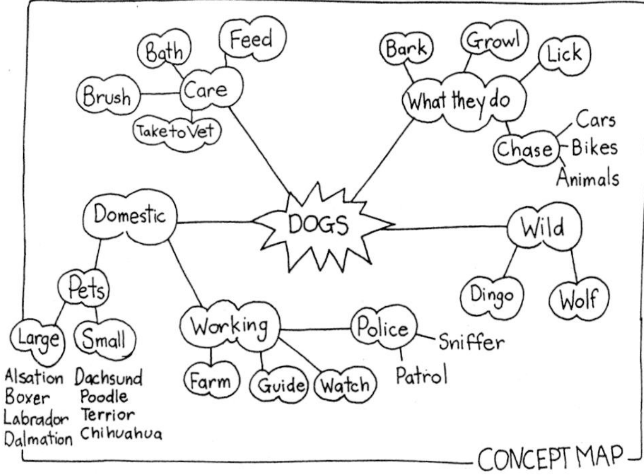

Concept map with several levels in the hierarchy

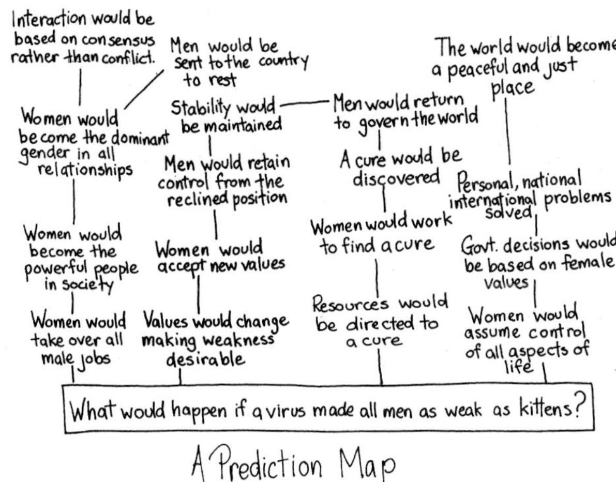

A prediction map

linked by intertwined lines and words which may make it difficult for students to use the map effectively. Because of the complexity of much learning, concept maps and networking may oversimplify relationships so that much important information is left out. Nevertheless, we believe that this approach is beneficial in facilitating learning and recall, and also helps learners to make clear to themselves what similarities there are between concepts, thereby improving generalisations of learning (Anderson, Reder & Simon 1996).

Question point: *Consider how a teacher could facilitate the development of memory skills in children by referring to the techniques that are discussed in this chapter.*

HOW SHOULD LEARNING STRATEGIES BE TAUGHT?

Strategic learners

When to be a strategic learner

As we have suggested above, cognitive strategies enhance learning. The appropriate use of strategies depends on how familiar the learner is with the material to be learnt, and is also domain specific (Garner 1990). The aim of strategy use is to minimise the demands on the working memory, and to make learning and responses as automatic as possible (Sweller 1993). When students already know a great deal about a topic they really don't need to use strategic routines for acquiring new concepts. Effective learners know when they need to be strategic and when they do not. Furthermore, strategies that are appropriate in one domain may be inappropriate in another. For example, it may be important to give extra attention to numerals in mathematics and history, but it would be unimportant in most language studies. Rehearsing information with attention to temporal or serial order may be useful in some domains (such as history) but inappropriate in others. Attention to the subjective content of some material may be essential (such as in literature) but in other areas it could interfere with processing information (such as physics). Weak strategies in particular domains may be strong strategies in others (Garner 1990).

In general, students (and adults, too) are not strategic learners. There are a number of explanations for this:

- students don't monitor their own learning and therefore don't really know when they are being ineffective;
- students resort to well-practised routines that get the job done even when these routines do not really enhance learning;
- students' meagre knowledge base about task demands blocks the appropriate use of strategies;
- students' inappropriate attributions (to ability rather than effort) and school/classroom goals, such as performance-based goals that do not support strategy use and greater involvement in deep rather than surface learning (Garner 1990).

Reasons why most learners are not strategic

Because children are not strategic learners they should be taught to monitor their use of strategies and their effectiveness. In line with this, children should be taught when and where to use particular strategies, and to be flexible—that is, if a particular approach is unsuited to a specific learning task, to adopt another strategy (Garner 1990; Paris, Lipson & Wixson 1983). It is also important to teach strategies within the context of real learning events such as mathematics, language and social science. Pressley et al. (1989) suggest the following points to guide the explicit teaching of a strategy. First, they suggest the teacher should describe the strategy to students and model its use. This modelling should include think-aloud statements about how to execute the procedure. These 'think-alouds' should also include important information on *why* and *when* the strategy could be used. Teacher-guided practice with the strategy should be given to students, followed by detailed feedback by the teacher on how individuals might improve strategy use. The practice–feedback loop continues until children can use the strategy efficiently. To facilitate acquisition, practice may begin with easier material and progress to harder tasks. To train for transfer of the strategy, the practice examples should be drawn from different content areas, and the strategy can be employed at various times during a day's instruction and as part of homework exercises. As you can see from this description, teaching effective strategy use to students should be explicit, intensive and extensive. The goal is for students to use the learned strategies autonomously, skilfully and appropriately.

Teaching strategies should be explicit, intensive and extensive

It is probably best to teach only a few strategies at a time and teach them well. Ultimately, the type of strategies employed by learners should be related to the amount of prior knowledge they possess, the nature of the material to be learned, and the kind of outcome the learner is trying to achieve (Garner 1990; Prawat 1989). At times simple mnemonics will be appropriate; at other times, concept maps will be more suitable.

Table 4.1 summarises the essentials for encouraging strategy development and use.

TABLE 4.1

ESSENTIALS FOR ENCOURAGING STRATEGY DEVELOPMENT AND USE

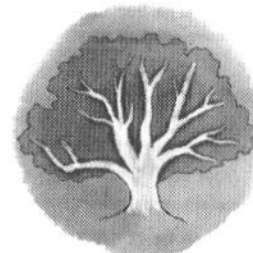

For teachers

- Describe strategies.
- Start with one or two strategies.
- Indicate why and when to use the strategies.
- Model strategy use with 'think-alouds'.
- Give guided practice in strategy use in varied situations.
- Give feedback on strategy use.
- Give autonomous practice in a variety of contexts.
- Motivate students to use strategies.
- Encourage positive self-beliefs by showing students how good stategy use prepares them better for everyday life and gives them an opportunity for self-advancement.

(based on Pressley & Woloshyn 1995)

Is strategy instruction a form of constructivism?

The teaching of cognitive strategies to students should emphasise that the learner must construct meaning from the material, otherwise strategies may become harmful and simply be used by students to commit facts and definitions to memory without any real meaning or applied value for the individual (Iran-Nejad 1990; see also Pressley, Harris & Marks 1992). Strategy instruction has been criticised as non-constructivist. Pressley, Harris and Marks believe that, while good strategy instruction incorporates features of behavioural and direct instruction approaches to teaching (see Chapter 6), which are considered by constructivist educators as mechanistic, good strategy instruction is anything but mechanical. They believe that strategy instruction is an extremely student-sensitive form of teaching designed to stimulate students to construct effective and personalised ways of tackling academic problems. In their article, *But good Strategy Instructors are Constructivists!*, they explore the constructivist principles that can be incorporated into strategy instruction. Table 4.2 presents a number of these key principles.

TABLE 4.2

ESSENTIALS OF INFORMATION-PROCESSING CONSTRUCTIVISM FOR EDUCATION

For teachers

- A focus on the child constructing knowledge in interaction with a more competent adult or peer.
- Instruction in groups, with students providing input and feedback to each other.
- Implicit monitoring of the child's progress by an adult, which determines future input.
- Non-scripted dialogues between teachers and students, characterised by meaningful adult reactions to student attempts to write, speak, or solve problems, followed by student reaction to feedback.
- Continual teacher encouragement of students to apply their knowledge to new situations.
- An acceptance of individual differences in the degree of assistance required and of rates of progress.
- Modelling and explanations given by teachers and peers that progress students along to greater competence through the creative transformation of teacher and peer modelled skills by students.
- An emphasis on learning through understanding.

For learners

- Practice in applying strategies to new situations or learning domains.
- Thinking 'deeply' rather than superficially about what they read.
- Consciously making connections to what they already understand or are familiar with.
- Monitoring performance of strategy use in a variety of tasks, some similar and some different.

(based on Pressley, Harris & Marks 1992 and Pressley & Woloshyn 1995)

Table 4.3 presents a taxonomy of learning strategies which you can use to guide your use of these strategies.

REMEMBERING

Our computer analogy highlighted the importance of disk storage space and procedures for making permanent records of our data processing. In this section we consider procedures that facilitate or inhibit the effective retention of human information processing. Much of the material presented to our senses each day is not remembered because we do not attend specifically to the stimuli. For example, who can recall the portraits on our currency? We remember on several occasions giving a listening exercise to a class, which then had to answer comprehension questions, only to be unable to answer the questions ourselves. Despite 'mouthing the words' our attention was obviously elsewhere.

How might counting on fingers be a great aid to remembering? Photo: authors

Factors that affect remembering in educational settings

Research into remembering and forgetting in educational settings indicates that students actually retain quite a lot of what is taught in the classroom (Semb & Ellis 1994). The long-term retention of school learning is quite complex and influenced by many factors. Among very important factors are the degree of organisation and structure of the material being learnt. In particular, if this structure relates to students' **prior knowledge**, retention should be enhanced. Practice, relearning, advanced

Why is it important to pay attention for effective information processing? Photo: Connie Griebe

TABLE 4.3 **A TAXONOMY OF LEARNING STRATEGIES**

Cognitive strategies	**Basic tasks (e.g. memory for lists)**	**Complex tasks (e.g. test learning)**
Rehearsal strategies	Reciting list	Shadowing Copy material Verbatim note taking Underlining test
Elaboration strategies	Keywork method Imagery Method of loci Generative note taking Question answering	Paraphrasing Summarising Creating analogies
Organisational strategies	Clustering Mnemonics	Selecting main idea Outlining Networking Diagramming

Metacognitive strategies	**All tasks**
Planning strategies	Setting goals Skimming Generating questions
Monitoring strategies	Self-testing Attention-focus Test-taking strategies
Regulating strategies	Adjusting reading rate Re-reading Reviewing Test-taking strategies

Resource management strategies	**All tasks**
Time management	Scheduling Goal setting
Study environment management	Defined area Quiet area Organised area
Effort management	Attributions to effort Mood Self-talk Persistence Self-reinforcement
Support of others	Seeking help from teacher Seeking help from peers Peer/group learning Tutoring

(based on Paul R. Pintrich's research on motivation and learning strategies, with permission.)

training and continued exposure to the content being learned also facilitate retention because they increase the degree of original learning. Instructional techniques also have an effect. In particular, research indicates that **mastery learning** approaches, which are highly structured around achievement goals and provide opportunities for practice, recall, feedback and review, produce superior academic performance (we discuss mastery approaches to instruction in Chapter 13). Instructional techniques that require the active involvement of the learner also facilitate remembering and recall. Finally, remembering is also affected by the nature of the assessment tasks. Tasks that call on recognition appear to stimulate remembering better than tasks that rely on recall. This is probably because the prompts for recognition are more explicit. Individual differences in ability also play a role in retention (Semb & Ellis 1994).

Research indicates that things to be recalled need to be consolidated in the long-term memory, and that a period of time is necessary for learning to become established. The actual physiological processes involved in this have attracted considerable attention from psychologists and physiologists, but are beyond the scope of this text (e.g. see Kantowitz & Roediger 1980). We will concentrate on the mechanics of learning for retention.

There are a number of techniques that may be used to enhance retention: whole and part learning, repetition and drill, overlearning and automaticity, and distributed practice.

Whole and part learning

Whole and part learning refers to the nature of the unit chosen for learning and memorising (Kingsley & Garry 1957; Seagoe 1972). With the whole learning approach, the integrity of the block of material to be remembered is maintained and encoded as a unit. With the part method, a large block is broken into smaller subsections and then put together again at the end. The most effective method is determined by the nature of the material to be learnt, and the age and ability of the learner. Whole and part learning approaches have implications for a range of learning activities such as learning the piano (should we learn one hand and then the other or both together?), poetry (stanza by stanza?), music (the whole piece or phrase by phrase?).

The author recalls having to learn the whole of 'The Rime of the Ancient Mariner' by heart. The whole class was expected to know it, word perfect, and each morning we were lined up around the wall to recite, in turn, stanza after stanza. Needless to say, with a poem this size, the part method was used and if the previous statement was accurate, the following student was prompted to make the correct response. Woe betide anyone who made an error! Not only did this cause a problem for the inaccurate student but following students also became confused.

On the other hand, when faced with learning a speech from Shakespeare the whole method often works better. There are no hard and fast rules, but there are some important principles when adopting one or other approach. The whole method binds material together at the outset into a meaningful whole; however, learning may seem slower. On the other hand, part learning supplies immediate goals, shows more rapid learning, and is therefore more satisfying. But part learning does not necessarily transfer to the whole, and too complete a learning of individual parts may inhibit later learning of the whole.

Repetition and drill

Repetition and drill are time-honoured practices among teachers, and are directed towards maximising the retention of learned material. Repetition, in itself, does not lead to greater retention; the important criterion for the usefulness of this as a technique is that it must be based on attention and understanding. The belief that if students do it often enough they will catch on is quite erroneous. Children can write out a list of spelling words many times without learning them; a child can practise some aspect of writing skills without improving in penmanship; and a child may do a series of exercises by following the steps indicated in the example without mastering the principles involved. Basically, repetition is useful if it has the interest, attention and purpose of the learner and is associated with meaningful learning; it is most useful in refining and improving the retention and recall of material already learnt.

Overlearning and automaticity

Continuing repetition of the material past the point of first mastery, called overlearning, is also beneficial in facilitating retention and recall. This repetition is also necessary for the development of **automaticity**. Automaticity refers to the status of a skill or behaviour that has been repeated to the point of being 'automatic'. That is to say the skill or behaviour can function automatically while other thinking occurs. Another characteristic of automaticity is that skills requiring several steps of behaviour are 'chunked' into a single unit. Consider a young man learning to play a musical instrument for the first time. He has to discern where the musical note is on the staff, what note it is, what position the hands must be in to create that note, and then execute the playing of the note. Early on, this process can fill the limited space in the working memory. Notes are produced slowly, deliberately and, occasionally, incorrectly. Repeated practice can lead to automaticity which connects all the steps necessary to produce the note into one process, thereby taking up less space in the working memory. This allows the musician to think about future notes to be played and the emotion that should be conveyed in the musical piece.

Another demonstration of automaticity can be seen in the efforts of a woman learning to drive a car with a manual transmission. The driver, faced with three pedals, two feet, five gears, steering and congested highways has her hands and working memory full. In the early stages of learning to drive, the car can lurch, the clutch is forgotten and gears grind: every bit of attention is necessary. After repeated experience the driving process becomes automatic. The shifting process occurs smoothly, effortlessly, and almost without thought. Robert Sternberg (1986) regards the ability to automatise as an element of intelligence (see Chapter 3). In his triarchic theory of intelligence, he describes the ability to deal with novel situations and the ability to automatise familiar experiences as one aspect of intelligence.

Distributed practice

Practice, like medicine, may be presented in small or large doses. It may be concentrated into relatively long, unbroken periods, or spread over several short sessions. When practice is concentrated in long periods it is called **massed**. When it is spread over time it is called **distributed**.

Almost without exception, the studies concerned with the relative effectiveness of distributed and massed practice, whether it is with motor skills (such as writing) or verbal learning (such as reading), show that practice should be spaced for the best results (e.g. Dempster 1988; Semb & Ellis 1994). A few words in spelling each day for a week will be mastered better than a large number bunched in one lesson.

It appears that when the amount of work involved in a task is great, and when the task is complex or not particularly meaningful, there should be regular practice periods separated by rest periods to allow for the consolidation of the material. This also applies to situations where a high level of attention or energy is required (such as learning to use complex machinery) and where the possibility of errors increases as individuals become fatigued. It also appears that the length of the rest period is not so crucial. A five minute 'breather' or 'smoko' (as they used to call it before the days of smoking bans) may be all that is necessary to allow the consolidation of information to take place, and an alleviation of potential fatigue effects.

When to use distributed practice

Massed practice periods are nevertheless very useful for tasks that are meaningful or already partially learnt. They are also useful for revising material or bringing the individual or group to a peak level of mastery on the material (Kingsley & Garry 1957; Seagoe 1972).

When to use massed practice

The author remembers rehearsals for a major drama production she was directing. Individual actors were given both extensive and short, focused practice sessions in their roles. Musicians also practised difficult sections of their scores individually. As the performance night drew closer, the pieces were fitted together and a whole-day dress rehearsal was held to 'get rid of the bugs'. That night, the final performance was held and, after all that massed and distributed practice, it was a great show, even if somewhat exhausting.

Serial position effect

It is an interesting fact that when faced with learning a list of things such as the alphabet, mathematical tables, spelling lists, historical dates, a long poem or a song, the material presented early is most easily remembered, material near the end is remembered relatively easily, but we often have great difficulty remembering the middle sections of the material. Children tend to make spelling errors in the middle of words and in the middle of spelling lists; they get up to 4 x 6 easily in their tables but forget the next in sequence until they sigh with relief at 4 x 10, 11 and 12. Children forget the middle of songs or poems, and pronunciation errors are made in the middle of words (e.g. chimbley). This fall-off in retention in the middle of the sequence is known as the **serial position effect**. It doesn't apply only to lists of things. Children have a tendency to listen to the beginning of the lesson, fall asleep in the middle, and wake up for the conclusion. It has been known to happen to students in lectures as well (Greene 1986; Rundus & Atkinson 1970; Stigler 1978).

This ability to retain and recall the first and last elements of a list more easily than the middle sections is referred to as the **primacy** and **recency effects** respectively. It appears that the serial position effect may be explained by a fall-off in attention in the middle, so encoding is therefore less effective and retention and recall are lessened.

Primacy and recency effects

In itself, this is no problem if precautions are taken to alleviate the effect. Important material should be presented at the beginning or end of the list. Less important or more easily remembered material could be included in the middle. If all material is of equal

Structure lessons to alleviate the serial position effect

importance, then the position in the list should be varied over a number of trials so that no item is located in the middle consistently. For example, spelling lists could be presented over three nights with a variation in word position each night. Alternatively, parts of the same list could be presented over three nights, with several words repeated in each until all words are included.

At times the sequence cannot be altered (as with a long soliloquy or a long song). However, we can effectively make the middle the start of a new learning episode by saying 'We are going to pay particular attention to stanza two today' or 'Let's go over the middle phrase of the song a couple more times'.

Simply drawing attention to middle items by saying 'I want you to pay special attention to this' can be effective, as is using variety throughout the learning episode. Students can also be taught to take extra care with particular aspects of learning tasks so that there is less variation in attention. You might say, for example: 'You might make mistakes in the middle section, so watch this carefully.'

Another problem with learning material in serial order for retention and recall is that the order in which we learn the material determines the order of easiest recall. In general, if we have slavishly learnt material in a serial form it is very hard to recall items without resorting to the whole list. For example, how many people have to go through a large part of the alphabet in order to recall a letter's position, or right through a multiplication table to locate a particular sequence? If we require flexibility of recall, items should not be learnt in a serial fashion.

Table 4.4 lists essential guidelines for using whole or part methods of learning.

TABLE 4.4

ESSENTIALS FOR USING WHOLE OR PART METHODS OF LEARNING EFFECTIVELY

For teachers

- When information to be learnt is highly unified and independent of other units, it is better for students to learn it as a whole.
- When information consists of many loosely related parts, which are in themselves unified, the part approach is perhaps better.
- Work from the whole to the part, for example, when teaching a poem, read through the poem several times as a whole before memorising individual stanzas. With vocabulary building, locate the words in a context before memorising a definition, and have children hear many stories before they are asked to write small sentences.
- Many exercises that are often taught partly can be taught wholly; for example, vocabulary, language and writing practice can be covered in the one exercise.
- Be flexible in approach.
- Give guidance in the use of the appropriate method as students do not always choose the best method.

Why do we have difficulty remembering some things?

Earlier we illustrated problems that can occur in accessing and retrieving information from computer files. Retrieval of information stored mentally also depends upon the effectiveness with which the information was encoded and the utility of the retrieval cues associated with the stored information. In this section we discuss some techniques to enhance memory retrieval.

We have seen that information in the working memory may disappear unless it is consolidated, and we discussed above some of the techniques for encoding and retaining material that should facilitate long-term memory and facilitate retrieval. Some researchers have suggested that the amount of effort put into encoding a memory may affect how long it lasts and how easily we can retrieve it.

There are four basic reasons why we forget.

Reasons for forgetting

1. The information in the working memory was never effectively transferred to the long-term memory.
2. Because the information is not used over a long period, the memory appears to fade.
3. We cannot retrieve the cues for information that is in the long-term memory.
4. Our retrieval of specific information is interfered with by similar information, causing confusion.

Obviously, in the first case, lack of attention or appropriate consolidation procedures, such as those discussed above, would prevent the effective encoding of information for retention and recall. We have all been pleased with ourselves for having remembered the names of people at a party while we are at the party, only to be embarrassed the next day by forgetting a name when we meet one of the party-goers at a local shop.

Some research indicates that our memories are encoded chemically in the brain, and if not reactivated periodically the memory traces simply fade with time. The third and fourth explanations are of more immediate interest to us. In our description of the encoding and retention processes we have emphasised the importance of encoding material in such a way that particular cues can be used to recall the information. Indeed, successful mnemonics depend upon cues that are easy to remember, acting as the trigger for remembering more difficult material. The effectiveness of retrieval cues depends on their relation to the nature of the stored material. For example, if you are given the word *violet* to remember, and it follows the words *daisy, tulip* and *zinnia* in a list, you are likely to encode it as a flower. Later, you are more likely to recall *violet* if you are given the retrieval cue *flowers* than if you were simply left on your own to remember the word. If you were given the word violet among a list of girl's names, such as *Bridie, Agnes* and *Beatrice*, and you were given the retrieval cue *girls' names*, you would probably also remember the word *violet* as belonging to the list. On the other hand, if the word was included in a list of girls' names and you were given the retrieval cue *flowers* you may very well have difficulty retrieving the word (Kantowitz & Roediger 1980).

Two further causes should be considered. First, much apparent loss of memory is simply the result of an individual's not associating the material with cues that can serve as triggers for the retrieval of the memory, and this is a memory skill that can be taught.

Second, apparent loss of memory may also be the result of the wrong retrieval cue being used. Some teachers go to considerable lengths to teach material to children in one context, only to require its recall in a context that does not present the relevant retrieval cues. For example, if children are taught a mathematical process such as multiple addition through drill and practice, but are examined for their recall of the procedures through a test where the procedures are buried in verbal problems, the children could very well appear to have forgotten how to do the procedure. In fact, what is happening is that the appropriate cue for recall is missing.

Interference effects Some argue that the basic reason we forget is not that we have lost the available information from memory, but that the memory is blocked from retrieval because of competing responses. In other words, events occurring before or after events that are to be remembered interfere with recall of the to-be-remembered events. One phenomenon that all teachers are familiar with is memory loss for student names at the beginning of a new term. We can remember each of the students' names in our class in a particular year. At the beginning of a new year we have considerable difficulty learning the names of our new class, but recall the names of our old class reasonably well. However, some time into the new term, we consolidate the names of our new class, only to be embarrassed when we can't then recall the names of our last class. This effect on retention is known as the **interference effect** and, depending on the direction of the interference, we have either proactive interference or retroactive interference.

Proactive interference occurs when earlier learning interferes with new learning; for example, a teacher learning the names of his new class may have difficulty because he confuses the names with those of an earlier class. In general, when we find it difficult to respond to new situations because of our established ways of responding, we have proactive interference. There are many examples of this effect—driving on the other side of the road in Europe, learning to touch type, correcting a well-established spelling error, driving an automatic car after a manual car. Recently a teacher relayed to us the difficulty children from a Lebanese background have learning our number system. It appears that, while the Western world borrowed many of the orthographic features of the Arabic number system, the numerical value, placement and way of reading them (right to left rather than left to right) were not retained. Can you imagine the trouble experienced by children who have an established Arabic number system, which is similar to, but confusingly different from, the system in use in our schools? This is a very good example of proactive interference.

Proactive interference: earlier learning interferes with new learning

When new learning impedes the retention of the old learning we have an example of **retroactive interference**. When we first started word processing on a computer we used the Macintosh format and became very adept at it. At a certain point we were provided with IBM machines for work. We found it inordinately difficult converting from the Macintosh to the DOS IBM, which is a good example of proactive interference. However, as we had no alternative, we persevered and became quite adept at using the IBMs. Now, when we return to the Macintosh we find it hard remembering exactly what to do, an equally good example of retroactive interference!

Retroactive interference: new learning impedes the retention of old learning

For educators the main implication of interference effects is to sequence learning experiences so that present learning does not inhibit the retention and recall of earlier or subsequent learning. For example, if we were to give children a spelling list that contained 'ie' words such as *achieve* and *piece*, any subsequent list should not contain 'ei' words, such as *conceive* and *receive*, until the earlier material is consolidated. We all use the rhyme 'i before e except after c' to try to sort this out. Knowing the problems most of us still have with ie/ei words indicates the power of the interference effects.

Proactive facilitation It should also be noted that learning one thing can often help a person learn similar material. For example, learning Spanish first may help a student learn Italian, a similar language. This is known as **proactive facilitation**. If we are teaching children how to spell 'ie' words and we follow up the initial learning with further lists containing 'ie' words, the earlier learning should be consolidated. This is known as **retroactive facilitation**. It is argued that the more similar the mother tongue is to English for ESL students the greater the help the mother tongue can give in acquiring the second language (Corder 1983, cited in Ringbom 1987). The difficulties in learning to understand any foreign language, for example, depend primarily upon the existence or lack of cross-linguistic and orthographic similarities to the native language, upon which the learner can draw. Many people find it helpful to recall the Latin roots of a somewhat obscure word to help decode its meaning.

There are a number of general principles regarding interference effects that will help you understand how they operate and suggest techniques for maximising facilitation while minimising interference:

- ☐ A task that is closely related to an earlier one, so that it is confusing, may interfere with the recall of the previous task; e.g. spelling list 'ie' words followed by 'ei' words would lead to confusion and neither list would be easily remembered or recalled.
- ☐ A task that is closely related to an earlier one, but reinforcing it, may facilitate recall—e.g. learning to drive a car, then a tractor; learning a list with silent ms and then one with other words with silent ms.
- ☐ A task unrelated to an original task may have no effect on the recall of the original task—e.g. following a maths lesson with an art lesson.
- ☐ A task which is extensive in nature may interfere with the consolidation and recall of an earlier task because of the fatigue induced.

Question point: Define and differentiate between retroactive interference and proactive interference. Discuss classroom examples. How can teachers use proactive facilitation to increase learning?

How do experts differ from novices in information processing?

In general, we consider adults more cognitively mature and capable of more sophisticated information processing than children. However, as illustrated earlier, when adults are given a mental task to perform in an area in which they have little knowledge, they often process the information less efficiently than children who have more knowledge in that area. This raises the question of the relationship between the amount of knowledge possessed and its impact on cognitive processing.

Increasingly, therefore, attention is being paid by researchers to the different cognitive characteristics of experts and novices in particular performance domains to find out how they differ in what they know, and the processes they use for performing a sequence of cognitive actions on the content (Chi, Glaser & Rees 1982; Shuell 1990; Sweller 1993). The findings from this research are thrown into strong relief when the experts are children and the novices adults.

TABLE 4.5

ESSENTIALS OF ENHANCING REMEMBERING

For teachers

- Provide opportunities for the active involvement of the learner.
- Provide multiple and varied learning opportunities.
- Provide opportunities for students to engage the material at higher cognitive levels to stimulate schema building and deep processing.
- Provide coherent and well-organised material relevant to students' prior knowledge.
- Provide corrective feedback.
- Provide recognition tasks to evaluate learning.

For learners

- Indicate whether understanding of new material has taken place ('Do I understand this?').
- Think of examples similar to the new material or procedure ('How is this similar to/different from what I already know about?').
- Try to relate the new information to prior understanding
('How does this connect to what I already know?').

Not surprisingly, the evidence shows that the expert knows more domain-specific concepts than the novice does, and that these concepts are more differentiated and interrelated, with each of the expert's concepts closely connected in **long-term memory** with many other concepts. Hence encoding, storage and retrieval are facilitated. Experts also appear to be more likely to use **cognitive strategies** such as planning and analysis before processing information. In many cases this simplifies the processing procedure as the experts call to mind appropriate

Experts know more domain-specific knowledge

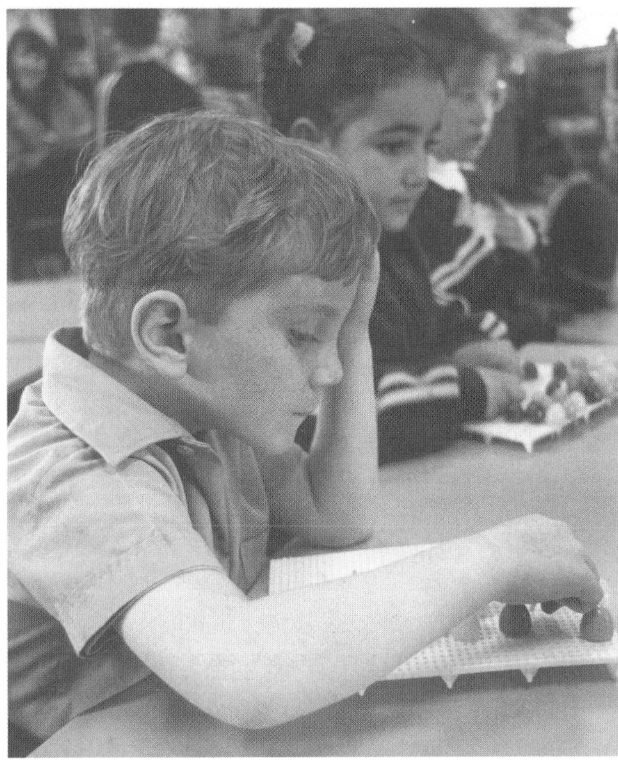

What elements are essential for the development of expertise by novices? Photo: authors

templates for cognitive action from their rich 'bank' of stored experiences and memories. In other words, the expert's response can be more automatic, unconscious and effortless (Shuell 1990; Sweller 1993). Nevertheless, if both adults and children are equally unfamiliar with the problem to be solved or the material to be learnt, adults generally may be expected to perform better because of their larger repertoire of experience-based learning, which will facilitate the solving of novel problems. It may also be that they have a greater store of strategies for learning new material than children.

By and large, the development of expertise in a domain area depends on experience and practice, but of course what individuals choose to, or have the opportunity to, invest time and practice in is subject to a wide number of environmental circumstances. One would expect that formal education at least makes all children expert in basic skills, with some measure of high-level, developmentally mature-looking cognitive performance (see Flavell 1985).

HOW IS KNOWLEDGE ORGANISED AND STRUCTURED?

Anderson's ACT*

A theoretical information-processing model of the learning process which has attracted a lot of attention from cognitive psychologists is John Anderson's Adaptive Control of Thought system (ACT*) which uses a computer program to mimic human cognition and problem solving (Anderson 1982, 1983, 1990; Lohman 1989; Shuell 1986). The system is too complex to describe in detail here but a few general points might give you an idea of how ACT* operates.

At its simplest, the model posits that the acquisition of new knowledge is related to three processes: the expansion of **declarative knowledge**, which deals with facts, the development of **procedural knowledge**, which deals with how to produce knowledge, and the transaction between the two.

Networks
Schemata

Declarative knowledge

Declarative knowledge is our knowledge about things (e.g. mathematical knowledge such as 7 + 3 = 10). This knowledge is hypothesised to be structured as an interrelated **network** of facts that exist as propositions. In other words, we don't know 'kangaroo' as a static concept, but rather we know about the concept 'kangaroo' because of its relationship to a number of other concepts such as animals, grass, hides, meat, farming and so on. Any one concept is networked with any number of other concepts, and it is this networking that ultimately gives the concept meaning and enables us to remember it. Furthermore, it is the richness of the networking that makes particular concepts more potent—that is, more easily retrievable from our long-term memory. Networks of connected ideas or relationships are referred to as **schemata** (a somewhat similar construct to that used by Piaget). We have presented, on the next page, a schema for the word 'kangaroo' to illustrate declarative knowledge.

Procedural knowledge

Procedural knowledge is knowing how to perform various cognitive activities, such as how to do addition sums and solve verbal problems. In this case, there is a transaction between the declarative knowledge and the actions performed upon it (procedural knowledge—which in ACT* theory is called a production system. You can see how this model of thinking originated in the development of computerised, artificial intelligence).

When new information is encountered it is coded into a network of existing propositions or ideas (schema). New information that fits into a well-developed and well-practised schema is retained far more readily than information that does not fit into a schema.

From this point the declarative knowledge is compiled into higher-order procedures (called *productions*) that apply the knowledge to solve problems. These productions are made in the format: if a certain condition

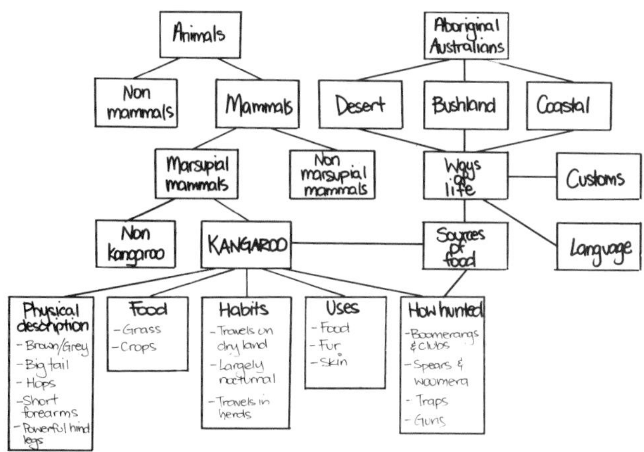

Declarative knowledge: a schema for the word 'kangaroo'

holds, then perform a certain action. For example, children acquire declarative knowledge about the number system through expository teaching. By linking the information they are receiving to already existing nodes, they develop a rather static understanding of mathematical concepts. Through a series of demonstrations by the teacher the students learn to manipulate the number system in the IF-THEN form. For example, IF the goal is to do an addition problem THEN add the numbers in the right-hand column. This sequence is called a **production**.

Productions

Productions are built up on one another; for example, a second production might be that IF the goal is to do an addition problem and the right-hand column has been added, THEN add the numbers in the second column. More and more sophisticated systems of productions are developed through processes of generalisation and discrimination so that increasingly difficult addition problems may be solved smoothly and efficiently (Shuell 1986). Depending on the positive and negative feedback that particular productions receive, better rules (higher-order processes) are strengthened and poorer rules are weakened.

The theory is useful for examining the differences in cognitive processing that characterise novices and experts in particular areas. The declarative knowledge of both groups may be equivalent but the procedural knowledge of the expert is more efficient. The theory is also useful for thinking about the ways in which children should be introduced to problem solving, and the relationship that exists between knowledge and procedures for operating upon this knowledge.

Question point: *Discuss the information-processing model of learning. What classroom implications can be drawn from this learning theory? How is the information-processing model of learning a constructivist one?*

ACTION STATION

Reflect on your own knowledge of study skills. What knowledge do you have about the best ways for you to study for an exam? What strategies do you employ to maximise your attention, concentration and memory recall when studying for an exam? Make a brief list of these and highlight those most frequently used.

In groups of three or four students, compare your study skills knowledge and behaviour, then discuss the following questions:

1. Do you have a well-developed knowledge of study skills behaviours? Do you regularly use these skills? Why or why not?
2. How did you acquire your study skills behaviours and knowledge?
3. The efficient and effective use of study skills requires considerable practice and effort. Do you consider this practice and effort to be worthwhile?
4. What encourages you to use particular strategies and discourages you from using others?

DEVELOPMENTAL IMPLICATIONS OF INFORMATION PROCESSING THEORY

As with all models of learning, information processing has limitations. For example, the model implies that thinking and learning occur in a serial (linear) processing form, whereas we know that thinking and learning are more complex than this (it is a recursive process). Furthermore, the model fails to take into account motivation, affect and social interaction as elements affecting learning processes (Mageean 1991).

Nevertheless, the model gives us many useful starters as teachers for considering how we might structure information in order to facilitate learning. Other essential elements of a full model of learning such as social interaction are examined elsewhere in the text. In any event, to the present, no theory has successfully combined all the possible components of learning into an integrated and holistic theory. It is our job as teachers to construct this integrated theory within the context of our classrooms from the information we have available.

Apart from the general description of key components of the model of information processing, a number of information-processing theories of development have been constructed (Case 1985a; Klahr & Wallace 1976; Siegler 1991; Sternberg 1985). It is beyond the scope of this text to describe these in detail. Table 4.6 summarises key elements of the theories and readers are recommended to read Siegler (1991) for further information.

As children grow older there is an increase in short-term memory capacity, and processing and encoding skills, an improvement in retrieval from long-term memory, and increasing development and use of cognitive strategies and self-monitoring metacognitive skills to enhance encoding, retention and retrieval. These developments occur as children are exposed to novel learning experiences, particularly modelling by parents, teachers and peers. At present it is not possible to say whether these changes reflect structural changes in the child's information-processing capacity (akin to Piaget's changes across stages) or whether they are functional capacity changes as the child becomes more expert in cognitive strategy use (Flavell 1985).

TABLE 4.6

OVERVIEW OF INFORMATION-PROCESSING THEORIES OF DEVELOPMENT

Theorist	Goal of theory	Main developmental mechanisms	Formative influences
Sternberg	To provide an information-processing analysis of the development of intelligence.	Strategy construction based on the use of knowledge acquisition components metacomponents and performance components. Also encoding and automatisation.	Information-processing theories' emphasis on encoding time course of processing and dividing thinking into components. Intelligence-testing emphasis on individual differences in intellectual ability.
Case	To unite Piagetian and information-processing theories of development.	Automatisation and biologically based increases in working memory, both of which increase processing capacity. Also strategy construction.	Piaget's emphasis on stages of reasoning and on between-concept unities in reasoning. Information-processing theories' emphasis on short-term memory limits automatisation and problem-solving strategies.
Klahr & Wallace	To formulate a computer simulation model of cognitive development.	Generalisation based on the workings of regularity detection, redundancy elimination, and the time line. Also encoding and strategy construction.	Piaget's emphasis on self-modification and on assimilation. Information-processing theories' emphasis on encoding and on computer simulation as a means for characterising thinking.
Siegler	To understand the adaptive character of cognitive development.	Choices among existing strategies and construction of new strategies. Also generalisation.	Piaget's emphasis on self-modification and equilibration. Information-processing theories' emphasis on adaptation to the task environment and on computer simulation.

(Reprinted with permission from Siegler, R. S. (1991) *Children's Thinking*, 2nd edn, p. 68, © Prentice Hall, Englewood Cliffs, NJ.)

WHAT WOULD YOU DO?

HE'LL SPEAK TO HIS BRAIN (continued)

Together Miss O'Brien and Andrew devised three ways to help.

First, they had a book of ideas which Andrew could carry around, and when he saw or did something interesting he could make a note of it. Second, he would 'speak to his brain' on a daily basis to explain to his brain that he was a writer. Third, they would celebrate his writing together and in front of the class.

Two days after this discussion Andrew came to Miss O'Brien and asked her if he could write a story on an idea that had come to him from the book they were reading in class.

What do you think of these solutions? Are they similar to any suggestions you made? How does this case study illustrate principles of information processing?

Case studies illustrating National Competency Framework for Beginning Teaching, National Project on the Quality of Teaching and Learning, Australian Teaching Council, 1996, p.10. Commonwealth of Australia copyright, reproduced by permission.

Recommended reading

Alexander, P. A., Kulikowich, J. M. & Jetton, T. L. (1994) The role of subject-matter knowledge and interest in the processing of linear and nonlinear texts. *Review of Educational Research*, 64, 210–52.

Anderson, J.R., Reder, L. M. & Simon, H. (1996) Situated learning and education. *Educational Researcher*, 25, 5–11.

Garner, R. (1990) When children and adults do not use learning strategies: Toward a theory of settings. *Review of Educational Research*, 60, 517–29.

Kail, R. & Bisanz, J. (1992) The information-processing perspective on cognitive development in childhood and adolescence. In R. J. Sternberg & C. A. Berg (eds), *Intellectual Development*. New York: Cambridge University Press.

Pressley, M., Harris, K. R. & Marks, M. B. (1992) But good strategy instructors are constructivists! *Educational Psychology Review*, 4, 3–31.

Pressley, M., Johnson, C. J., Symons, S., McGoldrick, J. A. & Kurita, J. A. (1989) Strategies that improve children's memory and comprehension of text. *The Elementary School Journal*, 90, 3–32.

Pressley, M. & Woloshyn, V. (1995) *Cognitive Strategy Instruction that Really Improves Children's Academic Performance*. Cambridge, MA: Brookline.

Rowe, H. (1989) Teach learning strategies. *SET Research Information for Teachers*, no. 1, item 14.

Rowe, H.A.H. (1988) *The Teaching of Critical Thinking: Assumptions, Aims, Processes and Implications*. Hawthorne, Vic. ACER.

Semb, G. B. & Ellis, J. A. (1994) Knowledge taught in school: What is remembered? *Review of Educational Research*, 64, 253–86.

Shuell, T. J. (1986) Cognitive conceptions of learning. *Review of Educational Research*, 56, 411–36.

Shuell, T. J. (1990) Phases of meaningful learning. *Review of Educational Research*, 60, 531–47.

Winne, P. H. (1995) Information-processing theories of learning. In L. W. Anderson (ed.), *International Encyclopedia of Teaching and Teacher Education*, 2nd edn. Tarrytown, NY: Pergamon, 107–12.

CHAPTER 5

Alternative cognitive views on effective learning

OVERVIEW

Cognitive psychology has influenced learning theory and classroom practice in several significant ways. Teachers influenced by cognitive theory view learning as an active, constructive process that involves higher-level procedures. Furthermore, cognitively oriented teachers believe that learning is cumulative and that the prior knowledge of the learner plays a fundamental role in the acquisition of new knowledge. Cognitive theories have also placed emphasis on the importance of the way knowledge is represented and structured in memory. Cognitively oriented teachers analyse learning tasks and performance in terms of the cognitive processes involved, and select content and instructional procedures to engage the psychological processes and knowledge structures appropriate for the students to achieve the desired learning outcomes. Throughout this chapter we emphasise that meaningful learning occurs when individuals are able to discover knowledge for themselves, perceive relations between old and new knowledge, apply their knowledge to solve new problems, communicate their knowledge to others and have continuing motivation for learning.

Teaching practices based on cognitive views of learning vary widely. In this chapter the perspective shifts from a cognitive constructivist view that emphasises the reproduction of knowledge in the form in which it was presented (the information-processing approach) to a constructivist view that emphasises the construction and reconstruction of knowledge as interpreted by an individual. As such, the construction and reconstruction of knowledge is personal and idiosyncratic. Indeed, from this perspective, true learning occurs when individuals are able to discover knowledge (both mental processes and content) for themselves. Discovering personal understanding becomes a very significant constructive process. In this context we discuss the cognitive theories of Gestalt psychology, and of Bruner, as examples of personal constructivism, and consider their teaching implications.

We compare Bruner's approach with that of Ausubel which is, in many ways, an example of information-processing constructivism. In Ausubel's theory, effective learning also occurs when learning is meaningful and students acquire personal understandings. However, in this case it is believed that the personal meanings can be achieved through transmission of information from the teacher to the learner. It is what the learner does with the information that is important. Classroom practices based on Ausubel's theory are discussed and compared with those of Bruner.

The ability to plan, monitor and regulate our cognitive processes while constructing knowledge is also considered in the context of research into metacognition and self-regulation of learning.

BOX 5.1 TEACHING COMPETENCE

The teacher structures learning tasks effectively

Indicators

The teacher:

- manages and paces teaching time to meet student learning goals;
- provides for individual differences in rates and styles of learning;
- links new content and processes with prior learning, contexts and interests;
- uses purposefully a range of material, human and technological resources.

Case studies illustrating National Competency Framework for Beginning Teaching, National Project on the Quality of Teaching and Learning, Australian Teaching Council, 1996, Element 3.4, p.49. Commonwealth of Australia copyright, reproduced by permission.

GESTALT PSYCHOLOGY AND PERSONAL CONSTRUCTIVISM

Gestalt psychology contributes to our understanding of how individuals personally construct meaning. Wertheimer, the founder of the Gestalt movement in Germany (Gillam 1992; Wertheimer 1980), was impressed by the fact that humans do not usually perceive events as

Human insight

'What'll we do?'

individual or disparate elements, but as whole, unified patterns, rather as the units of a motion picture (the individual photographs) are perceived as moving images when played at a particular speed. He believed that, because of the capacity of our perception, we always have a tendency to structure our world into meaningful patterns (the word 'Gestalt' means pattern), and that when we structure disparate elements the whole is greater than its parts. We are familiar with this principle whenever we listen to a musical composition composed of discrete notes, or view a work of art composed of discrete colours.

Gestalt organising principles

Pragnanz
Similarity
Proximity
Closure
Continuation

Koffka (1935; Wertheimer 1980) also did much to popularise Gestalt ideas and experimented with the organising tendencies of perception. These organising tendencies were grouped together as a series of 'laws', the most general of which was **pragnanz**—this refers to the tendency we all have to organise unorganised stimuli into patterns that make some sense to us. In other words, when faced with a problem we attempt to organise the features of the problem so that we have some insight into it. At a simple level this may be illustrated by our solving a jigsaw puzzle. In the first instance we may gather similar items together (e.g. all the pieces that have blue on them). This is referred to as the law of **similarity**. At other times, two or three connecting pieces may fortuitously lie together on the table and we perceive this and join them. This is referred to as the law of **proximity**. As we complete more of the puzzle we perceive spaces that may be completed by particular pieces with the appropriate shape or colour. This is called **closure**. And finally we organise pieces with flat edges along the outside. This is called the law of **continuation**. Using these perceptual processes helps us to solve the jigsaw puzzle. Gestaltists believe that we use these same processes naturally every day (although usually unconsciously) in our interaction with the world around us, and that they are the means by which we learn much about the world. At the moment of forming the good pattern, or realising the solution to the problem (e.g. in a crossword) we are said to experience an insight, colloquially referred to as the 'ah ha' experience. We hope that at least on some occasions while reading this text you will also have some 'ah ha' experiences.

As you have probably gathered, Gestalt psychologists view learning as a purposive, exploratory, imaginative and creative enterprise. The learning process is identified with thought or conceptualisation; it is, in fact, a change of insight. These theorists are concerned with important cognitive processes such as problem solving, decision making and perception. When faced with problematic situations, people bring an analytic ability to bear which enables them first to structure the problem and then to solve it through cognitive processes.

Learning viewed as purposive, exploratory, imaginative and creative

Classroom applications of Gestalt psychology

Gestalt psychology has had an impact on classrooms through the design and use of structural apparatus for the teaching of mathematics. The idea behind this type of apparatus is that by physically manipulating objects in patterns, children perceive the pattern of number arrangements as a meaningful whole. This perceptual learning, which evolves from the child's handling of the actual apparatus and from the child's physical experience of the relationship between quantities, develops into a mental activity in its final stages. Success depends on a wide variety of unstructured experiences gradually leading through structured activities to the necessary mental constructions required for mathematical thinking. The Gestalt approach has had a great impact on the world of education generally, with teachers implementing the principles shown in Table 5.1 which are drawn from this theoretical approach.

Question point: Constructivists believe that cognitive processes like perception and memory involve interpretation. Do you agree? In what ways are interpretative processes involved in perception and memory?

TABLE 5.1

ESSENTIALS OF A GESTALT APPROACH FOR EDUCATION

For teachers

- Provide for *insightful learning*, which is the key to effective meaningful learning.
- Structure the learning environment with materials necessary for satisfactory *discoveries* to be made, such as in learning centres.
- Motivate learners through their *intrinsic interest* in solving problems.
- Deal with *principles* rather than specifics.
- Provide imaginative and *exciting curricula*.
- Demonstrate how *abstract principles* can be drawn from *specific concrete examples*.

For learners

- Actively *search for patterns* in apparently unconnected materials.

- Brainstorm then *draw together ideas* into similar or dissimilar concepts.
- *Create puzzles* for others to solve.

Gestalt psychology was a forerunner of a number of other cognitive theories which have had significant impact on classroom materials and procedures. In the following sections we describe two key theories, and draw out those elements that have most clearly impacted upon classroom practices and the development of materials for learning and teaching.

BOX 5.2 **TEACHING COMPETENCE**

The teacher understands the relationship between processes of inquiry and content knowledge and uses educational processes appropriate to the curriculum and the field of inquiry

Indicators

The teacher:

- demonstrates the relationship between subject matter and appropriate modes of inquiry;
- encourages students to pursue processes of inquiry appropriate to curriculum content;
- utilises approaches to learning which explore the breadth of modes of inquiry;
- builds a repertoire of teaching approaches to facilitate and enhance students' knowledge and understanding;
- implements learning programs that enable students to learn from experience;
- uses resources to facilitate students' understanding.

Case studies illustrating National Competency Framework for Beginning Teaching, National Project on the Quality of Teaching and Learning, Australian Teaching Council, 1996, Element 1-2, p.30. Commonwealth of Australia copyright, reproduced by permission.

BRUNER'S THEORY OF COGNITIVE DEVELOPMENT AND LEARNING

Concept development

Conceptualisation
Categories

When a baby is born it is helpless, unable to make effective use of the environment around it. The stimuli in the baby's environment are largely meaningless, disorganised and undistinguished. For Bruner (1960, 1961, 1966, 1974) the process of intellectual growth and learning consists in children gradually organising their environment into meaningful units by a process called **conceptualisation.** These meaningful units are termed **categories** by Bruner. Depending on the number of effective categories an individual has, he or she is more or less a functional person in the environment. Through the process of conceptualisation young children begin to understand what food is, what clothing is, what danger is, what animals are and so on. The young child passes from the stage of having few functioning concepts and categories through to the adult who has many.

This process of conceptualisation does not stop as we get older and greyer. For example, we often find we are in new environments where we feel at sea because we do not have the appropriate categories for interpreting the environment. The process of forming categories and codes consists of linking ideas together because of common properties. By being exposed to a range of objects and experiences we begin to see these common properties emerge. According to Bruner, categorisation has four major advantages:

1. *Categorisation reduces the complexity of the environment.* For example, a person looking inside a car engine for the first time is struck by the array of different parts and is perhaps overwhelmed by this. An expert mechanic (who has a category for motors) sees the motor as an integrated system on which he can operate effectively.
2. *Categorisation permits the recognition of objects.* A car mechanic can work on a lawnmower engine because he can recognise the object in terms of the concept 'motor'.
3. *Categorisation reduces the necessity for constant learning.* We relate to new objects in terms of past experiences and concepts. We are also able to predict qualities of an object without actually testing them by saying that, because it belongs to a certain group, it should have certain properties. For example, general principles learnt in mathematics can lead to solving new problems. We don't need to approach each new problem in a totally fresh way.
4. *Categories provide directions for instrumental activity.* For example, a man lost in a jungle without food will come across a range of strange growing things. If he categorises an object as food, it will be used to stave off hunger. Indeed, if he is resourceful, he could use a log for floating down the river, a banana leaf for shade and shelter, an animal for meat and a stone for cutting. In a sense, categories define the use to which an object may be put. In learning categories we are learning uses.

Concepts are built up through experience and through a procedure Bruner calls **coding,** which refers to the relationship that exists between the general and specific categories. Education is concerned with helping children to encode their experiences, working from the specific to the general—that is, from particular examples to general principles.

Concepts formed by working from specific instances to general rules

In brief, this is the foundation of Bruner's theory. Bruner explains the way in which this procedure takes place both theoretically and practically. We are most concerned with describing the practical and less theoretical elements.

Bruner's stages of intellectual development

Bruner theorised that children go through three major stages of intellectual development. In the first stage, children learn about the world around them by acting on objects. In a sense, an object is what you can do with it. A glass is used to drink with, a bed is to lie in, clothing is to wear and so on. This stage is referred to as the **enactive** stage. Children progress from this stage to the **iconic** stage where experiences and objects are represented as concrete images. Children no longer need to manipulate objects in order to learn about them, but can learn through models, demonstrations and pictures. Children can operate mentally with pictures. Lastly, children enter the **symbolic** stage when they develop the capacity to think abstractly with symbols. In this stage individuals go beyond the present and concrete experiences to create hypotheses. For Bruner, it followed that instruction of children should also be sequenced. In other words, for learning to occur best, children should first experience it, then react to it concretely, and finally symbolise it. While progression is believed to be in order through these stages, more mature learners who are already at the symbolic stage often function best when two or more of the modalities are called upon when learning about something new.

Enactive: learning through actions on objects

Iconic: learning through seeing images

Symbolic: learning through abstract symbols such as words

If you wanted to learn how to use a new camera you could simply have the operations explained to you (symbolic explanation). Under this circumstance you would probably find it difficult to absorb the information and use it effectively. You might, alternatively, be shown a diagrammatic representation of the camera while being given the explanation (iconic explanation). In this case your understanding would be enhanced. However, you would probably feel most at ease and learn most efficiently if an explanation was given to you while you were handling the camera (enactive explanation). At a later time you might simply refer to the verbal instructions or pictures to refresh your memory about what you had been taught. Bruner's principle is that, at any age, teachers will get a better result with learners if they combine concrete, pictorial and symbolic presentations of the material. It should also be apparent that material that can be presented only in symbolic form should not be taught until children have acquired this mode of operation. A key to successful teaching is giving learners the opportunity to operate on material at appropriate levels of abstraction.

Personal constructivism and learning

Bruner's theory reflects many of the tenets of **personal constructivism**. Bruner believes that discovery of connections and patterns is central to meaningful learning and he emphasises the importance of imagination and discovery to effective learning. We look at each of these in more detail below.

Bruner believes that schools should structure learning experiences so that they are appropriate to each student's level of development. Schools should also facilitate the development of flexible thinking in children by encouraging intuitive thinking as well as analytic thinking. **Analytic thinking** characteristically proceeds step by step and the learner is, in general, aware of the information and operations involved. This is the type of thinking commonly encouraged in schools, and is most often used in mathematics and science. **Intuitive thinking** is characterised by hunches and solutions not

The need to develop flexible thinking

These children are fully involved in an enjoyable but challenging task, planned for their level of manipulative and problem-solving skills. Photo: Diane McPhail

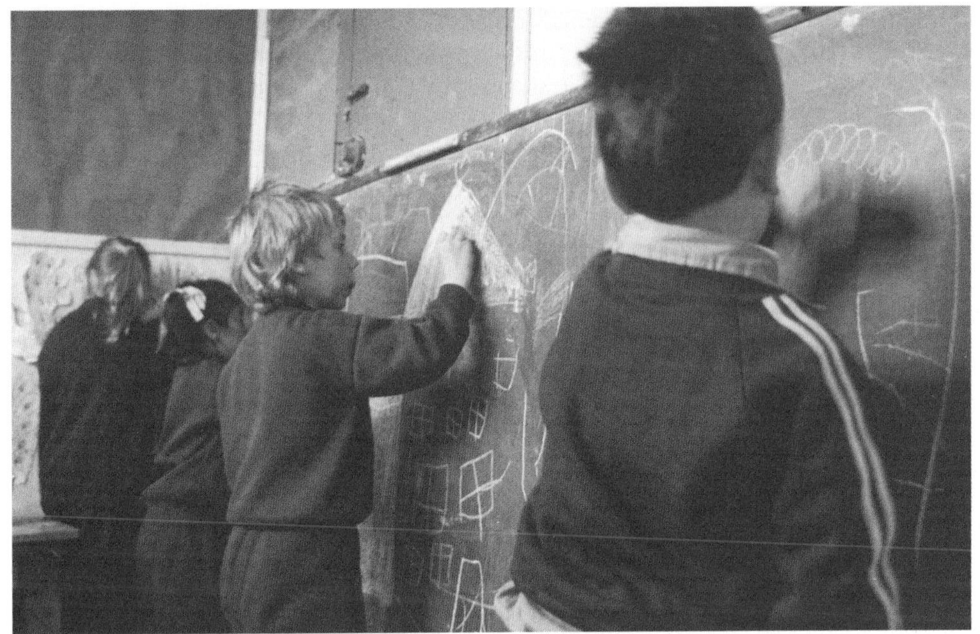

Children need to be actively involved in their learning. Photo: authors

based on work carried out with Dienes blocks. While the general principle of building on children's prior knowledge is a characteristic of most curriculum programs, few schools have implemented a fully integrated spiral curriculum. What would this involve?

based on formal processes of reasoning. Intuitive thought is based on a feeling one has for a particular subject in its wholeness. As a consequence it does not advance necessarily in carefully defined steps but tends to involve spurts and leaps reflecting the individual's perception of the total problem. Bruner believes that schools should establish an intuitive understanding of materials in children before exposing them to more traditional methods of deduction and proof.

Bruner believes that the basic ideas of science, maths and literature are as simple as they are powerful, and are capable of being translated to any level of experience. To this point he advocates the use of a **spiral curriculum** for developing concepts at increasingly higher levels of abstraction. If teachers of young children, for example, begin teaching the foundations of subjects in a manner appropriate for the pupil's intellectual development, the groundwork for later development is effectively laid. It is important that later teaching builds on earlier reactions and understandings, and that it seeks to create an ever more explicit and mature understanding of particular concepts. For example, understanding great human tragedy as reflected in the works of Shakespeare can be built on a young child's understanding of the concepts of happy and sad, developed through exposure to stories in kindergarten and primary classes and extended through later grades in moral dilemmas, re-creations through roleplay, or dramatisations and story writing. Understanding of complex mathematical concepts can be

Spiral curriculum: concepts presented at higher levels of abstraction as learning develops

Discovery learning

A number of principles may be deduced from the work of Bruner for application in classroom settings. Bruner believes learning should progress from specific examples to general principles by way of induction. One way to achieve this is through the use of **discovery learning** which refers to the learning of new information as a result of the learner's own efforts (Tamir 1995). The subject matter is not presented to the child in its final form, but rather the child, through his or her own manipulation of the materials, discovers relationships, solutions and patterns. Advocates of discovery learning believe that the following advantages characterise this approach:

- ☐ Discovery learning is more meaningful and hence results in better retention. Principles that emerge from the discovery method are significant because they come from the student's own work.
- ☐ Discovery learning enhances motivation, interest and satisfaction.
- ☐ Discovery learning enhances the development of intellectual capacities, information and problem-solving skills. Students learn how to discover, how to learn, and how to organise what they have learned.
- ☐ Discovery learning encourages transfer of skills to solve problems in new contexts.

Classrooms using discovery learning need to be resource-rich. Teachers need to abandon their role as purveyors of knowledge and become facilitators of children's learning. To perform this function well teachers need to be well prepared and competent in their understanding of the basic underlying principles of their discipline. This is particularly important in handling the range of 'discoveries' and personal proclivities that may characterise any one group of children in the classroom. Teachers must also be willing and able to try a variety of approaches to accommodate the varying needs of the children and their modes of cognitive reasoning (enactive, iconic and symbolic).

Far from being easy for the teacher, discovery-learning approaches are demanding of organisation and management skills. Novice teachers will need to anticipate thoroughly the sorts of needs the children will have in terms of movement around the learning space, noise and activity levels, resources, and guidance about the purpose of the learning activity. The **quality of learning** needs to be carefully monitored throughout, and interventions made to focus student attention on salient issues emerging from their discovery. 'Chalk and talk' approaches often appear far easier to manage, and to ensure that concepts the teacher feels are important are imparted in their entirety. What do you think?

Teaching through discovery is demanding on the teacher

Beware—young children do need considerable guidance in their discoveries because they have a developing knowledge base and are inexperienced in drawing 'scientific' conclusions on the basis of random pieces of evidence in the same way that adults do. Think back to Bruner's spiral curriculum and consider how you might structure their development of important concepts over a period of time.

Summarised below are some of the problems that have been associated with implementing effective discovery-learning environments. Table 5.2 lists the essentials for education of Brunner's discovery-learning approach.

- ☐ Lack of skills by teachers.
- ☐ Lack of appropriate resources.
- ☐ Time pressure to complete mandated curriculum.
- ☐ Difficulties encountered by students, especially slower learners.
- ☐ Failure by teachers to recognise the need to give individual assistance and guidance according to the abilities of the children.
- ☐ Can generate anxiety in students and teachers unsure of how to proceed.
- ☐ The challenge of discovery learning, especially in science, where many laws are counter-intuitive, may be too high and lead to failure and dissatisfaction.

(see Tamir 1995)

TABLE 5.2

ESSENTIALS OF BRUNER'S DISCOVERY-LEARNING APPROACH FOR EDUCATION

For teachers

- Redefine teaching role as *facilitator* rather than transmitter of knowledge.
- Stimulate learning and inquiry by setting *challenging problems* for students to solve.
- Provide *resource-rich* learning environments.
- Provide opportunities for students to *interact with material* enactively, iconically and symbolically.
- Allow for *individual differences* in ability, interest and prior experience.
- Monitor the *quality of learning* taking place in terms of students' ability, interest and experience.
- Revisit material at *increasingly higher levels of abstraction*.

For learners

- *Participate actively* in learning experiences—do not sit idle.
- *Ask questions* while investigating: 'What does this mean?', 'How is this similar to .../different from...?'
- Touch; draw pictures and diagrams; write summaries and descriptions of experiences.

WHAT WOULD YOU DO?

TAKING THE CLASSROOM OUTSIDE

Miss Black took her Prep/1 class on an excursion.
She included three parents and the school principal in her plan for the day. The children were divided into four groups and the parents and principal each selected to lead one of the planned learning experiences. Miss Black had planned learning activities in the historical building of the National Park where the children were required to look, listen to a commentary, touch various objects and talk about these experiences. Another group was to walk along a path in the bush, identifying favourite plant species and sketching them, and identifying the animals that also used the path by searching for droppings and footprints. A third group was to imagine that they were environmentalists and find a list of objects (e.g. someting that was once alive, something impossible to photograph, etc); and the fourth group played environmental games (e.g. 'hug a tree' and 'mini parks').

What types of learning might be expected from this excursion?

Case studies illustrating National Competency Framework for Beginning Teaching, National Project on the Quality of Teaching and Learning, Australian Teaching Council, 1996, p.8. Commonwealth of Australia copyright, reproduced by permission.

***Question point:** Discuss the advantages and disadvantages of discovery learning. Compare this with Vygotsky's notion of assisted discovery.*

WHAT WOULD YOU DO?

TAKING THE CLASSROOM OUTSIDE (continued)

The children (and parents) were fascinated by the number of living things they had never before noticed in a small area of grass; at how much evidence of animal presence they could find without seeing the animals; by the notion that someone lived alone among the mountains and had to walk for days to talk to another person; and at how aspects of the environment are interdependent. They also learned more about cooperating with each other and the responsibilities of bush walkers and visitors. Miss Black moved between groups asking questions and guiding discoveries. She was able to view her class outside the school environment and learn more about their personalities—one child who was quite dependent in the classroom surprised her by being able to locate and guide other children to public toilets and assume responsibility for garbage collection. She was also made aware of further things the children wanted to know, which they would research when back in the classroom.

How do the types of learning that the children experience relate to the theory of constructivism and especially to Bruner's theory of effective learning through discovery?

Case studies illustrating National Competency Framework for Beginning Teaching, National Project on the Quality of Teaching and Learning, Australia Teaching Council, 1996, p.8. Commonwealth of Australia copyright, reproduced by permission.

AUSUBEL AND RECEPTION LEARNING

As we have stated throughout this and other chapters, cognitive learning theorists have one central concern, and that is to make learning meaningful, rather than encouraging rote methods of learning. However, the range of beliefs as to how this is best achieved is vast. As evidenced above, Bruner believes that the most effective way is for learners to discover or induce principles from examples through the process of discovery learning. For Ausubel, however, concepts should be presented as principles embedded in meaningful examples. Ausubel believes that learning is most meaningful when new learning is effectively related to what children already know. This has long been a principle of good teaching: begin where the learner is at. This basic principle of Ausubel's was explored through his theoretical framework, the elements of which will be briefly described here.

How is cognitive structure developed in Ausubel's approach to learning?

For Ausubel (1963, 1966a, 1966b, 1968, 1977) cognitive structure (similar to Bruner's categories) is developed through a process of subsumption. There are three basic types of subsumption: derivative, correlative and obliterative. No one said the jargon was going to be easy, but the underlying concepts are actually quite easy to understand. **Derivative subsumption** refers to learning that occurs when a child builds upon concepts already mastered. For example, if children are learning about apples, they will compare characteristics of red and green apples, small and large apples, sour and sweet apples and so on, and build an overall concept of what apples are and what you can do with them.

Derivative subsumption: building on concepts already mastered

With **correlative subsumption**, concepts are extended. For example, children learn about apples, bananas and pears. In each case, comparisons are made and concepts extended. For example, children learn that some fruit skins can be eaten while others are best put on the compost heap. This may be best illustrated when children learn that certain things that look like fruit and vegetables (such as poison berries and toadstools) are to be avoided because they are dangerous. Subsumption reinforces an underlying principle of effective learning —to start with familiar material and extend it. For this reason general principles are often given which are then tested through examples.

Correlative subsumption: extending and developing new concepts

Obliterative subsumption refers to the distinguishability of the material to be learnt. If we want material to be remembered it must have some distinguishing characteristics, otherwise it will be forgotten. This is what is really meant by obliterative subsumption. Thus, with the apple example, it would be important to point out why some apples are best used for cooking and others for eating raw, as well as the cues that should be used to remember these differences. In other words similarities and differences should be highlighted, otherwise apples and apples are all just apples!

Obliterative subsumption: highlighting similarities and differences between concepts

How does reception learning operate in the classroom?

In reception learning the material to be learnt is presented to learners in a relatively complete and organised form. We have noted that in discovery learning learners are expected to discover much of the material for themselves and to organise it in their own way. Ausubel maintains that in most classrooms learning is through reception, and that discovery learning is inefficient and not necessary in most circumstances. The focus of attention should be on how to make reception learning most effective.

To this end, the teacher uses **expository methods** such as **demonstration, explanation** and **narration**. Practising skills in varied circumstances and revision are also important. Equally importantly, Ausubel warns against abuses of reception-learning techniques that lead to meaningless learning such as premature use of verbal approaches with cognitively immature learners; arbitrary presentation of unrelated facts without any organising or explanatory principles; failure to integrate new learning tasks with previously presented materials; and the use of evaluation procedures that merely measure ability to recognise discrete facts, or to reproduce ideas in the same words or in the identical context as originally encountered (Ausubel 1968, p. 18).

Demonstration

Explanation

Narration

To help children learn verbal material, Ausubel recommends what he calls **reception learning** in which material is organised from the top down, that is, from the most inclusive to the most specific. To prepare students for the material, Ausubel also advocates the use of **advance organisers** (1966b, 1978). As mentioned earlier, an organiser is a set of ideas or concepts that is given to the learner *before* the material to be learned. It is meant to provide the stable cognitive structure to which new learning can be anchored. Organisers can also be used to facilitate recall.

Advance organiser: a statement about a new topic providing structure for relating it to what students already know

Two types of organiser are suggested by Ausubel. The first is the **expository organiser** which is to be used with new material and presents an overview of the relevant concepts to attend to. For example, the teacher might say, 'Today we are going to learn about rats. I want you to notice the following aspects of …'. The second type, the **comparative organiser**, is used with material that is somewhat familiar. This type of organiser is likely to make use of similarities and differences between new material and existing cognitive structure. For example, the teacher might say, 'Today we are going to learn about green apples. Remember, yesterday we learnt that red apples had …'.

Expository and comparative organisers

Considerable research has also taken place into the effectiveness of advance organisers showing they are an effective teaching strategy when:

- ☐ they are presented as written analogies in paragraph form as diagrams and models;
- ☐ they are used with older students;
- ☐ there is sufficient time and help to use the organiser to make connections with previous understanding.

(Corkill 1992; Mayer 1989; Van Patten et al. 1986)

Table 5.3 summarises the essentials for education of Ausubel's reception-learning model.

Much ink has been used in debating the relative effectiveness of discovery versus meaningful reception learning and you will address some of the issues in activities related to this chapter.

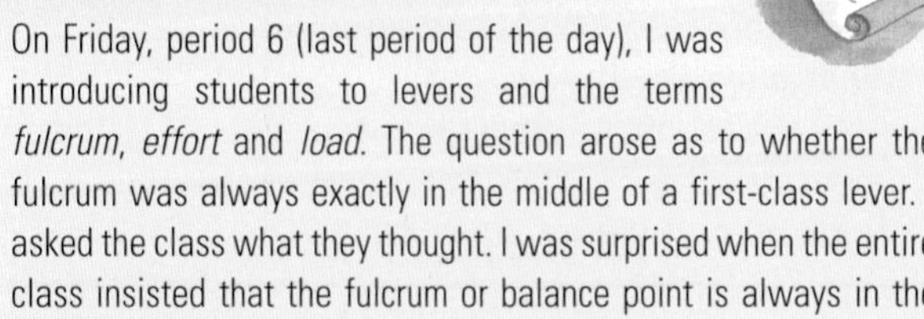

WHAT WOULD YOU DO?

FINDING THE BALANCE POINT

On Friday, period 6 (last period of the day), I was introducing students to levers and the terms *fulcrum, effort* and *load.* The question arose as to whether the fulcrum was always exactly in the middle of a first-class lever. I asked the class what they thought. I was surprised when the entire class insisted that the fulcrum or balance point is always in the middle of a lever or rod.

I went to the storeroom and obtained a metre ruler and three different brooms. I used a common method where you move your hands in from both ends to find the balance point. As expected, with the metre ruler the balance point or fulcrum was at the centre. Then I tested the broom. As I expected, the balance point was now closer to the broom head. The students did not believe me. They thought I was playing a trick on them. They were convinced the balance point would always be in the middle. The students' intuitive understanding of how things work was an impediment to their learning. I knew that misconceptions were common in science and very resistant to change. I asked a volunteer to run her hands along the broom until she found the balance point. She did so, but the rest of the class were still unconvinced. I encouraged students to try it with their pens. Unfortunately, some pens did have a balance point in the centre which they took as confirmation of their views.

How would you change student misconceptions?

Find out what the teacher did when we finish the case study on page 98.

Case studies illustrating National Competency Framework for Beginning Teaching, National Project on the Quality of Teaching and Learning, Australian Teaching Council, 1996, p.41. Commonwealth of Australia copyright, reproduced by permission.

TABLE 5.3

ESSENTIALS OF AUSUBEL'S RECEPTION-LEARNING MODEL

For teachers

- Logically *organise material.*
- *Link material* to what children already know.
- Relate material directly to *learner's existing concepts.*
- Use *effective expository teaching methods,* in particular explanation, narration and demonstration.
- Present *advance organisers* (expository and comparative) to the learner before the material to be learned is presented.
- Present material to be learned in a *variety of contexts.*

- *Review material* presented and learned and *provide effective feedback.*
- Apply acquired learnings in *novel situations* to demonstrate transferability.

For students

- Think about how the new information *fits in with what is already known.*
- *Ask questions* (of teachers and peers) to clarify understanding.
- *Think of examples* of principles given.

Question point: Consider Ausubel's notion of meaningful reception learning. Does the provision of guiding principles and analogies by the teacher reflect principles of constructivist learning?

WHAT WOULD YOU DO?

FINDING THE BALANCE POINT (continued)

I understood that each student would need to try the broom so I abandoned my planned lesson and let them all experiment with the brooms, metre rulers and pens. During the last 10 minutes we discussed our results and agreed that some rods do have a balance point at the centre, but not all. I described an example of a seesaw with a heavy handle at one end. If the seesaw is to balance, then the fulcrum must be moved towards the heavy handle. This same situation occurs when a heavy person moves towards the fulcrum when a light person is on the other end.

Even though the activity was not planned, I was pleased to see students actively engaged in experimenting, reflecting on and modifying their intuitive understanding.

Do you agree with this approach? How does it represent a discovery approach to learning? What might be some remaining problems with the students' understanding? What else might the teacher have done? In particular, consider how the teacher might have presented the material using effective expository teaching.

Case studies illustrating National Competency Framework for Beginning Teaching, National Project on the Quality of Teaching and Learning, Australian Teaching Council, 1996, p.41. Commonwealth of Australia copyright, reproduced by permission.

METACOGNITION AND CONSTRUCTIVISM

Our next Learner-centred Psychological Principle introduces the very important topic, metacognition: Why might the students' awareness of metacognitive processes promote more effective learning?

What is metacognition?

One of the key principles of constructivism is that

LEARNER-CENTRED PSYCHOLOGICAL PRINCIPLE 5

Higher-order strategies for selecting and monitoring mental operations facilitate creative and critical thinking.

During early to middle childhood, learners become capable of a metacognitive or executive level of thinking about their own thinking that includes self-awareness, self-inquiry or dialogue, self-monitoring, and self-regulation of the processes and contents of thoughts, knowledge structures and memories. Learners' awareness of their personal agency or control over thinking and learning processes promotes higher levels of commitment, persistence and involvement in learning. To foster this self-awareness of personal control, learners need settings where their personal interests, values and goals are respected and accommodated.

Reprinted with permission, APA Task Force on Psychology in Education (1993, January), p.7.

students are self-directed in their learning. Not only are educators interested in children acquiring the facts and figures of knowledge, but they are also interested in their acquiring the skills, strategies and resources needed to perform learning tasks effectively. Just as important is the ability to know when and how to use particular learning strategies. In other words, students need knowledge about how to monitor their cognitive resources (what we call metacognition) and how they learn (called metalearning) in order to learn more effectively (Brandt 1986; Costa 1984; Derry & Murphy 1986; Flavell 1976, 1979, 1985; McKeachie, Pintrich & Lin 1985; Marzano & Arredondo 1986a, 1986b; Shuell 1988; Thomas & Rohwer 1986; Weinstein & Mayer 1986). Many teachers, as part of their routine teaching, try to encourage the development of metacognitive skills in their students. Other teachers, however, emphasise content acquisition at the expense of learning skills acquisition and give very little attention to student needs in this area. Some simple techniques used by teachers to encourage the development of metacognitive skills are:

Metacognition: knowing about how one thinks and the ability to regulate it

- encouraging students to ask questions about processes;
- reflecting on their learning;
- problem solving by thinking aloud;
- being flexible in their approach to learning;
- developing learning plans;
- learning to summarise.

(Anderson & Hidi 1989; Costa 1984; Costa & Marzano 1987a; Dart & Clarke 1990; Derry 1989; Marzano & Arredondo 1986; Pressley et al. 1989;

Raths 1987; Volet & Renshaw 1990; Weinstein et al. 1989; Weinstein & Mayer 1986).

One very obvious feature of all classrooms is that some children seem to learn particular concepts and processes very easily while others make heavy work of the learning. Effective learners appear to have more knowledge about their own memory and are more likely than poor learners to use what they do know. This is sometimes referred to as **declarative knowledge**. Effective learners also have knowledge of a range of cognitive skills, using them strategically and automatically. This is referred to as **procedural knowledge**. Such students plan ahead, define goals and develop a strategy for reaching them. They monitor their performance while using that strategy, correcting errors and then checking at the finish to see that they have completed what they set out to do. Finally, effective learners know when and why to apply various cognitive skills. This is referred to as **conditional knowledge** (see Biggs 1987a, 1987c; Schraw & Moshman 1995; Shuell 1988; Thomas 1988).

Declarative knowledge: memory

Procedural knowledge: skills

Conditional knowledge: process

It is believed that metacognitive knowledge appears early and continues to develop at least throughout adolescence. Adults, because of their greater experience, tend to have more knowledge about their own cognition than younger people, and are also better able to describe it. However, children as young as six can reflect with accuracy on their own thinking, especially when asked to do it with familiar material (Schraw & Moshman 1995).

a

ACTION STATION

Reflect on your own study skills knowledge and behaviour. What knowledge do you have about the best ways for you to learn? What techniques and strategies do you employ to maximise your attention, concentration and memory recall when studying for an exam? Make a brief list of these techniques and strategies. How effective are they? Compare with others in your group.

Does metacognitive training improve student learning?

Considerable research in Australia and New Zealand, as well as internationally, has been directed towards understanding metacognitive and metalearning processes in the classroom and how these processes may enhance learning (Anderson & Walker 1990; Biggs 1987a; Bakopanos & White 1990; Dart & Clarke 1990; Mageean 1991; Swan & White 1990; Watkins & Hattie 1981; White & Gunstone 1989). Two programs that

Concentration and reflection are important components of metacognitive awareness. Photo: authors

are receiving quite a lot of attention in New Zealand and Australia are *The Project for the Enhancement of Effective Learning (PEEL)* and the *Study Habits Evaluation and Instruction Kit (SHEIK)* (Jackson, Reid & Croft 1980; White & Baird 1991).

Australian studies using PEEL show that students can improve in metalearning as a result of direct teaching of metacognitive skills. A study with nineteen 16-year-olds from Essendon Grammar School, Victoria, who were given training in reflective thinking, showed that those with such instruction increased in the quality of their learning as evidenced by the depth of their questions at the end of the study (Bakopanus & White 1990).

Another study (Swan & White 1990) investigated whether students could be trained to become more conscious, purposeful learners through writing statements about their learning processes in class. Students of a year 3 class were given an exercise book which they labelled 'Thinking Book'. The training involved a cycle in which:

- the children reflected on their learning each day and wrote in their thinking books;
- the teacher reflected on their entries and wrote a response in each book;
- the next day the child read the teacher's response and thought about it in making the next entry.

The teacher had two major objectives in writing the responses:

1. For the children to increase links between what they were learning, what they already knew, and their out-of-school experiences;
2. To become more active in learning through questioning things they did not understand, the purposes of classroom activities, and the effectiveness of their work habits.

The results indicated that the children increased markedly in their formation of links with prior knowledge and their own past experiences. It also showed that the students asked questions to find out more about the things that interested or puzzled them.

Both these studies illustrate the potential benefits to be achieved from training children in metacognitive skills. Both cases also illustrate, however, that interventions to increase metalearning cannot be brief and may have to alter the ingrained habits of years. As such, they have to be part of the normal program, not taught as separate lessons (Swan & White 1990).

RECIPROCAL TEACHING

Reciprocal teaching: A method to teach reading comprehension strategies based on modelling

Effective teachers promote learning by providing their students with strategies for monitoring and improving their own learning efforts as well as with structured opportunities for independent learning activities (Porter & Brophy 1988). As we have seen, students can be trained in the use of such metacognitive strategies as **planning, monitoring** and **evaluating,** which help them to control their own learning. One approach to such training is that developed by Palincsar and Brown (1984), called **reciprocal teaching**. This is a cooperative teaching method in which students are shown the processes involved in reading comprehension through teacher modelling, and then progressively trained in their use. For students with difficulty in reading comprehension, research has shown that this approach has significant benefits (Moore 1991). In reciprocal teaching the teacher, as expert, first models the strategies of:

- *summarising* a reading passage ('What is this passage about?');
- *predicting* ('What is going to follow?');
- *clarifying* ('What don't I understand?'); and
- *asking questions* about the main message of the passage ('What do I think this means?').

Students then practise these strategies aloud as the teacher monitors, providing feedback on the purpose of each strategy and the student's developing use of it, and gives encouragement (**scaffolding**) until they demonstrate they have mastered the strategies. This teacher support is gradually withdrawn as students transfer to cooperative peer groups in which they take on greater responsibility for using the skills with each other. Such active involvement by students in their own learning provides the motivation needed for the 'deep learning' of higher-order cognitive processes (Biggs 1991a).

Strategic questioning

This cooperative technique also provides students with a metacognitive strategy which develops their problem-solving skills. Alison King (1991; see also King 1992a, 1992b; 1994) has demonstrated that training pairs of children in **guided questioning** or the use of strategic questions (see below) improved their problem-solving ability over those children who were not given any structure for discussion. Students are given the following types of questions as prompts for discussion during problem-solving activities:

- *Planning*
  What's the problem?
  What do we know about it so far?
  What's our plan?
  How else can we do this?
  What should we do next?
- *Monitoring*
  Are we using our strategy properly?
  Is it time for a new one?
  Has our goal changed?
  What is it now?
  Are we on the right track to our goal?

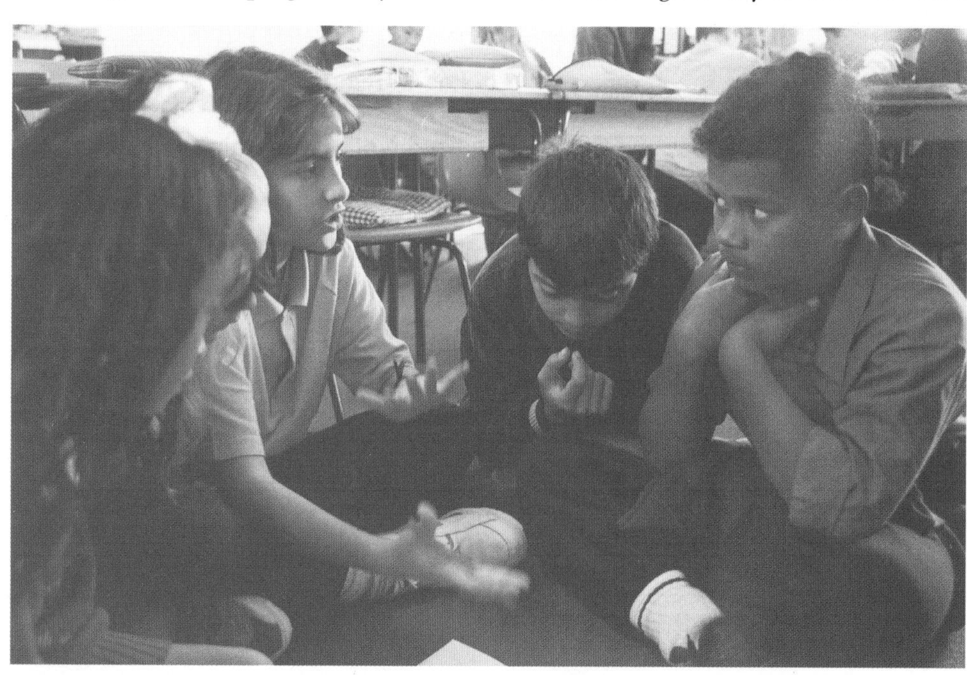

Reciprocal teaching has been shown to encourage the development of metacognitive strategies. Photo: authors

- ☐ *Evaluating*
  What worked and what didn't?
  How would we do it next time?

(adapted from King 1991)

Effective teachers can help their students become more effective learners by teaching them the strategy of **reciprocal peer questioning** (Rosenshine, Meister & Chapman 1996). In this technique, students are taught to use open-ended, generic question stems to create their own content-specific questions about expository material presented in classroom lectures. They then take turns asking these questions and responding to each other's questions in small cooperative groups, to help each other learn the material (King 1990, 1994).

Reciprocal peer questioning: Small groups ask and answer each other's questions about lessons

Examples of such question stems are:

- ☐ How are ... and ... similar?
- ☐ What is the difference between ... and ...?
- ☐ What do you think would happen if ...
- ☐ What is a new example of ...?
- ☐ Explain why ...
- ☐ What conclusions can you draw about ...?
- ☐ How would you use ...?
- ☐ What are the strengths and weaknesses of ...?
- ☐ How is ... related to ... that we studied earlier?

Using this technique, students are truly cognitively active in their own learning. They have to make mental connections among ideas and link this with previous knowledge. When students have to explain, elaborate or defend a point of view their learning is greatly improved. This is because of the active need to *construct* the material **cognitively** for themselves, and then reconstruct it in a way that is relevant and meaningful to another person. Much research has shown that, in peer tutoring and small group work, those students who do the explaining or summarising learn the most, compared with those who listen to explanations or check for errors (Brown & Campione 1986; Dansereau, 1988; Webb 1989; Webb & Farivar 1994). For older learners, cooperative group work in which generic question stems are used to assist revision of new material, achievement as well as self-concept and sense of mastery are enhanced (McInerney & McInerney 1996; McInerney, McInerney & Marsh, in press).

Table 5.4 lists the essentials of learning environments to encourage students to use metacognitive strategies.

Question point: *Should classroom learning be based on metacognitive principles? How might such classrooms operate? What might be the role of the teacher in a metacognitively oriented classroom?*

TABLE 5.4

ESSENTIALS OF LEARNING ENVIRONMENTS TO ENCOURAGE STUDENT USE OF METACOGNITIVE STRATEGIES

For teachers

- Provide an explicit *statement of goals, expectations and standards.*
- Provide *appropriate level of cognitive challenge* in tasks.
- Provide encouragement and support for *active engagement* of the learner in processing and cognitive monitoring of material.
- Provide latitude for *self-direction* in learning.
- *Reduce emphasis on performance-oriented tasks* and competitive grading.
- Provide support for the development of *self-efficacy* in students.
- *Think aloud* while demonstrating and have children talk their way through problem solutions.

For learners

- Develop appropriate content knowledge and *activate relevant knowledge.*
- Develop a realistic *assessment of capabilities.*
- *Plan* ahead by being aware of the purposes of the activity and the end-goals.
- *Monitor* progress or lack of progress in order to orient future activity.
- *Evaluate* alternative ways of handling the task and identify the ways that are likely to work best in the context.
- Know when and why to use various cognitive functions and *automate* these.
- *Predict outcomes* of stories.
- *Summarise* progressively the content of a lesson.
- Use colour to *highlight key points.*
- *Draw flow charts* to identify connections of ideas.
- Practise *self-questioning* while working though new problems.
- Practise *self-evaluation*: 'How could I complete this task differently?' 'How could this work be improved?'
- *Set goals* through the use of a learning diary of personal contracts.
- Utilise *learning strategies*; for example, in literacy: 'How can I make sense of this new material?'

(based on Biggs 1987a; Schraw & Moshman 1995; Thomas 1988)

a ACTION STATION

In groups of three or four, compare your knowledge and practice of effective learning strategies. Then discuss the following questions:

1. Do you have a well-developed knowledge of learning strategies? Do you regularly use them? Why or why not?
2. How did you acquire your knowledge of these learning strategies?
3. The efficient and effective use of learning strategies requires considerable practice and effort. How can the teacher ensure that students have this practice and make the necessary effort?

Question point: *What is metacognition? What are the generally accepted components of metacognition?*

Question point: *How do Vygotskian theorists explain the development of metacognitive processes? How does this view differ from the Piagetian view? (Refer to Chapter 2.)*

Teaching learning strategies

CAN STUDENTS CHANGE THEIR APPROACH TO LEARNING?

It is clear from research that both adults and children use learning strategies inadequately. For example, both adults and children often fail to monitor their cognitions. Such faulty monitoring is evidenced when children fail to listen to instructions, and when adults' minds wander while they are reading. Maybe this is happening to you at this very moment! How often do you stop and ask the question 'Am I understanding this?' It is also apparent that students don't utilise a range of cognitive strategies, such as summarising and reviewing, that could make learning more efficient and effective (Garner & Alexander 1989).

Teaching learning strategies

There is considerable evidence, however, that learning strategies can be taught and generalised beyond the original instructional context, and that study skills enhancement courses are successful in elevating student performance (Anderson & Hidi 1989; Anderson & Walker 1990; Dansereau 1985; Derry 1989; Derry & Murphy 1986; Idol, Jones & Mayer 1991; Kulik, Kulik & Schwalb 1983; McKeachie, Pintrich & Lin 1985; Thomas & Rohwer 1986; Weinstein & Underwood 1985).

In a study conducted with two Hunter Valley year 11 classes (Edwards, cited in Biggs 1987a), using the Study Habits Evaluation and Instruction Kit (SHEIK) (Jackson, Reid & Croft 1980), and a control class that continued with normal lessons, the experimental classes completed an evaluation of their learning processes using the Learning Process Questionnaire (Biggs 1987b) which gave students feedback on how they were going about their study in comparison with others. Students then individually discussed possible need for change in their learning strategies and ways of achieving this.

The students' approaches to learning were assessed on the Learning Process Questionnaire before and after intervention, and later the Higher School Certificate performance of both groups was followed up. It was found that the SHEIK groups both improved their deep approaches to learning and that their final examination performance was an average of 34 aggregate marks higher than the control group (Biggs 1987a; Biggs & Telfer 1987b).

This raises the issue of the usefulness of teaching learning and thinking strategies, and whether there is a 'best' way of doing this.

Many authors have turned their minds to developing effective means of teaching learning strategies (Ashman & Conway 1993; Jones 1981; Nickerson, Perkins & Smith 1985; Rowe 1988a, 1988b, 1988c, 1989a; Ruffels 1986; Sofo, 1988; Splitter 1988). In the next section we consider a number of the issues.

Thinking skills or content information first?

Authors package their thinking skills courses in many different ways. Idol, Jones and Mayer (1991) present a very thorough analysis of model programs and approaches to teaching thinking skills which include the Instrument Enrichment Program (Feuerstein 1978), Tactics for Thinking (Marzano & Arredondo 1986a, 1986b) and Reciprocal Teaching (Palincsar & Brown 1984) programs (see also Ashman & Conway 1993, for a description of their Australian Process-Based Instruction in the Classroom Kit). Reciprocal teaching is discussed earlier in this chapter together with reciprocal questioning strategies for enhancing the development of **self-regulated learning** and metacognitive skills in students.

Two basic approaches are possible. Proponents of the strategy/skill approach argue that it is difficult for most students, and especially for low-achieving students, to learn complex content and skills at the same time. Hence this approach provides explicit instruction of strategies and skills as an adjunct course with some attempt to transfer learning to content areas.

On the other hand, others argue that there should be a dual focus on content and skills. The primary focus should be content objectives, taught by the content teacher, but supported by a repertoire of specific strategies that will help students learn the new content (Idol, Jones & Mayer 1991). From our perspective the second approach seems more appropriate for use in the regular classroom.

Some authors argue that, as research indicates that most children are able to theorise about their own cognition by the age of four, and are able to use these theories to regulate their performance, it is reasonable to place some degree of emphasis on metacognitive training from the time children enter school, regardless of their basic skills level (Schraw & Moshman 1995). From this point of view, schools should actively promote the development of metacognitive skills among all students.

The following model (Rowe 1989a) illustrates the second approach and covers the major principles that underlie the practices and methods developed to teach thinking and learning skills. This model is a useful starting point for teachers and can be incorporated into the teaching of specific content.

Rowe's model of thinking and learning skills

How might teachers promote awareness of learning processes and strategies in regular learning settings? Teachers can encourage students to keep a daily **learning diary** in which students record their reflections on and reactions to academic activities. Such diaries can help identify points of confusion, help formulate questions for further clarification or investigation, and help students recognise important insights in their thinking. The diary shifts the focus of attention from getting the right answers from learning, to using the right processes in learning.

Learning diary

Teachers can also promote awareness of learning processes and strategies by the use of teacher and peer modelling. 'Thinking aloud' about processes and sharing different processes through peer interaction can be particularly effective. Rowe suggests that, after an assignment has been given, class discussion can focus on processes such as estimating task difficulty, identifying goals, choosing strategies, identifying a sequence of steps and planning for evaluation.

Thinking aloud

Finally, it is important for the teacher to encourage students to self-disclose what they know and the processes they use to think and learn so that teaching method and content can be adapted to cognitive needs. Because children have not been encouraged or taught how to disclose in this way in the past, they may be hesitant or incompetent at describing where they are coming from. In these circumstances, Rowe describes a number of direct and indirect techniques that can be used such as questionnaires, interviews and verbal reports obtained by the thinking aloud method, and teacher observation of spontaneous private verbalisations, the use of rating scales, performance and behaviour analyses, and task analyses.

Self-disclosure

FACILITATING CONSCIOUS MONITORING OF WORK

To promote conscious monitoring of their work, students must be given effective **feedback**. This feedback may come from teachers, peers or the material itself. Reciprocal teaching, where students take turns in adopting the role of the teacher and apply their knowledge to teach skills and strategies to others, can provide opportunities for students to receive feedback about their understanding.

Effective feedback and reciprocal teaching

Rather than encouraging students to complete their work as soon as possible, teachers can stimulate more active involvement with the task by training students in **self-questioning** and **monitoring**. Questions such as 'What am I asked to do here?' or 'Do I understand this?' or 'How else could I have gone about this task?' encourage students to take more personal control of, and responsibility for, their learning. Strategies such as re-reading, looking back for examples of similar questions and assignments, studying the examples provided and going back to assignment instructions for clues should become automatic.

Self-questioning and monitoring

Students should also be shown the effectiveness of **summaries** (as a form of self-testing) to analyse the state of their own understanding and determine what steps must be taken to improve this understanding. In particular, students must be encouraged to attempt to identify the reason (if one exists) for their difficulty in understanding. It might be an unfamiliar area, a new word in the text, or the unavailability of a rule. Difficulties may be caused by the manner in which the material was presented and/or organised. Once the source of the problem is identified, the teacher can guide the student to consider remedial activities.

Teachers can assist decisions about how to handle new learning by directing their students to consider the nature of the material to be learnt or the problem to be solved; the learner's current skills and knowledge relevant to the task; the strategies required from the student; and the criterion tasks or tests used to evaluate the degree of learning or correctness of the solution. Rowe suggests that the following four questions provide a useful approach:

Encourage a deliberate and systematic approach

1. What am I supposed to do?
2. What do I already know about this subject?
3. How could I start and how can I proceed?
4. How will I be evaluated?

Answers to these questions will lead to a plan for handling the task.

Finally, an overall plan for the study activity should be implemented. Before commencing, the student should have identified the purposes for doing it, with appropriate activities including browsing, skimming and posing questions that might be answered later. During the task the learner should consistently self-question about the processes involved, and after the task the student should review the processes used and question whether the goal(s) were achieved. Rowe believes that asking themselves these types of questions increases students' self-control, process and strategy awareness, executive control and independence in learning.

Develop an overall plan for study activity

Table 5.5 summarises the essentials of learning strategy instruction to encourage effective learning.

TABLE 5.5

ESSENTIALS OF LEARNING STRATEGY INSTRUCTION TO ENCOURAGE EFFECTIVE LEARNING

For teachers

- Model the effective use of *learning strategies,* particularly by means of 'think-alouds'.
- Complete *task analyses* of the content to be taught, in particular learning contexts, so that 'think alouds' are based on a thorough understanding of the nature and demands of the task.
- Apply strategies in a *variety of contexts* so that students learn to generalise their application.
- Commit *extensive time* to teaching the strategies, and *integrate strategy instruction* across the curriculum.
- Provide students with opportunities to practise the strategies they have been taught so that they eventually *become automatic.*
- Provide *guided practice and feedback* to students on their effective use of strategies.
- Let *students teach other students* how best to go about reading, problem solving, learning, and other cognitive processes.
- Provide *motivation* for the use of the strategies and show the links between strategy use and learning outcomes.
- Situate strategy instruction and use within a *mastery* rather than *performance* context.

(based on Garner & Alexander 1989 and Rowe 1989a)

Question point: *Is teaching students how to learn in a particular content area a constructivist approach? How can it be a powerful means of enabling students to construct their own effective ways of learning? Consider how the following teaching competence indicators might be achieved by teaching learning strategies.*

BOX 5.3 **TEACHING COMPETENCE**

The teacher fosters independent and cooperative learning

Indicators

The teacher:

- encourages students to take responsibility for achieving learning goals;
- encourages students to develop problem-solving and inquiry skills;
- develops student strategies in using learning resources and technology.

Case studies illustrating National Competency Framework for Beginning Teaching, National Project on the Quality of Teaching and Learning, Australian Teaching Council, 1996, Element 3.7, p. 52.

ACTION STATION

Can we teach children how to learn? It appears from research that one key to successful learning is a child's understanding of the learning process. In other words, successful learners are able to step back from their learning and monitor what they are doing. They appear to be strategic and can call upon a number of cognitive skills (such as story grammars and mnemonics) to assist with their learning. As it is clear that metacognitive skills are learned, greater attention is being paid by teachers today to the teaching of learning skills.

1. Discuss with teacher(s) how they teach children how to learn. In particular, make a list of techniques used (these may be quite formal, such as SQ4R, or informal, such as the use of mnemonics or underlining).
2. Interview two children while they are learning new material (which could be in mathematics, science or language) and ask them to describe in what ways they are trying to learn or solve a problem. Make verbatim notes and try your hand at interpreting each child's use of metacognitive skills (assuming they are using any!).

SELF-REGULATED LEARNING AND METACOGNITION

In earlier sections we discussed the components of metacognition. However, research indicates that young children often find it difficult to use their knowledge about memory and learning strategies to regulate their cognition (Flavell et al. 1993; Schraw & Moshman 1995). A reason for this is that children have not integrated their metacognitive knowledge and regulatory skills. As a consequence, many of the skills that might be used remain unused and difficult to apply. Educators seem unanimous that the most effective learners are also self-regulating. Self-regulated learners set goals for learning, decide on appropriate strategies, monitor their learning by seeking feedback (both self-generated and external) on their performance, and make appropriate adjustments for future learning activities. Self-regulated learners are thus aware of the qualities of their own knowledge, beliefs and motivation, and cognitive processing, and adjust their strategies and goals to make progress (Butler & Winne 1995; Winne 1995).

Feedback is very important in stimulating self-regulation and metacognitive behaviour. Information from self-generated and external feedback, particularly in terms of how one thinks progress is going relative to existing goals and strategies, orients the student's future choice of goals, and the strategies to achieve them. To be most effective, feedback should not only provide information about the mastery of material but also information for guiding the use of strategies for processing the information effectively—what we might term **cognitive feedback** (see Butler & Winne 1995).

TEACHER'S CASE BOOK

GOT IT, MISS!

Bronwyn's kindergarten class is involved in process writing. Steven raises his hand. 'How do you spell *walking*, Miss Letts?'

'What do you think goes on the end of it?' Bronwyn replies. Steven answers 'ing'.

'Yes,' says Bronwyn. 'Now you need to find what goes on the front. Maybe you could find the word in a book. Maybe *At the Park*.' Bronwyn indicates the bookshelf near Steven's desk.

Steven goes to the bookshelf and looks through the book, searching for the word. 'It's not in *At the Park*,' he tells Bronwyn. She does not hear him as she is engaged in conversation with another child.

Steven continues his search and triumphantly finds the word he is looking for on the cover of the book *Rosie's Walk*. He takes it to his desk where he copies *walk* onto his page and then adds *ing*.

'Got it, Miss!' he beams.

Case studies illustrating National Competency Framework for Beginning Teaching, National Project on the Quality of Teaching and Learning, Australian Teaching Council, 1996, p.8. Commonwealth of Australia copyright, reproduced by permission.

Case sudy activity

How does this case study illustrate the fostering of self-regulated learning by the teacher?

Recommended reading

Bruner, J. S. (1974) *Beyond the Information Given*. London: George Allen & Unwin.

Butler, D. L. & Winne, P. H. (1995) Feedback and self-regulated learning: A theoretical synthesis. *Review of Educational Research*, 65, 245–81.

Corkill, A. J. (1992) Advance organisers: Facilitators of recall. *Educational Psychology Review*, 4, 33–67.

Derry, S. J. & Murphy, D. A. (1986) Designing systems that train learning ability: From theory to practice. *Review of Educational Research*, 56, 1–39.

Garner, R. (1990) When children and adults do not use learning strategies: Toward a theory of settings. *Review of Educational Research*, 60, 517–29.

King, A. (1994) Questioning and knowledge generation. *American Educational Research Journal*, 31, 338–68.

Pressley, M., Harris, K. R. & Marks, M. B. (1992) But good strategy instructors are constructivists! *Educational Psychology Review*, 4, 3–31.

Pressley, M., Johnson, C. J., Symons, S., McGoldrick, J. A. & Kurita, J. A. (1989) Strategies that improve children's memory and comprehension of text. *The Elementary School Journal*, 90, 3–32.

Rosenshine, B., Meister, C. & Chapman, S. (1996) Teaching students to generate questions: A review of the intervention studies. *Review of Educational Research*, 66, 181–221.

Rowe, H. (1989) Teach Learning Strategies. *SET Research Information for Teachers*, no. 1, item 14.

Schraw, G M. & Moshman, D. (1995) Metacognitive theories. *Educational Psychology Review*, 7, 351–71.

Shuell, T. J. (1990) Phases of meaningful learning. *Review of Educational Research*, 60, 531–47.

Tamir, P. (1995) Discovery learning and teaching. In L. W. Anderson (ed.) *International Encyclopedia of Teaching and Teacher Education*, 2nd edn. Tarrytown, NY: Pergamon, 149–55.

CHAPTER 6

Behavioural and social cognitive perspectives on effective learning

OVERVIEW

It is an old piece of educational wisdom that no single method of instruction is the best for all students and for all learning goals. Even instructional procedures that are very effective in one context can be limited in others (Weinert & Helmke 1995). In our discussion so far we have emphasised learning as a constructive process in which there is an emphasis on self-regulated, contextualised learning which is intrinsically motivated. In this view of learning, the learner is perceived as predominantly active while the teacher is seen as a facilitator. This contrasts with the traditional view of instruction where there is more emphasis on teacher control. There appears to be a paradox here: research on learning suggests the importance of the active, transforming role of the learner, while research on teaching demonstrates the importance of direct instruction, which seems to suggest a passive role for the student (Shulman 1982).

As a framework for teaching and learning, constructivism presents a number of difficulties. Perkins (1992) lists three of these: cognitive complexity; task management and 'buying in'. Constructivist approaches demand a lot of the learner. For example, constructivist instruction may ask students to cope with cognitively complex situations for which they may not have the existing prerequisite understanding or schemas. Unless appropriate support is available through scaffolding or modelling, students may flounder. Constructivism also requires students to manage their own learning to a great extent. While this is important in enabling students to become autonomous learners, many students are unused to managing their learning. They need 'training' in task management. In many classes this is not forthcoming and so some students do poorly. Finally, some students ask the question, 'Why don't you just tell me the answer?' In other words, they see little merit in an approach that appears to have them doing double learning: learning the process and learning the content. In this case, they 'buy out' rather than 'buy in' to the instructional approach.

In this chapter we look at two forms of teacher-controlled instruction that can lead to active and successful learning and which appear to address the three potential problems of constructivism identified above. We first look at behaviourism and its implications for effective teaching and learning. Our major attention is given to operant conditioning and the work of Skinner. In particular, we explore the classroom applications of behaviourism by discussing the use of behavioural goals, reinforcement in the classroom, applied behaviour management, and direct instruction. Rosenshine's explicit teaching model is presented as a contemporary example of direct teaching and illustrates a movement that is occurring within the behavioural camp to include some cognitive elements in its approach.

Our second focus considers social cognitive theory. Key elements of social cognitive theory—modelling, inhibition, disinhibition, elicitation and facilitation—are explored. The four processes involved in social learning—attention, retention, reproduction and motivation—are described with examples. The emphasis that social cognitive theory places on self-efficacy and self-regulated learning is also emphasised.

BEHAVIOURAL VIEWS OF EFFECTIVE LEARNING

Some years ago we had a long-haired Persian cat called Tiffany. Tiffany was a wonderful cat, although her long hairs had a tendency to get attached to our noses, and cause sneezing fits. Tiffany had the habit of rushing to the kitchen whenever there were sounds of chopping on a board, or whirring noises from an electric can opener. While we were busily cutting up tomatoes or opening tins of soup, the cat would be purring and meowing, pawing at the cupboards, and becoming more agitated the longer we ignored her.

Why was Tiffany doing this? We remembered a time when we had been cutting up liver on the board and threw her the scraps. She was excited by the liver, and on subsequent occasions we also gave her scraps while cutting up the meat. Over time, just the sound of cutting on the board was enough to elicit the same desperate meowing. In effect, Tiffany had been taught new behaviour through conditioning.

Classical conditioning and simple learning

The early years of the twentieth century saw a growth of research interest in trying to explain how learning takes place by investigating the **observable mechanisms of learning**. This new scientific, physiologically based interest in learning contrasted with earlier mentalistic models of the learning process and concurrent cognitive models of learning represented by the European Gestalt school (Wertheimer 1980), Piaget and Vygotsky. Focus was directed on observable forms of behaviour which included not only bodily movement as seen by an observer watching a subject, but also the internal physical processes related to overt bodily movement, and how these could be modified. Ultimately, this

Observable mechanisms of learning

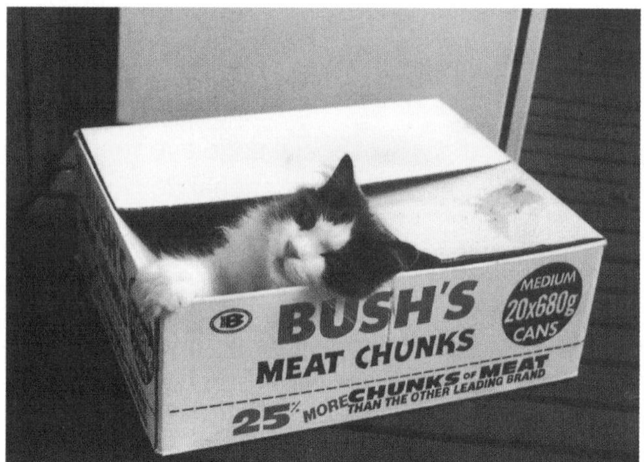

Tiffany trained us through behavioural conditioning. Photo: authors

model of learning developed into a theory of learning called **behaviourism.** Three early behavioural scientists were Pavlov (1849–1936), Watson (1878–1958) and Thorndike (1874–1949).

Pavlov demonstrated the simple relationship between stimulus and response in teaching (conditioning) an organism to modify its behaviour. Using the simple paradigm below, Pavlov conditioned a dog to salivate to the sound of a bell by linking a neutral stimulus to an unconditioned stimulus, meat powder.

Relationship between stimulus, response and learning

US (meat) ——————► UR (saliva)
CS (bell) + US ——————► UR (saliva)
CS (bell) ——————► CR (saliva)

By pairing the **neutral stimulus** (bell) on repeated occasions with the meat powder which automatically produced saliva in the dog, the bell became the new stimulus alone for the salivation. In general terms, this early research demonstrated that any stimulus that readily leads to a response can be paired with a neutral stimulus (one that does not lead to a response) in order to bring about the type of learning described. It is important to note that the learner is typically unaware of this growing association.

Table 6.1 lists the essentials of the classical conditioning process.

TABLE 6.1

ESSENTIALS OF CLASSICAL CONDITIONING

Conditioning (C)	a process of learning
Stimulus (S)	any change in the physical world eliciting a response
Response (R)	the response to the stimulus. This can be organic, muscular, glandular or psychic
Unconditioned stimulus (US)	a stimulus that produces a reflex or unlearned response
Conditioned stimulus (CS)	a stimulus paired with an unconditioned stimulus that becomes capable of producing a response
Conditioned response (CR)	a learned response resulting from pairing US and CS

Many years ago, one of us taught an educational psychology course in which we used to give students lecture notes on white paper. We also used to conduct occasional psychological exercises with the students, such as learning nonsense syllables, learning under various levels of distraction, mastering techniques to enhance learning, and so on. These exercises were usually presented on yellow paper. On one occasion the lecturer ran out of white paper and printed the lecture notes on yellow paper instead. When entering the room the lecturer noted a degree of disquiet. Without knowing it the students had begun to associate yellow paper with some sort of 'unpleasant' exercise in which they would have to participate, and subconsciously assumed that there was to be one in the session. The lecturer hadn't made a comment. Again, a **neutral stimulus**, yellow paper, had become associated with an **unconditioned stimulus**, psychological testing, and with the unpleasant feelings associated with this, and had acquired the same capacity to elicit negative feelings. To this day we surmise that some former students still have problems referring to the Yellow Pages!

Pavlov's apparatus for classical conditioning of a dog's salivation.

There are a number of ways of demonstrating the power of classical conditioning with humans. Two that we have conducted in the past with students are conditioning the **patellar reflex** (knee jerk) and the eye blink. In the former case, the 'teacher' rings a bell while

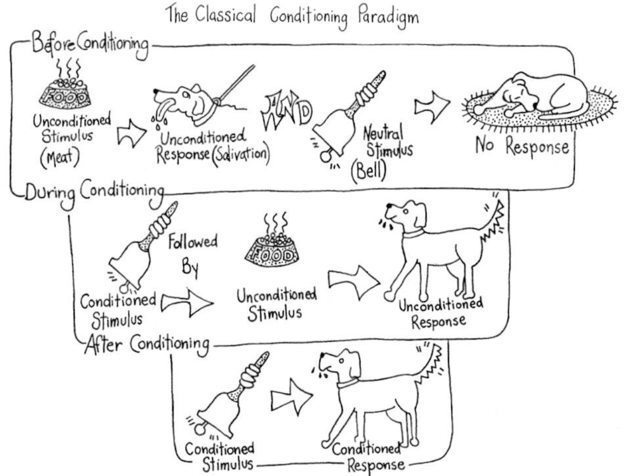

lightly tapping the tendon (don't hit it too hard, you don't want to bruise the subject!). After a number of trials the bell alone is sufficient to elicit the knee jerk. On one occasion we had a student so well conditioned that other students would sneak up behind him and ring a bell, screaming with delight when his leg jerked out involuntarily. Luckily for the hapless individual the conditioning fades with time if it is not periodically reassociated with the unconditioned stimulus, on this occasion the tap on the knee. The eye blink is exceptionally sensitive to conditioning; unfortunately, on most occasions when we demonstrated conditioning of the blink by pairing a bell with a light puff of air to the eye a lot of students ended up with conjunctivitis, so we abandoned this demonstration.

Patellar reflex and eye blink

Early behavioural views of learning

J. B. Watson (1913, 1916, 1930) further developed the concept of classical conditioning and was the person who coined the term **behaviourism** to denote this approach to exploring and describing learning. Watson drew heavily on Pavlov's work and became convinced that learning was a process of building conditioned reflexes through the substitution of one stimulus for another. Watson defined the human in mechanistic, behavioural terms and totally rejected any mentalistic notion of learning (Bigge 1971). His work was particularly concerned with the acquisition of affective responses such as fear.

Behaviourism: mechanistic behavioural view of learning

Thorndike (1913, 1931) made a very significant contribution to behavioural theory in exploring the effect of consequences of behaviour on subsequent behaviour. His findings were generalised as the *law of effect* which *proposes that a response is strengthened if it is followed by pleasure, and weakened if followed by displeasure (or pain)*. This principle has become a keystone of behavioural theory and is known now as **reinforcement**.

Law of effect Reinforcement

While early behavioural theorists such as Watson and Thorndike hoped that their explanations of learning would be useful in understanding the human learning process generally, their models fell far short of explaining the complex nature of learned human behaviour. However, within the classroom context, classical conditioning does help to explain why children behave the way they do in particular circumstances. For example, some children learn to dislike poetry or mathematics, not because of the nature of the subject per se, but because the subject has been paired with fear-producing stimuli such as belligerent teachers. In other cases, an unfortunate event accompanying an otherwise pleasant event can so alter the associations for an individual that the person avoids similar situations in the future at all costs. This process is known as **stimulus generalisation.**

Of course, classical conditioning can also be used positively. Having children work on difficult assignments under pleasant conditions will enhance children's positive attitudes. For example, many teachers play music while children complete assigned work. Classical conditioning can similarly be used to countercondition anxieties, fear responses and phobias. For example, children who are afraid of dogs may be counterconditioned through a carefully worked out procedure not to fear dogs, and children who fear particular school activities, such as forward rolls, can be **counterconditioned** not to be anxious. In these cases, the repeated association of non-threatening or pleasant experiences with the fearful object or experience serves to reduce the anxiety over time.

Positive use of classical conditioning

Operant conditioning and learning

B. F. Skinner (1948, 1954, 1968, 1971, 1986) has had a powerful impact on the world of education. Skinner's work is now commonly considered an extension of Thorndike's law of effect (Iversen 1992). Extrapolating from techniques that he found very successful in training animals, Skinner maintained that these same techniques should be highly effective when used with children. In general, Skinner believed that all animals, including humans, learn things by having certain aspects of behaviour reinforced while other aspects are not. **Reinforcement** occurs when something is added to the situation that makes the performance of the behaviour more likely in the future.

Early studies on the effectiveness of operant conditioning were conducted with animals. To train an animal such as a rat or a pigeon, Skinner devised an apparatus now called a **Skinner box**. The Skinner box enables the animal's behaviour to be observed and controlled so that particular behaviours are more likely to occur. When these behavioural units, called **operants**, are performed they are reinforced immediately by the application of a reward such as food. By progressively reinforcing operants that come closer to the goal behaviour, a process called **shaping**, the animal is gradually taught to perform quite complex behaviour. Hence, in the initial stages of conditioning an animal to press a lever or peck a button, the animal is reinforced each time it turns in the direction of the lever or button. This is called **continuous reinforcement**. Subsequently, reinforcement is only administered when the animal

Schedules of reinforcement: continuous and intermittent

adds to the response (e.g. by moving closer to the lever or button). Over a number of trials the animal progressively acquires the desired behaviour (e.g. pressing a lever). At this point reinforcement is moved to an intermittent schedule, and secondary reinforcers (such as lights and buzzers) may be introduced to facilitate behaviour when primary reinforcers are no longer effective (even rats become satiated with food pellets!). **Intermittent reinforcement** may be presented in a **fixed ratio**, that is, after a specific number of responses; at a **fixed interval**, after a specific period of time when a response occurs; or at a **variable interval**, at any time subsequent to a correct response. In general, continuous reinforcement is necessary to establish responses. Once the response is established, *an intermittent schedule enhances the retention of behaviour* (Iversen 1994). If a response is not intermittently reinforced it will gradually fade. Indeed fading behaviour is an important counterpoint to shaping behaviour, as we discuss later.

Why do you think an intermittent schedule of reinforcement would enhance the retention of behaviour? What would be some problems in applying only continuous reinforcement?

It is important that the goal behaviour is task analysed into those components that can be sequenced and successively reinforced. The complex behaviour of dolphins at Sea World is not conditioned in one go, but is the result of many hours of laborious training. Furthermore, unless the acquired responses are reinforced intermittently, the behaviour will fade and ultimately be extinguished.

Goal-directed task analysis

Similar results of training may be achieved using **negative reinforcement**. For example, the floor of the Skinner box may be mildly electrified. On the performance of the appropriate operant, the current is turned off. A bright rat would very quickly learn to sit on the lever! In general, positive reinforcement is found to be more effective than negative, and avoids deleterious side effects.

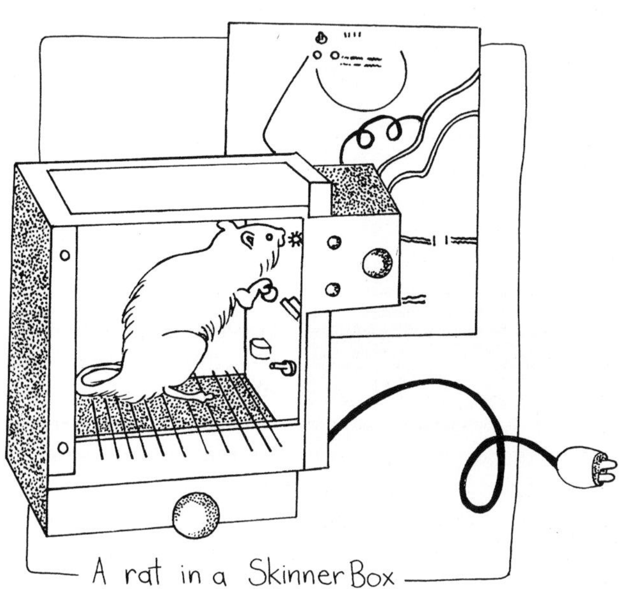
A rat in a Skinner Box

Table 6.2 summarises the essentials of operant conditioning.

TABLE 6.2

ESSENTIALS OF OPERANT CONDITIONING

Operants	the label used by Skinner to describe a behaviour not elicited by any known or obvious stimulus
Shaping	the continuous reinforcement of operants that become increasingly closer approximations of the desired behaviour
Fading	the eradication of a response through the withdrawal of reinforcement
Positive reinforcement	a stimulus that increases the probability of an operant recurring as a result of its being added to a situation after the performance of the behaviour. It usually takes the form of something pleasant
Negative reinforcement	a stimulus that increases the probability of an operant recurring when it is removed from the situation. It usually takes the form of something unpleasant
Punishment	the addition of an unpleasant stimulus to a situation as a consequence of behaviour that has occurred. The aim is to suppress behaviour rather than to establish new behaviour
Reinforcement schedule	the application of positive or negative reinforcement, continuously or intermittently, by time or ratio of responses

SKINNER, BEHAVIOURISM AND EDUCATION

Each of the principles of behaviourism, reinforcement, shaping and fading, can be applied effectively in human learning environments (Cairns 1995; Sladecz & Kratochwill 1995; Sulzer-Azaroff 1995). Skinner (1965; see also Merrett & Wheldall 1990, Sulzer-Azaroff 1995 & Wheldall & Merrett 1990) believed that learning in traditional classrooms was dominated by children trying to avoid unpleasant situations (such as punishment and negative reinforcement) rather than working for pleasant rewards. He also believed that there was too great a lapse of time between the performance of particular behaviour and its reinforcement.

In fact, Skinner believed that reinforcement of desired behaviour occurred much too infrequently and erratically. Furthermore, learning episodes were not sufficiently goal-directed in the sense that teachers did not adequately define the terminal behaviour desired as goals, or establish the steps that children needed to progress through in order to achieve these goals.

Behavioural goals

In applying Skinner's approach to the classroom, teachers need to establish the goal of a particular lesson in terms of **behavioural outcomes** and design a set of experiences that are tightly sequenced in hierarchical steps to achieve this goal. Furthermore, students should be placed in a situation where particular forms of behaviour (operants) are more likely to occur. For example, if a teacher wishes to teach mathematics then students should be put in a situation where mathematical behaviour is more likely to occur. If the teacher wishes to teach swimming then the logical classroom would be the local pool. Many teachers run into the difficulty of trying to teach behaviour in physical situations where inappropriate behaviour (operants) may be stimulated. Hence there is a strong argument for specialised resource rooms.

Reinforcement in the classroom

As we have noted, a key to the success of operant conditioning lies in the application of reinforcement and punishment. For children, reinforcers may be **material**, such as toys or some enjoyable activity; token, such as stamps and gold stars; or social, such as the goodwill and recognition of the teacher or competition. Often this style of reinforcement is called **extrinsic reinforcement** as it is externally applied, usually by the teacher. The teacher needs to decide what reinforcers are appropriate and available. The important point here is not so much what the teacher thinks is rewarding (or punishing) so much as the effect it has on later behaviour.

Material, token and social reinforcers

'I find that if I keep my performances intermittent, my staff are more motivated to control their tendency to overfeed.'

A number of studies show that pupils' opinions about rewards and punishments vary a lot from those of their teachers. There are many examples of things that teachers believe are positive reinforcers but which actually turn out to be negatively reinforcing or punishing, and examples of things that teachers believe are punishing actually acting as reinforcers and thus establishing behaviour (Merret & Tang 1994). Among some of these controlling or punishing strategies that teachers use are nagging, scolding and grumbling. But to the extent teachers use these constantly and persistently they are ineffective, and may in fact be shaping undesirable student behaviour. How do you think this occurs? Could you think of some examples?

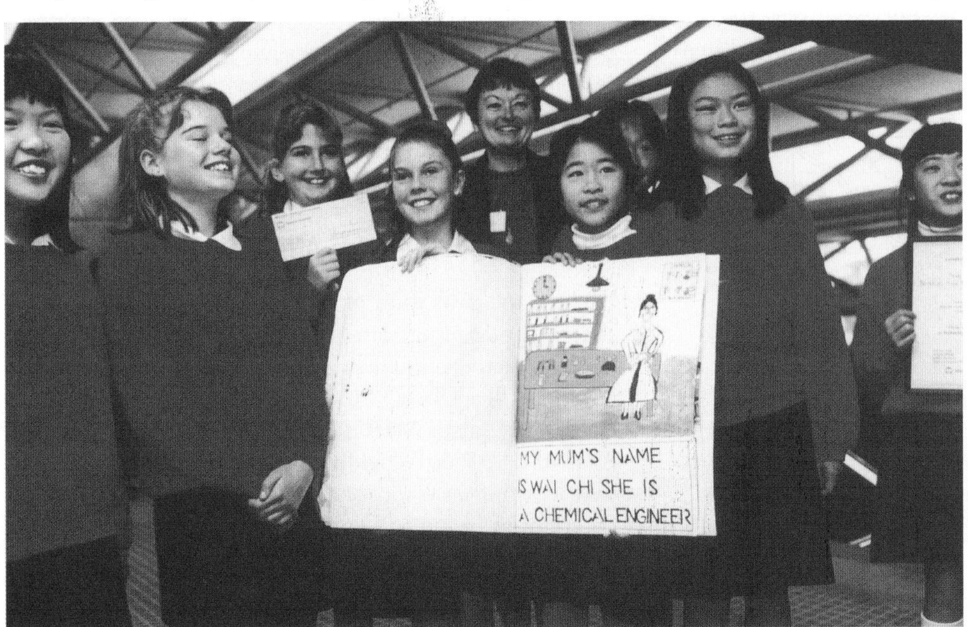

Extrinsic reinforcers can be an important element in motivating students. Photo: The Gen

Positive reinforcement is considered more effective than **negative reinforcement.** One could construct a classroom so that all the seats of the desks are connected to a mild electric current. When the children perform an appropriate behaviour, such as putting up their hands, the current would be switched off. No doubt the children would 'learn' the behaviour very quickly, but perhaps the cost in terms of parental complaints (and escalating electricity bills as the few wayward children persisted in not performing the appropriate behaviour) would not make it a viable approach. However, the use of negative reinforcement is common, if not quite as extreme. For example, some teachers have children stand up until they respond correctly by putting up their hands, after which they are allowed to sit down. Often children work hard not because of the inherent interest they have in the task, but to turn off the teacher's nagging!

Use of negative reinforcement

How many of us have sat in classrooms where our good behaviour or good work has gone unnoticed or ignored by the teacher? How many students have decided that it really isn't worth the effort if they are not getting appropriate feedback or reinforcement? Skinner wished to avoid such problems—caused by the erratic application of reinforcement by teachers—by the use of technology to assist learning. As we have noted, reinforcement in the classroom must be given immediately upon the performance of the behaviour, especially in the early stages of learning new behaviour. To ensure that reinforcement was immediate and contingent upon the correct response, Skinner advocated the use of programmed instruction in the form of 'teaching machines'. These delivered small amounts of information and exercises to which students would respond and for which they would receive prompt feedback (reinforcement) on their accuracy.

Effective reinforcement: immediate and contingent upon correct response

Question point: *Discuss the use of teacher attention and praise as reinforcement; include, especially, examples of when it is valuable, reasons that teachers find it difficult to use, the components of effective praise, and the mistakes that teachers often make in its use.*

ACTION STATION

Students benefit from positive reinforcement. Consider exciting, innovative and fun ideas for rewarding everyone—individuals or the entire class. Draft a pamphlet that presents your ideas on the use of creative reinforcement.

ACTION STATION

Make a list of potential motivators that seem appropriate for very young children, those in infants and primary school, high school students, and young adults. List both tangible and non-tangible rewards and motivators. Some people find it easier to generate reinforcers for certain ages than others. Which group was the most difficult? Why?

TEACHER'S CASE BOOK

I'M GLAD YOU'RE WATCHING NOW

The junior education support class sat closely around the concept keyboard, engaged in a reading task. Each child was taking turns at pressing the keyboard and carrying out the instruction, matching a drawing of an animal with the written work. After a short period of time, Miss Wild noticed that Brett's attention was wandering and he began to fidget.

Miss Wild then said to Troy, who was sitting beside Brett, and paying attention, 'Troy, I love the way you're watching what we're doing. You must want the next turn.'

Troy proceeded to have his turn. This caught Brett's attention and he immediately turned around and focused on the task.

Miss Wild was then quick to comment, 'Brett, I'm glad you're watching now. You'll be able to have the next turn.'

Case studies illustrating National Competency Framework for Beginning Teaching, National Project on the Quality of Teaching and Learning, Australian Teaching Council, 1996, p.28. Commonwealth of Australia copyright, reproduced by permission.

Case study activity

Why do you think Brett refocused on the task? What elements of reinforcement are illustrated in this case study?

Problems in the use of extrinsic reinforcement

The use of extrinsic reinforcers at school (and at home) is very widespread although, often, very poorly used from a theoretical point of view. Walters and Grusec (1977, p. 124) state:

We have good reason to suspect that agents of socialisation may well have diminished the effectiveness of social and material reinforcement by being too prodigal in its use, or at least by often administering it independent of the behavior engaged in.

Often, teacher education students have the feeling that the application of extrinsic reinforcement is not very different from bribery. Of course, from a theoretical perspective it can't be bribery because the knowledge of the reward is incidental to its effect. We see this clearly in the case of training animals and very young children. However, the knowledge of the reward does seem to 'contaminate' the effect of extrinsic reinforcement with older children. Under certain circumstances, extrinsic reinforcement can be detrimental to motivation and performance. Children begin to think: 'Am I being given enough stamps?'; 'Why did Johnny get two stamps while I only got one?'; 'Boy! the teacher is going to give us a chocolate bar for finishing this exercise—it must be more difficult than I thought'; 'I'm never going to get the reward, so why try?'; 'This must be a boring exercise because the teacher has to give us a reward for doing it'; 'Is that all I'm going to be given for all this work?' and so on. One child was heard to say with reference to a popular fitness program sponsored by a pizza company: 'If you don't get the reward the whole thing is a waste of time.' No doubt you can remember yourself saying these exact things.

A number of interesting research programs addressing this issue are presented in an appropriately titled text, *The Hidden Cost of Reward* (Lepper & Greene 1978). Recent reviews (Butler 1988; Boggiano & Barrett 1992; Kohn 1996; Lepper & Hodell 1989; Ryan, Connell & Deci 1985) re-emphasise the key findings of the earlier research but widen their analysis to include the effects of **external evaluation** and **performance feedback, social control, task design** and **task structure** on the student's *continuing motivation* for the task, problem-solving ability and creativity. They strongly suggest that extrinsic controls frequently have a negative effect on continuing motivation.

One study concluded that giving children extrinsic rewards for engaging in an interesting activity, regardless of whether the reward is accorded high or low value by the child, is not only superfluous, but may prove to be detrimental to subsequent interest. However, highly valued rewards may enhance subsequent interest in a relatively uninteresting activity (McLoyd 1979).

Another studied the effect of external reward on interest and quality of task performance in children of high and low intrinsic motivation, specifically with regard to drawing. Time spent drawing and 'quality' of drawing were measured both one week, and seven weeks after the activity. The group who showed initial high interest in the task and were rewarded had lost interest when observed one week later, with the reverse occurring for those with initially low interest. By seven weeks both groups had returned to their original levels. At the time of the reward, high-interest rewarded subjects drew more drawings, but of poorer quality, than did the unrewarded high-interest children. Low-interest children who were rewarded also drew more than their unrewarded counterparts, but the quality was not affected (Loveland & Olley 1979).

Counter views are expressed by a number of authors who believe that, in settings such as classrooms, the use of verbal rewards (praise and positive feedback) can be used to enhance intrinsic motivation. When tangible rewards, such as gold stars or money, are offered contingent on performance of a task, or are delivered unexpectedly, intrinsic motivation is maintained. A problem occurs when the rewards are offered without regard to the level of performance of the student. In this case, when rewards are withdrawn, students demonstrate diminished continuing motivation in the task. Rewards can be offered for work completed, solving problems successfully, or maintaining a predetermined level of performance without undermining intrinsic motivation (Cameron & Pierce 1994, 1996).

As you can see, the argument about the usefulness or otherwise of extrinsic rewards has not been resolved (Cameron & Pierce 1996; Lepper, Keavney & Drake 1996; Kohn, 1996; Ryan & Deci 1996).

Weiner (1990) believes that the simple theoretical notion that a reward automatically increases the probability of an immediately prior response occurring again does not stand up when applied to human motivation. Weiner (1990, p. 618) summarises this in the following way:

> ***... if reward is perceived as controlling, then it undermines future effort, whereas reward perceived as positive feedback is motivating ... Furthermore, reward for successful completion of an easy task is a cue to the receiver of this feedback that he or she is low in ability, a belief that inhibits activity, whereas reward for successful completion of a difficult task indicates that hard work was expended in conjunction with high ability, a belief that augments motivation. In addition, reward in a competitive setting is based on social comparison information, signaling that one has high ability and is better than others, whereas reward in a cooperative context signals that one has bettered oneself and has tried hard. Hence, it became recognized that reward has quite a variety of meanings and that each connotation can have different motivational implications.***

Appropriate uses of extrinsic rewards

As we have seen, the misuse of extrinsic rewards and sanctions can have a variety of detrimental effects on children's intrinsic motivation, task performance and learning. Under appropriate conditions, however, extrinsic rewards can enhance motivation and promote learning. Extrinsic rewards may be used to get children interested in tasks for which they have little interest or aptitude. Indeed, there may well be some tasks for which everyone needs a little prodding (how many of you learnt the mathematical tables with great intrinsic interest?).

Extrinsic rewards are also often used by teachers (and parents) to distinguish between valued activities and less valued activities (Lepper & Hodell 1989). For example, prizes may be awarded for maths and reading but not for art or PE. We are somewhat amused that at some schools the football team gets more rewards in the form of special uniforms, responsibilities and privileges than the school intelligentsia! One major problem with the application of such rewards is that, once children are removed from the particular circumstance under which the token system was used, there may be no transfer to a new situation. Many classes work well for their regular teacher, but misbehave for the relief teacher because he or she does not use the same extrinsic reward (and punishment) systems for specific behaviour.

Extrinsic rewards and valued activities

Extrinsic token rewards such as stamps, gold stars or certificates are often used successfully to indicate to children how well they have performed individually in comparison with others. As such, these rewards state something about the competence of the child, and may function as an effective motivator for further task involvement and striving for excellence in their work. Indeed, children may become 'turned on' to the task and not really require further token reinforcement once they have experienced some level of success. Among appropriate rewards for younger children are sweets, small presents, free time, teacher praise, house points, badges, stars, certificates or a letter home to parents and child saying how well the student has done. For older students, rewards that have been found to be effective are free time and a positive letter home. It appears that involving parents is very important in determining how effective rewards and punishments are at school (Merret & Tang 1994). However, for the children who don't receive rewards, such a system can lead to a reduction in their sense of competence and a subsequent loss of interest in the task.

Involving parents is important in determining the effect of reinforcement

We believe that extrinsic reward systems must be used with great care and not as a matter of course. At the very least, the teacher must consider the potential impact of such rewards for the individual involved in specific activities. Sadly, it appears that, despite the research evidence that the use of extrinsic motivation systems are fraught with dangers, they are still widely used in classrooms throughout Australia and New Zealand.

PUNISHMENT AND LEARNING

Reward and punishment and their relationship to the process of learning behaviour have long been the subject of much folklore. We have proverbs enshrining society's attitudes to these control devices:

Spare the rod, spoil the child.
You win more bees with honey than vinegar.

Western society has vacillated in its attitude towards reward and punishment to encourage behaviour. Through the early stages of mass education, good discipline and motivation were very much tied to severe punishment techniques—belting, starving, stuffing children's mouths with paper, pulling children's hair, shaking, ear pulling, detentions, loss of privileges and extra assignments (Maurer 1974). Many of these excesses continued into the second half of this century. The older author remembers vividly the leather strap that formed part of the essential accoutrement of his teachers at both primary and secondary school. A good day was when you and your friends avoided the belt.

A more 'enlightened' time saw the demise of some of the more extreme punishment techniques and the rise of the belief that reward is more effective in establishing desirable behaviour in children. Punishment was criticised as ineffective, productive of undesirable behavioural traits, immoral and inhuman. Baby books and psychology textbooks emphasised the use of rewards rather than punishments as the key to effective learning. This change was supported by early Freudian, behavioural and social learning theories.

The relative effectiveness of reinforcement and punishment has been subjected to research. Punishment is defined in this research as the application of something unpleasant to a situation to suppress behaviour (such as a sudden clip across the ear for talking out of turn), or the removal of something pleasant to suppress behaviour (such as a favourite activity—'you have been grounded'). A large body of research, all of it carried out with children, suggests that punishment for incorrect behaviour leads to faster learning than does reinforcement for correct behaviour, and a combination of reinforcement and punishment is no better than punishment alone (Constantini & Hoving 1973; Penney 1967; Walters & Grusec 1977; Witte & Grossman 1971). A possible explanation for this effect may be that reward is generally non-specific, pervasive and indiscriminate (associated with a general pleasantness of the teacher to children) while punishment is used most often for specific acts. The behaviour (or non-behaviour, such as non-completion of an exercise) responsible for the punishment is clearly associated with the punishment, and more specific information is communicated to the child by punishment than by reinforcement. One problem, however, with research such as this is the nature of the punishing stimulus that has been used. Typically, the use of punishment has not been like that in real classrooms and may not necessarily reflect the true impact of punishment. Without doubt, however, the evidence against the use of **corporal punishment** is very strong (Edwards & Edwards 1987).

Response cost

Response cost refers to the loss of positive reinforcers when particular behaviours are not performed. For example, teachers sometimes allocate individuals or groups 30 minutes of free time per day for their own chosen activities. Each time an individual or member of a group misbehaves, a minute is lost. As such, response cost acts as a punishment. One study of the effects of response cost (Constantini & Hoving 1973) found that the motivational effect of children losing marbles was greater than that of receiving them, even when the number of marbles retained or received by the students was the same! It appears from this study that the withdrawal of positive reinforcers as a method of controlling behaviour is effective for at least three reasons:

Response cost: removal of positive reinforcers as a punishment

1. It generates a weaker emotional effect than does the presentation of something unpleasant and tends to foster and maintain the subject's orientation toward the agents who control the positive reinforcers.
2. There is less recovery of the punished response when the contingency is removed.
3. It is more frequently used in naturalistic settings than punishment.

Parents often use response cost when they tell their children that they will lose particular privileges if they don't behave. This is often found to be more successful than smacking them when they are naughty. Some parents also believe that it is better than giving rewards to children for behaving and finishing their chores, for these behaviours are an expectation and should not be rewarded. What do you think?

Are there appropriate forms of punishment?

It appears that punishment can be an effective motivational agent for children in particular contexts. Punishment is, however, often criticised for producing too many unpleasant side effects to be really useful in the classroom. For example, punishment communicates more about what not to do than what to do; punishment may affect the attitude of the child to the teacher and, in some cases, punished behaviour, such as thumbsucking, bedwetting, out-of-seat behaviour, becomes more resistant to change. The following forms of punishment, nevertheless, may be valuable aids to socialisation and learning:

- ☐ verbal rebuke and social disapproval that do not attack a person's worth;
- ☐ withdrawal of privileges and material objects;
- ☐ occasional use of mild physical punishment contingent on specific behaviour.

Punishments at the secondary level that students think effective are an unfavourable note sent home to parents complaining about their child's behaviour, being put on report and detention, and being sent to the head teacher (Merret & Tang 1994). Private interviews with teachers (while not necessarily seen as punishment) are also considered very effective. Punishments that students consider less effective are 'being told off' and being sent to another teacher.

Student views on effective punishment

Research indicates that it is important for the child to be given an explanation for why a particular behaviour is being punished. There should also be consistency in applying the punishment. If the punishing agent is perceived by the child to be a nurturant person, there is less likelihood of negative consequences as a result of the punishment. Punishment that is extremely severe, administered randomly so that the relationship between the action and its consequences is not clear, or which is administered by a hostile and rejecting caretaker is to be avoided (Walters & Grusec 1977).

Importance of explanation for punishment

Whatever the case for punishment we must be careful not to return to the bad old days when often barbaric forms of retribution were visited on children. An early article (Maurer 1974), 'Corporal Punishment', shows how many thousands of children were subjected to cruelty under laws that were defended, at least in part, by research evidence that punishment can change behaviour. One apparent and unfortunate side effect of the use of corporal punishment in schools is that children subjected to it appear to become more tolerant and supportive of its use—surely not a good sign for socialising individuals as caring and loving parents, teachers and colleagues (see Ritchie 1983).

TEACHING STRATEGIES BASED ON BEHAVIOURISM

Skinner's approach is reflected in many teaching strategies from the use of programmed instruction materials such as DISTAR (Direct Instruction for the Teaching of Arithmetic and Reading), SRA reading laboratory materials, and computer-assisted instruction, through to the use of complete classroom and school procedures based on behavioural principles such as positive teaching, applied behaviour analysis (sometimes called behaviour modification), direct instruction, precision teaching and the personalised system of instruction (Merrett & Wheldall 1990; Sulzer-Azaroff 1995; Wheldall 1987).

> **BOX 6.1 TEACHING COMPETENCE**
>
> **The teacher encourages positive student behaviour**
>
> *Indicators*
>
> The teacher:
>
> - acknowledges appropriate student behaviour and fosters self-discipline among students;
> - uses an approach that emphasises consequences for inappropriate behaviour;
> - applies a variety of behaviour management strategies; e.g. negotiating rules, applying effective sanctions;
> - develops clear routines for managing student behaviour consistent with school policy;
> - takes appropriate action promptly, firmly, fairly and consistently.
>
> *Case studies illustrating National Competency Framework for Beginning Teaching, National Project on the Quality of Teaching and Learning, Australian Teaching Council, 1996, Element 2.4, p.40. Commonwealth of Australia copyright, reproduced by permission.*

Positive teaching

The basis of **positive teaching** is for teachers to identify what children find rewarding and then to structure the teaching environment so as to make such rewards dependent on both the social and academic behaviour that they want to encourage (Merret & Tang 1994). As we stated earlier, teachers have a great deal of control over many of the consequences they provide for their pupils but few use them consistently and well. Positive teaching shows teachers how to use behavioural techniques such as shaping, fading and reinforcement consistently and effectively.

Applied behaviour analysis

The conditioning of socially appropriate behaviour through the use of reinforcement and punishment has been used successfully in the modification of human behaviour, particularly in cases where the behaviour is very atypical and resistant to other forms of modification—for example, aggression in the class, day-dreaming and non-attention, out-of-seat behaviour and antisocial behaviour (such as spitting and verbal abuse) (Cairns 1995; Greenwood et al. 1992; O'Leary & O'Leary 1977; Wheldall 1987; Wheldall & Merrett 1990).

Timeout from reinforcement is used to reduce unwanted behaviour. In timeout, children may be removed to a room (or part of the classroom) where they cannot participate in the ongoing activities, nor be distracted by occurrences around them. The theory is that the withdrawal of positive conseqences will encourage the child to choose to behave in order to be returned to the more rewarding environment of the classroom.

Timeout

As with all behavioural approaches, applied behaviour analysis must be a carefully planned program designed to lead students to a predetermined goal through the use of rewards. The teacher needs to set up a situation that allows students to experience good behaviour, discriminate between acceptable and unacceptable behaviour, and associate their appropriate behaviour with a reward. The teacher also needs to praise students on how well they are doing when the agreed-upon reward is presented. Particularly important is the need to help students to become progressively less dependent on the extrinsic reward and to function in the regular classroom as well as in other settings.

TABLE 6.3

ESSENTIALS OF APPLIED BEHAVIOUR ANALYSIS

For teachers

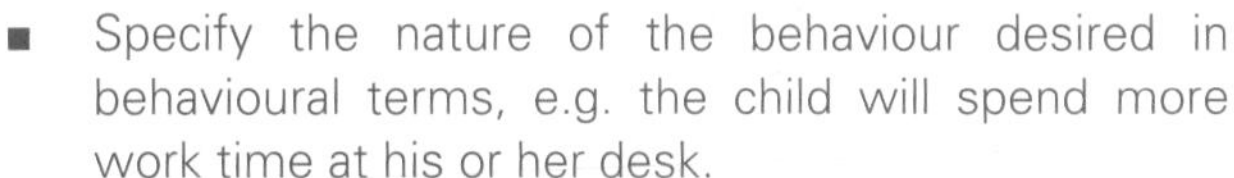

- Specify the nature of the behaviour desired in behavioural terms, e.g. the child will spend more work time at his or her desk.
- Set a level of behaviour that will be the goal for the behaviour, e.g. the child will work for 20 minutes at a time without leaving his or her desk.
- Instigate an effective reward-keeping procedure and assess the behaviour through direct observation, such as counting how often it occurs. This form of teaching is often called *precision teaching* and involves the use of stop-watches, graphs and charts.
- Work out appropriate reinforcing strategies; e.g. tokens will be awarded for the performance of the appropriate behaviour and on the cumulation of 20 tokens, a reward (lolly or free activity) may be traded for the tokens.

Direct instruction as a behavioural strategy

Direct instruction is a general term that has acquired a number of different meanings referring to somewhat different instructional practices (Rosenshine & Meister 1995). What they all have in

DISTAR

WHAT WOULD YOU DO?

A TICK FOR CHRIS

Chris had been disruptive during class on a few occasions and had already been in Timeout twice during the past two weeks. On this particular afternoon, the children were writing out their favourite recipes to make a class cookbook. Chris was slow in starting his work, spending his time talking loudly to the neighbouring children at his group table. Meredith, his new teacher, gave him one warning about the rule he was breaking but he did not change his behaviour. She was concerned about putting him in Timeout again because he seemed to be experiencing only failure lately, so she took him aside for a talk.

What do you think the talk consisted of? What actions do you think resulted, and can you predict their consequences?

Case studies illustrating National Competency Framework for Beginning Teaching, National Project on the Quality of Teaching and Learning, Australian Teaching Council, 1996, p.18. Commonwealth of Australia copyright, reproduced by permission.

WHAT WOULD YOU DO?

TAKING MY SAILS OUT OF THEIR WIND

Mr Sims' year 10 mathematics class contained several students who were achieving well below their ability level. Tony was a typical case: he showed no interest in school, dressed aggressively, and had a long history of exclusion from class, incomplete work and poor grades. His occasional flashes of brilliance sustained Mr Sims' efforts to involve Tony in class activities.

Mr Sims decided to shift Tony from the back row to the front row, but this was not without incident. Tony stomped on the floor, sulked, put his head on the desk and complained that 'life's not fair'. Mr Sims' reason for the move was that he could offer Tony the attention he craved in an acceptable context. 'It's not a discipline thing,' he said to Tony. 'I believe that you've got ability and I can help you get good marks; but if all I ever say to you is "Tony, be quiet", "Tony, get back into your seat", "Put that away", we don't stand much of a chance. Come up the front and I'll help you.'

Soon afterwards, at the beginning of a lesson, the blackboard ruler was lying on the front bench and Tony grabbed it and began fencing with it. Mr Sims saw this as a ruse to attract attention. Mr Sims asked 'Tony, can I have my ruler back?' and grasped the free end of the ruler. Tony replied 'No', and started to engage in a tug-of-war.

What would you do? ***Read what the teacher did on page 120.***

Case studies illustrating National Competency Framework for Beginning Teaching, National Project on the Quality of Teaching and Learning, Australian Teaching Council, 1996, p. 44. Commonwealth of Australia copyright, reproduced by permission.

BOX 6.2 **TEACHING COMPETENCE**

The teacher plans purposeful programs to achieve specific student learning outcomes

Indicators

The teacher:

- relates learning programs to educational goals and objectives;
- establishes clear purposes for learning programs in terms of agreed student learning outcomes;
- selects and sequences learning activities to achieve planned student outcomes;
- takes account of students' goals and prior learning;
- relates assessment processes and strategies to learning objectives, content and tasks.

Case studies illustrating National Competency Framework for Beginning Teaching, National Project on the Quality of Teaching and Learning, Australian Teaching Council, 1996, Element 3.1, p.46. Commonwealth of Australia copyright, reproduced by permission.

common however, is a teacher-centred control of presentation and evaluation of learning material; specifically, **delivery, scheduled practice** and **feedback.**

One form of direct instruction, based on behavioural principles, is a systematic, tasks-analysed teaching procedure (Maggs et al. 1980). Three examples of this approach to direct instruction have been used in Australia and New Zealand: the Direct Instruction System in Arithmetic and Reading (DISTAR); morphographic spelling; and corrective reading. Research here and overseas indicates that these direct methods of instruction can be quite effective with a broad range of children (Maggs et al. 1980). However, the approach generates as much heat as light in Australia and New Zealand where academics and teachers argue over the merits of a system that appears to guarantee student success, but is extremely teacher and content dominated. Key elements of this approach are listed in Table 6.4.

TABLE 6.4

ESSENTIALS OF DIRECT INSTRUCTION AS A BEHAVIOURAL STRATEGY

For teachers

- Develop an explicit step-by-step strategy.
- Ensure mastery at each step in the process.
- Provide specific corrections for student errors.
- Gradually fade teacher-directed activities towards independent student work.

- Provide adequate and systematic practice through a range of examples of the task.
- Provide for a cumulative review of newly learned concepts.

(based on Rosenshine & Meister 1995)

Direct instruction as a cognitive strategy

More recently, views of direct instruction have moved from the rather narrow definition of tightly sequenced instruction with constant feedback to definitions that emphasise the development of cognitive strategies. Key elements of this approach are:

- ☐ explicit strategy or skills instruction—teacher explanations of *what* the strategy is and *when*, *where* and *how* to use it, as well as *why* it should be used;
- ☐ the gradual transfer of responsibility for learning from the teacher to the student;
- ☐ a focus on constructing meaning and problem solving;
- ☐ both cognitive and metacognitive instruction involved (Idol, Jones & Mayer 1991).

In short, while appearing teacher-centred, the emphasis is on the student's needs and responses, with teacher awareness of student understanding a priority. The essentials of direct instruction as a cognitive strategy are given in Table 6.5.

TABLE 6.5

ESSENTIALS OF DIRECT INSTRUCTION AS A COGNITIVE STRATEGY

For teachers

- Begin the lesson with a short review of previous learning.
- Begin the lesson with a short statement of goals.
- Present new material in small steps, providing for student practice after each step.
- Give clear and detailed instructions and explanations.
- Provide a high level of practice for all students.
- Ask a large number of questions, check for student understanding, and obtain responses from all students.
- Guide students during initial learning phases.
- Provide systematic feedback and corrections.
- Provide explicit instruction and practice for seatwork exercises and, where necessary, monitor students during seatwork.

(based on Rosenshine & Meister 1995)

Do these approaches have elements in common? One element in common across these approaches to direct instruction is that students experience a *high level of success* after each step of the learning activity during both guided and independent practice. The amount of material presented, the extent of teacher-guided practice and the length of time spent on independent practice should be determined by the age of the students and their previous knowledge of the content. Other features in common are:

- ☐ presenting new material in small steps;
- ☐ modelling learning;
- ☐ guided practice;
- ☐ 'think-alouds' by teachers and students;
- ☐ regulating the level of difficulty in the task;
- ☐ cueing learning;
- ☐ providing systematic corrections and feedback;
- ☐ supporting student corrections;
- ☐ providing for independent practice.

Remember that these are the teaching functions that have been found to be most effective. However, they do not have to be followed as a series of prescribed steps: feedback to students, correction of errors and misunderstanding, and reteaching must occur as necessary.

For unstructured material where skills do not have to be sequenced, or where there is no general rule to be learnt that has to be applied, such as in problem-solving activities, writing essays, analysing literature or creative expression, explicit teaching is obviously less appropriate and less effective. For this type of material, indirect approaches such as brainstorming, guided questioning and cooperative group work are more appropriate.

Why is direct instruction successful?

Research demonstrates that direct instruction is a very effective instructional technique. Among the reasons for its success are the following:

- ☐ The teacher's classroom management is structured, leading to a low rate of student interruptive behaviours.
- ☐ The teacher maintains a stong academic focus and uses available instructional time intensively to initiate and facilitate students' learning activities.
- ☐ The teacher ensures that as many students as possible achieve good learning progress by carefully choosing appropriate tasks, clearly presenting subject matter, information and solution strategies, continually diagnosing each student's learning progress and learning difficulties, and providing effective help through remedial instruction (Weinert & Helmke 1995).

WHAT WOULD YOU DO?

A TICK FOR CHRIS (continued)

First, Meredith ensured that Chris understood the rule he was breaking. Next, she set him the task of taking responsibility for his behaviour by asking him how he could avoid distractions. He opted for moving away from the group he was working with and sitting alone on the floor in front of the chair. Meredith praised him for his solution and challenged him to complete his work by the end of the session, so that he could get his recipe into the book. She added that if he could do this task, he would be awarded a 'tick' on his merit chart. This reward system is part of the school's discipline code.

Chris worked diligently for the remainder of the session and handed over his completed recipe at the end. His smile conveyed the message that he was satisfied with his work so Meredith honoured their agreement and put a tick on his chart. Then she verbally praised him for his work once again before home time. The next day, Meredith had no cause to warn him about being disruptive.

Initially, Meredith was concerned about offering external rewards for work. However, she felt that if she could ensure his success in some way, then internal motivation might follow.

Did you predict the teacher's action and its consequences? What other alternatives might solve this and similar problems in the classroom?

Case studies illustrating National Competency Framework for Beginning Teaching, National Project on the Quality of Teaching and Learning, Australian Teaching Council, 1996, p.18. Commonwealth of Australia copyright, reproduced by permission.

WHAT WOULD YOU DO?

TAKING MY SAILS OUT OF THEIR WIND (continued)

Mr Sims said, 'I just let go and walked away; I let him have it. Where's his fun and attention if I refuse to wrestle with him? It took a lot for me to let go and walk away because I'm the teacher and it's my classroom but the disruption of the lesson just wasn't worth it.'

Mr Sims' attitude to his students is, in his words, 'I refuse to believe that any kid doesn't like success. They all like to feel they've achieved something.' Mr Sims' approach to Tony when he'd settled into the front row was to go out of his way to talk to Tony frequently. For instance, when Mr Sims asked the class to open their files, he'd chat to Tony for a moment—this ensured that Tony got his work out and, at the same time, satisfied Tony's need for recognition. Nevertheless, Mr Sims was careful not to become involved in power plays, such as the ruler incident, for which Tony was well known. When confrontation threatens, as Mr Sims put it, 'I take my sails out of their wind.'

Is Mr Sims' approach what you would have done? How does this case study illustrate principles drawn from behavioural theory?

Case studies illustrating National Competency Framework for Beginning Teaching, National Project on the Quality of Teaching and Learning, Australian Teaching Council, 1996, p.44. Commonwealth of Australia copyright, reproduced by permission.

CONSTRUCTIVISM AND BEHAVIOURAL APPROACHES TO TEACHING AND LEARNING

The emphasis of behavioural theorists on observable behaviour has led to many educational practices that focus on producing and evaluating specific kinds of overt behaviour, rather than other indicators of learning such as affect and insight. As we have seen in the discussion of constructivism, the emphasis is on developing students' understandings. Within a behavioural teaching context, 'understanding' may be less emphasised than performance. In this instance, students may be able to perform particular academic activities without really understanding the meaning behind them. It is not unusual to see children skilfully doing mathematical calculations without understanding place value, and teachers having to re-explain it with the introduction of each new operation because learners never understood it in the first place (Fosnot 1992). Many children can recite the multiplication tables without any idea of how tables are constructed (multiple addition). Children can perform chemical experiments and write up reports without understanding the basic science involved. These 'empty' learnings are not necessarily a by-product of behavioural teaching, but it is something that needs to be guarded against. In fact, if care is taken by the teacher to be aware of what students already know and monitor their progressive development of knowledge, understanding should take place.

For constructivist educators, tasks themselves should be intrinsically interesting, thus obviating the need for extrinsic motivators. Because the instructional sequence is of primary concern in a behavioural approach, teachers (and program designers) may take little care to develop programs that are also stimulating and interesting. Some behaviourally based teaching programs are so crushingly boring that the only recourse for the teacher to keep children motivated is the application of extrinsic reinforcers (such as moving up colour levels, achieving prizes, and so on). These reinforcers are often built into the programs themselves. We discussed earlier in the chapter the potential limitations of applying rewards to ensure children engage in learning.

Constructivist programs emphasise individual initiative and creative thinking in learning. In many behaviourally based programs there is little, if any, scope for individual initiative as students are locked into preprogrammed material to which they have to make a controlled (predictable) response. In saying this, we also need to emphasise that good behavioural programs are individualised.

Can behavioural approaches incorporate cognitive constructivist elements?

In classical behavioural theory, the centre of attention is clearly the teacher and the materials, with the student being a passive recipient of teacher management and behaviourally manipulated through the use of reinforcement. Little opportunity is given for students to construct their own learning (Mageean 1991). Nevertheless, **neo-behavioural theorists** believe that a cognitive element can be incorporated into their model and, increasingly, efforts are being made to demonstrate this (Wheldall 1987). We see the application of cognitive elements to behavioural interpretations of learning in the next section, on social cognitive theory.

SOCIAL COGNITIVE THEORY AND EFFECTIVE LEARNING

The original theory, called social learning theory, was based on a framework derived from operant theory. It has its roots in the early work of Bandura and Walters (1963) but is most closely associated with the work of Albert Bandura (1962, 1969, 1977a, 1977b). **Social cognitive theory**, as it now called, has grown beyond its roots to provide a view of learning which has much to offer educators. Bandura's learning theory (1986) differs from the traditional behaviouristic theories in that it emphasises symbolic representation and self-regulatory procedures (Holland & Kobasigawa, 1980) in addition to operant learning. As such, it reflects a number of important constructivist principles. In this theory the functioning of operant conditioning in a social context is examined, as well as the role of cognition in processing information. Three principles apply to social cognitive theory:

1. Much human learning is a function of observing the behaviour of others.
2. We learn to imitate by receiving reinforcement for performing a certain behaviour, and maintain this imitative behaviour through continued reinforcement.
3. Imitation, or observational learning, can be explained in terms of operant conditioning principles, provided it is correct to say that people can 'imagine' both the reinforcement and the behaviour of models.

Principles of social cognitive theory

Social cognitive theorists believe that much complex human behaviour, such as the acquisition of language, social behaviour and attitudes, can only be explained through **modelled learning**, and that little is really learned through operant conditioning or through purely cognitive means such as information processing. Social cognitive theory holds that if an individual pays attention to a particular behaviour in another, then the capacity to perform similar behaviour (with practice) is developed. This imitative behaviour can be developed through:

Modelling
Disinhibition
Elicitation
Facilitation

- ☐ **modelling**—when the individual acquires a new response by observation;
- ☐ **inhibition** or **disinhibition**—whether a behaviour acquired through observation is practised or not depends on the perceived rewards or punishments that would apply to the performance of the behaviour;
- ☐ **elicitation** or **facilitation**—when behaviour similar, but not identical to, the modelled behaviour is performed after a cue from a model. These effects are described in detail below.

Social learning experiences and modelling

Modelling has been shown to aid in the development of many social behaviours, such as moral judgments, altruistic behaviour, resisting and yielding to temptation, aggression, self-reward and social interaction. This has obvious implications for parents in their role as models.

As an example of the acquisition of behaviour through modelling, consider the growth of assertive and aggressive behaviour in males and females. Gender differences in the development of aggression can be related to the different social learning experiences of boys and girls (Sanson et al. 1993). A key element in this is the nature of the social role stereotypes that boys and girls experience. In Australia the predominant male stereotype continues to be the 'macho' image. This is reinforced through the aggressive sporting pursuits promoted for boys and the many aggressive toys and TV programs (including sporting programs!) designed for boys. All these factors serve to promote and reinforce the idea that male aggressive behaviour is appropriate, effective and rewarded. This may be coupled with a father model who demonstrates dominance and aggression within the home.

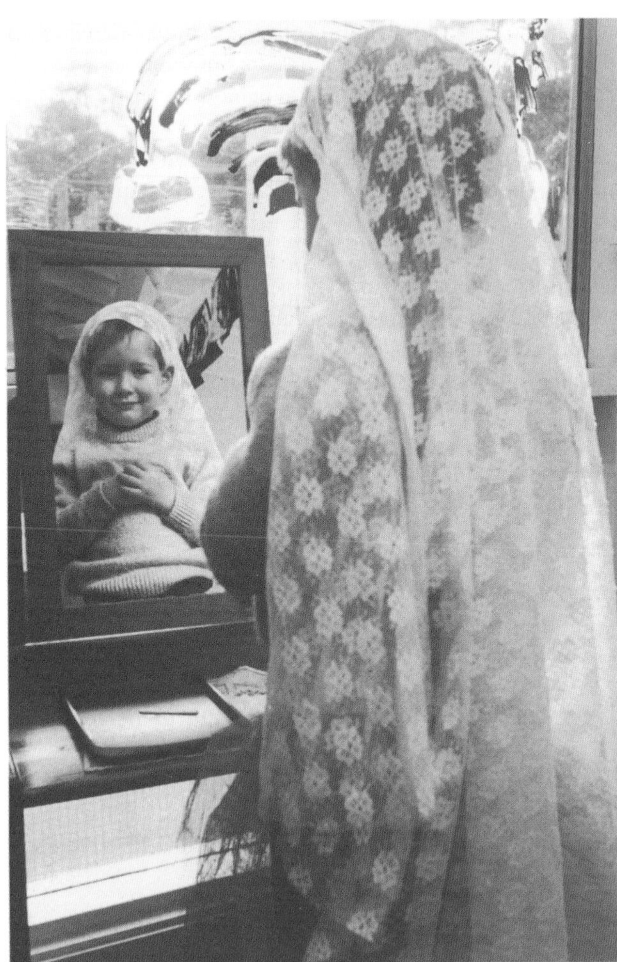

How might dressing-up and play-acting illustrate the modelling effect? Photo: The Gen

This social experience of boys stands in marked contrast to the experience of girls, who tend to receive reinforcement for exhibiting sympathetic, cooperative and nurturant behaviour, and are expected to be helpful and to take responsibility for the well-being of the family (Sanson et al. 1993). The increasing level of assertive behaviour among females, which for some spills over into aggression and violence, has been attributed to the effect of the broader range of models to which females are now exposed, and their increasing involvement in sports and activities that have stereotypically been viewed as male. Films such as the 'Aliens' trilogy, 'Terminator 2' and 'Barb Wire', and certain types of rap music, present females in violent roles. Apparently, this is having some type of modelling effect. What do you think?

Learned behaviour does not have to be implemented by the learner and, indeed, may never be implemented if environmental circumstances don't elicit its performance. We are all aware that we know how to perform particular actions as a result of observation even if we never actually perform them. For example, by observing violence we learn how to be violent; by observing loving behaviour we learn how to be loving; by observing the way people dress and speak we learn various ways of dressing and speaking. Sometimes we choose to imitate and practise particular behaviour as a result of our observations; at other times we don't. The theory states that this is because we develop various **outcome expectations** about the behaviour. The functional value of behaviour, whether it results in success or failure, reward or punishment, exerts strong motivational effects on observer modelling called—the **disinhibitory effect**. Modelled behaviours are more likely to be performed if they previously led to rewarding outcomes than if they resulted in punishment. This is regardless of whether individuals experienced the consequences directly or vicariously (Schun 1987). Rewards may be extrinsic (such as positive praise from parents, or a token such as pocket money) or intrinsic (the satisfaction of performing the action as well as the model). These reinforcers elicit the performance of the modelled behaviour.

The disinhibitory effect: outcome expectations and functional value of behaviour

Non-sexist education programs introduce children to a wider range of appropriate roles. Photo: The Gen

When we inhibit the performance of behaviour because we anticipate that its performance will lead to negative consequences and punishment, we see the **inhibitory effect** of perceived consequences of the act. For example, children learn to smoke and drink alcohol by observing others smoking and drinking (see, for example, Byrne, Byrne & Reinhart 1993; Ho 1994; McClellan 1989). On most occasions children do not do either because they are worried that parents or teachers will catch them at it; hence the behaviour is inhibited through fear of punishment. However, many children have smoked behind the toilet block when it was believed that the act was hidden, or raided their parent's liquor cabinet while the parents were out. The former case illustrates the *inhibitory* effect, and the latter the *disinhibitory* effect. The incidence of looting, arson and violent behaviour during periods of civil unrest or national disaster can be well explained by the disinhibitory effect.

The inhibitory effect: inhibiting behaviour to avoid negative consequences

Four principles governing social cognitive learning

According to social cognitive theory, learning through observation is governed by four processes:

1. attention
2. retention
3. reproduction
4. motivation.

People cannot learn effectively unless they *attend to* and *perceive accurately* the significant features of the modelled behaviour. Among the factors that influence attention are model characteristics, observer characteristics and features of the modelled behaviour.

Each of these characteristics can be illustrated effectively by many everyday examples. Film stars, sportspeople, teachers, parents and peers have a combination of model characteristics that at times make them very powerful models for young children—and also for not so young people!

Model characteristics

- ☐ *attractiveness* (physical and emotional)
- ☐ *social power* (over reward and punishment)
- ☐ *status* (perceived importance of the model)
- ☐ *competence* (specifically in the area of interest)
- ☐ *nurturance* (perceived concern for the observer)
- ☐ *interaction level with observer* (degree of contact, energy of contact)
- ☐ *similarity* (characteristics in common, such as sex, age, interests, between observer and model).

Apart from the power of the model, which is influenced by the above features, observer characteristics also have considerable impact on the attention brought to the model. For example, the perceived competence of a child in a particular activity, referred to as **self-efficacy**, and the activity's importance influence children's attention. Children attend to models of activities at which they feel competent, rather than activities at which they feel less competent.

Observer characteristics

- ☐ level of dependency
- ☐ socioeconomic status
- ☐ race and sex
- ☐ individual's perception of competence in the specific area
- ☐ relevance of incentives.

The learning activity itself must also be capable of attracting attention. In any learning situation the material to be modelled must be characterised by variety and distinctiveness. Material that is bland, presented too quickly or too slowly, or that is overly complex will not attract attention, and may lead to downright boredom or frustration, so potential for learning from such models is minimised. Those of you preparing to be teachers will be paying particular attention to these aspects in your lesson preparation.

Features of the modelled behaviour Learning is most effective when the modelled behaviour is coded symbolically in images and verbal codes. This basically means that individuals think about what they are doing and rehearse the behaviour mentally and with language before performing it overtly. *At this level the theory becomes explicitly constructivist in the sense that individuals interpret the modelled behaviour in terms of their existing mental schema.* Among techniques that have been found useful to facilitate retention are talking about the activity to oneself, labelling elements of the performance, or using vivid imagery to imagine the performance of the activity before the event. Many of you will have practised a speech in front of a mirror, or rehearsed a lesson mentally (and physically) before entering the classroom. Our daughter Laura often says to her father 'Daddy, what are you saying?' when he is talking to himself.

Retention facilitated through using images and verbal codes

The third component of modelling is to convert these symbolic representations into appropriate motor reproductions. When these actions are accompanied by *immediate corrective feedback* from the model or other source they become more accurate. Obviously, effective performance depends on appropriate motor skills being available to the individual. Where these are deficient, corrective adjustments must be made. For example, individuals with physical coordination problems or immaturity will have difficulty writing neatly even if they have learnt the modelled behaviour cognitively.

According to social cognitive theory, motivation is a function of personal expectations and goals, and self-evaluative processes (Bandura 1986, 1991; Schunk 1996). As people work to achieve goals they evaluate their progress. If the evaluation is positive, personal feelings of **self-efficacy** are enhanced, which sustains motivation. Social and contextual factors affect motivation through their influence on expectations, goals and self-evaluations of progress (Schunk 1989, 1996). Among the factors that have an impact are social comparisons, goals, rewards and reinforcement, classroom organisation and types of feedback. Aspects of classroom processes that enhance student self-efficacy (such as perceived similarity to the model, discussed earlier) can foster further motivation.

Self-efficacy and motivation

As with operant theory, the theory holds that observers are more likely to attend to the model's actions (thereby improving the potential for learning) and to adopt the modelled behaviour if the behaviour results in outcomes they value, or averts punishment. Observing consequences to the model (that is, **vicarious reinforcement** or punishment) similarly influences the learner's motivation. How many children have resisted the temptation to try a cigarette after witnessing an older sibling being reprimanded by irate parents for smoking?

Vicarious reinforcement: observing consequences to others

Social cognitive theory emphasises that reinforcement may facilitate but is not a necessary condition for observational learning to occur. In contrast to operant theory, **anticipated rewards** are thought to strengthen retention of what has been learned observationally by motivating observers to code and rehearse the behaviour they value. In this way, reinforcement is believed to be most effective when used as an incentive rather than a reward. In other words, informing observers in advance about the benefits of adopting modelled behaviour is considered to be more effective than waiting until they happen to imitate a model and then rewarding them.

The importance of anticipated rewards to motivation

Question point: *Discuss the potential strengths and weaknesses of using reinforcement as a reward for behaviour or a facilitator of behaviour in and out of the classroom.*

Question point: *Discuss, with examples, the four processes—attention, retention, reproduction and motivation—in the context of a classroom lesson. Illustrate how these processes may reflect constructivism.*

What are the sources of modelling stimuli?

Sources of modelling stimuli may be provided by parents, teachers and peers, or may be symbolic, such as films, television, books and verbal discourse. Much research has taken place into the effects of various types of symbolic models on the acquisition of behaviour (Friedrich-Cofer et al. 1979; Friedrich & Stein 1975; Galst & White 1976; Sanson & Di Muccio 1993). There is a continuing debate about the effect of television and film violence, with many arguing that violent crimes are committed by individuals whose acts have been elicited by viewing such violence (Hennigan et al. 1982; McCann & Sheehan 1985; Murray 1973; Sanson & Di Muccio 1993; Smith 1979). It is argued that in cases where the violence has been presented in a non-moral context, or where there are no punishing consequences attached to the performance of the violent act by a model, violent behaviours in the observers are disinhibited.

While research in this area is inconclusive, it does appear that television models can be used successfully to teach **prosocial behaviour** and to influence behaviour in general (Friedrich-Cofer et al. 1979; Friedrich & Stein 1975; Galst & White 1976). For example, Friedrich and Stein showed that young children watching prosocial television shows such as 'Sesame Street' and 'Mister Rogers' Neighbourhood' would learn and perform the modelled behaviours if they were aided by having the relevant behaviours coded verbally (e.g. Big Bird is helping the little boy) and then rehearsing the behaviour themselves through role play with puppets. 'Do the right thing' and other prosocial commercials on television are based on the belief that individuals do copy the behaviour of significant models. Many influential identities are involved in anti-smoking and anti-drink-driving commercials because it is believed that these individuals can effectively persuade members of the community not to practise these behaviours. The Australian Government's legislation banning the advertising of smoking and the sponsorship of a range of sports such as football and cricket by tobacco companies reflects the belief that the association of smoking with sportspeople is a powerful modelling influence on young children to take up smoking. The evidence on this is not clear and the debate is quite vociferous.

Modelling through prosocial television

A major emphasis of social cognitive theory is the individuality with which people observe aspects of observed behaviour and incorporate elements into their own behaviour. This individuality in attending to features of the modelled behaviour explains the great versatility and flexibility in human behaviour. There are ten children in the male author's family; each of these has his or her own particular behaviours and ways of doing things, despite the fact that they were exposed to the same parental models. However, with each successive child, new models were added to influence individual development in the form of the siblings and their influence on each other. As you can see from this example, the range of models, and what particular individuals observe from these models and then practise, is quite vast. It is a wonder that any of the children have any behavioural similarities! This aspect of social learning must be emphasised. There is great diversity in the way individuals relate to models and incorporate features of the modelled behaviour into their own behavioural repertoire. It is not a mechanistic theory which suggests a one-to-one relationship between modelled behaviour and the acquisition of this behaviour by the observer. Ultimately, this diversity may explain the development of creativity whereby individuals amalgamate features from a wide range of models in novel behaviour.

a

ACTION STATION

Select a boy or a girl for observation over a period of time, preferably a younger member of your own family. Consider the behaviour of that individual in various situations, at home and with friends. In particular, note participation, sharing, leadership, deference to others, defiance, and so on. Analyse specific aspects of the child's behaviour in objective terms using the following criteria:

1. What are the social influences operating on the child and how are they influencing the child's behaviour?
2. What appears to be reinforcing the behaviour, where does the reinforcement come from, and how frequently?
3 Which behaviours appear to be shaped by observational learning? How can you tell?
4. What behaviours appear to be modelled? What behaviours appear to be elicited? Have you seen any evidence of the inhibitory/disinhibitory effect?

ACTION STATION

a

Choose two or three television programs, some of which cater for adults, and others specifically designed for children. Note their titles, type (comedy, drama, nature, etc.), origin and duration. Make the following observations:

1. What types of models are presented?
2. What kinds of vicarious experiences are offered to young children?
3. Are there differences in the models that are presented to girls and boys, and to female and male adults?
4. What kind of vicarious reinforcers and punishers are presented?
5. Suggest some positive and negative aspects of television as a social influence on children.

CLASSROOM APPLICATIONS OF SOCIAL COGNITIVE THEORY

Social cognitive theory can be applied directly to the classroom (Yates & Yates 1978). The theory draws our attention to the power of models in the classroom, and to the effects of vicarious reward and punishment on the performance of behaviour. There is a rich research base that illustrates the power of modelling in shaping student academic, emotional and affective behaviour (Copeland & Weissbrod 1980; D. Deutsch 1979; Gresham 1981; King, Ollendick & Gullone 1990; Schunk 1987; Stoneman & Brody 1981).

All part of the same family but illustrating many individual differences. Photo: authors

Vicarious effects of reward and punishment

Social cognitive theory gives strong support for the use of **peer modelling**. Reinforcement given to one child may 'spill over' and serve as a cue to other peers that their own behaviour could attract the teacher's attention (Kazdin 1973). For example, when a teacher's attention is focused on the inattentive behaviour of one child, nearby peers actually increase their attentive behaviour. In other words, direct reinforcement or punishment of target children may have a vicarious effect on peers watching them. Observing others' successes, failures, rewards and punishments creates outcome expectations in observers that they are likely to experience similar outcomes for performing the same behaviours (Schunk 1987). However, a target child's reactions to the praise or punishment may serve to strengthen or weaken the intended effect of vicarious consequences. For example, a schoolchild ridiculed for asking 'stupid' questions becomes a negative model for his equally naive, though now inhibited, classmates. Children who revel in the attention of annoyed and angry teachers, or disparage the positive attention of teachers, act as negative models and undermine the intended effect of the vicarious reward or vicarious punishment (Yates & Yates 1978).

Spill-over effect

It is important to ensure that children who do perform appropriate modelled behaviour after witnessing vicarious consequences are themselves directly rewarded, at least intermittently, otherwise these behaviours will not be performed, even though learnt.

Peer models and self-efficacy

Peers may be effectively used to demonstrate classroom procedures. A teacher may call upon children in his class to demonstrate how to do a forward roll, or draw a bushfire, or complete a mathematical exercise. University students may be asked to demonstrate aspects of good teaching practice to their peers. These motivational effects are hypothesised to depend, in part, on perceptions of self-efficacy, or personal beliefs about one's capabilities to perform the desired behaviours to the same level of proficiency as demonstrated (Bandura 1986; Schunk 1987, 1996).

Peer demonstrations

Teachers use peer modelling for a variety of purposes. One common use is to illustrate that activities shouldn't be sex stereotyped: thus we have girls and boys alike emptying the school bins, learning bush dancing, and doing cross-stitch and embroidery. Teachers use symbolic models such as literature, pictures and posters, or video to illustrate and emphasise the models. Observational learning principles and, in particular, **peer modelling**, are used with children who experience various forms of social anxiety such as social withdrawal and isolation. Typically, the isolate child is required to observe peers engage in the requisite behaviours. This modelling process may be achieved through the use of live or video models. In one experiment young isolate children viewed a film depicting several peer models engaging in a variety of social activities. In contrast to a control group of children who viewed a film about dolphins, these children showed substantial increases in peer interactions after viewing the film (King, Ollendick & Gullone 1990).

One important aspect of peer models is that they can supply a realistic gauge of what is potentially possible for children who lack a sense of self-efficacy. Adult models may be perceived as possessing a level of competence that children are unlikely to attain whereas peer models may be more successful. Same-sex models do not appear to be any more successful than different-sex models except in those behaviours that relate to gender appropriate behaviour. Sex of model seems less important in general learning contexts.

Teachers as models

Teachers are highly influential models in establishing and maintaining students' attitudes towards their studies. Teachers' expressed attitudes towards dress, television, morals and so on can greatly influence children. Children can also learn attitudes towards school: cheerfulness, enthusiasm, patience, fairness, consistency and optimism. If teachers fail to display these qualities, they are unlikely to see them in their students (Yates & Yates 1978).

Student attitudes towards school

In order to function as effective models of academic skills, teachers should make use of effective demonstrations. Table 6.6 illustrates some features of effective demonstrations from a social cognitive perspective.

Teacher demonstrations

How might peer group modelling be a powerful influence on children? Photo: authors

How can peer models enhance feelings of self-efficacy in other children? Photo: authors

Children are inclined to model equally the behaviour of peers and adults, depending on two criteria: first, the modelled behaviour must appear to be instrumental in achieving goals; second, the model must appear competent. Where peers are viewed as being as competent as adults, the behaviours of both are likely to be modelled. When children question the competence of peers, they tend to model the behaviour of adults. When same-sex peers are viewed as less competent than younger peers, children pattern their behaviour after the competent but younger children rather than age-mates of lower competence than themselves (Schunk 1987).

Factors influencing the impact of the model

MODELLING THOUGHT PROCESSES AND CONSTRUCTIVISM

Modelling of thought processes does not mean explaining how something is done—modelling is thinking aloud to express the thoughts, feelings and attitudes of teachers as they figure something out, with all the stops and starts, puzzlements, revisions and on-line processing of thinking that occur in reality (Idol, Jones & Mayer 1991). Modelling of thinking aloud is particularly important in teaching students how to construct meaning (especially because of the non-linear aspect of thinking), how to monitor one's thinking, and how to answer a question through reasoning. Modelling also demonstrates how people may construct somewhat different meanings because they have different prior knowledge and perspectives about a specific topic (Idol, Jones & Mayer 1991).

TABLE 6.6

ESSENTIALS OF A SOCIAL COGNITIVE APPROACH FOR EDUCATION

For teachers

- *Focus attention* on a specific area or task and ensure that all students are paying attention.
- Give a *general orientation* or overview—explain what is to happen.
- *Label* verbally and visually any new concepts or objects, and have students repeat these.
- *Verbalise thought processes* involved in problem solving or performing behaviours.
- *Model methods of gathering information* through questioning so that students can learn these cognitive strategies themselves.
- *Proceed step by step*—break each complex behaviour into smaller operations and demonstrate processes by thinking aloud.
- Perform actions with appropriate pace to *maintain attention.*
- Provide student opportunity for *guided practice:* e.g. through teacher mentoring or peer tutoring, so that corrective feedback can be given by the teacher.
- Provide opportunity for *independent practice.*
- *Do not emphasise mistakes*—redemonstrate and encourage another attempt.
- *Provide antecedent reinforcement* for efforts and achievements.
- *Use valued models* to demonstrate behaviours, skills and attitudes.

For learners

- Pay attention.
- Check to see if you understand what is to be done: ask questions if you are unclear.
- Draw or write a description of a new idea or procedure to show that you understand what to do.
- Talk out loud/describe what you are doing or thinking while working out a solution or doing an activity.
- Copy the teacher or other students who show you good ways to find information.

- Practise what you have been shown and try again if you make a mistake.
- Think about how you can break down a large piece of work into a series of small tasks.
- Observe what happens to other students when they do a task or solve problems. Do they get rewards or feel good about themselves?
- Think about what might encourage you to work hard on a task.

Scaffolded instruction and mentoring for apprentices

New learners in a particular area are often referred to as apprentices. The learning of apprentices can be facilitated by mentoring and scaffolding. Both mentoring and scaffolding of apprentices involve observation of models, guided practice by the model, and feedback on the efforts of the apprentice that is progressively reduced. For Idol, Jones and Mayer (p. 80), the hallmarks of successful models of teaching thinking skills are presented in Table 6.7.

TABLE 6.7

ESSENTIALS OF MODELLING EFFECTIVE THINKING SKILLS

For teachers

- Modelling, especially thinking aloud about how to apply strategies or skills.
- Coaching, which involves diagnosing problems, prescribing corrections and providing feedback.
- Articulation, getting students to articulate their knowledge and thinking process.
- Reflection about the process of thinking.
- Exploration—that is, pushing students to extend their learning.

(based on Idol, Jones & Mayer 1991)

TEACHER'S CASE BOOK

THAT WAS FUN. LET'S DO IT AGAIN.

Nicole teaches Japanese to year 8 students at a metropolitan high school. In their eighth Japanese lesson Nicole was teaching the students to respond appropriately to simple classroom instructions given in Japanese. She used a series of games to help her students overcome their resistance to speaking a new language in front of their peers. The lesson was started with students listening to the instructions and mimicking the teacher's actions.

Tatte kudasai (stand up). Suwatte kudasai (sit down).
As practice time continued, the teacher stopped doing the actions herself and allowed the students to determine the responses. At this stage some students merely copied the responses of others. They were shy and reluctant to participate.

The next stage was to play a game of 'Simon Says' in Japanese. Students who were 'out' helped to judge who was slowest or who did the action incorrectly. At this stage, unwilling students were still not fully involved as they copied others and were quickly eliminated from the game.

Saimon wa tatte kudasai, to iimashita (Simon says 'stand up').
The class was then divided into 4 teams for a new game. One member from each team came to the front of the class. The teacher then gave an instruction to the 4 students at the front.

Mite kudasai (Please look). Kiite kudasai (Please listen).
The first person to respond won a point for their team. All students were encouraged by their team-mates and were participating in the class. When students were given a quiz at the end of the lesson most of the class gained 100%, and, as one of the students said as he left the room, 'That was fun. Let's play again.'

Case studies illustrating National Competency Framework for Beginning Teaching, National Project on the Quality of Teaching and Learning, Australian Teaching Council, 1996, p.50. Commonwealth of Australia copyright, reproduced by permission.

Case study activity
In what ways does this case study exemplify social cognitive theory?

SOCIAL COGNITIVE THEORY AND SELF-REGULATED LEARNING

Self-managed reinforcement

In an attempt to answer criticisms that reinforcement is too externally controlled and denies children the opportunity to develop self-management of their own learning and behaviour, a number of theorists and researchers have explored the use of reinforcement as a self-managed aspect of learning (Bandura 1986; Hayes et al. 1985; Rhode, Morgan & Young 1983; Schunk 1990, 1991; Zimmerman 1990, 1994).

Even within a behaviourally oriented classroom children may still be involved in goal setting, monitoring their own work, keeping progress records and evaluating their work. They may also be involved in selecting their own rewards and punishments and administering them. Obviously, the developmental level of the children has much to do with the successful implementation of such a plan. The ability of children to set goals is very important to self-management and motivation. Children who successfully set goals and can communicate them to others (e.g. the teacher) perform better than those who have vague goals (Hayes et al. 1985). With appropriate training children can monitor their own work and keep progress records, which should also foster their motivation to learn. Some suggest that they can also be taught to evaluate their own work adequately (Rhode, Morgan & Young 1983; Paris & Oka 1986), although monitoring by the teacher is important to validate the accuracy of the evaluation. **Self-reinforcement** is the final step. Bandura (1986) argues that giving oneself rewards on the basis of good performance enhances future performance, although other psychologists maintain it is unnecessary. (See also Schunk 1991.)

From social cognitive theory has developed the **self-regulated learning** model (Corno 1992; Zimmerman 1990; Zimmerman & Schunk 1989). In this model, self-regulated learners view learning as a systematic and controllable process and accept responsibility for their achievement outcomes. Self-regulated learners approach tasks with confidence, diligence and resourcefulness, and proactively seek out information when needed, attempting to take the necessary steps to master it. Self-regulated students are metacognitively, motivationally and behaviourally active participants in their own learning (Winne 1995b; Zimmerman 1990, 1994). In terms of metacognitive processes, self-regulated learners plan, set goals, organise, self-monitor and self-evaluate at various points during the learning process. Because of this they are self-aware, knowledgeable and decisive in their approach to learning. Self-regulated learners appear to be self-motivated and report high self-efficacy (i.e. a belief in themselves as learners) and self-attribution (i.e. they accept responsibility for successes and failures); they value the importance of effort, and intrinsic task interest (Pintrich & De Groot 1990).

Self-regulation: resonsibility for learning outcomes

Metacognition: plan, set goals, organise, monitor, evaluate

Self-reinforcement for a job well done!
Photo: authors

Self-regulated learning may be domain-specific. This means that learners who have learned to self-regulate in a particular activity such as reading may need to learn self-regulation in another activity such as essay writing (Alexander 1995; Boekaerts 1995). The skills of self-regulation detailed above don't occur naturally or spontaneously in learners. Indeed, the development of such skills is complex and long-term. Teaching episodes need to be developed to encourage learners to develop these skills across a range of subjects so that, in the long term, self-regulating becomes a generalised capacity (see Pressley 1995).

SOCIAL COGNITIVE THEORY AND SELF-EFFICACY

In social cognitive theory there is an emphasis on **self-efficacy**. Self-efficacy refers to individuals' belief that they can exercise control over their own level of functioning and over events that affect their lives. Efficacy beliefs influence how people feel, think, motivate themselves, and behave. Albert Bandura believes that *students' beliefs in their efficacy* to regulate their own learning and to master academic activities determine their aspirations, level of motivation and academic achievements. *Teachers' beliefs in their personal efficacy* to motivate and promote learning affect the types of learning environments they create and the level of academic progress their students achieve. Bandura also believes that whole-school beliefs in their collective instructional efficacy contribute significantly to the schools' level of academic achievement (Bandura 1986, 1993; Schunk 1991b). Our own research (McInerney 1993; McInerney & Swisher 1995) with Aboriginal and Navajo children suggests that self-efficacy for the task of school learning is one of the most important determinants of school motivation.

Student and teacher self-efficacy

Bandura believes that the higher individuals' perceived self-efficacy is, the higher the goal challenges they set for themselves and the firmer their commitment to them. It is believed that children base their appraisals of ability on a wide range of sources including their performance, feedback from others, and vicarious (observational) experiences such as seeing others performing in a like manner being praised, ignored or ridiculed. High self-efficacy for a particular activity, does not in itself, necessarily lead to motivated behaviour. The perceived value of the activity, and outcome expectations also influence level of motivation. However, without a sense of self-efficacy it is unlikely that children will engage in activities, irrespective of whether they are perceived as important or not.

Helping students to develop self-efficacy

Important ways of helping to develop and maintain self-efficacy among students include teaching goal setting and information-processing strategies, using models and providing attributional rewards (Schunk 1991b).

The setting of challenging but attainable goals and the achievement of these goals enhances self-efficacy and motivation (Schunk 1990; Zimmerman, Bandura & Martinez-Pons 1992). Teachers need to assist students to set both **proximal**, or **short-term**, **goals** and **distant**, or **long-term**, **goals**. Among techniques suggested by Schunk are setting upper and lower limits on students' goals and removing them when students understand the nature of the task and their immediate capabilities; using games (such as shooting for goals in basketball) and goal-setting conferences where students learn to assess goal difficulty and their present level of skill in collaboration with the teacher. As students become more self-regulated they will be more adept at setting their own goals. Short-term goals are important, particularly for younger or novice learners, as progress is more noticeable. However, the achievement of long-term goals is ultimately more important for the development of self-efficacy as it offers more information about developed capabilities.

Setting short- and long-term goals

Associated with this point is the notion that, if students feel they have control over their goal setting and learning, self-efficacy is enhanced.

If children are taught how to learn (i.e. their **metacognitive** and **metalearning** skills are developed) they are more likely to feel competent in a range of learning situations, and, therefore, more motivated to continue in these activities. We have discussed the importance of teaching thinking skills, and ways of achieving this in Chapter 4. Classroom models (both teachers and peers) may also be used to demonstrate that particular tasks lie within the range of ability of particular students. Observing others succeed can convey to observers that they too are capable, and can motivate them to attempt the task. We have also dealt with the importance of modelling in our discussion of social cognitive theory.

Information processing and using metacognitive skills to enhance self-efficacy

We need to guide children to see the relationship between *ability*, *effort* and *success*, and in particular to encourage them to attribute their failures to factors over which they have some control. When a child feels in control motivation is enhanced. In this context, it is worth remembering that this sense of control as a function of effort may come from mastering strategies for learning and problem solving. Indeed, even in the face of failure, effort attributions, for example, can encourage a child to try again. At other times, attributing success to ability enhances self-efficacy and motivation. This has important implications for children with learning disabilities who may develop a sense of helplessness about their lack of ability relative to others.

Providing attributional feedback to enhance self-efficacy

To enhance self-efficacy, feedback should also emphasise goals achieved or gains made rather than shortfalls in performance. For example, we can tell students that they have achieved 75%, emphasising progress, or we can highlight the 25% shortfall in their performance. Accenting the gains enhances perceived self-efficacy, while highlighting deficiencies undermines self-regulative influences with resulting deterioration in student performance (Bandura 1993).

Probably the most important source of feedback for younger children is the teacher. As children become more self-regulated they will self-evaluate their performance in terms of their perceived ability and effort and the appropriateness of particular goals, and will modify their involvement accordingly. Under these circumstances motivation is channelled into achieving goals that are perceived as attainable and worthwhile.

Finally, rewards may be used to indicate that a goal has been achieved, and hence enhance self-efficacy and motivation. The strengths and weaknesses of reward use have been discussed earlier.

Providing rewards

INSTRUCTIONAL DESIGNS AND THEORIES

We began our discussion of effective learning by asking a basic question: How do people learn? In our analysis of this we have covered a broad range of theoretical perspectives. Among other questions we have addressed are the following:

- ☐ What are the influences that determine teaching practice?
- ☐ Are some teaching practices more effective than others? Why?

- ☐ Are some teaching practices more suited to particular activities?
- ☐ Are some teaching practices more suited to particular students?

Perhaps Bruner's insights on the best way to foster learning will give you food for thought:

> ***Any model of learning is right or wrong for a given set of stipulated conditions, including the nature of the tasks one has in mind, the form of the intention one creates in the learner, the generality or specificity of the learning to be accomplished, and the semiotics of the learning situation itself, what it means to the learner …***
>
> ***It was a vanity of a preceding generation to think that the battle over learning theories would eventuate in one winning over all the others. Any learner has a host of learning strategies at command. The salvation is in learning how to go about learning before getting to the point of no return. We would do well to equip learners with a menu of their possibilities and, in the course of their education, to arm them with procedures and sensibilities that would make it possible for them to use the menu wisely.***
>
> *(Bruner 1985, pp. 5–7)*

The current status of learning theories

What is the current status of these theories, and what evidence is there that models derived from them are effective? Each of the theories covered in Chapters 4, 5 and 6 has generated a vast amount of research. A review of some aspects of this research conducted since 1977 yields impressive evidence for the effectiveness of a variety of innovative teaching practices drawn from *cognitive, behavioural* and *social cognitive* theories (Joyce, Showers & Rolheiser-Bennett 1987). With regard to social cognitive theory, cooperative learning approaches which represent social models of teaching appear effective in producing positive outcomes in higher-order thinking, problem solving, social skills and attitudes. The use of advance organisers (derived from Ausubel's theory) and other cognitive tools for learning (such as mnemonics), on the other hand, can help students remember learned material with long-lasting effects. Research on DISTAR, an example of the behavioural family of models, is similarly associated with increased achievement, and influences aptitude to learn.

As mentioned previously, when these models and the strategies derived from them are combined, they have even greater potential for improving student learning. We should use a variety of models because certain models are more appropriate to particular pupil needs; certain models are more appropriate to particular subjects; models can be adapted and combined to increase effectiveness; a multiplicity of school and classroom objectives requires a variety of models; and, lastly, the effective use of a variety of models enhances flexibility and the professional competence of the teacher (Brady 1985).

Table 6.8 presents a comparison of four major learning theories covered in the text.

Question point: *Using the information contained in this and earlier chapters discuss how particular pupil needs may best be met by a particular teaching model or combination of models.*

Question point: *Discuss how the demands of particular school subjects make one teaching model more suitable than another.*

ACTION STATION

Observe a teacher over a period of a day (or several days). Make notes on the teacher's use of instructional designs for teaching. For what purposes were they used? When were they used? How were the designs combined? In what ways did learner characteristics influence the choice of instructional approach?

Prepare a timetable of the teacher's day and indicate the material or topic being taught, the time and length of the session, and which particular design or combination of designs was used by the teacher.

ACTION STATION

Select a topic from a curriculum area in which you are specialising. Write three separate lesson plans for the presentation of this material, one reflecting a behavioural approach, one a cognitive approach, and one a social cognitive approach. You will need to describe the age and ability levels of the children for whom the lesson is being prepared. Compare and contrast the different approaches. You might like to trial each during practice teaching.

TABLE 6.8

A COMPARISON OF FOUR MAJOR LEARNING THEORIES

	Behaviourist	Humanist	Social cognitive theory	Cognitive
Means of introducing material	1. Limiting stimuli to those strictly relevant to task (Skinner box). 2. 'Engineer' initial operants appropriate to task. 3. Presentation of structured materials (e.g. DISTAR). 4. Teacher-cented. 5. Specification of ends of exercise (behavioural objectives).	1. Part of ongoing self-selected work (e.g. projects). Student-centred. 2. Relation of material to some event or experience of interest in children's lives. 3. Student self-selection of time and materials to work with (perhaps in consultation with teacher). 4. Supply large range of interesting materials. Focus attention on what is happening here and now by creating moderate novelty.	1. Display of models, e.g. teacher demonstration, audiovisuals, peer performance, guest speakers. Material should be relevant and interesting to children if the model is to gain attention. 2. Child-centred. Directed at gaining and maintaining attention.	1. Advance organisers and problem setting. 2. Integration of new material with pre-existing knowledge. 3. Establish procedures to assist encoding, retention and retrieval of material presented.
Activities/ Methodology	1. Individualisation of task assignment, of rewards and discipline. 2. Detailed methods to develop skills, and use of technology. 3. Linear progression in teaching content and skills—emphasis on mastery. 4. Emphasis on content rather than process of learning.	1. Based on needs and individuality of each child. 2. Integrated approach—emphasis on 'real' experience related to child's personal needs. 3. Emphasis on insight learning and under-standing (not mere acquisition of skills). 4. Emphasis on the process of learning rather than content of learning. 5. Emphasis on effective interpersonal skills.	1. Detailed method—step by step following of model. (Model methods of working process.) 2. Explanations and verbal cues given. 3. Instructional material well structured and of interest to children. 4. Opportunity for children to code and rehearse material.	1. Hierarchical order of concepts and skills emphasised. 2. Emphasis on 'insight' learning and understanding (not mere acquisition of skills). 3. Emphasis on process of learning rather than content of learning. 4. Development of metalearning and metacognitive skills.
Motivation and goals	1. Extrinsic, through reinforcement, consequent on act being performed. 2. Mastery of specific skills—competence.	1. Intrinsic, satisfaction of needs, self-fulfilment and understanding. 2. Social and personal develop-ment; communication skills, sensitivity to group and individual needs. 3. Acquisition of self-learning skills and responsibility (self-reliance). 4. Development of affective attitudes. 5. Self-evaluation.	1. Reinforcement—antecedent to task being performed (anticipated reward). 2. Intrinsic and vicarious reinforcement emphasised. 3. Acquisition of modelled behaviour and its transfer to new situations.	1. Intrinsic—task involvement, solving problems. 2. Learning through discovery. 3. Mastery of processes.
Evaluation	1. Constant formative evaluation. 2. Formal summative evaluation (perhaps a pretest/post-test arrangement). 3. Completion of set task at a specified level of mastery (e.g. the students will complete 10 sums correctly)	1. Observation checklists; interest shown in task. 2. Self-chosen enrichment work. 3. Completion of contract work. 4. Conferences with teacher, skill checklists, record folders, diary accounts, etc. 5. Peer acceptance and classroom adjustment. 6. Effective adult interaction.	1. Constant formative evaluation—immediate and positive corrective feedback. 2. Satisfactory motor reproduction of acquired behaviour. 3. Use of acquired skills in new but similar situations (transfer). 4. Effective peer and adult interactions.	1. Self-evaluation. 2. Mastery of process and quality of insights. 3. Ability to transfer learning. 4. Use of higher-order cognitive strategies. 5. Understanding of 'how to learn'.

Recommended reading

Bandura, A. (1986) *Social Foundations of Thought and Action*. Englewood-Cliffs, NJ: Prentice Hall.

Bandura, A. (1991) Self-regulation of motivation through anticipatory and self-regulatory mechanisms. In R. A. Dienstbier (ed.) *Perspectives on Motivation: Nebraska Symposium on Motivation*. Lincoln, NE: University of Nebraska Press. Vol. 38: 69–164.

Bandura, A. (1993) Perceived self-efficacy in cognitive development and functioning. *Educational Psychologist*, 28, 117–48.

Cameron, J. & Pierce, W. D. (1996) The debate about rewards and intrinsic motivation: Protests and accusations do not alter the results. *Review of Educational Research*, 66, 39–51.

Merrett, F. & Wheldall, K. (1990) *Positive Teaching in the Primary School*. London: Paul Chapman.

Perkins, D.N. (1992) What constructivism demands of the learner. In T.M. Duffy & D. H. Jonassen (eds) *Constructivism and the Technology of Instruction*. Hillsdale, NJ: Lawrence Erlbaum: 161–5.

Pressley, M. (1995) More about the development of self-regulation. Complex, long-term, and thoroughly social. *Educational Psychologist*, 30, 207–12.

Rosenshine, B. V. (1986) Synthesis of research on explicit teaching. *Educational Leadership*, 43, 60–9.

Rosenshine B. E. & Meister C. (1995) Direct Instruction. In L.W. Anderson (ed.) *International Encyclopedia of Teaching and Teacher Education*, 2nd edn. Tarrytown, NY: Pergamon: 143-9.

Sulzer-Azaroff, B. (1995) Behavioristic theories of teaching. In L.W. Anderson (ed.) *International Encylopedia of Teaching and Teacher-Education*, 2nd edn. Tarrytown, NY: Pergamon: 96–101.

Ryan, R. M. & Deci, E. L. (1996) When paradigms clash: Comment on Cameron and Pierce's claim that rewards do not undermine intrinsic motivation. *Review of Educational Research*, 66, 33-38

Schunk, D. H. (1987) Peer models and children's behavioral change. *Review of Research in Education*, 57, pp. 149-74.

Sladeczek, I.E. & Kratochwill, T. R. (1995) Reinforcement. In L.W. Anderson (ed.) *International Encyclopedia of Teaching and Teacher Education*, 2nd ed. Tarrytown, NY: Pergamon: 224–7.

Wheldall, K. (ed.) (1987) *The Behaviourist in the Classroom*. London: Allen & Unwin.

Winne, P.H. (1995b) Inherent details in self-regulated learning. *Educational Psychologist*, 30, 173–87.

Zimmerman, B. J. (1994) Dimensions of academic self-regulation: A conceptual framework for education. In D. H. Schunk & B. J. Zimmerman (eds.) *Self-Regulation of Learning and Performance: Issues and Educational Applications*. Hillsdale, NJ: Lawrence Erlbaum: 3–21.

Zimmerman, B. J. (1995) Self-regulation involves more than metacognition: A social cognitive perspective. *Educational Psychologist*, 30, 217-221.

CHAPTER 7

Information technology: implications for effective learning

OVERVIEW

Nowhere in educational circles is there more disagreement than about the impact on the learning, minds and futures of young people of the adoption and perceived 'best' uses of technology in today's and tomorrow's classrooms. Many of you will be standing in front of a classroom of students in the near future making decisions about whether to teach in a 'traditional' way, probably the way that you were taught (and you turned out all right, didn't you?), or whether to incorporate computer-based technology which will supposedly help you teach better and enhance the learning experiences that you provide for your students. The issues you will need to confront with regard to information technology are more complex than merely how to use equipment; they have to do with questions of the nature of students, your role in their learning and socialisation for the future, and the philosophy of learning and teaching that you adopt. In all of this, you need to ask yourself: '(How) do I need computer technology in my classroom? Do I have a real choice about its use? Will I and my students be better or worse off for its introduction?'

CONSTRUCTING LEARNING AND INSTRUCTION IN THE NEW INFORMATION TECHNOLOGY ERA

In its potential for interactivity with the learner and its ability to be individually customised, the computer can clearly provide the means by which students can *construct their own knowledge*. Three rationales for using computers within education have been tentatively posited (Finger & Grimmett 1993):

- ☐ as a personal *amplifier* to enhance the productivity of the learner—for example, software such as spreadsheets, databases and word processors take over many of the intellectually demanding tasks such as mathematical calculations and editing, freeing the user to develop other skills;
- ☐ as an educational *actualiser* to extend and enrich the school-based experience of learners; simulations, multimedia and graphics programs can provide this opportunity;
- ☐ as an *intellectual tool* to empower the learner; the use of programming languages such as LOGO, the exploration of microworlds, and the creation of programs through authoring tools such as HyperCard enhance learning significantly.

How might this use of technology enhance the personal construction of knowledge? Photo: The Gen

The potential learning uses of computers

There are widely differing ways in which the computer can be used in the classroom. Typically these are categorised as **tutor, tool** or **tutee** (Taylor 1980).

Computer as tutor As tutor, the computer presents instructional material to the student whose responses are 'evaluated' by the program. The ongoing presentation of material is determined by these responses. In other words, the control of the student's learning is determined by the computer program or, more accurately, by the developer of the program (software). This approach to instruction is a behavioural one in that student responses determine the reinforcement that follows. (We discuss this type of learning in the context of Skinner's programmed instruction in Chapter 6.) The term frequently used to refer to this model of computer use is **computer-assisted instruction** (CAI). One of the frequently cited claims for the advantages of CAI over traditional classroom teaching is its interactive nature. The student's active participation in learning activities is required. Additional positive aspects are the facility for students to proceed at their own pace with the computer remaining 'patient' and non-judgmental while providing immediate feedback when responses are made.

Computer as tool The use of the computer as a tool is probably its most common use in education and business alike. Here the computer has practical value in saving time and expenditure of intellectual energy (Adams 1992). An increasing array of software is available that demonstrates the utility of the computer in this form: databases; spreadsheets; word processors; desktop publishing programs; utility software such as dictionaries, spelling checkers, thesauruses and calculators; graphics ('painting') packages; and information resources (e.g. multimedia encyclopaedias and atlases); not to mention the uses that have been designed for those with physical and learning disabilities (we talk more about this later in the chapter). Some would include adventure games within the category of tool software (Adams 1992), arguing that their educational potential is for extending a range of skills including mapping, vocabulary, problem solving and cooperative interaction.

Computer as tutee The third model of educational computing use is that of tutee, where the computer is the 'student' providing an interactive medium or stimulus for developing the user's personal knowledge (Loader & Nevile 1993). Here the student has control of the computer and, depending on the software employed, may learn through exploration and discovery (as with LOGO, microworlds and simulations). In this context, the computer is a vehicle for **personal constructivism**. Through computer-based scaffolding and modelling—such as the metacognitive skills training programs of the cognitive apprenticeship style (Scardamalia et al. 1989; Collins et al. 1991)—the computer provides a medium for learning as seen from a social constructivist perspective (see also Chapters 5 and 6).

The computer and personal and social constructivism

Computers and higher-order thinking skills It is argued that the computer not only increases the effectiveness of traditional instruction but can also provide opportunities for learning powerful intellectual skills such as problem solving and higher-order thinking skills. Open-ended, exploratory learning environments can be provided by simulation software, such as those of scientific laboratories where students can perform 'experiments' too complex or too dangerous for them to undertake in reality. Most recently, the development of interactive **hypertext** and **hypermedia** programs enable students to seek information on a multitude of topics unable to be dealt with by a single teacher in a short period. Even more liberating is the potential for students and teachers to create their own programs using a variety of computer-mediated tools.

Computers as multi-purpose tools As a multi-purpose tool, computers can help students accomplish a number of academic and creative goals: word-processing programs reduce the drudgery of writing and, with the use of some programs, can help students to learn to organise their thoughts before beginning to write. With the use of database programs, students can organise their knowledge of a topic or integrate it with that of others. Not only can the computer amplify or extend our capabilities to do traditional tasks but, more significantly, can provide us with the medium to explore new ways of thinking and of using computers to solve problems (Pea 1985). Computer-based spreadsheets, for example, enable users to perform calculations that might otherwise be beyond their capabilities, while, more importantly, encouraging them to make and test hypotheses in the form of 'living plans' which can compare the outcomes of crucial variables.

However, computers and their software may add little to the learning environment if they are poorly used. An article in the American national publication, *Business Week* (1989), presented the following pessimistic outlook: 'Chalk-age' teachers and dull software mean many PCs serve as typewriters and flash cards (p. 108). The author goes on to point out that much that professes to be 'educational' software is no better than textbook material represented on screens and with the same impact on students—boring. Software that has potential to extend students' creativity and thinking is extremely expensive to develop and produce due to its complexity. Publishers, therefore, tend to place their efforts elsewhere, namely in the drill and practice or arcade-type games (such as Math Blaster) or adventure games with mass appeal (such as the Carmen Sandiego series), which are often touted as fostering problem-solving skills. In reality, such 'popular' software is frequently used by teachers to entertain or motivate students, while the educational purpose to which teachers put them may be either resented by students, or minimally achieved (Downes 1993). Even where software tools are of a high quality they may be poorly used by teachers and students who do not understand their capabilities.

DISTRIBUTED LEARNING AND INFORMATION TECHNOLOGY

When the learning environment exists among a population of students separated by physical distance, it is said to be a **distributed learning environment** (Oblinger & Maruyama 1996). While such a learning environment retains many traditional school-like functions such as a library and a classroom, these are not defined by physical place or time: the needs of the learners determine the structure of the environment and the way it is accessed. Both teacher and students can participate from different locations and at different times: a class is made up of a virtual community of learners who may enter the learning environment when they are sufficiently prepared and may leave when they have reached a

Distributed learning not defined by place or time

required level of mastery. For a distributed learning environment to be achieved, information technology and a networked system that allows for both synchronous (at the same time) and asynchronous (delayed) communication are necessary.

One such global network, known as **I*Earn** (Copen 1995), has students from kindergarten through senior high school participating in joint social and environmental projects to raise intercultural awareness and understanding of international problems such as hunger, increasing population and environmental degradation. Traditional distance education has been reshaped through 'knowledge webs' which provide opportunities for distributed access to information by learners across the globe (Dede 1996).

Distributed cognition: social constructivism and technology

The current **personal constructivist** philosophy of learning argues that knowledge is most effectively constructed by individuals actively participating in developing their own understanding. **Social constructivists** (Rogoff 1990, 1995; Davydov 1995) would go further and insist that this process occurs best through social interaction, where cognitions are distributed between those involved in the interaction. In this context, the computer can be a vehicle for distributing cognition in one of two ways: the first is by reducing some of the mental processing for the user and, in doing so, freeing up processing space for higher-level mental activities; the second is as a mediating artifact through which communities of learners can interact intellectually to construct knowledge jointly in a dynamic way (Salomon 1993). In the first way, mental effort is divided between the user and the machine itself, while, in the second, cognitions of the various users build on each other in a 'self-scaffolding' way (Hewitt & Scardamalia 1996; see also the section on CSILE later in this chapter). Rather than existing within each individual in a fixed and final form, knowledge is said to be 'in between' individuals (Lave & Wenger 1991), emerging jointly from a partnership with appropriate 'intelligent' computer software, and social interaction (Salomon, Perkins & Globerson 1991). Distributed learning, therefore, can take place in settings where **cooperative goal structures** operate. (For more on cooperative learning, see Chapter 10.)

Personal tools for learning: notebook computers at Melbourne's MLC school. Truly a community of learners!
Photo: McKenzie & Associates P/L

Distributed teaching: managing classroom activities

Distributed teaching can similarly occur when the computer is used to manage classroom activities, thereby freeing the teacher to engage in higher levels of teaching with individuals or small groups. One example of educational software that has been designed to facilitate such management while fostering the development of cooperative learning is the *Decisions, Decisions* multimedia series (Tom Snyder Productions). In this program, students organised into groups with a computer to share, are managed by the computer through a number of role-playing simulation games where they gain experience in problem solving. The teacher is freed to work with the group on the ideas that emerge through their computer-mediated interaction while the computer directs the game and provides feedback on student decision making.

Cognitive apprenticeship

Learning can be very effective if it occurs in the context of cognitive apprenticeship (Collins et al. 1991); that is, the personal construction of understanding, and the process of acquiring knowledge and skills should occur in the social and functional contexts of their use. In their natural learning environment outside school, children learn more in groups than they do individually. They use tools and resources that are related to specific situations (such as washing up, skateboard riding or origami). School learning, however, frequently focuses on abstract concepts presented in symbolic forms (Resnick 1987). DeCorte (1990, p. 78) summarises the cognitive apprenticeship approach in the following way:

... constructive learning processes should be embedded in contexts that are rich in resources and learning materials, that offer opportunities for social interaction, and that are representative of the kinds of tasks and problems to which learners will have to apply their knowledge and skill in the future.

Situated cognition In what ways can the computer enhance learning in a social context? First, the tasks and problems that students are given must reflect the way that they are useful in real life—learning that is called **situated cognition** by Brown, Collins and Duguid (1989) Greeno (1997) and Anderson, Reder & Simon (1997). The computer can provide instructional environments that imitate situations in the real world that are difficult to create in a traditional classroom: databases, microworlds, multimedia and 'virtual reality' are some of the approaches with the most obvious application. Furthermore, other tool software such as spreadsheets, word processors and graphics packages can provide opportunities for 'intellectual partnerships' between human user and computer (Salomon, Globerson & Guterman 1989) as we describe later in a discussion of computer-scaffolded reading and writing development.

Observing experts

Second, opportunities for observation of 'experts' in an area must occur. Here again, the computer can provide rapid access to vast knowledge bases (domain-specific expert knowledge) as well as models of the cognitive and metacognitive strategies that experts in a field use to solve problems. Especially here, computerised multimedia technology, which combines voice, text, graphics and animation, can add clarity to the explanation of a complex process (Collins 1991).

STUDENT-CENTRED LEARNING

CSILE

Procedural facilitation

Scardamalia et al. (1989; see also Scardamalia & Bereiter 1995; Hewitt & Scardamalia 1996) firmly advocate the view of education that puts control of the learning process in the hands of students, and have designed computer software to this end. Theirs is an example of the **cognitive apprenticeship** model of learning, mentioned earlier in this chapter. The Computer-Supported Intentional Learning Environments (CSILE) approach that Scardamalia et al. have been researching for some time is an example of what is referred to as **procedural facilitation.** This is an instructional approach that provides students with temporary supports or cognitive prompts that give them guidance while they learn more complex strategies for themselves. Such supports include menus under which students organise the type of cognitive activities they engage in during a task. For example, they might draw icons that depict 'confusion' or 'new learning' and, as they proceed through the task, any concerns, discoveries or new hypotheses that emerge are entered into the appropriate files for their own retrieval later, or that of their teacher and class peers. In this way, normally covert thinking processes ('knowledge-construction activities', as Scardamalia et al. refer to them) are made overt.

Currently, the CSILE model is being extended to facilitate 'knowledge-building communities' in which a whole class can contribute to communal knowledge building on a common problem. In this context, CSILE is used to place individual student thinking and discussion on a common screen for all members of the class to read and react to as they build on each others' ideas. As with hypertext, the role of the teacher in such classroom knowledge building is vital. A number of important strategies for using such technologies as CSILE have been identified. Key features of using information technology effectively are indicated in Table 7.1.

TABLE 7.1

ESSENTIALS OF DEVELOPING A KNOWLEDGE-BUILDING CLASSROOM USING INFORMATION TECHNOLOGY

For teachers

- Provide a supportive social climate by teaching students how to respond constructively to each other's ideas and work on screen.
- Focus students on communal problems of understanding through answering each other's questions, and clarifying and refining ideas. Teach students how to redirect their efforts to a single focus, namely, the solution to a specific problem, rather than diverging into broad topics.
- Encourage students to read each other's work as valid sources of knowledge and ideas.
- Encourage connectivity among ideas by teaching students how to ask questions, offer opinions, and extend others' ideas.
- Emphasise the work of the community over the work of the individual. Students who work on a shared problem should view their own writings only in the context of all other knowledge partners: a 'knowledge map' is an important class tool in this regard.

(based on Hewitt & Scardamalia 1996)

Surface and deep learning

CSILE takes into account the cognitive strategies employed by novices such as focusing on *surface* not *deep* features of a task; organising thinking by topics, not goals; using a linear approach through a task rather than a recursive one (i.e. one in which the learner comes back to revise, following further insights into the problem); and adding to an original solution rather than transforming it afresh. This program provides students with the structure for the development of the type of cognitive goal setting (metacognitive skills) used by experts in problem solving, such as learning, finding out and planning, rather than the task goals that novices adopt such as scoring a certain number of points or finding the treasure, as in most adventure games. Such support should be withdrawn as the learner becomes more proficient.

Using computers to enhance and facilitate thinking processes

In this context, students can use a 'scratchpad' into which data can be copied and reprocessed to add new material, ideas and graphics, ask questions or make summaries. The main point here is that the computer supports different ways of organising knowledge which are not necessarily linear or hierarchical. Thus, narrative or expository text could be re-presented by students in a variety of forms—such as a concept map, table, timeline, causal chain or flow chart, for instance—which encourages the use of divergent and higher-order thinking skills. Such use of the technology depends, of course, on the ways in which the teacher structures the learning activities. But then this holds for the use of any resources in the classroom, doesn't it?

Using computers to organise ideas

Most recently, another valuable (personal constructivist) tool for helping students develop their thinking has emerged. This is 'ThinkSheet' (Acorn) which is designed to assist students to record and see their ideas as they occur in their heads. These ideas are recorded on 'cards' which can be arranged in a linear way (as with a word processor) or rearranged and grouped in a non-linear, branching fashion (as with hypertext, on which we will elaborate later), in whichever direction their thoughts take them. Such software can be used to prepare and analyse a piece of writing, as well as to plan a research project and organise collected material (e.g. compile a database). A particular strength of this type of tool is that it can support group discussion and the planning of cooperative problem-solving tasks by recording ideas during brainstorming and organising them in tree form for subsequent analysis. As such, it supports a social constructivist approach to learning that is facilitated by information technology.

COMPUTERS AND CONSTRUCTIONISM

Constructionism is based on Piaget's constructivism in which learners build knowledge from their experiences in the world rather than having it supplied by the teacher (alive or machine; see Chapter 2). Papert extends this concept a step further by maintaining that such construction, which takes place 'in the head', often happens particularly effectively when it is supported by actual construction of a personally meaningful product. In Seymour Papert's view this construction is of a public sort: something concrete such as a sand-castle, a cake, a poem, a LEGO machine, a computer program or virtual objects such as a MOO ('a constructionist playground' according to Bruckman & Resnick 1996, p. 220) which can be shown, discussed, probed and admired (see Papert 1993).

The importance of concrete thinking

Papert's focus on the concrete constructions that children need to make in order to learn is a strong reaction to what he believes is wrong with education today: 'the mistaken belief that children's learning should be "advanced" to higher order, abstract reasoning as soon as possible, using concrete means briefly as stepping stones. Such misplaced emphasis results in teachers spending minimal time where the most important work is to be done' (p. 143). Among the important contributions that Papert made to illustrate the relationship between concrete manipulation of materials and the development of higher-order thinking was his development of LOGO and Turtle Graphics.

LOGO

LOGO is a computer programming language originally designed 20 years ago to teach mathematics but considerably modified since then for general educational applications. The vision that Papert (1980) had of LOGO in his famous book, *Mindstorms: Children, Computers and Powerful Ideas*, was to provide an environment in which the act of programming the computer to do something was an opportunity to make explicit the thinking and problem-solving tasks involved. Using LOGO, the child can plan, devise procedures, use problem-solving techniques such as iteration and recursion, make mistakes and search for 'bugs' in reasoning, devise new hypotheses and test them. Most importantly, learning with LOGO is a discovery-learning approach in which the child builds on simple cognitive structures in the process of developing more complex ones (Adams 1992). The environment in which this building takes place is the 'microworld', a simplified model of the real world.

Turtle Graphics

Despite the power that it gives children to create and explore as well as to develop problem-solving skills, LOGO is not as appealing or as important, according to Papert, as the 'turtle' into which Papert has transformed the cursor on the computer screen (Papert 1988). Papert's turtle was created to represent an *object* which a child can use to think about problems (Adams 1992). The turtle has two properties, position and direction, just as a point in geometry. These properties of the turtle give it a lifelike quality that children can identify with as they control its movements (Turtle Graphics): the turtle faces a direction and walks that way as if the child were doing it, thus allowing the working out of problems in a 'real' space (although restricted), rather than an abstract concept of space. In addition, children need to *represent* their intentions for the turtle's movements in terms of explicit (LOGO) programming commands for the manner in which this must occur. From their practical manipulations of the turtle, therefore, children come to understand geometric principles.

Research findings on the cognitive effects of LOGO programming have produced varied results. As Adams (1992) points out, however, despite the meagre positive evidence of its benefits, LOGO still captures a devoted international following of educators who want to put the control of learning in children's hands and who persist in the slow process of creating educational change. Although, as yet, nothing has replaced LOGO, BOXER is emerging from it as a new approach to programming, one from a powerful computational environment for abstracting and representing ideas at a number of levels (diSessa 1987). The educational applications of BOXER are currently being developed at the Sunrise School at the Royal Melbourne Institute of Technology (RMIT) in Australia and at the University of California, Berkeley.

The clearest evidence for the value of using LOGO as a tool for developing children's problem-solving skills has been provided by research at the State University of New York (Swan 1991). Used alone in a discovery-learning approach, LOGO was not found to be effective. However, when combined with explicit instruction and mediated practice, programming with LOGO supported both the development of problem-solving strategies and their transfer to new situations.

Similar research has also pointed out the interaction between LOGO and instructional method (Au & Leung 1991). Students trained to use LOGO through a process-oriented approach have been shown to develop general problem-solving strategies which they can transfer to new tasks more than those who receive content instruction on LOGO commands and the basic syntax of the programming language. The process-oriented approach has four important elements:

1. A focus on the *metacognitive strategies* of students by encouraging them to actively explore their ideas and monitor their own solutions. In particular, emphasis is placed on the skills of planning, analysis, monitoring and evaluation.
2. *Structured guidance* is provided through the use of increasingly difficult activity sheets which help students to keep metacognitive strategies in mind.
3. *Questioning techniques* are used by teachers to remind students of the problem-solving skills they are to apply: the emphasis is on guidance, not content instruction and the giving of answers.
4. A *socially interactive* and reflective learning environment.

THE COMPUTER AS A ZONE OF PROXIMAL DEVELOPMENT

Scaffolding through the use of a computer

According to Lev Vygotsky (1978), teaching/learning environments should be aimed at the child's *zone of proximal development* (i.e. what the child is able to achieve with the support of an adult or peer), rather than matching what the child is currently able to do independently (see Chapter 2). Salomon, Globerson and Guterman (1989) have shown that the computer tool can also provide the intellectual 'scaffolding' that an adult or peer might supply. With the aid of a computerised 'reading partner' which presented reading principles and metacognitive guidance for reading, it was shown that children's understanding of text could be greatly improved, along with their essay writing skills, to which their new learning transferred. As Salomon, Perkins and Globerson (1991, p. 5) point out:

The partnership with the technology is like the one with a more capable peer: It allows mindful learners to engage in cognitive processes that are of a higher order than the ones they would display without that partnership ... to stretch their cognitive muscles to the maximum.

Computers and modelling

Salomon et al. point out that the computer can readily be used to provide **models** of the ways in which information can be represented, as well as to enable the learner to **activate higher mental operations** by removing many tedious, time-consuming lower-level mental chores and drains on memory. However, they stress that, for the computer to act effectively in leaving a 'cognitive residue' in the learner's thinking—that is, something that transfers to new situations—it must provide the equivalent of 'explicit humanlike guidance' in the intellectual partnership (p. 621). In other words, the computer should be programmed to act as a more capable peer, in Vygotsky's terms, in order to provide guidance in self-regulatory metacognitive strategies that would become internalised by the learner, who could then proceed to perform at a higher cognitive level independently. Thus the 'reading partner' provided eleven pieces of text (from 150 to 350 words) accompanied by:

- ☐ *self-guiding questions that good readers use while reading;* e.g. 'Think about what message the text is trying to convey to you.' 'Think what thoughts the text brings to your mind.' 'Ask yourself whether you understand the text.'
- ☐ *specific reading principles*—such as the inferences that can be drawn from a title, images that can be conjured up, and the intermediate summaries that can be made while reading.

These elements were then presented at the bottom of the computer screen in the form of guiding metacognitive-like questions (p. 622) such as: 'What can I learn from the title?' 'What thoughts does this bring to my mind?' 'What are the key sentences in the text?' 'How might I summarise what has happened in the text so far?'

Question point: The work cited above serves to highlight a number of significant questions with regard to the use of computers as tools to think with:

- ☐ *Can the computer provide a stronger aid or intellectual partner for crossing the zone of proximal development than peer or teacher guidance?*
- ☐ *Can it be used to best advantage in a complementary role with the teacher?*
- ☐ *Will some students benefit more from computers than from teacher-mediated learning because of their own learning styles?*

What is important to note here is that the mere use of the computer is not sufficient to create a positive cognitive change—in this case, a generalised ability for self-reflection. Just sitting children in front of an intelligent computer program in a natural school setting will not necessarily lead to transfer of skills to the learner. The evidence does show, however, that such cognitive effects can be 'engineered' (Salomon, Perkins & Globerson 1991) to focus the user's mental efforts on abstracting thinking skills and strategies while engaging in the learning activity.

STUDENTS CONSTRUCTING LEARNING

In line with the philosophy of children constructing their own learning through interaction with experiences in which they struggle to find equilibrium between their current level of understanding and that of the next, we would argue that it is not the computer that should do the tutoring, provide the knowledge, structure the learning process and guide the student through a program; it is the student. What a powerful computer environment provides is the tool for empowering students to engage in **cognitive struggle** with a new learning situation, allowing them to take control of their own learning, reflecting on their thinking and on the consequences of choices they make, all of which are factors in developing metacognition (Sewell 1990; see Chapter 5). In particular, as we have pointed out, the computer can provide situated learning contexts and the opportunity to observe expert models of particular skills.

Metacognition

The computer can also provide rapid access to vast knowledge bases (domain-specific expert knowledge) as well as models of the cognitive and metacognitive strategies that experts in a field use to solve problems. Especially here, computerised multimedia technology, which combines voice, text, graphics and animation, can add clarity to the explanation of a complex process.

Domain-specific expert knowledge

Increasingly students are encouraged to become self-regulated learners. How might the use of technology facilitate this?
Photo: McKenzie & Associates P/L

Computers and motivated learning

Many argue that traditional educational tools (the teacher and soft technology such as books) are not sufficiently motivating for today's students, who are accustomed to the pace of electronic entertainment and instant access to information. Nor can traditional approaches provide the challenge and consistent 'success' experiences that computer programs profess to—an even greater indictment of the education system, especially for the student who has low self-confidence and self-esteem at school as a result of repeated failure experiences with learning. The computer used in a self-paced, individualised tutorial mode can 'diagnose' the level at which a student is currently capable of working and then customise the delivery of instruction from this point by monitoring errors and periodically reviewing concepts, as well as advancing the student to the next phase of mastery as appropriate. This behaviourist model focuses on individualistic goals and is comparable to that of Rosenshine's direct instruction approach (discussed in Chapter 6).

INTERACTIVE MEDIA AND EFFECTIVE LEARNING AND TEACHING

Hypertext and hypermedia

Advances in the use of computer-based technology as an entertainment medium and a learning tool have been mind-bogglingly rapid over the past decade. The areas of most recent expansion are those of **hypertext** and **hypermedia**.

Typically, traditional print media require the reader to follow information from 'beginning' to 'end' in a linear fashion. Of course, alternative paths are possible if readers choose to refer to diagrams, definitions, footnotes, glossaries and the index as they are reading (Rouet & Levonen 1996). Hypertext, in contrast, is an on-line computer environment in which electronic links allow the user to make connections to blocks of text in whichever order they wish to explore and present the information.

Non-linear thinking

With hypertext, therefore, the student reads the first screen of information and then branches to other screens as interest or needs for further explanation dictate. Information is stored in stacks which can be likened to electronic index cards, each linked to other cards through encoded information (Vockell & Schwartz 1992). These 'cards' can contain a variety of different media, including printed text, numerical data, pictures (both still and moving), animation, sound and virtual reality. Stacks of such cards are collected as hypermedia packages. It is becoming increasingly common for large, commercial hypermedia databases to be stored on CD-ROM disks which may either be connected to the computer from a separate player, or built into the hardware as a separate drive. The term 'hypermedia' describes a hypertext system that is extended to include a range of other media along with text (Layman & Hall 1991).

Hypertext is emerging as a new literary genre: one with no centre, no end, and probably multi-authored (Snyder 1996). As yet, there are few expert 'hyper-readers' who have had sufficient practice in devising effective navigational strategies through non-linear material (Rouet & Levonen 1996). Although, at present, there is little documented research on the use of hypermedia in education, Vockell and Schwartz (1992, p. 301) conclude their discussion of hypermedia with the following enthusiasm:

As hypermedia applications become more common, it is likely that users will become accustomed to the idea of non-linear thinking, and students will begin to think non-linearly. This could be perceived as a problem by teachers who invest huge amounts of energy in getting students to follow a clear, systematic line of thought—why encourage them to jump around in their thought? However, the non-linear thinking of hypertext is by no means haphazard. Since hypermedia applications require careful planning and complete sets of information, hypermedia programmers and users will learn to incorporate these characteristics in their own thinking and presentations.

Hypertext as a tool for constructing learning There are several ways in which effective use of hypertext materials can enable the learner to construct knowledge in a meaningful way. Table 7.2 presents some of these.

TABLE 7.2

ESSENTIALS OF USING HYPERTEXT TO ENABLE THE LEARNER TO CONSTRUCT KNOWLEDGE

For teachers

- ☐ Diminish teacher authority and *share knowledge construction* with students.
- ☐ Use *multilayered learning approaches* in which interdisciplinary boundaries are crossed in making hypertext connections.
- ☐ Allow students the opportunity to *assume responsibility for accessing information and sequencing their exploration*, based on whatever meaning they derive from it.

- ☐ Encourage students to be more *independent and active* in their building of knowledge.
- ☐ Encourage *student collaboration* by the use of hypertext.
- ☐ Guide the development of *critical thinking and creativity*.

(based on Snyder 1996)

For learners

- ☐ Feel free to explore the hypertext information at first. Remember that it is natural to feel overwhelmed if you are unfamiliar with a particular domain.
- ☐ Brainstorm your ideas for what you are seeking and the procedure you will adopt. Share your ideas with others.
- ☐ Collaborate with another user to plan a navigation route through the information. Draw a visual map of your strategy.
- ☐ Ask for guidance from the teacher as to suggested structures for exploration, selection of significant material, and collection, recording and presentation of information.

Cognitive research into the ways in which humans process information has highlighted the associational nature of **memory** (Anderson 1983). In other words, by making associations with other material already in memory, retention and retrieval of the new information is facilitated. The use of multi-relational semantic maps may help students to learn and recall information better than more traditional presentations (Lambiotte et al. 1989). Computer-generated hypertext, therefore, which allows the user to follow semantic associations, would appear to provide an effective environment for enhancing meaningful retention of information. Of course, by this we mean the associations created by the learner, not those of the author of the software.

Is hypertext an effective learning tool? As for research findings relating to the use of hypertext as a learning tool, the little that is available appears to support its educational value, although not without qualification. While there are advantages in allowing the user to branch at will through a hypertext or hypermedia system, there may be a real danger of getting lost in the process of exploring: 'On the one hand, the construction or adaptation of text to one's own purpose is useful. On the other hand, following one's associations can create such a micro-view that the overall sense of where a particular bit of knowledge fits into the macrostructure is lost' (Reynolds et al. 1991, p. 169).

In this context, research has been conducted on the use of non-linear, knowledge 'hypermaps' and 'hypertexts' for learning new material in which they compared computer screen versions with those presented on paper (Reynolds et al. 1991). Interestingly, these were placed in a cooperative learning setting where one student took the role of 'pilot' (the one who used the computer), and the other, that of 'navigator' (who used the paper version). These roles were scripted, as previous research has shown the benefits on processing of information of using scripted cooperation together with concept maps.

The results showed that those who used the computer version were far less frustrated than those who used paper versions of the hypermaps and hypertext. Both forms, however, were valuable for learning: the maps enabled the users to recall main ideas better, while the text assisted the recall of details. The computer clearly reduced the cognitive load on students by presenting smaller chunks of information on the screen than were on the paper version. In this study, the 'navigation' through concepts was automated by the computer rather than in the control of the learner.

The role of the teacher in using hypertext. Hypertext is the basis for the **World Wide Web** on the **Internet**, which is fast becoming an educational tool for rapid access to vast stores of information and specialist communities. Given its importance, we feel that a close look at the role of the teacher in using hypertext is warranted. Strategies for navigating hypertext can be taught effectively, even with young students (Rouet 1990). The role of the teacher, therefore, is to help students by training them in hypertext literacy skills, such as using structural cues and making mental efforts to find coherence while reading hypertext. How can this be done? Most of the evidence suggests that structure can be provided in two ways: the hypertext material itself may provide the reader with a map of its hierachical organisation—the key concepts and the links that have been coded by the writer; or readers should keep a running record of their current location in the network and keep track of previous steps in the navigation (Rouet & Levonen 1996). Coherence, on the other hand, emerges from mental representations that are made while reading—for example, when making lateral moves through material rather than hierarchical ones, it is important to teach students to go back to the section where they made their digression in order to reestablish the context in which they were thinking (see Foltz 1996). We continue to explore ways of navigating hypertext and hypermedia later in this chapter when we talk about the Internet.

Tolhurst (1993) suggests that, for effective use of hypertext presentations, the general reading skills required for gaining information from traditional linear presentations need to be expanded to include such new skills as making associations by semantic links. How can teachers do this? Table 7.3 lists some useful strategies.

TABLE 7.3

ESSENTIALS OF TRAINING LEARNERS TO USE HYPERTEXT EFFECTIVELY

For teachers

- Design off-computer lessons that complement the use of hypertext material. For instance, teachers might develop activities that prepare students in a topic (thereby building prior conceptual understanding), which would assist them in making sequencing choices once they began using hypertext.
- Have pairs or small groups of students evaluate strategies they have used for locating information with hypertext, and then plan a range of possible paths for their next computer session.
- Design worksheets that will guide hypertext users in making effective sequencing choices in line with desired learning goals. Such an approach is in keeping with the 'guided discovery' approach advocated by Jerome Bruner (1971) in which the teacher's role is to facilitate student problem solving by providing some structure.
- Use approaches such as prediction and concept mapping to facilitate the development of skills needed for effective hypertext use.

Reading skills and hypertext There is one very important point to keep in mind when you are planning to use hypertext with your students: their degree of reading skill with linear text is a determinant of their ability to read hypertext. Poor readers who depend on context to help them decode meaning will be disadvantaged by hypertext unless a map of its structure is provided, or information is given by the teacher about the way the content has been structured, and the link nodes that have been programmed (Foltz 1996). Another concern with such students is that the mental effort to process unstructured material is far greater than for skilled readers who are better at parallel processing. What is the message here for teachers? Practise yourself, first with the material you are asking your students to use, so that you can anticipate their experiences and difficulties.

Skill in linear reading affects ability to read hypertext

Multimedia

The advent of multimedia in the classroom has brought with it mixed reactions. At one extreme is the grave concern expressed by educational philosophers like Chris Bigum and his colleagues at Deakin University in Victoria at the creation of 'monstrosities' as a function of the current multimedia wave. At the other extreme is sheer excitement at the awesome power of technology to provide access to vast amounts of information at lightning speeds in forms that are available to teachers and students. In fact, the number of curriculum-specific CD-ROM multimedia packages is currently mushrooming, with the computer industry, both alone and in collaboration with education consultants from Departments of Education, designing interactive databases for the educational market. For example, at present, there are choices for schools from such packages as:

- ☐ Bodyworks (Softkey) which features 3-D models of the human body in virtual reality, together with 50 films that illustrate the workings of the body;
- ☐ Compton's Interactive World Atlas (Learning Company);
- ☐ Ultimate Children's Encyclopedia for grades 2 to 5 (Learning Company);
- ☐ Dictionary of the Living World (Media Design Interactive);
- ☐ downUNDER (NSW Board of Studies)—interactive Australian geography for high school students;
- ☐ ENCARTA (Microsoft), the Funk and Wagnalls Encyclopaedia series;
- ☐ FlashBACK (NSW Board of Studies)—interactive Australian history for primary and lower high school;
- ☐ OZ I.D. (NSW Board of Studies)—an interactive search for Australian heritage and identity through an examination of visual primary sources;
- ☐ Shakespeare (Dataflow).

Multimedia and multisensory presentations There is no doubt that such multimedia packages provide vast stores of information in a compact form that is both stimulating and motivating for students as a function of their use of multisensory presentations. Animals move and make sounds; people from the past talk in radio broadcasts or film clips; students enter places in present and past times to which they would otherwise not have access.

To use multimedia effectively, learners need some structure (a map) through such vast information resources as are stored in multimedia packages (Downes 1993). The analysis skills needed for effective exploration of multimedia/hypermedia software do not come naturally to either teachers or students. There needs to be classroom-based training in research strategies, such

Analysis skills required to use multimedia effectively

as the use of index systems and cross-referencing, and these guidelines need to be included in the packages themselves. Without such skill development and clear procedures for charting progression through hypermedia, students and teachers alike merely browse haphazardly in the material or, worse, get hopelessly entangled and confused (Fraser 1993).

Although there is clearly much opportunity for exploration—and it is in this sense only that the material can be called interactive—many students are unable genuinely to interact with the information presented in order to construct their own meanings from it. Students are restricted to examining the information as presented and 'cutting and pasting' pieces from it (which they can print), rather than re-presenting it in other forms such as graphs or diagrams. Most of the multimedia software available does not permit students to add any text of their own, nor alter the information to suit their own research purposes—neither truly interactive nor encouraging of creative information-handling skills.

Virtual reality

The most recent development in computer technology of some interest to educators and the general public alike is 'virtual reality'. The term **virtual reality** (VR) typically refers to three-dimensional interactive computer imaging or simulated models implemented with devices that track the movement of the user's eyes, hands, head or body. This can be achieved through a variety of hardware such as stereo viewing **goggles, helmets** or **head-mounted displays** (which provide auditory input to the user as well as three-dimensional perceptions), and **datagloves** and **datasuits**, which contain fibre-optic receptors that respond to the user's movements and transmit these to the computer via cable (Krueger 1991). As for what it does, Sherman and Judkins (1992) emphasise the capability of VR to immerse the user:

VR allows you to explore a computer-generated world by actually being in it ... It has three components: it is inclusive, it is interactive, and it happens in real time. That is to say you become part of the world, you can change it, and the changes occur as you make them.

The user of VR perceives certain experiences that have been programmed into an artificial (virtual) environment through their senses of sight (goggles) and sound (helmet), and which they can control through their gloves or suit.

VR and constructing learning There are two important elements of virtual reality that appeal to an educator with a constructivist philosophy of learning. The first is the potential for students to genuinely interact with their learning environment, and the second is the facility provided by VR technology for turning abstract concepts into concrete ones. The theories of Piaget, Vygotsky and Papert can each strongly support such use in the following ways: Piaget's belief in the importance of *experience with the world* for a child's intellectual growth; Vygotsky's emphasis on the role of *active involvement in learning* and *the value of auxiliary stimuli* in mastering the environment (Archee 1993); and Papert's constructionism, which stresses the *role of computers as a medium through which learning can occur*, rather than as a mere tool. Most importantly, Papert's emphasis on the child's active participation in the creation and dissemination of knowledge for real purposes, through the use of technology and in collaboration with teachers as mentors, admirably supports the application of virtual reality to the classroom, according to Archee (1993).

Special educational needs and VR Although, at present, VR has not made inroads into Australian or New Zealand schools, it seems certain that, as the entertainment industry increasingly promotes its commercial versions for children and adults, VR will find its way into educational applications. For those involved in teaching children with special educational needs, those with physical or learning disabilities, VR technology holds great promise in providing experiences (albeit, in artificially created environments) that may otherwise be unavailable to them. Sherman and Judkins (1992), who have conducted some of the early research on the educational use of VR with children, described a number of positive outcomes:

1. Children (between 9 and 15 years) worked successfully in five cooperative groups to design and create virtual worlds.
2. The children learnt how to use the technology far more quickly than the researchers expected.
3. Motivation to participate was high.
4. In completing their projects children learnt how to program, network and design.
5. Girls especially flourished through the experience. 'They "loved it" ... the process, rather than goal-oriented system ... they were more creative, more whimsical. They produced non-violent worlds, no blowing up of anything!' (Meredith Bricken, coordinator, cited in Sherman & Judkins, p. 89). This is not surprising given the frequent anecdotal evidence from classroom teachers that girls are motivated and challenged more when working with multimedia, HyperCard and graphics programs than with more abstract programming forms.

Advantages of using VR in the classroom The following features of VR present potential advantages of the technology for classroom use:

- ☐ The immersive quality of virtual worlds engages the student affectively and cognitively.
- ☐ The nature of interaction in virtual worlds is intuitive—children are able to point, touch and manipulate naturally.
- ☐ Guidance for student use of virtual worlds can be programmed at various levels.
- ☐ Students can relate virtual worlds to their own previous experience as objects retain the same properties in both worlds.
- ☐ It is possible to re-enter virtual worlds any number of times in order to clarify concepts.
- ☐ As with computer technology in general, basic procedures can be automated in virtual worlds so that the student can be freed to focus on higher-order functions.

(Winn & Bricken 1992)

The long-term effects of using VR Despite the optimistic views of VR for educational use expressed above, there are still unknowns about the long-term effects of the immersive process on the user's perception or cognitive functioning. Will repeated experiences of virtual worlds have damaging effects comparable to those produced by perception-distorting drugs, for example? As VR is still in its infancy, research on such potential dangers does not yet exist, or has not yet been published.

As virtual reality operates in real time, it appears to be instantaneous. It is important to bear in mind, however, that the reality of the experiences provided in VR are nonetheless programmed by the developers of the virtual worlds. Even with software that allows the user to program while within the virtual world, the ultimate limits are set by the technology. As with simulations, such limits may have advantages educationally in focusing attention on particular aspects of experiences. On the other hand, as we have mentioned before, there may also be a risk that young school students in the future will become increasing unable to separate reality from simulated reality. This is a significant matter for the attention of present and future educators.

Simulations

What are simulations and when would you use them? Computer simulations are applications that enable the teacher to provide students with opportunities to perform particular activities they are to learn in a context that closely resembles the real world (Alessi & Trollip 1991). **Computer simulations** have significant advantages over real-life experiences for a number of reasons that make them worthy of consideration for classroom use. Simulations can:

Uses of simulations

- ☐ *Reduce the complexity of variables being addressed at any one time in a situation*, allowing the teacher to use the simulation to focus student learning on particular aspects. Thus, within a social studies unit on the development of cities, a program such as SimCity or SimTown (Maxis) enables students to control selected variables that highlight the important decisions involved in city planning and the environmental effects of 'real' neighbourhoods.
- ☐ *Be less expensive, more convenient and repeatable than their real counterparts*; for instance, when learning to drive a car, manipulate equipment or dissect animals.
- ☐ *Speed up the passage of time* when studying such topics as the laws of genetics or ecology. SimLife (Maxis) has been developed for such a purpose and allows the user control over individual components of the environment so that the repercussions of particular changes (such as the destruction of species of animals or plants, climatic variations, or toxins and mutagens) are demonstrated.
- ☐ *Eliminate dangers* associated with scientific experiments in chemistry or experiences such as operating a nuclear power station. WhatWatts? (Dataworks), for instance, gives students the chance to 'control' the supply of an electricity plant and to experience the consequences of particular decisions from the perspectives of consumer, planner and controller.

There are two types of simulation—those that teach *about something* in the world, and those that teach *how to do something* (Alessi & Trollip 1991). For maximum effectiveness, teachers should make the learning purpose of simulations clear to students.

Simulations and motivation Simulations are, without doubt, motivating and fun ways for students to learn. As for their cognitive benefits, opinions vary (Morton 1993). The research evidence for simulations is strong with regard to the affective domain, especially in motivating students, improving attitudes towards teacher and subject matter, and developing confidence in making judgments. This is not to deny their cognitive value, as positive attitudes and a sense of control are clearly fundamental to effective learning and classroom management, as we have said throughout this book. Nonetheless, it is worth looking briefly at the evidence for the cognitive effects of simulations. A number of researchers have demonstrated that computer simulations

Why is it that boys tend to be more interested in computerised adventure and skill games than girls?
Photo: authors

encourage the development of **problem-solving skills** in students, which transfer to new situations (Collis 1987; Pollin 1989). Research has also indicated that it is the lower-achieving students who benefit most from simulations (Morton 1993).

Cognitive gains are most likely to be made if teachers *structure the learning activity* so that sufficient time is provided for students to reflect on and discuss information gained from the simulation. Furthermore, *it is important that the purpose of the simulation is clearly understood by students and that they are shown how to integrate the data with existing knowledge.* This merely reinforces the obvious point that it is the teacher who must plan the learning activity thoroughly, knowing how computer software can contribute to student understanding and making this known to students. Otherwise, the technology exists in the classroom only as expensive entertainment (Stead 1990).

Need for planning, relevance, reflection and discussion

THE INTERNET AND LEARNING

The most significant educational tool in our time, or just another wizz-bang technology that will fade from view eventually? How do you see the role of the **Internet** in education today and in the future? The popularity of the Internet undoubtedly reflects the sense of liberation that this apparently 'democratic' tool provides with its universal access to information. All you need to be connected to vast storehouses of material, special interest groups and individuals from all corners of the globe is an up-to-date computer, a modem and lots of time to 'surf', or explore. Of course, if you don't have the facilities, the time to play, or the money to pay for access and on-line time you cannot participate. In reality, this may exclude a host of groups from the network of users, although in theory, access to the information web is available for all.

Books, learning and the Internet

As the focus of this book is on learning, we explore here the possibilities for 'playing' on the Internet as one means through which learning can take place, as well as the more obvious school-based uses of **global telecommunication**. As the Internet is still in its infancy, it is not surprising that there is not yet a strong research pool from which to draw evidence on the educational benefits of Internet use. Nevertheless, there is much that has been explored and there are a number of perspectives on its educational implications emerging. One of these is the concern about whether the electronic media will be replacing the print media in the future. This possibility has important implications for schools as we know them today and for the publishing of books in general. Will it mean the demise of reading and literature, as some fear (Munter 1996; Spender 1995)? Will the young book readers of today expect their words to be accompanied by pictures and sounds in the future? And what will become of famous authors who 'had something important to say' and whom we studied for that reason? Perhaps the author of the future will become more of a team leader of a multimedia production (Hiley 1993; Spender 1995).

Internet implications for books

Another major concern is that, with increasing use of technology in education, students will spend most of their time learning to use and keep up with computer tools, rather than concepts; accessing information per se will take precedence over learning how to use the information to make 'educated' decisions (Stoll 1995). Furthermore, there is the danger

Internet implications for learning

of virtual teaching and virtual learning, which take place in a shared synthetic world, increasingly replacing human interaction in real-life communities.

ACTION STATION

Think for a moment about how the separation of message from owner and context, as on the Internet, impacts on our traditional notions of classrooms. Discuss the potential positive and negative outcomes.

Cognition and the Internet

Are the **cognitive processes** involved in learning from electronic media different from those for conventional print? Does regular use of multimedia change the way that we think, or does multimedia merely mimic the non-linear form in which humans think? In other words, if we think through associations, then doesn't the increased facility and range of media through which we make these associations increase our capacity to think? As John Warren from the School of the Future (Adelaide, Australia) says, 'Print in our era has bound us into thinking in a rigid, linear way; the technokids of today and the future will be far more comfortable thinking divergently and on a number of levels at the same time' (Warren 1996).

Does using multimedia for learning change the way we think?

Non-linear thinking While traditional literature such as novels and poetry provides us with the opportunity to reflect on ourselves and the human condition, the Net encourages users to **scan information rapidly**, jumping from one 'hot-link' to another as the impulse takes them. Some argue that this (progressively) may lead to a reduction in reflective and higher-level **critical thinking** (Birkerts 1994). Others suggest that the ability and patience of learners to engage in sustained inquiry will suffer as a consequence of interactive relationships with material presented in multimedia environments and in hypertext format—that is, on the Net or on CD-ROMs (Munter 1996). What do you think?

Scanning information rapidly

Although it is fun to explore the Net, it can also be extremely frustrating and even stressful because of the mass of hot-linked information 'out there'. As already discussed in relation to hypertext, effective searching for information should be planned using a strategy such as the one shown in Table 7.4.

The need to have a **search strategy** and to keep a record of the direction that the search follows in case you need to replicate it has been demonstrated to us through our own explorations on the Net. Using Netscape as a 'navigator', we have found ourselves leaping gleefully into cyberscape and skipping around when something looked as if it might be relevant or interesting. Of course, it was not always easy to retrace our steps other than to rely on the 'Back' command provided by the navigator. The logic of what we were doing was sometimes lost in the excitement of new 'finds', and our memories became overloaded with the cognitive effort of making progressive, rapid associations. In our enthusiasm about the apparent wealth of information accessible, it was tempting to print out or download what seemed as though it might be useful, rather than run the risk of losing the sites and the pathway there (or collecting an endless list of 'bookmarks' along the way). Needless to say, the mass of reading and paper that results can be daunting and frustrating when it is found to be largely irrelevant. The compulsion to search that little bit more for the latest information from the most comprehensive sources is known to be a factor in the increasing stress associated with regular Internet use. We are guilty of this—what about you? Think about the implications of such haphazard and somewhat frantic collecting of information by children in educational settings.

Need for a search strategy

TABLE 7.4

ESSENTIALS OF USING THE INTERNET EFFECTIVELY

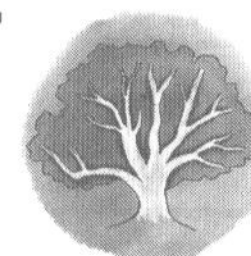

Search step	Things to consider
Reflect	■ Consider why you need to use the Internet as a resource. What is the purpose of the search? ■ List what is already known about the area of information being sought. ■ Choose the software that suits the location and type of information being sought. Is the search feasible?
Select keywords	■ Begin with broad general terms and refine concepts if there are too many locations. Narrow terms if necessary. ■ Develop lists of successful keywords. Use a thesaurus to find keywords.
Search	■ Be purposeful but be open to chance location of suitable information. ■ Internet searching is dynamic and can easily become random 'surfing'.

Retrieve	■	This involves locating, accessing, downloading, viewing and saving. Consider the cost of transfer and the storage medium.
Reflect	■	Is this the information that was being sought? Should the search continue? Are other resources likely to be more effective now?
	■	List useful locations with bookmarks.

(adapted with permission from Nanlohy & Howe 1996)

Electronic mail Electronic mail (**e-mail**) has proved to be one of the most popular first experiences for users of the Internet. Traditional mail is now referred to as 'snail mail' by e-mail users, a term that mocks the slowness of handwritten messages delivered by a postperson in comparison with those that are sent electronically. Already, in some schools, such as Reece High School in Devonport, Tasmania, students have their own individual e-mail accounts for communicating with each other locally, with other students across the world, and with their teachers. Through electronic mail, individuals can take part in discussion groups. Some participate silently by just reading the mail; others are more active and contribute to the ideas that emerge over time. In our experience, there can be some shyness about making such contributions if one feels an outsider; it is worth encouraging students to enter a group as many new opportunities can emerge.

One warning, however: e-mail can become very time-consuming as the immediacy of the comunication sets up expectations in the users that a response should follow the message very quickly. We have noticed in our workplace that some people feel obliged to check their e-mail as soon as they arrive in the office, while others have their e-mail 'open' as a window on their screen all day while they are working, so that new mail is announced the instant it arrives (sometimes with musical bells on it!).

MUDs and MOOs The term 'MUD' stands for vitual social space which many computer users can share and interact in simultaneously, thus its full name of Multi-User Domain or Multi-user Dimension. MUDs are also known as Multi-User Dungeons. This reference to 'dungeon' arose in the early days of computer game development because of the similarity between the kind of virtual place created by users in the present day MUDs and those of the pre-computer era game Dungeons and Dragons. In this game, a dungeon master created a magical world in which characters took on fictional roles and acted out exciting adventures in labyrinthes of mazes. Essentially, a MUD is a computer environment in which users play text-based games in 'real-time'—that is where there is no inbuilt delay between sending an electronic message and receiving a response from other players. It is a form of **Internet Relay Chat** (IRC), which literally allows people to 'chat' using their keyboard live across the Net (Lowe 1996). For the most part, MUDs are used for entertainment and provide an opportunity for highly developed social interaction. They allow and encourage the enactment of multiple identities on the computer screen in the context of games played in virtual worlds made up of words in cyberspace (Turkle 1995). MOOs (MUDs of the Object Oriented

'You're trying to contact who?'

variety) are a form of MUDs in which the players can metaphorically 'build' their own objects and architecture, such as a room in a house. To do this, they write their own set of commands for building their scene using the computer's (object-oriented) programming language capability (Turkle 1995).

In our explorations, we have found that access to MUDs and MOOs requires one to learn a set of programming instructions for how to communicate, as well as to agree to the code of ethics that has been developed for players logging on to the site. In fact, one such MOO created for children, *MOOSECrossing*, requires written consent forms signed by both child and parent to be sent by traditional post to the developer before access is granted.

MUDS, MOOS and imagination

While not apparently educational, IRC provides a platform for very personal styles of communication and authoring. Some would argue that, by encouraging uncensored, 'unstructured ramblings' (Lowe 1996), IRC channels on the Internet do not really produce communication of any real quality. Others would say, however, that MUDs and MOOs are environments in which users can be as creative as their imagination allows. Cyberion City, for example, is an educational cyberspace run by the MediaLab at MIT (Massachusetts Institute of Technology) in which children can jointly author extended stories on screen, interacting with other users to provide feedback as their stories progress (Kelly & Rheingold 1993; Spender 1995). We note that the recent educational MOO, *MOOSECrossing* (MediaLab, MIT, at **http://lcs.www.media.mit.edu/groups/el/elprojects.html**), aims to provide a learning environment in which children can construct a virtual world collaboratively while they develop their reading, writing and programming skills. It is also intended to provide a context in which girls may interact more readily with computers (Bruckman 1996; Bruckman & Resnick 1996). 'If the power of this (virtual reality) technology is to be unleashed, users need to be the creators and not merely the consumers of virtual worlds' (Bruckman & Resnick 1996, p. 221).

The MUD environment also allows for the exploration of human identity in a way that has not been possible before. There is a surrealism about some aspects of MUD life: Sherry Turkle, for example, relates an interview with an 18-year-old student who lives his life through multiple windows left open on his computer screen: physics homework on one window; sexual interactions with an unknown girl via a MUD on the second; a heated debate with someone on yet another MUD; and messages in real-time on the last window which he calls his least interesting, 'RL' (real-life) window (Turkle 1995). The potential of the MUD as a constructivist learning tool and learning environment for children and adults alike, appears strong.

Redefining oneself as a multiple system

The long-term use of Windows technology may encourage users to redefine themselves as a multiple system, distributed over many roles at the same time: a decentred self, any one version of which may be as 'real' as the others (Turkle 1995). From a psychological point of view, the roles people play on the screen may represent who they are or would like to be, or even be an outlet for enacting who they don't want to be. We wonder about the long-term effects of disembodied virtual experiences (even MUD weddings take place for those who cannot engage in real-life experiences!) on social and emotional development, especially during the adolescent period and **identity formation.** What is fascinating to contemplate is that, for many devoted players of such games, the distinction beween play and reality disappears: what is real is what is in the imagination and happening now.

ACTION STATION

Imagine you are in a setting where your students have a lab of networked computers, access to the Internet and electronic mail. Would you use such a technology-rich resource in the design of educational experiences for your students? If so, how would you prepare your students for the most efficient and educationally worthwhile use of the technology?

Question point: *What are your thoughts on the notion of children as programmers of their own virtual worlds?*

WORLD-WIDE INFORMATION NETWORKS AND MULTIMEDIA

Increasingly, value is placed by the present generation on the 'latest' information, rather than on knowledge that has stood the test of time (Spender 1995). With the easy access to the Net, there is the danger that only the most recently published material will be considered reliable and desirable. Future educators will need to avoid falling into the trap themselves, and take care to teach their students to be discriminating users of electronic information, evaluating it in the same way as they would the mass media.

One noted educational psychologist, Gavriel Salomon (1996), who has been concerned with the impact of technology on learning and teaching, anticipates a number of negative effects of the World Wide Web on education:

- ☐ Increased preference for undisciplined thinking based on associations of fragmented pieces of information, multimedia-like.
- ☐ Intellectual shallowness in the place of systematic and in-depth development of disciplined knowledge.
- ☐ A feeling of confusion in a sea of unorganised information which may become increasingly devalued.
- ☐ A growing sense of social alienation:

The Internet, ... the present day campfire around which we all gather once in a while to reiterate our shared culture, will now turn into a thousand, nay, a million separate and unrelated campfires with no center to hold them together. With each hobby club, interest group, collection of tennis or jeans lovers having their own Home Page, that is their own camp fire, alienation is likely to follow. (Salomon 1996, p.11)

Desktop videoconferencing

Despite the possible dangers of social alienation described above, **videoconferencing** from desktop computers will increasingly allow users to communicate in real-time to a person at the other end of their computerised connection, using moving pictures and sound (Lowe 1996). Videoconferencing has great potential in the distance education of children in remote areas, as did the earlier 'School of the Air', which based its communication on radio technology. Already, videoconferencing is being used in the United States by the Global Schoolhouse/Global SchoolNet Foundation (**http://www.gsn.org/gsn/cuseeme.schools.info.html**) to link both primary and secondary school students around the world so that they can collaborate on mutual projects (Fetterman 1996).

Learning and collaboration on the Net

The possibilities for collaborative, international research by both students and academics, via the Internet and videoconferencing, are now extensive. What is especially exciting is the ease with which material can be shared among members of a particular educational or research community, so that the focus of research is increasingly shifting from the publication of findings as if these were definitive, to the dynamic process of interaction. In fact, so strong is the belief in the importance of currency in some fields such as science that the print publication merely affirms one's recognition; being seen to be at the cutting-edge is critical, and is available only through the electronic information network (Spender 1995). The advantages to be gained through this type of interaction and collaboration apply to all levels of education.

ACTION STATION

a

The use of virtual worlds for teaching should be aimed at helping students function in their real-world, and the application to everyday life of what is learned through their virtual, distributed communities needs to be a focus of instructional design (O'Neil 1995). How might this be accomplished?

ACTION STATION

a

As an aspiring teacher or parent-to-be you should be aware of what is available commercially in the area of computer hardware and software. Visit a computer shop and find out:

1. What the latest computers can do that would make your teaching life easier in terms of lesson preparation and daily teaching tasks.
2. What types of software are available for children at various ages. Note down those that are designed to enhance student learning and those that are for entertainment. What about the range of applications that are available, such as spreadsheets, databases, word processors and creativity and productivity tools? Which of these have a place in your classroom? For what purpose?
3. Who are reputable educational software suppliers (try Microsoft, Dataflow or Edsoft, as well as Departments of School Education). Familiarise yourself with the range of software available. Perhaps you can form a group and organise a free demonstration. Present an information workshop to the rest of your class.

EFFECTIVE LEARNING AND TEACHING USING THE COMPUTER

As mentioned before, in educational circles, internationally, there has been a consistent movement away from behaviouristic approaches to learning and teaching to cognitive and sociocultural approaches (see Chapters 2, 4 and 5). This shift is paralleled by the ways in which many educators discuss the optimal use of the computer in the classroom, namely, that of a technological medium through which individuals can think and learn within their own individual representations of reality (O'Shea & Self 1983). The **pedagogical role of computers** is that which we will turn to next.

Lindsay Greig, coordinator of Carnarvon School of the Air, talks to a student by phone as he teaches.
Photo: WA Education News

Cooperative learning and the computer

Theoretically, the computer is an ideal medium for individualisation by adapting the pace of instruction to differing student needs, allowing for privacy, varying presentation modes, encouraging interactivity rather than passivity, and providing the potential to change instruction on the basis of individual performance. However, truly individualising instruction by creating 'intelligent' computer programs which can adapt curriculum to individual student needs is hugely expensive in terms of both money and time because of the complexity of programming involved (Carrier & Jonassen 1988). It is, therefore, not an option for most classrooms. The reality of the lack of sufficient computers for individual use in many Australian schools makes the collaborative use of the technology more likely and, perhaps, more valuable in terms of situating learning in a social context for cooperative task performance and **cooperative learning** (Murray 1988).

The importance of social interaction to learning

Computer-based peer-directed group work

The importance of social interaction for knowledge acquisition and cognitive development has been highlighted in Vygotsky's work (1978) and more recently by Perret-Clermont and Schubauer-Leoni (1989). (See also Chapter 2.) Furthermore, there are beneficial effects of computer-based peer-directed group work on student learning. In particular, verbalising planning and 'debugging' strategies to other group members, giving explanations, and making suggestions about what to input into the computer were shown to make significant contributions to learning during programming (LOGO and BASIC) activities (Webb & Lewis 1988).

Using cooperative learning software packages

The importance of mutuality and equality in problem solving

Cooperative learning through problem solving in small groups in which mutuality and equality are both high is particularly favourable to fostering learning (Collins et al. 1991; Damon & Phelps 1989). **Mutuality** refers to the degree of engagement between group members, which has an effect on the level of interaction achieved, whereas **equality** refers to the degree of equity between them. There are many so-called cooperative learning software packages on the market. However, unless their use is placed within a cooperative learning structure by the teacher, they may not function as anything more than just another small group activity where there can be loafers and free-riders who can lower the group's motivation to work and learn cohesively (Hooper 1992a; see Chapter 10). In other words, so-called cooperative learning software is not usually designed to foster positive interdependence of the group's members, nor to require individual accountability—and these are criteria that proponents of cooperative learning agree determine how effective the group's learning will be. Of course, much depends on the way in which the teacher structures the activity cooperatively.

Software and criteria for cooperative task structure

Given the research evidence for the beneficial effects on learning of computer-based cooperative grouping (Carrier & Sales 1987; Dalton, Hannafin & Hooper 1989; Hooper 1992b; Shlechter 1990), we consider it a worthy goal for the classroom teacher to search out software that fulfils the criteria for the cooperative task structures referred to above.

Of particular importance in the instructional use of technology is classroom discussion that centres on students' problem-solving approaches. Here the teacher should lead students to examine the decision-making processes they adopted during cooperative problem-solving activities. The teacher (or specialist experts) may model one approach and then encourage students to reflect on their own collective and individual performances. These can then be compared to broaden understanding of how different students and more expert performers solve the same problem (Collins, in Idol & Jones 1991).

Planning the use of instructional technology in a social context

Social interaction, peer tutoring and cooperative group work is easily promoted at the computer. Databases, simulations, LOGO, microworlds, word processing, desktop publishing and adventure games readily lend themselves to collaborative interaction. It is up to the teacher to plan carefully the use of the **instructional technology** within the context of desired learning outcomes for particular tasks, as these are derived from the social and academic values of cooperation. Ideally, the use of the technology in this way will be a natural part of a classroom in which learning is truly placed in its social context: children and teacher learn together and from each other. As discussed in Chapter 10, cooperative learning activities must be structured and students given guidance and training in what it means to 'cooperate' during an activity. In the initial stages of establishing cooperative learning structures, the teacher should act as model to demonstrate and reinforce the social and cognitive elements of communal interaction.

Social interaction promoted at the computer

Some software packages come with particular roles for children already defined, or with the interaction manipulated to varying degrees; many others, probably a preferable approach, allow teachers flexibility to adapt their use according to their goals. With greater experience of cooperative task performance and learning, students should increasingly be encouraged to design jointly their own strategies for the use of particular programs as tools for accomplishing specific learning tasks.

Social benefits of sharing computer equipment

Apart from the cognitive benefits of cooperative computer tasks, extensive qualitative research into computer use in primary classrooms in North America and Australia highlights the overwhelmingly competitive and individualistic use of computers (Gloet 1992), despite the reality of limited computer access in many schools which may require students to share the equipment. Such 'egocentric' use encourages the continued design of computer software which supports such teaching approaches.

Given the extensive research literature on the social benefits of cooperative classroom structures, such as heightened self-esteem, interdependence, empathy, improved interracial and interethnic relations, and enhanced peer group support (Hertz-Lazarowitz 1985; Kagan 1985; Slavin et al. 1985; Johnson & Johnson 1989a, 1989b, 1989c; Berrell 1993), it would appear beneficial to use computer equipment and programs in a cooperative way. Typically, teachers do not preplan and organise computing activities based along cooperative lines. Instead, their efforts are frequently absorbed by the need to instruct and monitor students in the mechanics of computing. Classroom interaction patterns do change in cooperative settings from those in teacher-dominated ones: teachers may express fears of losing classroom control when students are free to move around and talk, or of losing their traditional image as disseminator of knowledge. Pairing or grouping students is often the closest approximation to cooperative computer use, but this is merely collaboration and a far cry from cooperation. A range of classroom activities can be readily adapted to cooperative computer uses: group reports, computer conferencing, electronic penpal schemes, desktop publishing and small-group problem solving.

Question point: *You have just been appointed as the new principal of a small primary school or country high school. The previous principal ensured that there was one computer in each classroom, but no school policy on computer use exists. Teachers can choose how, when and if they want to use the computers. You feel that computers have an integral role in children's learning and should be used across the curriculum. What strategies will you use to implement your philosophy?*

ACTION STATION

Cooperative use of computers has been shown to have social and academic benefits for both boys and girls. Design a series of lessons for a particular grade that will require cooperative group work around the computer. Make your first plan for a one-computer classroom and the second for a computer laboratory of 15 machines. You will need to decide on the purpose of the learning task and the software that will facilitate cooperative interaction.

ACTION STATION

Despite otherwise harmonious cooperative relations in structured group-work activities, 'mouse war' (Miller & Olson 1995) can erupt among younger children who are required to take turns in pairs using the computer to input their ideas or to interact with a multimedia CD-ROM. Sometimes the dominant personality or more able student will take over, sometimes it will be the boy taking control away from the girl. What procedures would you put into place to ensure that 'mouse war' doesn't break out?

Recommended reading

Copen, P. (1995) Connecting classrooms through telecommunications. *Educational Leadership*, 53, 2, 44–7.

Fetterman, D. M. (1996) Videoconferencing on-line: Enhancing communication over the Internet. *Educational Researcher*, 25, 4, 23–7.

Foltz, P. W. (1996) Comprehension, coherence, and strategies in hypertext. In J. Rouet, J. Levonen, A. Dillon & R. J. Spiro (eds) *Hypertext and Cognition*. New Jersey: Lawrence Erlbaum.

Miller, L. & Olson, J. (1995) How computers live in schools. *Educational Leadership*, 53, 2, 74–7.

Papert, S. (1980) *Mindstorms: Children, Computers and Powerful Ideas*. Brighton, UK: Harvester.

Papert, S. (1993) *The Children's Machine. Rethinking School in the Age of the Computer*. New York: Basic Books.

Rogoff, B. (1995) Observing sociocultural activities on three planes: participatory appropriation, guided appropriation and apprenticeship. In J. V. Wertsch, P. Del Rio & A. Alverez (eds) *Sociocultural Studies of the Mind*. Cambridge: Cambridge University Press: 139–64.

Rouet, J. & Levonen, J. J. (1996) Studying and learning with hypertext: Empirical studies and their implications. In J. Rouet. J. Levonen, A. Dillon & R. J. Spiro (eds) *Hypertext and Cognition*. New Jersey: Lawrence Erlbaum.

Salomon, G., Perkins, D. N. & Globerson, T. (1991) Partners in cognition: Extending human intelligence with intelligent technologies. *Educational Researcher*, 20, 2–9.

Spender, D. (1995) *Nattering on the Net: Women, Power and Cyberspace*. North Melbourne: Spinifex Press.

Turkle, S. (1995) *Life on the Screen: Identity in the Age of the Internet*. New York: Simon and Schuster.

CHAPTER 8

Information technology: applications for effective teaching

OVERVIEW

Advertisements in the national media about the arrival of virtual reality entertainment and promotions in major metropolitan shopping malls fuel visions and fears of what sorts of experience young people will 'normally' have (or are already having) that serve to distance us (educators) and make us 'strangers in our own classrooms and in postmodern culture more generally' (see Green & Bigum 1993, p. 21). Will schools, as we know them, become 'effectively extinct' as a function of their lack of participation in the technological revolution? Or will schools of the future serve as havens from the assault of technology and its constant flux of electronically produced sounds and images (Sachs, Chant & Smith 1989)?

It would be foolish to suggest that most teachers use computer technology in their classroom let alone have expertise in the multiple uses to which it can be put. Nevertheless, there is little doubt that the present technological trends are destined to make a lasting impact on the way that teaching occurs in classrooms as we know them today. In Chapter 7 we examined a range of implications of information technology and the evidence for their value in enhancing learning. While recognising that learning can occur without direct teaching, in this chapter we consider the ways in which teachers can use computers and telecommunications to enhance their teaching and provide access to a greater range of students than might otherwise be possible.

THE COMPUTER AS A POSTMODERN 'OBJECT TO THINK WITH'

In the early days of personal computing the computer was seen as an object that you could understand if you were prepared to 'open the box', so to speak, and analyse the programming on which particular applications were based. For example, it was relatively easy to master a Microsoft-DOS-based word processing package if you spent time learning all the commands and typing them in: there was a logical, linear rule-driven style of design. With the growing popularity of the Macintosh approach to computing, however, the mechanical aspects of computing became increasingly hidden. The user was presented with a surface layer of 'icons' which visually represented or simulated the tools that underlay its workings, and a 'mouse' which allowed the user to access the various tools by using an arrow icon to track their physical movements on screen. Today, this style of human-computer interaction has evolved into a 'culture of simulation' (Turkle 1995) where the mechanics of computing are hidden and there is, as a result, greater freedom to extend the workings of the mind as well as one's physical presence across distances. It also represents the **postmodern** philosophy that understanding of the self and the social world is not possible—certainly not by reducing the complex to the simple as in the modernist belief of looking analytically and logically 'inside the box' of what is to be understood.

What has all this to do with education? Where, previously, the 'educational' use of computing was limited to those students and their teachers who wished to learn how to program the computer (largely within the physical sciences and mathematics), the present-day computer with its access to multiple 'windows' encourages a focus on functional use and exploratory learning, even though the MS-DOS operating system is still accessible beneath the iconic surface of the new Windows programs. Increasingly, therefore, students and teachers are engaging in the use of a wide range of programs that encourage great interactivity and exploration.

Truly, the computer has become a constructionist object to think with.

CLASSROOM APPLICATIONS OF COMPUTERS

Multimedia software

Reference software

Reference software, such as the *ENCARTA* annual encyclopaedia and atlas, and the *Australian Infopedia*, which contains the Macquarie Dictionary and Thesaurus as well as an encyclopaedia of Australia, allows students access to a wide variety of information presented in dynamic visual and

Will computers as personal resources replace traditional pens and paper at school? Photo: McKenzie & Associates P/L

aural forms. Personal construction of knowledge for specific purposes is fostered by such resources.

Hypermedia authoring packages

Hypermedia authoring packages, based on scripting or programming languages, allow users to design their own hypermedia with tools such as *Toolbook* (for Windows), *HyperCard* (for Macintosh) and Linkway (for MS-DOS).

Interactive adventure games

Interactive adventure games, like *Myst*, foster the development of problem-solving skills through totally unguided exploration. *Myst* does not come with a set of rules; it is for the users to discover the secrets of the deserted island from clues they pick up and explore: magical maps, segments of books, and hidden rooms. Simulations such as *SimCity* and *SimLife* are also examples of open-ended, problem-solving games where users construct their cities or their life forms by taking into account a range of complex, interrelated factors (as in the 'real' world), such as population, traffic, disease and climate.

'Edutainment'

'Edutainment', or interactive educational games like the *Reader Rabbit* (K-3) series, Treasure MathStorm (1–3), and the Where in the World is Carmen Sandiego? series teach various concepts in the context of adventure games and playlike formats. Interactive stories, like those in the Living Book series (Just Grandma and Me, Arthur's Teacher Trouble, the Tortoise and the Hare), allow children to hear the words being spoken as they read along, and to interact with pictures on the screen by clicking on various parts.

Interactive stories

Productivity and presentation software

Productivity tools such as those in *Microsoft Office, Lotus Smartsuite* or *ClarisWorks* include a word processor, spreadsheet and database to assist with business work. Some schools have based their whole curriculum around the use of such business software, believing that 'educational' software is second-rate compared with that designed for business, and that high school students should be equipped for the future by incorporating these tools into their everyday learning across all curriculum areas. An instance of such school-wide adoption is that of Trinity Grammar in Kew, Melbourne, a boys' school, where the Principal undertook in 1993 to ensure that his students had access to the high quality, Windows-based *Microsoft Office* software that was used in business. To support its school-wide adoption, all teachers were provided with a computer and professional development courses at no charge. It was felt that such an approach would minimise the resistance-to-change attitude that emerges out of a perceived need to 'survive' in teaching, as well as communicating that if teachers did not develop proficiency with the new technology, they would be ill-prepared for their teaching in the public eye. This was an effective strategy, as most teachers pride themselves on being well prepared (Crawley 1996).

Presentation software

Presentation software such as *HyperStudio, Kid Pix Studio* and *PowerPoint* allows users to create their own presentations, incorporating a range of media (video, sound, graphics, animation and text) and designing these to appear with special effects such as fade-ins and time-delay, as they wish.

Graphics, painting and design software (*SuperPaint, TruboCAD, Flying Colors*) takes the tedium out of drawing, painting and designing images. This powerful software presents the user with professional-looking finished products while demanding little computer expertise.

The future: Newton 'pen-down' technology, Newton e-Mate

Apple Computers has designed a new Newton, the *e-Mate 300*, which retains the features of the original hand-held appliance (i.e. its portability and the ability to write on the screen with a stylus) but adds a keyboard, touch screen and the facility to draw directly on the screen. With the additional use of multimedia and access information tools, the *e-Mate 300* has been specifically targeted for educational use, as their press release states:

> ***Apple's support of the 'distributed learning environment' concept is based on its commitment to four critical elements of successful learning: information access, wherever it resides; communication and collaboration with other students, teachers, experts, anytime and anywhere; multisensory tools that facilitate diverse learning styles, creativity and understanding; and access to personal learning materials—books, supplies and technologies.*** *(Apple Computer 1996).*

In addition, the *e-Mate 300* has taken the needs of children's use into account: it is both lightweight and small enough to fit into a backpack, and durable enough to take sudden impact, being encased in a thick plastic 'clamshell' reinforced with a steel frame and suspension mounted. Sounds like they've thought of everything, doesn't it?

The games people play

The wealth of software available today, packaged as computer games for home education, reinforces what educators have known for a long time—that learning can emerge from play; in some games there are no apparent rules, so the only way to learn how to play them is through the process of immersion in the game. This is an example of the role of **discovery** in learning and the principle of inductive reasoning, where individuals construct hypotheses or rules from examples collected from their experiences.

Even kindergarten children today are encouraged to engage in exploratory play with specially designed software such *as Paint, Write and Play, Reader Rabbit* (The Learning Company) *and Millie's Math House* (Dataflow).

The challenge exists for both teachers and parents to understand the nature of these games and evaluate whether they are truly educational or just gimmicky and attractively presented to appeal to children and to sell.

EDUCATIONAL USES OF COMPUTERS

From the educator's perspective, computer software exists to enhance a large range of pedagogical functions that are relevant to the classroom teacher (Vockell & Schwartz 1992). A number of these are summarised below.

Mastery learning and direct instruction

The theory of mastery learning maintains that, given enough time and effective instruction, most students can master learning objectives (Guskey & Gates 1986). The appropriate selection of computer software can provide those students who require it with the extra help and practice needed to master the objectives, as well as enrichment and stimulation for those who reach their learning goals early. If teachers clearly specify the learning objectives to students, demonstrate with examples and non-examples, provide guided practice, and give feedback and correctives as in Rosenshine's (1986) direct instruction model, effective learning of basic skills can occur. Computer-based tutorial programs that can also promote such learning should adopt this model.

Direct instruction

Basic facts and skills need to be practised past the stage of mastery (overlearned) in order for them to be accessed automatically. Tutorial (games) software can be used to give students self-paced, individualised practice in particular skills while maintaining their motivation and interest where otherwise practice might become boring.

Overlearning

Peer tutoring and cooperative learning

Research shows that in peer tutoring interactions there are social and cognitive benefits for both tutor and pupil (Magolda & Rogers 1987). Computer programs can be used to facilitate peer tutoring when student-tutors are trained in the skills of effective tutoring, such as speaking clearly, telling tutees when they are right, correcting mistakes, praising good work, and recording the lesson outcomes (Sulzer-Azaroff & Mayer 1986). The research of Alison King (1990) on reciprocal questioning and the development of metacognition through peer tutoring is a good example of such computer use (see also Chapter 5).

There is much evidence of the advantages of cooperative learning structures over those that are competitive and individualistic (Johnson & Johnson 1975). It is important to provide opportunities for students to work in cooperative groups at computers, as well as to find programs that promote cooperation. Of course, students will need guidelines for cooperative roles at computers, and monitoring by the teacher to ensure effective interaction is taking place.

Cooperative learning

Monitoring student progress

Monitoring of student progress enables students, teachers and parents to identify the strengths and weaknesses of learners. There are several record-keeping programs that are effective for recording student progress.

Behavioural theory has demonstrated the power of feedback that comes quickly after a response. To establish confidence and motivation in areas that are weak, or to develop basic skills in some areas, computer programs that provide immediate and corrective feedback are effective.

Providing immediate feedback

Facilitating learning

As discussed elsewhere in this book, students differ widely in their preferred learning environments and styles of learning (Dunn, Beaudry & Klavas 1989) (see Chapter 11). There may be advantages for some students in presenting material via programs that match their preferred learning style. Especially where teachers' teaching styles do not coincide with the ways in which some students learn best, using multimedia programs and hypermedia authoring tools (such as HyperCard) may be particularly beneficial ways of accommodating individual differences.

Learning styles

Just as higher-level thinking skills and meta-cognition can be fostered through the teacher's use of higher-order questions and sufficient wait-time (at least three seconds), computer programs that include higher-level questions or prompts can achieve the same result. It is important to select software that has these features, such as the Computer-supported Intentional Learning Environment developed by Scardamalia et al. (1989) or the Reading Partner (Salomon et al. 1989).

Teacher questions

Programs that provide 'concrete' examples of topics being dealt with by the classroom teacher can enhance student understanding. In the context of science, computer simulations and graphics are ideal tools. Furthermore, database applications can encourage students to make hypotheses, and collect and record data that may answer their particular research questions. As for mathematics, there is an increasing number of software programs that claim to deliver quality education while maintaining the fun. For younger learners, these programs place mathematical concepts in the context of adventure games. For the adolescent and young adult learner, programs are designed to encourage the user to 'explore and learn' without the mental effort of performing calculations or drawing maps, which are done automatically by the program.

Learning mathematics and science

Much has been written about the advantages of using word processors as a tool for writing. Bangert-Drowns (1993) has examined the question of whether the word processor can enable students to learn new skills from their partnership with this specialised writing device. In doing so, he reviewed 32 studies that examined the effects of the word processor as an instructional tool. In each of these, two groups received identical writing instruction initially but only one group was allowed to use the word processor to complete their writing assignments. On the basis of his analyses, Bangert-Drowns concludes that word processing:

Word processing and writing

- ☐ frees the writer from the mechanical concerns of poor handwriting, corrections and spelling, thereby encouraging a more fluid conceptualisation of text;
- ☐ improves the quality of written work, especially for weak writers—that is, those who had previously demonstrated difficulty with writing (this effect was apparent for both short-term and long-term exposure to the word processor, suggesting that there was a strong, positive *motivational* impact on the user);
- ☐ encourages the writing of longer documents.

Australian longitudinal research supports these claims. A detailed investigation over a school year, comparing two classes of year 8 girls who received the same form of genre-based writing instruction (narrative, argument and report) from the same teacher, but who used either pen or word processor for the completion of their written work, found that for the writing of argument and report texts, significantly higher quality was associated with word processors rather than pens (Snyder 1993). Why was this so?

It was found that the teaching/learning contexts differed significantly in quality between the two groups. In the computing context the teacher acted more as 'expert learner' in a learning community, one who modelled the learning process; and as a facilitator, adviser and editor in a student-centred classroom. In the non-computing context, on the other hand, learning was teacher-directed and more time was spent actually teaching the genre-based writing strategies. Students seemed to be less intensely engaged in the writing process compared with those in the computer context where, overall, the development of a more interactive cooperative and collaborative atmosphere was observed.

In summary, the evidence is clearly in favour of using the word processor for developing writing skills and quality texts, particularly those that require the student to conceptualise, synthesise and abstract ideas (Snyder 1993). Seen from a constructivist perspective, using the computer as a writing tool changes the traditional writing instruction to one of greater student independence and initiative, mediated by a skilled teacher and peers—a Vygotskian (dialectical) approach to learning. Furthermore, it encourages greater spontaneous collaboration and cooperation between peers in the writing process as a function of the 'public nature of computer writing' (Snyder, p. 21).

The management of teaching

We have spoken at length about the potential for the use of the computer to enhance student learning and as a pedagogical tool. What about its use as a tool to facilitate the management of teaching? The amount of classroom time available for learning is determined to a great extent by the teacher's instructional and management skills. Teachers with efficient management skills have more time to devote to teaching than those who lack these skills.

Many management functions can be handled effectively by computers, thereby freeing the teacher from numerous non-instructional tasks. For example:

- ☐ keeping records of student progress;
- ☐ drafting and keeping a record of individualised correspondence to students and parents;
- ☐ keeping attendance records;
- ☐ maintaining inventories of classroom equipment and materials;
- ☐ designing tests, answer sheets, worksheets and individualised learning contracts;
- ☐ producing posters, calendars and class awards;
- ☐ generating student reports to parents.

Schools and the Internet

Increasingly, schools around Australia and New Zealand are being connected to the Internet and are even setting up their own Web pages. One of the first in Australia to do so was the City Beach Senior High School, Perth, which can be located at the following Internet address:

http://www.citybeach.wa.edu.au. The school has published an extensive Weblist for teachers which provides immediate links to educational (and some not so obviously 'educational') sites in Australia and overseas (we found, for example, The Simpsons, Triple J radio station, the Science Museum of London, the Houses of Parliament, Mathematics on the Web, Virtual School, and the Global Schoolhouse). We recommend that you take a look yourself as it is regularly updated. Other excellent Australian sources can be found at the *Aussie SchoolHouse/oz-TeacherNet* (**http://www.ash.org.au**) and *BushNet* (**http://www.bushnet.qld.edu.au**). Both have extensive networks in place and *Bush Net* has even developed a BushMOO to encourage social interaction and rudimentary programming experience for primary school children in remote areas.

SCHOOLS, CLASSROOMS AND MULTIMEDIA

In Chapter 7, we discussed the use of multimedia and hypermedia software in terms of student learning. We described the commercially produced multimedia information packages that are commonly used in schools. There is also available what is known as *presentation software* which allows the user to create multimedia information 'stacks' that can include the spoken word (via microphone), music, photographics, videos and text. This type of software provides the 'interactivity' in learning that we have referred to so often in this book. In other words, it is the students (preferably in cooperative learning groups that have received guiding principles from their teacher) who take charge of their own learning, making it relevant and personal. Using multimedia presentation software, therefore, students, rather than the program designer, have the option and potential for exerting control, both in the design and in the delivery of the presentation (Dockterman 1991). The most effective use of hypermedia and multimedia tools is for the teacher to put them into the hands of students themselves while providing the instructional scaffolding that will enable them to create their own materials.

Multimedia and individual learning styles

It is frequently cited in the promotional literature accompanying multimedia software that it provides a means of adapting instruction to individual learning styles (see also Chapter 11). This is true to the extent that those who respond more readily to visual and auditory presentations of information are better catered for than if forced to learn from print alone. Some learners like a faster pace while others like (or need) to take their time. In the context of how computers can improve learning by accommodating individual differences in learning styles, Geisert and Dunn (1991) have designed a program ('*Thinking Networks*') to teach reading and writing to students who are achieving poorly in these areas. Their program is based on earlier findings that students learn new and difficult material when it is introduced through their primary sensory strength (auditory, visual or tactual), and then *reinforced* through their secondary or tertiary modality. *Thinking Networks* is based on the whole-language approach and is designed to be particularly responsive to global thinkers by incorporating non-verbal graphic features such as 'maps' or semantic networks to help them develop holistic models of various styles of writing such as narrative, sequential or content-specific. To date, the results of this program for significantly improving the reading comprehension and writing skills of low achievers have been very positive, especially when employed consistently over a period of time. The difficulty faced by the classroom teacher in choosing the 'right' software for all students and curriculum needs becomes very real if one takes the evidence from such research to indicate that all learners would benefit from multimedia software. The best advice is to avoid falling into the trap of believing that computers in the classroom are *the* answer to true individualisation. As we have said elsewhere in this book, provide a variety of activities and resources, and present new information in a variety of forms so that all students can benefit in some ways.

One warning, however: as stated above, multimedia presentations have been touted as the best method for involving students through all their senses. It is certainly true, in theory at least, that students have the option of interacting with the material through whichever (sensory) path they choose. Research on cognitive style suggests that not all students would benefit from such freedom. Impulsive students, for example, will be tempted to rush around, getting lost in the mass of detail in the information. These children tend to look at the big picture, and perform better on tasks that require global interpretations; in multimedia there is no 'big picture'. Reflective children, on the other hand, do better when required to analyse details.

USING COMPUTERS TO ENHANCE CONSTRUCTIVE LEARNING

If learning is to be truly constructive, then teachers must evaluate their teaching practices to ensure that they support student construction of knowledge. The 'What would you do' box looks at the efforts of one teacher to design a constructive learning environment in which computers can play an authentic part.

The role of the computer in teaching

As you can see from George's experience and from earlier discussions in this chapter, there are many roles that teachers must play to incorporate computer technology effectively into their teaching. We suggest the most important ones in Table 8.1. Are there others you can think of?

TABLE 8.1

ROLES TEACHERS PLAY INCORPORATING COMPUTER TECHNOLOGY EFFECTIVELY INTO THEIR TEACHING

Planner

- Considers the place of computer software in relation to educational aim
- Establishes clear purpose for computer use
- Allocates time at the computer

Facilitator

- Contributes prior knowledge
- Researches the quality of available software
- Ensures appropriate focus on the software

Manager

- Negotiates with relevant experts to provide support for novices and for technical difficulties
- Ensures all students have appropriate access to resources

Guide

- Asks key questions
- Coordinates student efforts
- Helps but doesn't 'tell'
- Oversees student collaboration
- Structures effective group work
- Motivates and remotivates as necessary

Model

- Confident
- Encouraging
- Flexible
- Sensitive
- Humorous

(*adapted from* The role of the teacher in computer education. *Computers in Education Development Unit, Department of Education, Wellington, New Zealand 1987*)

Computers as school resource

Not only is the variety of computer uses considerable in Australian and New Zealand schools today, but access to computers is also very variable. Some schools have a small number of computers that are shared by classes (wheeled around on trolleys) on a rostered basis. Others have all their computers in a central laboratory where classes are brought to work on projects or to receive 'doses' of computer instruction (Loader & Nevile 1993). Fortunate schools have both. These variations on computer access are based on the model of the computer as a *school* resource.

WHAT WOULD YOU DO?

SETTING UP AN EFFECTIVE COMPUTER LEARNING ENVIRONMENT

George has been teaching geography at a private girls' school in a large city for two years, his first appointment since he completed his teacher training. While he has not used computers much himself, he feels that he would like to incorporate information technology into his teaching to make his lessons more meaningful and challenging, and less a matter of the students just learning information given. The school has a lab of 15 networked computers with access to the Internet, a stand-alone computer on a mobile trolley, and a laptop and modem available to staff for home borrowing.

Before he begins planning, he asks the students in each of his classes to tell him if and how they use computers. Their answers range from no computer use at all, through games at home and CD-ROM reference use in the school library, to regular Internet explorations for assignments.

How might George incorporate computer use into his teaching with such a mixture of expertise among the students?

Computers as personal learning resource

A strikingly different model is exemplified in a school like the Methodist Ladies' College in Melbourne where the goal is for every student to have a computer as a *personal* resource (Loader 1997). Every student at the school from years 4 to 12 is required to own her own laptop computer. At present, there are 1200 laptops and 300 additional desktop computers.

Why encourage such a huge investment in terms of financial, psychological and energy expenditure? The philosophy underlying the MLC Laptops across the School Project was one in which computers were seen as merely resources for enhancing the process of teaching and learning, as common and indispensable as pencil and paper, but not objects of study themselves. The project initiators stressed the important role of the computer as a very personal learning tool; not in the sense of enabling the student to be more productive and efficient, which is the business metaphor often used for the computer, but, rather, 'as a convivial tool with which (they) can develop their personal knowledge' (Loader & Nevile 1993, p. 31). This personal knowledge must necessarily be idiosyncratic as 'what is "knowledge" for one person may not be for another' (p. 31). Thus, the advantage of the laptop to the student is seen to be its personal nature and portability.

Question point: *What are the advantages and disadvantages of laptops across a school? Consider the perspectives of parents, students and teachers. Does it make a difference whether it is primary or high school?*

GENDER DIFFERENCES IN SCHOOL COMPUTING

Considerable research over the past decade has shown that females have less self-confidence and greater anxiety about their ability with computers, irrespective of their actual levels of achievement, than do males (Chen 1986). Attitudinal differences are not related to a perception by girls that computers are a sex-typed domain (Durndell et al. 1995). The lack of willingness by girls to engage in computing activities at school may be attributable to the influence of the peer group in socialising males and females towards different interests. Boys are more likely to report that skill with computers is a source of respect from friends and parents (Chen 1986), and tend to hold more strongly sex-stereotyped views about computer use than do girls (Yelland 1995).

In an early Australian study of primary school children, Clarke (1987) found that, for girls, the perceived attitudes of parents and **peer group interest** were the most important predictors of initial interest in learning computing. Even after a substantial period of experience with classroom computing, extrinsic reinforcement from peers and parents remained an important influence in their final interest.

Ensuring equity

Appropriate experiences for boys and girls

For classroom practices to ensure equity, it may be inadequate to suggest that teachers should simply provide the same experiences for boys and girls in the (maths, science and computing) classroom, but, rather, that they adjust classroom activities and teaching methods to accommodate the differences in customary behaviour patterns of boys and girls. Evidence exists which shows that boys are more likely to have their own computers than girls and to use them more outside school.

Girls and LOGO

LOGO-based activities have been cited as best advancing girls in computer learning because of their interactive nature and potential for collaborative use, which girls reputedly prefer (Johnson, Johnson & Stanne 1986; Sanders & Stone 1986). Louie (1985), for example, found that after LOGO word processing experience in groups, students' (aged 9 to 15) level of internalised locus of control increased, which is associated with feelings of

WHAT WOULD YOU DO?

SETTING UP AN EFFECTIVE COMPUTER LEARNING ENVIRONMENT (continued)

George decided to take the laptop and modem home each weekend for four weeks and try out a bundle of CD-ROMs that he received 'on approval' from an educational software distributor. He also experimented with the Internet and had a 'surf' around, exploring what was available. Before he did this, however, he arranged for a private tutorial with the school's computer coordinator to get her to show him how to connect to the World Wide Web.

On the basis of his homework, George decided to design a series of topics from which pairs of students could choose to research and present to the class. Double periods would be allocated each week for four weeks to allow students to rotate through three activities: work in the computer lab in pairs to conduct their Web search, to explore possible databases and collect suitable information (after brainstorming ideas and planning their search strategy in class); library research using CD-ROM references (encyclopaedia and atlas) as well as text material; and classwork time for collaboration with other students and the teacher on the progress of their work. In this class time, George also planned to work with groups of six students at a time around the mobile computer, addressing such issues as how they will become part of a virtual community using e-mail to talk to other students in remote sites: would they set up a geography discussion group themselves, or find a school with whom they could become 'e-mail pals'?

George planned to use those students within the class with greatest computer proficiency to act as peer tutors for those who were relatively inexperienced. What he aimed to do later in the year was to get all the girls to contribute in some way to a virtual school such as Aussie SchoolHouse or the Global Schoolhouse. In the meantime, he was going to join a teacher network (oz-TeacherNet) so that he could ask virtual colleagues to share their experiences with him and act as guide along the way.

Can you see any problems in implementing George's plans?

We feel that the first thing George should consider is what he wants to achieve by using technology: how does it fit with his personal beliefs about teaching, and what limitations will the curriculum place on his ambitions? These will influence the second consideration—how he chooses to use computers. Evidence shows that teachers' prior practice determines what they use technology for rather than the technology leading them into new ways of teaching (Miller & Olson 1995).

self-confidence, self-esteem and achievement. In a more recent study, Clements and Nastasi (1988) found that (for first and third grade children) paired training in LOGO programming produced a significantly higher percentage of problem-solving behaviours than did the drill-and-practice treatment (in aspects of the reading and arithmetic curriculum), as well as a higher occurrence of behaviour that indicated **metacognitive processing.** In terms of enhancing the ability to be self-directed (believing that one is in control and able to effect change in one's environment), the evidence from this study was that the LOGO group showed a greater frequency (six times more) of such metacognitive behaviour than the drill-and-practice group. This was measured as working independently of adult direction, showing persistence and determining rules. Fostering metacognitive skills of this kind for girls may well be the key to reducing gender differences in the interest, self-confidence and achievement in computing activities, especially by developing their independence and adaptive abilities.

Single-sex versus co-ed classes

With regard to computing, single-sex classes have been suggested as remedies for the access difficulties experienced by girls in co-educational classes so that 'girls can claim a fair share of teachers' time, discussion, questioning and presenting of ideas as well as access to equipment and resources, in an environment where they are not harassed or denigrated by boys' (p. 63, Education for Girls, 1985). In her report on the Girls and Computing Project in South Australia, Reimann (1985), for example, wrote that the self-esteem of girls placed in a single-sex class for English and social science lessons using computers (word processor and database) increased while that of girls in a mixed class markedly decreased. Similarly, those in the latter group reported fewer opportunities for involvement in class activities and for being able to use their initiative. This was despite apparently equitable access to computers for both genders, as reported by the teachers.

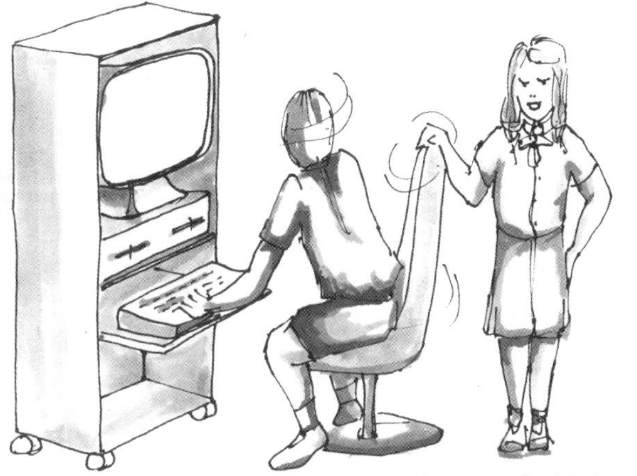

'Excuse me! I believe this is the "girls-only" time slot! It is my turn.'

It is important to keep in mind that such segregation should be adopted only as a short-term measure (Moore 1986; Sanders & Stone 1986). The question of what degree and types of computer experiences girls need in order to establish a firm perception of their self-efficacy, one that will not be influenced by mixed-sex contact later, must also be considered carefully.

Teachers clearly need to be sensitive to computer access problems and to be aware of harassment, inequitable student participation, and withdrawal, which may be passive and easy to overlook.

Boys have been observed to monopolise computer use in schools, sometimes by bullying or belittling girls' accomplishments: 'Is that *all* you can do?'

TABLE 8.2

ESSENTIALS OF OVERCOMING ACCESS AND EQUITY PROBLEMS IN COMPUTING

For teachers

- Be aware of sexist, cultural and racial bias in software and computer literature.
- Monitor classroom computer interaction, access and participation.
- Involve girls in problem-solving tasks with the computer rather than tutorial packages or tasks that merely involve recall.
- Begin computing activities with girls at an early age (at beginning of primary school) to avoid sex stereotyping, and maintain continuous involvement to increase mastery.
- Organise furniture in computing areas so that desks are equally close to teacher for help, and conducive to group discussion.
- Select 'neutral' software that can be used equally by both genders in different ways to accomplish different individual goals (i.e. adapted to individual interests).
- Use LOGO-based activities collaboratively.
- Extend the use of the computer across the curriculum, especially in traditionally female subject areas (e.g. English) and those that are not gender-specific (e.g. social studies and music).
- Use computers in a practical, purposeful way, making use of graphics, word processing and spreadsheets; for example, the design and printing

Should girls work with other girls rather than with boys when using computers? Photo: authors

of a school newspaper or the creation and maintenance of files for sport teams will demonstrate the utility of the computer as a tool.

- Invite women in computing careers to talk to girls about career options.

For administrators

- Locate computers in easily accessible positions such as libraries and multipurpose work areas.
- Encourage female staff members to attend computer training courses in release time from school.
- Hold all-female inservice sessions for beginning computer training.
- Allow staff to borrow laptop computers overnight and at weekends and ensure that a contact resource person is available for solving problems. This will enable them to work at their own pace and build up confidence by making their mistakes in private.
- Organise computer open days/nights where all students can introduce and coach parents in computer use.
- Provide parents with access to computers after school or borrowed to take home.

a

ACTION STATION

During an extended practice teaching period, record gender differences in computer use. Consider the following issues:

1. Do girls and boys prefer different types of computing activities?
2. If given a choice, do they prefer to work individually, in (same-sex?) pairs or in small groups?
3. How does the teacher interact with the boys and the girls during computing activities?
4. Does access to the computers vary according to gender?
5. What strategies does the school have in place to ensure equity of computer use?

Record your findings in report form. What recommendations for action would you make on the basis of your findings?

Note: You could conduct the same type of research focusing instead on cultural background and ethnicity. Do these factors influence computer use at school? Remember to consider both compulsory and voluntary activities.

SPECIAL LEARNING NEEDS AND TECHNOLOGY

There are many ways in which computer-based technology can help overcome educational disadvantages such as physical or behavioural disablement. The special learning needs of gifted students can also be met by many current 'open-ended' software packages (e.g. applications such as authoring programs, desktop publishing, hypertext/hypermedia and simulations). Technology can provide the means for students with a wide range of special needs to have greater control over their own learning and to progress at their own pace

Children with special learning needs can experience so much more through computer tools such as the concept keyboard. Photo: Special Needs I.T.

with a degree of anonymity. Those who would otherwise be inhibited by the possibility of publicly making mistakes, as in face-to-face learning, are more likely to take risks when working with computers, thereby developing both intellectually and personally. Even students who cannot speak or write can now learn to communicate via the computer; visually impaired students can access information by computers linked to **speech synthesisers** and **braille printers**; and those with hearing impairments can develop language skills through computers linked to videodisks. The benefits to all learners with disabilities in terms of self-confidence, self-esteem and self-image arise from the greater independence and autonomy that they can experience through computers and appropriate software.

TEACHER'S CASE BOOK

HELPING LEARNING-DISABLED CHILDREN WITH COMPUTERS

Geoff, aged 5, has cerebral palsy. He does not talk. For the first six months of his schooling, Geoff cried constantly. He would not participate in any of the class activities or interact with any of the staff or other children. Near desperation, the teacher introduced Geoff to the computer. She showed Geoff that by touching the concept keyboard (a flat A3-size board), a picture of a tree or a boat would appear on the screen. She waited. Slowly, Geoff's hand reached out to touch the concept keyboard. He looked at the screen. He smiled. Success at last! The staff were in tears. The computer had been successful in facilitating Geoff's first smile and response.

Geoff continues to enjoy the computer sessions. According to his teacher, Geoff tries to communicate with her and the other children. He even takes her hand, indicating that he wants her to touch the keyboard. Next, the teacher wants to try a micro-mike to encourage Geoff to verbalise.

Brian (aged 15) writes to a female penpal in England, who is also physically disabled, using electronic mail. Because of his physical problems, Brian initially produces his letter on the word processor. The teacher then helps him to activate the modem. Through his writing, Brian states that he has discovered some interesting facts about England (such as the difference in time and season compared with Tasmania).

Case study reported by Cuthbert (1988)

Case study activity
Highlight the powerful impact of computer use for the special needs of these two disabled children.

FACTORS RESTRICTING THE ADOPTION OF TECHNOLOGY

Given the range of computer uses outlined in this chapter and Chapter 7, why is it that the majority of teachers are not using computer technology in the classroom, even when it is available?

There is a range of reasons. The origins of educational computing in Australia were somewhat elitist, the driving force behind the push for technology in schools coming from (mostly male) specialist computer teachers who were often untrained in its use but who were themselves computer hobbyists or graduates of computer science courses. Many of these teachers have now reached managerial positions within educational systems, where they are now in a position to influence major policy (Adams 1992).

Inexperience and anxiety

Lack of teacher familiarity and training in the use of technology tends to limit its impact on students' lives in school settings. While those involved in computing policy and consultancy positions may be highly experienced and confident, the average classroom teacher is, for the most part, inexperienced and lacks formal training in the use of technology, except, perhaps, for word-processing applications. Such unfamiliarity with technology may be both real and perceived.

Research (Heller and Martin 1987), for example, shows that even after formal training in the use of computers teachers still regard themselves as beginners. This study reported that of 495 teachers using computers in their first year, *all* exhibited the *non-user* profile. Although these teachers were actually using the computers, their personal concerns about the new technology outweighed their concerns about implementing the innovation in their classrooms. These personal concerns existed universally irrespective of years of teaching experience, amount of computer training or level of use of microcomputers in classroom instruction. Similar concerns were found among Australian teachers who were in the early stages of introducing computers into their teaching (Sinclair & McKinnon 1987). Uncertainty and adequacy in coping with the demands of the innovation were among the highest-rated areas of concern.

Such findings may not be surprising given the rapidity of technological change and the 'panic' induced by media and industry spokespeople about redundancy of equipment and teaching approaches (Tobias 1993). Many teachers feel that they must respond to technology as a 'given', rather than something over which they have influence. Government educational authorities are increasingly modelling such an approach in their planning for teacher training in using technology. The TILT (Technology in Learning and Teaching) initiative of the NSW Department of School Education is one example of an attempt to expand the expertise of cohorts of teachers who are not currently using technology in their classrooms. Despite such efforts to expand the use of technology in schools, some teachers may make the choice to turn a blind eye to using information technology altogether, because it is too time-consuming to design learning experiences based around computer software with which they are relatively unfamiliar, and which is being constantly updated and becoming more complex.

Teacher workload

Teachers are very busy people. They do not have a great deal of time to explore, let alone evaluate, new hardware and software packages, or to begin to think creatively about how to incorporate them into their daily teaching lives. Nor are they sufficiently qualified to do so. Rather than risk failing with technology in the public eye and in their self-estimation, they are more likely to resist the temptation and pressure to be liberated, and to stay with what already seems to be working (Cooley 1992). Alternatively, many simply restrict computer use to what are fairly safe word-processing packages for writing activities, and games that students can operate themselves either for entertainment (reward) purposes, or as motivating babysitting activities that free the teacher for tasks such as marking or preparing lessons.

Question point: *The Parents and Citizens Association at your high school has just voted to direct any future fundraising efforts towards playground renovation and beautification (removing asphalt, planting trees for shade and environmental reasons, etc.). The staff, however, have a strong commitment to updating the computer equipment and networking if possible. They need the financial support of the energetic P & C Association. As head computer coordinator, what will you do?*

ACTION STATION

Imagine that you have one computer with access to the World Wide Web in your classroom (the national average) and that you are programming your teaching at the beginning of a new year. Devise a range of ways in which you would incorporate the computer into the learning experiences of your class: in infants, primary or high school subjects.

LEARNING AND THE FUTURE—A FINAL SCENE

How much has computer technology infiltrated and radically altered our lives over just the last decade? Are there many of us in Western society who do not know about, or use, automatic bank-teller machines or EFTPOS outlets to pay our bills, for example? Home fax and photocopying machines, modems, cellular car phones, answering machines, pagers, digital watches and clocks, programmable microwave and conventional ovens, dishwashers and video machines, Sega and Nintendo electronic games are commonplace in a great number of middle-class homes in Australia and New Zealand today. Do we stop and think about the ways in which changes in technology are shaping our daily domestic, educational and professional lives? Don't we, as educators for the future, need to?

Will the technologically rich of the future be educated outside school by accessing massive information databases on the Internet and using individualised 'intelligent tutoring' programs that develop their thinking skills? Will schools exist merely as socialising agents that focus on 'living' and physical skills? Or does the teacher of the future have an integral part to play in the construction of students' learning? Certainly, computer technology frees the teacher to interact more with individual students as they are involved with their particular learning activity, rather than with whole groups; unless, of course, they are using integrated learning systems which are whole-class, teacher-directed, computerised packages of integrated curriculum materials.

As with all professions, there are those who are dedicated and those who are just doing a job. Teachers who are committed to student learning will use computer technology as an opportunity to provide the scaffolding for learning that Vygotsky talks about in many key learning areas of the curriculum. In other words, they will use the individualised teaching opportunities provided by computers to interact with all students to find out what they already understand and what their abilities are in the area of study, so that they can determine the most effective pace and mode of presentation. On the other hand, those teachers who are lazy or unprepared will take advantage of the technology to leave students to their own devices while they catch up on marking or administration. Where will you be?

Recommended reading

Durndell, A. et al. (1995) Gender and computing: Persisting differences. *Educational Research*, 37, 219–27.

Yelland, N. (1995) Young children's attitudes to computers and computing. *Australian Journal of Early Childhood*, 20, 20–5.

PART 2

Managing effective learning

CHAPTER 9

Motivation for effective learning: cognitive perspectives

OVERVIEW

We all know what it means to be motivated, particularly to go on a holiday, buy a new dress, or play a round of golf. We also know what it is like to be unmotivated (perhaps you are feeling this way as you begin to read this Chapter, though we hope not!). In this chapter we consider theories which attempt to explain why people are motivated to do some things but not to do others. We have selected cognitive theories that have particular relevance to educational settings.

As you will recall, behavioural approaches to learning emphasise reinforcement as the primary means of controlling and maintaining student motivation. Many cognitive theorists believe that this approach places too much emphasis on external control, denying the opportunity for individuals to be self-directed. In particular, cognitive psychologists believe that any theory of motivation must consider the psychological processes involved in our decisions about which activities to invest our energies in. An increasingly important theme in the literature on motivation is the role played by thoughts and perceptions in guiding and directing behaviour. This chapter explores cognitive views of motivation and draws out their implications for classroom practice. In particular, we consider intrinsic motivation, achievement motivation, expectancy x value theory, attribution theory and goal theory.

Using a model of motivation drawn from goal theory we consider ways in which a school's psychological environment may be changed so that it facilitates the motivation and achievement of all children. We also consider the nature and importance of teacher expectations for student motivation and achievement.

As a final theme in the chapter we consider the relationship between arousal, anxiety and motivation and give suggestions for alleviating school anxiety and stress.

WHAT IS MOTIVATION?

What is motivation? All teachers are familiar with classes and individuals that are highly motivated. There is a zing in the air. No work seems too hard or too much or too boring. Teacher and students work harmoniously and energetically. Students are alert, attention is focused. Highly motivated individuals and classes persist at the task, desire high levels of performance, and come back to the task time and time again voluntarily. Perhaps you have experienced such a class as a student, or as a teacher? Or perhaps you have been in classes where the absence of such motivation was evident.

We are also aware that within any class there is great variation among individuals in the level of motivation for particular tasks (and this applies equally to students and teachers). Sometimes this variation appears to reflect interests and values, ability and effort. Sometimes the variation seems to relate to sex differences (e.g. girls appear more motivated in language activities and boys in construction activities); sometimes the variation appears to reflect ethnic differences (e.g. Aboriginal and Maori children appear less motivated for academic work than Chinese or Eastern European children); and sometimes the variation seems to be connected with socioeconomic and family background variables.

One of our major concerns as teachers is why so many children who have such a zest for learning language, play and social skills before beginning school appear to lose motivation for learning while attending school (Lepper & Hodell 1989; Ryan, Connell & Deci 1985). What is it that schools and teachers do or don't do that seems to demotivate so many children? Why is it that some children maintain motivation even in difficult circumstances, while others give up?

If we knew with certainty what motivated individuals in particular situations and could package this information, we would make a fortune. Alas, no one has come up with the magic formula. Nevertheless, research and theory have yielded many insights helpful to us in our quest for the answer. We will share them with you in this chapter.

LEARNER-CENTRED PSYCHOLOGICAL PRINCIPLE 6

The learner's creativity, higher-order thinking and natural curiosity all contribute to motivation to learn. Intrinsic motivation is stimulated by tasks of optimal novelty and difficulty, relevant to personal interests, and providing for personal choice and control.

Positive affect, creativity, and flexible and insightful thinking are promoted in contexts that learners perceive as personally relevant and meaningful. For example, learners need opportunities to make choices in line with their interests and to have the freedom to change the course of learning in light of self-awareness, discovery or insights. Projects that are comparable to real-world situations in complexity and duration elicit learners' higher-order thinking skills and creativity. In addition, curiosity is enhanced when learners can work on personally relevant learning tasks of optimal difficulty and novelty as well as in interaction with others.

Reprinted with permission, APA Task Force on Psychology in Education (1993, January), p. 7.

BOX 9.1 TEACHING COMPETENCE

The teacher designs teaching programs to motivate and engage students

Indicators

The teacher:

- knows and uses a wide range of teaching approaches;
- sets and maintains explicit teaching and learning goals;
- relates content and teaching approaches to student learning goals and needs;
- selects and adapts content, resources and activities to suit the students and the context of teaching;
- recognises learning opportunities in issues raised by students.

Case studies illustrating National Competency Framework for Beginning Teaching, National Project on the Quality of Teaching and Learning, Australian Teaching Council, 1996, Element 3.3, p. 48. Commonwealth of Australia copyright, reproduced by permission.

DEVELOPING SELF-MOTIVATED LEARNING

Essential to the cognitive perspective on motivation is the concept of intrinsic motivation. Generally referred to as the motive that keeps individuals at a task through its own inherent qualities intrinsic motivation is a complex concept with many interpretations of what constitutes it and what its underlying processes are (Heckhausen 1991). These issues are beyond the scope of this book. We will, however, pick up a number of theoretical notions of motivation which have as their basis cognitive processing of thoughts about self in a learning environment and some concept of intrinsic motivation.

WHAT WOULD YOU DO?

THEY'RE JUST NOT WRITING

Christine teaches years 1 and 2 at a remote community school. It is not her first year teaching in an Aboriginal community, but it is her first year at this school.

Comparing this year's year 2 students with the students in her last school, she was very concerned. What was happening? What had gone wrong? 'I'd put a piece of paper in front of them and they wouldn't do it. They wouldn't touch it.'

What would you do? Find out what the teacher did on page 175.

Case studies illustrating National Competency Framework for Beginning Teaching, National Project on the Quality of Teaching and Learning, Australian Teaching Council, 1996, p. 32. Commonwealth of Australia copyright, reproduced by permission.

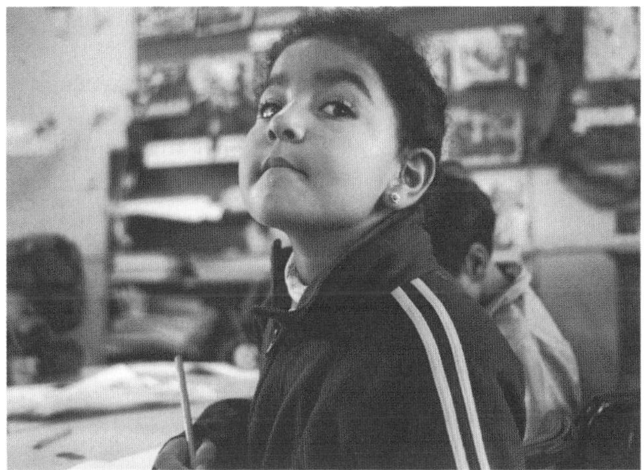

Young children are intensely interested in learning. How can we foster this intrinsic interest? Photo: authors

Cognitive theories of learning, in general, suggest that the key to people's motivation lies their desire to solve problems, have insight and gain understanding, particularly in ambiguous or problematic situations (Andre 1986). Elements of intrinsic motivation include task involvement, desire to experience adventure and novelty, striving for excellence in one's work, trying to understand something and wishing to improve, and goal direction (i.e. seeing a purpose in what one is doing). For Piaget, intrinsic motivation involved the feelings of satisfaction at resolving incongruities; for de

Elements of intrinsic motivation: task involvement

adventure and novelty

striving for excellence

goal orientation

These children have developed their own mathematics games in English and Spanish. The activity has encouraged a sharing of cultures and ideas, and has motivated the children to produce attractive and enjoyable learning aids. Why is this an example of intrinsic motivation? Photo: Diane McPhail

Charms (1968), feelings of personal causation were important for motivation; for Heckhausen (1991), the valuing of the activity for its own sake was particularly important. For Deci & Ryan (1991), intrinsically motivated behaviours are those that the person undertakes out of interest. In this regard, interest and intrinsic motivation are virtually synonymous (Deci & Ryan 1991; Tobias 1994). One definition that we particularly like is that intrinsic motivation is the joyous absorption in the activity which characterises truly motivated persons (Csikszentmihalyi 1975; Csikszentmihalyi & Nakamura 1989). The nexus between intrinsic motivation and cognitive theories of learning is neatly highlighted by the definition offered by Corno & Rohrkemper (1985): 'a facility for learning that sustains the desire to learn through the development of particular cognitive skills'.

The contrast between intrinsic and extrinsic approaches to understanding motivation is neatly put by Csikszentmihalyi and Nakamura (1989, p. 69):

If we conceive of human behaviour mechanistically and explain phenomena in mechanistic terms, we stand to treat people accordingly. On the other hand, if we conceive of humans as intentional agents, who sometimes choose to act for the sake of intrinsic enjoyment alone, we might be able to facilitate people's enjoyment of the activities in which they engage.

Students who are intrinsically motivated—that is, who think a task is useful and important—are more likely to persist with it and more willing to try different strategies to achieve their goals (Pokay & Blumenfeld 1990). Recent research indicates that both **intrinsic** and **extrinsic motivation** can be experienced simultaneously depending on the nature of the task. Can you think of occasions where intrinsic and extrinsic motivation were both important to your motivation? What about a time when you were motivated intrinsically with no extrinsic motivator being present? What was it like when you worked only for the extrinsic reward?

How can we engage the interest of the learner intrinsically?

Research indicates that the features of activities and learning environments discussed below are most likely to engage the interest of the learner intrinsically (see Brophy 1987; Lepper & Hodell 1989; Ryan, Connell & Deci 1985).

Level of challenge

For individuals to be motivated in a particular task the task must involve a **level of challenge** that is suited to their perceived capacity so that their skills are put to an appropriate test. This challenge level needs to increase as the individual becomes more proficient. Teachers should help children therefore to set realistic and challenging goals.

Curiosity and motivation

Curiosity is also a major element of intrinsic motivation. **Curiosity** is stimulated by situations that are surprising, incongruous or out of keeping with a student's existing beliefs and ideas. An enthralling display was given by a student teacher motivating a class to write a creative composition. He had a large black box of furry, feathery, squishy, squashy, hard, long and thick objects. Each child had to put his or her hand through a small hole, feel an object, and then go back and write a short story on what had been felt. The pupils were spellbound and couldn't wait to have their turn and write their story. On another occasion the same student teacher had a large treasure chest in which there was an assortment of items. He drew out one at a time while telling a pirate story. Each item was part of the story. Interest was very high as students were asked to predict what would come out of the box next.

Sense of autonomy

Also important is a child's feeling of having a **choice** in and **control** of an activity. The busy, productive work of children in groups working on projects is a measure of their intrinsic interest. It is a truism that we work best at things we are interested in and have control over.

Fantasy, make-believe and simulation games

Fantasy, make-believe and simulation games can also help children to become intrinsically interested in learning (Lepper & Hodell 1989; Parker & Lepper 1992). The success of the ABC television program 'Play School' illustrates this. Young children spend a lot of time reciting nursery rhymes and singing songs heard on 'Play School', their only reward being the joy of singing and knowing that they are learning new things. Often classrooms are set up as shops to teach about money, or students prepare a class newspaper to learn about journalism. Many of the computer software programs now available capitalise on fantasy and simulation to captivate the interest, attention and motivation of the user. Curiosity, fantasy and simulations elicit what has been termed **situational interest** in the task, which facilitates motivation (Tobias 1994). Children's play is a clear opportunity to observe intrinsic motivation at its best. In fact, if the teacher structures the play by telling children what to do or what resources to use, it may no longer be intrinsically motivated and, therefore, no longer 'play'.

Other classroom practices that have been associated with developing students' intrinsic motivation include giving children the opportunity to be actively **involved** in the lesson through manipulation of objects, cooperative group work and presentations; providing **immediate**

feedback to students on their work so that they see how well they are going; allowing students time to complete their products and **achieve goals**, and providing students with the opportunity to **interact with peers** in a variety of learning situations such as role plays, dramas, debates and simulations.

Active involvement, immediate feedback, finished products, peer interaction

Teachers should model an *interest in learning* and a *motivation to learn* by being enthusiastic, interested in the tasks being presented, and curious. They should also show interest (and, dare we say, excitement) at what children initiate, and indicate to children that they expect them both to enjoy their learning and to be successful. Students' natural motivation to learn will also be enhanced if teachers provide a safe, trusting and supportive environment. This would be characterised by quality relationships in the classroom, learning and instructional supports that are tailored to individual needs, and opportunities for students to take risks without fear of failure (McCombs & Pope 1994).

Teachers as models

Question point: How realistic is it to tell students that they should not be working for marks? Can a school subject ever be made interesting for its own sake?

Cautions about the use of intrinsic motivation

It is important to note that the use of highly motivating techniques should not be at the expense of the substance of learning. In other words, a lot of razzmatazz may be highly interesting and motivating, but unless it is used to support meaningful learning activities then such techniques are educationally valueless. Furthermore, techniques used to enhance the presentation of a learning activity should not be so distracting as to conflict with the purpose of learning. For example, when a teacher sets up a competition to stimulate interest, some children become more concerned with the competition and scoring points for their work than with the quality of work they are completing. Often children enjoy participating in an educational game without trying to derive any academic benefit from it (Blumenfeld 1992; Brophy 1983, 1987; Corno & Rohrkemper 1985). Many multimedia computer software programs are very entertaining but provide

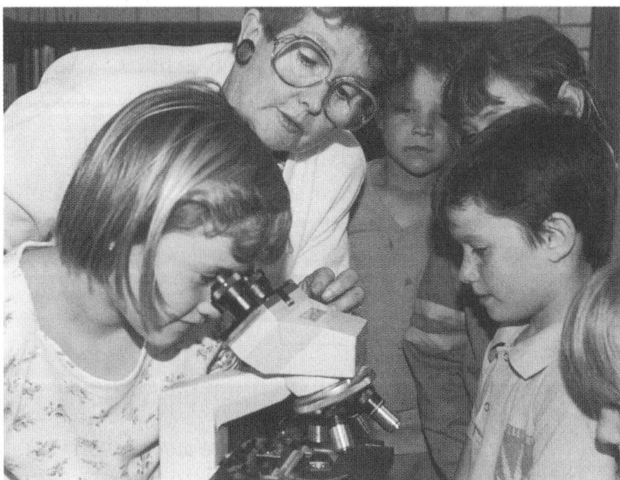

Why is student motivation enhanced through hands-on activities? Photo: WA Education News

Motivation — and leading by example!

WHAT WOULD YOU DO?

THEY'RE JUST NOT WRITING (continued)

Christine spoke to the principal, Paul, complaining that 'they're just not writing'. His response was to ask her to focus on what the year 2s could do, not what they couldn't do. They might not be ready for formal writing, but were they ready to role play writing at a writing table?

So Christine set up a big writing table with paper, crayons, textas, magazines, telephone books, telephones, a blackboard and a shop. For half an hour each morning Christine's students had free time at the writing table. They played and drew pictures, and Christine used the writing materials for her own telephone messages and shopping lists.

It was just amazing. They weren't afraid to write because it was so informal. It wasn't 'Here's a piece of paper, off you go'.

Did you suggest this solution? If not, what solution did you suggest?

Case studies illustrating National Competency Framework for Beginning Teaching, National Project on the Quality of Teaching and Learning, Australian Teaching Council, 1996, p.32. Commonwealth of Australia copyright, reproduced by permission.

little in the way of 'educational content'. It is important, therefore, that situational interest generated by such techniques be converted to topic or task interest that will be relatively enduring for the students. In particular, this is related to the acquisition of knowledge.

TABLE 9.1

ESSENTIALS OF PROVIDING A LEARNING ENVIRONMENT TO STIMULATE INTRINSIC MOTIVATION

For teachers

- Establish a *level of challenge* suited to individual student capacity.
- Build on students' *prior knowledge and interests.*
- Stimulate *curiosity* in classroom activities.
- Utilise *fantasy, make-believe and simulation games.*
- Engineer *active involvement* in the learning activities.
- Provide *meaningful feedback.*
- Allow sufficient time for students to *complete products* and *achieve goals.*
- Provide opportunity for students to *interact with peers.*
- Provide opportunities for students to develop *autonomy* in their learning.
- *Model* an interest in learning and a motivation to learn.
- Provide a *safe, trusting and supportive environment.*
- Communicate *an expectation of student success.*

For learners

- Look for ways to make a task interesting.
- Reinvent a learning experience, if necessary, to create interest and challenge in it.
- Expect success and work towards this.
- Ask for feedback on learning progress.
- Be curious: ask questions about what you are doing.
- Don't wait to be told what to do: take the initiative to make it interesting, fun and worthwhile for yourself.
- Make sure you allow plenty of time to finish what you start.
- Set both short-term and long-term goals that are realistic.
- Share ideas and tasks with others.
- Don't put up with feeling uncertain—express your concerns, clarify, and get help.

ACTION STATION

Of central importance to motivation is interest in the learning exercise. Interest may be generated in a number of ways. For example, relating new material to a student's needs and existing capabilities often fosters interest. Moderate levels of challenge, relating learning experiences to the 'real world', and the perceived importance and relevance of the learning to the individual also facilitate interest.

Observe and *discuss* with a classroom teacher the ways in which interest is gained and maintained in the classroom. *Record* your observations.

BOX 9.2 TEACHING COMPETENCE

The teacher matches content, teaching approaches and student development and learning in planning

Indicators

The teacher:

- balances the curriculum and process goals of teaching and learning;
- selects or devises content and activities appropriate to student learning needs, strengths and interests;
- caters for individual differences within the group in terms of teaching approaches and learning materials;
- anticipates and prepares for situations that may arise incidentally;
- organises resources (human, material and technological) that facilitate achievement of learning goals.

Case studies illustrating National Competency Framework for Beginning Teaching, National Project on the Quality of Teaching and Learning, Australian Teaching Council, 1996, Element 3.2, p. 47. Commonwealth of Australia copyright, reproduced by permission.

ACTION STATION

Observe a range of television programs aimed specifically at children and adolescents (such as 'Sesame Street', 'The Simpsons', the 'Science Show', 'Neighbours'). Also observe a range of commercials directed at the same age groups.

List the elements of motivation you see demonstrated in these programs.

What principles of motivation seem to be used most often in these programs to engage, maintain and increase interest and attention? Do these vary according to the age group targeted? Illustrate how these same principles may be used effectively in the classroom.

MOTIVATION—EXPECTING AND VALUING SUCCESS

To this point we have been talking about behaviour motivated by interest and expectations of success. Important insights about expectations of success have come from the expectancy x value theory. In particular,

WHAT WOULD YOU DO?

WE'VE LOST THE PLOT

Mrs Chalmers found that teaching the novel *The Shiralee* to grade 8 students as a recommended text proved to be one of those classroom experiences that caused her to wonder about her teaching and the appropriateness of the choice of text. During class the students were very clearly uninterested. They were reluctant to listen, discuss or participate in any written activities. Was it her teaching? Was it her reading? She thought it was a great novel but it wasn't until they were some way through the story that it occurred to her that the problem wasn't necessarily the way she was teaching but, rather, the language of the text. It came from a different era and, as far as the kids were concerned, it might as well have been written in Russian. The structure was too complex and the idiom, although Australian, was unfamiliar. It was beyond their experience and age level.

What would you do? Read the teacher's solution on page 179.

Case studies illustrating National Competency Framework for Beginning Teaching, National Project on the Quality of Teaching and Learning, Australian Teaching Council, 1996, p. 44. Commonwealth of Australia copyright, reproduced by permission.

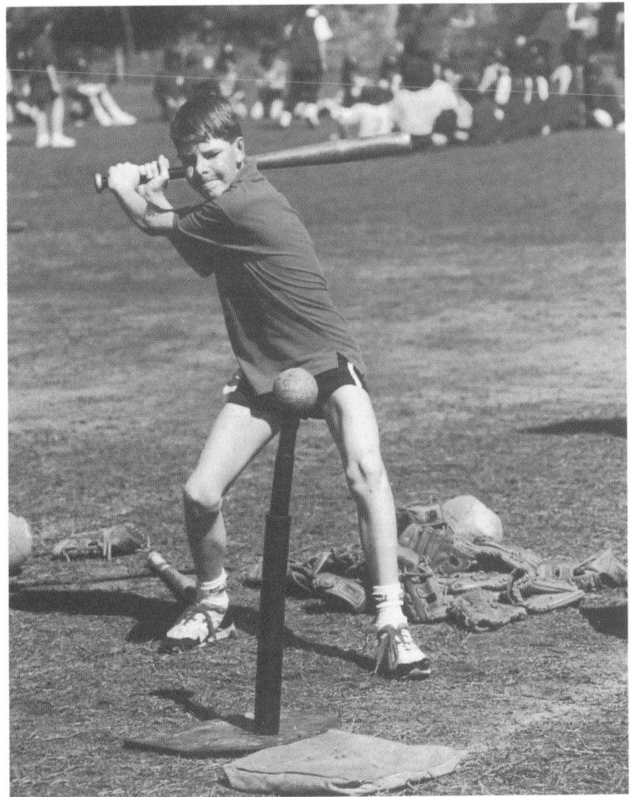

Some of us get 'fired-up' to achieve. Photo: authors

the early work of Atkinson (1958, 1964; Atkinson & Feather 1966; Atkinson & Raynor 1974) highlighted the interaction of personality and environment in determining motivated behaviour. Atkinson proposed that each individual has a tendency to achieve success and a tendency to avoid failure. This tendency is moderated by the individual's expectation of success or failure with a particular task and the incentive value of the task. The disposition an individual has to seek success or avoid failure is considered to be relatively stable, but the actual playing out of this mix depends on the two variables that are subject to environmental variation—the value of the task to the individual and the individual's expectation of success.

In short, this theory tries to explain what it is that causes some individuals to perform certain behaviours and others not to, when both are equally able to do so. Not only is the *expectation of success* important, but also the *value of that success* in terms of anticipated rewards or punishments. For example, we probably all know of someone who has tried to give up smoking. The motivation to persist at this difficult task over a period of time is very much influenced by how successful they feel they will be, and how personally valuable that success will be in terms of its rewards—pleasant breath, greater social acceptability, and less risk of serious health problems—versus its negative consequences—unpleasant withdrawal side-effects, the increased hunger and potential weight gain, and the sense of bowing to social pressure.

High-need achievers and low-need achievers

Atkinson proposed two theoretical personality types: the person for whom the need to achieve is greater than the fear of failure, and the person for whom the fear of failure is greater than the need to achieve. The first group are labelled **high-need achievers** and the second **low-need achievers**. For the high-need achievers, situations of intermediate challenge are most motivating. However, for the low-need achievers, tasks of intermediate challenge appear most threatening. In this case, low-need achievers choose tasks that are far too hard, so that failure can be excused because of task difficulty, or tasks that are so easy that success is guaranteed. The figure on p. 178 depicts the situations.

According to this theory the individual's subjective experience of success or failure will vary according to the person's level of need achievement and will further influence later goal-setting behaviour. For example, a high-need achiever who perceives a task as easy, but fails, is likely the next time round to reassess the task as more difficult than at first anticipated and persist with it. On the other hand, a low-need achiever who perceives a task as easy and fails will reassess it as moderately difficult and withdraw from it completely. Even when low-need achievers succeed with a task perceived as very difficult, they are still likely to withdraw from it, judging that in the future failure is highly likely. Best to stop while ahead.

Attainment value, intrinsic value and utility value of success

Expectancy × value theory has been developed from its original conception by Eccles and Wigfield (Eccles 1983; Wigfield 1994). They have explored three components of the value of a task: **attainment value**: that is, the importance of doing well on the task; **intrinsic value**: that is, the inherent, immediate enjoyment one derives from the task; and **utility value**: that is, the perceived importance of the activity to a future goal such as advancing one's career prospects. Research by Eccles and Wigfield has shown that the value of a task is positively related to achievement. However, when expectancy for success and value of the activity are used to predict success, it is a person's expectancy beliefs that are significant predictors, not the values. It appears, therefore, that while values may be important in the initial choice of activity (we don't usually get involved in activities that have little value or interest), expectancy of success is more important to motivation than values after that.

Classroom applications of the expectancy × value theory

One of our functions as teachers is to assist students to set realistic and challenging goals and to ensure that students experience success at least a lot of the time. In terms of expectancy x value theory, this will reinforce the student's perception that success for effort can occur, even if tasks may appear difficult. Of course, there needs to be appropriate incentives for the student to make the effort: these should be negotiated with the student and may be designed as individual contracts.

It is worth keeping in mind that students with a low expectancy of academic success often defy classroom and school rules, because the value of academic achievement is also low relative to the value of status among their peers. For such students, threats of detention,

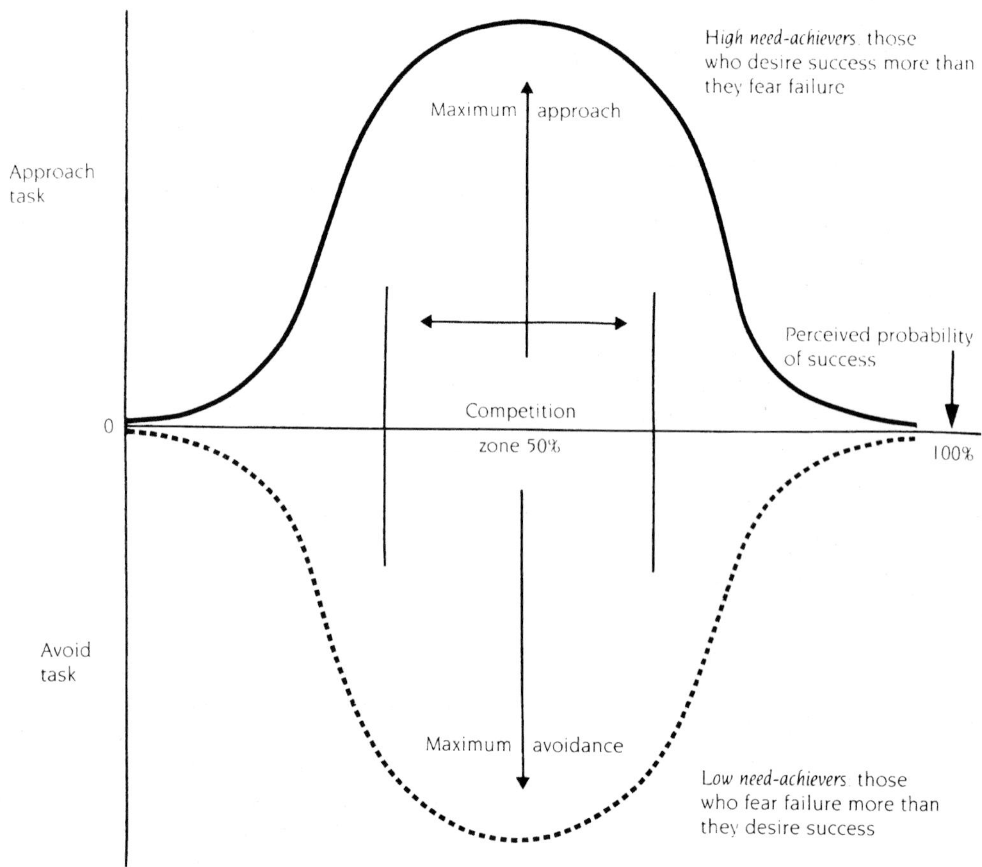

WHAT WOULD YOU DO?

WE'VE LOST THE PLOT (continued)

Mrs Chalmers decided to discuss with the class why they were responding to the novel in this particular way. Through discusson and reflection they were able to come to an understanding of what was causing the difficulties.

The class watched a video of the novel and Mrs Chalmers found it very interesting to notice how attentive the students were when they were viewing as compared to when they were reading. When she discussed why this happened it seemed to be that they could more easily make links between the language and the action and plot with a visual medium. They found it difficult to visualise anything when reading the novel because of the language and the complexity of the time frame structure of the novel. They had been so busy deciphering the language that they had lost the plot and then simply lost interest. Mrs Chalmers found this to be a good learning experience for her. She had misjudged both the referential and structural reading experience of the class. They needed to be led through other reading experiences before being presented with *The Shiralee*. Abandoning the reading of the novel at this stage seemed to be the best course of action.

Do you agree with this solution?

Case studies illustrating National Competency Framework for Beginning Teaching, National Project on the Quality of Teaching and Learning, Australian Teaching Council, 1996, p. 44. Commonwealth of Australia copyright, reproduced by permission.

suspension, or even expulsion from school are not a disincentive: it is more motivating to have the (negative) attention of teachers and schoolmates than to try to achieve academically and fail publicly.

This approach to describing motivation in the classroom is valuable for interpreting the behaviour of children in achievement situations. Children with a low need for achievement, faced with possible failure, may adopt a range of coping strategies to minimise the effect of failure on their self-esteem; this is considered by Covington (1984, 1992; Harari & Covington 1981) as either **failure-avoiding** behaviour or **success-guaranteeing** behaviour (see also Rohwer, Rohwer & Howe 1980; Thompson 1993).

Coping strategies: guaranteeing success and avoiding failure

TABLE 9.2

FAILURE-AVOIDING AND SUCCESS-GUARANTEEING STRATEGIES

Failure-avoiding behaviour

- *non-attendance*—just don't turn up;
- *non-participation*—'nothing ventured, nothing failed';
- *false effort*—apparent effort such that the child will get praise for busy work or effort, and at least avoid substantial reproof for failure;
- *irrationally high goals*—'no one can be blamed if the task is obviously too difficult';
- *lack of effort*—'if I'd tried harder I could have done it'; avoids personal criticism of the student's ability, and also avoids any real test of ability.

Success-guaranteeing strategies

- *low goal setting*—the selection of simple tasks so that success is certain: 'anyone can pass this easy task';
- *academic cheating*—success is guaranteed through cheating. This presents a great problem for the student: how to maintain the success when the possibility for cheating is removed. The child may go to great efforts to conceal the cheating, to often using quite extravagant subterfuges;
- *overstriving*—expenditure of extravagant effort to achieve success and avoid failure.

Coping strategies are used to preserve our sense of self-worth in competitive situations. They are commonly used by students in our classrooms. We should show students the value of learning ways of dealing with difficulty and temporary failure. The author recalls one student, who was able, but not brilliant, preparing for the final high school exams. Over the months leading up to the exams he became seriously fatigued. On talking to him the author discovered that the student was getting about three hours sleep per night. The rest of the time was spent in study to ensure he would not fail in the levels he had chosen to do for the final high school examinations. With considerate advice and parental consultation, the student reshaped his expectations and work schedules so that he could cope with the task of preparing for the tests in a more healthy fashion. This meant a reassessment of the need for success and the fear of failure for that individual—not an easy personal readjustment in a competitive academic climate such as final exams.

ACTION STATION

Consider your own motivation and performance levels in particular activities and relate this to the high- and low-need achievement profiles described in the text. How adequate is the expectancy model as an explanation of your personal motivational level?

TABLE 9.3

WHAT TEACHERS CAN DO TO INFLUENCE STUDENT MOTIVATION: INSIGHTS FROM EXPECTANCY THEORY

Expectancy *'If I try hard, what are my chances of success?'*

Teacher's actions

- help students identify the behaviours associated with successful learning; e.g. asking questions, searching for answers from knowledgeable sources, and reflection on learning progress (i.e. understanding);
- teach strategies for learning and metacognition; bolster expectation of success as a result of personal actions;
- provide support if learner will benefit; tutor individually or use alternative materials (e.g. computer-based).

Utility value *'To what extent will I get something I want, or avoid something I don't like, if I do this?'*

Teacher's actions

- help clarify with students the relationship between actions and consequences;
- provide appropriate rewards and recognition for effort and achievement in a number of areas;
- provide rewards equitably across the class;
- counsel students on the long-term consequences of effort and academic achievement;
- support students in long-term success goals in situations where parental support may be lacking.

Attainment value *'If I work hard and reach the desired standard, do I really care?'*

Teacher's actions

- diagnose the values that students place on academic achievement;
- relate this knowledge to the effort expended by students;
- reinforce students' self-awareness of negative consequences for not making efforts in learning;
- model positive consequences for effort and achievement; reward with desirable reinforcers.

(based on Hancock 1995)

MOTIVATION—ATTRIBUTING SUCCESS AND FAILURE TO THE RIGHT CAUSES

It is implied in expectancy x value theory that individuals must feel some ownership of, and control over, their successes if they are to be motivated. The motivational importance of such perceived causal control over one's successes and failures has been made a focus of the work of Bernard Weiner (Weiner 1972, 1979, 1984) in relation to **attribution theory**. The hub of attribution theory is that individuals seek to explain and interpret (what we call 'attribute') their successes and failures in activities in terms of causes. In other words, individuals ask questions such as 'Why did I fail the exam?' or 'Why did my team lose?' or 'Why did I achieve so well?' It is, however, more likely that these types of questions are asked after failure rather than after success. In answering these questions, people attribute their successes and failures to various causes, some of which can be personally controlled, while others lie outside of personal control. Depending on the nature of the attribution made, motivation may be more or less enhanced (Heckhausen 1991; Maehr 1989).

Basic assumptions of attribution theory

Attribution theory rests on three basic assumptions. First, it assumes that people attempt to determine the causes of their own behaviour and that of others. In other words, people are motivated to seek out information that helps them make attributions about cause and effect, particularly in situations where the outcome was unexpected or negative. Second, attribution theory assumes that the reasons people give to explain their behaviour govern their behaviour in predictable ways from one situation to the next: they do not occur at random. The final assumption is that causes attributed to a particular behaviour will influence subsequent emotional and cognitive behaviour.

Weiner originally postulated four causes that are perceived as most responsible for success and failure in achievement-related contexts:

Four attributional causes

1. ability
2. effort
3. task difficulty
4. luck

Ability refers to a person's perceived performance capacity in a particular activity; for example, some people feel they are good at tennis, others at mathematics, others at drama and so on. **Effort** refers to the energy expended on a task (whether that effort is general and typical or specific to the task). We have all experienced times when we put a lot of effort into completing a task, or achieving a goal. We have also experienced times when we really put little effort into our work. **Task difficulty** refers to the parameters of the task. Tasks that most people can perform are labelled easy, while tasks that few can master are labelled difficult. **Luck** refers to the variables that lie outside personal control that may affect the behaviour (other than the first three mentioned). Things like being unwell, or suffering a flat tyre on the way to an exam could affect performance.

Each of these 'causes' of success and failure can be further categorised along the following dimensions: **locus of control: internal/external** (referring to the degree of personal influence involved); **stable/unstable** (referring to the perceived constancy of the factors over time); **controllability/uncontrollability** (referring to the perceived element of personal responsibility and intentionality involved); and **globality** (referring to the general feelings of success or failure the person experiences, over a range of events, i.e. some people are generally success or failure oriented, while others are oriented more by specific tasks).

Dimensions of causes: locus of control: internal/ external Stable/unstable Controllable/ uncontrollable Globality

Each of these dimensions is presumed to influence a person's interpretation of the significance of success and failure. The stability dimension affects the individual's expectancies for future success or failure on a given task, while the internal/external dimension affects the individual's feelings of self-esteem. We feel more guilty if we fail for reasons within our own control. Table 9.4 illustrates the way in which the attribution model may be used to analyse the impact of success and failure on an individual's motivation for future tasks. Consider some of your own success and failure experiences in this context.

Table 9.4 shows the attributions as a function of stable and unstable, external and internal causes.

Importance of attributions to future motivation

The first element in the mental processing of success or failure on a particular task for the individual is an *affective* one. When we are told we have failed something we are generally flooded with feelings of disappointment and frustration. These affective reactions to the outcome gradually become moderated or intensified as we begin to attribute the failure to external or internal causes that are either stable or unstable. In other words, there may be a change in emotions depending on the attributions made. The individual who fails in a maths test may attribute the failure to lack of preparation. In this instance, the effect on future motivation will be considerably different from the individual who attributes the failure to lack of ability. If the failure is attributed to bad luck (such as illness), future motivation may not be affected; however, if the failure is attributed to task difficulty, the individual may withdraw from involvement in the task in the future.

Affective reaction to success or failure

This process of attribution can also be illustrated with a success example. While a student will initially feel pleased that she has successfully passed a test or performed an activity, further affective feelings and motivation will be influenced by whether the success is attributable to ability, effort, task difficulty or luck. Whether the task was perceived as easy or difficult, or whether the student was lucky will have a considerable impact on how she feels and on later motivation. The student might consider that her success was not really in her control (not related to her effort), so motivation would drop. If, on the other hand, the student felt that the task was easy because she had put a lot of effort into preparation, then her motivation would remain high because of pride in her achievement.

Antecedents of student attributions

What factors are known to influence attributions for performance? The *performance of others relative to our own* is one important factor. For example, if students perform much the same as others they are more likely to attribute their success or failure to external causes (such as task difficulty. On the other hand, if a student's performance varies from others, and is significantly better or worse, the individual is likely to attribute it to internal factors (such as ability or effort).

A person's *history of performance* also affects attributions as it is associated with the stability dimension. Outcomes that are consistent with previous performances are likely to be attributed to stable causes ('I always fail in reading'). Outcomes that run counter to previous patterns are likely to be attributed to unstable causes (such as effort or luck).

Beliefs about competence also influence causal attributions. Individuals who believe they are competent, and also perform well, have this competence confirmed and are likely, therefore, to attribute their success to stable causes (such as ability). Students who believe they are competent, but fail, are likely to identify their failure in terms of unstable causes (such as effort or luck). Conversely, students who believe that they lack competence are likely to attribute their successes to unstable causes (such as luck) which is consistent with their perception of themselves as incompetent. *Teacher feedback* is also important, and we consider this in a later section of this chapter.

Characteristics of good attributions

In achievement tasks it is important that individuals attribute the success or failure in previous performance to causes that will positively motivate future performance, and not to dysfunctional ones that will discourage

Differences between high and low-need achievers

TABLE 9.4

ATTRIBUTIONS AS A FUNCTION OF STABLE AND UNSTABLE/EXTERNAL AND INTERNAL CAUSES

Type of cause	Locus of control	Failure experience Outcome attributed to		Success experience Outcome attributed to	
UNSTABLE	EXTERNAL (uncontrollable)	**1. Bad LUCK**		**5. Good LUCK**	
		AFFECTIVE REACTIONS	Disappointment, annoyance, little shame	AFFECTIVE REACTIONS	Pleasure, surprise, thankfulness, relief, decreased pride
		MOTIVATIONAL IMPACT	Possible change in future performance, but not highly motivational	MOTIVATIONAL IMPACT	Possible change in future performance, but not highly motivational
	INTERNAL (controllable)	**2. Insufficient EFFORT**		**6. Sufficient EFFORT**	
		AFFECTIVE REACTION	Disappointment, regret, guilt, some shame	AFFECTIVE REACTION	Pleasure, relief, satisfaction, augmented pride
		MOTIVATIONAL IMPACT	Expectation of possible change in future performance with increased effort. Probable increase in achievement behaviour	MOTIVATIONAL IMPACT	Possible change in future effort Maintenance of, or increased probability of, achievement behaviour
STABLE	EXTERNAL (uncontrollable)	**3. Difficult TASK**		**7. Easy TASK**	
		AFFECTIVE REACTION	Disappointment, little shame, possible frustration	AFFECTIVE REACTION	Little pride, reduced pleasure and satisfaction
		MOTIVATIONAL IMPACT	Withdrawal from task with expectations of similar peformance outcome in future	MOTIVATIONAL IMPACT	Little motivational impact
	INTERNAL (controllable)	**4. Low ABILITY**		**8. High ABILITY**	
		AFFECTIVE REACTION	Disappointment, increased shame, anxiety, embarrassment	AFFECTIVE REACTION	Pleasure, confidence, satisfaction, competence, pride
		MOTIVATIONAL IMPACT	Avoidance of task in future with expectations of similar performance outcomes	MOTIVATIONAL IMPACT	Increased probability of achievement behaviour

(adapted from Weiner, 1972, 1979, 1986, 1994; Bar-Tal, 1978; Biggs & Telfer 1987a)

further involvement. It has been found through a number of research programs (Dweck & Repucci 1973; Kukla 1972; Nolen & Nicholls 1993; Weiner 1972; Weiner & Kukla 1970) that people high in achievement motivation generally attribute their successes to ability and effort (internal causes) and failures to lack of effort or external factors, while those low in achievement motivation generally attribute their successes to external causes (such as the ease of the task or luck) and thereby discount the extent that their ability and effort are responsible for their success. Hence, this group experiences less pride for their successful performance. These students also attribute their failures to lack of ability rather than to external factors, or to lack of effort (Bar-Tal 1978). Weiner suggests that the major differences between individuals high and low in achievement needs are that individuals in the former group are more likely to *initiate* achievement activities; work with greater *intensity*; *persist* longer in the face of failure; and *choose* more tasks of intermediate difficulty than persons low in achievement needs (Weiner 1972). Among variables that have been found to influence achievement motivation and attributions are sex differences, ethnic differences, achievement needs, self-esteem, emotional state, reinforcement schedules and internal/external control perceptions (Bar-Tal 1978; Biggs & Telfer 1987a).

How might teacher attributional beliefs influence student motivation?

The primary focus in attribution theory is on the individual's reaction to success or failure in terms of the personal attributions made. As discussed above, when an individual's failure is attributed to lack of ability,

If I try my hardest, I'm sure I'll do well!
Photo: authors

which is *uncontrollable*, shame and embarrassment may lead to a decrease in performance. On the other hand, failure attributed to lack of effort, which is *controllable*, may provoke guilt feelings in the individual and lead to an increase in performance. However, Weiner (1994; see also Graham 1988) points out that the reaction of the teacher to a child whose failure is perceived to be the result of either lack of ability or lack of effort has significant implications for the child's future motivation for the task.

Research indicates that when teachers perceive that students' failures are due to lack of ability, they often express sympathy and offer no punishment. On the other hand, when teachers perceive that students' failures are due to lack of effort, they often express anger and punish the student (e.g. through verbal reprimands). Weiner believes that, in the first instance, expressed sympathy and lack of punishment will lead students to believe that the teacher ascribes their failure to uncontrollable causes (e.g. low ability), increasing those students' personal beliefs about lack of controllability and non-responsibility. Shame and reduced performance will be the result. On the other hand, when teachers express anger towards students for exerting insufficient effort, and that anger is accepted by the students, then there should be increased inferences of self-responsibility which raise guilt and lead to improved performance of these students.

Research certainly tends to support these notions. For example, it appears that teachers give negative feedback to failing students whom they perceive have ability but have not put in sufficient effort, yet give little or sympathetic feedback to students whose ability they doubt. One study (Graham 1988) showed that when teachers communicated anger to children following their failure, using cues such as loud voice, children tended to ascribe their poor performance to lack of effort. This was subsequently related to high expectancy of success and increased performance.

It would appear from this information that communications of anger and punishment for failure will prove more effective in stimulating further motivation to improve performance than sympathetic feedback and the absence of reprimand. This is certainly the case when the teacher perceives that the students are capable of the task. However, Weiner warns that this principle should not be accepted without considering qualifying conditions and mitigating circumstances. In particular, as teachers we must be very certain that increased effort will, in fact, lead to improved performance. As Weiner points out, persistence in the face of failure in some instances may not be the best approach to achieve long-term success, and it would be beneficial for the learner to alter the direction of his or her energies. In this case, being sympathetic and withholding punishment may be the appropriate methods of producing achievement change.

Relationship of anger and punishment to motivation

Attributional retraining

Where motivation to achieve is severely lacking, **attributional retraining** has been shown to be very successful. The essence of attributional retraining is to train individuals to change their patterns of attributions so that lack of motivation, perceived lack of self-efficacy and perceived states of learned helplessness are reduced. The assumption is that encouraging students to attribute their poor performance to temporary causes over which they have control, such as lack of effort or inappropriate strategy use, should increase their expectations of future performance, reduce anxiety and feelings of helplessness, and lead to better motivation and task performance in later activities (Ho & McMurtrie 1991; Weine 1994). Furthermore, particularly for failure-oriented students,

Goal structures and self-worth

it is important to teach them to accept credit for success rather than to concentrate only on training them to substitute lack of effort attribution following failure for inability attribution (Thompson 1993).

In one study (Ho & McMurtrie 1991) 45 junior high school students who were identified as underachieving, received training in organisational skills, editing and planning strategies. During this training they periodically received either effort attributional feedback, ability plus effort feedback, or no attributional feedback. Children in both feedback groups successfully substituted adaptive causal attributions for those that were dysfunctional. In other words, they learned to reattribute their success and failure more to their effort (or lack of it), and less to the causal factor of luck. As well, both effort and ability plus effort feedback conditions were found to be equally effective in raising the children's success expectations. The results clearly indicate the importance of emphasising effort as a source of success for underachieving children as the effort plus ability feedback was no more effective (see also Forsterling 1985). In this case, success perceived as a function of effort can exert motivational effects on future achievement behaviour. For children who are not underachievers, effort and ability feedback might lead to greater feelings of *self-efficacy*, and as a consequence to enhanced motivation (Ho & McMurtrie 1991) (see Chapter 6 for a discussion of self-efficacy).

It is important that teachers acknowledge positive effort rather than emphasising lack of effort, which can be counterproductive. For example, it is useful for teachers to comment, when appropriate, that they can see that certain students are putting a lot of effort into their work, and associate this effort with the better achievement resulting from this. Teachers can also comment, with good effect, on the attitude of students, for example, by commenting on their thoughtfulness and the interest they are showing in their work (Nolen & Nicholls 1994).

Classroom applications of attribution theory

Research into attribution theory indicates that the attributions an individual makes influence task choice, need for and type of feedback sought, persistence and performance outcomes (Heckhausen 1991; Weiner 1979, 1984). Success-motivated individuals strive for information about their proficiency and prefer moderately difficult tasks, while failure-avoidant individuals try to avoid such feedback and therefore choose tasks that are too easy or too difficult.

It is important that students attribute their successes and failures to factors that will enhance further motivation. If students attribute failures to stable causes, whether internal or external (ability or task difficulty) there is little perceived point in trying again at the task.

Success helps you feel good about yourself, doesn't it?
Photo: Connie Griebe

Indeed, such future efforts will simply confirm the situation and reduce the individual's self-esteem. Generally, teachers should encourage and teach children (particularly low-achieving children) to attribute their successes and failures to the factors over which they have most control—that is, personal effort or strategy use. In particular, it is important for teachers to modify children's dysfunctional attribution patterns for failure and success. Among techniques that have been found valuable are persuasion, providing opportunities for meaningful success experiences, exercises and demonstrations through role models, and training in appropriate strategy use (Forsterling 1985, 1986).

Enhance motivation through the use of attributions

We must caution here about ascribing inappropriate attributions with the intention of improving student motivation. For example, the attribution to effort can be a double-edged sword (see Covington & Omelich 1979). Imagine that Johnny has a perceptual motor problem and his writing is very untidy. He receives feedback from his teacher that he needs to improve, and that the best way to do this is by increasing his effort. Well, Johnny puts in more effort ... and more effort ... and more effort, to no avail. The teacher says his writing is still very sloppy and he needs to put in more effort and practice. What can Johnny do? He will probably withdraw from the task and become alienated from writing. In Johnny's case, the poor writing should have been attributed to a motor skill deficiency and the problem addressed through a restructuring of the task or special remedial programs rather than insisting on more effort.

Avoid inappropriate attributions

Teachers often inappropriately ascribe poor performance to a child's supposed lack of ability. For example, teachers may ascribe low ability to a child in mathematics when, with a restructuring of tasks so that they are appropriate to the child's capacity, along with increased effort on the part of the child, success will be achieved. In many cases situations need to be restructured so that individuals see the link between effort and success. The experience of success alone may be sufficient to effect positive changes to learning motives and strategies, and be the most salient factor in promoting positive emotive responses. These feelings may, in their turn, result in alterations to behaviours designed to increase the probability of further success. What do you think?

Restructure learning situations to guarantee success

Research indicates one interesting crossover effect of ability and effort relating to self-esteem (Covington 1984; Nicholls 1976). Younger children generally equate ability and effort. In other words, they believe bright kids work hard, dumb kids loaf. Adolescents, however, are likely to maintain that, if students are putting in a lot of effort, they are probably not so bright. In their view, students with a lot of ability appear to achieve success effortlessly. Many adolescents go to a great deal of trouble covering up the effort they put into achieving success. It is not unusual even for university students to be dismissive of any effort they have put into exam preparation. Perhaps you have heard students bemoaning their lack of preparation for an upcoming test, while in reality they have secretly studied very hard (see Covington 1984). Mind you, this might also be an example of a failure-avoiding strategy.

Developmental relationship between effort and ability attributions

What is **learned helplessness**? In much of what we have stated above we have suggested that children should be guided by teachers towards a belief in themselves as **constructive** forces influencing their own successes and failures in the classroom. De Charms (1968) introduced the notion of pawns and origins when describing individuals' perceived level of control in particular challenging situations. To the extent that students believe their successes and failures are subject to external forces (such as the teacher setting easy or hard tasks), or that their successes and failures are a matter of luck, they are acting like **pawns**, as in a game of chess (de Charms 1968). In other words, they feel powerless and ineffective in particular circumstances. If this feeling of powerlessness generalises to a range of behaviours, children may demonstrate **learned helplessness** (Diener & Dweck 1978; Johnson 1981; Thomas 1979; Tiggemann & Crowley 1993; Zuroff 1980). In other words, they lose the capacity to be accountable for their own behaviour and performance, and learn to be helpless. On the other hand, children who seize the initiative, perceive the relationship between success and effort, restructure situations to maximise chances for success, as far as circumstances permit, and have a realistic view of their abilities, are **origins**.

Learned helplessness

Student accountability

Success and failure

Origins and pawns

The two dimensions, origin and pawn, lie along a continuum, and individuals are neither one nor the other exclusively. In certain situations children may be origins, while in others they may be pawns. Some children, for example, are very much pawns in the classroom, while origins on the sporting field.

Children are not born as origins or a pawns. They develop these characteristics through socialisation in various circumstances. Teachers can act as effective agents in developing origin characteristics in children.

Question point: *Define motivation and differentiate between behavioural, cognitive and social learning approaches to its interpretation.*

Question point: *Success and failure are both important motivating agents. How can teachers use these to maximise motivation in the classroom? What might be the effects of repeated success and repeated failure on level of aspiration and self-concept?*

Question point: *Some teachers rationalise: 'Why should I break my neck to teach children who just do not want to learn?' How might the impasse be resolved? Do some teachers operate under misconceptions of their role?*

LEARNER-CENTRED PSYCHOLOGICAL PRINCIPLE 7

What and how much is learned are influenced by the learner's motivation. Motivation to learn, in turn, is influenced by the individual's emotional states, beliefs, interests and goals, and habits of thinking. The rich internal world of beliefs, goals, expectations and feelings can enhance or interfere with learners' quality of thinking and understandings created. The relationship among thoughts, mood and behaviour underlies individuals' psychological health and ability to learn. Learners' interpretations or constructions of reality can facilitate or impede positive motivation, learning and performance. Positive learning experiences can help reverse negative thoughts and feelings and contribute to positive motivation to learn.

Reprinted with permission, APA Task Force on Psychology in Education (1993, January), p. 7.

THE GOALS OF SCHOOLING

How do the goals of schooling affect motivation? The theories covered so far emphasise the importance of children's beliefs about themselves as constructive, active agents. Mention has also been made of the importance of motivated learning to valuing the task. Students ask the question: Why am I doing this task? and the answer to this question influences their motivation to continue. The measures of achievement used in schools communicate to students the value placed on particular tasks and are represented as **goals of schooling**. The goals stressed by schools have dramatic consequences for whether children develop a sense of efficacy and a willingness to try hard and take on challenges, or whether they avoid challenging tasks, giving up when faced with failure (see Ames 1984, 1992; Covington 1992; Elliott & Dweck 1988; Maehr 1989; Maehr & Midgley 1991).

Mastery, performance and morality-based goals

Goals represent the purposes that students have in different achievement situations, and are presumed to guide students' behaviour, cognition and affect as they become involved in academic work (Ames 1992; Pintrich, Marx & Boyle 1993). Two academic goal structures have received considerable attention from researchers: **mastery goals** (also called learning goals) and **performance goals** (sometimes called ego goals). Central to a mastery goal is the belief that effort leads to success: the focus of attention is the *intrinsic value of learning*. With a mastery goal, individuals are oriented towards developing new skills, trying to understand their work, improving their level of competence, or achieving a sense of mastery. In other words, students feel successful if they believe they have personally improved, or have come to understand something. Their performance relative to others is irrelevant; of greater importance is the task.

In contrast, central to a performance goal is a *focus on one's ability and sense of self-worth*. Ability is shown by doing better than others, by surpassing norms, or by achieving success with little effort. Public recognition for doing better than others is an important element of a performance goal orientation. Performance goals and achievement are 'referenced', against the performance of others or against external standards such as marks and grades. Consequently, 'self-worth' is determined by one's perception of ability to perform relative to others. Hence, when students try hard without being completely successful (in terms of the established norms) their sense of self-worth is threatened (Ames 1992; Covington 1992; Dweck 1986; Nicholls 1989).

Research evidence suggests that students adopting a mastery orientation focus on learning, understanding and mastering the task, while those who adopt a performance orientation appear to focus on getting a good mark or doing better than other students. One of the major offshoots of this is that mastery-oriented individuals appear to use deeper processing strategies like elaboration as well as more metacognitive and self-regulatory strategies (Nolen 1988) (see Chapters 4 and 5). It also appears that mastery-oriented students can retrieve information more effectively from long-term memory (Graham & Golan 1991). Research has further shown that mastery goals increase the amount of time children spend on learning tasks and their persistence in the face of difficulty.

In contrast, performance-oriented individuals appear more likely to use surface level strategies such as rote memorisation and rehearsal (see Chapter 5). Furthermore, because this approach is linked with social comparison, it has been associated with both avoidance of challenging tasks (particularly with those students who have a low self-concept of ability, and withdrawal from tasks after an initial failure (why continue if one lacks ability?).

In addition to academic goal structures, individuals can also have **morality-based goals**. By this we mean a motivational system in which the goal is to help others in a cooperative group work situation in the hope of increasing the group's achievement (Ames 1984).

The importance of effort

When the focus of attention is effort, as with mastery-oriented and morality-based learning, pride and satisfaction are associated with successful effort, and guilt with inadequate effort. As the relationship between ability and outcome is not an issue the student is encouraged to expend greater effort to improve performance next time round. In this sense the utility of the mastery goal approach fits within the attributional framework discussed earlier in the chapter. Mastery-oriented students are more likely to be tolerant of failure (Ames 1992) and see it as a necessary condition for further effort in learning. Similarly, with morality-based motivation, individual effort is seen in terms of contribution to a group product and helping others, as in cooperative teamwork. The *intention* of group members to help or expend effort takes priority over their actual ability to do so, irrespective of group success or failure (Abrami et al. 1992; Abrami et al. 1995).

How do schools communicate achievement goals?

There is considerable research directed at examining ways in which schools and teachers implicitly and explicitly communicate various achievement goals.

TABLE 9.5

BEHAVIOURAL AND AFFECTIVE COMPONENTS OF MASTERY AND PERFORMANCE GOALS

Behavioural components of mastery goals

Students motivated by mastery goals:

- take extra effort in class even when there are no marks for it;
- seek challenging work for the sake of it;
- ask for additional work;
- ask more than the usual number of questions about their work;
- make applications of school knowledge to the real world.

Affective components of master goals

Students motivated by mastery goals:

- are pleased when they find the solution to a problem;
- enjoy challenging work even though it is more difficult;
- are pleased when extra effort leads to a good result;
- want to understand things even if it requires extra effort or explanation from the teacher;

Behavioural components of performance goals

Students motivated by performance goals:

- ask questions often about the teacher's expectations related to assignments;
- ask questions about the structure of assignments, especially how many marks are awarded to each section;
- do work beyond the usual expectations to get more marks;
- question the distribution of exam and assignment marks.

Affective components of performance goals

Students motivated by performance goals:

- get upset when their academic results are not as good as expected;
- are never satisfied with anything less than their very best;
- are constantly concerned about relative performance.

(based on Dowson & McInerney 1996, 1997)

There are many ways in which schools communicate achievement goals to students: through the **tasks** that are set, the **assessment** and **evaluation** policies implemented, and the **distribution of authority** within the school and classrooms (Ames 1992 Blumenfeld 1992).

The nature of the tasks set

Clearly, the nature of the tasks set for children will influence whether they are likely to become intrinsically interested or strive for extrinsic goals (such as grades and marks). Among key aspects of tasks that have been found to be related to interest and intrinsic motivation are *variety, diversity, challenge, control* and *meaningfulness*. We have made many suggestions throughout this and other chapters about how student interest in learning tasks may be enhanced by developing these task dimensions. When motivation is intrinsic, social comparison and other performance criteria become less salient to the student.

The type of evaluation conducted

The way in which schools and teachers evaluate and recognise student performance also establishes both overt and covert goal structures. For example, if teachers structure learning episodes so that students engage in intrinsically motivated learning and they are then evaluated through non-competitive means (such as portfolios), students are likely to be mastery-oriented. On the other hand, if teachers structure learning episodes so that students experience intrinsically motivated learning and then evaluate them through formal normative testing, students are likely to be performance-oriented. In this case, the covert goal established through the assessment process is performance-based. Whenever evaluation is based on social comparison, performance goals are established: the overt mastery goals established through the structure of the learning episodes are thereby undermined. We deal with this issue in some detail in Chapter 13.

As discussed earlier, the use of extrinsic reward systems may also undermine mastery orientation under certain conditions (see Chapter 6).

Distribution of shared authority

Another powerful factor that will influence whether children perceive the classroom as mastery or performance oriented relates to who holds the power to make decisions in the classroom. The extent to which children perceive that they genuinely share authority and have significant levels of autonomy in making choices appears to be a significant factor in their engagement in learning and the quality of their effort. To the extent that external controls are reduced and children have some meaningful level of control over the selection of tasks, materials, method of learning, product, pace and assessment, they are more likely to be mastery-oriented than performance-oriented. Again, this issue is dealt with in a number of chapters.

Question point: What is the importance of goal structure in influencing motivation and relationships with others? Differentiate between and give examples of cooperative, competitive and individualistic goal structures.

Expanding goal theory to other dimensions of importance

Recent theorising and research suggest that performance and mastery goals are not opposites and that individuals may hold both, varying in importance, depending on the nature of the task, the school environment and the broader social and educational context of the school (see e.g. Blumenfeld 1992; McInerney 1989, 1991b; McInerney & Sinclair 1992; Pintrich & Garcia 1991; Urdan & Maehr 1995; Wentzel 1991a, 1991b). Furthermore, students may hold multiple goals such as a desire to please their parents and teachers, to be important in the peer group (especially for girls in some cultures), to preserve their cultural identity, each of which may impact upon their level of motivation for particular tasks in school settings. Indeed, these multiple goals interact providing a complex framework of motivational determinants of action. A child from a minority group especially for girls in some cultures, for example, may feel strong conflicting pressures to maintain cultural values which may not foster academic achievement, and to achieve in a school context, strongly expressed in teachers' values. Meanwhile, yet another pressure is operating, that of being accepted and liked by one's peers, which may further influence whether doing well at school is seen as appropriate or not.

Personal investment in achieving goals

Schooling does not consist solely of learning academic material. Indeed, the social dimension of schooling (including the influence of parents, teachers and peers) may be equally important, and extremely influential in affecting children's attitudes towards schooling in general, and learning in particular. A goal model of motivation which considers other relevant and interacting goals has been used in a number of studies of student motivation. This approach is called the **personal investment theory of motivation**. This model is helpful in conceptualising motivation as it highlights, first, that students may hold multiple goals, each of which may impact upon their level of motivation for particular tasks, and, second, that there is a potential interaction between a variety of important goals for students in school-related areas.

In the personal investment model the goal structures are described as task, ego, social solidarity and extrinsic rewards. **Task goals** emphasise the intrinsic interest of the learning exercise where the goal of learning is to gain understanding, insight or skill. Learning in itself is valued, and the attainment of mastery is seen as dependent on one's effort. **Ego** and **extrinsic goals** emphasise individual comparison and competition, and achievement is seen as the means of obtaining external rewards. **Social solidarity goals** emphasise the cooperative and affiliative dimensions of learning. Among social goals that have been found influential in determining a student's motivation at school are approval, responsibility, welfare, affiliation and survival (Dowson & McInerney 1997).

Each of the goal structures described in the personal investment model impacts upon an individual's sense of competence, sense of autonomy and sense of purpose in learning, and contributes to the motivational orientation of the individual. Our own research indicates that classrooms and schools should emphasise task and social solidarity goals. Unfortunately, many schools emphasise ego and extrinsic goals through competition and social comparison, ability grouping and tracking, public evaluation of performance and conduct based on normative standards of performance. Such schools give children little opportunity to cooperate and interact with other children, and little opportunity to choose the tasks that are of most interest and relevance to them. There are, of course, classrooms and schools that emphasise task and social solidarity orientations and give opportunities for peer interaction and cooperation; they group students according to interest and needs, allow flexibility in choice of activities and opportunities for student initiative and responsibility, define success in terms of effort, progress and improvement, and put emphasis on the value and interest of learning. Children in these classrooms are likely to be highly motivated, to set themselves meaningful and challenging goals of achievement, and to persist at school for the perceived benefits that will accrue to them.

We consider personal investment theory in more detail when we discuss motivation in a cross-cultural context in Chapter 12.

TABLE 9.6

BEHAVIOURAL AND AFFECTIVE COMPONENTS OF SOCIAL GOALS

Behavioural components of social goals

Students motivated by social goals may:

- ask about marks and grades on behalf of parents;
- work hard at school to please parents;
- make opportunities to talk to teachers;
- work hard at school to please teachers;
- become involved in charity/fundraising activities;
- volunteer for activities that help the class to run well, such as book and lunch monitoring;

- pass notes in class;
- stake out an area in the playground;
- want to work only with particular people;
- interact with peers beyond the immediate school situation;
- be upset when friends are reprimanded;
- become involved in peer tutoring;
- voluntarily help special needs children in the class/playground;
- volunteer to be a buddy or peer adviser;
- promote the social development/interaction of less accepted peers;
- make other students aware of school rules and conventions.

(based on Dowson & McInerney, 1996, 1997)

Question point: *Competition is a powerful incentive since it brings the full force of group pressure to bear upon the learner. On the other hand, it can be dangerous and should be used judiciously. How might competition be used judiciously and effectively?*

Question point: *Discuss the potential effects on students of each of the following classroom procedures. In particular, discuss the effects on high- and low-need achievers of:*

(a) streaming
(b) open classrooms
(c) mastery learning
(d) competitions.

ADOLESCENCE AND SCHOOL MOTIVATION: ARE THERE SPECIAL ISSUES?

It is a common experience of teachers that it is easier to motivate younger children academically than adolescents. There is clear evidence that there is a decline in school motivation for many students as they move from primary grades to high school (Anderman & Maehr 1994). Research tends to support the view that motivation is a serious issue during adolescence, and whether adolescent students are motivated academically may have major consequences for later life choices.

What are the causes of this decline in school motivation? Studies suggest that declines in motivation during adolescence are associated with contextual/environmental factors and are not simply the result of pubertal changes (Anderman & Maehr 1994; Eccles & Midgley 1989). There is a direct link between changes in classroom learning environments as children move into secondary grades and the decline in motivation, with a number of researchers suggesting that the instructional practices and educational policies of secondary schools may be inappropriate for maintaining student motivation.

Contextual and environmental factors

Secondary schools, for example, emphasise comparative student performance through exams and assignments much more than primary schools. As children grow older they become more convinced that ability is relatively fixed and that expenditure of effort, particularly in an activity in which they are not very successful, demonstrates their lack of competence to others. Consequently, many individuals avoid putting in effort simply to avoid being labelled ‘dumb’. Through their assessment and evaluation policies and practices, many secondary schools do not encourage adolescents to become academic ‘risk-takers’.

Relationship between ability and effort

Adolescents seek opportunities for developing a sense of self-efficacy and autonomy. We see this commonly demonstrated by the way in which adult power is constantly challenged by adolescents. Secondary schools, by and large, are very regimented places in which the power hierarchy is quite explicit, both within and outside the classroom. With little opportunity to take charge of their own learning and motivation in such a context, many adolescent students simply oppose or withdraw from engagement (see, for example, Eccles & Midgley 1989; Eccles et al. 1993).

Self-efficacy and autonomy

Many primary classrooms emphasise the fun of learning and thus captivate students intrinsically in activities. Who said that adolescents no longer want or need to be captivated? Yet many secondary classrooms are crushingly dull places in which to learn. It is still common to hear of teachers who engage their students in monotonous rote recall activities such as copying notes off the whiteboard. With little real stimulation in many classrooms, students will engage in a diverse range of more stimulating, non-academic activities. It is not a case of adolescents lacking motivation but, rather, of them investing their motivational energy in the wrong activities for the lack of something better at school.

Fun and intrinsic motivation

The next section addresses the question of how schools can more effectively fit the needs of students so that motivation is enhanced.

CHANGING A SCHOOL’S PSYCHOLOGICAL ENVIRONMENT TO ENHANCE STUDENT MOTIVATION

It is clear that to enhance students’ motivation we must improve school and classroom practices. Maehr has called this changing the school’s ‘psychological environment’ (Anderman & Maehr 1994; Maehr, Midgley &

Urdan 1992). There is a need to change a lot of the messages that classrooms and schools communicate to children about the purposes of schooling—messages that are communicated through policies and practices related to rewards, praise and recognition, the nature of school tasks, grouping and evaluation practices, and resource allocation. A number of these topics have been covered in earlier sections of the chapter. Our research, and that of an increasingly large group of educators, has shown that the personal engagement of children in learning seems to be most affected by the sense of self that students have in the school context. The expectations that students hold for themselves as they generalise from past experiences and incorporate the more immediate expectations of parents, teachers and peers profoundly affect motivation and performance level. Children's sense of self, reflected through a sense of competence and a sense of the purpose of schooling, is critical to their motivation, academic achievement and retention at school.

Sense of competence

Sense of competence relates to students' self-concept for the task of learning: how they assess their capacity to learn. A sense of competence is a major determinant of children's school confidence, how much they like school, their level of attendance, and the goals they set for themselves while at school and later. Our research has shown that children who feel incompetent dislike school, have limited occupational aspirations, have high absenteeism and lower classroom grades (McInerney 1993; McInerney & Swisher 1995).

Sense of purpose in schooling

Students who have a strong sense of the purpose of schooling value school more, intend to complete school, perform better academically at school, and desire more prestigious occupations after leaving school than those who do not see a purpose in schooling. Clearly, those students who set academic goals and see a purpose in schooling are more likely to be successful in that context.

Achievement motivation

In all the studies conducted by the author, level of intrinsic motivation, such as striving for excellence in one's work and desiring improvement against personal standards, strongly predicted a student's commitment to learning. In contrast, competition and extrinsic rewards were either unimportant or contrary to the best interests of the children. For example, in our Australian study, extrinsic rewards only appeared to be important to children already determined to leave school! In a Navajo study we conducted, the extrinsic dimension was excluded from the final profile for these students as it appeared to be culturally irrelevant! With regard to competition, all groups appear to be competitive to some degree, but competitiveness does not seem to be related to school motivation and achievement.

Diagnosing current school practice

As we have suggested, many schools and classrooms do not implement policies and practices that are in the best interests of motivating children, and in some cases school practices actually run counter to effective motivation strategies within classroom settings. For example, a teacher may work very hard to encourage children's intrinsic interest in reading only to have the school executive decide to implement a commercial program, such as that presented by a particular pizza company, where rewards and incentives become a goal. Or a teacher may decide to grade according to improvement, only to have this undermined by a normed assessment program across grades. Teachers may provide recognition on the basis of progress, improvement and effort, while the school rewards relative ability. Obviously, best practice must be introduced consistently, across classrooms and across the school as a whole.

Target the problem

Borrowing an acronym (TARGET) from Epstein (1989), Maehr (Buck & Green 1993; Maehr & Midgley 1991; Maehr & Anderman 1993) has developed a framework that can be used to guide the development of a schoolwide emphasis on task goals in learning rather than ego goals (see Table 9.7). TARGET is a process for effectively assessing current practices within a school, and planning future directions in order to integrate and implement the findings, discussed above, on what practices are most likely to engage the intrinsic motivation of children in learning (Ames 1990). The acronym stands for:

Task	Grouping
Authority	Evaluation
Recognition	Time

Within each of the TARGET areas, teachers and administrators can use strategies that either focus on task and social solidarity goals, or on ego and extrinsic goals. Maehr (Maehr & Midgley 1991, p. 404) makes the following points:

Teachers can and do define the nature of academic **Tasks**. *Thus, they may make specific attempts to give their students challenging learning experiences. They may attempt to select activities that are interesting and intrinsically engaging. Similarly, teachers make significant decisions regarding how they will share* **Authority** *or distribute responsibility; they* **Reward** *and* **Recognize** *students for different reasons, for improvement, progress, or for comparative performance; they* **Group** *children differently and thereby emphasize or de-emphasize interpersonal competition and social*

TABLE 9.7

GENERAL FRAMEWORK EMPLOYED IN THE DEVELOPMENT OF A SCHOOL-WIDE EMPHASIS ON TASK GOALS IN LEARNING

TARGET Area	Focus	Goals	Strategies
Task	Intrinsic value of learning	■ Reduce the reliance on extrinsic incentives ■ Design programs that challenge all students ■ Stress goals and purposes in learning ■ Stress the fun of learning	■ Encourage programs that take advantage of students' backgrounds and experience ■ Avoid payment (monetary or other) for attendance, grades or achievement ■ Foster programs that stress goal setting and self-regulation/management ■ Foster programs that make use of school learning in a variety of non-school settings (e.g. internships, field experiences and cocurricular activities)
Authority	Student participation in learning/school decision making	■ Provide opportunities to develop responsibility, independence and leadership skills ■ Develop skills in self-regulation	■ Give optimal choice in instructional settings ■ Foster participation in cocurricular and extracurricular settings ■ Foster opportunities to learn metacognitive strategies for self-regulation
Recognition	The nature and use of recognition and reward in the school setting	■ Provide opportunities for all students to be recognised ■ Recognise progress in goal attainment ■ Recognise efforts in a broad array of learning activities	■ Foster 'personal best' awards ■ Foster policy in which all students and their achievements can be recognised ■ Recognise and publicise wide range of school-related activities of students
Grouping	Student interaction, social skills and values	■ Build an environment of acceptance and appreciation of all students ■ Broaden range of social interaction, particularly of at-risk students ■ Enhance social skill development ■ Encourage humane values ■ Build an environment in which all can see themselves as capable of making significant contributions	■ Provide opportunities for group learning, problem solving and decision making ■ Allow time and opportunity for peer interaction to occur ■ Foster the development of subgroups (teams, schools within schools, etc.) within which significant interaction can occur ■ Encourage multiple group membership to increase range of peer interaction
Evaluation	The nature and use of evaluation and assessment procedures	■ Increase students' sense of competence and self-efficacy ■ Increase students' awareness of progress in developing skills and understanding ■ Increase students' appreciation of their unique set of talents ■ Increase students' acceptance of failure as a natural part of learning and life	■ Reduce emphasis on social comparisons of achievement by minimising public reference to normative evaluation standards (e.g. grades and test scores) ■ Establish policies and procedures that give students opportunities to improve their performance (e.g. study skills and classes) ■ Create opportunities for students to assess progress toward goals they have set
Time	The manage-ment of time to carry out plans and reach goals	■ Improve rate of work completion ■ Improve skills in planning and organising ■ Improve self-management ability ■ Allow the learning task and student needs to dictate scheduling	■ Provide experience in personal goal setting and in monitoring progress in carrying out plans for goal achievement ■ Foster opportunities to develop time management skills ■ Allow students to progress at their own rate whenever possible ■ Encourage flexibility in the scheduling of learning experiences

(reprinted with permission from Maehr & Midgley 1991)

comparison; they certainly Evaluate *in various ways and on various bases. Finally, teachers choose to use* Time *allotted to them in certain ways and, of course, significantly control the scheduling of learning. To some degree all of these factors seem to contribute to an overall sense of what learning in a particular classroom, at least, is about. Such strategies as those grouped in the so-called TARGET categories serve to communicate to students the purpose for learning in a given situation. (p. 404)*

LEARNER-CENTRED
PSYCHOLOGICAL PRINCIPLE 8

Acquisition of complex knowledge and skills requires extended learner effort and guided practice. Without the learner's motivation to learn, the willingness to exert this effort is unlikely without coercion.

Educators must support and develop learners' natural curiosity or intrinsic motivation to learn, rather than 'fixing them' or driving them by fear of punishment. Also, both positive interpersonal support and instruction in self-control strategies can offset factors that interfere with optimal learning—factors such as low self-awareness; negative beliefs; lack of learning goals; negative expectations for success; and anxiety, insecurity, or pressure.

Reprinted with permission, APA Task Force on Psychology in Education (1993, January), p. 7.

Some students become anxious in a testing situation. How might we structure tests to alleviate anxiety? Photo: Connie Griebe

ANXIETY AND SCHOOL MOTIVATION

Many children experience moderate to severe anxiety within the school setting. Such anxiety can be general (i.e. an overall feeling of unease while at school) or it can be more specifically related to particular subjects, teachers or school practices (such as testing and evaluation). It appears that general forms of anxiety increase as students move from primary into secondary grades. This has been associated with changing school environments. Secondary schools are more evaluative and social comparisons become more prevalent. Other factors that are thought to increase school anxiety are moving from a smaller to a larger school, having different teachers (and classmates) throughout the school day, experiencing ability grouping, and having fewer opportunities for decision making and less autonomy (Wigfield & Eccles 1989). One specific form of anxiety we will consider is test anxiety.

Test anxiety

What is test anxiety? Does it affect all students? How does test anxiety affect motivation and learning, and what can the teacher do to prevent or minimise any negative effects?

Research in the area of anxiety has differentiated between individuals who show **state anxiety** (which is experienced only in certain situations such as exams or learning to use a computer) and those for whom anxiety is a **trait** (which generally affects much of what they do in their lives). **Test anxiety** (Wigfield & Eccles 1989) is an example of state anxiety—specifically, it is a state of anxiety about not performing well when being evaluated in a test situation. The anxiety is experienced by those for whom the test situation involves a perceived threat to their self-esteem, sometimes referred to as 'ego-involvement' (Heckhausen 1991).

State and trait anxiety

Final phase of preparation for an exam.

Why do some students become more test-anxious than others? There are two current theories about the causes of test anxiety; let's have a closer look at them.

Types of test anxious students

The first theory suggests that students find it *hard to focus attention* on the task at hand because of self-doubting and task-irrelevant thoughts generated in the evaluative situation (e.g. worrying about how one is doing rather than concentrating on the task). It is argued that these thoughts interfere with the retrieval of learned material and that students perform poorly as a consequence (Wigfield & Eccles 1989; Wine 1971).

Attention interference theory

A more recent theory regards the *ineffective information-processing skills* of some highly test-anxious students as the main factor in their anxiety and poor academic performance in test situations. Naveh-Benjamin (1991), for example, demonstrated that, for highly test-anxious students who had poor study habits, a training program in study skills reduced anxiety and improved performance in a test situation. Prior to such training, these students had performed poorly in both take-home tests (with no external pressure) and written (essay and short-answer) questions under test conditions. This type of evidence suggested that *initial* learning and organisation of material was ineffective, thereby making retrieval of complex learning material difficult, rather than a problem of blockage during recall. As Covington and Omelich (1987) suggest: 'Simply put, learning must be present for it to be interfered with' (p. 393). The cause of anxiety for these students is their **metacognitive awareness** of their inadequate knowledge (Tobias 1985a).

Information-processing skills theory

The evidence strongly suggests, therefore, that there are two types of test-anxious student: those who have good study habits but who suffer from interference (through negative cognitions) at the retrieval stage of information processing; and those who have poor study habits which prevent them from learning material effectively at the outset (Wigfield & Eccles 1989). (See also Chapter 4 for a thorough description of the elements of information processing.)

Are there effective means of alleviating text anxiety?

Naveh-Benjamin (1991) found that, for the first type of student, the most effective treatment was a program which **desensitised** the student to the anxiety-producing elements of the exam situation so that attention could be focused on the task itself. For these students, strategies that taught them how to deal with their interfering thoughts were most effective. In particular, training in **relaxation techniques** paired with **visualisation** of anxiety-producing test situations (such as entering the exam room, seeing printed exam questions, and receiving grades) was beneficial.

Relaxation and desensitising techniques

For the second type of anxious student (with poor study skills), **improvement in study habits**, such as training in the **PQ4R technique** (Thomas & Robinson 1972), improved performance in situations perceived as evaluative, because knowledge of material was increased, and anxiety decreased because of greater metacognitive awareness of improved mastery. (See Chapter 5.)

Improvement in study habits

Bandura believes an individual's perceived coping self-efficacy regulates anxiety arousal. The stronger people's belief that they can cope, the bolder they are in taking on threatening situations (Bandura 1993). Students who have a low sense of efficacy at managing academic demands are expecially vulnerable to achievement anxiety. Bandura suggests that the best way of alleviating this is to develop in students cognitive capabilities and self-regulative skills for managing academic task demands and self-debilitating thoughts.

Enhancing self-efficacy

There will always be a number of students in your care who are anxious about evaluation. It is important that you identify and address the source of their anxiety before motivation to achieve becomes seriously affected. Knowing that for highly test-anxious students, grading and testing may reduce their performance or even debilitate them, you need to consider the matter of assessment carefully.

Effective reduction of anxiety involves the use of coping strategies to remove or circumvent the cause of stress and to deal with the reactions and emotions that are experienced. Coping strategies can be categorised in three ways (Zeidner 1995):

Coping strategies in exam situations

1. *Problem-focused* coping, which tries to manage or solve the problem by dealing with the source of the stress in a positive way; e.g. through planning, collecting resources, studying hard;
2. *Emotion-focused* coping, which tries to reduce the emotional symptoms associated with stress; e.g. talking to friends to gain reassurance, crying, denying the importance of the situation;
3. *avoidance-oriented coping*, which tries to avoid the stressful situation; e.g. by isolating oneself from others, wasting time on irrelevant tasks, watching television excessively.

The evidence is clear that, while emotion-focused or avoidance coping might help the individual keep an emotional balance for a short time, they may become maladaptive or even dysfunctional over time (Wills

1986). There are plenty of examples of the negative long-term effects of ventilation of emotions, mental disengagement, binge eating and the use of tension-relieving substances such as alcohol and drugs, where the maladaptive nature of such coping strategies becomes evident (Carver, Sheier & Weintraub 1989).

With important tests or exams, the stressor cannot be removed. However, reducing the perceived threat that it poses can be achieved by planning a study schedule, increasing study time, and working with a friend or parent to revise important material. Such coping strategies are adaptive in that they are problem-focused and provide a sense of mastery over the stressor. This sense of personal control over the situation changes the perspective, diverting attention in a positive direction. It also helps to reduce the physiological and emotional reactions that initially build up at the anticipatory stage: 'What am I going to do to cope? There are all these demands on me.'

One method of helping students for whom the test situation is debilitating is to reduce the perceived threat of evaluation. Covington and Omelich (1987), for example, provided opportunities for students to resit an exam with unlimited time in which to complete answers. They found that, for students who were well prepared, this opportunity disinhibited anxiety and allowed original learning to be effectively retrieved. Not surprisingly, for those who were poorly prepared (although anxious) the disinhibition did not improve performance.

Failure-avoiding and failure-accepting students

Researchers distinguish between **failure-avoiding** and **failure-accepting** students. Students who are failure-avoiding (highly anxious with good study skills) are motivated to achieve in order to maintain their sense of personal value which is judged by external performance. However, they are anxious that, if they fail despite all their efforts, they will be seen as lacking in ability. On the other hand, students who fail repeatedly because of poor study skills will be anxious but failure-accepting, believing that their failure is an indication of low ability. Over time, such students will become resigned to defeat, having little or no motivation to achieve, akin to learned helplessness (Abramson, Seligman & Teasdale 1978).

TABLE 9.8

ESSENTIALS OF REDUCING STUDENT ANXIETY

For teachers

- Teach effective study habits to students and review them periodically.
- Teach relaxation techniques.
- Utilise desensitisation strategies such as exposure to 'mock' exam situations, as appropriate.
- Reduce time pressures in evaluative situations.
- De-emphasise the evaluative nature of the task in test situations. Emphasise the nature of the task and self-evaluation (relative to previous performance) rather than competition and student–student comparison.
- Whenever possible, give students feedback on their performance that is task-related (such as comments) rather than ego-related (such as grades and praise). In this way, intrinsic motivation will be fostered and concerns about self-worth will be minimised.
- Provide opportunities for overstriving (well-prepared), anxious students to meet as a group with the teacher to share concerns. Often this reassurance will reduce anxiety considerably.
- Provide models of anxious individuals engaging in successful task-completion strategies.
- Provide more organised instructional material for highly anxious students.

For learners

- Recognise signs of anxiety such as negative self-talk ('I can't do this'; 'I'm going to fail'), fearfulness, irritability, avoidance and worry.
- Practise positive self-talk ('I can do this if I try/ask for more help/work harder/manage my time better/don't allow myself to be distracted').
- Learn and use relaxation techniques: deep breathing, muscle contraction and relaxation, brisk exercise, conscious 'emptying' of mind and focusing on a positive image.
- Set short-term achievable goals rather than global, long-term goals.
- Learn study skills (from teachers, friends, books) and reward yourself with special privileges when you practise them successfully.
- Practise working to a time limit for some tasks.
- Ask the teacher for feedback on your work.
- Talk to others who tend to be anxious and share your worries; talk to your teacher about your concerns; listen to others' advice.
- Confide in significant adults (parents or other family members) and encourage them to show interest in your work.

(based on Butler 1987; Nicholls 1984; Sarason 1972, 1975; Wigfield & Eccles 1989)

AROUSAL THEORY AND ITS RELATIONSHIP TO MOTIVATION AND ANXIETY

An optimal level of arousal is required for active attention and involvement in specific activities. For example, the arousal level for an exam needs to be higher than the arousal level for quiet reading, but less than the appropriate arousal level for finding one's house on fire (although the way some students go on at tests you would think that their house was indeed on fire!). If arousal level is too low for a given activity students become bored, and perhaps even fall asleep; if it is too high, students may panic or freeze. The figure below illustrates the continuum from less effective to very effective behaviour, depending on appropriate arousal level for a given activity.

Arousal level and effective action

To a large extent, teachers control the arousal level in a classroom through the use of media, variability of presentation, challenging questions and so on. However, for the effective use of such stimulating strategies the arousal level of particular students needs to be taken into account.

Arousal level and variabilility

The author recalls a graphic example of arousal in the classroom. A student teacher had had considerable trouble motivating her year 4 class to be actively involved in her lessons. He had a 'heart to heart' with her and suggested a number of ways in which she could generate greater enthusiasm (in effect, to arouse the children). The next day he turned up to supervise the lesson. The student teacher was to give a creative writing lesson on ghosts and had gone to considerable trouble darkening the classroom, hanging creepy things from the ceiling, and making a recording of ghost-like noises. When the children entered the classroom they were bombarded by the highly novel stimulation and spent the rest of the period running around on desk tops making **'WHOOOO'** noises and scaring the living daylights out of each other. The teacher was beside herself—so much for arousal.

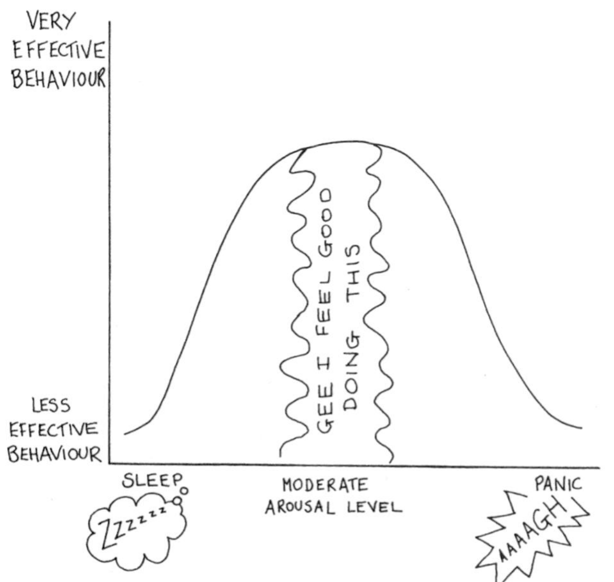

'Weave the cane around the basket.' Hmmm, perhaps the clarity of the message got lost in the excitement of the task.

Closely aligned with arousal is anxiety. As we suggested earlier, if the level of arousal for a given activity is too high then an individual may panic or freeze. This is particularly likely to occur when a person's performance is to be evaluated in some way. Public performances such as giving a speech, appearing on the stage, demonstrating a skill, or completing a test or exercise are potentially capable of creating anxiety rather than optimal arousal.

Classroom applications of arousal theory

Teachers would dearly love to be able to 'switch on' the optimal level of arousal for students in particular learning activities. Our experience is that in some activities students become aroused too quickly (how many teachers give up taking art and craft lessons because the children become too excitable?), while in other activities they show no interest at all. It is not an easy task to manipulate arousal levels in the classroom so that they are optimal, for this needs to take into account individual student differences in susceptibility to stimulation, the characteristics of the material or experience that students are being exposed to, as well as teacher characteristics.

Variability

For Berlyne (1960) the primary determinants of arousal are novelty and change, surprisingness, complexity and ambiguity. A number of teaching texts (Cole & Chan 1987; Barry & King 1993; Turney et al. 1985a,

WHAT WOULD YOU DO?

REBIRTH OF A GRADE 8 CLASSROOM

At Mr Daniels' school it is a customary policy for teachers to view how another teacher is developing students' reading, writing, speaking, listening and critical thinking skills. The school is a district high school and it was decided that a primary teacher would work with a secondary teacher. This structured collaborative program continued for four weeks.

Mr Daniels felt there were so many things that he could learn from the primary area that he continued to visit the Prep/1 class at the end of the four-week structured program. Each time he went there he was struck by the stimulating and aesthetically pleasing environment, and reminded of the sterility of his own room. So with the cooperation of the Prep/1 teacher, a deal was struck!

What do you think the deal was and how would Mr Daniels' secondary classroom be affected? Read what actually happened on page 197.

Case studies illustrating National Framework for Beginning Teaching, National Project on the Quality of Teaching and Learning, Australian Teaching Council, 1996, p. 11. Commonwealth of Australia copyright, reproduced by permission.

1985b) translate these into principles of variability which are intended to maximise students' attention to and interest in the learning activity. Key aspects of variability according to Turney et al. are:

- **variations in teacher's manner or style**
  voice
  focusing and pausing
  eye contact
  gesturing
  movement
- **variations in the media and materials of instruction**
  visual
  aural
  tactile
- **interaction variation**
  teacher–pupil interchange variations
  pupil activity variations

More recently, this notion of variability has been related to task-oriented (sometimes called mastery-orientated) motivation which can foster positive achievement activity (Ames 1992). We dealt with task-oriented motivation earlier in the chapter. However, more knowledge is needed about how variability can truly promote mastery orientation rather than simply induce short-term attention. In the latter case, the attention may be a necessary precursor of, but not synonymous with, intrinsic motivation. There is a danger that, unless it is carefully designed, task variety can heighten interest and attention at the expense of cognitive engagement (Blumenfeld 1992).

Two aspects of arousal theory which have implications for classroom management are **overstimulation** and **understimulation.** Overstimulation may lead to disruptive behaviour (such as the children pretending to be ghosts) or even anxiety and panic for some individuals. It is not unusual to have children 'freeze' when they are asked to read in public, or 'forget' all they have learnt when they are faced with an impromptu exam. When children are understimulated they may engage in 'diverse exploration' (Heckhausen 1991) whereby they seek out stimulation regardless of content and source. This behaviour is not related to curiosity but is frequently motivated by boredom. So children daydream, misbehave, pass notes, poke other children in the back and in general become obnoxious to the teacher (and often to each other).

Overstimulation and understimulation

As teachers we will, from time to time, be confronted with classroom problems stemming from under- and overstimulation. In Chapter 10, which deals with classroom management, we address this issue and give some practical hints on how to handle the situation.

ACTION STATION

Even when students are initially interested in a topic, attention may flag at times. Observe how classroom teachers maintain student attention during a lesson or group work. Techniques might include variability (such as the use of aids, group dynamics and sensory modalities), attention cues (such as 'this is very important', or bells and claps), accountability (such as structured cooperative activities involving designated roles), questioning (general question to whole class before directing to specific student). There are many others. Remember that the most important element in motivation is the initial interest. Attention-gaining techniques may simply be reduced to razzmatazz unless the learning activity itself is meaningful, relevant and interesting to the children.

Observe and *discuss* with teachers the ways in which attention is gained and maintained in the classroom. *Record* your observations.

Question point: *Do you know what the interests of the learners in your class are? How might you find out what their interests are? How would you use this knowledge in planning your teaching/learning activities?*

WHAT WOULD YOU DO?

REBIRTH OF A GRADE 8 CLASSROOM (continued)

Mr Daniels would do English/Social Science work with Mrs Wilson's children, and she would assist him in the overhaul of his box-like room. It took them six weeks, but now the changes include a large work board to celebrate outstanding student work; a reading corner containing numerous texts (students can borrow these); copious amounts of student work displayed around the room; a games area with educational work and thinking games for early finishers or as a reward; a knowledge area where students are kept informed about world issues—that is, writing letters to the President of Bosnia condemning the mass rape of women by soldiers; and learning centres or independent working areas, with activities related to core work.

Mr Daniels believes that his teaching and the students' learning have changed in quite significant ways. He now has a stimulating, informative environment which enhances the quality of his teaching. The efforts put into the classroom environment are recognised by the students. He feels that the new organisation of his classroom makes a strong statement about quality learning and about the value he places on this learning place. The students feel comfortable in the classroom and they take pride in its appearance for they feel a sense of ownership. Mr Daniels is able to employ a diverse range of teaching methodologies. Students are immersed in written language every time they enter his classroom and reluctant learners are motivated to pick up things to view and read.

How many of the features of Mr Daniels' reborn classroom illustrate principles of learning and motivation covered in this and other chapters? Should secondary classrooms become more like good primary classrooms?

Case studies illustrating National Competency Framework for Beginning Teaching, National Project on the Quality of Teaching and Learning, Australian Teaching Council, 1996, p.11. Commonwealth of Australia copyright, reproduced with permission.

TEACHER EXPECTATIONS AND EFFECTIVE MOTIVATION

How do teacher expectations influence motivation and achievement?

'*We have no stars at our school.*' In her capacity as university adviser for practice teaching, the author was visiting a school located in a multicultural and lower socioeconomic area. She was holding a meeting with school staff to explain the involvement that student teachers would have at the school, and how they should be given opportunities to interact with teachers and pupils. The discussion moved to the area of exposing the student teachers to a range of pupil abilities and aptitudes, when one senior teacher stated 'We have no stars at our school'.

Positive expectations are important to the success of all children. Photo: WA Education News

The self-fulfilling prophecy effect

Pygmalion in the classroom

Implicit in much of what has been written so far is the notion that the beliefs that students hold about themselves and the expectations they have for their academic performance are strong influences on their school motivation. Where do these beliefs and expectations come from? One source, of course, is the classroom teacher. Significant research has been conducted into teacher expectations and their effects on learning, attitudes, beliefs, attributions, expectations, motivation and classroom conduct (see Brophy 1983, 1985 for a review). In an early study, *Pygmalion in the Classroom*, Rosenthal and Jacobson (1968; also Rosenthal 1973) demonstrated the effects of what has become known as the **self-fulfilling prophecy**, in which initially false expectations held by teachers set in motion a chain of events that cause the expectations to come true (Brophy 1985a, 1985b; Good 1995).

Four factors are believed to produce the Pygmalion effect (Rosenthal 1973): **climate, feedback, input** and

'My dad says the way Sir treats us kids is like something out of Shakespeare—whatever that means!'

output. Teachers who have been led to expect good things from their students appear to do the following.

1. *Climate:* they create a warmer social-emotional mood around their 'special' students.
2. *Feedback:* they give more feedback to these students about their performance.
3. *Input:* they teach more material and more difficult material to their special students.
4. *Output:* they give their special students more opportunities to respond and question.

A model of how expectations become self-fulfilling

Good and Brophy (1990; see also Good 1995) propose the following model to explain how teacher expectations become self-fulfilling:

- ☐ The teacher expects specific behaviour and achievement from particular students.
- ☐ Because of these expectations, the teacher behaves differently towards different students.
- ☐ This treatment by the teacher tells each student what behaviour and achievement the teacher expects, and it affects the student's self-concept, achievement motivation and level of aspiration.
- ☐ If this teacher treatment is consistent over time, and if the student does not actively resist or change it in some way, it will shape the student's achievement and behaviour. High-expectation students will be led to achieve at high levels, but the achievement of low-expectation students will decline.
- ☐ With time, the student's achievement and behaviour will conform more and more closely to that expected by the teacher. (p. 445)

In both of these models the student appears to be a relatively passive element in the process, and teachers appear to be relatively inflexible once they have embarked on an expectation-'driven' course of action. Much research since the original Rosenthal and Jacobson study has indicated that the process is far more complicated than this (see Brophy 1983; Goldenberg 1992; Good 1987). Good now talks of both the **self-fulfilling prophecy effect**, in which an originally *erroneous* expectation leads to behaviour that causes the expectation to become true, and the **sustaining expectation effect**, in which teachers expect students to sustain previously developed behaviour patterns, to the point that teachers take these behaviour patterns for granted, and fail to see and capitalise on changes in student potential. There are many examples of this latter effect, such as the class clown always being typecast, and the uninterested mathematics student not being actively encouraged to be involved despite his renewed interest. Good suggests that the sustaining expectation effect may be more pervasive than the self-fulfilling effect.

The sustaining expectation effect

The sources of teacher expectations

Some common sources of erroneous expectations that may influence teachers are **socioeconomic status** (children from public housing don't have the same ambitions as children from affluent suburbs, or children from professional homes are more motivated to achieve at school than children from working-class homes); **sex differences** (girls are less interested and able in maths than boys, girls are better behaved than boys, boys are better at mechanical activities than girls); **physical appearance** (good-looking children are more motivated and better behaved than unattractive children); **racial grouping** (Maori children are lazy while Asian children are very studious; Aboriginal children are less academically motivated and able than non-Aboriginal children). Among other sources of expectations are **student profiles** passed on from teacher to teacher, the individual's demonstrated **personality** (e.g. introvert, extrovert), apparent **achievement orientation and prior behaviour patterns** (Braun 1976).

Sources of teacher expectations
Socioeconomic status
Sex differences
Physical appearance
Racial stereotyping
Student profiles
Personality
Behaviour

An extensive literature review (Dusek & Joseph 1983) examined whether or not expectations based on some of the above assumptions were, in fact, related to various indices of student academic performance and social/personality behaviours. *Physical attractiveness* (usually measured by facial attractiveness) was found to be a determinant of teacher expectations for both academic performance and social/personality attributes. However, while expectations may initially be based on physical features in lieu of any other information, as other more academically pertinent information becomes available these expectations are modified by teachers. Despite research evidence suggesting that teachers interact differently with girls and boys in the classroom, this review concluded that student gender is not a basis of teacher expectations for general academic performance. However, student gender was related to expectations for classroom behaviour.

Information, such as *cumulative record files* and more informal sources of information (such as corridor talk), was found to be strongly related to teacher expectations. It is important to note here that teachers apparently distinguish between reliable and unreliable information, and that this more reliable information is used as a basis for developing programs for the individual. In this context the expectations may be highly valid and useful. Social class and racial stereotypes were also examined, and both were found to be significantly related to the formation of teacher expectations—for example, students from a lower social class were expected to perform more poorly than the higher social class students, and students who were black or Mexican were expected to perform less well than white students.

Sibling and family profiles

Other possible sources of expectations studied were whether teachers held expectations of siblings after experience with an older brother or sister, and whether expectations were based on family profiles, such as single parenting. In the first case there is some evidence that an older sibling's previous performance (with the same teacher) is related to the formation of teacher expectations, while family situation does not appear to be systematically related to the development of expectations. No doubt some of you can recall anecdotal stories of these expectations in operation. Table 9.9 summarises the findings from the Dusek and Joseph study.

TABLE 9.9

SUMMARY OF BASES OF TEACHER EXPECTATIONS

Student characteristics related to teacher expectations

- attractiveness
- student classroom conduct
- cumulative record folder
- race
- social class

Student characteristics not related to teacher expectations

- gender
- one-parent family situation

Student characteristics on which there is questionable evidence

- older sibling's previous performance (with same teacher)
- sex-role behaviour
- name stereotypes

Disconfirmations of teacher expectations

Expectations, even erroneous ones, are only likely to have an effect when the teacher holds them consistently and implements practices in line with these expectations which are not challenged by changes in student behaviour or other environmental events. Most of us have been guilty of expecting poor assignments and test results from particular students because they are inattentive, or appear non-involved in our particularly interesting lessons, only to be surprised when the student performs exceptionally well in a particular task. It is amazing how we look upon the student in a new light! Children who are perceived as disruptive will at times be 'little angels'; 'rude' children bring the teacher a Christmas present; children from low-income areas have professional parents; students we think of as academically hopeless are highly thought of by other teachers, and so on. These types of disconfirmation of expectations happen all the time in the classroom. Furthermore, particularly in high school, children have a variety of teachers over a school day, and so the impact of any one teacher is lessened. It should also be noted that many of the expectations that teachers have of students are based upon good understanding of the individual, are accurate, and are used to facilitate the effective development of the child. Indeed, one of the tasks we have set ourselves in this text is to give prospective teachers the information needed to make informed decisions about the likely needs of individual students, and to act appropriately to set up the best possible educational environment for them.

So perhaps the impact of inappropriate and inaccurate expectations of students is not as destructive as the theory of the self-fulfilling and self-sustaining prophecy would suggest. However, we must emphasise that the effect of expectations on student motivation and performance is quite pervasive. At times, expectations become detrimental to the effective learning of many children perceived by teachers to be low in motivation or low in ability because the expectations themselves become associated with *poor teaching*. Expectations can affect the type of groups that teachers establish, the type of questions asked and the wait time given for pupils to respond, the type of reinforcement and feedback given, the different activities that children are allowed to be involved in, and the general quality of interaction (Braun 1976; Good 1995). In general, high-expectation children are taught more effectively. They receive more positive and warm contact from the teacher. They are given more opportunities to learn new and more difficult material, and are given more clues and wait-time than low-expectation children. High-expectation children receive more praise and recognition for correct responses and less criticism for incorrect responses than low-expectation children (Brophy 1983; Good 1995). However, what really matters for student achievement is what teachers do or don't do, despite their expectations. In other words, if a teacher holds low expectations of a student but nevertheless takes strong corrective action, the chances of student success increase, despite low expectations. Conversely, if a teacher fails to teach effectively, even children for whom high expectations are held may perform poorly (Goldenberg 1992).

Classroom implications of teacher expectations

Teachers and positive expectations

While teacher expectations may affect a range of behaviours, our particular focus in this chapter is motivation. It would seem likely that when teachers expect learners to be interested in their work, productive and capable, and demonstrate this in their own preparation for teaching, they are more likely to find that learners make efforts to be so than if they expect the reverse. Several studies have shown the beneficial effects of such positive expectations on children (Andrews & Debus 1978; Dweck 1975; Schun 1982, 1983).

While teachers should hold positive expectations that children will want to learn, enjoy learning and be successful at learning, these positive expectations need to be tempered by a sense of reality. Teachers should seek to communicate a confidence that accurately reflects the student's actual ability and potential. Students need to be taught to monitor their own learning and achievements towards desired learning goals as well. Positive teacher and student expectations need to be buttressed by effective teaching. Even low-achieving students in such contexts improve their academic performance (Good 1995).

Question point: *Researchers have examined the effects of teacher expectancies on three factors: kinds of questions asked, quality of interaction, and reinforcement. Discuss the findings, indicating how high achievers and low achievers would be differentially treated in each area.*

Question point: *What unfounded assumptions are often held of students at school that might affect their self-concept and performance at school? What action should be taken to alleviate the negative effects of such assumptions?*

TEACHERS' COMMON KNOWLEDGE AND THEORY ABOUT MOTIVATION

We have covered a range of potential sources of classroom motivation and have suggested that motivators that arise from a child's inherent interest in the task and desire to master new information are probably more potent and effective than those derived from external influences such as a teacher's application of rewards and punishments, or social comparison. But what do teachers actually believe as part of their common knowledge and what do they actually do?

It appears that teachers have a good knowledge of, and preference for, strategies to stimulate and maintain motivation that are not dissimilar to those proposed by research as useful (Nolen & Nicholls 1994). The most preferred strategies for enhancing motivation are showing interest, giving responsibility, attributing thoughtfulness and improvement, promoting cooperation, selecting stimulating tasks and giving choice of tasks. Among strategies rejected by teachers as less useful are attributing failure to low effort alone and publicising superior performance. Teachers are divided on the value of entrinsic rewards, although more appear to consider them harmful than consider them useful (Nolen & Nicholls 1994).

What motivators do teachers use?

What strategies do teachers actually use? It appears that teachers restrict their use of motivational strategies to a limited range that includes strategies not considered the most desirable (Newby 1991; Nolen & Nicholls 1993 1994). One study investigated the quantity of motivational strategies used, the types most frequently used, and the relationship between strategy use and student behaviour in the classrooms of 30 beginning elementary teachers in the United States. The findings indicate that these teachers directed a lot of effort into motivating their students and used a range of strategies reflecting those covered in this text. For example, teachers used attention-focusing strategies such as dividing the class into four work groups and switching them to a new location and task on the sound of a bell (representing arousal techniques); relevance strategies such as using familiar past experiences to introduce a subject (representing cognitive approaches); confidence-building strategies such as minimising the feelings of failure, and demonstrating and modelling performance (representing social cognitive and attributional approaches); and, lastly, satisfaction strategies such as giving verbal reinforcement, tangible rewards or taking away privileges (representing a behavioural approach). *The majority of strategies used, however, were based on supplying or restricting extrinsic reinforcers!* Although not as frequently used as satisfaction, the attention-focusing strategies were used to a much greater degree than the relevance and confidence-building strategies.

The extensive use of extrinsic reinforcers and attention-focusing strategies by these teachers may reflect the age of the children taught and the perceived need for frequent changes of activity. However, the small percentage of confidence and relevance strategies used may be an indication of:

- ☐ the limited knowledge these teachers had about implementing such strategies;
- ☐ the difficulty they found in building students' confidence or in making the instructions relevant to the students;
- ☐ the attitude that such motivation should be the responsibility of the student, not that of the instruction or the teacher;
- ☐ increased individualisation that is required for such strategies, which may be inhibitory on the teacher's time or which may require more experience to implement effectively. (Newby 1991)

Of most importance from this research was the finding that there was a significant positive relationship between the teachers' use of relevance strategies and the observed on-task behaviour of the children. Those classrooms in which there was a higher incidence of giving reasons for the importance of the task or in which students were encouraged to relate the task to their personal experiences showed a higher rate of on-task behaviour (see also Marshall 1987). Students in classrooms in which higher levels of either rewards or punishments were delivered were observed to have lower levels of on-task behaviours. This latter case could illustrate that the reinforcers and punishments were losing their effect, or that the teachers involved perceived that students were getting off-task and increased the rewards or punishments in an attempt to get the class back on-task. In both cases the motivational outcome is unsatisfactory.

A further study (Nolen & Nicholls 1994) also found a discrepancy between what teachers believed were effective strategies and what they actually practised. Among the reasons suggested for this situation are the coercive influences of mandated curricula and accountability constraints, which induce teachers to use strategies that ensure output irrespective of whether they encourage intrinsic motivation.

There are a number of messages coming from this research. What do you think are the implications for teachers, students and administrators?

Question point: Teachers who fail to ensure the frequent and continued success of their pupils should be regarded as negligent. Discuss.

THE RELATIONSHIP BETWEEN MOTIVATION AND CONSTRUCTIVISM

When looking back over the content of this chapter, what elements appear to reflect a constructivist approach? Clearly, whenever the focus shifts to what the student does to interpret and become engaged in learning experiences (i.e. motivated to learn) we have elements of constructivism. So when teachers foster intrinsic motivation, autonomy, self-regulation and self-management, and stress meaningful learning, prior knowledge, real world problems, authentic tasks and social interaction as sources of motivation and student engagement in problem solving, we have evidence of a constructivist approach. The application of extrinsic or performance-based motivators are largely irrelevant to this approach.

Recommended reading

Ames, R. A. & Ames, C. (eds) (1984) *Research on Motivation in Education: Vol. 1. Student Motivation.* Orlando: Academic Press.

Ames, C. & Ames, R. (eds) (1985) *Research on Motivation in Education: Vol. 2. The Classroom Milieu.* Orlando: Academic Press.

Ames, C. & Ames, R. (eds) (1989) *Research on Motivation in Education: Vol. 3. Goals and Cognitions.* Orlando: Academic Press.

Anderman, E. M. & Maehr, M. L. (1994) Motivation and schooling in the middle grades. *Review of Educational Research*, 64, 287–309.

Bandura, A. (1993) Perceived self-efficacy in cognitive development and functioning. *Educational Psychologist*, 28, 117–48.

Corno, L. (1992) Encouraging students to take responsibility for learning and performance. *The Elementary School Journal*, 93, 69–83.

Covington, M. L. (1992) *Making the Grade. A Self-Worth Perspective on Motivation and School Reform*. New York: Cambridge University Press.

Eccles, J. S. (1983) Expectancies, values, and academic behaviors. In J. T. Spence (ed.) *Achievement and Achievement Motivation*. San Francisco: Freeman: 75–146.

Good, T. L. (1995) Teacher expectations. In L. W. Anderson (ed.) *International Encyclopedia of Teaching and Teacher Education*, 2nd edn. Tarrytown, NY: Pergamon: 29–35.

Maehr, M. L. & Buck, R. M. (1993) Transforming school culture in M. Sashkin & H. Walberg (eds) *Educational Leadership and Culture: Current Research and Practice*. Berkeley, California: McCutchan.

Maehr, M. L. & Midgley, C. (1991) Enhancing student motivation: a school-wide approach. *Educational Psychologist*, 26 (3 & 4), 399–427.

Maehr, M. L. & Anderman, E. M. (1993) Reinventing schools for early adolescents: Emphasizing task goals. *The Elementary School Journal*, 93, 593–610.

McCombs, B. L. & Pope, J. E. (1994) *Motivating Hard to Reach Students*. Washington, DC: American Psychological Association.

Nolen, S. B. & Nicholls, J. G. (1994) A place to begin (again) in research on student motivation: Teachers' beliefs. *Teaching and Teacher Education*, 10, 57–69.

Schunk, D. H. (1991) Self-efficacy and academic motivation. *Educational Psychologist*, 26, 207–31.

Urdan, T.C. & Maehr, M.L. (1995) Beyond a two goal theory of motivation and achievment: A case for social goals. *Review of Educational Research*, 65, 213–43.

Weiner, B. (1994) Integrating social and personal theories of achievement striving. *Review of Educational Research*, 64, 557–73.

Wigfield, A. (1994) Expectancy-value theory of achievement motivation: A developmental perspective. *Educational Psychology Review*, 6, 49–78.

Wigfield, A. & Eccles, J. S. (1989) Test anxiety in elementary and secondary school students. *Educational Psychologist*, 24, 159–83.

Zeidner, M. (1995) Adaptive coping with test situations: A review of the literature. *Educational Psychologist*, 30, 123–33.

CHAPTER 10

Classroom management and cooperative group work for effective learning

OVERVIEW

The author well recalls her first teaching experience while finishing her Diploma in Education, about 24 years ago. The only advice or preparation given for 'managing' students was 'start tough, you can always smile later'. So there she was, a slim, slightly built, long-haired 20-year-old, about to enter one of the toughest, all-boys secondary schools in a poor, industrial area of Sydney. Armed only with determination to 'survive' at all costs (meaning maintain her dignity and authority while controlling the students) but completely ignorant of basic classroom management skills, she agonised over how she was supposed to dazzle her supervisor with her teaching brilliance while these adolescents (larger than she) were obviously plotting to sabotage whatever she did, to 'test her out'.

How many times have young student teachers, academically well prepared and sincere in their commitment to teaching, been reduced to near nervous wrecks at the prospect of standing before a classroom full of smaller, or at least younger, human beings with their disparate needs, talents, weaknesses and socioemotional backgrounds, in order to prepare them for their place in society?

This chapter will provide practical ideas for managing instructional activities and preventing discipline problems, as well as means of dealing with misbehaviour should it occur. Well-established theoretical perspectives on management and discipline will be discussed as they illuminate these practical suggestions. In particular, the ideas of Kounin, Gordon, Glasser, Dreikurs and the Canters will be covered. However, rather than seeing the different views on management and discipline as being in opposition, we believe it is more profitable to take the best ideas from each and show how they can provide the most effective resource 'package' for beginning teachers. In this context, we will present the behaviour management approach of Bill Rogers as one which integrates many of the powerful strategies from each model.

The effectiveness of cooperative learning models will also be highlighted and related to principles of classroom management.

We hope that the range of ideas presented will assist you in developing effective classroom management skills.

GOOD TEACHING MINIMISES DISCIPLINE PROBLEMS

Discipline problems just don't seem to occur in classrooms where students are engaged in activities that they find absorbing or meaningful. What is meaningful to children is what they feel excited about learning, discovering or experimenting with, and which they feel they can master. Learning activities must be seen as purposeful, and the procedures and expectations for completing them must be clearly understood by all students (Jones & Jones 1995). If schools are boring places, out of touch with young people's interests, their challenges, and the pace of the rest of the world outside school, then the classroom will be a place for dissension and disorder, quelled only by an authoritarian regime. Schools can no longer guarantee students a successful future and a job as a reward for compliance with whatever policies and curricula they impose. Difficult economic times have shown that this is not the case.

The design of effective learning experiences in

What potential classroom management problems are illustrated in this picture?
Photo: authors

which *all* children can experience success is at the heart of managing student behaviour in classrooms. We suggest that you refer to Chapter 1 in which we talk about the many elements of effective teaching.

It is worth noting at this point that *nearly all classroom misbehaviour is of a minor nature*, rather than aggression or violent defiance. The sorts of 'discipline problems' that we face daily as teachers should be kept in perspective as merely nuisance behaviour, often annoyingly repetitive, and certainly not conducive to either student learning or the teacher's peace of mind. However, there is a real danger of over-reacting to such minor misbehaviour out of our own frustration and weariness, of labelling children as having 'behaviour problems' and, as frequently happens, of taking the easier course of ignoring the offenders and excluding them from class activities. As one beginning teacher put it, after her efforts to conduct a lesson on the sinking and floating of objects with second grade children resulted in a number of wet children and little learning:

This experimentation activity was performed at the end of the day because I felt tired and thought that it would be an easy one to supervise. It turned out to be not as easy as I first thought. I didn't predict how some children would react; that instead of doing the set task, it was a play period for them to splash water over themselves and the floor. I was annoyed that these children didn't want to learn and were spoiling it for the other children. I won't tolerate such poor attitudes to learning. In future, these children will be banned from all water activities.

Avoiding minor disruption through effective management

In this instance, the teacher was quick to assign blame for 'poor attitudes' to the children when there were a number of factors operating that contributed to the misbehaviour. It was late in the day (both children and teacher are tired); the children may be too young to conduct small group discoveries without considerably more structure and supervision, perhaps with the aid of parents or senior buddy-classmates; the procedures for water activities need to be defined by the teacher at the outset and repeated by the students; consequences for appropriate and inappropriate behaviour need to be pointed out as well; and, most importantly, students should have a clear understanding of the purpose of the activity, its relevance and usefulness, so that their attitude is one of excitement for learning, rather than for playing.

Much of what causes disruption to learning in classrooms *can be avoided*. In this chapter, a range of approaches will be presented that will help you to prevent or nip in the bud a large number of discipline problems, or deal with them once they have erupted. A range of discipline models from preventive approaches through supportive to corrective ones will be considered. In what ways are these methods different? We can characterise discipline as **preventive discipline** when we implement strategies to prevent misbehaviour occurring, **supportive discipline** when we prevent misbehaviour developing any further, and **corrective discipline** when we implement strategies to stop misbehaviour when it has occurred and redirect behaviour into positive channels. The eclectic approach of Rogers (1995) integrates elements of all these models and presents **positive behaviour management** as an integrated set of practical strategies for beginning and experienced teachers alike, grounded in a philosophy of respect for human dignity.

Positive behaviour management

Preventive discipline

Supportive discipline

Corrective discipline

SOCIAL RESPONSIBILITY, ACHIEVEMENT AND DISCIPLINE

Schools and classrooms are characterised by rules and regulations. The excerpts from *Cole's Funny Picture Book* illustrate some earlier views of rules, regulations and punishments. On a superficial level these rules are in place to keep children 'in line' so that schools and classrooms appear orderly, well-disciplined and characterised by harmonious interpersonal relationships. However, there are more important reasons for the implementation of rules and regulations.

Schools and social values

Schools are a major institution for the socialisation of children into our society. They are key players in passing on the mores of social behaviour from one generation to the next. Ideally, they are structured so that progression through a school exposes children to a range of personal and social rules, norms and roles that characterise interpersonal communication and activity in the wider society. Because the development of social responsibility and moral character is a matter of great concern to parents, teachers and students themselves, most school systems formulate policies that define the manner in which they should foster the adaptation and integration of children into social settings. Hence rules are developed that reflect cooperation, respect for others, and positive forms of group interaction, as well as those relating to facilitating academic learning and performance. Producing socially responsible students is seen as a valuable outcome in its own right, irrespective of achievement (Doyle 1986).

Snooks' Patent Whipping Machine for Flogging Naughty Boys in School.
"The Snooks' Whipping Machine has proved a total failure."–"Times."

DECLARATION OF A DISTRACTED SCHOOLMASTER

A year ago I took charge of a school of 1000 boys. They were a very bad lot indeed, and I could do nothing with them. Being of a mild disposition, I attempted to reason with them; but I might as well have reasoned with the pigs. I then thought of punishing them, but what mode of punishment should I adopt? In my utmost perplexity I wrote to the principal headmasters in the world, and the following are the replies:

From the High School of Eton wrote headmaster, Mr Squeers:
'If they don't behave as they should do, why, soundly box their ears.'

From the Grammar School of Harrow wrote headmaster, Mr Phfool:
'If they do not behave themselves, expel them from the school.'

From the Training School at Rugby wrote headmaster, Mr Wist:
'Just take a handful of their hair, and give a sharp, short twist.'

From the College School of Oxford wrote Professor Rarey Hook:
'Instead of nearly killing, overawe them with a look.'

From the Bible School of Cambridge wrote Professor William Brying:
'Well whip them with a birchen rod, and never mind their crying.'

From the Blue Coat School of London wrote Professor Rupert Gower:
'At arm's length make them hold a book the space of half-an-hour.'

From the Naval School of Liverpool wrote headmaster Mr Jointer:
'Just rap them on the knuckles with a common teacher's pointer.'

From the People's School of Sheffield wrote headmaster, Mr Clay:
'If the boys are disobedient, do not let them out to play.'

From the District School of Edenburgh wrote headmaster, Mr Glass:
'The naughty boys should all go to the bottom of the class.'

From the Latin School of Dublin wrote Professor Patrick Clayrence:
'If the boys are very bad boys, write a letter to their parents.'

From the Lyceum of New York wrote Professor Henry Buthing:
'Take delinquent boys one hour and make them sit on nothing.'

From the Public School, Chicago, wrote headmaster, Mr Norrids:
'If they will not behave themselves, why, just you slap their foreheads.'

From the Academy of San Francisco wrote headmaster, Mr Power:
'Make them stoop and hold their fingers on the floor for just an hour.'

From the King's College, Lisbon, wrote Professor Don Cassiers:
'If you want to make them good boys, pull, pinch, and twist their ears.'

From the Cadets' School of Paris wrote Professor Monsieur Sour:
'Just make them hold their hands above their heads for one full hour.'

From the Royal School of Amsterdam wrote Dr Vander Tooler:
'If they will not behave themselves, just trounce them with a ruler.'

From the Model School of Peking wrote Professor Cha Han Cox:
'Just put their hands into the stocks and beat with a bamboo.'

From the Muslim School of Cairo wrote the Mufti, Pasha Saido:
'Upon the bare soles of their feet give them the bastinado.'

From the Common School of Berlin wrote Professor Von de Rind:
'Just lay them right across your knee and cane them well behind.'

At last, as I was thinking deep how puzzling all this looks, I had a tempting offer from a certain Mr Snooks. His 'great machine to whip with speed' I bought with flusteration.

To see how it succeeded you must view the illustration.
And then look at 'Professor Cole's Gentle Persuader,' next page.

Responsible behaviour and academic achievement are related. Behaving in a responsible way may also be a critical student characteristic that directly contributes to learning and academic performance (Wentzel 1991).

Relationship between academic achievement and responsible behaviour

Correlational studies in the United States have shown a relationship between intellectual outcomes in elementary school with prosocial behaviour, classroom conduct and compliance (Entwisle, Alexander, Cadigan & Pallas 1986; Feshbach & Feshbach 1987). A study with high school students, for example, showed that students have a better chance of achieving success in high school if they (and their parents and peers) believe in the value of 'good' behaviour (Hanson & Ginsburg 1988).

How does behaving in a socially responsible way contribute to achievement at school? Wentzel (1991) suggests three reasons. First, a socially responsible student would adhere to student role requirements such as paying attention, keeping to the task and completing work, qualities that are related to academic achievement.

Social responsibility and positive social interaction

Second, socially responsible behaviour can play a role in facilitating positive social interactions with teachers and peers which may enhance the learning process. It appears that teachers may give less attention to students who misbehave and don't adhere to norms for responsible student behaviour. Hence these students do more poorly academically. It also appears that peer groups can influence classroom performance and learning outcomes in positive ways (see McInerney 1991b), and that they can complement teacher behaviour in ways that support the instructional process (Wentzel 1991). Consequently, strong peer group ties, particularly with peers who value education, enhance the individual's motivation and achievement (Hanson & Ginsburg 1988).

Third, the motivation underlying socially responsible classroom behaviour may influence the degree to which students become engaged in academic work. This is particularly the case if learning and social responsibility goals are pursued at the same time. The question about which causes the other remains, however. Does social responsibility affect learning and achievement in the sense that socially responsible children feel guilty if they are not working hard at school and achieving as well as they can? Or does being successful at school subjects promote socially responsible behaviour? Clearly, the two interact. If a person is performing poorly academically, the chances of misbehaviour are increased and social rejection is more likely.

For the reasons we have outlined, our perspective on the role of rules, routines and discipline should take on a broader focus than simply using them to facilitate an orderly and well-managed class. This broader perspective should be considered when you evaluate the techniques for management and discipline discussed below.

Cole's Patent Whipping Machine for Flogging Naughty Boys in School.

TESTIMONIAL FROM A SCHOOLMASTER

(To Mr Cole, Book Arcade, Melbourne)

Sir,

This remarkable machine proved highly efficacious from the first day it was put into service, when it effectively punished the following bad boys for the reason given.

John Hawking, for talking
George Highing, for crying
Edward Daring, for swearing
Henry Wheeling, for stealing
Peter Bitting, for spitting
Robert Hoaking, for smoking
Luke Jones, for throwing stones
Matthew Sawter, for squirting water
Nicholas Storms, for upsetting forms
Reuben Wrens, for spoiling pens
Samuel Jink, for spilling ink
Simon McLeod, for laughing aloud
Timothy Stacez, for making faces
Caleb Hales, for telling tales
Daniel Padley, for writing badly
David Jessons, for cribbing lessons
Edmond Gate, for coming late
Ezra Lopen, for leaving doors open
Edwin Druent, for playing truant
Charles Case, for eating in school
Francis Berindo, for breaking a window
Harold Tate, for breaking his slate
Jacob Crook, for tearing his book
Conrad Draper, for throwing chewed paper
Cyril Froude, for speaking too loud
Elijah Rowe, for speaking too low
Gregory Meek, for refusing to speak
Hannibal Hartz, for throwing paper darts
Jonah Platts, for hiding boys' hats
Aaron Esk, for cutting the desk
Alexander Tressons, for talking in lessons
Alfred Hoole, for eating in school
Ambrose Hooke, for blotting his book
Ambrose Grace, for making a face
Anthony Sands, for clapping his hands
Benjamin Guess, for untidy dress
Humphrey Proof, for stoning the roof
Jonah Earls, for grinning at girls
Jonathan Spence, for climbing the fence
Philip Cannisters, for sliding down bannisters
Lambert Hesk, for crashing a desk
Lawrence Storm, for breaking a form
Lazarus Beet, for stamping his feet
Leopold Bate, for riding a gate
Norman Halls, for writing on walls
Stephen Platt, for teasing a cat
Rupert Keats, for glueing the seats.

In conclusion, I can vouch for the fact that, thanks entirely to Cole's Whipping Machine, I no longer have a single bad boy in my school.

A HEADMASTER
(Name and address supplied.)

(From *Cole's Funny Picture Book No. 1*. Reprinted with permission from Cole Publications.)

BOX 10.1 TEACHING COMPETENCE

The teacher establishes clear, challenging and achievable expectations for students

Indicators

The teacher:

- establishes a positive learning environment oriented towards achieving learning objectives;
- maintains a secure environment in which expectations for student learning and behaviour are clearly understood and reinforced;
- develops routine procedures to manage recurring tasks;
- fosters and positively reinforces responsible student behaviour.

Case studies illustrating National Competency Framework for Beginning Teaching, National Project on the Quality of Teaching and Learning, Australian Teaching Council, 1996, Element 3.6, p. 51. Commonwealth of Australia copyright, reproduced by permision.

CLASSROOM MANAGEMENT: THE TEACHER AS CLASSROOM LEADER

At this point, it would be useful to distinguish between **classroom management** and **discipline**. Classroom management is a broad term which refers to everything that teachers do to establish and maintain an environment in which effective learning takes place (Copeland 1987). Discipline, therefore, is only one aspect of classroom management, and relates specifically to methods adopted to manage student behaviour and involvement in school-based activities. It is an important aspect of teacher leadership in that the teacher leads students towards particular positive goals.

Goals of discipline

We would strongly agree with the goals of discipline that Bill Rogers (1990) proposes (see Table 10.1.)

TABLE 10.1

ESSENTIALS OF THE GOALS OF DISCIPLINE

For teachers and students

- Self-discipline and self-control
- Enhancement of self-esteem
- Respect for others' rights
- Cooperation
- A positive classroom atmosphere
- Fairness and honesty

(adapted from Rogers 1990)

BOX 10.2 TEACHING COMPETENCE

The teacher encourages positive student behaviour

Indicators

The teacher:

- acknowledges appropriate student behaviour and fosters self-discipline among students;
- uses an approach that emphasises consequences for inappropriate behaviour;
- applies a variety of behaviour management strategies; for example, negotiating rules, applying effective sanctions;
- develops clear routines for managing student behaviour consistent with school policy;
- takes appropriate action promptly, firmly, fairly and consistently.

Case studies illustrating National Competency Framework for Beginning Teaching, National Project on the Quality of Teaching and Learning, Australian Teaching Council, 1996, Element 2.4, p. 40. Commonwealth of Australia copyright, reproduced by permission.

Prevention is better than cure

The 'good old days'?

On arrival at his first teaching position, the author was presented with a box of chalk and a cane, and admonished to 'wallop the living daylights out of the kids to keep them in order'. Furthermore, it was bluntly communicated to him that the measure of a good teacher was how well he kept the class quiet.

No longer is the classroom a place where the teacher, armed with chalk, duster and cane or strap, dispenses knowledge like an interactive textbook. Today's classrooms are places where the teacher serves as a highly knowledgeable guide who leads students to sources of factual information, but who also encourages shared problem solving and reasoning through talk and group work. Children are encouraged to express opinions, clarify values and critically think through problems. Media models of assertive, even defiant, behaviour by young people, uncertain economic and employment futures, universal recognition of the rights of the individual—child, disabled or minority group member—along with the abolition of corporal punishment in schools in Australia in the 1980s, have encouraged children to be more outspoken and far less submissive to adult authority.

Effective teaching and classroom management

Nowhere is it more obvious than in a classroom 'out of control' that preventing the occurrence or development of misbehaviours is preferable to trying to regain order from pandemonium. It should be strongly emphasised at the outset that no classroom management strategies will

As well as the cane, the chalkboard eraser was also a marvellous management too!

prevent discipline problems if effective teaching is not taking place. When children are motivated because what they are learning is interesting, exciting and relevant, when they feel respected and cared for by their teacher even if they are not always able to get all the answers right, when they feel they have a legitimate place in *our classroom*, then inattentive, problem behaviour is most unlikely to occur. This is not to say that children won't have 'off days' when they don't feel like complying or getting involved in learning activities; after all, there is much more to their world than just academic learning—a fight with a best friend or parent, an impending attack of influenza, a hormone-led growth spurt with consequential embarrassment and touchiness, parental marital friction—any number of factors may be responsible. An effective teacher will have a repertoire of strategies on which to call. Let's have a look at these now.

Planning for good classroom management

Teachers who successfully prevent misbehaviour and foster learning have an effective management system which consists of three phases: before the school year starts (planning), the first few weeks of school (developing), and throughout the year (maintaining) (Evertson & Emmer 1982).

Effective classroom managers anticipate problems

The planning stage involves deciding on preventive measures that will *minimise potential problems.* Organising the physical space of the classroom is an important place to start in planning for a new year. Will the children sit individually, in pairs or groups? Where will the teacher's desk be best placed to allow for easy student access and monitoring? How will classroom supplies be stored and distributed? Other important management decisions involve planning an integrated set of rules and procedures to be taught to the new class in the development stage of the year.

Organising the physical setting of the classroom

Table 10.2 presents a number of the most important aspects of the physical working environment that an effective teacher would prepare for before teaching begins.

TABLE 10.2

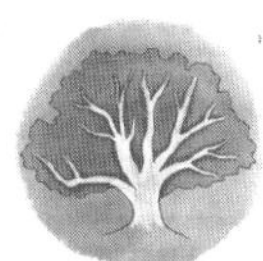

ESSENTIALS OF EFFECTIVE PLANNING OF THE CLASSROOM ENVIRONMENT

For teachers

- *High-traffic areas free of congestion.* Wherever possible, make sure that students do not have to crowd or negotiate other students' desks in order to leave or enter the room, consult the teacher, or gain access to materials or their belongings.
- *Students and teacher able to see each other easily.* Check that all students can be monitored from the locations at which the teacher will be teaching and interacting with students.
- *Ready accessibility to frequently used teaching materials and student supplies.* Use shelves to store and display books, storage trays to hold and distribute materials, hooks to keep bags and coats tidy and accessible, and trolleys to move overhead projectors and computers around the room.
- *Students able to see/hear instructional presentations and displays easily.* Check that all students will be able to participate in whole-group instructional activities without having to move their furniture or themselves excessively. If students have to strain to see or hear, or have to turn around or leave their seats, the opportunity for inattention and disruption increases.
- Students able to interact in small-group activities without major reorganisation of the furniture. If not, can furniture be easily rearranged ?
- Adequate seating for the age and size of the students.
- Effective classroom lighting, ventilation and heating.

(based on Evertson et al. 1989)

Developing appropriate behaviours during the first few weeks

The first few weeks of school are a time of uncertainty for all students as to what the teacher's expectations for behaviour and classwork will be. Considerable research has demonstrated that effective teachers have a framework of appropriate classroom behaviours (rights, responsibilities, rules and routines) and devote the beginning of the school year to ensuring that there is no ambiguity about their expectations (Doyle 1986). Consequences associated with these behaviours are also planned for in advance. This 'establishment phase' (Rogers 1994, 1995), with its preventive focus, is crucial to effective teaching and learning later in the year (Kyriacou 1986, 1991). With younger children, it has been shown that teachers who have little difficulty throughout the year in managing their classroom, *actually teach* rules and procedures to the class on the first day of school and during the next few weeks, rather than merely explaining them in words or listing them on the wall (Evertson et al. 1989). As with any effective teaching, there are three important steps here: describing and demonstrating the desired behaviour, rehearsal and feedback. **Describe** in specific terms what you expect and **demonstrate** with actions (or allow students to do so) what behaviours are desirable. Don't assume that students know precisely what you want them to do or that they can actually perform the procedures correctly. Rules such as 'Students may whisper during group work', 'Enter and leave the classroom in an orderly fashion' and 'Get on with something quiet when you've finished your set work or you are waiting for the teacher' should be clearly demonstrated and then rehearsed. **Practising** the desired behaviours ensures that rules and procedures are understood. **Feedback** to students on their performance is very important in shaping future behaviour. For example, 'I am very pleased that you all lined up outside the classroom door as soon as the bell rang, but I was not happy about the talking' gives clear guidelines as to what is considered appropriate behaviour and what is not.

Describe and demonstrate desired behaviours

Provide for rehearsal and feedback

For secondary school students, it is preferable to explain rules, procedures and consequences (sometimes referred to as 'expectations' with senior students), and to discuss their necessity in a positive way. Rules and procedures that are presented as a means of ensuring a fair and productive classroom learning environment for all students, rather than as idiosyncrasies of the teacher, will be accepted more readily. Such an approach is supported by the Australian research of Lewis and Lovegrove (1984) who found that secondary school students prefer teachers to establish clear and reasonable rules that are based on the teacher's desire to ensure that effective learning takes place rather than on the teacher's authority. Table 10.3 lists some procedures that will provide a sense of order and calm at the start of a new year when nerves are likely to be strained.

Explain rationale for rules

TABLE 10.3

ESSENTIALS OF ESTABLISHING GOOD CLASSROOM MANAGEMENT

For teachers

- Being prepared: have name tags made and ready to wear (as well as extra labels for unexpected students). Label students' desks for at least the first few days in the earlier grades. Older students may be left to choose their own seats.
- Greeting each student as they enter the room (and taking the younger ones to their seats).
- Introducing yourself briefly and having the students do so as well, perhaps with a few words about themselves ('My favourite hobby is … ').
- Using an 'ice-breaker' activity to reduce inhibitions and establish the classroom as a warm cooperative environment. One such activity we have had success with at all age levels is 'Tangles' (or 'Human Chain'). You need to divide the class into groups of about 6 to 8 and have them cluster together with both hands streched up. Each child takes the hand of one person with their left hand, and of another person with their right hand. The aim is to form a circle after untangling the chain without breaking hands. There is usually much laughter, the beginnings of cooperative group work and evidence of potential group dynamics—those who are 'leaders' will give directions to the others.
- Presenting and discussing rules, procedures and consequences.
- Being available to all students: move around checking on student progress and avoid sitting at your desk for the first few days. Make it obvious that you are *interested, aware and in charge*.

(adapted from Evertson et al. 1989)

The four Rs: rules and routines expressed as rights and responsibilities

The next aspect of an effective management plan is to decide what sorts of behaviour the teacher requires to

Sunblock time at this pre-school occurs each day before morning tea and outdoor play. Why is it essential to teach the procedures for such activities to young children in a group setting?
Photo: authors

ensure a smoothly functioning classroom that is conducive to learning: movement around the room, talking to the teacher and peers, marking of work, requesting help, and treatment of others. Can you think of other areas where you would want to establish your standards and expectations of students at the start of the year? Such guidelines can be imposed top-down by the teacher, or negotiated with the students. They will be expressed as **rules** and **routines** (along with their corresponding consequences) which will vary as a function of teacher personality (e.g. some teachers tolerate more student noise and movement than others), student age and school policy. Just a brief pause for definitions here. **Rules** define general standards for behaviour and often indicate what constitutes unacceptable or prohibited behaviour—for example, students must stay in their seats unless they have the teacher's permission to move around. A positive classroom climate will be fostered more by rules that are positively worded than those that prohibit behaviours (McDaniel 1983). **Routines** refer to behaviours that relate to specific activities or situations. For example, how will students enter and leave the classroom? What are students to do when you are called from the room or when someone becomes ill? If, in line with the current philosophy of democratic classroom management, students are encouraged to design their own classroom rules and routines, a sense of ownership of learning and of 'their' classroom will be engendered.

In contrast, we can all probably remember our primary school days when rules were presented as dictates from higher authority and included some of the following:

- ☐ Don't speak in class.
- ☐ Don't get out of your seat until the bell goes.
- ☐ Don't talk in lines or in the corridors.
- ☐ Wear your school uniform in its entirety at all times to and from school.
- ☐ Don't play in the 'out of bounds' areas in the playground.

And as for consequences, detention was the penalty for everything. A number of afternoons were wasted in the senior years of the then-teenage-girl author's school life sitting in a schoolroom for half an hour or more for the 'crime' of wearing nailpolish and no gloves or hat on the way to school. Detention time was spent just sitting (with hat and gloves on) without speaking, presumably meditating on what had been done wrong. Of course, the real crime was in being seen and reported by the prefects whose duty it was to enforce the rules when teachers were out of sight.

From punishment to rights and responsibilities—'the fair rule'

These so-called rules said nothing about rights or responsibilities, let alone about effective learning, nor did the punishment particularly fit the crime. Let us consider this recent transition in thinking about discipline a little more closely.

Collaborative democracy

As pointed out by Bill Rogers in his eminently sensible and humanitarian book, *You Know the Fair Rule* (1990), classroom and school-wide rules should not be imposed arbitrarily from above, but should evolve from commonly held values. These community values are expressed as **rights** which have associated **responsibilities** that protect them. Rules that are equitable are derived from these rights, and indicate the due responsibilities of students, teachers, and parents or education system where appropriate. Rogers refers to this approach as

collaborative democracy and argues that the 4Rs focus (rights, responsibilities, rules and routines) is not only an effective basis for determining equitable classroom management policies, but also prepares children 'for participation in and enjoyment of the benefits of a social group' (p. 109).

Let us illustrate this process with an example. A fundamental value of Western democracy and, many would argue, of humanity in general is that of equality and fairness of treatment. Thus, irrespective of background, ethnicity, colour, gender or disability, all children should be treated equally and have equal access to educational opportunities. This value is expressed as the *right of children to learn in a warm, supportive and encouraging environment*. Similarly, *the teacher has the right to teach in a positive environment, and one that is physically and emotionally safe*. Both parties, therefore, have the responsibility of being considerate and supportive. Student responsibility includes being cooperative and completing work as requested, while teachers must provide support and guidance at all stages of learning, encouraging effort and being fair in discipline. Parents must also support both children and their teachers in fulfilling their responsibilities.

The right to learn

Box 10.3 presents an illustration of a list of classroom rights and responsibilities designed by a year 6 class.

If you adopt the rights and responsibilities approach to classroom management, then rules will emerge as logical ways of protecting the rights of the participants in the education process, and will be seen as acceptable means of enforcing the responsibilities that accompany them. Clearly, positive and negative consequences follow naturally from choices made to observe the rules or not.

Rules outline one's responsibilities and allow the enjoyment of rights

How many, and which rules?

Rules are, therefore, preventive measures, logically derived from agreed-upon rights of both teacher and students, and are most effective if they are:

- ☐ *Expressed positively*: 'Hands up before you speak' rather than 'Don't call out', or 'Walking in corridors' rather than 'Don't run'.
- ☐ *Kept to a minimum number:* No more than five to eight rules should be needed for defining acceptable student behaviour. In fact, any more than this can be difficult for younger children to remember, and appear very authoritarian to older students.
- ☐ *Unambiguous*: Specify, clearly, exactly *what* students are to do and *when*. 'Respect other people's property' or 'Don't steal' may be worthwhile principles to teach but do not tell students, especially young ones, precisely what behaviour you expect in your classroom. A better rule is 'Ask first before you use another person's things'. Similarly, 'Be polite', 'Don't run', 'Don't call out', are neither positive directions for how to behave nor specific to particular situations. Do children know what being polite means? Are they *never* to run or call out in school time?

Here are some commonly used rules:

- ☐ Raise your hand before speaking to the teacher.
- ☐ Listen quietly while others are speaking.
- ☐ Walk in the classroom.
- ☐ Leave toys and games in schoolbags for lunchtime play.
- ☐ Discuss problems after the bell goes.

BOX 10.3 CLASSROOM RIGHTS AND RESPONSIBILITIES

Rights	Responsibilities
To discuss openly with teachers any aspect of class management that we feel is unfair or a problem	To abide by the decisions made by the parties involved
To be treated with dignity and respect always	To treat others with dignity always
To work in the tuckshop	To be honest and accurate when giving change
To use things in the classroom	To take care of things and put them back in their proper place
To help and show small children the right thing to do in the playground	To set a good example and not to yell or scare them
To be able to eat at our desk on cold days	Not to make a mess, and to put rubbish in the bin
To write on the whiteboard	To use the pens carefully and only for school-related things
To have a neat, clean classroom	To clean up after ourselves; to cooperate with each other and finish the job
Not to have weekend homework	To finish off all other work during the week
To sit next to who we like	To work well together

In your explanation of this last rule you might specify the exact procedure: disputes are negotiated between the participants in the first instance, and then with the teacher if necessary.

The 'golden rule'

With older age groups, the 'golden rule' may be the only one you need: '*Do unto others as you would have them do unto you*' or '*Treat others as you would like to be treated*'.

Involving students in designing rules

Some teachers like to involve students in designing rules, believing that personal 'ownership' will help develop a positive classroom climate and that peer encouragement to uphold them is preferable to teacher enforcement alone. Rogers (1990, 1995), for example, suggests that children from grades 3 or 4 should be encouraged to write out classroom rules in their own words. He also advocates the use of general labels for easy reference to rules as the occasion arises, especially for younger children. For instance, you might have these categories:

- ☐ communication or 'talking rule'
- ☐ fair treatment rule
- ☐ conflict or 'problem-fixing rule'
- ☐ movement rule
- ☐ safety rule
- ☐ learning rule.

Better than drafting general rules in 'neutral language' is wording class rules in 'inclusive' language (Rogers 1995): 'In *our* class, we ... '; '*Our* rule for ... is'. A useful strategy, therefore, in the establishment phase is to have a general rule-reminder before on-task activity begins: 'Before we begin our work/our discussion, I want you to remember our communication rule. Hands up, thanks.'

In cases of misbehaviour, therefore, such as an argument over who 'stole' whose ruler, the question can be asked, 'Monica and Tom, what's our problem-fixing rule?' Answer: 'We talk about it after the bell goes, and then come to you if we can't sort it out.' The teacher can reply: 'Thank you. Now would you both go on quietly with your work, please, and wait behind at recess?'

It should be pointed out here that research on effective management shows that it is not always necessary to have younger students negotiate class rules. More important is that the teacher presents the rules clearly and concisely with explanations for their need and then allows for student discussion (Evertson et al. 1989). It is perhaps more important for older students, whom we are training for civic responsibility, to be involved in writing and negotiating class rules (see Brophy & Evertson 1978; Eccles & Midgley 1989; Ericson & Ellett 1990).

Consequences for rules and procedures

Consequences should be logical, applied calmly, and consistent

In the context of classroom management, consequences for behaviour emerge from classroom rules which are established to protect the rights of individuals in that class. As well as defining rules and procedures, therefore, teachers must plan the consequences for following or neglecting to follow them. These should be 'logical', that is, they should relate as closely to the behaviour as possible so that students can see a connection between them (Dreikurs 1968; Dreikurs & Pearl 1972). In this way, students are taught to foresee the outcome of their behaviour (Rogers 1994) and to develop an ownership of it. We have often used the term **YOYOB—You Own Your Own Behaviour—**from Bill Rogers in our own upbringing of children. For consequences to be effective, it is important for them to be understood and agreed to by the students. *Logical consequences are not punishments*; they are not imposed by the teacher as authority but are a conscious 'choice' made by the student about how to behave; in other words, consequences demonstrate that one must be accountable for one's behaviour. They must be applied calmly (never in anger) and consistently (the same consequence for every student, every time), thus encouraging the development of responsible self-discipline: bad choices of behaviour *always* result in unpleasant, but just, consequences, and vice versa.

Include positive and negative consequences

It never ceases to amaze us how easily teachers can dream up creative tortures (contrived consequences) for misbehaving students, such as writing a thousand lines of promises of good behaviour in a lunch hour; standing in a dark storeroom to learn not to fidget; or picking up leftover food scraps and litter in the playground (including used

This child is looking forward to the positive consequences of finishing work and packing up – an 'early mark'.
Photo: authors

tissues and deteriorating fruit, which our eldest daughter Ali was once made to collect as punishment for talking in lines), yet how difficult it seems to be to design consequences that are logical—especially positive ones—and reward students for actually adhering to the desired rules. Some examples of logical consequences are:

- ☐ Students who work quietly without disturbing others may work with a group of friends.
- ☐ Students who damage school property must repair or replace it.
- ☐ Students who constantly leave their seats should be made to do without one until they decide that they need one, and will stay in it!
- ☐ Students who regularly hand in their work on time may be excused from submitting the next piece of homework.
- ☐ Students who keep their work area clean may bring something to beautify their desk (pot plant, favourite ornament).
- ☐ Students who hurt someone on purpose, for example, by kicking or name-calling, are to do two things for the hurt child to make them feel better (write an apology; make something for them). (Rogers 1995).

Table 10.4 suggests how poorly expressed rules and consequences may be reworded positively and logically.

TABLE 10.4

IMPROVING RULES AND CONSEQUENCES

Poor (vague)	Negative rule	Positive rule	Contrived punishment	Logical positive and negative consequences
1. Respect each other	Don't hit classmates	Settle arguments by discussion	Detention	Timeout from reinforcement (to make a plan or contract) 'Peacemaker' award.
2. Be co-operative	Don't call out	Put up your hand when you wish to speak	Lines: 'I shall not call out in class'	Teacher ignores calling-out behaviour. Teacher praises and responds to student with raised hands.
3. Be prompt	Don't be late to class	Come to lessons on time	Detention	Make up missed work at recess, lunch-time or after school. Privilege such as 'early mark' before the bell.
4. Work hard	Don't leave homework unfinished	Complete all homework	Teacher lecture or nagging	Finish homework in recreation time at school. Letter sent to parents. Exemption from a particular piece of homework. Letter of praise sent home.
5. Be honest	Don't cheat	Do your own homework	Teacher lecture or sent to the principal	Work redone in class recreation time. 'Honour' award.

Maintaining effective management throughout the year: Kounin's approach.

Once a system of rules and procedures is in place, teachers should monitor the behaviour and work habits of students by using the strategies discussed below (Kounin's preventive measures): withitness, overlapping and group focus.

It is equally important to monitor the impact of teaching styles and work demands on individual students, as it is more likely that students who are having difficulty coping with lesson content or meeting teacher expectations for achievement will be predisposed to misbehave. Such difficulties need to be diagnosed for what they are: learning ones. Perhaps peer and cross-age tutoring, an individualised program of work, enlisting parental support for extra practice at home, or a contract negotiated with the student that sets out short-term mastery goals are preferable alternatives to dismissing such students as 'behaviour problems', and inflicting penalties on them.

Obviously, dealing with misbehaviour or unproductive work habits is the final component of maintaining effective classroom control. A number of powerful means of doing this will be considered in detail later in this chapter. For now, it would be valuable to look at one other approach to preventing discipline problems, that of lesson management.

Jacob Kounin's (1970, 1977; Copeland 1987) research on group management, based on analysis of

TEACHER'S CASE BOOK

TIMEOUT

It's last period on Friday afternoon and Peter Firth's year 9 model-making class has been busily painting, gluing and wiring models for about 20 minutes. Suddenly, over the top of the low hum of industry, someone calls out: 'Hey, Graeme, chuck us that blue tube, will you?' Peter looks up just as Graeme's misdirected paint tube whizzes past and smacks Michael Travers' unsuspecting ear.

There is a tense pause. A golden rule of the practical arts centre about throwing objects has been broken. Peter, a high-profile local basketball player, stands, motions to Graeme and calls 'foul', using a basketball umpire's familiar hand signal.

'How many's that you've got?' someone asks Graeme.

'Four.'

A buzz goes round the room. Five fouls in a week means temporary suspension from the game. The team checks out each other's foul count. Time to settle down.

Case studies illustrating National Competency Framework for Beginning Teaching, National Project on the Quality of Teaching and Learning, Australian Teaching Council, 1996, p. 47. Commonwealth of Australia copyright, reproduced by permission.

Case study activity
How effective is this teacher's management policy in terms of fostering student responsibility and accountability in this educational setting? What approach would you use?

thousands of hours of videotaped classroom interactions, has provided teachers for two decades now with insights into powerful strategies for preventing misbehaviour. The central focus of Kounin's research findings is that good classroom behaviour depends on effective lesson management. Especially important are appropriate reactions to misbehaviour, maintaining activity flow in lessons, smooth transitions between activities, group (whole class) alerting, and individual student accountability. Some of Kounin's key concepts will be examined in greater detail.

Kounin's preventive measures

Teachers should be aware of what is going on in all areas of the classroom at all times. The term Kounin uses to describe such awareness is withitness and is like the popular expression, 'having eyes in the back of the head'. The 'withit' teacher is always visually scanning the room even when working with an individual child or small group of students and will act promptly (timing is very important) to prevent any potentially disruptive behaviour from developing. An important proviso for 'withitness' is that the action taken does not interrupt the flow of the learning activity for the rest of the class.

Withitness and visual scanning

Let us illustrate this technique with an example. The scene is an art lesson where the teacher is outlining the procedure for blending primary colours to create secondary ones, before letting the class experiment for themselves. During the explanation, the teacher sees two children snatching at the same box of craft equipment in order to have the first pick of the paint pots. Without stopping the lesson, the 'withit' teacher moves towards the offenders and either makes stern eye contact with both of them or taps one on the shoulder while gesturing to stop the misbehaviour. The 'non-withit' teacher, on the other hand, would stop the lesson saying, 'Would both of you stop fooling with the craft box until you are told what to do, otherwise you will be doing your maths homework while the rest of the class paints! Now what was I

Hands on heads can be a prompt to appropriate behaviour.
Photo: Connie Griebe

'Miss Jones, I thought you were supposed to have eyes in the back of your head!'

saying before?' Needless to say, the other students have now become uninvolved with the lesson content and there is potential for new misbehaviour.

Remember also that a 'withit' teacher does not wait too long before taking action; children may interpret your hesitation as weakness and take advantage of your apparent lack of awareness. Behaviourists might recommend the technique of *tactically ignoring* behaviours in order to avoid reinforcing them (see Chapter 6 for an explanation of behavioural theory). Experience has shown us that such a choice by the teacher depends heavily on the nature of the situation—some obvious but 'mild' form of attention-seeking behaviour, such as calling out, pouting and refusing to speak, or clowning, may be consciously ignored as long as the child is reinforced for on-task behaviour as soon as it occurs. Of course, any serious or potentially dangerous off-task behaviour—fighting, swearing, rude calling out—cannot be ignored. The strategy of ignoring is discussed in greater detail in the section on models of discipline, below.

Two additional, important features of 'withitness' need to be highlighted. The first is that of making sure that the right culprit is chosen for the disciplinary action: a teacher's credibility can be rapidly diminished if an 'un-withit' accusation of misbehaviour is made. Negative student attitudes to teacher and to schoolwork are related to incorrect targeting, either by choosing the wrong student, or by blaming the wrongdoings of one individual on a group (Lewis & Lovegrove 1984, 1987). The second feature to remember is to attend to the more serious misbehaviour when two problems occur at the same time. Thus, intervening swiftly in a potential fight in the playground takes precedence over reprimanding children for dropping their lunch scraps.

Choose the right culprit

Attend to more serious behaviour

Skilful classroom managers are expert at dealing with two issues at the same time. For example, while working with a small group of readers, the teacher looks up to see two children bobbing under their desks to look at a 'forbidden' comic. A number of *overlapping responses* are possible: 'Keep reading, John, that's fine. Julia and Mario, put the magazine away (or on my desk) and get back to your work.' Another method would be to encourage the reading group to continue while silently moving to the offending children. With a light tap on one of the children's shoulders, or stern eye contact, remove the magazine and gesture to the culprits to resume their work.

Overlapping

A teacher who stops a learning activity to berate naughty children causes a loss of **momentum** which is hard to restore and which can encourage restlessness and boredom among other class members.

Momentum

Kounin's research shows that student misbehaviour is closely related to the way in which lessons flow (momentum and smoothness). Momentum refers to pacing and is evident in lessons that move briskly. **Slowdowns,** which encourage students to lose interest in the main idea of an activity, are frequently caused by teachers giving directions in a laborious, detailed way, nagging when correcting students, and having students wait for each other before moving from one activity to the next. For example, during a science lesson a teacher may slow down a lesson by saying, 'Students in the first row may come up and collect their equipment. Now those in the second row. Those in the third row may come up next.' With better planning, this teacher could prevent student boredom and inattention by not fragmenting the lesson into unnecessary steps—for example, each member of a group could have a role such as collecting the paper for the group.

Movement management

Where teachers are able to move smoothly from one activity to the next, student attention is maintained. For instance, a teacher who is giving a maths lesson glances at her watch and realises that she has forgotten to collect permission notes and money

Smoothness

for the class excursion, which must be sent to the office for filing and banking before the lunch bell. She will be guilty of poor **movement management** ('jerkiness') if she interrupts the lesson and says, 'How many of you are coming on the excursion? I had better finalise numbers as soon as I have finished explaining this problem.' Even worse, in Kounin's estimation, would be the abrupt cessation of the lesson to attend to the administrative matter immediately.

Group focus

A skilful classroom manager must be able to direct the activities of the whole class while ensuring that its individual members are all engaged in the lesson. Kounin suggests two major techniques for achieving this **group focus**: group alerting and individual accountability.

Group alerting

It is of paramount importance to have the attention of all students at the start of any learning activity. Always *wait* for full student attention while visually scanning the room and making direct eye contact with each student. This group alerting communicates to the students both that you are in control and that you are sufficiently interested in them to wish to teach effectively.

After gaining the full attention of the class, there are a number of effective ways of keeping all students attentive. These are listed in Table 10.5.

Group alerting is reduced by calling on a particular student before asking a question, or discussing an answer at length with only one student. Let's have a look at a situation where group focus is lacking. Having just read a story with the class, the teacher says, 'Max, why do you think that the character ...?' Max says, 'Because he ...'. The teacher continues. 'What did the writer say that gives

We all sit down on the steps when the teacher is busy. Photo: authors

We all do our part when the teacher begins. Why is it important for a 'withit' teacher to have effective group-management skills for whole class activities? Photo: authors

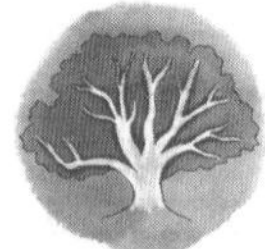

TABLE 10.5

ESSENTIALS OF MAINTAINING STUDENT ATTENTION

For teachers

- Pausing (for at least three seconds) after asking a question to allow students thinking time, then naming a student to answer.
- Calling on students at random.
- Creating suspense by saying things such as, 'I wonder if anyone will have heard of this?' or 'This is going to be a tricky one.'
- Asking students to listen carefully because they might be asked to contribute something to another student's answer.
- Looking at other students at the same time as calling on one student to answer a question.
- Teaching active listening.

you that idea, Max?' Meanwhile, what do you imagine is happening to the involvement of the rest of the class? How could the teacher have maintained group focus more effectively?

Following the reading the teacher could say, 'Think about why the main character ... '. Now the teacher pauses to allow for *wait time*—students need at least three seconds to be able to formulate a verbal response from their thoughts—then, 'All right, we should be ready now to hear what you think. Why did the main character ...?' Pause. 'Max, what do you think?' Following the answer, the teacher keeps the group's attention by asking, 'What did the writer say that gave Max that idea? Sandra?' Sandra responds, and so on.

Students will be kept accountable for their learning if the teacher communicates that their participation will be monitored and their performance evaluated in some way. This can be achieved by:

Individual accountability

- ☐ asking all students to write their answers on a card and hold them up;
- ☐ having the students write their answer to a question in a special notebook which is checked while the teacher circulates;
- ☐ asking all students to work out a solution to a problem in their books at the same time as one student is asked to solve it on the board; answers are then compared;
- ☐ asking students to write a summary of what they have been doing;
- ☐ having students record reflections in a diary or journal.

In cases of misbehaviour, asking a student to answer a question is a sure way of regaining his or her attention. This is provided that it is done in such a way as to avoid embarrassing the student or creating an opportunity for argument—that is, by phrasing the question in such a way that the inattentive student can once again participate: 'Jane, Sam says that cars contribute to the destruction of the ozone layer ... what do you think?' rather than 'Jane, tell me what Sam just said.'

ACTION STATION

Discuss the range of strategies that you could adopt in situations of minor student misbehaviour where you keep the intervention private and minimise disrupting the lesson as much as possible.

MODELS OF DISCIPLINE

The degree to which students and teachers should share responsibility for, and have control over, discipline in the classroom has been the focus of a number of writers. In the next section we explore a range of models of discipline, from student-centred approaches to teacher-centred approaches.

Gordon's counselling approach

Thomas Gordon's **humanistic** approach (Gordon 1974), fully expressed in his book, *Teacher Effectiveness Training*, encourages the creation of a warm supportive relationship between teacher and student where the teacher is sensitive, accepting and non-critical. Above all, Gordon's approach stresses that the teacher uses minimal control and seeks to *understand* the student and the source of the problem. How?

Who 'owns' the problem?

First, teacher and student clarify the source of their dispute: who 'owns' the problem, the teacher or the student? In other words, is the student having a problem that is the cause of the misbehaviour or does the teacher own the problem because the student's behaviour is having a direct and concrete effect on him or her? If the problem is the student's then the teacher's role is to listen critically in order to understand the 'real message' underlying it. This should be done in the first instance by non-verbal encouragement such as nodding or gestures (**critical listening**), followed by non-directive statements (**active listening**) which summarise and repeat or mirror what the student is saying to confirm that the student's real message and feelings are being clearly understood.

Let us look at an example of this approach in practice. The problem is one of a student who is pushing others and defiantly refusing to join the rest of the class in gymnastics.

Teacher: Abdul, I would like you to line up with that group at the floor mats, please. We will be doing some tumbling.
Student: I'm not going to!

At this stage, the teacher has to decide whether the problem is the student's and should be worked out without any influence from the teacher, or whether the teacher is having a problem with the student's behaviour and, therefore, 'owns' the problem. The following dialogue illustrates Gordon's approach.

Teacher: Abdul, when you refuse to join in, I get annoyed that I have to spend extra time with you when other students need my help. I'm also worried that someone might get hurt because I'm not watching them.
Student: I hate gym ... I can't do all the things you want.
Teacher: Uh, huh (nodding while listening critically). You don't like gym because you feel that you can't do it? (active listening)
Student: Yeah.
Teacher: Why? (door opener)
Student: All the other kids laugh at me because I can't do the cartwheels and tumbles properly.
Teacher: You feel that the other kids will laugh at you if you can't do everything in gym and that's why you don't want to join in?
Student: Uh, huh. They all say I'm hopeless.

Here it is clear that the student and teacher *both* own the problem and it is up to the teacher to help Abdul explore some solutions to the problem.

Teacher: Abdul, I need to be able to concentrate on helping everyone in the gym or accidents will happen. I want you to join in the activities willingly, but you're not happy to because kids tease you. What do you think you can do about it?
Student: I suppose I could practise a bit more.
Teacher: Mmm. What else?
Student: Maybe I could get George (a more proficient friend) to show me how to do some of the gym.
Teacher: Any other ideas?
Student: Not really.
Teacher: Okay I'm sure your ideas would help. I could also give you some coaching at lunch time when none of the class was there, if you would like. Maybe George could come too? What do you think?
Student: I'd like you to show me what to do by myself first, and then me and George could go to the gym later to practise until I get good at it.
Teacher: Sounds like we've got a plan to work with, Abdul. Next week, we'll see how much the practice and extra coaching has helped. Okay?

If the teacher owns the problem, he or she gives a **directive 'I-message'** which has three components: a description of the student's behaviour which does not judge or blame the student; the negative effect the behaviour is having on the teacher; and how the teacher feels about the behaviour. These three aspects of an effective I-message are seen in the following example:

Directive 'I-messages'

'When you forget to bring your homework in, I can't check all the work at the same time to see if everyone is ready for me to teach the next topic. This makes me feel very frustrated at the waste of time.'

The I-message thus allows the teacher to prompt appropriate behaviour without negative evaluation of the student, nor issuing a direct command (Weinstein & Mignano 1993). Of couse, the responsibility for changing the behaviour rests with the student. However, there is a greater likelihood of this happening than if an accusatory 'you-message' is given ('You are being very inconsiderate when you don't hand in your homework on time').

At times, active listening and I-messages are not enough to solve problems between teacher and student. When both own the problem, Gordon advocates the use of a **no-lose** approach to conflict resolution where neither teacher nor student is winner or loser, but rather both are winners. In other words, the emphasis is on cooperation, not power. How is this done? In the earlier example of Abdul, the teacher adopts a problem-solving strategy that follows these steps:

No-lose approach to conflict resolution

1. Define the problem.
2. Brainstorm possible solutions.
3. Evaluate the solutions.
4. Select one solution that is mutually acceptable.
5. Decide how to put the solution into practice; establish an agreement as to who will do what and when.
6. Assess how successful the solution was.

For communication with students to be effective, Gordon insists that at no stage should the teacher put up **'roadblocks'** such as **moralising** ('You should know what happens if you ...'); **judging** ('That wasn't a very smart thing to do'); **stereotyping** ('That's typical behaviour for someone like you!'); **advising** ('What you need to do is ...'); or **sympathising** ('I always found gym difficult when I was your age, but if you really practise, you'll find it gets easier.'). These impose teacher control and prevent students from solving the problem themselves.

As you can see, Gordon's approach will not always be easy to implement: time pressures may prevent extended conferences with students; their language development may limit how effectively they can express thoughts and feelings; and the age and reasoning ability of children may restrict the extent to which the teacher can use logical argument. Furthermore, one needs to be patient and committed to genuinely empathising with students in order to hear their messages. Even more difficult for a teacher is the ability to admit to 'owning' a problem rather than seeing blame as originating with the student, especially when faced with hostility or defiance. The approach requires a good rapport between teacher and students to be already in place, or some students, especially adolescents, may find it patronising rather than sincere.

The conflict resolution approach may be best used with students who have chronic behaviour or personality problems rather than as a general classroom approach (Good & Brophy 1990, 1991). Such a student-oriented approach may also be well suited to follow-up interactions with students who have been placed in detention or extended timeout (Lewis 1992). It is during this time that teachers have the opportunity to use active listening to help students formulate a solution to their unacceptable behaviour.

Glasser's interactionist approach

Glasser's philosophy is a blend of **humanist** and **behaviourist** approaches. Although it was intended to be used with students who persistently violate rules, Glasser's approach has been adopted by a number of Australian schools as their whole school discipline policy (Lewis 1991).

There have been two stages in the development of Glasser's theory. The focus of the first stage (Glasser 1969) was on the **power sharing** between teacher and student(s), and especially the responsibility of the group for the behaviour of its members. Glasser encouraged the use of regular **classroom meetings** to deal democratically with issues that are most relevant to the group: class rules, appropriate behaviour (of particular class members, as well as the whole class) and discipline. A brief look at how these meetings should be run may give you a better insight into whether you feel such an approach could be added to your management repertoire.

Power sharing and classroom meetings

Holding classroom meetings

1. Teacher and students sit in a closed circle.
2. The length of meeting should depend on the age of the children: for early grades 10 to 30 minutes; for older grades 30 to 45 minutes.
3. Problems and topics for discussion are those that emerge from the needs of the group.
4. Students should feel free to express their opinions and feelings without fear: there are no right or wrong answers.
5. The teacher leads the discussion but does not make evaluative comments; it is important for the teacher to keep the discussion focused by summarising or paraphrasing what students say.
6. The goal of the meeting is to solve the problem in a positive way and come up with a plan of action that is agreed upon by all participants—this may need a couple of meetings.
7. *Action* is important following the discussion. There should be no 'letting off the hook'. Teachers and students see that what is decided actually occurs.

Where a student has broken rules, Glasser recommends a technique called **reality therapy**. This is based on the premise that each individual has a need for self-worth and that, in order to feel worthwhile, he or she must maintain a satisfactory standard of behaviour (Wilkins 1987). Using this approach, the teacher focuses on helping the student evaluate his or her behaviour and make some efforts to improve it. When a student misbehaves, therefore, the teacher must avoid making judgments and assigning blame; instead, the teacher should use direct questioning to encourage self-evaluation and accountability in the student in the following way:

Reality therapy

1. The student is confronted and told to stop the misbehaviour: 'George, sit back down in your seat.'
2. The student is then asked to *explain* the behaviour that was occurring. The teacher uses 'What' questions, not 'Why': 'What are you doing?' This prevents the student from finding excuses, such as 'I had to get up because he stole my pencil', and draws attention to the **cause** of the problem (self-evaluation).
3. If the rule-breaking behaviour continues, step 2 is repeated, adding 'Is it against the rules?' Here the emphasis is on the **consequences** of the behaviour (student responsibility): 'If you continue to do this what will happen?'
4. The teacher asks the student to make a **plan** or

TEACHER'S CASE BOOK

LET'S MAKE OUR OWN RULES

Miss Langridge is a year 7 homeroom teacher. At the beginning of the year the students and Miss Langridge decided to come up with a set of class rules. They brainstormed together and the students really enjoyed having a say in how 'their' classroom should operate. Once they had finished brainstorming and come up with a set of class rules, they compared them with the school rules and discovered that they had devised rules totally consistent with the school rules.

Miss Langridge then posed the question: 'Okay, we now have some class rules which we have devised and agreed about. What do we do if one of us violates one of the rules?' They brainstormed again and some students came up with some innovative strategies, and after seeing the school discipline policy again decided that they would like to use that. However, one student suggested that this was not enough and some other means of punishment was necessary to prevent further unnecessary behaviour. Susan suggested that violation of rules should result in that person forfeiting participation in the end-of-term activity days. There were some people who opposed this so a secret ballot was held. There was more support for Susan's suggestion than not, so her motion was carried.

Miss Langridge asked the students if they thought that a note should be written home in their diary to let parents know of a rule violation. Once again a group vote was taken and this was agreed upon. Angela asked a very good question: 'How will you know that the note has been seen by the parent?' Miss Langridge suggested that they could have it signed by a parent and there was general consensus for this suggestion.

After all these decisions had been made, Miss Langridge typed them up in the form of a contract and had each individual student sign this contract to endorse the agreed set of rules and consent to abide by their agreement. Miss Langridge has found this to be most successful in encouraging positive student behaviour and fostering personal development, for the students take responsibility for their own actions.

Case studies illustrating National Competency Framework for Beginning Teaching, National Project on the Quality of Teaching and Learning, Australian Teaching Council, 1996, p. 44. Commonwealth of Australia copyright, reproduced by permission.

Case study activity

As a group, discuss this teacher's democratic, interactionist approach to establishing a classroom management policy with high school students. Is it an approach that you would use and, if so, in what circumstances?

commitment to finding alternatives: 'What are you going to do about your behaviour?' or 'What is your plan so that you don't break the rule again?'

5. Sometimes the student may be asked to go to the 'castle' (Glasser's term for **isolation** desk or corner in the classroom) until the problem is worked out. This isolation is a logical consequence of breaking the class rules. This step is vital as it places responsibility with the student for his or her own behaviour and for finding alternatives (accountability).
6. If the rule-breaking behaviour still persists, steps 2–5 are repeated but the teacher indicates that support will be provided: 'We have to work it out.' The teacher arranges a specific time and location in the near future to help in the development of the plan and to provide encouragement for it to work. The student is allowed to return to the class after a solution has been arrived at.
7. If the student fails to fulfil his or her commitment and plan, the next step is **isolation to a designated room** (Principal's office or special isolation room). Steps 2, 3, 4 and 5 are repeated by the Principal, grade supervisor or school counsellor, who has been notified earlier. Parents may be involved in solving the problem.
8. Finally, if the student is out of control, the parents are notified and asked to collect the student immediately. The student may return to the school when he or she is able to obey the rules.
9. If all else fails, the parents and student are referred to an outside agency to 'work it out'.

As for the notion of punishment, Glasser sees that the use of teacher-imposed punishment for failing to keep to a plan is counterproductive to students' development of a sense of self-control. He sees it as more beneficial for them to suffer the logical consequences of not abiding by class rules for behaviour—that is, exclusions from the class—together with the natural consequences of failing to follow their plan—that of having to start all over again on a new one.

The teacher's role in reality therapy

One of the most important features of Glasser's discipline plan is his emphasis on the need for the teacher to give positive attention to students when they are *not* breaking the rules: wish them 'Good morning' when they arrive at school, reward them for effort, simply acknowledge them in a pleasant manner when they are around. In other words, develop a positive relationship with students, letting them see you as genuinely warm, as well as firm in your resolve to have them abide by the rules. Furthermore, it is vital that you examine what *you* are doing to cope with discipline problems and how effective your methods are: do you ridicule or threaten students? Does this work, or does it merely encourage hostility and further misbehaviour?

Since 1985, Glasser has adopted a different philosophy to discipline called control theory (Glasser 1992). As with reality therapy, the focus in control theory is on the *causes* of misbehaviour. However, whereas reality therapy places these causes with the student, control theory maintains that it is the school's responsibility to prevent student misbehaviour. Specifically, Glasser has advocated in his new theory that discipline problems will not erupt if schools fulfil powerful student needs for belonging, power, fun and freedom. In other words, student behaviours, in fact, all our behaviours, are efforts to control our lives. His approach should be compared with that of Maslow (see Chapter 15). Certainly, in some schools the importance of fulfilling student needs has been demonstrated in the establishment of breakfast programs for primary school children. Glasser maintains that the major problems in schools are not defiance or hostility from students, which require teacher control, but rather apathy and unwillingness to participate in learning activities through boredom. His philosophy is a **humanistic** one: motivation cannot be coerced or manipulated externally as the **behaviourists** would argue—it comes from within the individual.

Control theory school's responsibility to prevent misbehaviour by fullfilling student needs

Three basic notions stand out in control theory:

1. Schools must meet the basic psychological needs of students for **belonging** (security, comfort and group membership), **power** (importance, status, being taken into account by others), **fun** (having an emotionally and intellectually good time), and **freedom** (being able to choose, to be self-directed and to have responsibility).
2. The way in which curriculum material is presented in teacher-directed methods must be replaced by 'quality' schoolwork in which skills are developed not facts learned, and learning that has been traditionally evaluated by achievement tests alone should incorporate **student self-evaluation** as well.
3. Teachers must become 'lead-managers' who make learning interesting and help students, rather than 'boss-managers' who dictate in their teaching and discipline (Glasser 1992). Boss-managers turn students into adversaries by relying on coercion and criticism which are not conducive to encouraging high-quality work in students. Lead-management, on the other hand, is non-coercive; it encourages cooperative learning which gives students power and, therefore, the incentive to work harder.

The teacher's role in a '**quality school**' is to use the skills of problem solving and persuasion to show students how it is in their best interests to produce high-quality work. Of course, the school environment must provide the tools (**curriculum** and **resources**) and the atmosphere (**non-coercive** and **cooperative**) for this to be feasible (Glasser 1992).

The quality school

Question point: *What are your thoughts on this approach to teaching and management—to what extent are you prepared to organise your teaching and the class to meet students' psychological needs; or do you believe that students should fit in with your needs as the teacher?*

How do these children illustrate the important elements of Glasser's control theory?
Photo: authors

Looking at the two approaches advocated by Glasser, we feel that both offer valuable insights for managing student learning and behaviour. Control theory is an ideal that may genuinely foster **intrinsic motivation** in students, thereby preventing much misbehaviour. Reality therapy gives the teacher an organised and proven method for encouraging the development of student self-management, and for dealing with problems once they erupt. **Cooperative learning strategies** (see later in this chapter) provide ideal opportunities for students to satisfy their needs and gain a sense of control at school. How is this so?

- *Belonging* By working together in teams on learning tasks, students develop a sense of mutual interdependence and motivation to achieve.
- *Freedom and power* Students who are academically more able gain a sense of power from helping those in their group who are less able. All students gain a sense of importance and self-worth from their contributions to the group project. Later in this chapter we describe in greater detail how to structure cooperative tasks so that each member of a group has an equally valuable part to play.
- *Fun* When students work cooperatively together on exciting projects, 'fun' is guaranteed.

Dreikurs' democratic classroom

Logical consequences

Rudolf Dreikurs (Dreikurs 1968; Dreikurs, Grunwald & Pepper 1982) has much in common with the approach of Glasser. He believes that teachers should be involved in the ongoing process of helping students develop *inner control of their behaviour*, rather than imposing control externally during conflict. In a classroom where the teacher is seen as a firm but kind friend who does not patronise students and treats them with respect, discipline problems will be prevented, according to Dreikurs. In true democratic style, teachers and students should decide together on class rules and the logical consequences for keeping or breaking them. You will remember that we have already discussed such an approach earlier in the chapter (see The Four Rs).

Misbehaviour reflects a need for recognition

Dreikurs firmly believes that student behaviour is motivated by a need to be recognised and to belong, and that misbehaviour is the product of efforts to achieve this recognition by satisfying four mistaken goals: *attention getting, power seeking, revenge seeking* and displaying *inadequacy*. Students choose to misbehave because socially acceptable means to achieve recognition have failed them. What help does this give the teacher in dealing with misbehaviour? If a student tries to get attention, for example, by clowning, asking incessant questions or annoying other children, Dreikurs believes that the teacher should *avoid* responding in the way the student expects. In fact, his advice is that teachers must always resist their first impulse in cases of misbehaviour, whichever mistaken goal is being expressed, as this is precisely what satisfies the student's goal.

Motives for misbehaviour: attention power revenge recognition

To deal effectively with misbehaviour, in Dreikurs' view, teachers should determine which of the four goals of misbehaviour is being satisfied by their reaction. By not reacting in the expected way, the teacher can help the student begin to eliminate the destructive behaviour, and substitute other means of developing a sense of belonging. In the case of a student seeking **attention** by being late, for example, the reaction should be to ignore the lateness, but to point out calmly that the missed work must be made up in the student's own time (a logical consequence). A student who seeks **power** by being defiant and argumentative should have no one to fight with; it is futile arguing if there is no response. When a student shows **revenge** by destroying property or stealing, the consequence is not retaliation by the teacher, but, rather, restitution. As for the individual who is attempting to gain **recognition** by being 'inadequate', the teacher should withhold giving help constantly as this merely serves to reinforce the hopelessness. Instead, setting short-term, achievable goals for which encouragement can be given is preferable (Balson 1992).

WHAT WOULD YOU DO?

ENOUGH IS ENOUGH

Darryl was a 12-year-old student who came from a very unfortunate background. Consequently, he was a difficult and obstinate student who abused other children as well as teachers and would simply refuse to do things. During the first month of term 1, when Darryl encountered a situation which displeased him, he would pack his schoolbag, swear and go home. This was becoming a real problem and nothing Miss Jordan had been doing was working. She tried pleading with him, growling at him, joking with him and adopting a calm and rational approach aimed at trying to get him to see the importance of remaining at school.

What would Dreikurs say about the range of responses that the teacher has made to the student? What other strategies might be useful in this situation? Consider further the teacher's response on page 225.

Case studies illustrating National Competency Framework for Beginning Teaching, National Project on the Quality of Teaching and Learning, Australian Teaching Council, 1996, p. 46. Commonwealth of Australia copyright, reproduced with permission.

The Canters' assertive discipline model

Lee and Marlene Canter (1976, 1990, 1992) have developed a program for *corrective* classroom control known as **assertive discipline** (or positive behaviour management) which is widely used in many schools today. Teachers find its approach appealing because it allows them to use class time more productively for teaching; it can prevent discipline problems from occurring because students have a clear understanding of the consequences of keeping and breaking the rules; it can also provide supportive control when a warning may be all that is needed.

Assertive discipline: protecting and restoring order in classrooms

We look first at the important features of the approach and then consider some of the major criticisms of it made by educational experts. Think about whether this is the approach that best suits your views of classroom management.

First, the notion of 'assertiveness' is clarified. The Canters distinguish between non-assertive, hostile and assertive teachers:

- ☐ *Non-assertive* 'For the sixth time, boys, will you please try your best to stop talking and finish your work?' (Doesn't really convince students that the teacher expects them to change their behaviour.)
- ☐ *Hostile* 'Okay. I've had it! The next person who opens their mouth will have the whole class staying back after school to clean up the playground!' (Communicates teacher dislike of students and establishes an atmosphere of mutual mistrust and vengeance.)
- ☐ *Assertive* 'John, you know it's against the rules to talk when I am teaching. This is the second time: please move to the timeout desk.' (Business-like communication of reasonable teacher expectations and disapproval followed by a clear indication of what the student is to do.)

The Canters' aim is to establish a positive discipline system that reinforces the teacher's authority to teach and to control in order to ensure an environment that is optimal for learning. They recommend that this be done in the following way.

Establishing a positive discipline system

At the outset

1. Select the behaviours expected of the students together with the positive and negative consequences.
2. Seek the Principal's support for the list of rules.
3. Discuss the expected behaviours and their consequences with the students in the first class meeting.
4. Have students write the rules and consequences on paper and take it home for parents to read and sign.
5. Emphasise that the rules have been made to ensure effective learning and appropriate behaviour.
6. Teach the behaviours that you want from students in particular situations. For example, if you require students to stay seated during group work but will allow 'quiet talking', then you must explain the directions for this behaviour clearly and teach these by modelling and checking for understanding: students can demonstrate the correct behaviour by practising in an actual example. Have the students repeat orally what the rules are and their consequences.

Once introduced

1. Use positive repetition to reinforce students when they are correctly following the directions: 'Joanna put her hand up before she spoke. Thank you.'
2. Apply positive and negative consequences, which have already been defined and communicated to the students earlier, as appropriate.

You will notice that these are not 'logical' consequences, as described earlier in the chapter. In effect, the 'consequences' advocated by the Canters are rewards and punishments in the behavioural sense (Cairns 1995).

The Canters believe that positive consequences are more powerful in shaping student behaviour than negative ones. If students deliberately violate the rules, they suggest that the

Positive consequences

WHAT WOULD YOU DO?

ENOUGH IS ENOUGH (continued)

Finally, the turning point came one day. Things were not going Darryl's way and he stood up, swore at Miss Jordan and went to the cloakroom, packed his bag and said 'I'm f...ing going home and you can't make me stay here'. She had had enough, she was frustrated by this child's constant interruption of the class. She managed to stay calm and said, 'Fine, Darryl, you're right, I can't make you stay and frankly I'm not even going to bother. You've been annoying me and the children, and interfering with their learning—and we'd all be better off without you. So just go and we'll see you later.' She requested politely, 'Can you please shut the door after you?' and turned back to the class and ignored him.

Out of the corner of her eye she could see that Darryl hadn't moved. He eventually put his bag down and came and sat on the mat. Darryl never threatened to go home again, and he has ceased to be such a problem. Miss Jordan is no longer playing his game. She has stated clearly what is acceptable behaviour in her classroom and has taken unmistakable control of the situation. Those who do not choose to accept these conditions will not be missed; threats will no longer be effective.

What are some of the principles of effective classroom management that the teacher appears to have used with success here?

Case studies illustrating National Competency Framework for Beginning Teaching, National Project on the Quality of Teaching and Learning, Australian Teaching Council, 1996, p. 46. Commonwealth of Australia copyright, reproduced by permission.

negative consequences that result should be graded in severity, according to the number of times the offence is repeated during the lesson or day (each day starts afresh):

1. First offence—a warning (name recorded privately not publicly, such as on the chalkboard, as this can either humiliate students or, in some cases, serve to feed their attention-seeking needs). This should be done without interrupting the lesson.
2. Second offence—10 minute timeout (within-class isolation).
3. Third offence—15 minute timeout.
4. Fourth offence—parents contacted.
5. Fifth offence—sent to Principal.

For students who are very disruptive, the Canter approach recommends two control techniques: 'moving-in' and the 'freeze' approach. **Moving-in** involves the teacher walking up to the student, using eye contact, touch and gesture when speaking to the student, and stating the consequences that the student has chosen with his or her behaviour ('By throwing your books around the room, you have chosen to go to detention after school'), and warning of the consequences for further disruption. The **freeze** technique has the teacher saying 'freeze' to the offending student in an assertive tone, and then stating the rules that should be followed in this instance. Sometimes the **broken record** method is also used in cases of misbehaviour. This is merely the repetition of the rules and consequences in the face of persistent argument:

Control techniques for disruptive students

Teacher: Kate, either stop speaking or choose to do your work at lunchtime.

Kate: That's not fair, Mario and Peter were talking too!

Teacher: You will stop speaking now or spend 15 minutes at lunchtime.

Kate: I can't stay in at lunchtime because I have drama practice.

Teacher: You have now chosen to stay in the classroom for 15 minutes at lunchtime to finish your work. If you continue to speak now, you will be choosing to stay for half an hour.

Some argue that the assertive teacher (in the style of the Canters) is too dominant and harsh, and focuses more on preventing undesirable behaviour than on

WHAT WOULD YOU DO?

A TICK FOR CHRIS

Chris had been disruptive during class on a few occasions and had already been in Timeout twice during the past two weeks. On this particular afternoon, the children were writing out their favourite recipes to make a class cookbook. Chris was slow in starting his work and he was spending his time talking loudly to the neighbouring children at his group table. Meredith, his new teacher, gave him one warning about the rule he was breaking but he did not change his behaviour. She was concerned about putting him in Timeout again because he seemed to be experiencing failure only lately so she took him aside for a talk.

What do you think the talk consisted of? What action might the teacher take next and with what consequences? Consider what Meredith did on page 227.

Case studies illustrating National Competency Framework for Beginning Teaching, National Project on the Quality of Teaching and Learning Australian Teaching Council, 1996, p. 18. Commonwealth of Australia copyright, reproduced by permission.

providing opportunities for students to develop responsibility for their own behaviour, an important social skill, particularly as students get older. Another criticism is that teachers make excessive use of rewards and punishments with the effect that motivation is externally controlled, not intrinsic to the students. In other words, students are trained to respond to anticipated positive and negative consequences rather than being taught the value of responsible behaviour. What are your feelings on this?

Criticisms of assertive discipline

Despite the longevity of assertive discipline and its widespread use by classroom teachers (McCormack 1989), Render, Padilla and Krank's (1989) review of research concluded that it may be appropriate to use assertive discipline 'in severe cases where students are behaving inappropriately more than 96 per cent of the time' (p. 72). Anecdotal Australian evidence exists, however, that the Canter approach is less successful in 'difficult' schools than in 'middle-of-the-road' schools. However, as a policy to be adopted school-wide, it is not strongly supported by research evidence.

In the final analysis, the 'success' of any student discipline policy should be measured by the extent to which it supports teaching and learning, rather than the degree of order and quiet in the classroom (Evertson 1995).

Question point: *Of the approaches to classroom management and discipline that have been described to this point, which appeal to you the most? What is your own personal philosophy on the approach that would best support your teaching and the learning of your students?*

COOPERATIVE LEARNING AND CLASSROOM MANAGEMENT

Classroom goal structures

Both locally and internationally there is a growing interest in the educational benefits of grouping children for learning. Classroom grouping is an important management function which has implications for effective learning and classroom management. Typically, classrooms and lessons can be structured in one of three ways: individualistically, competitively or cooperatively. In **individualistic** goal structures, the student is expected to do the very best that he or she can, alone. Achieving individually does not interfere with the achievement of others. Rewards are based on the extent to which a student's performance meets specified standards, not on how well or poorly the student performs in comparison with others. When **competitive** goal structures are used, success and rewards are determined by others' 'failure', by 'beating' other students: for there to be a winner (the scorer of the 'A' grade) there must also be a loser, or many losers. Currently, there is considerable interest in the use of **cooperative** goal structures in which students work together to achieve or complete shared or common tasks. The success of group members depends on the success of *all* members of the group: helping each other in groups to achieve ensures both individual and group rewards.

Typically, teachers report that cooperative group work is most effective when student interaction will enhance learning such as in learning complex conceptual material. There is no advantage for students, in using cooperative learning structures for activities that involve completing merely factual or computational tasks where the fastest worker or the one who knows the answers will 'share' with the rest of the group (Cohen 1994a). This isn't to say that cooperative learning approaches are not effective for lower-level tasks such as recall of factual information, decoding and motor skills: they are (Slavin 1990). Probably of greater interest to us as educators is the very strong

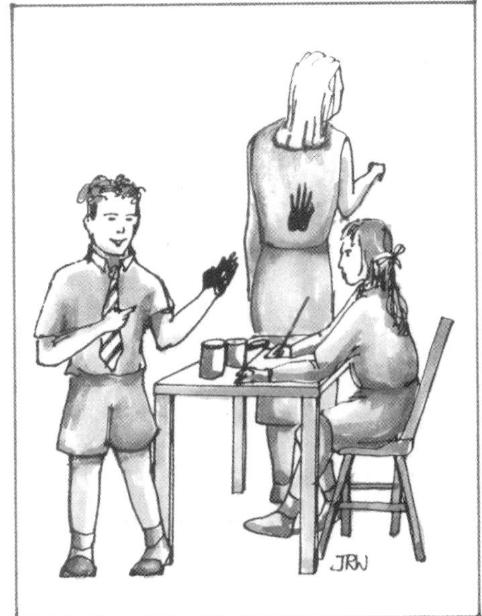

'I think it improves her dress'

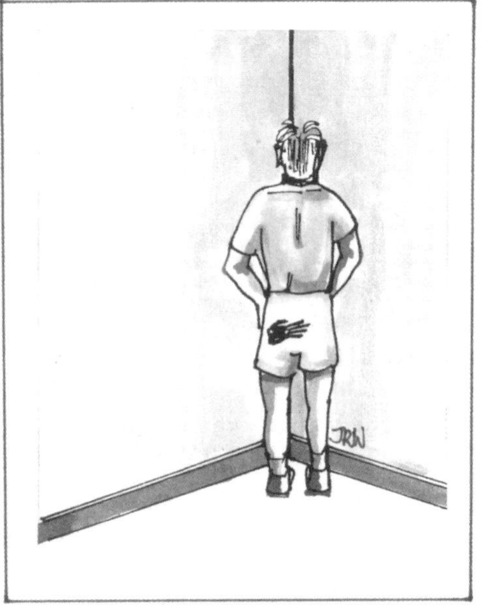

'I think it improves my behaviour!'

WHAT WOULD YOU DO?

A TICK FOR CHRIS (continued)

First, Meredith ensured that he understood the rule he was breaking. Next, she set him the task of taking responsibility for his behaviour by asking him how he could avoid distractions. He opted for moving away from the group he was working with and sitting alone on the floor in front of the chair. Meredith praised him for his solution and challenged him to complete his work by the end of the session, so that he could get his recipe into the book. She added that if he could do this task, he would be awarded a 'tick' on his merit chart. This reward system is part of the school's discipline policy.

Chris worked diligently for the remainder of the session and handed over his completed recipe at the end. His smile conveyed that he was satisfied with his work so Meredith honoured their agreement and put a tick on his chart. Then she verbally praised him for his work once again before home time. The next day, Meredith had no cause to warn him about being disruptive.

Initially, Meredith was concerned about offering external rewards for work. However, she felt that if she could ensure his success in some way, then internal motivation may follow.

What are your thoughts on the solution taken by the teacher in the context of the literature on classroom management and motivation?

Case studies illustrating National Competency Framework for Beginning Teaching, National Project on the Quality of Teaching and Learning, Australian Teaching Council, 1996, p. 18. Commonwealth of Australia copyright, reproduced by permission.

research evidence that cooperative efforts at higher-level tasks such as problem solving are superior to competitive ones for individuals of all ages from pre schoolers to adults (Qin, Johnson & Johnson 1995). Specifically, for problems expressed in words, such as discussion and essay questions; mathematical problems, figures, mazes and puzzles; and creative problems requiring imagery or novel representations, cooperative groups are better able to find solutions than those who work competitively and alone.

Social value

If, on the other hand, the goal is the development of harmonious interpersonal relationships, especially of an intercultural nature, the research evidence for the use of team-based approaches (such as STAD, TGI, Jigsaw and Group Investigation, described later in the chapter) also shows strong positive effects (Slavin 1990). In addition, low-achieving students find that their achievement is enhanced because they must seek to clarify any lack of understanding in order to contribute to the group goal. This is more motivating than merely performing a task because the teacher says so. Also, the low expectations held by and of low-status students are dissipated as group members discover similarities other than academic ones, and also find that the final product of collaboration is far richer than any one individual could produce.

Planning to use cooperative learning in the classroom

If you think you would like to try a cooperative learning approach to a learning activity, Abrami et al. (1995) recommend that you ask yourself the following questions first. Can this work be done better in a group than individually? That is, will the mix of different abilities, viewpoints and creative talents be an advantage? Is the task so large or complex that only a group can handle it? If the answers are 'yes', then you have a recipe for success. If, on the other hand, you have answered 'no', then it is unlikely that students will put a great deal of effort into a group project in which they feel that they would do better or enjoy independently. Group tasks must be carefully planned and structured by the teacher so that cooperative interaction between students is required for successful completion: students must understand what the objectives are, what their individual responsibilites are, and how these are interrelated with those of other team members. In fact, research has shown that the most effective cooperative learning techniques incorporate both group goals and individual accountability (Abrami et al. 1995).

Question point: *What are the types of management issues that you would need to consider when planning to make cooperative learning activities a regular part of your classroom?*

Group work and classroom management

Needless to say, students who are productively engaged are unlikely to cause discipline problems. In the traditional classroom, where the teacher directs the flow of student interaction and conversation, management of behaviour is less complex than in the cooperative classroom. Ideally, in terms of enhancing student learning outcomes, cooperative techniques (carefully structured so that students *are* productively engaged) enable the teacher to spend more time giving direct instruction to specific groups as needed, as well as to act as a consultant to all groups. However in relation to cooperative learning, the question is often raised: 'If students are allowed to argue or debate among themselves while they work on group projects, won't serious management problems develop that will be too hard to control?' We would be lying if we said that you will not find the implementation of cooperative strategies demanding in terms of management, at least until the students have become accustomed to the skills required in collaboration. Nonetheless, the evidence is clearly in favour of the benefits of consistent use of cooperative learning approaches over a period of time, especially in terms of social skills which contribute to improved classroom behaviour (Jordan 1997). In Table 10.6 we list some helpful hints which can get you started and minimise potential problems. Before that, what were some of those classroom management issues you were thinking of?

Those that generally present themselves as problems are the following:

- ☐ noise
- ☐ seating arrangements
- ☐ presenting students with directions
- ☐ accessing materials for collaborative use
- ☐ dealing with inappropriate behaviours that violate the norms for cooperation—not helping others, putdowns, arguments, bullying and loafing.

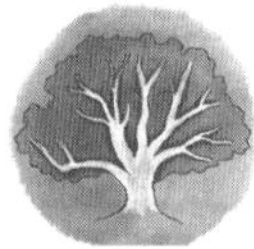

TABLE 10.6

ESSENTIALS OF GETTING STARTED WITH COOPERATIVE LEARNING IN THE CLASSROOM

For teachers

- Planning well ahead: set realistic and attainable goals for the activity and communicate these to the students.
- Beginning with topics or groups with which you are likely to be successful: don't be too ambitious at the start.
- Using very small groups (pairs) at first and increasing size to threes or fours later.
- Restricting the first cooperative activity to less than 15 minutes.
- Designing the activity to require group processes.
- Using a 'quiet signal' or 'noise meter' to help students monitor and control noise levels.
- Reflecting on the outcomes of the group collaboration in terms of your planning and your learning objectives. Have the students do the same.
- Persisting with a variety of cooperative approaches: it takes a lot of practice to master any teaching approach. Students also need to learn how to work collaboratively: it will come with time.

(adapted from Abrami et al. 1995)

Establishing cooperative learning in the classroom

As indicated in the earlier part of this chapter, the establishment of clear behavioural and learning expectations by the teacher is critical for effective classroom management. The same principle applies to the use of cooperative learning approaches. The first few weeks of the year are the ideal time to begin. During this period, the teacher should establish a cooperative learning atmosphere in which students develop a sense of trust in and appreciation of each other. Fear of making mistakes or of not being 'the best', competitive concerns which inhibit collaborative interaction and learning, should be progressively eliminated through class-building and team-building activities such as those described in the excellent resource book of Spencer Kagan (1994), *Cooperative Learning*.

Kagan also recommends that rules for cooperative behaviour, even better described as 'class norms', should be formulated by the students where appropriate, rather than presented by the teacher. One way of doing this is to have the students reflect on how they feel when participating in group work themselves. What feels good? What makes it work? What spoils it? Perhaps you can also think about that now, from your own experiences? The norms can be broken simply into two categories: those that relate to personal responsibility (I am responsible for these types of behaviours: ...); and those that relate to team responsibility (We are responsible for these types of behaviours: ...).

Box 10.4 illustrates the types of class norms that are useful.

BOX 10.4 **CLASS NORMS FOR COOPERATIVE BEHAVIOUR**

Personally, I am responsible for:

- Helping my team-mates
- Asking for help
- Putting in my best effort
- Being polite
- Encouraging and praising

As a team, we are responsible for:

- Using quiet working voices
- Figuring out our own problems
- Asking each other before the teacher
- Helping other teams

ACTION STATION

Imagine that you have a year 9 English class of boys for the year which is composed of a number of ethnic groups who do not work collaboratively in class, and call each other names or even fight in the playground. You are going to begin a six-week unit of work on the theme of 'What it is to be an Australian' after the next school holiday, and have decided to adopt a cooperative learning approach instead of the traditional lecture and group discussion method.

Your aim is to improve the interpersonal relations between the students by devising activities that will help them: recognise their similarities; understand and appreciate their differences; and begin to develop a class identity. What will you do when you first begin and then progressively over the six weeks?

Working with a group, brainstorm some of the possible ways in which this teacher's goals may be fulfilled.

Cooperative learning encourages individuals to learn at their own pace, within the support of a sharing group. To be successful, all group members must understand the relevant group processes. Photo: Diane McPhail

The benefits of cooperative group learning

What are the positive outcomes, both cognitive and non-cognitive, that have been claimed for cooperative structures? As well as being an effective method of managing students (once they have learned the skills of collaboration), cooperative learning structures have been shown to improve academic achievement for students of a range of ability levels at primary and secondary school level, irrespective of subject area and type of school (Slavin 1991, 1995). Particular achievement gains have been shown in mathematics (Davidson 1991), verbal skills in social studies, reading, language arts and English (Winitsky 1991), and computer-based learning (Rysavy & Sales 1991).

Positive outcomes of cooperative structures: classroom management student achievement social relationships and enhanced self-esteem

As for non-cognitive outcomes, it has been demonstrated that cooperative learning produces positive attitudes towards learning, raises self-concept and self-esteem, improves relationships between students, increases feelings of social support, and enhances acceptance of 'difference' such as minority group membership, gender or disability (Johnson & Johnson 1989–90; Wilkinson 1988–89). In fact, the evidence in favour of adopting cooperative learning as a method of improving non-academic classroom outcomes is far more clear-cut than that for academic achievement, where the research findings are not always consistent (Good & Brophy 1991). The reason for this lies not so much in the strategy but in the methods used to synthesise the results of the many different research studies on the effects of cooperative strategies on achievement (Abrami et al. 1995).

Why does cooperative learning work?

There are two broad theoretical perspectives on why cooperative learning works: cognitive and motivational. Within the cognitive viewpoint, there are those (followers of Piaget and Vygotsky) who support a **cognitive-developmental** view in which they argue that the cognitive benefits of cooperative learning derive from peer interaction around cognitive tasks. Damon (1984), for example, argues that student learning increases as a consequence of the cognitive conflicts that occur when discussion takes place between students who are at slightly different levels of cognitive development. The use of language during student–student interaction is a critical factor in enhancing thinking: when children argue their point of view with other children, verify it and criticise the opinions of others, they are engaging in ideas generation.

Cognitive-developmental perspective

In addition, there those who argue for a **cognitive-elaboration** explanation of the cognitive processes underlying small-group cooperative interaction (Dansereau 1985). They maintain that for learning to take place, there must be some form of cognitive restructuring in the mind of the learner. One way in which this takes place in a group learning situation is when concepts are elaborated, such as when explaining something to others who ask for help or clarification (Webb 1989; Webb & Farivar 1994). In the cognitive-elaboration view, both the person providing the elaborated explanation and the recipient of the help benefit cognitively. You have probably experienced this yourself—teaching something to someone else helped you learn the material even better yourself. Why do you think that might be so?

Cognitive-elaboration perspective

Finally, Johnson and Johnson (1992, 1994) advocate cooperative learning as a constructivist method for fostering cognitive processes. They support this assertion with the following reasons:

Cognitive constructivist perspective

- ☐ *Rehearsal*: peer discussions help the coding of information into memory through the need to explain, elaborate and summarise to group members.
- ☐ *Mixed groups*: the mix of abilities, learning styles, and viewpoints towards the learning task within groups fosters divergent thinking.
- ☐ *Varied perspectives*: the need to take different perspectives on the task results in better understanding of their ideas.
- ☐ *Feedback*: peer feedback regarding the contributions of others is regularly provided throughout a group project. This may challenge group members to consider the value of their contribution in terms of its relevance and quality.
- ☐ *Conflict*: different opinions which may erupt into controversy promote critical thinking.

The second theoretical perspective is a **motivational** one. This focuses on understanding why individuals within a group are motivated to work interdependently for a common goal. We look here at three motivational approaches to cooperative interaction: cooperative rewards, morality-based cooperation, and social interdependence. Some proponents of a motivational view of cooperative group interaction maintain that rewarding the group on the basis of individual achievements is a powerful way to motivate individual learning. **Cooperative reward structures** (extrinsic rewards or recognition based on the group's performance as a sum of individual achievements) can be gained only if the entire group is successful. Slavin (1987c, 1992), for example, would argue that building group incentives into the cooperative activity will motivate students to contribute and do their best. Theoretically, individual accountability for learning is encouraged by this approach.

Motivational perspective

As discussed elsewhere in this book, there is concern about the detrimental effects of extrinsic motivators on interest and intrinsic motivation (learning for its own sake). Slavin maintains that incentives need to be used when the material to be learned would not otherwise be found interesting nor be engaged in willingly by students. However, he feels that any potential harmful effects of individual competition or motivation are compensated for by the encouragement and help of team members working for group rewards.

Should rewards be built into cooperative activities?

Question point: *What do you think about learning for group rewards? What are some of the potential difficulties that may emerge when students are not of the same ability or equally disposed to work together? What strategies need to be adopted to protect against difficulties?*

As described in the chapter on motivation (Chapter 9), Ames (1984) suggests that individual effort in cooperative interaction is motivated by a wish to help the group achieve its goal and to help others in order to do so. One's ability is less important in this situation than one's genuine attempts to contribute. Research has shown that when groups do not achieve well, however, those of low ability feel that it was their lack of ability rather than effort that was to blame (Abrami et al. 1992). When the group is successful, on the other hand, effort is considered more important. How might you prevent feelings of failure lowering the motivation of less able students if their group performs less successfully than others? Abrami et al. (1995) suggest three ways: one is to make sure that teams are not put in competition with each other; another is to have groups reflect on the process used to set goals and to achieve them ('What worked and what didn't?'); and the last is to allocate group improvement points to encourage effort and persistence in addition to individual improvement points.

Morality-based motivation

Not only do they argue for a cognitive rationale for cooperative learning, Johnson and Johnson also put forward a strong motivational perspective on why some groups are successful in terms of learning (Johnson & Johnson 1992, 1994). This approach proposes that cooperative groups who are cohesive and work well together are motivated by the understanding that the success of the group is positively related to how well they work as a team and help each other. This positive social interdependence is a function of trust and can be

Positive social interdependence

fostered through many team-building activities, such as those developed by Kagan and his colleagues (1994). Once this interdependence is established, the Johnsons believe that motivation to learn together follows and is shown in helping and negotiation behaviours.

FOUR GENERAL APPROACHES TO LEARNING IN COOPERATIVE GROUPS

While teachers have typically grouped students informally for discussions, projects and problem-solving activities, these group structures have not necessarily been 'cooperative'. Structured cooperative learning methods, which have particular defining characteristics, have been developed as a result of research over many decades. We will consider now some of the approaches to cooperative classroom organisation that have been shown to be effective for developing cognitive and social skills.

To give you insight into the range of approaches that are available to you together with their advantages and disadvantages, we focus on four major models of cooperative learning:

1. Learning together (Johnson & Johnson);
2. Student team learning (Slavin);
3. Structures (Kagan);
4. Group investigation (Sharan & Sharan).

The choice of approach to cooperative group work that you adopt will depend on the purpose of the task and the degree of student familiarity with the social skills involved in cooperative interaction.

Learning together (Johnson & Johnson)

According to Johnson and Johnson (1989c, 1994), for a lesson to be described as truly 'cooperative', there are certain criteria that apply.

- ☐ positive interdependence;
- ☐ face-to-face interaction;
- ☐ individual accountability;
- ☐ collaborative skills;
- ☐ group processing.

Positive interdependence

Positive interdependence means that students must demonstrably function as a group with a shared goal; one that 'sinks or swims together'. No individual who is more able or more assertive should be able to dominate the group. Such interdependence may be expressed in a variety of ways: a common product or goal; assignment of unique roles (task specialisations) that combine to form a whole; shared resources; and shared rewards for a group effort (the motivational perspective) which provide incentives for all members to help each other.

Face-to-face interaction

It is important that tasks be set that require group members to have **face-to-face interaction**, rather than allowing for independent completion of discrete components which are merely combined as separate pieces at the end. Students must be able to reach consensus on what the task entails and how they can best help each other achieve the group goal. They must encourage and support each other's efforts to learn.

Individual accountability

Cooperative learning strategies vary in the extent to which they use rewards based on group performance. In some approaches, group rewards are given only when all members of the group achieve their individual learning goals. The onus is on each member of the group to master his or her own particular material (which may be at a different level from other members), and to be responsible to the group for doing so: each individual is accountable for his or her performance. The essential element here is that *the individual must feel a responsibility to participate*, either through intrinsic motivation, or extrinsic individual or group rewards based on the sum of all the individual parts.

In other methods, rewards are given on the basis of a single group product. As mentioned earlier, developmentalists would reject, outright, the notion of extrinsic rewards for group learning (Damon 1984), maintaining that peer interaction alone is enough to increase student learning. Those who take a humanistic stand argue that intrinsic motivation for the task is destroyed when rewards are used to 'bribe students to work together' (Kohn 1991). Research conducted on cooperative learning approaches that use rewards has not shown this to be the case. Cooperative strategies that intentionally avoid using rewards have been shown to be no more effective than traditional classroom structures, which are competitive and individualistic, in terms of increasing academic achievement (Solomon, Watson et al. 1990).

Collaborative skills

Collaborative skills are crucial to effective cooperative learning. Students need to develop the skills required for working cooperatively. Not all students know how to work and to learn collaboratively; for that matter, probably a large proportion of the adult population could benefit by being taught such skills. Increasingly, employers are looking for individuals who can work as part of a team. Students need to be trained in the necessary social skills of listening, asking and answering questions, giving and receiving explanations, sharing, helping and treating all group members with respect (Webb 1982, 1985a, 1985b,

Collaborative skills are crucial to effective cooperative learning. How can these be taught? Photo: authors

1987, 1989, 1994). This should be done through teacher modelling, examples and reinforcement of the behaviours that demonstrate cooperative group interaction. We give examples of some of these behaviours later in this chapter.

Group processing

Groups need to evaluate how well they are achieving their goals, how their group is performing, and how best to maintain productive working relationships between all members of the group. Time must be made available for **group processing** or reflection to occur and assistance should be given by the teacher, initially, in suggesting ways of giving constructive feedback to group members on their participation. Individual students should also evaluate their personal achievement and contribution.

This model takes time for the teacher and students to master and use but is well worth the effort for learning tasks that focus on concepts and skills.

Student team learning (Slavin)

The research focus of Robert Slavin has been in the use of cooperative learning strategies for the acquisition of basic skills. The following three types of activity are characteristics of his approach.

Teams-Games-Tournament

1. In the **Teams-Games-Tournament** (TGT) the teacher presents first to the whole class material which heterogeneous teams of four to five members then proceed to help each other master during the rest of week, until they compete against other teams on the Friday. These competitions take the form of 'tournaments' at which three students of similar previous performance sit at tables and attempt to gain the most points for their group by answering as many questions on the material as they can from a teacher-prepared handout. Each tournament winner brings the same number of points (six) back to his or her team, irrespective of initial level of ability. Thus, all members have an equal chance of success and of a boost in self-esteem when they contribute to the group total. It is clearly to everyone's advantage in the group to help their team-mates learn. TGT has the advantage of being adaptable to any age group or curriculum area.

Student Teams-Achievement Divisions

2. **Student Teams-Achievement Divisions** (STAD) is a simpler version of TGT that replaces the tournaments between students with individual quizzes. Individual quiz scores are compared with previous averages and points are given based on how much a student meets or improves on past performance. Thus, this method de-emphasises competition between classmates and focuses instead on self-improvement. The sum of individual points is the team score, and teams compete to gain the highest total, for which they are rewarded by the teacher.

Jigsaw

3. One of the earliest approaches to cooperative learning was **Jigsaw**, developed by Aronson and his colleagues (1978). In this method, students are assigned to six-member teams of mixed ability, gender and ethnicity. The material to be learnt is divided between the members of the team. Each team has the same material to learn. Individuals with the same section combine to form 'expert' groups who study their part together. They then return to their original groups to teach these parts in turns to the other team members. Finally, all students are tested on the complete material. Subsequently, Jigsaw II has been modified by Slavin (1985a) so that all students read the entire assignment and are then allocated particular topics on which to become 'experts'. As with STAD, grades are awarded on the basis of individual quizzes to assess individual improvement, and then combined to give a team score.

The student team learning model is an easy one to use but requires good classroom management skills on the teacher's part and students who are well behaved or who have developed the cooperative learning ethic. According to Dalton (Bellanca & Fogarty 1991), the Australian approach to integrating curricula and focusing on developing intrinsic motivation and control over their learning in students is at odds with the competitive, content-specific emphasis of this model.

The structural model (Kagan)

Spencer Kagan's (1994) structural approach has successfully translated the abstract concepts of positive interdependence and individual accountability into practical lesson plan formats for teachers. These allow the teacher freedom to use a variety of **content-free** cooperative learning 'structures' with any subject matter to help provide different ways of organising cooperative interaction between students. Kagan provides activities for six categories of structures which can be adapted to any number of content areas, according to the teacher's objectives. These are:

1. thinking skills
2. communication skills
3. information sharing
4. mastery
5. class building
6. team building.

We will take two examples of popular structures to show you how they can apply to any number of classroom situations.

Numbered Heads Together

In **Numbered Heads Together,** students form teams of four, each student with a separate number. All team members work together to answer the teacher's questions, although only one number will be called from each group to reply. These students will represent their groups but are individually accountable for their answers as there is no prior warning as to which number will be called. Such a structure can be used to check for understanding of content and review of previously learned material (Weinstein & Mignano 1993).

Think-Pair-Share

Think-Pair-Share has been designed to encourage the development of thinking skills. In this structure, a problem is posed which students think about alone, initially, for a specified period. They then pair up with someone to discuss the question. At this stage, careful listening to each other is important as students may be called on to explain their partner's answer during the final stage when all pairs come together to share their answers with the whole class. One interesting variation of this method is to substitute reporting to the whole class with joining another pair in the **Think-Pair-Share** structure to make a team, which can further extend the students' thinking and discussion.

The group investigation model (Sharan & Sharan)

Group investigation

Group investigation is a model for classroom organisation derived from John Dewey's view that children should have some responsibility for directing and influencing their learning, as well as a sense of belonging to social groups while retaining their individuality (Sharan & Sharan 1992). Furthermore, it encompasses a constructivist philosophy that cognitive development involves actively building understanding from personal experiences, not from information being presented by external sources.

According to Sharan and Sharan, there are four critical components of group investigation:

Four critical components of group investigation

1. *Investigation* This refers to the way that classroom learning is organised to enable inquiry-based (project method) learning to occur. It involves changes in student attitudes as much as physical changes in classroom organisation.
2. *Interaction* Sitting students together in small groups does not guarantee that cooperative interaction will take place. They need to be shown the ways in which to talk and work with each other for academic purposes.
3. *Interpretation* Students will interpret both their interpersonal relationships and the information they are studying. There needs to be an opportunity for reflection by students (individually and as a group) and by the teacher.
4. *Intrinsic motivation* This is an essential component of effective group investigation as there are no extrinsic rewards provided. Students need to be personally interested in the topic and their part in its study.

Let us see how *group investigation* operates. Two to six students (heterogeneous in ability and ethnicity) combine to choose a section of a topic from a general unit of work being studied by the class. They then break down this subtopic into individual activities which the members set about completing. It is important that students determine their own learning goals, what to study, and how. Students carry out their individual tasks, discuss and synthesise their findings as a group, and present their final product to the entire class. In this way all groups contribute cooperatively to a broader understanding of the original unit.

The teacher's role in the group investigation approach is very important as students need to be guided and monitored through each stage of the inquiry process (Bellanca & Fogarty 1991). An essential component of this approach is the evaluation at the end of the project by both students and teacher. Students evaluate their own learning and affective experiences, as well as the dynamics of the group's participation in the investigation.

This model is ideal if your aim is to develop student inquiry and creative problem-solving skills while exploring concepts (Kagan 1992). It is not effective for covering specific curriculum content nor when students are inexperienced in communication skills such as asking questions and reaching consensus (Bellanca & Fogarty 1991).

COOPERATIVE GROUP WORK IN AUSTRALIA AND NEW ZEALAND

Although the four models discussed above have considerable research support and are widely used in the United States, the cooperative learning model typically adopted in Australia and New Zealand is a 'holistic' one. By this we mean that it begins from a whole school perspective which then flows into classrooms, with all school members becoming a 'community of learners' (Graves & Graves 1990). The difference is that the emphasis in Australia is on cooperation as a **social value** with social skills being emphasised and explicitly taught (Dalton 1985, 1992), while in the United States cooperative structures are more commonly used for curriculum-based team activities, often for mastery of lower-level cognitive objectives such as knowledge or comprehension. Content-free structures such as those of Kagan, however, have the advantage of enabling the teacher to quickly incorporate cooperative group work into any classroom or curriculum, and can be used across a whole school to encourage the development of problem-solving skills, teamwork, social skills and curriculum content mastery. We are impressed with the versatility of this structural approach, which allows the teacher to set learning objectives across the range of levels in the cognitive and affective domains. Above all, the approach is truly constructivist in that the students are largely in control of both the interaction within the group and the group outcome. Just one final note: for benefits to accrue in personal, social and cognitive terms, cooperative structures should become a regular part of each week, and not relegated to 'Friday afternoon fillers' as play activities (Bellanca & Fogarty 1991).

THE DIFFICULTIES IN USING COOPERATIVE LEARNING STRATEGIES

Teachers face several problems when attempting to introduce cooperative goal structures into their classrooms. Cultural differences, for example, may inhibit some students from wanting to share their ideas, as competitive rather than cooperative goal structures are common in many of our students' cultures.

Cultural differences

Teachers have also traditionally cautioned students to keep their eyes on their own work; not to speak to their neighbour while solving problems; to ask the teacher for any help needed; and to do their own work (Weinstein & Mignano 1993). Such warnings are clearly not conducive to developing a spirit of cooperation in task performance and learning.

Teacher traditions

Teachers who have themselves been taught by teacher-centred methods, or believe they are the fount of all knowledge, will find it difficult to 'let go' the control of instruction. Parents may also question the educational value of cooperative learning.

Teacher-centred methods

Teachers who first introduce cooperative strategies into their classrooms frequently report disappointment: students are noisy in talk and movement; arguments erupt over who will work with whom, and what responsibility each will have; some students dominate, others are ostracised; time is wasted with little accomplishment; cooperative social behaviours are lacking.

Student disruption

The four problems most commonly associated with the use of cooperative groups are:

1. segregation of particular groups on the basis of disability, ethnicity or gender;
2. unequal participation of group members either by dominance or 'freeloading';
3. lack of achievement as a result of socialisation and noise;
4. lack of cooperation because of lack of understanding of cooperative behaviour and inexperience in cooperative groupwork. (Weinstein & Mignano 1993)

Overcoming difficulties in introducing cooperative learning

How can such difficulties as these be overcome? For cooperative learning activities to be successful, there are two simple things to remember: first, plan the activity, specifying exactly what is to be done, why, and by whom; and second, teach the 'rules' and procedures for cooperative interaction, publishing the guidelines in written form for each student to see. There are also several practical approaches for avoiding difficulties.

First, start with very simple, brief group activities (not necessarily cooperative ones) until students have mastered some of the important skills required —asking others for assistance; helping one another; explaining; checking for another's understanding; providing support; active listening without destructive comments; taking turns in expressing an

Start with simple group activities

opinion or contributing to a task; and reaching consensus (Cohen, 1994a).

Second, as mentioned ealier, classroom control may be difficult to maintain when students are not stimulated by the learning task. In other words, the content of their learning must be relevant and interesting to students, as well as at the appropriate level of difficulty, *before* considerations of grouping or other structures are considered.

Design stimulating learning activities

Third, for cooperative techniques to be effective, the teacher must ensure that students have the skills necessary to engage in cooperative group learning. As Cohen (1986) points out:

Train cooperative skills

> ***There is no point to a discussion that represents collective ignorance. Furthermore, there must be some way to be sure that people will listen carefully to each other, explain to each other, and provide some corrective feedback for each other. All this is unlikely to take place by magic; the teacher has to lay the groundwork through meticulous planning. (p. 11)***

Ways of introducing cooperative interaction

How can you introduce students to cooperative interaction and minimise classroom management problems while maximising student learning?

Johnson and Johnson (1989–90) suggest that an effective way of making cooperative behaviours clear to students is by describing what the particular behaviours look like and sound like—that is, making the behaviours explicit. This should be done as part of class discussion. Thus, a list of behaviours for taking turns, for example, might look like this:

Make the behaviours explicit

Taking turns

Looks like:

- ☐ Eyes look at eyes
- ☐ People wait until the speaker has finished
- ☐ Nodding head as you listen

Sounds like:

- ☐ 'Have you finished?'
- ☐ 'Do you want to say anything else?'
- ☐ 'Can I say something now?'

(adapted from Hill & Hill 1990)

Role plays that demonstrate cooperative behaviours in action can be of great value, especially when introducing the behaviours for the first time or with younger students. The teacher acting as model will add even more to the demonstration (Hill & Hill 1990). In fact, in terms of cooperative behaviours generally, it is recommended that the teacher demonstrate and role play what is meant by particular cooperative behaviours such as being part of a team, rather than merely describing it (Kagan 1994).

Demonstrate desired cooperative behaviours

It is also important for students to gain experience in these behaviours through regular practice. Dalton (1985) suggests that, until cooperative skills are learnt, practice should be given to a portion of the class at a time moving gradually to include the whole class. This can best be done through work with a partner—for example, in 'listening pairs', where students first take alternate roles as listener and talker and then begin to introduce the skills of responding and questioning. With practice, these pairs can be extended to include another pair and then another until groups are formed.

Farivar and Webb (1993) point out that asking for help is not cheating or dependency, but is instrumental to learning. However, most students (and adults as well) do not naturally have 'helping skills' and must be taught them. Some suggestions from Farivar and Webb are:

Teach helping behaviours

For the help-receiver

- ☐ Recognise that you need help.
- ☐ Decide whom to ask for help.
- ☐ Ask clear and precise questions.
- ☐ Ask questions until you have definitely understood.

For the helper

- ☐ Be aware when other students need help.
- ☐ Do not just give the answer; explain how to do the problem, or why.
- ☐ Correct the other student's errors with explanations.
- ☐ Follow up the explanation with additional questions to check for understanding.
- ☐ Give praise for effort.

Research has clearly demonstrated that in mathematics, for example, unless specific instruction is given by teachers in cooperative methods of working, particularly in what constitutes 'asking for help' and 'giving help', low-achieving students (especially low-achieving girls) will typically be those requesting help and withdrawing effort from group tasks (Mulryan 1996).

For cooperative group interaction to be productive, equal participation of all members needs to be ensured. An effective way to do this is through **role-taking**, an important skill in itself, and one that also fosters the development of individual accountability within a group. Teachers can help students practise different roles by

Assign roles to all members of cooperative groups

Cross-age tutoring has social and academic benefits for both tutor and tutee. What might some of these be? Photo: Leo Kiriloff

- ☐ *Timekeeper:* makes sure the group completes the task on time.
- ☐ *Challenger:* asks group to justify decisions /actions.
- ☐ *Observer:* checks participation and roles—gives feedback to group.
- ☐ *Noise monitor:* keeps group noise level within acceptable limits.
- ☐ *Gopher:* collects all materials needed by the group.
- ☐ *Reporter:* reports group findings.

(based on Graves & Graves 1990)

assigning them at the outset of a group project and ensuring that they are rotated each new lesson. Tactfully done, it is also an important strategy to use when trying to restrain domineering students (allocating them to the role of observer, for example) or assisting shy students to have more authority within the group (as reporter of group findings, for instance) (Abrami et al. 1995). Graves and Graves (1990) provide details of a number of roles that children might play in cooperative groupwork:

- ☐ *Initiator:* gets things going.
- ☐ *Clarifier:* checks that everyone understands.
- ☐ *Contributor:* makes active contributions to the task.
- ☐ *Listener:* models active listening techniques.
- ☐ *Summariser:* sums up ideas and contributions.
- ☐ *Encourager:* encourages all team members to participate.
- ☐ *Evaluator:* checks that the team has completed the task.
- ☐ *Tension reliever:* identifies humour in situations, suggests compromises.
- ☐ *Checker:* checks for accuracy.
- ☐ *Reader:* reads problems to the group.
- ☐ *Explainer:* paraphrases contributions and explains tasks.
- ☐ *Praiser:* gives positive feedback to group members.
- ☐ *Mover/organiser:* organises furniture to enable all group members to participate.

It is vital that you do not assume that students, especially young ones, will know what a particular role entails. Discuss what each student's role involves, model it, or even make a chart with explanations on it. For example: 'The encourager's job is to get everyone in the group to talk and share ideas. What are some of the things the encourager might say and do?' (Dalton 1985, p. 14).

The teacher should decide on group composition in order to overcome segregation. You might well wonder, however, which method of grouping works best? Research by Noreen Webb (1985a) suggests that groups of four students at two levels of ability are most successful: either high and low, or medium and low combinations, because when high, medium and low ability students are grouped, those with medium (average) ability are frequently excluded from the interaction. Homogeneous groups are successful only for those with average ability who interact energetically and help each other. High achievers tend to remain independent, assuming, perhaps, that no one needs help, while low achievers become frustrated because they are unable to explain material effectively to each other (Good & Brophy 1991). The practical implications of such findings is that mixed groups have the most potential for learning; however, effective *training* of students in group interaction is essential.

Allocate students to their groups

We do not wish to imply that teachers should always control group composition. Indeed, this could breed resentment in students. Other techniques, such as random assignment by number to groups, is often seen as fairer by students. Student-selected groups may be most appropriate when students are used to group work and, in particular, when students are working on projects where common interests are important.

One danger of using group methods for learning is what Slavin (1990) calls the **'free rider' effect.** By this, he means the tendency for some students to be allowed to 'come along for the ride' and not contribute or learn anything, either by choice or accident. This can occur when the group has a single product to present—in other words, where individual accountability is not required. Some group members who are considered less capable of a task than the rest of the group may be perceived as a liability and ignored, to the detriment of their learning. High-achieving students, on the other hand, may find the group task unstimulating and remain passively uninvolved. Of course, shy students may also prefer to be uninvolved as this means that they are not obliged to speak in public.

Ensure equal participation

Free rider effect

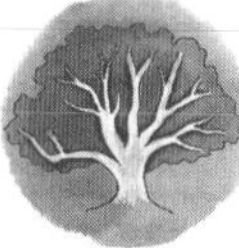

TABLE 10.7

ESSENTIALS OF ENSURING THAT ALL STUDENTS PARTICIPATE IN COOPERATIVE LEARNING ACTIVITIES

For teachers

- Assign active roles of responsibility to the uninvolved students (e.g. group reader, spokesperson or scribe).
- Ensure that the roles assigned to high achievers are challenging ones—that is, roles with which they may be unfamiliar, such as that of facilitator. Reward them for helping others to solve problems.
- For the 'free-riders' promote individual accountability by issuing bonus points for improvement and for individual contributions to group scores and rewards.

(adapted from Graves & Graves 1990)

Some students (sometimes the more able ones) just don't want to be part of a cooperative group, at least initially. Others may refuse to work with particular students or leave the group without participating. For the former, it may be helpful to discuss the academic and social benefits of group learning and the importance of acquiring teamwork skills for their future role in the workplace (Abrami et al. 1995). For disruptive students, however, it is most effective to use behavioural strategies of reinforcement for the desired cooperative behaviours (Graves & Graves 1990). For instance, individual and group rewards may be tied to a particular behaviour such as 'working with everyone in the group' so that every time the student (or the others) works appropriately (or approximates it) they are able to score a point.

There will always be those who don't want to join in

Of course, you may already be thinking that an obvious solution is to try to organise an activity that capitalises on the special interests or abilities of the more difficult students, thereby letting them feel successful. This is certainly helpful as long as it is done with subtlety—making such students feel obvious may be counterproductive in a number of ways. Can you think of reasons why?

Efforts on the part of the teacher to develop active listening skills and the use of non-aggressive 'I-messages' among *all* group members would have obvious benefits for cooperative interaction generally, but particularly for disruptive students who would learn how their behaviour affects the rest of the group (refer to the earlier discussion of Thomas Gordon's counselling approach to discipline problems). If there is little improvement in the behaviour of the disruptive student it may be wise to pair him or her with one other student only until cooperative behaviours can be developed (Graves & Graves 1990).

A common complaint by teachers introducing cooperative learning structures into their classrooms for the first time is the increase in the level of classroom noise and apparent lack of accomplishment. It is important to differentiate between the sound of busy and exuberant interaction and the noise of students out of control. Young children will certainly need to have demonstrated to them what you mean by 'quiet voices' and to have an opportunity to practise speaking this way simultaneously, yet so that groups cannot hear each other.

Cooperative group work can be noisy: a busy hum or chaos?

A tangible signal is also necessary for any age group. Many forms of signals have been used with success: timers, noise meters, noise monitors, coloured cards to indicate degree of noise, bells and gestures. The **'quiet signal'** (Kagan 1994) is a very useful gesture as it is non-intrusive and allows students to exercise some responsibility for controlling their noise. The teacher raises one hand and those nearby signal others until all students progressively raise their own hands, stop talking and working, and give their full attention to the teacher. Of course, the teacher will have previously introduced this signal by explaining that when groups talk to each other, noise

Quiet signal

levels can rise progressively and the teacher will need to indicate that this is happening and regain order. The signal and procedure will then be modelled and practised until it is learned. Have you seen or thought of your own alternatives to the 'quiet signal'?

It is important for the teacher to circulate during groupwork in order to monitor individual efforts and progress. Providing students with a list of expected progress markers is a useful way of keeping them on track. Another is to stop group work periodically to ask groups for progress reports. If projects are large, break them into smaller components that are checked daily (Weinstein & Mignano 1993).

Monitor individual effort and progress

A final word of warning. Despite their obvious effectiveness, cooperative learning methods should not be overused as students will find it monotonous to work in teams on all learning tasks. It goes without saying that effective classroom managers vary their teaching approaches according to the nature of the task and the students involved. Some would argue that enabling students to take responsibility for their own learning as well as for their behaviour, by substituting direct supervision with authority delegated by the teacher, is the most important aim of education. Certainly, well-designed and monitored cooperative learning activities provide students with the opportunity to gain experience in taking such responsibility.

Question point: *Individual achievement and competition is what we (educators) practise; cooperation is what we preach. How can we be teaching the social skills and values of cooperation in learning when we continue to assess children's individual academic performance and grade them accordingly? What do you think?*

TEACHER'S CASE BOOK

HOW DID IT GO?

Children in Sylvia's family-grouped class of 5–8 year olds have been working in groups making a timeline of Australia. Each group has worked independently, organising materials and sharing ideas. Sylvia has been circulating the room assisting if needed, questioning, encouraging and extending the children's experience. At the conclusion of the activity, she brought the children together.

Sylvia: I was really impressed with how you worked in the group and the work you produced. I would like some feedback on how your group worked.

Charles: I liked how none of my group wandered off and did other things. They did look at other things but they came back.

Sam: I think our group worked well. Everyone had something to do.

Daisy: Our group was sensible. They did not muck up.

Sylvia: That's fantastic.

Case studies illustrating National Competency Framework for Beginning Teaching, National Project on the Quality of Teaching and Learning, Australian Teaching Council, 1996, p. 18. Commonwealth of Australia copyright, reproduced by permission.

Case study activity

Design a series of generic group evaluation questions that students may respond to orally or in written form both during and at the completion of a cooperative learning activity. Specify the age and experience level for which you would target this evaluation schedule.

Teachers need to monitor children's engagement in the task of learning, both in individual and cooperative activities.
Photo: authors

Recommended reading

Abrami, P. C., Chambers, B., Poulsen, C., de Simone, C., d'Apollonia, S. & Howden, J. (1995) *Classroom Connections: Understanding and Using Cooperative Learning*. Ontario, Canada: Harcourt Brace.

Balson, M. (1992) *Understanding Classroom Behaviour*, 3rd edn. Hawthorn, Vic. ACER.

Charles, C. M. (1992) *Building Classroom Discipline*, 4th edn. White Plains, NY: Longman.

Cohen, E. G. (1994b) Restructuring the classroom: Conditions for productive small groups. *Review of Educational Research*, 64, 1–35.

Dalton, J. (1992) *Adventures in Thinking: Creative Thinking and Cooperative Talk in Small Groups*. South Melbourne, Australia: Thomas Nelson.

Evertson, C. M. (1995) Classroom rules and routines. In L. W. Anderson (ed.) *International Encyclopedia of Teaching and Teacher Education*, 2nd edn. Cambridge, UK: Pergamon.

Graves, N. & Graves, T. (1990) *A Part to Play*. Melbourne: Latitude Publications.

Johnson, D. W. & Johnson, R. T. (1994) *Learning Together and Alone: Cooperative, Competitive, and Individualistic Learning*, 4th edn. Boston, MA: Allyn and Bacon.

Kagan, S. (1994) *Cooperative Learning*. San Juan Capistrano, CA: Kagan Cooperative Learning.

Kyriacou, C. (1991) *Essential Teaching Skills*. Oxford: Basil Blackwell.

Lewis, R. (1994) Classroom discipline: Preparing our students for democratic citizenship. Paper presented at the Annual Conference of the Australian Association for Research in Education, Newcastle, November.

Qin, Z., Johnson, D. W. & Johnson, R. T. (1995) Cooperative versus competitive efforts and problem solving. *Review of Educational Research*, 2, 129–43.

Rogers, B. (1995) *Behaviour Management: A Whole-School Approach*. Gosford, NSW: Ashton Scholastic.

Slavin, R. E. (1995) Cooperative Learning. In L. W. Anderson (ed.) *International Encyclopedia of Teaching and Teacher Education*, 2nd edn. Cambridge, UK: Pergamon.

Webb, N. M. & Farivar, S. (1994) Promoting helping behaviour in cooperative small groups in middle school mathematics. *American Educational Research Journal*, 32, 369-95.

Special needs and effective learning

CHAPTER 11

OVERVIEW

There is one incontrovertible fact of education and that is that our classes are full of individuals, all of whom have their special differences. Children bring a range of personal packages—physical, behavioural, social and cultural—to the learning situation which affect their learning and motivation in the classroom. In the next two chapters we focus on the individual qualities of learners that demand the attention of educators in making adaptations to the educational environment of such learners in order to facilitate their learning.

Our first focus concerns learning and cognitive styles and the links between these, academic achievement and classroom practice. We then take a detailed look at special needs education and discuss mainstreaming children with disabilities. In this context we discuss a range of physical and intellectual disabilities and draw out the educational implications of these disabilities for educators. We also consider the educational needs of children who might be considered gifted, talented or creative, and suggest adaptations that might be made to educational environments in order to support the development of these children. An important point made here is that all children have talents and that disabled children can also be gifted, talented and creative.

Finally, we consider ways in which teachers and schools can adapt the educational environment to suit individual student needs. We discuss adaptive education and illustrate forms of micro-adaptations, which may be introduced into the classroom or school with little difficulty, and macro-adaptations, which might require greater system resources. In effect you will see that most of these adaptations are processes that are discussed throughout our text.

LEARNER-CENTRED PSYCHOLOGICAL PRINCIPLE 9

Learners have different strategies, approaches and capabilities for learning that are a function of prior experience and heredity.

The same basic principles of learning, motivation and effective instruction may apply to all learners. However, individuals are born with and develop unique capabilities and talents and have acquired through learning and social acculturation different preferences for how they like to learn and the pace at which they learn. Also, learner differences and curricular and environmental conditions are key factors that greatly affect learning outcomes. Understanding and valuing cultural differences and the cultural contexts in which learners develop—including language, race, beliefs and socioeconomic status—enhances the possibilities for designing and implementing learning environments that are optimal for all learners.

(Reprinted with permission, APA Task Force on Psychology in Education (1993, January), p. 9.

DO STUDENTS DIFFER IN THEIR APPROACH TO LEARNING?

We are all different as learners. One of the authors can work with interruption and noise, while the other prefers quiet (with perhaps a little soft music); one doesn't like the distraction of eating and drinking while working, while the other author nibbles and drinks coffee constantly; one author likes to sit and work for long periods, uninterrupted, while the other prefers to pace, and occasionally take a walk to break the monotony. One of us likes to study when feeling a little cool, the other likes to feel warm; one refers to one resource at a time, while the other covers the floor with resources that are referred to simultaneously; one likes to write off the top of the head, the other likes to plan and organise before committing material to a final form; one likes to work into the night, the other prefers to work in the morning (and use the evening for sipping red wine!). We are all different! Think for a moment about your preferred learning styles.

Sources of individual differences

Where do these differences come from? Perhaps some of them are biological (the one who prefers to work in a warm environment is thinner than the one who can tolerate cold);

BOX 11.1 TEACHING COMPETENCE

The teacher recognises and responds to individual differences

Indicators

The teacher:

- identifies and fosters student learning strengths;
- uses students' social and cultural backgrounds to enrich the learning process;
- uses strategies that assist students to overcome individual learning difficulties;
- uses support services where appropriate.

Case studies illustrating National Competency Framework for Beginning Teaching, National Project on the Quality of Teaching and Learning, Australian Teaching Council, 1996, Element 2.3, p. 39. Commonwealth of Australia copyright, reproduced by permission.

perhaps some of them are the result of social conditioning (the one who can work with noise and distraction is one of ten children, the other who prefers quiet is one of two); the one who likes to nibble to maintain concentration has a racing metabolism, the one who finds eating a distraction wouldn't lose weight in a month of fasting! Children in our classrooms similarly have different preferences for modes of learning.

Three learning styles

Learning styles: cognitive, affective and physiological behaviours influencing learning

Meaning style

Reproducing style

Achieving style

Learning styles may be considered as characteristic cognitive, affective and physiological behaviours that serve as relatively stable indicators of how learners perceive, interact and respond to the learning environment. They are demonstrated in the pattern of behaviour and performance with which individuals approach educational experiences (Butler 1986; Keefe & Ferrell 1990; Messick 1995; Perry 1996; Kolb 1976). Learning styles include factors such as perceptual modality preferences, group or individual work preferences, and environmental preferences (relating to factors such as light and heat) (O'Neil 1990).

Three styles of learning that relate closely to learning tasks have received attention from researchers interested in the effect they have on learning outcomes. These three are **'meaning'**, **'reproducing'** and **'achieving'** orientations (Biggs 1987; Messick 1995). Students with a **meaning orientation** adopt deep processing strategies to maximise personal understanding. Students with a **reproducing orientation** tend to adopt a shallow processing approach such as rote learning and memorisation. Students with an **achieving orientation** will utilise whatever approaches lead to high grades and are rewarded, so both deep and shallow processing strategies may be used. The style adopted will often reflect the achievement goals and tasks established in the classroom (see Chapters 4 and 9), and each may be useful, given specific circumstances.

Sixteen elements of learning styles

A number of models of learning styles have been developed including those of Kolb (1976), Gregorc (Butler 1986) and Dunn and Dunn. Dunn and Dunn (Brandt 1990; Care 1996; Dunn & Dunn 1972, 1979; Dunn, Beaudry & Klavas 1989; Keefe & Ferrell 1990; Kidd 1996; O'Neil 1990) have listed 16 elements of learning style under four global headings (see Table 11.1).

TABLE 11.1

ELEMENTS OF LEARNING STYLE

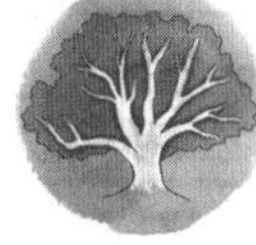

The environmental elements

1. sound
2. light
3. temperature
4. design

The emotional elements

5. motivation
6. persistence
7. responsibility
8. need for structure

The sociological elements

9. working alone
10. working with peers
11. working with an adult
12. working in a combination

The physical elements

13. perceptual strengths
14. intake
15. time of the day
16. need for mobility

Individualising instruction

This model outlines the environmental, emotional, sociological and physical preferences that children might have which potentially influence their learning and motivation. For example, when is the student most alert? What level of noise can the student tolerate? How does the student work best—alone, with one person, or in a larger group? Where does the child work best—at home, in learning centres, in the library? What type of physical conditions suit the child best—floor, carpet, reclining, table lighting? How does the child learn most easily—visual materials, sound recording, printed material, tactile experiences, kinaesthetic activities, multimedia packages, combinations? What type of learning structure suits this student most of the time—strict, flexible, self-determined, self-starting, jointly arranged with teacher? What type of assignments suit the student best—contracts, totally self-directed projects, teacher-selected tasks? (Dunn & Dunn 1972). Dimensions such as these are assessed via observation and the use of a learning style inventory (Dunn, Dunn & Price 1985). Dunn, Dunn and Price then advocate individualising instruction to accommodate these various needs.

Matching learning and teaching styles

Individualisation also takes into account teaching styles and attempts to make the best match possible between what the teacher (and, more broadly, the educational environment) can offer and what the individual student needs (Dunn & Dunn 1979). When there is a best match between the needs of the student and what the environment provides, learning and motivation (according to the advocates) are enhanced (Dunn, Beaudry & Klavas 1989). Other instruments for measuring learning styles have also been developed (e.g. Keefe & Ferrell 1990).

However, matching teaching and learning styles may not be very effective, for the following reasons (adapted from Good & Stipek 1983):

1. There is no single dimension of learners that unambiguously dictates an instructional prescription. Effective learning is the result of a number of variables such as level of prior knowledge and ability.
2. There are higher levels of interaction between learner characteristics and instructional treatments such as the relationship of the teacher to the learner, the time of the year, and the nature of the learning task.
3. Most students are adaptable to a variety of instructional modes, even if they are not preferred. The major concern is how well the instruction is designed to motivate the learner to attend. More important instructional qualities may be task clarity, importance of the goals, effective feedback and opportunities for practice.
4. Teachers have particular skills and certain approaches may be more compatible with these skills than other approaches. Effective teachers use a variety of presentations to help all individuals see the material from a variety of perspectives.

Criticisms of learning styles

There is an inherent attractiveness about learning style inventories such as those proposed by Dunn and Dunn, Kolb, and Gregorc, as they provide a rich resource for considering potential influences on children's learning and motivation. However, at the practical level, the sheer diversity of possibilities creates great problems for the classroom teacher coping with such diversity (Doyle & Rutherford 1984). A major concern really has to be: What difference do the differences make? In other words, which differences among learners have consequences for the outcomes of instruction? Some educationalists believe that there are other important factors that are more likely to impact on student learning than those suggested in such inventories. Furthermore, they argue that the research evidence supporting such micro levels of adaptation to individual differences is quite equivocal (Curry 1990; Dunn 1990; Karvale & Forness 1987, 1990).

Probably the best strategy is to ensure that any educational setting includes a variety of approaches to teaching and learning to account for all the possible preferences in learners.

Question point: *To what extent can individualisation of instruction take into account all the possible learning and cognitive styles of students?*

COGNITIVE STYLE AND EFFECTIVE LEARNING

While learning style generally refers to that vast range of internal and external factors that may influence our learning and motivation in a given situation, **cognitive style** more specifically refers to the stable perceptual and thinking processes by which individuals within a culture comprehend their world, conceptualise meanings, learn a task, solve a problem and relate to others (Entwistle 1991; Messick 1976, 1984, 1995; Tiedemann 1989; Wolman 1989). Cognitive styles are generally considered to be information-processing habits: individually characteristic ways of interpreting and responding to the environment (Shipman & Shipman 1985). Many cognitive styles are talked about in the literature: category width; cognitive complexity versus simplicity; levelling versus sharpening; scanning; automatisation versus restructuring; converging versus diverging. Only three have been subjected to significant empirical research, namely, field dependence versus field independence, cognitive tempo, and locus of control (Messick 1995; Tiedemann 1989).

Cognitive style: stable perceptual and thinking processes

Field dependence and field independence

Witkin and his colleagues (1977; Kogan 1971) focused on the dimensions of field dependence and field independence or *global* versus *analytic perceptual style*. **Field dependence** refers to a type of cognitive perceptual processing in which stimuli are perceived as parts of a whole, while **field independence** refers to a type of cognitive perceptual processing in which stimuli are differentiated and then organised on the basis of structural differences and similarities (Witkin, Moore, Goodenough & Cox 1977). Witkin et al. conclude that while field-dependent and field-independent students don't differ in learning ability or memory, they do differ in the kinds of material they learn most easily, and the strategies they use for learning. For example, it appears that field-dependent students have difficulty isolating independent elements of a problem or situation. They are easily affected by manipulations of the surrounding contexts. In contrast, field-independent individuals are able to 'dis-embed' parts of a task from its organisational framework and devise alternative organisational patterns, if necessary, to understand information and solve problems. It is thought that field-independent students learn better under intrinsic motivation and low structure (e.g. open classrooms, discovery learning and problem solving) although the differences between field-independent and field-dependent learners can be altered by various interventions such as pointing out salient cues and directly teaching particular problem-solving skills to field-dependent children.

Field-dependent

Field-dependent individuals appear to be more influenced by the social circumstances of their learning; for example, they spend more time looking at faces, pay more attention to statements with social content, are more influenced by the opinions of prestigious others, and prefer shorter physical distances between themselves and others (Shipman & Shipman 1985). As a consequence, field-dependent people appear to be more socially competent, better liked and more sociable than their field-independent peers (Witkin et al. 1977; Shipman & Shipman 1985).

Teachers as field-dependent/field-independent

Of course, teachers can also be categorised as field-independent or field-dependent, and perhaps an individual teacher's cognitive style might have an impact upon the way he or she structures learning experiences for children. For example, field-dependent teachers may be more concerned with structure and interpersonal relationships in the class, while field-independent teachers may be more concerned with lecturing and discovery learning (Entwistle 1991). Some research has been directed to examining what happens when there is a match/mismatch between learning and teaching styles and student achievement, but as yet there are no definitive findings (Shipman & Shipman 1985). Your training as a professional should equip you to teach using approaches attractive to both groups of students.

Field-independent

Conceptual tempo

Reflective and impulsive students

Kagan (1965, 1966; Kagan & Kogan 1970) concentrated on **conceptual tempo**, which refers to the degree to which people are cognitively **reflective** versus cognitively **impulsive** in deciding on a response when two or more alternatives are plausible. Impulsive learners give the first answer that occurs to them and are often inaccurate. Reflective learners, on the other hand, examine alternative hypotheses and attempt to validate their answers before responding. They take longer to respond but are often more accurate (Entwistle 1991; Messer 1976). Children who are classified as reflective (slow and accurate) in reading, for example, tend to be better readers than impulsive children of equal IQ (Kagan 1965, 1966).

However, we must caution here against adopting a too simplistic view of what this means in real life. For example, there are individuals who make up their minds quickly and are right, and others who make up their minds slowly and are wrong. Hence, speed at a response may indicate level of background knowledge rather than impulsivity. Furthermore, impulsive thinkers are not necessarily impulsive people generally. Kagan & Kogan (1970) suggest that reflective children may have been taught to regard absence of errors as a mark of competence, and as such become anxious over making mistakes, which slows them down. Impulsive children, on the other hand, might have learnt that being quick indicates competence, and therefore become anxious about responding slowly. Other reasons for impulsivity/reflectivity in particular situations may be the degree to which an individual needs to pay attention to detail (i.e. the degree of complexity of the task), the description of the task and the degree of accuracy implied for satisfactory completion of the task.

In general, research indicates that impulsives perform more poorly on a variety of academic tasks. Research has been directed towards teaching such children to be less impulsive and some techniques for this are covered in Chapter 10.

Reflective thinkers

Impulsive thinkers

Locus of control

Locus of control: internal vs external

When individuals think that they are responsible for their success and failure and believe they have substantial control over their learning, they are said to have an **internal locus of control.** On the other hand, individuals who believe that they have little control over their own learning, and that their successes and failures are due to forces outside their control (such as teacher control) are said to have an **external locus of control.** Locus of control forms a major component of Weiner's attributional model of motivation discussed in Chapter 9.

As well as these delineations of various cognitive styles there are numerous others discussed in the educational literature, so many in fact that they become quite confusing in their overlap (e.g. see Messick 1995). We have chosen just a few to indicate the diversity of constructs used to describe various forms of cognitive functioning.

Are there problems with cognitive style approaches to student learning?

Cognitive styles are dynamic, that is, they might be task-specific or reflective of an individual's stage of development and experience, and, most importantly, they act in concert with other cognitive styles for a given person in a given situation. The notion, therefore, that we can identify an individual's cognitive style and design educational experiences based on this style is far too simplistic.

Dynamic nature of cognitive styles

While each of the styles (such as locus of control) is described as a continuum from one dimension to the other (e.g. internal to external), in effect they are often seen as polarised—for example, internal versus external. Individuals are grouped as belonging to one or the other classification (Entwistle 1991). The dichotomising of cognitive styles also suggests that one pole is good and the other bad. Indeed, the terms used (such as dependent, external and impulsive) predispose us to think this way, although the terms themselves are not meant to be value-laden. Within particular situations some cognitive styles may be more useful than others and it is not simply a case of one end of the continuum being more positive. Nevertheless, within a Western-oriented school system, field-independent characteristics, such as a high valuation of independence, individualism and a desire for personal rather than group achievement and success, are considered most valuable (Nedd & Gruenfeld 1976).

Artificial dichotomies

Culture and cognitive style

In societies as culturally diverse as Australia and New Zealand, groups that manifest the opposite qualities, such as **collectivism** and **group orientation**, are often believed to be poorly suited to a Western education system. This notion is currently being challenged by a number of authors (McInerney 1991; McInerney & Swisher 1995; McInerney et al. 1997; Ogbu 1983, 1992; Ogbu & Matute-Bianchi 1986). We take up this issue a number of times throughout our text.

There have been so many difficulties in cognitive style research and application that Tiedemann (1989, p. 273) was moved to say that '... the cognitive style concept has to be considered a failure on the diagnostic level and, therefore, the empirical level as well'. He recommends we abandon it as a fruitful source of information on individual differences. This is a controversial view. What do you think?

WHAT WOULD YOU DO?

GIRLS DON'T MAKE CARS

The year 2 children were happily engaged in a construction project during a maths activity session when Mrs Arturo overheard Ben make a sexist remark to another student: 'You can't use those wheels, Kelly, because girls don't make cars, so give them to me,' said Ben.

This placed Mrs Arturo in a dilemma. She always tries to accept the home values of each child, but she also wants to support community standards of gender equity. Mrs Arturo stood outside the group and listened to the children's response to Ben.

'Girls do,' replied Kelly. 'I'm allowed to'.

'No, you're not,' replied Ben. 'My sister's not allowed to play with my Lego at home.'

'She can make cars,' said Michael, 'because my sister does.'

'Yes, I think she can too,' added Josh.

How would you deal with Ben's sexism?

Case studies illustrating National Competency Framework for Beginning Teaching, National Project on the Quality of Teaching and Learning, Australian Teaching Council, 1996, p. 13. Commonwealth of Australia copyright, reproduced by permission.

ARE THERE SEX DIFFERENCES IN LEARNING AND ACHIEVEMENT?

Sexism in the classroom

There are important school achievement differences between boys and girls, although over the last few years the gap has been closing. Among major concerns are the disproportionate number of males that are placed in special educational settings, and the differential in achievement levels between girls and boys in language, mathematics and science (Bailey 1993; Barnes & McInerney 1996; Fennema and Peterson 1987; Kahle et al. 1993).

Table 11.2 summarises some of the factors that have been shown to contribute to these differences.

TABLE 11.2

WHY GIRLS AND BOYS MAY ACHIEVE DIFFERENTLY AT SCHOOL

- Teachers often hold expectations about individual students and groups of students. These expectations, sometimes based on gender differences, may limit the opportunities that teachers present to students.
- Teachers treat boys and girls differently in many learning contexts: boys participate in more interactions with teachers, receive more feedback, help and praise from teachers, and are reprimanded more (thereby receiving more attention) than girls. It should be noted here that not all boys receive this attention. It is more often the case that a few 'star' male students receive the bulk of the teacher's attention to the exclusion of all other pupils, male and female (Bailey 1993).
- Teachers initiate more low-level and high-level interactions with boys than girls—for example, calling on boys to answer word problems and to give their explanations. It is important to note that the direction of interaction is *from teacher to student.* Both boys and girls ask the teacher questions with the same frequency. However, it has been found that when boys call out answers the teacher responds more often than to girls and, in fact, girls are often reprimanded for calling out (Bailey 1993; Kahle et al. 1993). It is often the level of interaction between the teacher and males and females that is used to explain the imbalance in student performance in science and maths.
- From the early grades boys and girls develop friendship groups along gender lines. As a result, boys and girls develop different modes of operating in the

educational environment. When they are put together in mixed groups it is thought that boys dominate discussion and monopolise equipment and materials, to the disadvantage of girls. In particular, girls may be 'silenced' or relegated to gender-stereotyped roles. While girls proffer assistance to boys, this is not reciprocated. So boys 'win out'.

- Boys appear to benefit more from competitive learning structures, while girls seem to benefit from more cooperative learning structures. Many classrooms, however, emphasise performance goals in a competitive setting which advantages boys.
- Some boys tend to 'throw their weight around' which can intimidate girls and other boys. This form of bullying can occur during classroom activities, negatively impacting on the work of other children (see, for example, Kahle et al. 1993).
- Some curricula are gender-stereotyped. For example, schools and teachers might construct gender, science and achievement in ways that define achievement and the study of science as masculine.
- Much curricula material is specifically single gender-stereotyped. For example, many computer activities based on 'warring' analogies are of little interest to girls; and literature that deals with topics such as dancing, friendships or animals is of little interest to boys. Much material also provides sexual stereotypes of appropriate behaviour for boys and girls (such as women being 'homemakers' and men being 'breadwinners') which further limits opportunities.
- Society as a whole reflects value systems that are embedded in gender stereotyping. Appropriate activities for girls and boys, appropriate career aspirations, appropriate behaviour and values are often sharply delineated and reinforced by families, peer groups and organisations such as churches and clubs. These values, which are passed on to children through socialisation (much of which occurs before children begin school) are quite resistant to change, irrespective of what the school and teachers do.

What, then, are the implications of this research for the effective teaching and learning of girls and boys? Table 11.3 details some of these.

TABLE 11.3

ESSENTIALS OF A NON-SEXIST CLASSROOM

For teachers

- Monitor interactions with girls and boys to see that they are equivalent.
- Implement classroom practices to facilitate equal opportunity for responses—e.g. greater wait-time after questions (to facilitate responses from girls and shyer boys) and deliberate turn-taking.
- Organise practical activities so that all children have equal time with equipment and materials. Learning centres and rosters might help.
- Model problem solving rather than giving the answer or strategy.
- Emphasise divergent and independent thinking.
- Stress cooperative activities more than competitive ones.
- Proscribe any form of bullying or gender harassment.
- Provide curricula materials that are of interest and relevance to girls and boys in all academic areas.
- Provide models of women in mathematics, computing, science and politics, as well as in the humanities. Have real-life guest speakers, visits to workplaces, and video library material.
- Include social and real-life contexts in as many activities as possible.
- Vary assessment tasks and modes.
- Provide opportunities for student choice of assessment mode.

(based on Bailey 1993; Munter 1993; Fennema & Peterson 1987)

For learners

- Be confident about asking the teacher for help with work or answering questions.
- Ask for opportunities to experience a range of activities, computer software, and books (irrespective of whether you are a boy or a girl).
- Offer opinions in small groups or whole-class discussions—be an active listener; ask questions; encourage others to speak.
- Do not allow anyone to intimidate or harass you—enlist the help of others or the teacher.
- Be an active participant in cooperative activities—remember, your role is important to the whole group achieving its goal.

CHILDREN WITH SPECIAL NEEDS IN MAINSTREAM CLASSROOM SETTINGS

In this section we consider the special needs of children with disabilities.

As mentioned earlier, we describe categories of disability for the sake of clarity. However, categories blend for all children, and it is important to keep this in mind while reading the following sections.

Some children have sensory disabilities, motor disabilities, health impairments or emotional disorders

WHAT WOULD YOU DO?

GIRL'S DON'T MAKE CARS (continued)

Mrs Arturo then joined in the discussion and it was agreed finally that anyone could make a model car and that girls were certainly capable of doing so.

Do you think this response is adequate? What else could be done to ensure that similar sexist values are challenged? Give some further examples of family values that might run counter to broader community standards. Consider Mrs Arturo's dilemma: is it inappropriate to challenge family values within the classroom and school?

Case studies illustrating National Competency Framework for Beginning Teaching, National Project on the Quality of Teaching and Learning, Australian Teaching Council, 1996, p. 13. Commonwealth of Australia copyright, reproduced by permission.

TEACHER'S CASE BOOK

SEXIST REMARKS

Nancy was concerned about remarks she heard Thomas making in her second class. 'Girls can't do computers!' 'I don't have to do a project with her, she's just a girl.'

She had tried chatting quietly with him about these opinions, but had found him resistant to her point of view. Subsequently, during a parent–teacher interview, Nancy felt she needed to tell Thomas' parents that their son had a tendency to make genderist remarks to the other children. Nancy knew from a previous experience that such remarks were acceptable at home.

She explained to the parents that children, particularly girls, did not like to work with their son because of his remarks, and that because of this Thomas was beginning to miss out on some things. The parents became quiet and left shortly after.

Nancy continued to seek informal opportunities to follow up her concerns with Thomas and his family. She also started to collect magazine articles, books and photographs which showed men and women involved in and excelling in a range of sports and occupations. She planned to include them in her teaching.

Case studies illustrating National Competency Framework for Beginning Teaching, National Project on the Quality of Teaching and Learning, Australian Teaching Council, 1996, p. 13. Commonwealth of Australia copyright, reproduced by permission.

Case study activity

Consider Nancy's approach. How effective do you think it would be? Will classrooms and schools ever be able to alter children's values that are the product of socialisation within the home?

that require special attention from parents, teachers and other professional groups involved with children. The causes and nature of these disabilities are usually well described in developmental psychology and special education texts, and will not be discussed in detail here. Our major focus is to highlight some of the more common disabilities and their implications, and some of the supports available for these children and their teachers. Further details can be found in Ashman & Elkins (1990), Butler (1990) and Cole and Chan (1990).

Among the common disabilities that children have are learning disabilities (such as attention deficit hyperactivity disorder), intellectual disabilities, autism and cerebral palsy. Others suffer from behavioural, physical, hearing and visual disabilities.

Keeping in mind that we don't advocate a categorical approach (i.e. categorising children with disabilities), for purposes of description we give a brief survey of a few of the indentifiable characteristics of a number of these disabilities.

Attention deficit hyperactivity disorder

Among the student disabilities that teachers are most likely to encounter in the regular classroom is **attention deficit hyperactivity disorder** (ADHD). The title of the disorder really sums up the symptoms—namely, children characterised by low attention to task, and high physical activity levels. By physical activity we mean intensity level, frequency, and duration of small motor behaviour such as fidgeting, body ticks, tapping of feet and hands, and excessive locomotion (Pelligrini & Horvat 1995). Children with high rather than low physical activity levels are typically low achievers at school and often experience such social problems as peer rejection and teasing. Inattention to task has obvious implications for academic achievement. When both these characteristics occur together they can cause profound problems for the children concerned.

American data suggest that ADHD is a significant educational problem and we have no reason to suspect that the situation is not the same in Australia and New Zealand. Data from the United States indicate that about 4% of the primary school population have ADHD and that, of these, about 80% are boys (Pellegrini & Horvat 1995; see also Chess & Gordon 1984; Kelly 1988). The onset of ADHD appears to occur in first grade and remains relatively stable after that. Symptoms of what appears to be ADHD in a range of settings, including school, are assessed using a diagnostic manual.

No one is certain of the cause of ADHD. Biological causes are implicated, and ADHD has been related to both **minimal brain dysfunction and attention deficit disorder** in which inattention and impulsivity are key symptoms. However, it is very likely that, while biology might explain the initial occurrence of ADHD, later social experiences within the home and school probably contribute to its maintenance and development (Bailey 1992).

It is not unreasonable to speculate that children who exhibit 'problem' behaviour at both home and school may be subjected to coercive socialisation and educational practices which exacerbate the 'problem'. Pelligrini and Horvat (1995) suggest that it might be issues such as this which explain the difference in the diagnosed incidence of ADHD between boys and girls, and between older and younger children. Many of the behaviours that are considered 'normal' for younger children, such as high levels of exploratory activity and energetic, lively play and movement, are considered undesirable, or even 'abnormal' in primary grades. These behaviours are actively fostered by the adult caregivers and teachers of younger children. In contrast, primary and high school are often regimented places which demand particular behaviours of children that are in marked contrast to their established behaviour patterns. In other words, ADHD may be compounded by the lack of fit between expected classroom routines and children's individual temperament.

For many teachers, children diagnosed as ADHD can be particularly difficult to handle although behaviour modification programs and an increasing use of drug therapy have helped to alleviate their symptoms. In some cases, dietary changes (e.g. eliminating food dyes and additives from the child's diet) have also reduced the level of hyperactivity in some children (Pelham & Murphy 1986; Walden & Thompson 1981). Some would argue that it is possible that a better matching of children's temperaments to educational experiences may alleviate the problem for many children (see Pelligrini & Horvat 1995, for a discussion of this issue). Others believe that ADHD may be related to the unpreparedness of some children for particular learning activities and advocate further learning experiences to improve these inaptitudes (see the section on aptitudes later in this chapter). For example, Laszlo (1996) suggests that giving ADHD-diagnosed children extra visual-motor coordination training should enhance their school behaviour and performance.

Intellectual disability

Intellectual disability is a very broad term encompassing a wide range of disabilities within two basic categories: mild intellectual disability and moderate to severe disability. Two criteria are usually employed to classify children as intellectually disabled: first, their intellectual functioning must be significantly below average and, second, their adaptive behaviour (i.e. their ability to be personally and socially independent) must be severely impaired. You will appreciate the danger inherent in classifying individuals in terms of their IQ score alone.

Research has consistently shown that either changing environmental conditions or increasing environmental stimulation for the intellectually disabled enhances development, and in some cases quite dramatically (Balla & Zigler 1975; Dennis 1973; Horn 1983; Nelson, Cummings & Boltman 1991; Scarr & Weinberg 1983; Turkington 1987). Behavioural disorders, which are often manifested by intellectually disabled children, create further management difficulties for teachers and parents, and limit the placement of such children in regular school settings. However, there is sufficient evidence to indicate that intellectually disabled children benefit from the experiences that characterise a normal child's lifestyle, even though the stresses on the caregiver may be high.

Increased educational opportunities for the academically disadvantaged

Autism

Autism relates to an individual's extreme inability to relate to other people, and a tendency to withdraw from real life and indulge in day-dreaming and bizarre fantasies (Jones 1988; Wolman 1989). Autistic children often display symptoms such as repetitive rocking, head banging, apathy, fear of change, insistence on preservation of sameness, lack of interest in people, severe speech disorders with frequent mutism, and extreme aloneness (Wolman 1989). The educability of these children depends on the severity of the symptoms as well as their level of intelligence. When severity is less, and the individual has a reasonable level of intelligence, parental and educational interventions can enhance the child's development so that he or she becomes able to socialise and engage in productive work (Chess & Gordon 1984; Jones 1988).

Cerebral palsy

Cerebral palsy is a form of paralysis resulting from brain injury (Wolman 1989). In addition to the motor dysfunction caused by the paralysis, cerebral palsy may also include learning difficulties, psychological problems, sensory defects, convulsions and behavioural disorders (Bigge & Sirvis 1982; Chess & Gordon 1984). As with the other disabilities we have discussed, there is a great range in severity and manifestation. While intellectual disability may be associated with cerebral palsy, not all cerebral palsied children are intellectually disabled (indeed, some are in the higher levels of intellectual functioning). Furthermore, it is not certain whether some who are classified as intellectually disabled really are, or whether the tests used to measure level of intellectual functioning have been inadequate to assess their true potential (Cruickshank, Hallahan & Bice 1976). Due to the neurological damage, even cerebral palsied children with normal intelligence suffer significant difficulties with perceptual and language disorders, poor manual control and visual-motor ability, distractability and lessened physical vitality. Associated emotional problems together with absenteeism further exacerbate their educational problems (Kirk & Gallagher 1983; Chess & Gordon 1984).

Visual impairment and hearing impairment

While there are clinical definitions of both visual and hearing impairment, such definitions, unfortunately, do not allow for the diversity in the manifestation of either condition, nor indicate appropriate remedial action that will alleviate the condition and allow the mainstreamed student to benefit from education in a regular classroom. Added to this are complications arising from the time of onset of the disability and its association with other disabilities. For example, many children who suffer visual impairment also suffer multisystem disorders that involve other parts of the brain as well (Chess & Gordon 1984).

Visual impairment

As indicated in Chapter 2 much of the early learning of a child is sensorimotor-oriented. Children who are blind from birth, therefore, may have limited opportunity to test themselves out in the physical world (parents may be hesitant to allow the visually impaired child to explore in case it hurts itself). Consequently, the gross and fine motor skills, perception and perceptual-motor integration, which are so important for development will not be acquired. Furthermore, such restricted experiences ultimately limit cognitive development. Visually impaired children may also develop mannerisms such as rocking or tilting the head which can be disturbing to parents and other people, such as teachers (De Mott 1982).

Often children only need small adjustments to their environment (such as eye glasses) to stride ahead with their learning.
Photo: Natalie Thew

Hearing impairment

A general term, *hearing-impaired*, is often used to describe children with all levels of hearing loss. However, there is great diversity within this group related to the degree and nature of the hearing loss, the age of onset of the loss (e.g. prelingual or later), existence of other disabilities, and the nature of the infant care and socialising experiences of the child (among a host of other things). To highlight one of the complexities here, we note that some hearing-impaired children might not learn to speak as a result of intellectual disability that is also manifested in hearing impairment, while in other cases children may fail to speak simply because they have never heard the spoken word.

In general, hearing-impaired children with no other handicap have essentially the same distribution of intelligence as hearing individuals. The use of hearing aids and knowledge of speech reading help many of these children to develop well. There is some debate as to whether signing should be taught or whether children should be taught speech reading exclusively. However, today the trend is to teach sign and speech reading as part of a total program that also includes gestures and facial expressions (Hallahan & Kauffman 1988).

Other disabilities

Behaviour problems

Speech disorders

Motivation and attention problems

Asthma and epilepsy

Within any classroom there are children who suffer a range of disabilities that have an impact on their learning and motivation. For example, you will teach children who have **behaviour problems, speech disorders** (such as poor articulation, stuttering and delayed language development), motivation and attention problems, and psychological problems such as excessive fear and **anxiety disorders** (e.g. test anxiety and school phobia). Increasingly, children with even severe physical impairments, such as being restricted to a wheelchair or walking with the aid of callipers, are being mainstreamed (see Butler 1990; Cole & Chan 1990; King, Ollendick & Gullone 1990).

We also note here a range of other debilitating conditions such as **asthma** and **epilepsy** which may impede children's education. These health impairments should cause few problems if the teacher is fully aware of the child's condition, and physical and medical requirements. Schools today request emergency contact phone numbers and procedures from all children on enrolment. Medications, if required, should be clearly labelled and stored in an accessible place. Teachers should have a **peer support system** to operate in case of emergency. Children need to be trained in procedures involving illness or emergency. We remember one class we visited in which a child was prone to sudden and severe epileptic seizures. The third grade children were well aware of the child's behavioural and facial changes, and had been trained to notify the teacher promptly and to clear furniture away from the child so that injury would be minimised. The sense of responsibility and care for the disabled child was very obvious.

MAINSTREAMING AND EFFECTIVE LEARNING

The least restrictive environment

As a flow-on from the civil rights movement in the United States, educators and parents became more concerned with the rights of children with disabilities. Foremost among these was the right to an education that took into account the individual differences characterising disabled children and which would maximise the quality of their lifestyle. As a result, a significant law called the *All Handicapped Children Act, Public Law 94-142 (PL 94-142)* was enacted by Congress in 1975 (Gallagher 1989; US Congress 1975). This law guaranteed the right of a disabled child to an appropriate public education in the 'least restrictive environment', in other words, children with disabilities were to be schooled along with their regular peers unless their disabling conditions were so severe as to make this undesirable or impracticable. In the latter case, special educational provisions were to be made available, such as special classes and special schools (Alper & Ryndak 1992; Madden & Slavin 1983). To enable the effective **mainstreaming** of disabled students, an **individualised educational plan (IEP)** was prescribed for each disabled student who was to be educated within

IEP: individualised educational plan

Increasingly, children with disabilities are being mainstreamed. When effectively handled, this enriches the experiences of the abled and disabled children alike. Photo: authors

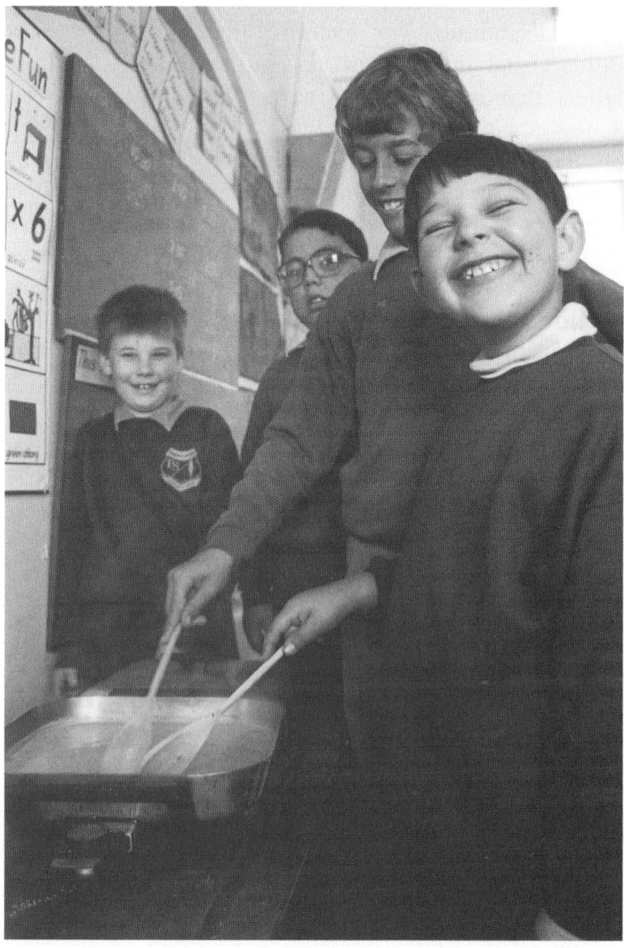

Integration is to help children with disabilities feel positive about themselves in the wider community. Photo: authors

the regular school and classroom. There were levels of restriction (referred to as the *cascade of services* model) which reflected the potential of the individual (Reynolds 1984). The following list is one form of the cascade model (Fuchs, Fuchs & Fernstrom 1993). On the successful accomplishment of tasks at one level children were to be moved into the next level of least restriction.

- Regular classroom
  - Regular classroom with consultative assistance
    - Regular classroom plus part-time resource room
      - Regular classroom plus part-time special class
        - Full-time special class
          - Full-time special day school
            - Homebound instruction
              - Hospital or residential placement

The passing of PL 94-142 had a significant effect on provisions for disabled children in Australia and New Zealand (Bailey 1992; Gow 1989; Levin 1985; Rietveld 1988). There is wide consensus throughout Australia and New Zealand that children with disabilities have the same basic rights to a full education as all other children. There is also general acceptance of the notion of integration. This is reflected in goals of the national and state Departments of Education which typically include statements on the integration of all students with disabilities into regular classroom environments whenever practicable, and the necessity of providing high-quality services, sufficiently diverse and flexible to meet the educational needs of all students (Gow 1989). The **least restrictive environment** (sometimes referred to as the *most advantageous environment*) concept has been the guiding principle in the development of programs across Australia and New Zealand over the last two decades. And, as noted earlier, this model allows for the placement of people with disabilities along a continuum of services ranging from the least restrictive to the most restrictive (Gow 1992).

Zero reject model: despite disabilities all children are educated in local schools

As a result of these initiatives in special education children with disabilities are being integrated increasingly into regular classrooms and schools. As a teacher, you will probably face the added challenge (characterised by joys and frustrations) of teaching children with disabilities in your classroom. There are significant differences, however, between Australian states in their interpretation and implementation of mainstreaming. Within Australia, Victoria comes closest to the **zero reject model** in which all children, irrespective of disability, are educated within the environment of the local school (Grbich & Sykes 1992; see, however, Marks 1992a, 1992b). New Zealand is also strongly committed to this model (Harvey & Green 1984), and because of its unified system of education has been more successful in applying mainstreaming.

Arguments for the least restrictive environment Many educators argue that labelling and segregated schooling restrict the educational opportunities made available to disabled children, as teachers fail to appreciate the potential of these individuals and teach to limited expectations. There is also limited opportunity for disabled children to interact with their age peers, which reduces their opportunity to learn much normal behaviour modelled by their peers, and restricts the opportunity of non-disabled children to learn from the disabled (Atkins & Lewis 1982; Casey, Jones, Kugler & Watkins 1988; Grbich & Sykes 1992; Jenkins, Odom & Speltz 1989; Madden & Slavin 1983). Furthermore, the labels used to describe disabled children are considered to be detrimental to their sense of self as humans and learners, making it difficult for them ever to enter the mainstream (Gow et al. 1992; Elkins 1987).

TABLE 11.4

ESSENTIALS OF A LEAST RESTRICTIVE ENVIRONMENT FOR CHILDREN WITH DISABILITIES

- Providing educational services in the regular classroom.
- Providing services in a more restrictive setting only when necessary and moving people to the next level when they are 'ready'.
- Meshing special and regular education services as indicated by students' needs.
- A special-needs perspective which supports the notion that curricula and instructional procedures should meet individual needs.
- Encouraging a sharing of responsibility by special and regular educators.
- Enhancing the likelihood that the child will function more appropriately in society-at-large.

(based on Gow et al 1992)

Positive effects of integration

There is no doubt that integration has been successful for many children (Center et al. 1989; Gow 1989; Jenkinson & Gow 1989; Madden & Slavin 1983). There is a general consensus that integration leads to either improved academic and/or social progress for children with special needs, or at least to the same outcomes as those experienced by children who are segregated (Jenkins et al. 1985; Wang, Reynolds &

Walberg 1988). Furthermore, well-designed mainstreaming also appears to benefit the non-disabled peers of disabled students. Among the benefits cited are: the opportunity for non-disabled students to learn new skills and new values and attitudes about human differences; the opportunity for non-disabled students to develop a greater sense of responsibility and to assume new social roles; the opportunity for non-disabled students to develop valuable social, emotional and personal perspectives; the opportunity to make friends with and learn from people who are different from themselves (Alper & Ryndak 1992).

As well as these important considerations, effective instructional methods developed for the learning-disabled are equally likely to be effective with non-disabled students. All children should do better academically and socially in classrooms where the focus is on individual needs (Schloss 1992).

Alternative models of mainstreaming

Gow and others argue that we should be moving to a new model of integration, the **all-inclusive collaborative school** model. The basic notion here is that all children have special needs of one kind or another, and all teachers should, in a sense, be special educators. As such it is a matter of degree, and all disabled children should be accommodated in regular schools and classrooms (especially equipped to integrate the children effectively) as a matter of course, and only be restricted when it is demonstrated that such integration is not appropriate. In the all-inclusive school the arbitrary distinction between those children who receive 'special help' because they are labelled 'special', and those who don't, is broken down.

The all-inclusive collaborative school model

The learning experiences of this Down Syndrome child are so much richer with a caring teacher and an appropriate environment. Photo: Special Needs I.T.

Similar calls for what has been termed the **regular education initiative (REI)** are being made in the United States. Advocates of REI argue that all students, whether or not they have been identified as having disabilities, should be educated together (Alper & Ryndak 1992; Fuchs, Fuchs & Fernstrom 1993; Gallagher 1990; Lipsky & Gartner 1989; Schloss 1992). This movement addresses the right of each student who lives in the catchment area of a school to be included in all aspects of life at that school. It also affirms the right of those students with disabilities to participate fully in that life alongside their non-disabled peers who attend the school.

Regular education initiative

Problems of implementing the least restrictive environment

There is opposition to mainstreaming from some academics, teachers and parents who fear the burden will be too great for schools to carry, and that children who need specialised attention will not receive it adequately in a mainstreamed setting (see, for example, Bradshaw, in press). Bain (1992) argues that because there is no legislative equivalent of the PL 94-142 determining entitlement to special education in Australia, and there is little commitment to resource mainstreaming effectively, the policy has the potential of returning special education to what it was like 50 years ago—that is, severely disabled students placed in highly restrictive settings and more moderately disabled individuals in regular classes with minimal support from untrained personnel.

Opposition to mainstreaming

Some academics (e.g. Chapman 1988; Bornholt & Cooney 1993; Marsh 1984; Marsh & Johnston 1993) argue that children's self-concepts as learners are more likely to be positive when their frame of reference for comparison are children of like ability. Placing these children in a situation where their limitations are more obvious in comparison with others who have greater apparent skills and talents may cause a decline in perceived competence, and a decline in academic and physical self-concept. Consequently, mainstreaming may have more harmful side effects for children with disabilities than the labelling that occurs when children are put into special classes and schools (Marsh & Johnston 1993). (See also Cole, Vandercook & Rynders 1988 and Chapter 16.)

Frame of reference effects

Question point: *Consider the potential problems with mainstreaming outlined above. How would you address such issues?*

ACTION STATION

Consider a range of individual education programs (IEPs) in schools. Discuss, with those responsible for their development, how particular IEPs were designed. Using information provided about a particular student, and classroom observation over a period of time, if possible, design an appropriate IEP.

WHAT WOULD YOU DO?

PHYSICAL REARRANGING OF THE LETTERS HELPS HIM LEARN

Billy, in Miss Clifford's class, struggles with his work in all areas. He has a lot of trouble picking up on new ideas that are presented in a written or verbal way. Through observation and working intensively with him, Miss Clifford discovered that the easiest way for him to learn was to use concrete tactile aids and provide him with many practical experiences.

One example of this was when she was working with him on spelling. They were looking at a particular word family and Billy was having trouble recalling what he was doing. Miss Clifford started working with letter tiles with the individual letters on them and played a variety of games which involved arranging the letters to form different letter patterns. This physical rearranging of the letters really seemed to help Billy clarify his understanding of what they were doing.

What other modifications could be made to the teaching program to enhance Billy's learning? Consider the teacher's reasons for making modifications to her program on page 256.

Case studies illustrating National Competency Framework for Beginning Teaching, National Project on the Quality of Teaching and Learning, Australian Teaching Council, 1996, p. 9. Commonwealth of Australia copyright, reproduced by permission.

What are some classroom implications of mainstreaming?

Early identification

At times there will be children in your classroom with very mild forms of disabilities which may not have been identified in the home. Observant educators take note of unusual behaviour of children, such as holding books too close to the eyes, or turning one ear in the direction of the teacher, and refer any child suspected of having a disability to a health specialist. Early attention, even at this stage, will help avoid more severe problems developing, and may have positive consequences for behavioural and learning outcomes.

Children of migrant parents

The early identification and treatment of problems may be hampered in a number of ways. For example, children of migrant parents who speak little or no English may have disabilities which are not diagnosed before the child begins school owing to the parents' lack of awareness, and lack of information on sources of health monitoring (Masselos & Hinley 1981). When at school the problems may continue to be undetected for a period because of the child's lack of English. In other cases, isolation may be a confounding factor in the early identification and treatment of problems. For example, Aboriginal children living in remote areas may develop eye problems that go undetected and untreated because of geographic isolation.

At other times, parents may fail to perceive or acknowledge that their child has a disability, hence delaying and frustrating attempts by other caregivers to assist their child. This can be made worse if parents spend little time with their young children and don't want to acknowledge 'problems'. Such situations occur if both parents work and leave the child for long periods in the care of untrained caregivers rather than family members (Judge 1987; Masselos & Hinley 1981) or leave them by themselves. It is important to note that certified early childhood caregivers are trained to take note of developmental anomalies in young children.

When children with disabilities are mainstreamed there are several implications for the schools and teachers charged with their care and education. To assist schools and class teachers a number of resources are made available by education departments to service students' and teachers' needs. These include special facilities, support teachers, specialist advisers, special classes and placements. Each school will have a list of the relevant services available.

Teacher concerns

You may feel a little daunted by the prospect of having to teach children with disabilities in your classrooms and wondering how will you cope. You are not alone in these concerns. A study of students with severe intellectual disabilities who had been mainstreamed found that school personnel involved in integrating these students were concerned by their own lack of knowledge and skills necessary to modify the curricula; their need for more specialist support; the lack of positive evidence of academic progress for the integrated student; timetable problems; lack of time, and lack of resources (Grbich & Sykes 1992; see also Harvey & Green 1984 and Madden & Slavin 1983). Other less frequently reported concerns were student resentment and teasing (by students without disabilities), and staff resentment of the presence of a student with disabilities. Among the advantages mentioned were improved social benefits for all, improved confidence, and sometimes improved academic performance for the student with disabilities.

It is important that those who work with children with disabilities see those children as individuals first and as children with disabilities second. Throughout this text we emphasise the need for teachers to design educational programs with an eye to individual differences in the classroom, and have considered a range of topics related to this such as team teaching, mixed ability teaching, cooperative learning, peer tutoring, teaching for diversity, individualising instruction through special programs and the use of technologies, and a variety of evaluating and reporting schemes. You will find specific suggestions to enable you to help the child with disabilities in your classroom at the end of this chapter in the section on adaptive education. The chapters on learning, motivation, classroom management, effective teaching and instructional technology will also be of considerable help. Educational programs that are effective in promoting academic achievement for students with disabilities in mainstream educational settings are effective for all students. To the extent that teachers apply good teaching practice in regular classrooms they are already in a strong position to teach students with disabilities effectively. Further sources of information on this important topic may be found in Ashman and Elkins (1990), Butler (1990) and Cole and Chan (1990).

How do attitudes towards disability impact on children's motivation and learning?

An attitude is a disposition to respond favourably or unfavourably towards some person, thing, event, idea, place or situation (Wortman & Loftus 1992). These thoughts and feelings encourage us to act as if we like or dislike something. Psychologists believe that attitudes have three components: what you think or believe about something (the cognitive component); how you feel about it (the emotional component); and how you act towards it (the behavioural component) (Wortman & Loftus 1992). Often these three components are consistent, but at other times conflicting, and competing demands may produce behaviour inconsistent with thoughts and emotions. At times, individuals hold attitudes that need to be changed or modified.

WHAT WOULD YOU DO?

PHYSICAL REARRANGING OF THE LETTERS HELPS HIM LEARN (continued)

The content that Miss Clifford plans for him is different from the rest of the class because he is a delayed learner and she has to match the content of her teaching program specifically to him to accommodate his learning needs. Making ongoing observations has allowed Miss Clifford to track Billy's development over the year and to continually modify her approach to his needs as they have arisen. This has involved making many new resources and trying to focus on his interests to increase his motivation towards learning.

What solutions did you come up with? How does this case study illustrate a number of the features of effective teaching of children with disabilities?

Case studies illustrating National Competency Framework for Beginning Teaching, National Project on the Quality of Teaching and Learning, Australian Teaching Council, 1996, p. 9. Commonwealth of Australia copyright, reproduced by permission.

TABLE 11.5

ESSENTIALS OF AN EFFECTIVE SCHOOL FOR CHILDREN WITH DISABILITIES

For teachers

- Adopt a philosophy, state it and plan for it strategically.
- Remove labels such as 'Special Education' from doors, from children and teachers and especially resource rooms.
- Make resource rooms open to all children and teachers; a place where all children can go for more assistance, and a place where teachers can go to consult collaboratively with their colleagues.
- Plan according to the needs of the individual children, not for administrative expedience.
- Collaborate with special educators and resource teachers, parents, guidance officers and other professionals.
- Use an integrated, multidisciplinary team approach.
- Create a more caring school environment where diversity is celebrated and not merely accepted. Help all teachers, students and parents feel that they belong by working to establish a school policy of caring.
- Make use of the special resources in your region.

(based on Gow 1992)

Family attitudes towards disability

Children with disabilities come from families that have varying attitudes to disability. While many come from supportive homes, others come from homes characterised by blame and superstition, by a belief that the disability results from curses, evil spirits or even a punishing god (Smith & Smith 1991; Judge 1987). These attitudes towards the cause of the disability and the disabled provide a less than ideal environment. Some parents want to hide their disabled child. Some remain in a state of grief and don't establish an effective relationship with the child. Others resent the attempts made by educators and health professionals to rehabilitate their children if this is seen to run counter to cultural beliefs.

A further problem for many children with dis-

TEACHER'S CASE BOOK

PLAYGROUND INSULTS

When I heard some of my year 3 students using the word 'spastic' as a playground insult, I was offended. I told them the comment was completely inappropriate, and we had several class discussions about the terms 'spastic' and 'cerebral palsy'. Most of the children agreed that the word 'spastic' should not be used as a derogatory comment towards someone. However, I observed that there were still several individuals who persisted in using the word as an insult. After discussion with some colleagues during a break it was obvious that the problem did not exist exclusively within my class, and so it was decided to invite some guest speakers from the Cerebral Palsy Association to address the students.

The two visitors, both sufferers of cerebral palsy, spoke frankly and openly to the students in each class at the middle and senior school levels. Their honest and humorous presentation was well received by the students, many of whom were keen to ask questions of the speakers throughout the sessions. I particularly observed the thoughtful questions and comments made by some of the former perpetrators from my class both during and after the talk. It was clear that the visitors had some effect on the attitudes of these students.

Case studies illustrating National Competency Framework for Beginning Teaching, National Project on the Quality of Teaching and Learning, Australian Teaching Council, 1996, p. 22. Commonwealth of Australia copyright, reproduced by permission.

Case study activity
Why did the presentations by the two cerebral palsy visitors have a more positive effect than teacher admonition?

abilities lies in their physical appearance and perceived incompetencies which can be disconcerting, both to other children and teachers in the regular classroom, as well as to parents and the community in general. The spasticity and abnormal speech patterns characteristic of some disabled children readily set them apart, and often, sadly, provoke negative attitudes and social rejection by peers and teachers. This in its turn can cause psychosocial development problems that have little to do with the original condition (Lewandoski & Cruickshank 1980). Clearly, as teachers, we must be prepared to change our own attitudes and to assist students who hold negative attitudes to change them.

Peer and teacher attitudes towards disability

Strategies to improve and develop positive attitudes

Not being able to 'get into the mind' of those with apparently severe disabilities, it is natural for many to feel profound sympathy for those afflicted, and to want

Why are positive expectations of teachers towards children with disabilities so important to their success at school?
Photo: authors

to do things for them. This can be very damaging to the self-esteem of a disabled person who may well want to make the effort (albeit very laborious and even painful) to function as 'normally' as possible. Be prepared to feel helpless and confused as to what is acceptable, and do not hesitate to ask the disabled person what they would like you to do. Such respect is appreciated and deserved.

Part of our role as teachers of disabled children in regular classrooms is to educate ourselves and others (children and parents) to accept children with disabilities as individuals with strengths and talents. Furthermore, we need to educate children with disabilities to be adaptive to society, to help them to develop the personal skills to cope with the good and bad that society will present, and to become socially integrated (Fisher, Monsen, Moore & Twiss 1989; Harvey & Green 1984; Paterson 1992; Rietveld 1988; Stephens & Stephens 1986).

Our role as educators

How attitudes can be changed has been the subject of much research which is beyond the scope of this book. However, **persuasive communication** involving an expert source of knowledge, honesty and sincerity, importance and relevance, can be most effective. Having individuals experience unpleasant tension (sometimes called **cognitive dissonance**) by confronting incompatible thoughts (such as the belief that one doesn't want to associate with disabled individuals and the belief that disabled individuals are entitled to normal respect and treatment) can lead to a shift towards behaviour consistent with more positive attitudes.

In addition to such programs, which are designed to improve attitudes and behaviour, the following strategies are important: school authorities need to support fully the notion of integration; children with disabilities must be considered part of the normal student body; planning should be effective and include input from students, family members, teachers and others involved in the placement; there must be effective communication before and during the integration between concerned parties; schools and classrooms should be mastery- oriented rather than performance-oriented to alleviate the negative effects of social comparison (Alper & Ryndak 1992; Cole, Vandercook & Rynders 1988; Madden & Slavin 1983).

ACTION STATION

Discuss the arguments for and against the mainstreaming of children with disabilities. Does the type of disability make a difference?

WHAT WOULD YOU DO?

WE'D LOVE TO HELP MICHAEL

Michael was a new student, arriving in week 9 of term 3 in Miss Ingram's grade 5 class. Michael was 12 years old; he had extremely poor reading and writing skills and, basically, he was illiterate. Miss Ingram was really at a loss to know where to start with him. Eventually, after a shared reading and writing session, it became apparent that he did not know any sounds or letter blends—the obvious place to begin.

Because the rest of the children were progressing nicely, a lot of Miss Ingram's time was focused on Michael, which was not fair to the other students. She needed Michael to be able to continue with his work, but she didn't want to spend every minute of her day with him.

What would you do? Read what the teacher did opposite.

Case studies illustrating National Competency Framework for Beginning Teaching, National Project on the Quality of Teaching and Learning, Australian Teaching Council, 1996, p. 10. Commonwealth of Australia copyright, reproduced by permission.

GIFTED AND TALENTED CHILDREN AND EFFECTIVE LEARNING

Ability in various academic, creative and social domains lies along a continuum. We have spent some time discussing the needs of children with various forms of disabilities that affect their effective learning; we now move to the other end of the continuum to consider the special needs of children who are gifted and talented.

Who are the gifted and talented?

Among the characteristics of gifted individuals are above-average intelligence, above-average problem-solving ability (particularly in their use of metacognitive strategies), an emotive interest in their work, motivation and persistence (e.g. see Reis 1989; Renzulli 1986; Hoge & Renzulli 1993; Shaughnessy 1993; Tannenbaum 1986). However, gifted and talented students do not form a homogeneous group. They can display many different talents and come from many different backgrounds. We also realise that children who are quite gifted across a number of areas may nevertheless require remediation in certain subject areas, and that various talents may become evident as children grow older (Cropley 1993; NSW Department of School Education 1991; Reis 1989; Sternberg & Davidson 1985; Torrance 1986; Weill 1987; Yewchuk 1993).

Broader perspectives on giftedness and talent

The issues of the definition and measurement of giftedness, and the identification of gifted and talented children are enormously complicated (see Hoge 1988). In the past, children who scored an IQ of 130 on the Binet performance test were considered gifted (Shaughnessy 1993). However, the specific attributes assessed by such a single measure often bore little relationship to the cluster of qualities more broadly characteristic of the gifted individual. Today, a more thorough screening process, based on a wider conceptualisation of giftedness, is used to identify gifted and talented children for

Identifying gifted and talented children

WHAT WOULD YOU DO?

WE'D LOVE TO HELP MICHAEL (continued)

After much experimentation, Miss Ingram came up with an individual spelling and reading program for Michael, where everything was written on cards so that he could physically manipulate any words he was attempting to make. It was a very simple system: matching sounds and blends, making words, etc. The system was carefully explained to Michael. Miss Ingram also asked the class if anyone would be interested in becoming a peer tutor to Michael. She had heaps of volunteers. She chose five responsible students and explained how Michael's spelling and reading system worked.

The system is working well. Michael can now work more independently, his knowledge of sounds, words, blends of letters is improving all the time, and not only has it released Miss Ingram to work with other children, but she has noticed positive improvements in the learning and behaviour of the peer tutors.

Using Michael's case study as an example, discuss the usefulness of IEPs within the regular classroom.

Case studies illustrating National Competency Framework for Beginning Teaching, National Project on the Quality of Teaching and Learning, Australian Teaching Council, 1996, p. 10. Commonwealth of Australia copyright, reproduced by permission.

'So there you are, Leonardo! Will you stop that infernal doodling and get yourself down to the footy field where a boy of your size belongs!'

purposes of special educational programs. Among the measures that may be used are standardised tests of creative and general ability, behavioural checklists, anecdotal records, interviews, products and performance, class grades and multidimensional testing (Frasier 1989; NSW Department of School Education 1991; Reis 1989; Sternberg & Davidson 1985). As with any assessment of students' abilities, we should consider the evidence from a number of sources.

Programs for the gifted and talented

The all-inclusive school

We have maintained many times throughout this text that teachers of the regular classroom should be competent to facilitate the learning of all children in their classroom. The previous section, dealing with learning-disabled children, indicates that there is some movement towards inclusive schooling and mainstreaming educational opportunity for these children. It would appear a little odd, therefore, to argue here that the gifted and talented should be educated in special schools or special classrooms isolated from the mainstream. One objection to special programs is that they neglect the important fact that all children can be talented and gifted to a greater or lesser degree, and well-trained teachers should endeavour to maximise the talents of all children.

Special classes for the gifted

Many people argue that the gifted and talented child's educational needs are not being met adequately in the regular classroom and, because of this, they are a disadvantaged group (Cropley 1993; Horowitz & O'Brien 1986; Relich & Ward 1987). Some argue very strongly for the establishment of special classes, schools and programs for the gifted. Selective high schools and gifted classes are designed to meet the needs of the gifted student. Research generally indicates that grouping gifted students facilitates their cognitive and social development while having no impact on the achievement or attitudes of the children remaining in the regular heterogeneous classroom (Feldhusen 1989; Urban 1993).

Classroom provisions

There are, nevertheless, a number of provisions that can be made to facilitate the education of these children which can be provided within the context of the regular school and regular classroom (Urban 1993). Regular classes can give enough room to improve the achievement of gifted children by reshaping teaching methods, grouping with differing levels of difficulty, encouraging creative thinking, and well-designed and organised extracurricular activities. Indeed, we have argued strongly that schools need to be adaptable to the special needs of all children. This is particularly important when we consider the fact that

Giftedness knows no bounds. A child with a disability paints with his feet. Photo: WA Education News

very few potentially gifted individuals will ever find themselves in a special program for the gifted. Provisions that can be made within the regular school context are shown in Table 11.6

TABLE 11.6

CLASSROOM PROVISIONS FOR THE GIFTED AND TALENTED

- *Teaching strategies* that involve the implementation of appropriate and specific strategies in the regular classroom to stimulate the development of gifted and talented children. These strategies could include self-directed and independent study, and individual education plans (IEPs) (e.g. see Treffinger 1982; Urban 1993).
- *Flexible progression,* which involves the promotion of a child to a level of study beyond the usual one for his or her age group. This flexible progression may take one of the following forms:
    - *Early enrolment*;
    - *Early completion* of a stage and entry into the next stage in one or more subjects;
    - *Early entry to tertiary education*;
    - *Compaction of course content* (e.g. see Brown 1982; Feldhusen 1989; Rogers & Kimpston 1992; Stanley 1978, 1980; Kulik & Kulik 1984; Torrance 1986; Urban 1993).
    - *Vertical grouping,* which may involve grouping students by ability across age ranges or stages of development (e.g. see Maxwell et al. 1989).
- *Enrichment,* which is a process of adaptation of the curriculum to enable gifted and talented students to pursue study of a particular topic at greater depth and breadth. It might include special tasks, projects, freely selected activities, interest clubs, resource rooms, seminars, independent study and field trips (e.g. see Maker 1987; Print 1981; Urban 1993).
- *Mentor programs,* whereby gifted and talented children are matched with mentors with expertise and ability to foster the development of the children (see Urban 1993).

Many schools run camps, clubs or extension programs where courses of study are provided in one or more areas for gifted and talented students so that the children may extend their talents while working with similarly talented and focused youngsters (McKeith & Daniel 1990; Rickard 1981; Torrance 1986). Various states in Australia and schools in New Zealand have applied different policies governing these practices (Braggett 1987; Smith 1987).

Coping with giftedness

Apart from the academic issues, teachers of gifted children need to help them cope with the special problems that might arise from their giftedness (Hoge and Renzulli 1993). Cropley (1993) suggests that teachers and counsellors should help gifted children with special problems such as: perfectionism and fear of failure; ambivalence about themselves (i.e. a concern over whether they are really gifted or not, and whether they want to push themselves); arrogance or its opposite, self-doubt; deviation from family or peer norms; and social isolation associated with being different. Many gifted children develop interests and ambitions that are wildly different from the expectations held by parents and peers, and this may cause them to become isolated. Cropley also suggests that educational and career guidance take on additional dimensions with gifted children: linking children up with out-of-school programs or mentors; finding teachers who display special sympathy or skills with gifted children; and so on. Personal counselling is needed to help gifted children set realistic goals, accept and live with the consequences of giftedness on social relations, come to grips with the social and emotional situation within the family, and develop a strong self-concept and identity.

The effects of teacher and parental expectations on gifted students

In general, teachers hold expectations of gifted and talented children that facilitate their development. Good and Brophy (1990), however, appropriately caution teachers about holding expectations of gifted children that may cause problems. High-achieving students are often expected to do too much too soon, and are 'not allowed' to make mistakes, 'slacken off', or be reflective. They are expected to be deeply knowledgeable, but are often given too little opportunity to develop and deepen their understanding before being pressured to move on (see also Horowitz & O'Brien 1986).

Family pressures may create difficulties

Family pressures may also create difficulties for the gifted. Problems can be caused by overambitious parents determined to push their children to the limits, or by parents who are afraid that their children may 'get above' their station in life and therefore doom themselves to isolation from family and friends. In some cases, parents become overawed by the child's talents and expect the child to become the emotional support for the family. Accumulated pressures may lead to gifted adolescents feeling they have been robbed of their childhood (Cropley 1993).

Question point: What special precautions should be taken by schools and teachers to identify the gifted and talented among minority groups and children with disabilities?

Question point: Should there be special educational programs for the gifted and talented?

CREATIVITY AND EFFECTIVE LEARNING AND TEACHING

The author collects brooches, and the other author has given up counting the number of brooches she now has (but it must be approaching a Guiness Book of Records record). There is one thing in common about these brooches and that is that they are all quite unusual. There are glass brooches, wire brooches, clay brooches, big brooches, little brooches ... and each appears to be the product of a creative mind. Within any classroom there will be creative children and some who appear less creative. Teachers often find it difficult teaching the more creative. In the following sections we explore aspects of creativity in the classroom and the adaptations teachers can make to enhance its development.

What is creativity?

As with intelligence, there is no agreed-upon definition of creativity. Some definitions of creativity emphasise personality characteristics, while others focus on the process of thought. Still others emphasise the product of effort as the criterion of creativity (Feldhusen 1995; Logan & Logan 1971; Perkins 1981, 1988).

Characteristics of creative people

Torrance (1962, 1986) found that the creative children he studied had a reputation among their peers for having 'wild' or 'silly' ideas, and their work was atypical, characterised by humour, playfulness relaxation and lack of rigidity.

MacKinnon (1962) found that the more creative individuals described themselves as inventive, determined, independent, individualistic, enthusiastic and industrious, while less creative individuals described themselves as responsible, sincere, reliable, dependable, clear-thinking, tolerant and understanding.

Getzels and Jackson (1962) found that personality characteristics such as relative absence of repression, openness to experience, sensitivity, lack of self-defensiveness, and awareness of people and phenomena in the environment were related to creativity.

Research into the personal characteristics of creative people supports many of these stereotypes

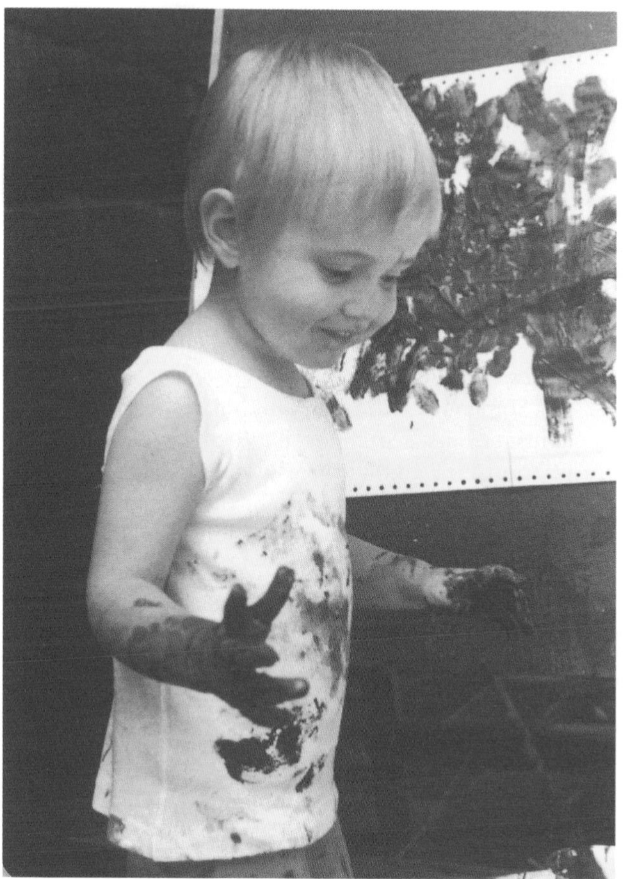

Being creative starts early! How can creativity be stimulated by parents and early childhood educators?
Photo: authors

(Perkins 1981). A person can't be very creative without seeing things in unusual ways, accepting unconventional thoughts, or exhibiting independence of judgment. Other personal characteristics, such as being highly observant or tolerant of ambiguities, also seem to play clear supporting roles in creative effort.

Stages in creative thinking

Stages in creative thinking may also be looked at as a cognitive process involving various stages of mental processing by which individuals discover something new (at least for themselves), or rearrange existing knowledge, a rearrangement that might involve an addition to knowledge (Frederiksen 1984). Many techniques have been used to uncover elements of the creative process including retrospective self-disclosure by creative people, tracking through 'hard data' such as drafts of stories, paintings and other compositions, psychological monitoring of the process while it is occurring (such as having people report on their thoughts during or right after a mental activity) (Perkins 1981).

Among the stages that might characterise creative thinking are the following suggested by Wallas (1926).

1. *Preparation*—intense study of the problem at hand; involves assembling all the available information and working through it so that it is clearly understood.

   Often the creative individual becomes so immersed that he or she won't even break for refreshment. We have all heard of the artist hidden away in a garret producing the definitive poem, novel or musical score.
2. *Incubation*—a period of rest and reflection, engagement in an activity not related to the work under consideration.

   Somehow, during this period, the mind continues its search as it seeks to uncover new relationships among the assembled facts.
3. *Illumination*—flash of insight that puts the various elements into their proper relationship. Distractions at this time can be disastrous as they disrupt the flow of thought.
4. *Verification*—a period of intense, systematic work during which the poem is written down and polished, the theory tested or the machine built.

It is at this time that the idea must be tested against the cold reality of fact. Will it work? Does the building stand up? Does the audience applaud? This stage is very irksome for many individuals who like to pass the baton on to someone else to continue with the work while they move on to other endeavours.

Do you go through these stages when you are 'being creative'?

The creative product

What makes a truly creative product? This is highly contentious as the judgment of creativity is so subjective. Some products achieve fame because general consensus holds that they are creative. But once we move outside the area of general consensus it is extremely difficult to judge what is truly creative. One of us has been standing admiring Jackson Pollock's 'Blue Poles' only to hear passers-by comment how a class of preschoolers could have produced as good. We are not particularly impressed by gallery collections that include crumpled garbage cans, or large canvases filled with various shades of white (called 'Illumination in white'). Creative products appear, nevertheless, to be characterised by competence, originality, scope and significance.

How do we assess creativity?

Tests of creativity

Given the complexity of understanding what creativity is across many diverse domains of human activity, the assessment of creativity is equally complex. Tests have been designed to measure the person, process and product components (Feldhusen 1995).

J. P. Guilford (1967, 1985; see also Meeker et al. 1985), whom we discussed earlier in the context of intelligence, devised a series of tests of creative thinking based on his model of intelligence, which attempt to tie together the qualities of the creative process and the creative person. The traits that Guilford believes are related to creativity are the **ability to see problems, fluency of thinking** (i.e. coming up with a lot of ideas), **originality** (no one else thinks of the idea), redefinition and **elaboration** (describing the features of the solution in detail). Guilford believes that these elements may be measured through a series of tests:

- ☐ *Word fluency*—how many words ending in 'ion' can you think of (the divergent production of symbolic units)?
- ☐ *Ideational fluency*—think of as many words as you can that refer to things soft, white and edible (the divergent production of semantic units).
- ☐ *Originality*—unusual and clever responses, such as the consequences test: What would happen if everyone in the world doubled in size? What would happen if all teachers had a strike for twelve months?
- ☐ *Spontaneous flexibility*—freedom from inertia in giving a diversity of ideas, such as in the uses test: How many uses of a housebrick can you think of (the divergent production of semantic classes)?
- ☐ *Adaptive flexibility*—the tricky problems test where solutions require ingenuity and unconventional responses. This involves lateral thinking, that is, seeing a number of possibilities and evaluating them.

The more creative the individual, the higher the score on each of these tests.

Fluency *Flexibility* *Originality* *Elaboration*

Paul Torrance (1962, 1966, 1973, 1986) believes the creative process to be characterised by **fluency**, a fertility of ideas, **flexibility**, the ability to abandon old ways of thinking while initiating new ones, **originality**, the ability to produce uncommon responses and unconventional associations between ideas, and **elaboration**, the capacity to use two or more abilities for the construction of a more complex object. His thoughts have also been reflected in a series of tests. One common type of test is the circles test (see Logan & Logan 1971). For this test individuals are given a series of empty circles (see the following diagram) and invited to use the circles to complete as many objects as possible in ten minutes. By objects we mean such things as a fried egg, or a pair of glasses. A circle must be a main component of each drawing and individuals are encouraged to put as many ideas into each drawing as

CIRCLES See how many objects you can make from the circles. Add lines to complete your picture, inside, outside or both. Try to be original. Make as many ideas as you can.

they can think of. We have had many university students complete this test, and it is very illuminating! Why don't you try it?

The 'test' is scored for the number of responses made (fluency); the number of idea changes that occur (flexibility)—(some individuals have a one-track mind and simply draw lots of objects related to food while others move rapidly across a range of objects); the amount of detail in the drawing (elaboration)—(some people present just an outline of a pair of glasses, while others draw a full face with glasses, including eyebrows, hair, etc.); and, finally, originality—that is, the number of ideas that rate as unique (based on surveys of the most common responses). This last one always gets us into trouble with individuals arguing that drawing a fried egg is highly creative!

Guilford, Torrance and others maintain that tests of creativity measure ability for creative thinking. However, some authors believe that, to the extent such tests have time constraints, involve some level of anxiety, and are conducted in an artificial atmosphere, they really don't measure creativity as it occurs 'in the real world'. They believe that creativity occurs only in open, stress-free situations, and basically the response made must be to a real situation. What do you think?

The validity of creativity tests

Less formal means of assessing creativity may be through teachers' ratings of children and pupils' ratings of each other. You will find that some children in a class will be very popular during composition time as their stories are always interesting, full of action and humour. The other children will love listening to them. Others will produce paintings and craftwork that the class really appreciates. And of course there are always the children who are great at theatrics (both wanted, and unwanted!). Using this information it is relatively easy to assess individual levels of creativity without resorting to formal tests. Torrance suggests the following clues to help a teacher decide when creative behaviour is taking place:

Teacher and pupil ratings

- ☐ intense absorption in listening, observing or doing;
- ☐ intense animation and physical involvement;
- ☐ use of analogies in speech;
- ☐ tendency to challenge ideas of authorities;
- ☐ taking a close look at things;
- ☐ eagerness to tell others about discoveries;
- ☐ continuing in creative activities after time allocated;
- ☐ showing relationships among apparently unrelated ideas;
- ☐ various manifestations of curiosity;
- ☐ spontaneous use of discovery or experiments;
- ☐ habit of guessing and testing outcomes;
- ☐ independent action, boldness of ideas;
- ☐ manipulation of ideas and objects to obtain new ones.

How can we develop creativity in the classroom?

Many of our classroom activities are concerned with developing conventional ways of doing things. Teachers really don't want students to invent new tables and spellings, or ways of doing long division. Many classrooms supply little opportunity for the development of creativity.

Quashing creativity

Torrance has listed the common educational hindrances to creative thinking, including attempts by adults to eliminate fantasy; restriction of the child's manipulativeness and curiosity; overemphasis or misplaced emphasis on gender roles; overemphasis on prevention, fear and timidity as control measures; misplaced emphasis on certain verbal skills; emphasis on destructive criticism; and coercive pressures from peers to conform.

Potential hindrances to the development of creativity

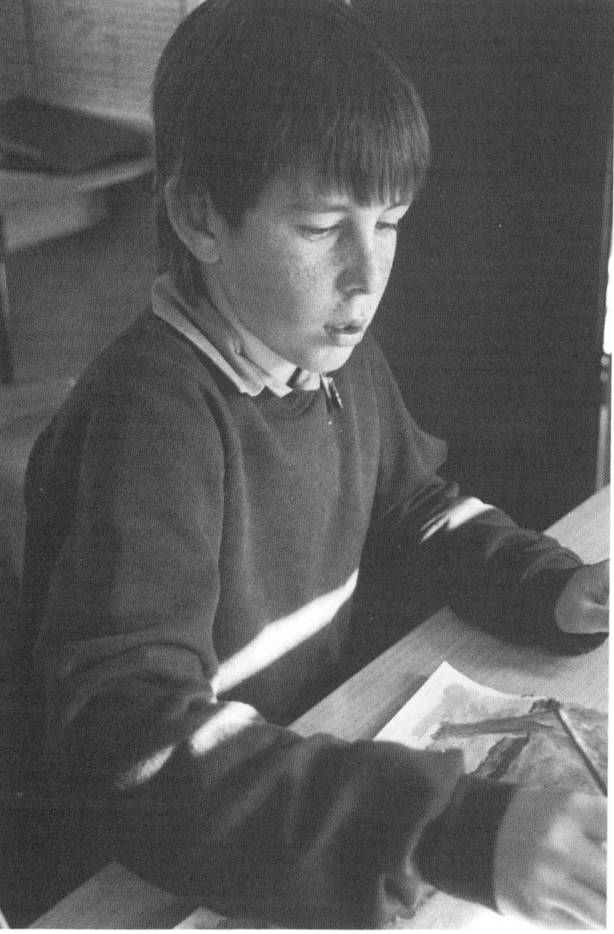

Creative self-expression is the ultimate example of constructive thinking. Photo: authors

What we envisage to address this situation is a total approach to teaching which does not divide the creative, intuitive and divergent from the convergent, deductive and logical. The responsible teacher should develop an approach that integrates all modes of thinking and, most importantly, should model these in the classroom. A number of formal programs have been developed to help teachers stimulate children's creativity. Among these are de Bono's CoRT program and the Purdue Creativity Thinking Program. Reviews of research on the effectiveness of creativity enhancement programs suggest that creativity can be taught effectively (Feldhusen 1995).

Holistic approach to teaching and learning

What does this mean in practical terms? The acrostic in Table 11.7 presents a number of ideas for stimulating creativity in the classroom. Being creative is the ultimate in constructivism, and teaching to stimulate

TABLE 11.7

FOSTERING CREATIVITY IN THE CLASSROOM

Confidence: Instil in children a confidence in their abilities in all activities. Many children believe that they just aren't any good at writing, art, music, performance, and general problem solving. Creativity can be shown across the curriculum and children must be encouraged to try their skills at everything. There are many under-achievers in creative behaviour, but few over-achievers. The challenge for teachers and parents is to discover ways of equalising creative potential and creative achievement. Confidence in themselves as learners and creators is an essential element of this.

Respect: Respect children for all their ideas and contributions. Show that you value creation. Encourage students to think of knowledge as incomplete, to ask questions, to look beyond given facts.

Enjoy: Learning and creating is fun! Far too many adults have lost their joy in creating. Recapture in your classrooms the energy and joy that characterises young children learning and discovering in the natural world. Abandon the distinction between work and play in the classroom. Provide opportunities for children to explore and create in a non-evaluative atmosphere.

Activity: Provide opportunity for unstructured and active involvement in learning and discovering. Excessive seatwork and formal exercises can stultify creativity.

Time: Allow time for children to reflect; this will allow ideas to incubate. Rather than expecting immediate responses and disciplined schedules of production, encourage children to research, think, rest and then come back again to the task with new insights. Show children how to use time effectively for reflection—model it yourself!

Integrate: Design learning experiences that integrate formal logical thinking with the opportunity for divergent thinking. Show how they work in tandem to produce really important knowledge. Show that information from a variety of sources can and should be used to solve problems. Show how there is maths in music and science in art!

Value: Reward and praise the unusual and unconventional as much as the conventional and convergent. Show that you value the creative contribution made by individuals whether it be in academic, social, interpersonal or performance areas. There should be a place where children can exhibit their art, display their stories, demonstrate their abilities. Treat children's ideas with respect as indifference or ridicule will stifle children's creativity.

Invite: Members of your school's community have many talents. Invite them into your classroom as colleagues to motivate children to be creative.

Tolerate: Be prepared to tolerate disorder and messiness during the creative process. If you insist on neatness and everything being done in the 'right' way at the 'right' time, you will stifle creativity. At the appropriate time children should be disciplined to 'verify' their production according to the appropriate criteria for presentation. Remember that being creative is not an excuse for a sloppy final product, but a certain level of disorder is essential to the creative process. You must also be prepared to tolerate a certain level of the unexpected, whether it be in behaviour or product. When children are given the opportunity to create they will also set out to shock.

You: Yes, *you* play a very important role in developing the creative powers of children in your care. Through your expectations, modelling, designing of appropriate educational experiences, valuing and enjoying what your children produce, you are a major player in the child's development as a creator and thinker.

creativity is the ultimate in being a constructivist teacher.

a

ACTION STATION

Consider the options for stimulating giftedness and talent presented on page 260. Arrange these in order of acceptability and practicality. What can you do personally to encourage the development of giftedness and talent in children who you teach?

ADAPTING SCHOOLS AND CLASSROOMS TO INDIVIDUAL DIFFERENCES

As we have seen throughout this chapter, children in any one classroom differ from one another in many ways, although there are broad similarities that make it reasonable to group them as a cohort. Providing they are not extreme, some individual differences, such as levels of physical and motor development, and behavioural and personality differences, can be adequately catered for in any well-organised classroom. Tolerance and understanding on the part of the teacher, as well as some level of individual attention and individualising of instruction, is often all that is needed for most children to thrive.

At times there will be children in our classrooms whose special needs require a little more attention at either the classroom, school or system levels. There is a continuum; all children have special needs of one kind or another at some time or another, and all children have normal needs of one kind or another.

Adapting teaching programs

While the thought of adapting your teaching program to suit each individual in your classroom may appear daunting, we have already covered many of the essential features of adaptive education. All the chapters in this text give perspectives on how you might function effectively as an adaptive teacher, whether in terms of presenting material programmatically for some children and through discovery learning for others; the nature of the resources you choose; or the way you evaluate. As well, you will attempt to foster intrinsic motivation and to teach metacognitive and self-regulating skills to children. In other words, you have knowledge which should enable you to adapt your program of teaching to the special needs of all the children in your class, and to assist individual students to adapt to particular forms of instruction.

Adaptive education refers to educational approaches aimed at effectively accommodating individual differences in students while helping each student develop the knowledge and skills required to learn particular tasks. Adaptive education is characterised by flexibility in instructional procedures and resources so that students can take various routes to, and amounts of time for, learning (Brophy 1988; Corno & Snow 1986; Wang & Lindvall 1984).

Adaptive education

One of the first things you need to do as a teacher is to assess the special strengths and weaknesses of individuals in your classroom in terms of the learning outcomes to be achieved. Particular learning goals will call upon different student strengths (in a number of places these are called *aptitudes*), while particular student weaknesses (often called *inaptitudes*) will inhibit the attainment of specific goals (Corno & Snow 1986). Aptitudes may be **cognitive** (such as intellectual abilities and prior knowledge), **conative** (such as cognitive and learning styles) or **affective** (such as academic motivation and related personality characteristics). Aptitudes interact in a complex way to facilitate or inhibit learning particular tasks.

Student aptitudes and inaptitudes

Depending on your assessment of the relevant aptitudes of each child in your classroom, you can begin to develop programs that either build on existing aptitudes, or that remediate or circumvent inaptitudes. In other words, you need to devise instructional alternatives that are matched to the performance and needs of the learner.

Another consideration when developing individual programs for children is whether or not the goals being set are common educational goals that are to be met by each individual in the educational system (to a greater or lesser extent) or goals that might more appropriately be individual. Teachers often confuse the two and give themselves endless problems trying to get all their students to master the same goals. For example, aspects of literacy and numeracy are common, socially desirable goals. In contrast an ability to play the recorder may be an individual goal. When we look at the curriculum from this perspective it gives us a better sense of where our efforts should lie in helping children learn.

Common goals and individual goals

Many adaptations can be made in the classroom, some can be made by the school, or indeed by the educational system as a whole. Adaptations that can be made in the classroom may be termed **microadaptations** while larger school or system adaptations may be termed **macroadaptations** (Corno & Snow 1986). Table 11.8 presents ideas on some of the adaptations that may be made to individualise instruction in your classroom, while indicating how these overlap with school and system adaptations. Many of these adaptations are discussed in this text.

TABLE 11.8

ADAPTING EDUCATION TO SUIT INDIVIDUAL NEEDS

MICRO/ADAPTATIONS	using a variety of teaching skills; variability, questioning, reinforcement giving students the time needed to learn providing flexibility in classroom rules and organisation monitoring and processing student feedback and other environmental cues—modifying instruction as required modelling thinking and learning processes using a variety of lesson formats and resources for presenting material, e.g. programmed instruction lecture, self-directed guided learning, ICAI—Intelligent Computer Assisted Instruction, parent educators and excursions structuring lessons through the use of advance organisers, headings, reviews using a variety of styles of discourse
MICRO/MACRO	providing for individualised goals and programs, e.g. negotiated curriculum providing flexible teaching/learning spaces, e.g. individual study spaces, clustered desks, interest centres, resource centres using group work—student collaboration, cooperative learning, provisions for students to seek help and give help, peer and cross-age tutoring using task analysis and matching student characteristics (such as competence, attitudes, values) with task demands e.g. IEPs teaching thinking/learning skills to provide the student with skills to adapt to the demands of the material/course to be learnt implementing enrichment/remediation programs implementing intervention strategies to develop in students a positive sense of self as a learner, and self-regulatory and self-management skills providing flexibility in assessment and reporting criteria
MACRO/ADAPTATIONS	providing appropriate physical (such as ramps and special equipment) and educational (a variety of teaching aids and materials) resources providing elective as well as core subjects implementing streaming by ability and needs implementing vertical grouping and semesterisation providing opportunities for accelerated promotion implementing special programs aimed at providing for students' individual differences e.g. PLAN—Program for Learning in Accordance with Needs, PSI—Personalised System of Instruction, IPI—Individually Prescribed Instruction, TAI—Team Assisted Individualisation, IGE—Individually Guided Education, ML—Mastery Learning providing resource personnel (such as support teachers), special curriculum advisers, and teacher aids providing effective guidance counselling adopting a whole-school approach, e.g. ALEM—Adaptive Learning Environment Model, establishing special schools/centres, e.g. selective high schools, hospital schools, extension programs, intensive language centres implementing bilingual and community language programs

TABLE 11.9

ESSENTIALS OF AN ADAPTIVE LEARNING ENVIRONMENT

- Instruction based on the assessed capabilities of each student.
- Materials and procedures that permit each student to progress at a pace suited to his or her abilities and interests.
- Periodic evaluations that inform the student about mastery.
- Student assumption of responsibility for diagnosing present needs and abilities, planning learning activities, and evaluating mastery.
- Alternative activities and materials for aiding student acquisition of essential academic skills and content.
- Student choice in selecting educational goals, outcomes and activities.
- Students' assistance of one another in pursuing individual goals and cooperation in achieving group goals.

(from Wang & Lindvall 1984)

***Question point:** How can schools and classrooms best adapt to the wide range of individual differences among children in our classrooms?*

ACTION STATION

Consider Table 11.8. In this table we have listed adaptations that can be made within schools and school systems to cater for the individual needs of students. Using this framework as a guide, consider ways in which adaptations for students have been made in schools with which you are familiar. Highlight adaptations that are micro, macro, and a combination of each. Consider adaptations that have not been made. Why is this so? Are they potentially useful? Could they be introduced?

Recommended reading

Ashman, A. F. & Elkins, J. (1990) *Educating Children with Special Needs*. Sydney: Prentice Hall.

Bailey, J. (1992) Australian special education: Issues of the eighties. Directions for the nineties. *Australian Journal of Special Education*, 16, 16–25.

Bailey, S. M. (1993) The current status of gender equity research in American schools. *Educational Psychologist*, 28, 321–39.

Butler, K. (1986) *Learning and Teaching Style*. Melbourne: Hawker Brownlow.

Cole, P. G. & Chan, L. K. S. (1990) *Methods and Strategies for Special Education*. Sydney: Prentice Hall.

Corno, L. & Snow, R. E. (1986) Adapting teaching to individual differences among learners. In M. C. Wittrock (ed.) *Handbook of Research on Teaching*, 3rd edn. New York: Macmillan.

Cropley, A. J. (1993) Creativity as an element of giftedness. *International Journal of Educational Research*, 19, 17–30.

Cropley, A. J. (1993) Giftedness: Recent thinking. *International Journal of Educational Research*, 19, 89–97.

Dunn, R., Beaudry, J. S. & Klavas, A. (1990) Survey of research on learning styles. *Educational Leadership*, 47, 50–8.

Entwistle, N. J. (1991) Cognitive style and learning. In K. Marjoribanks (ed.) *The Foundations of Students' Learning*. Oxford: Pergamon.

Feldhusen, J. F. (1995) Creativity: Teaching and Assessing in L.W. Anderson (ed.) *International Encyclopedia of Teaching and Teacher Education*, 2nd edn. Tarrytown, NY: Pergamon: 176–481.

Messick, S. (1995) Cognitive style and learning. In L. W. Anderson (ed.) *International Encyclopedia of Teaching Education,* 2nd edn. Tarrytown, NY: Pergamon: 387–90

Hoge, R. D. & Renzulli, J. S. (1993) Exploring the link between giftedness and self-concept. *Review of Educational Research*, 63, 449–65.

Messick, S. (1984) The nature of cognitive styles. Problems and promise in educational practice. *Educational Psychologist*, 19, 59–74.

Pellegrini, A. D. & Horvat, M. (1995) A developmental contextualist critique of attention deficit hyperactivity disorder. *Educational Researcher*, 24, 13–19.

Perry, C. (1996) Learning styles and learning outcomes based on Kolb's learning style inventory. *SET Research Information for Teachers*, 10 (1), 1–4.

Shipman, S. & Shipman, V. C. (1985) Cognitive styles: Some conceptual, methodological, and applied issues. In E. W. Gordon (ed.) *Review of Research in Education* (vol. 12). New York: AERA.

Smith, N., & Smith, H. (1991) *Physical Disability and Handicap*. Melbourne: Longman Cheshire.

Tiedemann, J. (1989) Measures of cognitive styles. A critical review. *Educational Psychologist*, 24, 261–75.

CHAPTER 12

Cultural dimensions to effective learning

OVERVIEW

A complex and interactive relationship exists between schooling and culture. This becomes all the more complicated within societies characterised by ethnic diversity. For many children in our schools the language of the home is not English, and the culture of the home often reflects the parents' culture of origin. Consequently, many of these children are brought up in a culturally different environment until they first go to school and thus have similar experiences to overseas-born children on entry to school. The female author, although born in Australia, was the child of Ukrainian immigrants. She spoke no English until she attended Newtown Infants School at five years of age.

In this chapter we highlight the importance of cultural context for effective schooling; the importance of teachers, parents and schools in developing learners' life chances and the relevance of mainstream psychology and cross-cultural psychology in understanding the special needs of culturally different learners. The implications of these factors for educators are discussed in particular.

Among issues examined are the nature and importance of multicultural education, the importance of home language maintenance, and the roles of bilingualism and English as a second language. Special attention is given to indigenous minority education and the needs of non-traditional and traditional Aboriginal and Maori learners. Creative responses to these needs in the form of bilingual/bicultural education, two-way schools and two-way learning, and *kohanga reo* are described. Finally, we consider the issue of classroom management in ethnically diverse classrooms.

The material in this Chapter will help you to implement Learner-Centred Psychological Principle 10 and the teaching competencies in Box 1.1.

LEARNER-CENTRED PSYCHOLOGICAL PRINCIPLE 10

Learning is most effective when differences in learners' linguistic, cultural and social backgrounds are taken into account.

Learning is facilitated when the learner has an opportunity to interact with various students representing different cultural and family backgrounds, interests, and values. Learning settings that allow for and respect diversity encourage flexible thinking as well as social competence and moral development. In such settings, individuals have an opportunity for perspective taking and reflective thinking, thereby leading to insights and breakthroughs to new knowledge.

Reprinted with permission APA Task Force on Psychology in Education (1993, January), p. 8.

EDUCATION IN MULTICULTURAL SOCIETIES

Individual respect for children's backgrounds

Children like to know that the things they value (whether they are as important as language, religion and family values, or as simple as a salami sandwich) are respected. All of us need to feel respected for who and what we are. It is important, therefore, for schools and classrooms to demonstrate a respect for the cultural background and characteristics of the children they serve.

Culture and the zone of proximal development

The manner in which children respond to school and benefit from the experiences presented will reflect the cultural environment in which they are socialised. Language and conversational forms, and children's familiarity or lack of familiarity with the use of various conventions (such as questioning) and tools (such as computers) within the school context must be considered by teachers if they are to make education relevant (Smagorinsky 1995). Teachers need to build on the experiences of children in order to advance their academic and social development. In other words, as we suggest in Chapter 2, effective education from a Vygotskian

BOX 12.1 TEACHING COMPETENCE

The teacher values diversity and believes that all students can, and have the right to, learn

Indicators

The teacher:

- values and uses the gender, and cultural and linguistic backgrounds of the students;
- encourages students to value the cultural backgrounds of other students;
- designs programs that are sensitive to individual students' backgrounds;
- recognises own cultural assumptions and biases and those within the school's curriculum and practices;
- ensures that students' learning is not limited by expectations based on stereotypes and prejudices;
- acts equitably towards all students.

Case studies illustrating National Competency Framework for Beginning Teaching, National Project on the Quality of Teaching and Learning, Australian Teaching Council, 1996, Element 1.7, p. 35. Commonwealth of Australia copyright, reproduced by permission.

What do you think about children participating in cultural displays such as this at school?
Photo: WA Education News

Vygotskian perspectives have strongly influenced educators' ideas of effective learning in cultural settings. In particular, the sociocultural milieu of learning (see Chapter 2; also Rogoff & Chavajay 1995) affects the following:

- ☐ the way children go about learning;
- ☐ values and goals appropriate to learning;
- ☐ definitions of meaningful learning;
- ☐ definitions of intelligence and intelligent behaviour;
- ☐ the importance of individual versus group activities;
- ☐ appropriate measurement and evaluation.

perspective must be situated within the zone of proximal development for children. Generally, school practices are consistent with how mainstream students have been socialised in their home culture and with the learning preferences and strengths they have developed. However, effective teaching also requires that teachers make linkages between all students' home culture and classroom practices even when the students are non-members of the mainstream group (Hollins 1996).

WHAT WOULD YOU DO?

JULIO CAN DO IT

Sixteen-year-old Julio had recently arrived from South America, where English was his second language. He was placed in Miss Miley's grade 7 English class at the beginning of the year. Mr Cugliari, his ESL teacher, his grade 7 English teacher and Miss Blainey, who taught the grade 8 English class, met to discuss the possibility of Julio being placed in grade 8 for third term.

Imagine you are Miss Blainey. What arguments would you present for keeping Julio in year 7? What arguments would you use to support his move to year 8? Read what happened** **on page 272.

Case studies illustrating National Competency Framework for Beginning Teaching, National Project on the Quality of Teaching and Learning, Australian Teaching Council, 1996, p. 49. Commonwealth of Australia copyright, reproduced by permission.

In the following sections we discuss some of the features that characterise children who are socialised in cultural contexts different from the mainstream, and how these need to be considered by effective teachers.

Taking into account our students' cultural background

Australian and New Zealand schools are characterised by ethnic diversity, and both countries have introduced legislation that fosters multiculturalism in general and multicultural education in particular. There is a significant political agenda related to multiculturalism and the role education has to play in the development of multicultural societies (Bullivant 1986, 1988a; Castles, Kalantzis, Cope & Morrissey 1988; Corson 1993; Foster 1988; Goodman, O'Hearn & Wallace-Crabbe 1991; Irwin 1991; Kalantzis & Cope 1987, 1988; McInerney 1987a, 1987b, 1987c; Partington & McCudden 1992; Polesel 1990; Poole 1987; Smolicz 1991) which is beyond the scope of this book. Instead, our focus lies on the dictum that *good teaching starts where the child is*. Whether particular societies are interested in social engineering of the type leading to multiculturalism or pluralism, or are interested in developing a monistic society from the diversity of its citizens, good teaching must pay heed to the cultural characteristics of its students.

WHAT WOULD YOU DO?

JULIO CAN DO IT (continued)

Miss Blainey felt very hesitant and unsure about this proposal. Surely this was unwise since Julio was having difficulty with English.

However, during the discussion, Miss Miley and Mr Cugliari spoke of the importance of this move for Julio's social development, of the tremendous staff support for both Julio and Miss Blainey and of the boy's own determination to do well, and Miss Blainey changed her opinion. Julio moved to her class.

One day, a number of weeks later, Miss Blainey asked Julio to read a passage aloud from the class novel. He approached this task in a very positive fashion and read clearly and slowly. When he came upon a word that he was unsure of, he successfully worked out the correct pronunciation. Miss Blainey felt very pleased and proud of Julio's achievement. She was grateful to her fellow staff and for their insistence on giving the boy the opportunity to develop and fulfil their expectations of him.

Case studies illustrating National Competency Framework for Beginning Teaching, National Project on the Quality of Teaching and Learning, Australian Teaching Council, 1996, p. 49. Commonwealth of Australia copyright, reproduced by permission.

MULTICULTURAL EDUCATION—AUSTRALIAN PERSPECTIVES

Multicultural education policies

Officially, all schools in Australia are called upon to implement *multicultural education policies* that have been mandated by state and national governments (Alcorso & Cope 1986; Brentnall & Hodge 1984; Office of Multicultural Affairs 1990). These policies emphasise teaching for intercultural understanding and, in schools where need demands, developing the English language competence and preserving the ethnic traditions and language of children from non-English-speaking backgrounds.

In schools with large numbers of NESB children, school-based multicultural policies and practices were in place well before the rise of multiculturalism as an official policy, and have continued to flourish. In these schools, need was the mother of invention. However, the impact of multicultural education policies has been less than anticipated on schools where there does not appear to be any significant migrant presence. Many of the notions underpinning multicultural education (culture, ethnicity, equity, participation) appear somewhat vaguely defined in the policy documents (Poole 1987; Sachs 1989). Perhaps as a result of this, the attitude of many teachers (and the community at large) is somewhat ambivalent to multiculturalism.

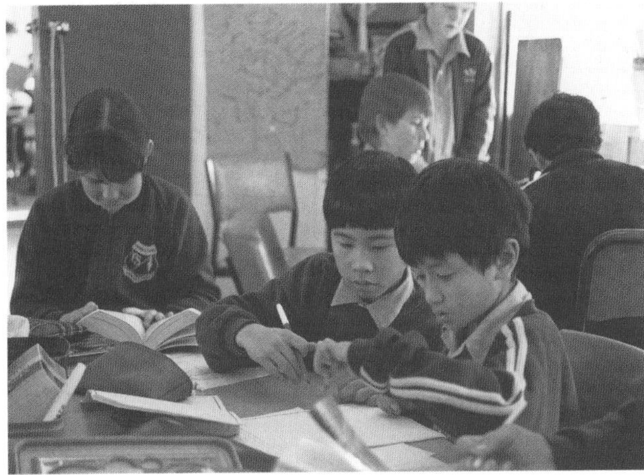

Our multicultural classrooms bring many teaching challenges. Photo: authors

Potential problems of children of migrants

In a survey in the Metropolitan South West Region of the New South Wales Department of School Education (McInerney, 1979) teachers identified the significant problems of children of migrants. The findings are given in Table 12.1.

TABLE 12.1

POTENTIAL PROBLEMS OF CHILDREN OF MIGRANTS

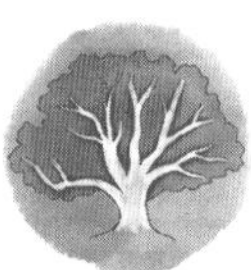

In society as a whole

- Loss of close family ties. Loss of peers of the same nationality, and the difficulty of making friends outside the ethnic group.
- Inability to communicate basic emotional needs.
- Understanding the rules of the new society with the insecurity of not knowing what is acceptable behaviour.
- Conflict between parental ideas and the developing ideas of the children regarding food, dress, excursions, dates, responsibilities, and male and female roles.
- Inability or reluctance of some members of the family to change to new language and customs. The hesitancy of most parents to assimilate as quickly as their children would like them to.
- Protective ethnic grouping resulting in confrontation between groups and a consequent refusal to assimilate.
- Sudden change from a low socioeconomic group to an affluent society.

Within schools

- The demand by schools and other institutions for children to be more responsible and independent of the family than is expected at certain ages in other cultures.

- The problem of cutting ties with mothers who insist on bringing children to school and waiting at school for them all day.
- Adjusting to different ideas of schooling; frequently, antagonistic attitudes of teachers who do not welcome migrants.
- Being labelled 'unintelligent' throughout school years when the problem is basically one of language.
- Ostracism by Australian children and the feeling that they are never going to be like Australians.
- Parental insistence on their mother tongue at home. Parents do not often have the same opportunities for learning English as their children; consequently they often speak only the mother tongue at home which makes it difficult for migrant children to practise at home what they have learnt at school.
- The reluctance of some migrant parents, particularly non-English-speaking women, to venture near the school for fear of non-acceptance or being misunderstood.

These perceptions of teachers give us much food for thought when we consider ethnically diverse classrooms, particularly ones in which there are large numbers of new arrivals and/or refugee children.

Question point: Discuss the list (in Table 12.1) of adjustment difficulties faced by children from other cultures. What can we do as teachers to alleviate the potential stress caused to our NESB students by these adjustment difficulties?

Children from a non-English-speaking background (NESB)

Intensive language programs

At the most obvious level, children who arrive at school unable to understand or speak the language of instruction suffer a double jeopardy. At the time they are expected to master new cognitive skills, they are also expected to master a new language in which these skills are encoded (Diaz 1983; Garcia 1993; Guthrie & Hall 1983; Snow 1992). Most schools have made provisions for these children to learn English through intensive language programs in ESL and follow-up classroom-based programs.

There is considerable debate, however, over the appropriate and best ways to teach children the second language (Benton 1989; Garcia 1993; McCroarty 1992; Snow 1992; Pease-Alvarez & Hakuta 1992). One argument holds that children learn best in intensive language centres where the emphasis is clearly on the acquisition of English. In this case there is a belief that the real goal of education for NESB children should be their social and economic advancement in mainstream society, not the preservation of their native language and culture (Porter 1990). The school's focus should be on equipping children with fluent English as quickly as possible, thereby empowering them with the tools to enter the mainstream, namely the English language and mainstream curriculum (Pease-Alvarez & Hakuta 1992; see also Hollins 1996).

Bilingual/bicultural education

Another argument holds that English should be learned in a bilingual/bicultural context (Benton 1989). Much of this debate is philosophical/socio-cultural/human rights oriented. For example, Cummins (quoted in Pease-Alvarez & Hakuta 1992, p. 5) says:

Educators who see their role as adding a second language and cultural affiliation to students' repertoires empower students more than those who see their role as replacing or subtracting students' primary language and culture in the process of assimilating them to the dominant culture.

In this case the linguistic and cultural differences of the students are seen as both individual and societal resources not to be wasted (Cziko 1992; Smolicz 1991). Many NESB immigrant communities are reluctant to see their children lose their community language through immersion in intensive English courses, although individual members of particular communities may have little interest in preserving their home language.

Significant educational issues in second language teaching

Much of the language debate highlights significant educational issues, such as whether the cognitive development of a child is delayed while learning a new language to label old concepts. In this case people argue that it is better to keep cognitive development on track by teaching in the children's first language while gradually introducing English as the medium of instruction. If and when appropriate, English can become the dominant medium of instruction (Diaz 1983; Smolicz 1991). Others argue that there is inhibition from one language to another, and that children faced with learning two languages and two sets of labels for new concepts at the same time are jeopardised (McCroarty 1992).

Another aspect of this issue relates to the extent to which a child's **sense of self** is inextricably interwoven with culturally mediated experiences. Language is considered an essential element in the development of a sense of self (see, for example, the discussion of

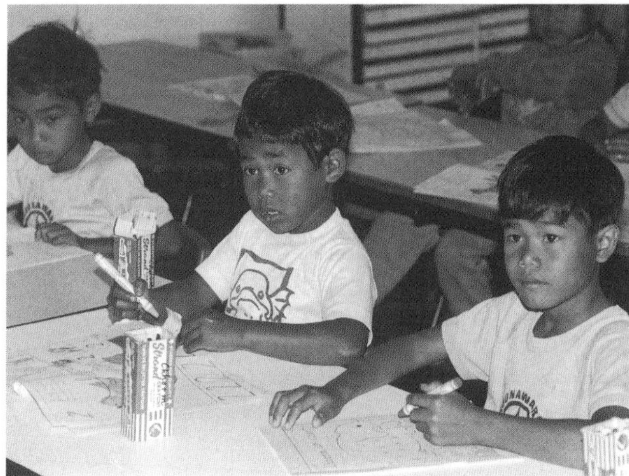

ESL classes are essential for new arrivals who speak no English. Photo: WA Education News

Vygotsky in Chapter 2). This is one of the strongest arguments for bilingual education and community language programs in our schools. Furthermore, as language is one of the major vehicles for the preservation of a culture, multicultural education programs that are designed to preserve ethnic diversity should have a significant language component. If they do not, they are tokenistic (McInerney 1987; Smolicz 1991).

Sense of self and language acquisition

Snow (1992) answers a number of questions regarding the acquisition of a second language that are helpful for us as teachers to consider. Table 12.2 presents a summary of her answers.

TABLE 12.2

COMMON QUESTIONS ABOUT THE ACQUISITION OF A SECOND LANGUAGE

- *Is there a best age to start second-language acquisition?* As children get older, their capacity to benefit from formal second-language teaching gradually increases. However, fluency depends on using the language in a range of social interactions. Younger learners should be exposed to the second language in relatively unstructured and unthreatening 'real-life' language situations.
- *How long does it take to learn a second language?* One can learn enough of a second language in a few hours to perform some tasks in it. Other tasks (including some academic and literacy related tasks) may take years to master. Even native speakers continue to acquire fluency as they encounter new language situations [e.g. the language of educational psychology].
- *How can second-language acquisition be facilitated?* Real-life language encounters with native speakers are most important. Positive regard for the culture of the language also helps, as do well-designed curricula and good teachers.
- *Can learners function as effectively in communicating, learning, reading and talking in a second language as in a first?* Learners can become better in their second language than in their first. Fluency in either or both language(s) depends on exposure to a full range of language experiences in the languages.
- *Does acquisition of a second language have any positive or negative consequences for the learner?* Acquiring a second language can give young learners some advantage in metalinguistic and analytic tasks but it can also increase processing times slightly for both languages. Both of these effects are quite small, and the costs in processing speed do not outweigh the advantage of knowing two languages.
- *Why do some people have so much trouble with second-language acquisition, when it is relatively fast and easy for others?* Differences in aptitude, motivation, opportunities to communicate in the second language effectively and pleasantly, as well as teaching effectiveness, influence the ease with which an individual will learn the second language.
- *How should we test for language proficiencies of second-language learners?* There is a range of domains of language proficiencies. Tests should relate to the goals of the instruction. For example, if oral acquisition is important then this should be assessed. Good oral language does not predict academic performance in the language. If command of academic language is the goal, this should be assessed.

ACTION STATION

a

Authorities argue about the merits of bilingual/bicultural education versus concentrated ESL for new NESB arrivals to our country. Conduct a debate which examines the arguments for and against these options.

Teacher attitudes to community language maintenance and bilingual education

A review of the Commonwealth Multicultural Education Program (Phillip Institute of Technology 1984) found that teachers' general knowledge about Australia's ethnic groups was seriously deficient and that there was little support among teachers for the proposal that the Australian school system should develop bilingualism. While teachers were generally in favour of multicultural education there was a widespread lack of understanding that the policy was appropriately applied to all schools whether or not they had significant numbers of migrant background children. One study (McInerney 1987a) indicated that 84.5% of 800 teachers surveyed in south-west Sydney agreed that it was important for children to retain their mother language and 77.9% thought that schools should encourage children to retain their mother language. However, only 23.4% of the teachers believed that schools should assume responsibility for language maintenance. There was little commitment to the notion that ethnic languages should be used as a medium of instruction for part of the day in schools with large numbers of non-English-speaking background children, and indeed 22.1% of the teachers surveyed believed that NESB children should not be encouraged by the school to retain their ethnic language.

Ambivalent attitudes to multicultural education

National policy on languages

Despite this rather ambivalent attitude to community language maintenance and bilingualism within the schools surveyed, there has been considerable progress in developing community language programs within Australian schools. Indeed, Australia is at the forefront of international developments in the area of language teaching. In 1987 an official national language policy was adopted (Lo Bianco 1987). This *National Policy on Languages* seeks to establish a framework for the teaching of languages of relevance to Australia and is based on four broad strategies:

- ☐ the conservation of Australia's language resources;
- ☐ the development and expansion of these language resources;
- ☐ the integration of Australian language teaching and language use efforts with national economic, social and cultural policies; and
- ☐ the provision of information and services in languages understood by clients.

(National Languages & Literacy Institute of Australia 1993)

It is the intention of the *National Policy on Languages* to provide English for all; to maintain and develop Aboriginal and Torres Strait Islander languages; to provide the opportunity for all to learn a language other than English; and to provide language services in languages other than English.

While the importance of English as the national language has been maintained, the position of **community languages** has been strengthened on two fronts. First, native speakers of community languages now have official support for their preservation through Australia's schools. Second, non-native speakers are encouraged to learn a language other than English. The implementation of this policy is directed towards:

Community languages

- ☐ the overcoming of injustices, disadvantages and discrimination related to language;
- ☐ the enrichment of cultural and intellectual life in Australia;
- ☐ the integration of language teaching/learning with Australia's external (economic and political) needs and priorities;
- ☐ the provision of clear expectations to the community about language in general and about language in education in particular;
- ☐ support for component groups of Australian society (ethnic communities, the deaf, Aboriginal groups for whom language issues are very important) with recognition and encouragement, and guidance in attempts to link technology and language use and learning.

(National Languages & Literacy Institute of Australia 1993)

School achievements of the children of migrants

Despite the difficulties faced by many children of immigrant parents there is no indication that the immigrant groups, in general, are disadvantaged in Australian schools. The evidence supports the belief that many students from NES and Asian backgrounds (including recently arrived groups) are succeeding in our schools (Bullivant 1986, 1988b). Among the reasons given for this success are their capacity for hard work, academic motivation, self-discipline, good behaviour and reliability in class, high-achievement orientation and aspirations, coupled outside the school with parental support and choice to put in long hours of work. In particular, students who are backed by strong motivation from their families perform well at school and may become outstanding students (Bullivant 1988b; see also Marjoribanks 1980; McInerney 1988a, 1988b).

MULTICULTURAL EDUCATION—NEW ZEALAND PERSPECTIVES

The notion of multiculturalism is quite different in New Zealand. Within New Zealand, mandated multicultural policy development is largely synonymous with the development of bilingual/bicultural programs for

Attending to cultural needs is an important aspect of effective teaching. Photo: authors

Community language teaching, such as the teaching of Arabic, is now a common part of the curriculum0

Maori and Pakeha (European) students (Corson 1993; Irwin 1989). Other ethnic groups, such as Pacific Island and Indo-Chinese groups (as well as more established European immigrant groups) are largely ignored in official legislation and policy.

There are important historical reasons for this, including the dominance of the Maori group within New Zealand society (Maoris make up approximately 15% of New Zealand's population of 3.5 million) from early settlement days, and the Treaty of Waitangi. Because of this the Maori are accorded the most prestige in the initial development of multicultural curricula. However, it is envisioned that the Maori-Paheka base will be the first step in the development of a full multicultural program to serve all cultural groups within New Zealand (Irwin 1989). We discuss elements of this bilingual/bicultural response to multicultural education later in this chapter.

It is interesting to note the difference in the development of multicultural policies for Aboriginal, migrant and Maori communities. Within Australia, multiculturalism is identified with immigrant settlers. The indigenous Aboriginal groups consider that it is inappropriate to have their special needs lost within curricula developed for the wider group. Instead, a separate set of policies has been mandated for Aboriginal groups that seeks to foster the development of Aboriginal identity and achievement. These policies have been introduced with considerable vigour in many Aboriginal and non-Aboriginal communities.

Cultural background is only one factor influencing achievement at school. What are some of the others? Photo: authors

TEACHER'S CASE BOOK

HE JUST WON'T ANSWER

Carl, a teacher at Railway Fields Primary School, was concerned about the progress of Mikael, one of the NESB children in his mainstream class. Mikael spoke some English, but his schooling had been in Finnish until eighteen months previously. When Carl asked some of the other students about Mikael, one class member said: 'Mikael won't answer you if you talk to him. Often he understands but he just won't answer, so we walk off.'

A few days later, when Carl was visiting Mikael's ESL withdrawal class, he heard the ESL teacher asking the children to examine the processes they went through when they listened. A typical response was: 'Well, first I translate what is said into my own language, then I think of the answer in my own language, think of the English words, put the words into the right order for the English way to say it, and then I say it.'

Carl could not help but think that the mainstream students would benefit from hearing this explanation. Instead of walking off on Mikael as he was struggling to frame a response, they might learn to give him some 'wait-time'. Carl introduced his class to this idea of wait-time for translation—along with a number of other initiatives designed to heighten students' awareness of cultural and linguistic differences—and was very pleased by their response.

Comments in Carl's journal a few months later summarise the changes:

Children seem to be more eager to listen to Mikael and to discuss differences between their cultures. The (mainstream) children seem to be displaying more interest in listening to and learning about how other people live.

Case studies illustrating National Competency Framework for Beginning Teaching, National Project on the Quality of Teaching and Learning, Australian Teaching Council, 1996, p. 52. Commonwealth of Australia copyright, reproduced by permission.

Case study activity
Discuss other potential problems between students and new arrivals. What solutions might work to alleviate these?

APPLICATIONS OF MULTICULTURAL EDUCATION

Apart from mandated educational policies which come with a number of support documents to assist with the implementation of multicultural programs, and an extensive range of resource materials available through various educational resource centres, the following points represent school practices aimed at adapting the school and classroom environment to the needs of these children. All these practices are in place in particular schools and are found to be very helpful:

- ☐ School notes and reports written in several languages (especially important notices such as immunisation papers).
- ☐ Use of community and ethnic services (e.g. interpreting and translation services).
- ☐ Meetings with migrant parents where school procedures and programs are explained via an interpreter. Interviews with parents carried out through an interpreter.
- ☐ Children encouraged to welcome their parents to the school, and parent/child excursions arranged.
- ☐ Community times organised when parents teach all children crafts, cooking and dancing.
- ☐ ESL classes held for adults on school premises. Pupils and parents attend.
- ☐ Playgroups established and migrant mothers encouraged to attend with their younger children, to foster an interest in the school.
- ☐ Use of Australian parents in home tutor plans.
- ☐ Parents involved in teaching community languages.
- ☐ School staff encouraged to take an interest in ethnic functions in the district.
- ☐ Teachers visit parents personally in their homes.
- ☐ Migrant Parents and Citizens Associations.
- ☐ Ethnic aides appointed to help solve problems and to translate.
- ☐ 'Shopping centres' established where parents are guided on buying habits and currency usage in their new country.

INDIGENOUS MINORITY EDUCATION

Within the wider multicultural context of Australia and New Zealand, two indigenous minority groups are making significant educational progress, despite the economic and educational disadvantage they have suffered historically. Much of the important progress with Aboriginal Australians and Maori communities is the result of creative initiatives currently being taken by the communities to develop educational programs that are culturally relevant and appropriate, but that look ahead to future possibilities.

The notion of what is culturally relevant and appropriate in the modern world is complex, however, and this is particularly the case with Aboriginal and Torres Strait Islander communities which are characterised by great diversity. Some Aboriginal groups live very traditional lifestyles in isolated communities; some live semi-traditional lifestyles on the outskirts of country towns; others participate fully in the urban life of city communities. Clearly, one form of education cannot be culturally relevant and appropriate to all Aboriginal and Torres Strait Islander communities (see

TEACHER'S CASE BOOK

THE MISSING HUMAN ELEMENT

Mr Kirkwood teaches in a district high school. The student intake is from the surrounding farming area and the people living in the area are concerned with their own lives and the local activities. Strangers are looked upon with suspicion and students who attend the school have limited knowledge of, and little interest in, the world beyond their own community.

Last year Mr Kirkwood was dissatisfied with the grade 10 Social Science Asian Studies unit. The students were uninterested. What was more disconcerting was their failure (and he realised it was his failure also) to see Asian people as people. The human element was missing.

This year he was fortunate enough to work alongside an Indonesian lady. Bingo! They decided they would team-teach the grade.

Mrs Varido talked informally about her experiences and reasons for coming to live in Tasmania. Once a week for four weeks students cooked food from China, India, etc. Primary students joined the grade 10 lessons, giving the senior students a chance to show leadership skills. This was videotaped and photos were taken.

The students collected and posted a variety of materials to an international school in Japan. Groups of students built up folders of materials on Asian people and they added information to a class map. At the end of the unit Mr Kirkwood asked the students to write a personal opinion of the issue of Asian migrants living in Australia.

Because students had experienced this human element and had interacted with Mrs Varido, they were able to provide a more balanced, reasoned and informed view on the question. Even though a majority found it difficult to give a 'yes-no' answer, they were able to discuss advantages of having Asian migrants living in Australia.

Case studies illustrating National Competency Framework for Beginning Teaching, National Project on the Quality of Teaching and Learning, Australian Teaching Council, 1996, p. 43. Commonwealth of Australia copyright, reproduced by permission.

Case study activity
How would you handle the situation faced by Mr Kirkwood if you did not have a co-teacher of Asian origin?

Jordan 1984). Furthermore, there is great diversity of opinion among Aboriginal and Torres Strait Islander groups as to what constitutes relevant and appropriate education for their children. For example, some urbanised Aboriginal people who do not have any language other than English, vehemently support the concept of bilingual education, while there are traditionally oriented Aboriginal people who reject the

Inviting the wider cultural community to share its knowledge in schools is enlightening to all children.
Photo: WA Education News

need for bilingual education for their children (see Gale et al. 1987; Williamson 1991).

Effective education for non-traditional urbanised Aboriginal groups

Urban Aboriginal communities

In a survey of Aboriginal parents in urbanised Aboriginal communities in New South Wales (McInerney 1989b), parents clearly indicated that mainstream education is very important and thought that it should provide a good education in the basics, a grounding in social skills and personal development (in particular, life skills such as a sense of autonomy and self-understanding), and improved employment prospects. These goals of education were very similar to those given by the non-Aboriginal parents interviewed at the same time. Surprisingly, few Aboriginal parents mentioned that it was important for their children to learn about Aboriginal culture within schools. Some parents indicated that they thought the difficulties experienced by Aboriginal children within schools could be attributed to a curriculum that was not appropriate to Aboriginal needs, and that schools were discriminatory when they did not give enough individual attention to Aboriginal children. Doing badly at school was perceived by these Aboriginal parents as radically diminishing an Aboriginal child's self-esteem within the school context, the child's motivation to continue with school and, consequently, the child's life chances.

Reasons for the poor achievement of many Aboriginal children

As well as school-related reasons for the poor performance of many urbanised Aboriginal children in this survey, such as poor teaching, insensitive and uncaring teachers, inadequate curriculum, and inadequate teacher and school support, the Aboriginal parents also suggested poor parental encouragement, bad home life and little parental understanding of the value of schooling.

The pupils themselves also attracted some blame for being lazy and poorly motivated. It should be noted that similar reasons were also given for the poor performance of non-Aboriginal children.

Our own research has indicated that lack of motivation or laziness is not the major influence on poor school performance. Rather, the key factors influencing Aboriginal school children's performance and motivation in mainstream school settings are the children's perception of themselves as competent learners, their level of confidence in school settings, their level of intrinsic motivation and how much they like and value school (McInerney 1991, 1992b, 1993; McInerney & Swisher 1995). It is unlikely that the performance of Aboriginal children will improve unless they are encouraged to believe in themselves as effective learners who can be successful within a Western education system. We develop this notion further in the chapter on motivation (Chapter 9). Aboriginal education programs, Aboriginal resource centres, and Aboriginal teacher assistants are part of the initiatives that have been introduced into mainstream schools to enhance the confidence of Aboriginal children.

Question point: *Consider the special educational problems of remote and traditional Aboriginal children. What role should/could non-Aboriginal teachers play in designing a relevant education for these children?*

Educational initiatives among remote and traditional Aboriginal groups

Clearly, the results of our survey apply only to a particular group. Other surveys and studies have indicated a need for education to be radically reshaped to focus on the special needs of remote and traditional groups, as well as those communities that are re-establishing their cultural identity within the wider social milieu (e.g. see Jordan 1984; Folds 1987). In particular, attention has been directed within many of these communities towards developing curricula and school structures that give access to Western knowledge, while rebuilding, fostering and preserving cultural values and traditions important to the identity of the people. On this level there have been some exciting developments.

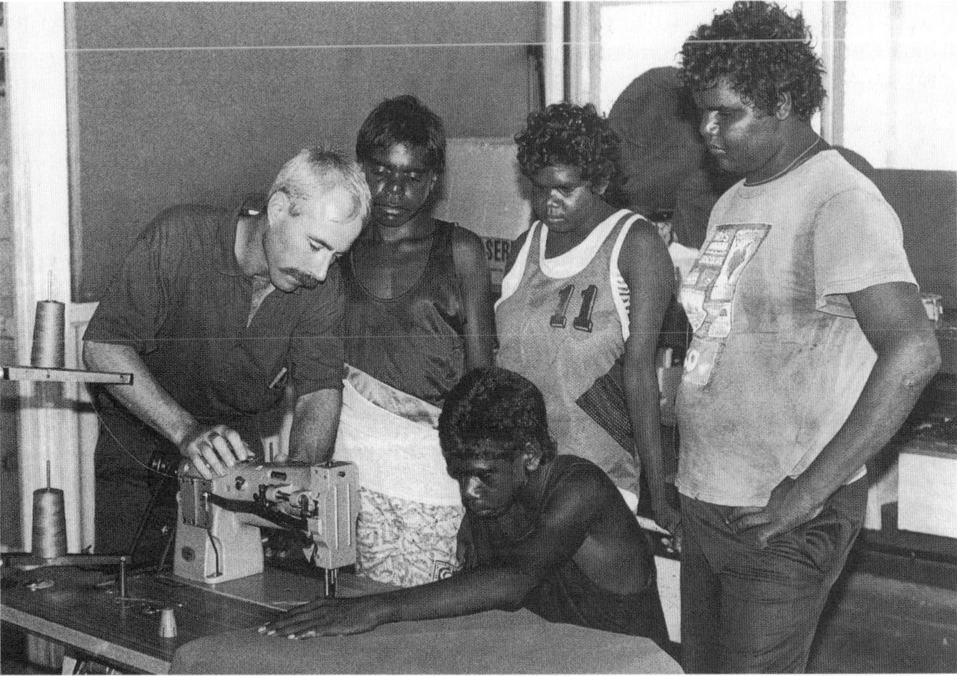

What is relevant and meaningful education for remote Aboriginal communities?
Photo: Mark F. Pearce

Bilingual/bicultural education for Aboriginal children

There has been a significant growth of bilingual/bicultural Aboriginal education throughout Australia. The Northern Territory began developing these programs in 1973 (Allen 1986; Benton 1989; Gale et al. 1987; Folds 1987) and other states have also implemented programs. Bilingual programs have been difficult to establish because of the number of Aboriginal languages and the fact that the languages are unwritten. Hence extensive preliminary work has to take place to establish the written characteristics of each language. From this point it is necessary to develop written curriculum materials and train bilingual teachers. Despite these extensive problems, bilingual programs are flourishing.

As an example of this development, Yipirinya School in Alice Springs uses Aboriginal culture, knowledge and language as the starting point for all learning. Aboriginal culture and language are never phased out to enable transfer to an English language and Western culturally dominated curriculum. Learning begins with the known and gradually introduces the unknown by relating Western concepts to Aboriginal concepts.

In a number of communities, Aboriginal people have established their own schools or taken control of existing facilities. Within Western Australia, for example, a network of Aboriginal schools that share a number of common features has been established (Teasdale & Teasdale 1993, 1994; Vallance & Vallance 1988):

1. They are fully controlled and administered by the local Aboriginal communities, funding being provided by a system of State and Federal grants that are paid to all non-government schools in Australia.
2. Although trained non-Aboriginal teachers are employed, they are expected to work at all times under the direction of community leaders.
3. Community observations of and participation in all school activities is encouraged; community ownership of the school is stressed.
4. In general, children are taught in kin rather than age groups, taking account of mutual obligation and avoidance relationships.
5. Traditional authority structures are maintained by first presenting curriculum materials based on Western knowledge to the older members of the community.
6. Strong emphasis is placed on maintenance of traditional languages; vernacular literacy programs are given high priority.

The concept of the **two-way school** has been developed at Yirrkala, a large community in north-west Arnhem Land where the government school is staffed and administered largely by Aboriginal teachers. Two-way schools attempt to introduce Western knowledge while at the same time taking active steps to promote culture maintenance. The main features of the school are:

Two-way schools

1. The Aboriginal ownership of the school program is recognised.
2. Aboriginal people are taking the initiative in shaping, developing and implementing the program.
3. Clan elders come into the school to teach, thus reaffirming relationships between older and younger generation levels.
4. Children are organised by clan and family relationships and by separating boys and girls.
5. Flexible structures allow for recognition of traditional ceremonial obligations, especially during initiation.
6. Equal respect is given to Aboriginal and Western knowledge; the exchange of knowledge is stressed.

Schools in the Kimberley region in the north of Western Australia have evolved a concept of **two-way learning** that underlines all curriculum planning. It emphasises the need for children to learn both Aboriginal and mainstream ways of life by sharing and exchange. Implementation involves Aboriginal decision making, integration of school and community, the strengthening of teaching/learning relationships between older and younger members of the community, and the development of flexible school structures (Teasdale & Teasdale 1993).

Two-way learning

A number of Aboriginal communities have opted out of Western education almost entirely and established **homeland schools**. These schools have an element of formal structure but there is little emphasis on learning Western knowledge or language. Some communities have opted for voluntary exclusion and have no formal schooling at all for their children. The focus of these communities is clearly on re-establishing the identity of the groups as a cultural entity (Folds 1987; Teasdale & Teasdale 1993).

Homeland schools

Educational initiatives among Maori

As with many indigenous minority groups, the Maori has typically been disadvantaged in mainstream educational settings (Cazden 1990; Fergusson, Horwood & Shannon 1982; Fergusson, Lloyd & Horwood 1991; Sultana 1989). Ranginui Walker (cited in Irwin 1989) identifies variables that he considers are the major problems of Maori education. The first is that the teachers in New Zealand are, by and large, Pakeha (European), monocultural people who lack the skills, sensitivity and knowledge to be able to teach effectively in multi-ethnic classrooms. Because education is geared to this monocultural, Pakeha frame of reference, Maori children see little of relevance to them at school. Success is limited to those stereotyped areas that Maoris are good at, such as sport and music. Maori peoples have

WHAT WOULD YOU DO?

ABORIGINES ARE AUSTRALIANS, TOO

Miss Gray always approaches parent–teacher evenings with a certain feeling of apprehension despite being reassured by other members of staff that it is worse for the parent. Her fears were justified when at the most recent parent–teacher evening a parent seriously questioned her teaching of Aboriginal studies as part of the grade 7 Social Science course. 'Haven't you done enough? Why focus on the Aborigines?'

What would you say in this situation? Read about the teacher's reaction on page 281.

Case studies illustrating National Competency Framework for Beginning Teaching, National Project on the Quality of Teaching and Learning, Australian Teaching Council, 1996, p. 48. Commonwealth of Australia copyright, reproduced by permission.

learnt to have an ambivalent attitude towards education because success in Western schools appears to run counter to important cultural values, and the schools themselves do little to encourage and develop the cultural qualities that Maoris consider very important.

Others argue that the reason for the disadvantage and underachievement lies in the socioeconomic differences between Maori and Pakeha, rather than a cultural mismatch between Western schooling and Maori cultural values (Fergusson, Lloyd & Horwood 1991).

In contrast to the Aboriginal Australians, Maori peoples form a relatively homogeneous group sharing the one language and many cultural traditions. This has facilitated, in recent years, the development of educational initiatives to preserve Maori language (*te reo Maori*) and Maori culture (*taha Maori*) within and outside the regular school system (Irwin 1989, 1991, 1992; Corson 1993).

One exciting development is the *kohanga reo* (language nests) movement, which began in 1982. This offers a preschool all-Maori language and culture immersion environment for children from birth to school age, aimed at developing children within a context replicating a Maori home, where only Maori language is spoken and heard. The *kohanga reo* are open to all children from all cultures, and have proved to be very popular. Following on from this is the increasing provision of bilingual/bicultural education for children at the primary level, ultimately through to secondary school. There are also several Maori language and culture immersion primary schools (*kura kaupapa Maori*) (Corson 1993; Irwin 1991, 1992; Irwin & Davies 1992), and these are becoming increasingly common.

Kohanga reo

The importance of these schools lies in their attempt to situate learning in the appropriate cultural context. Corson (1993, p. 56) says:

Situating schools in their cultural context

The new schools try to restore* mana *[*mana *means status, prestige, power] to the Maori learner in a meaningful way by creating an environment where Maori culture is the taken-for-granted background against which everything else is set. For the pupils, being Maori in* te kura kaupapa *Maori is the norm; the school and classroom environment connects with the Maori home; cultural and language values are central; Maori parents make decisions for their children unimpeded by majority culture gatekeeping devices; and the* whanau *(extended family group) assumes responsibility for the education of their children along with control and direction of the school itself. At the same time, these schools are concerned to teach a modern, up-to-date and relevant curriculum, following national guidelines set by the state, whose outcome will be the production of bilingual and bicultural graduates.

A study of Maori culture has been included in the curriculum of New Zealand state schools (Townsend, Manley & Tuck 1991). This has met with about the same level of success as the multicultural education initiatives within Australian schools. In many schools *taha Maori* has been enthusiastically endorsed; in others the program has been poorly implemented. The nature of the program as well as its method of implementation are controversial, however, which has handicapped its effective implementation. The issue is beyond the scope of this book. Interested readers should refer to Corson (1993).

Maori cultural studies

Question point: How important is language to identity? Discuss the merits of ESL versus bilingual/bicultural education for NESB children. In particular, consider the possible ramifications of each for cognitive development and learning. In this context also discuss the bilingual/bicultural schools established by Aboriginal and Maori communities.

WHAT WOULD YOU DO?

ABORIGINES ARE AUSTRALIANS, TOO (continued)

After her initial shock, Miss Gray tried to explain to the parent the importance of Aboriginal culture and heritage in students' understanding of the history of Australia. The parent was not completely convinced, although she seemed reasonably satisfied with Miss Gray's approach.

Miss Gray finished the meeting by focusing on what topics were to be covered in the following term and highlighting the fact that the course covers a broader curriculum, of which Aboriginal studies is a part.

Is Miss Gray's response adequate? What would you have added to the discussion?

Case studies illustrating National Competency Framework for Beginning Teaching, National Project on the Quality of Teaching and Learning, Australian Teaching Council, 1996, p. 48. Commonwealth of Australia copyright, reproduced by permission.

Educational implications for indigenous minority education

In much of what has been discussed it is evident that Aboriginal and Maori communities are repossessing education and making it more culturally relevant and appropriate for their children. In some cases this is happening outside the regular school settings and under the control of community leaders and teachers. Regular teachers may have little input into these developments. What then is the role of mainstream teachers? And how does a knowledge of educational psychology prepare them for assuming this role?

Implications for mainstream teachers

First, we have argued many times throughout this text that, for education to be meaningful, it must take notice of the learner's background. This applies to all children, but in some cases the mismatch between teachers' understanding and the children's backgrounds and culture can be so vast as to impede effective schooling. Obviously, therefore, we must support wholeheartedly attempts by these, and other cultural communities, to restructure schools and teaching so that the community's culture becomes an essential basis from which to develop educational programs for the community's children. Schooling must be situated within the appropriate cultural context.

Schools and cultural context

Second, schools should be concerned with more than simply passing on information and academic skills. They should also be concerned with developing **life chances** for the children they serve (e.g. see Evans & Poole 1987). There are two basic types of life chance: those that relate to increasing social options for children (such as employment and further education), and those that relate to helping children establish themselves within a social framework that acts as a personal network for the development of a sense of identity. On the whole, schools don't do very well on the first kind of life chance for Aboriginal, Torres Strait Islander and Maori children, and perform poorly on the second. Many mainstream schools ignore the community element of education, namely—situating education within the context of mutually respectful relationships where children can develop the social bonds and a sense of identity that bind them to each other and to their family community. Many schools also foster values (such as individualism and competitiveness) that are in conflict with community values. This has the potential to set up a personal (and often unresolvable) dualism for the children. (See Folds 1987; Hohepa, Jenkins & McNaughton 1992; Jordan 1984; Malin 1990; Watts 1982; Williamson 1991.) As Folds (1987, p. 34) states:

Schools and life chances

In practice,* as anangu *are well aware, most school activities exclude community concerns and inevitably make Pitjantjatjara youth dissatisfied with their own society and culture. What most school activities have in common is that they are precisely the opposite to the bicultural ideal. Few activities at any grade level embrace community experiences, start where the children are or reinforce a positive Pitjantjatjara self-image. Most do nothing to contribute to community feeling that the school is 'theirs'. On the contrary, they reinforce beliefs among the older generation that school remains whitefella business.

The dilemma of mainstream schools is how to enhance the options for indigenous children in the wider community (i.e. giving them Western literacy and numeracy skills and work values such as competitiveness, independence, individualism, responsibility and punctuality) while also fostering values important to growing Maori or Aboriginal children (such as family ties, community bonds and cooperation) (see Teasdale & Teasdale 1993, 1994).

What can mainstream psychology contribute to our understanding?

Much mainstream psychological theorising on the importance of self-concept, identity formation, learning and cognitive styles, information processing and effective teaching (and many other factors) for effective learning can supply valuable insights in our attempt to understand the needs of these children for an education that is culturally relevant, yet appropriate to the modern world of which these communities are now a part.

In our modern theorising about the most effective ways to facilitate learning for all children, we can also learn from models characteristic of traditional Maori and Aboriginal learning styles and settings. Traditional emphases on learning through real-life performance, learning through observation and imitation, constructing knowledge holistically rather than through decontextualisation and fragmentation, and learning through cooperation and group work are not far removed from the notions of effective learning and teaching models currently being developed and fostered within Western education settings. Furthermore, the emphasis on community involvement in educational programs, a major element in Maori, Aboriginal and Torres Strait Islander schools, is being strongly encouraged in mainstream schools through the establishment of school councils (see also Townsend, Manley & Tuck 1991).

It is unlikely, in the foreseeable future, that most Aboriginal and Maori children will be educated in other than mainstream schools. Consequently, many teachers trained for mainstream schools will have the opportunity to teach Maori and Aboriginal children. How can these schools and teachers best assist these children to achieve?

Serving the needs of indigenous pupils

For schools to serve the needs of Maori children more adequately, Corson (1993) argues that they need to provide an atmosphere that encourages a sense of belonging, a family feeling of physical closeness where each student is given personal attention, praise, encouragement and the daily experience of success and accomplishment. Teachers should pay attention to the preferred learning approaches of the students so that the self-esteem of the students is enhanced. Because learning is a cooperative exercise, children, teachers, parents and *whanau* should all be involved. As oral communication is so important to traditional Maori education, opportunities should be given for oral language interaction; older children should be given the chance to assist and care for younger children within school, as they are expected to in the community at large. Schools should emphasise collaboration, cooperation and group benefit and de-emphasise competitive individualism and individual gain. Assessment and evaluation need to be designed with these collaborative goals in mind. These points also have great relevance for Aboriginal education and, in our opinion, mainstream education could equally benefit from such values.

The importance of self-esteem

As indicated above, self-esteem and confidence is an important element in orienting a child's attitude towards school. Children's sense of confidence in the school context is influenced by their expectations of success and by their performance in key academic areas. Schools, through their policies, programs and administration, must be places where indigenous minority children can experience academic success. This success, however, must not be at the expense of significant cultural values. The definition of success must be broadly based and inclusive of the cultural values of minority groups (such as cooperation and affiliation). The chapters on motivation and effective teaching supply a number of suggestions on how this might be achieved.

The role of the teacher

Positive teacher support is also very important. We believe that teachers can most help these children by giving effective feedback and recognition to students in line with their performance and by helping the students develop a sense of competence, confidence and a positive self-image within the school context. Fundamental to this is the need for teachers to have cross-cultural awareness (Bell 1986; Malin 1990).

The role of parents

Parental support and encouragement for children to do well and to continue with school is perhaps one of the most important factors influencing children's attitudes towards school. Obviously, community values are of paramount importance. If children receive messages from their cultural community that it is good to do well at school, and that their life chances will be enhanced by successful schooling, they will stand a greater chance of success. Conversely, if the community's messages indicate that success at school is at best irrelevant, and at worst inimical to their cultural identity, children will not look to the school as the arena in which to demonstrate their successes (McInerney 1993; McInerney & Swisher 1995; Folds 1987).

When indigenous children are encouraged to feel that their efforts are going to be worthwhile, when they receive support from parents and teachers, and especially when they feel capable of success, their performance improves dramatically. We all have a role in this! Throughout this book we discuss many ways of restructuring educational experiences for children so that the experiences are more sensitive to individual needs, and we emphasise the active role played by learners in constructing their knowledge of how the world works. Many of these suggestions have particular relevance for restructuring educational experiences to make them more culturally relevant and appropriate to Aboriginal, Torres Strait Islander and Maori children.

ACTION STATION

a

In groups of three or four, review a number of multicultural or bicultural education policy documents. Discuss the philosophy or rationale underlining each policy and identify the assumptions implicit in the document. Relate your findings to issues raised in this chapter.

Using this information as a basis, translate these general policy statements into specific aims suited to a school with particular characteristics (region, size, pupil/teacher characteristics to be determined by your group).

Discuss how these aims can be put into practice. This will involve a consideration of suitable content and techniques, and an evaluation of existing resources and programs.

GIFTED AND TALENTED MINORITY CHILDREN

Sternberg and Davidson (cited in Reis 1989) state that giftedness is a concept that we invent, not something we discover. As such, it is whatever a society wants it to be, making it subject to change according to time or place. Very often we think of giftedness and talent from a limited cultural perspective. Some cultures even refuse to accept the notion of giftedness (Shaughnessy 1993). As teachers we need to be very sensitive to cultural variations in the meaning and demonstration of talent and giftedness. As a simple example, from a Western cultural perspective, giftedness may be recognised in those children who are competitive and verbally fluent. Other cultural groups may not value these qualities, but rather value an individual's capacity to coordinate and lead a group while remaining in the background.

Cultural facilitation or inhibition of the development of talent

Our cultural and socioeconomic group may either facilitate or inhibit access to the means of developing particular talents. For example, children with the capacity to be gifted writers, musicians and sportspeople may be limited in their access to opportunities. Some cultural groups give little freedom to females to engage in sport or a wide range of social activities, consequently limiting the opportunity for the development of talent (Cropley 1993).

Under-representation of minority groups in programs for the gifted

Minority groups, whether they are cultural, socioeconomic or gender based, are often under-represented in special programs for the gifted (Boyd 1993; Frasier 1989). We should assume that giftedness and talent are normally distributed and we must ensure, therefore, that our methods of identifying the minority gifted and talented are not biased (Brown 1983; Feldhusen 1989; Frasier 1989). The Implementation Strategies for the Education of Gifted and Talented Students (NSW Department of School Education 1991) suggest that a wide range of methods is needed to ensure that all students who are gifted and talented are identified, particularly when identification is generally difficult. There are many reasons for this. Students, for example, may be:

- ☐ from non-English-speaking backgrounds
- ☐ Aboriginal or Maori
- ☐ disadvantaged by gender inequity
- ☐ socioeconomically disadvantaged
- ☐ disabled physically or in terms of sensory functions
- ☐ diagnosed as intellectually disabled
- ☐ conduct-disordered.

As you can see from this list, special needs blur across categories. Further complications are introduced when we realise that some students may actively disguise their giftedness and talents to maintain peer acceptance. It is commonly believed that Aboriginal students cover up their talents so that they are not perceived to be 'better than their mates'. Some students just don't like to appear different.

A CROSS-CULTURAL PERSPECTIVE ON CLASSROOM MANAGEMENT AND DISCIPLINE

In Chapter 10 we looked at general models of management and discipline. It is important at this point to pause and reflect on the extent to which these apply to a classroom that is not homogeneous in cultural background or is culturally different. In other words, how do you, if at all, modify your discipline approach to accommodate the ethnic composition of your class group? According to Partington and McCudden (1992, p. 159):

'The purpose of an effective management program should be to accommodate the needs of students in a supportive manner, not punish them for behaviours which are a consequence of their different upbringing and different perceptions of issues that gave rise to the disruptive behaviour'.

What are some of the differences that teachers may need to be aware of?

Communication with parents

Here is an example from our own experience. It was pick-up time for young Nicholas who had just started in grade 4 after moving to a new school. To his mother's polite inquiry about Nicholas's behaviour for the first week, his new young female teacher's response was that Nicholas had 'been a bit cheeky at lunchtime today', claiming that he didn't have to pick up a juice carton and put it in the garbage bin because it wasn't his. The next day Nicholas arrived at class badly bruised about the body and face, having been punished at home by his migrant parents for speaking rudely to the teacher (the bruises were the result of his insistence at home that he merely told the teacher that the carton was not his and that he had not been cheeky).

The incident sadly demonstrates how cultural background can contribute to discipline problems. Nicholas's socialisation had encouraged him to feel confident in his (male) right to assert a point of view, as did his two older brothers, especially in response to a directive issued by a female (his mother is always submissive to her husband's authority). His parents saw the incident primarily from the perspective of family dignity—in this case it was very important for the family to be accepted in the new school community, largely upper middle class Anglos (Nicholas's father was a builder and keen to make business contacts). Doing what the teacher says was one way of earning a good reputation.

The lesson learned by the teacher? To be very careful about communications given to parents about students' misbehaviour, and to be aware of the cultural 'baggage' that students bring with them to school.

Expectations about authority

Different expectations exist with regard to teacher authority. There is a danger of government policies on classroom discipline running counter to the cultural values of a number of minority groups (Lewis 1993, personal communication). For example, orthodox Jews, New Zealand Maoris and Arabic-speaking groups may take exception to the teacher engaging in dialogue with students about the rules for classroom control. After all, the teacher is expected to lead and control the classroom, and students are required to be obedient. Like the elders in these cultures, teachers represent authority. In these cultures, the philosophy is that teachers and parents must be strict and not enter into any discussion with students over misbehaviour. The authors' first-born child Alexandra, for example, is considered by her Ukrainian grandmother to be showing lack of respect to her elders when she wants to discuss the 'fairness' of a dictate: all children should show respect to authority as they did when grandmother grew up in the former USSR over 50 years ago. Today, young people are bombarded with messages that exhort them to demand an equal hearing. Conflict is often the result of the mixture of expectations that children receive from school and home.

The role of females

In some Middle Eastern and other cultures, females are traditionally accorded lower status in society and, consequently, female teachers may not be recognised as authority figures, particularly in upper primary and high school grades. Among orthodox Jews, the role of women in the decision-making process is quite clearly defined. Although the female has status and power in family matters, it is the male who makes and enforces laws (Lewis 1993, personal communication). Jewish parents may be very concerned, therefore, about their daughters being encouraged to be involved in making classroom rules—for example, in Glasser's (1992) democratic classroom meeting approach.

Teacher as educational expert

Some cultures expect the teacher to be the fount of all knowledge from whom students should receive constant help and regular homework. In a classroom where the teacher tries to encourage students to learn independently through guided discovery or inquiry-based approaches, students may feel confused about how to respond to the freedom, and react in a disorderly way. Because of their affiliation orientation, groups such as Aboriginal Australians may prefer collaboration to individualised work where students sit one to a desk. Teachers may respond to the 'sharing of ideas' by some groups of students as plagiarism. Negative comments from parents regarding the appropriateness of various 'new' teaching strategies may also undermine teacher authority.

There may also be a clash when the teacher, perceived as an expert in a limited area (formal school curriculum), presumes to act as an expert in culturally sensitive areas. For example, while the Pitjantjatjara are willing to accept the prerogative of teachers in English and maths, they are very resentful of teachers attempting to teach the Aboriginal languages and cultural traditions, which they believe is their prerogative. Furthermore, they ultimately believe that they have the right to authorise the content of much that is taught in the school so that it does not conflict with cultural values. The tension existing over who is the appropriate expert at particular times can flow over into classroom interactions between teacher and students, with students disparaging the teacher's efforts and expertise (Folds 1987).

On the other hand, parents of some groups such as Arabic-speaking children do not believe it is their place to question the teacher about class or school issues; in fact, they may feel quite inadequate educationally to do so. As Campbell et al. (1992, p. 62) comments, 'a lack of understanding of the Australian school system makes [Arabic-speaking parents] reluctant to be directly involved with the school'. This attitude may translate to Anglo teachers as lack of interest and set the stage for poor communication.

Some students may have been socialised not to 'argue' with the teacher nor to indicate that they are having difficulty. These students may not give explanations for incomplete work nor show that they are confused.

'Good manners' and proper behaviour

Differences in values and the nature of interpersonal communication resulting from socialisation within particular cultural groups can lead to severe clashes between teacher and students (Malin 1990). Values such as autonomy, social equality and affiliation may be demonstrated quite differently across cultural groups. Teacher-established behavioural norms for these values may conflict with those of culturally different students. As Malin (p. 318) states:

The autonomous and affiliative orientation of many of the Aboriginal students [in her study] was evident in their responses to classroom life in quite remarkable ways. The unfortunate thing was that the teachers were largely unaware that they were witnessing culturally based expressions of a particular competence which

had been valued in these children's previous four years at home. Instead some expressions of this autonomy were interpreted, by one teacher in particular, as disrespect for her, as defiance, and as a lack of acceptance of the legitimacy of her role as teacher.

Illustrating from her case study, Malin goes on to say that the autonomous orientation of many Aboriginal students means, at times, that they ignore teacher directives, either by delaying their response, not responding at all, or walking away from teachers while they are in the process of addressing them. The children are oblivious initially to the teacher's expectations that they maintain eye contact while being addressed and then acknowledge that they have heard and understood what was being said to them. These behaviours are not meant to be disrespectful, but rather illustrate the children's need for a degree of self-regulation, and their feeling of proprietorship for their classroom. Their slowness at complying carries the assumption, brought from home, that within certain bounds, adults and children hold mutual respect for each other.

The manner in which students respond to a teacher's question may also be a reflection of cultural background and this can get them into trouble. For example, in Pitjantjatjara society respect is shown to another person by inclining the head away and making infrequent eye contacts (e.g. see Folds 1987). Teachers, however, may regard the downcast eyes as an indication of insolence and insist that the student 'Look at me when I speak to you!'. The teacher's response may compound the problem so that, in retaliation, students may engage in a highly exaggerated form of avoidance, characterised by a complete lack of eye contact or any other form of recognition (Folds 1987; Malin 1990).

Folds (1987; see also Munns 1996) highlights forms of behaviour that Aboriginal students engage in when attempting to resist culturally different expectations of behaviour—absenteeism, and classroom resistance consisting of ridicule and disruption, and the 'wall of silence'. The most pervasive form is the 'wall of silence' when students refuse to communicate with the teacher, failing to respond to the teacher's solicitations or directions to do something.

Forms of resistance behaviour

Language and effective communication

Students who come to school with little or no English can become uncooperative and troublesome if they experience ridicule for mistakes with language. It is desirable for such students to be allocated a 'buddy' who is prepared to offer friendship and who will encourage conversation that focuses on meaning rather than correctness. Teachers should take care with polite expressions they may use in the classroom which really communicate a more assertive message. For example, saying 'You might like to finish this ... for homework' may be taken literally by some students who are less familiar with subtleties of the language.

'Well, Eddie, I was speaking figuratively when I said to get out there and tear them apart.'

It is important to remember that many minority group students who come in as refugees, especially the older ones, have already received a significant proportion of their education before their arrival in our schools and, in some cases, this may have been at a standard in advance of the rest of their class. It can be very demoralising and frustrating for these students to find, for example, that numerical notation or the direction of writing and reading have to be unlearned or, at least, relearned in a new form. (The division symbol in Vietnam is (:), the multiplication sign in Chile is (.) and the decimal marker in Laos is (,).)

Frustration felt by such students, aggravated by teacher impatience and student ridicule, can erupt into misbehaviour. Sometimes these students are inappropriately placed into lower ability groups on the basis of achievement and psychological tests. It is important to make an accurate diagnosis of the 'slow learner' as distinct from the student with 'inadequate English'. Research on the factors contributing to Aboriginal and ethnic

Inappropriate streaming of minority children

minority group disenchantment and dropping out of school has shown that incorrectly streaming minority group children into low ability groups is one of the major contributors to their entry into the cycle of self-defeating problem behaviours in school (McInerney & McInerney 1990; see also Simkin 1991).

Taboos

Many groups have cultural **taboos**. The head is considered by a number of Asian cultures as an altar to their ancestors and the fount of the mind or soul. Thus, patting the head of a student or waving something over it would be regarded as disrespectful, as would standing over someone who is seated. Others consider the left hand the 'toilet' hand and its use in handing something to another person in class or at meal times would be seen as quite vulgar (NSW Department of School Education 1990).

In some cultures, such as the Muslim, females are strictly constrained and not permitted to expose their bodies in public. This creates difficulty in a number of school-related areas to do with participation in sporting activities such as swimming and those involving contact with males, as well as participation in sex education lessons and excursions.

ESTABLISHING EFFECTIVE MANAGEMENT IN CULTURALLY MIXED CLASSROOMS

Some words of qualification should be noted about the concerns expressed above. It is clear that significant cultural differences may exacerbate discipline and management problems in some classrooms. There is a danger, however, in making generalisations about groups based on stereotypes.

Some minority group students (such as Aboriginal and Maori), who may have little confidence in themselves as students in the mainstream educational system, and who see little value in education generally, may be predisposed to misbehave or drop out. In these cases, discipline based on the behaviourist model of reward and punishment will be ineffective as this focuses on the end product, the problem behaviour or lack of it, rather than the cause of the problem.

Fostering a positive classroom climate

What is the answer to the dilemma of establishing effective discipline in culturally mixed classrooms? The teacher's task in the first instance is to foster a classroom climate that is responsive to differing student learning styles. This can be achieved by systematically varying teaching methods and activities to accommodate student differences. In this way all students can experience cooperative grouping, individual work, peer tutoring, structured and informal discussions, and questioning in accordance with their cultural expectations (Simkin 1991). In cross-cultural classrooms, cooperative learning structures are superior to those that focus on competition and individualistic goals in fostering positive relationships between different groups (Johnson & Johnson 1989b). Where such positive attitudes and relationships flourish, discipline problems will diminish (Abrami et al. 1995)

There needs to be a compromise between the teacher adopting a laissez-faire policy which allows all forms of behaviour in the classroom and an autocratic one in which the conventions of the majority culture rule (Simkin 1991). This compromise is reached through negotiation within the classroom as to the rules that are acceptable and that will encourage harmony and effective learning. This is preferable to forcing students into behaving in ways that they see as culturally 'wrong', wherein lies the potential for tension and hostility.

Establishing mutual respect

For successful management in culturally diverse classrooms, the effective teacher must establish an environment built on genuine mutual respect where difference and similarity are equally valued. An important factor in this process is that of building self-esteem in all students, regardless of cultural background. The teacher fosters the development of positive attitudes in a variety of ways: by acting as a model for positive behaviour through avoiding ridicule and punishment; by providing opportunities for all students to demonstrate proficiency in some area that is not necessarily academic; by the use of cooperative grouping for class activities (Cohen 1994) as well as other means of ensuring interaction between students such as shared interests; and by establishing rules for class behaviour, ideally derived from democratic classroom decisions. The difficulties in actually implementing such an approach have been examined earlier.

Consulting with parents

It is strongly recommended that opportunities be made for consultation between school and parents about the issues of greatest concern with regard to classroom discipline. As Lewis recommends, both groups need to identify which cultural values are 'not negotiable' (the complexity of this becomes obvious when there are many minority groups within the one school). Both sides must resolve a way of accommodating such values. One option is separate schooling, which has been suggested by some Maori and Aboriginal groups as the most effective solution for their dissatisfaction with the mainstream education system (Folds 1987; Lewis 1990; Teasdale & Teasdale 1993).

Separate culturally based schools

It is interesting to note here that by far the majority of Arabic-speaking parents choose to send their children to single-sex schools (Campbell, personal communication, March 1992) rather than having to compromise on cultural ideas. This is in keeping with one interpretation of what a multicultural society is: one within which cultural groups have the right to maintain their individual identity, and not have to adopt the ideals of the majority. Another view is that a truly multicultural society is one in which 'intercultural' understanding and interaction takes place and, as such, all groups give some ground. When applied to the area of classroom discipline, this approach would mean that minority and majority groups alike need to expose students to all the options, even if one is more strongly endorsed. Thus, Muslim and Jewish girls may be prevented from participation in decision making if this is requested by parents; however, they should be made aware that the process of democratic decision making is the one that is endorsed by the state in the country in which their parents have chosen to settle.

Are there universals to guide teachers in ethnically diverse classrooms?

There has been considerable research over the last two decades seeking evidence for (or against) the existence of psychological universals—for example, universal patterns in cognitive development, learning strategies and motivation (Thomas 1994; Keats 1994; McInerney 1994; McInerney, McInerney & Roche 1994a, b; McInerney et al. 1977). We have reviewed some of this research in other chapters. The value in seeking for universals is that, if it can be demonstrated that similar psychological features apply to groups irrespective of ethnic background, universal educational practices can be applied. This is, of course, controversial. Some argue that such an approach would inevitably lead to the diverse needs of students being masked or neglected. What do you think?

The present authors and colleagues have attempted to establish whether there are universal characteristics of school motivation (McInerney & McInerney 1996; McInerney, Roche, McInerney & Marsh 1997; McInerney, Hinkley & Dowson 1996). Our findings suggest that the motivational profiles of the diverse groups studied are more similar than different. We also found that key variables used to distinguish Western and indigenous groups (such as level of competition and affiliation) do not appear to be salient in the school contexts studied.

As a result of our work we suggest that classrooms and schools will be effective for all children if they emphasise mastery goals, encourage the development in individuals of a positive sense of self as a student, and foster programs that stress goal setting. In particular, schools and classrooms should provide their students with experience in personal goal setting and in monitoring progress in carrying out plans for goal achievement. Unfortunately, many schools and classrooms emphasise performance and extrinsic goals through competition and social comparison, ability grouping and tracking, public evaluation of performance and conduct based on normative standards of performance, and give children little opportunity to cooperate and interact with other children or to choose the tasks that are of most interest and relevance to them.

In contrast, classrooms and schools that emphasise mastery are likely to group students according to interest and needs, allow flexibility in choice of activities and in opportunities for student initiative and responsibility, define success in terms of effort, progress and improvement, put an emphasis on the value and interest of learning, and give opportunities for peer interaction and cooperation. Ethnic minority children in these classrooms are likely to be highly motivated, set themselves meaningful and challenging goals of achievement, and persist at these tasks for the perceived benefits that will accrue to them.

TABLE 12.3

ESSENTIALS OF CLASSROOM PRACTICES TO ENHANCE THE LEARNING OF CHILDREN FROM DIFFERENT CULTURAL BACKGROUNDS

For teachers

- Empower students to direct their own learning.
- Facilitate meaningful parent and community participation in decision making.
- Embed learning within culturally valued knowledge and experiences (such as learning historiography through a study of one's own group, or music from one's culture).
- Situate learning within culturally appropriate social situations (such as teacher/student interactions that are consistent with cultural values and practices).
- Establish an environment built on genuine mutual respect where difference and similarity are equally valued.

- Foster a classroom climate that is responsive to differing student learning styles (in particular, ways of knowing, understanding, representing and expressing typically employed in a particular culture).
- Include culturally appropriate curriculum content and instructional processes.

(based on Hollins 1996)

Question point: What might some essentials be from the learner's perspective?

Recommended reading

Corson, D. (1993) Restructing minority schooling. *Australian Journal of Education*, 37, 46–68.

Folds, R. (1987) *Whitefella School*. Sydney: Allen & Unwin.

Garcia, E. E. (1993) Language, culture, and education. *Review of Research in Education*, 19, 51–98.

Hollins, E. R. (1996) *Culture in School Learning. Revealing the Deep Meaning*. Mahway, NJ: Lawrence Erlbaum.

McInerney, D. M., Roche, L., McInerney, V. & Marsh, H. W. (1997) Cultural perspectives on school motivation: The relevance and application of goal theory. *American Educational Research Journal*, 34, 207–36.

McInerney, D.M. (1987) Teacher attitudes to multicultural curriculum development. *Australian Journal of Education*, 31, 129–44.

Malin, M. (1990) The visibility and invisibility of Aboriginal students in an urban classroom. *Australian Journal of Education*, 34, 312–29.

Partington, G. & McCudden, V. (1992) *Ethnicity and Education*. Wentworth Falls: Social Science Press.

Rogoff, B. & Chavajay, P. (1995) What's become of research on the cultural basis of cognitive development? *American Psychologist*, 50, 859–77.

Smolic, J. J. (1991) Language, culture and the school in a plural society: An Australian perspective for the 1990s. *Migration Monitor*, 23–24, 3–15.

Thomas, E. (1994) (ed.) *International Perspectives on Culture and Schooling: A Symposium Proceedings*. University of London Institute of Education: Department of International and Comparative

Measurement and evaluation for effective learning

CHAPTER 13

OVERVIEW

Measurement and evaluation are integral parts of the teaching and learning process. In this chapter we address such important questions as:

- What is measurement and how does it differ from evaluation?
- Why do we measure and evaluate student learning?
- What are the available methods of measurement and evaluation, what are their strengths and weaknesses, and how do we report the results?

With increasing concern over educational standards, quality assurances and accountability, teachers and schools are obliged to implement strategies of measurement and evaluation that are based upon the best available information. We hope to present you with such information in this chapter , equipping you to choose from a wide range of sound measurement and evaluation practices. In particular, we aim to help you develop a critical and reflective attitude to measurement and evaluation.

This description of measurement and evaluation reflects our view that education must be matched to individual needs. Clearly, both processes need to take into account the diversity of our students and the diversity of educational goals.

LEARNER-CENTRED PSYCHOLOGICAL PRINCIPLE 11

Setting appropriately high and challenging standards and assessing the learner as well as the learning progress—including diagnostic, process, and outcome assessment—are integral parts of the learning process.

... (T)o improve educational outcomes for all learners, one has to create a learner-centred assessment system that requires high standards for each student for each goal, individually negotiated by the student and the teacher. Also, a classroom instructional program is needed that helps students to achieve learner-centred standards. Assessments can be based on a variety of evidence about student achievement, which might include folios, projects, and performance. The critical differences between (a) a learner-centred assessment system based on goals and (b) standards established by the local community and implemented by teachers is that by involving learners in the process, only the learner-centred system promises consideration of the diversity of the nation's communities and school children in the redesign of schools. In this context, assessments are products—ways students have chosen to demonstrate their developing competencies and achievement of learning standards.

Reprinted with permission, APA Task Force on Psychology in Education (1993, January), p. 15.

BOX 13.1 TEACHING COMPETENCE

The teacher knows the educational basis and role of assessment in teaching

Indicators

The teacher:

- justifies assessment processes and strategies in terms of planned student learning outcomes;
- uses assessment procedures consistent with content and process goals;
- values collaborative approaches with parents and others in assessing student progress;
- plans and conducts assessment in accordance with school policies;
- is aware of ethical and legal issues relating to the collection and use of assessment data.

Case studies illustrating National Competency Framework for Beginning Teaching, National Project on the Quality of Teaching and Learning, Australian Teaching Council, 1996, Element 4.1, p. 55. Commonwealth of Australia copyright, reproduced by permission.

MEASUREMENT AND EVALUATION—GENERAL PRINCIPLES

Measurement: collecting data

Evaluation: qualitative judgments on data

In Western societies the measurement of children begins early. From infancy onwards, caregivers and other concerned people weigh, measure, poke and prod youngsters to assess whether or not they are growing and developing according to norms or other expected standards. In this sense the process of **measurement** relates to collecting specific quantitative data which might be in centimetres, kilograms, number of erupted teeth, heart rate or visual acuity (Gronlund 1985). In the context of education, measurement usually refers to marks obtained on tests or other pieces of work set by the teacher. In this context these measurements are often referred to as *assessment*. **Evaluation**, on the other hand, refers to the quality, value or worth of the information gathered (Gronlund 1985; Mager 1990a, 1990b). So while a child might weigh 15 kilograms (an objective measurement), he or she might be evaluated as being scrawny or pudgy (a subjective, 'evaluative' judgment). To make the interpretation less subjective other criteria (such as age norms) need to be applied to make the evaluation. Within a class, an individual's score of 80 on a mathematics test may indicate average, below average or above average performance (relative to the rest of those being tested or to some other criteria).

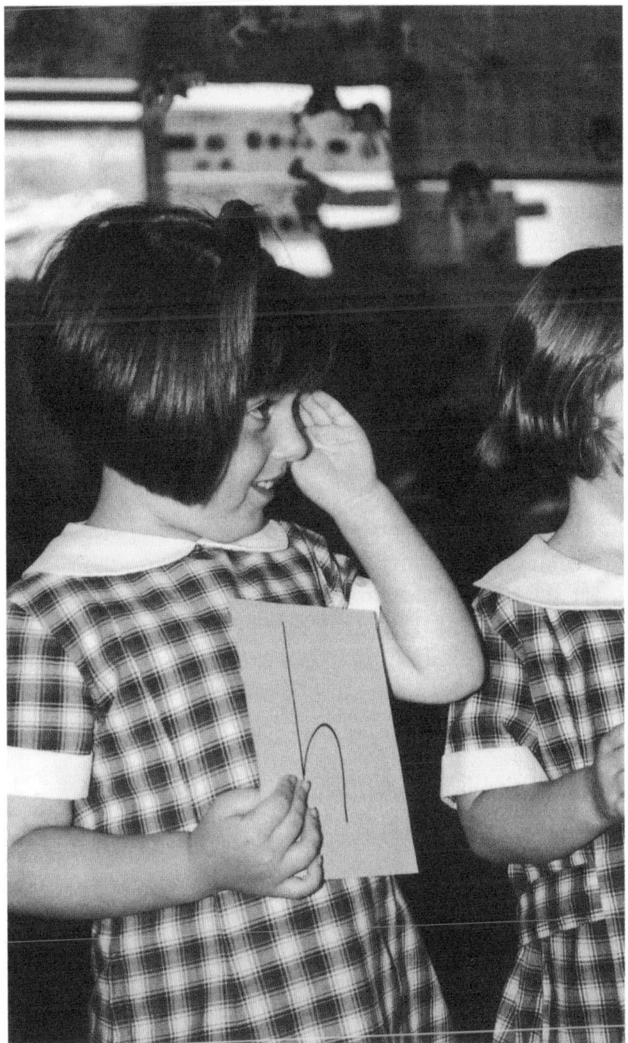

In Western society the public evaluation of learning begins early. Photo: authors

Furthermore, the score may be interpreted in terms of the individual's perceived ability and motivation, such that the performance may be evaluated as representing under-achievement for a child who was expected to do much better, irrespective of class norms. In this latter case we are talking about the evaluation based on the measurement. It is clear that it is the evaluation element that is of most importance, but this must be based on valid and reliable measurement.

What is validity in measurement?

We generally use the term **validity** in measurement to refer to whether we are indeed *measuring what we intend to measure*. More importantly, validity refers to the *appropriateness* of a measure for the specific inferences or decisions that result from the scores generated by the measure (Griffin & Nix 1991; McMillan 1992; Messick 1989; Moss 1992). If we wish to describe pupil achievement we should be confident that our interpretations are based on a dependable measure, do not exceed the limits of the measure, and are appropriate to the intentions of the measurement's use.

Validity: appropriateness of measure

Various types of evidence may be accrued to support the validity of measurements (Gronlund 1985; Messick 1989; Moss 1992; Shepard 1993). Among the evidence that may be used to support the validity of a particular measurement are face, content, criterion and construct evidence.

Face validity evidence indicates that the assessment task, at least on the surface, measures what it purports to measure (Sprinthall, Schmutte & Sirois 1991). It is a relatively low-level indicator of validity, but it is, nevertheless, an important starting point. Imagine answering a test on your mathematical knowledge in which all the questions seemed to relate to issues only tangentially connected with mathematics. You would probably question the usefulness and relevance of the test in terms of its expressed aims, and perhaps not answer it seriously or carefully.

Face validity evidence: making the test look right

Content validity evidence is provided when measurement activities reflect the appropriate domain of study. In other words, the activity should match as closely as possible the objectives of the teaching for which it was designed. If a teacher wishes to test mathematical reasoning, the questions should be selected from the same content and examples covered in the teaching.

Content validity evidence: choosing assessment items from the appropriate domain

Criterion validity evidence is provided when the results of specific measurement tasks converge with the results of other measurement tasks. For example, we might be interested in comparing individual performances on a particular test with other evidence of performance—completion of a practical activity, position in class, teacher rankings—to see if our test is measuring the same underlying quality. In each of these cases we are establishing a benchmark with which to assess how well our measurement techniques 'measure up' (McMillan & Schumacher 1989). If the data from our measurements are compared at the same time and lead to the same conclusions about the individual's performance, the evidence from each is called **concurrent validity**. When the data are able to predict a criterion such as school performance or job promotion we can say that the measurement provides **predictive** evidence for its validity.

Criterion validity evidence: comparing results with other evidence

At times, educators and researchers design questionnaires to measure psychological constructs such as competitiveness, self-concept, figural intelligence, creativity or computer anxiety. When researchers wish to establish that the questions designed to measure a dimension such as self-concept do measure this underlying theoretical construct in a systematic way, they may use a statistical procedure called factor analysis. When procedures such as factor analysis are used to support the underlying dimensions being measured by a test, we speak of establishing **construct validity** evidence. **Factor analysis** is a statistical procedure used to discover a structure within a larger number of variables. It does this by reducing the larger set of variables to a smaller number of more basic composite variables called factors. These resulting factors summarise the essential information contained in all the original variables (Ferguson & Takane 1989; Kleinbaum, Kupper & Muller 1988).

Construct validity evidence: what construct underlines the test?

Factor analysis is well beyond the scope of this book. For our purposes a simpler method of establishing construct validity of assessment tasks in the classroom context might be used. For example, if we design a test to measure mechanical aptitude we should be able to use the data obtained from testing individuals to classify them as either more or less mechanically able. To the extent that our classification is supported by external evidence (such as performance in mechanical tasks), we have evidence of the construct validity of the test (Tuckman 1988).

What is reliability in measurement?

As well as being concerned with issues of validity in measurement and evaluation, teachers must also be concerned that their measurements and evaluations of students are reliable—that is, stable and consistent over time.

Reliability: consistency and stability of measure

There are four common methods used to assess reliability: measures of stability, equivalence, internal consistency and intermarker reliability (Collis 1989; McMillan & Schumacher 1989; McMillan 1992). A coefficient of **stability** is provided by testing and retesting the same individuals after a period (so that the second results are not affected by practice). If the correlation between the two tests is high, it shows a consistent response by the individuals to the test on two separate occasions. In other words, those who scored high on the first occasion also scored high on the second, and so on.

Methods of assessing reliability

Stability: are similar scores obtained on separate testings?

When two equivalent or parallel forms of the same test are administered to a group at about the same time and the scores are related, the reliability that results is a coefficient of **equivalence**.

Internal consistency may be established by splitting the items in a test into comparable halves and correlating individuals' performances on both halves of the test. If students perform comparably on both halves of the test then the test has high reliability. Other forms of the internal consistency measure, such as the Kuder-Richardson techniques and the Cronbach Alpha, measure the degree to which the individual item responses correlate with the total score. The score is considered reliable if a high index is obtained as this indicates that each item is contributing to the total score (Collis 1989).

Internal consistency: are scores on comparable halves of the test similar?

When the scores of two markers are correlated (or the judgment of one person on the same test on two separate occasions is correlated), we have an index of **intermarker reliability**.

Intermaker reliability: are scores obtained from different, markers similar?

Each of these forms of reliability has strengths and weaknesses that are well described in introductory educational research texts. If a test is unreliable it cannot be valid. Can you suggest why?

CLASSROOM IMPLICATIONS OF MEASUREMENT VALIDITY AND RELIABILITY

As we have stated, teachers and educators must be concerned that the measures they use are both valid and reliable. Commercially available testing instruments (such as those supplied by Australian Council of Educational Research (ACER) and New Zealand Council of Educational Research (NZCER) and basic skills tests used by some education departments are usually rigorously tested for validity and reliability. Some of these tests may be administered only by qualified counsellors or psychologists. Other tests may be administered by classroom teachers. ACER and NZCER will supply a catalogue of tests to interested parties. If we choose to use one of these commercial tests then we must make sure that we use it according to the instructions supplied and interpret the results within the constraints of the test protocols.

Many standardised tests have fallen into disfavour because they are perceived as invalid for particular classroom use. The real problem often lies in their inappropriate use and the inappropriate (invalid) interpretations that result (Griffin & Nix 1991). Standardised tests can, however, play a useful role in student measurement and evaluation.

Teacher-made measurement tasks: issues of validity

Teachers in Australia and New Zealand more often depend on teacher-made tests and measurement tasks to measure student learning than on commercially available ones (Stiggins 1985). Unfortunately, many teachers develop these tests and measurement tasks without giving much thought to issues of validity, and fall into the trap of relying on the face validity of their tests and measurement procedures (Stiggins 1985). Teachers should evaluate the content and, where appropriate, the criterion validity of their tasks (Griffin & Nix 1991). What does this mean in practice? Let's look first at content validity.

Measurement and context

Learning is situated in a particular context. A teacher may, for example, wish to teach the addition of two and three digit numbers. Various practice examples, such as 356 + 21 are given, with additional drill exercises completed by the students. In order to measure the students' mastery of this particular addition process the teacher may set a number of problems of the kind: 'John was building a rectangular wall with a length 150 metres and a width 38 metres. How far was it around the wall?' On the face of it the problem involves simply the addition of two and three digit numbers, the process already drilled by the children. The poor performance of the children on this and similar problems may not reflect their lack of understanding of the addition process, but rather indicate that the test lacks instructional content validity. In effect, there are dimensions to the task in the test of the process that were not part of the original teaching procedure—dimensions such as the verbal presentation of the problem, and the extra calculation required to measure the length of the perimeter. In another example, if a final test uses essay questions to assess higher-order thinking skills, then similar essay questions should have been used throughout the learning program. Imagine you have just completed twelve practical lessons on how to swim freestyle. As the final test to accredit your achievement, you are given a written theoretical test on correct strokes, breathing, kicking and mouth-to-mouth resuscitation. How valid would you consider the test?

The measurement activities must be relevant to the teacher's goals of measurement and evaluation. For example, if you wish to sort out students who can write fluently and stylishly about current affairs, it would be inappropriate to examine their knowledge of current affairs by a multiple choice test (Biggs & Moore 1993).

Teacher measurement and criterion validity

Teachers should also use **criterion validity** to evaluate their measurement activities. It should be common practice for teachers to cross-reference results on a particular activity or task with a variety of other information available on the students' performance. In other words, a particular measurement should be validated against other criteria. Criteria may include other tests and assessments already completed by the children, as well as former reports and results. Any anomalies such as a poor result in the face of generally good performances should be carefully scrutinised to evaluate whether this reflects a truly poor performance or a poorly designed measurement activity.

Measurement tasks and predictive validity

When relevant, indicators of **predictive validity** may also be used. For example, there should be a relationship between the school-based marks obtained by students in the final school examination and those obtained in the external examination. When there is a gross difference, one could suspect that the school-based procedures used to assess the students are not valid for the purpose. There may be occasional discrepancies when a particular individual performance is affected by sickness, nerves or (hopefully more likely) an extra spurt of motivation at the end. In general, however, there should be a considerable degree of concurrence between school-based measurement and that achieved in the external exams.

RELIABILITY IN THE CLASSROOM CONTEXT

Teacher biases and marking

We would be very concerned if we tested children one day with a particular test and, on a subsequent occasion, using the same or a similar test, found that the

'Before we begin the task, Miss, the class wants to know if it comes with a guarantee?'

results were wildly different. We would also be concerned if different markers varied widely in their marking of similar pieces of work. A series of classic studies (Starch & Elliott 1912, 1913, cited in Biggs & Telfer 1987a) investigated the reliability of English, history and geometry assessment through tests. A total of 180 teachers graded two English papers per student on a 100-point scale, with 75 as a pass mark. The range in marks for one of the English papers was 47 points (50% to 97%). Similar results were found in the marking of geometry and geography papers. In effect, teachers were looking for different evidence of achievement (e.g. neatness, spelling, punctuation, showing calculations) and hence the measurements were quite unreliable. One of the most important findings from these studies was the discovery that subjectivity in marking was not confined to a particular subject. Individual grades tended to reflect the individual standards of the marker, and the unreliability of the scoring procedure.

Frame of reference effect and marking

In a study of the interaction between markers' handwriting clarity and the neatness of examination papers, the researchers found that markers with neat writing downgraded untidy essays heavily, while markers who were untidy writers were not influenced by the neatness of the essays (Huck & Bounds 1972). We are also aware that a **frame of reference effect** operates for markers and that the one marker can vary substantially in applying criteria of assessment depending on the number of pieces of work being assessed and the quality of surrounding work. For example, if a piece of work is marked in the context of very good pieces of work it may be graded down; on the other hand, if the same piece of work is graded in the context of poor pieces of work it might be graded up (Hales & Tokar 1975).

Naturally, we would want to have some faith in the consistency of the measures we take. If we are measuring students' learning for the purpose of academic ranking or streaming of some kind it is essential that we take more than one measurement to ensure that the results are consistent from one test to the next (or from one marker to another). When results are consistent (within an acceptable range) we can be happy that our measurements are reliable and proceed with the ranking. On the other hand, if there are considerable differences, we must question whether we are using reliable measuring devices and continue with further measurement. Note, even when the two measurement devices produce the same results, we cannot be sure that they are valid—validity depends on other criteria. However, when measurements produce inconsistent student results, as well as being unreliable, they must also be invalid. Can you see why? Appropriate measures of reliability that can be used in the classroom are measures of stability, equivalence and interjudge reliability.

It is not unreasonable to have another teacher periodically check on our measurement of students' work in order to evaluate how reliable we are. We often 'double mark' student work in a team and compare our ratings on important measurement tasks. Across-the-grade marking of standardised measurement tasks can also alleviate marker subjectivity. Remember, our measurements, and the evaluations we make on the basis of them, have a profound impact on children; we owe it to them to be reliable and valid in our measurement.

Collaborative checks on teacher measurements

WHY AND HOW DO WE MEASURE AND EVALUATE STUDENTS?

By now you are familiar with some of the technical issues associated with valid and reliable measurement, but we haven't directly addressed the issue of *why* teachers need to measure and evaluate. Perhaps this seems too obvious; after all, as teachers we want to know whether we are being successful and whether the children in our care are learning. Table 13.1 outlines some of the reasons typically given for measuring and evaluating our students.

TABLE 13.1

REASONS FOR MEASURING AND EVALUATING STUDENTS

- Measurement and evaluation help to clarify goals and objectives and can serve as a means of improving learning and instruction and as an incentive to increase student effort.
- Measurement and evaluation enable the teacher to give feedback to students, in particular about strengths and areas where further study is needed. It provides a record of achievement.
- Measurement and evaluation enable teachers to determine whether the processes of teaching and learning are effective, and whether other approaches to teaching and learning should be introduced or whether there should be a change in goals.
- Measurement and evaluation give information to parents. Teachers are accountable to parents for the quality of education their children are receiving.
- Measurement and evaluation are used to assist with the selection and certification of students for special

classes and programs. They are also used to predict later scholastic and career performance.

- Measurement and evaluation are used by teachers and schools as a performance indicator to the funding and employing bodies. As such, they serve an administrative function to help to determine the competency of teachers and to evaluate schools.

(see Gronlund 1985; Natriello & Dornbusch 1984; Slavin 1989, 1991; Withers & Cornish 1985)

What do you think of these arguments for measurement and evaluation? In relation to grading, some educators believe that grades have only a limited value as motivators, and are only really effective with those students who receive good grades (Yelon & Weinstein 1977; see also Airasian 1995). Low grades can be interpreted as a form of punishment, or can become a source of anxiety and frustration, and, as such, turn many children off school. The scramble for good grades (when only a few can achieve them) may result in unhealthy competition and cheating. Grades, as a form of extrinsic motivation, may diminish the student's desire to learn for its own sake (see Chapter 9).

Formative and summative measurement and evaluation

Measurement and evaluation may be either formative or summative (Scriven 1967). **Formative measurement** and evaluation refers to the continuous monitoring of the teaching/learning process to ensure its effectiveness, and to ascertain whether other approaches to teaching and learning should be introduced, or whether there should be a change in goals. Hence, the **process of learning** is of central importance, and rapid feedback is given to students to facilitate their mastery of the material to be learnt, where appropriate, or scaffolding by the teacher in the case of exploratory learning. Essentially, formative evaluation asks the questions:

Formative evaluation: emphasis on the process of learning

- ☐ How well are the students learning?
- ☐ What are they learning?
- ☐ What do they need to know?
- ☐ What can they do?
- ☐ What do they appear not to understand?

Key elements in the process are listed below:

Observe

- ☐ Are students asking questions and answering questions?
- ☐ Are students completing the assigned work in the set time?
- ☐ Are students showing interest and involvement in what they are doing?

Listen

- ☐ What is being said to you and other students about the learning tasks?
- ☐ What is the relevance and depth of the questions that students ask, and what is the nature of the answers that they give?
- ☐ Is there a voluntary contribution of ideas, and how do these relate to what the students are doing?

Test

- ☐ Can the students do what is required?
- ☐ What shortcomings are there in students' understanding and achievement?

Questionnaires

- ☐ What do students say when they are given an opportunity to evaluate the learning experience?
- ☐ How do students rate various aspects of the instruction, such as teacher performance, materials, assessment?

Summative measurement and evaluation refers to the process of determining whether or not learners have achieved the ultimate learning objectives that have been set up in advance. As such, summative measurement will typically consist of assessment items such as a test, assignment or presentation that represents what the student has learnt to that stage. At this point the emphasis is placed on the achievement of the student rather than the process of learning and teaching that lead to it. Unfortunately, many teachers overemphasise summative measurement and evaluation and fail to monitor the teaching/learning process adequately. As a consequence, opportunities to make corrective adjustments to teaching practices, which may have facilitated a better performance, are missed.

Summative evaluation: emphasis on the product of learning

We add here that, while evaluation tends to emphasise the student learning component, formative and summative evaluation should also apply equally to the teacher's role, materials used and goals set.

Norm-referenced measurement and evaluation

At times, educators may need to compare the achievement of students with other students or with established norms of achievement. This occurs, for example, when large numbers of students are ranked for specific purposes such as access to special school programs. When this is done it is an example of **norm-referenced measurement and evaluation.** Most commercially available achievement tests are norm-referenced. During the construction of these tests

Norm-referenced: comparing student achievement with other students

large numbers of students (similar to those on whom the tests are later to be used) are tested, and norms representing average performance by age or grade are developed so that individuals sitting for the test at a later time can be compared with these averages. Because these tests represent standards with which individuals can be compared (and the scores obtained by individuals are directly comparable to one another) they are often called **standardised tests.** Standardised tests are carefully constructed to provide accurate, meaningful information on students' levels of achievement or performance relative to the standardising group. The process of standardising such tests is beyond the scope of this text and interested readers are referred to texts such as Aiken (1979).

An important element of these tests is that the distribution of performance is often constrained by statistical procedures so that it follows a **normal distribution.** Simply speaking, this means that there is a large number of students who perform in an average fashion with decreasing numbers performing very well and very poorly. The normal distribution follows a bell-shaped curve and a particular student's score is plotted against this curve to indicate whether he or she is performing about average, above average or below average. Judgments based on standardised tests are used for selection and placement of students, diagnosis of learning difficulties, evaluation of achievement and, increasingly, as indicators of school and teacher performance (a form of accountability measure). The figure below indicates the normal curve and the distribution of scores that are located at various standard deviations from the mean.

Apart from commercially available tests, teacher measurements may also be norm-referenced. Whenever a teacher compares an individual's score with the average score of the class on an activity, he or she is using a norm-referenced approach. The focus is on relative performance and, as such, the definition of a good performance or a poor performance is determined by the group's mean and standard deviation (which is a measure of the dispersal of scores around the mean). Hence, a score of 70% on a maths test may represent a relatively good or poor score when compared with the average.

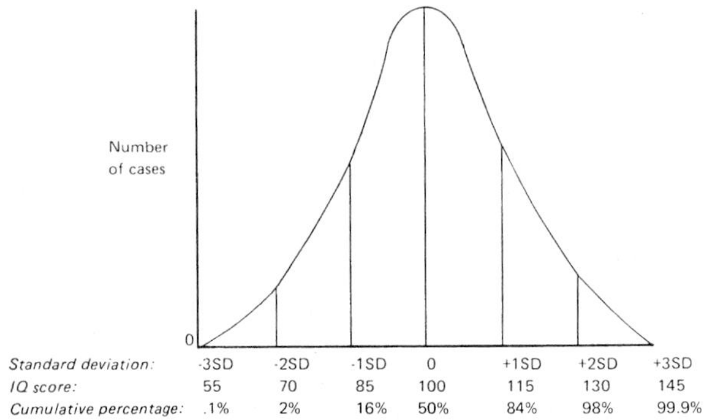

The normal curve

Are there problems with norm-referenced measurement and evaluation? Standardised tests have a number of potential problems relating to their norms. First, it is important that norms be continually updated so that the measurement obtained appropriately reflects what the children know. Second, it is important that norms reflect the background cultural and social experiences of the children being tested. Unfortunately, some standardised tests are not frequently updated and therefore, the interpretation of the measurement scores obtained by children must be interpreted with care. The norms in some tests are not sensitive to cultural backgrounds, so children from culturally different backgrounds may be disadvantaged. Furthermore, the manner in which these tests are conducted (e.g. in English, and usually through a paper and pen format) may be inappropriate for some children.

Teacher-produced norm-referenced measurement and evaluation may present a number of problems for the teacher, particularly when a procedure called **grading on the curve** is used. With this procedure, an implicit assumption is held that the distribution of grades should follow a normal distribution. For example, we are all aware that classes vary in ability from year to year, and we are also aware that so-called parallel classes are often anything but equivalent in ability. So we can have the anomalous situation of children who perform objectively no worse than other children (in previous years or in parallel grades) being graded lower because their particular reference group scores higher. Statistical procedures are available to moderate this potential problem.

Grading on the curve

In relatively homogeneous classes where there is little difference in achievement or ability among the children (they may all be high achievers or slow learners), the application of grading on the curve is not appropriate. In such cases, we may be constrained to award low grades to some children irrespective of what they have actually achieved. Very few classes are large enough or diverse enough in ability for grading on the curve to be defensible.

A further problem or limitation results from the fact that, in general, grades derived from typical norm-referenced measurement techniques (such as aggregated test marks) cannot be used to describe the specific competencies a student may or may not have. This is particularly the case when measurement procedures sample only a small area of the subject domain, and often in an haphazard fashion.

As a result of these and a number of other reasons, the use of norm-referenced testing has declined considerably over the last 20 years, particularly at the primary level.

Criterion-referenced measurement and evaluation

An alternative to norm-referenced evaluation, increasingly popular with many teachers, is **criterion-referenced measurement and evaluation.** Here the focus is not on an individual student's comparative performance against norms established by a group of students, but rather on *the comparison of an individual's performance against achievement goals*. Very often the criteria are relative to the student's individual performance standards. In other words, goals and their timing can be individualised to take into account a range of individual characteristics including ability and motivation (Docking 1986).

Criterion-referenced: comparing student performance with achievement goals

In criterion-referenced measurement and evaluation, achievement goals (such as learning to spell ten words or mastering two-digit addition) are clearly specified. The goals may be target goals for the entire class (this is appropriate when the skills are determined to be essential for all children) and the children keep at the task of learning until they have mastered the goals to a particular level of achievement (e.g. spelling all ten words correctly, or completing 90% of the additions correctly). At other times the goals may be individual, and programs of learning devised to assist the child to achieve the target.

Clearly, criterion-referenced measurement and evaluation approaches should be less competitive than norm-referenced ones. All children achieving a particular goal are graded as having satisfactorily completed the work at a particular standard. It is important here to note that the achievement of a particular grade is not determined by the distribution of grades that applies within norm-referenced measurement and evaluation. In the criterion-referenced system, all students can be graded an A or, conversely, if none of the students achieves mastery to appropriate standards, they may all be graded a failure. Teachers may, however, apply a grading system to criterion-referenced evaluation, grading mastery at particular levels with As, Bs and Cs. For example, mastery of 85% or more of the material may entitle the student to an A, 80% to a B, and so on.

One of the complex issues in criterion-referenced measurement and evaluation is the setting of appropriate criteria. At times it may be necessary to establish that the criterion for successful mastery is 100% accuracy. Can you think of examples where 100% accuracy should be required? Theoretically, these criteria should be set before the learning takes place and the task completed, and students should be made fully aware of what they are. However, often they are set after the task is completed and the teacher has evaluated performance. In this case, the criterion becomes less of a criterion than a norm. Why?

Why are more teachers using criterion-referenced measurement and evaluation? There are three reasons why more teachers are using criterion-referenced measurement and evaluation (Biehler & Snowman 1990). First, educators and parents complain that norm-referenced measurement and evaluation provides little information about what children can or can't do. The approach indicates where a student's performance lies relative to other students, but, as already indicated, everyone within the group may be performing relatively strongly or weakly. Little information is communicated regarding individual strengths and weaknesses.

Second, as many educational objectives are clearly specified in performance terms, the criterion-referenced approach appears most suitable for measuring the achievement of these performance objectives. Criterion-referenced tests are constructed in such a way that individual scores yield some 'direct meaning' or are directly interpretable in terms of specified performance standards (Haertel 1985). Last, and associated with the previous point, contemporary theories of school learning claim that most, if not all students, can master most school objectives under the right circumstances. Consequently, a system that de-emphasises performance based on competition, while emphasising individual goal achievement, appears more appropriate (see Chapter 9). In effect, criterion-referenced evaluation focuses attention where it belongs: on whether or not the learner has learnt what he or she was intended to learn (Airasian & Madaus 1972, cited in Biggs & Telfer 1987a).

In an education system in which the focus is truly on student learning, criterion-referenced evaluation gives greater opportunity for student involvement in their own assessment. This can have benefits both for the student through improved self-monitoring, and for the teacher in reducing the need for constant supervision (see Docking 1984, 1986).

TABLE 13.2

ESSENTIALS OF NORM- AND CRITERION-REFERENCED MEASUREMENT AND EVALUATION

Norm-referenced measurement and evaluation:

- compares students against norms of performance that have been established by other groups;
- assesses the range of abilities in a large group;

- ranks and selects the best students for competitive placements;
- typically covers a large domain of learning tasks with a few items measuring each specific task.

Criterion-referenced measurement and evaluation:

- measures mastery of specific skills;
- determines whether students have the prerequisite skills to start a new unit of work;
- assesses psychomotor skills;
- groups students into relatively homogeneous groups for instruction;
- is typically used for guidance and diagnosis;
- typically focuses on a limited domain of learning tasks, with a relatively large number of items measuring each task.

***Question point:** Discuss the advantages and disadvantages of norm-referenced and criterion-referenced measurement and evaluation.*

***Question point:** Consider a number of learning activities such as learning to swim, learning to drive a car and learning to speak a foreign language. Discuss the relative merits of norm-referenced versus criterion-referenced evaluation in regard to the activities. What reference standards should apply?*

LEARNING OBJECTIVES AND LEARNING OUTCOMES

The primary purpose of measurement is to monitor progress in students' learning and to measure students' achievement against learning objectives (Australian Teaching Council 1996). Teachers need to devise measurement strategies which are closely related to learning objectives, reflect the nature of students' programs of work and allow them to provide appropriate feedback on progress. An important aspect of the measurement and evaluation of learning is that it enables teachers, students and their parents to contribute to ongoing learning (Australian Teaching Council 1996).

Today it is more common to speak of desired learning outcomes than teacher-set objectives. Nevertheless, learning objectives strongly influence learning outcomes and, therefore, the course of study to be evaluated. There is, of course, a need to retain a degree of flexibility in evaluation so that, at the end of a program of learning activities, teachers can look back and evaluate the learning that occurred irrespective of whether it was prescribed by objectives.

In order to measure how well particular learning outcomes or objectives have been mastered, objectives must be clear. Robert Mager (1990a) outlines three characteristics of good objectives which facilitate effective assessment and evaluation (Table 13.3). The point of these characteristics is to clarify instructional objectives so that they can be identified ('the child will recognise time'), related to a context ('when given a clock-face with Arabic numerals'), and evaluated according to an appropriate and relevant criterion ('to a criterion of 100% correct responses').

TABLE 13.3

ESSENTIALS OF GOOD LEARNING OBJECTIVES

- A statement of what the learner will be able to do.
- A statement of the relevant conditions under which the performance is expected to occur.
- A statement of the quality or level of performance that will be considered acceptable.

(based on Mager 1990a)

Norman Gronlund (1985) takes a slightly different approach. He believes that it is best to state a general learning objective first that is broad enough to encompass a number of general learning outcomes (which direct our teaching), followed by a number of specific learning outcomes, which relate to the types of learning performance we are willing to accept as evidence of the attainment of the objective. This is then followed by assessment tasks which obtain samples of pupil performance like those described in the specific learning outcomes.

The following two examples taken from Gronlund (pp. 41–3) illustrate his approach.

1. *General objective*

☐ understands scientific principles

Specific learning outcomes related to this general objective

☐ describes the principle in own words;
☐ identifies examples of the principle;
☐ states tenable hypotheses based on the principle;
☐ distinguishes between two given principles;
☐ explains the relationship between two given principles.

2. *General objective*

☐ demonstrates skill in critical thinking

Specific learning outcomes related to this general objective

☐ distinguishes between fact and opinion;

- ☐ distinguishes between relevant and irrelevant information;
- ☐ identifies fallacious reasoning in written material;
- ☐ identifies the limitations of given data;
- ☐ formulates valid conclusions from given data;
- ☐ identifies the assumptions underlying conclusions.

The Mager and Gronlund approaches both focus on learning outcomes or instructional objectives and matching measurement techniques to the types of performance specified by the intended outcomes. If you are preparing to become a teacher you will have many opportunities to practise writing instructional objectives.

TAXONOMY OF EDUCATIONAL OBJECTIVES

Cognitive domain

Many teachers refer to taxonomies of educational objectives for writing their own teaching objectives (see Bloom 1956; Krathwohl et al. 1956; Simpson 1972). Three basic taxonomies have been developed covering the cognitive, affective and psychomotor domains. Within each domain there is a hierarchy of categories. For example, within the cognitive domain, educational objectives may relate to **remembering** material (which may or may not demonstrate an understanding), to **comprehending** (which requires an ability to interpret what the material means), to **application** (which requires working over the material in new contexts), to **analysis** (which requires breaking down material into its component parts), to **synthesis** (which requires working over disparate material to combine it into an intelligible whole), through to **evaluation** (which requires judging the value of material). As you can see, there is a progression here from low-level learning outcomes to higher levels. Many teachers teach with an eye to leading children through these various levels, as appropriate to the material being taught and the ability of the children. A criticism often levelled at some teachers is that their teaching and the educational objectives they set for learners become fixed at the lower levels (knowledge and comprehension), rather than extending to the higher levels of understanding.

Cognitive domain: dealing with thinking

Affective domain

Major categories within the affective domain are **receiving** (that is, the individual is willing to receive or attend to particular stimuli, events or information), **responding** (referring to the active participation on the part of the student in the experience), **valuing** (referring to how much the student values the experience), **organisation** (referring to integrating values across a range of experiences into a philosophy of life), and **characterisation** (referring to the individual's behaviour that reflects value systems incorporated into a consistent lifestyle).

Affective domain: dealing with feeling

As you have probably guessed, the writing of objectives reflecting levels within the affective domain, and the evaluation of these, is more difficult than with the cognitive domain. Nevertheless, there are many opportunities for teachers to use dimensions drawn from the affective domain when writing objectives in such areas as multicultural education and environmental education. Indeed, student growth in the affective domain—that is, in the development of attitudes and values—is a component of many syllabuses. For example, Aim 1 of the NSW Science 7–10 Syllabus (1989) is to foster the development of values that will provide a context for students to make informed and reasoned decisions about issues concerning science, technology and society. The objectives derived from this aim require students to demonstrate that they have a lively interest in natural phenomena, and that they value a scientific approach to problem solving.

Psychomotor domain

The psychomotor domain moves through simple objectives such as **perceiving, readiness for,** and **guided response to particular motor actions.** Higher levels are concerned with **establishing motor responses as habitual behaviours** that can be performed with some degree of skill, and the **combining of motor movements into complex motor actions.** The higher levels are concerned with adapting well-developed skills to meet new situations, and originating new motor skills based on those already learnt.

Psychomotor domain: dealing with action

None of these domains stands alone. In most learning experiences the cognitive, affective and psychomotor domains are intertwined, and each of the levels should also be intertwined. Thus, a range of assessment methods needs to be utilised appropriately.

Table of specifications to guide instruction and evaluation

Bloom, Hastings and Madaus (1971) and Gronlund (1985) indicate how these domains may be used to develop a **table of specifications** to guide instruction and evaluation. The notion is quite simple. A two-way matrix is constructed with content forming one axis and objectives forming the other axis, as indicated below.

	Objectives
Content	

Table of specifications matrix

Listed under 'Objectives' are those of relevance to the particular topic. If we were concerned with the cognitive domain they would range from knowledge to evaluation. Underneath 'Content' we would list the material to be covered. In a unit for primary children on how people work we might list the following content: tools of trade, clothing, location, grouping, transport and hours. The table of specifications would then look something like Table 13.4.

Within each cell we might list one or more specific learning objectives (some cells may have no entries). At a glance such a table of specifications indicates the material to be covered and the relative weighting to be given for particular objectives. This weighting should

TABLE 13.4 **TABLE OF SPECIFICATIONS**

TOPIC: HOW PEOPLE WORK

	OBJECTIVES					
Content	Knowledge	Comprehension	Application	Analysis	Synthesis	Evaluation
TOOLS OF TRADE	What tools are used? STATE/LIST	Describe different tools of different jobs. DESCRIBE	Explain why we have different tools for different jobs. SOLVE		Invent a new tool for a certain job. INVENT	Why do people need tools? ASSESSING/DECIDING
CLOTHING	Make a list of working clothes. LIST		Make a piece of clothing. UNDERSTAND/ DEMONSTRATE	Is the clothing practical? INVESTIGATE	Imagine you are a clothes designer and design a uniform for a specific job. DESIGN	Positive/negative characteristics of work clothes/ uniforms. JUSTIFYING
LOCATION	Survey and list the location of people's workplaces. LIST	Draw conclusions from the survey. Explain findings. EXPLAIN	Graph the findings. Plot locations on map. SHOW	Compare/contrast the location with the profession. COMPARE/CONTRAST	Construct a workplace diorama. CONSTRUCT	
GROUPING	Speaker on employment 'hierarchy'. ■ other countries ■ slavery RETELL/REMEMBER	Explain the duties within each level of personnel. EXPLAIN	Report on duties. Role play staff and duties. DEMONSTRATING/ APPLYING			Argue/debate the social structures in society and their relevance to work. ARGUE/DEBATE
TRANSPORT	Name the different types of transport used to get to work. NAME	Interview working people to find out why they choose that method of transport. EXPLAIN	Report findings of the interviews. REPORT	Analyse the information. ANALYSE		Debate the best way of getting to work. DEBATE
HOURS	List, e.g. 24 hours, ■ night shift ■ afternoon shift, etc. LIST	Explain why there are different shifts. EXPLAIN	Demonstrate concept of time-tabling, rostering. DEMONSTRATE		Design a timetable or roster for jobs. DESIGN	Evaluate the effectiveness of the timetabling. EVALUATE
TALLY	6	5	6	3	4	5

then be reflected in the number and kind of tasks used to measure how well students have mastered the material. Indeed, some teachers list within each cell the number of items to be used to test that particular objective. Such a system brings to a teacher's mind the full range of objectives possible so that simple knowledge and comprehension objectives are not focused on exclusively.

***Question point:** Discuss why instructional objectives are desirable from the teacher's point of view. What difficulties might arise in formulating objectives and what are possible strategies to counteract these difficulties?*

***Question point:** Demonstrate your understanding of Bloom's taxonomy by listing and defining levels in each of the domains. Discuss where various domains and levels may be most appropriate.*

WHAT IS MASTERY LEARNING?

A number of educational innovations are based on the criterion-assessment model, perhaps the most common being Benjamin Bloom's **mastery learning** model (Bloom 1984, 1987; Guskey & Gates 1986; Guskey 1995). Within these mastery learning programs a criterion of mastery is established, the progress of students towards the mastery of a given skill or concept is regularly assessed, and there is provision for corrective feedback and for opportunities to achieve mastery for students having difficulties. The expectation is that all students will achieve mastery of the given skill or concept.

Under the group-based mastery learning program designed by Bloom, a formative test is given to the students every two to three weeks, followed by feedback/corrective instruction and then a parallel formative test. The feedback corrective process begins with the teacher noting the common errors of the majority of students and designing instructional approaches to remedy these common errors. After this, small groups of students (with or without teacher guidance) work through the items they missed in the test, referring back to the original instructional materials to see where problems occurred. Finally, students attempt a parallel test to confirm that they have mastered the material to the mastery standard. Reviews of mastery learning indicate that, in general, mastery learning can be an effective approach to ensuring a large number of students achieve educational goals (Guskey & Gates 1986; Walberg 1984) although some debate exists over the level of its effect on student achievement, particularly when it is group-based rather than individualised (Slavin 1987b, 1989b).

TABLE 13.5

ESSENTIALS OF A MASTERY APPROACH TO INSTRUCTION

For teachers

- Specify what is to be learnt as learning outcomes.
- Motivate pupils to learn it.
- Provide appropriate instructional materials.
- Present materials at a rate appropriate for individual students.
- Monitor students' progress and provide corrective feedback.
- Diagnose difficulties and provide remediation.
- Give praise and encouragement for good performance.
- Give review and practice.
- Maintain a high rate of learning over a period.
- Provide challenging and rewarding extension and enrichment activities upon mastery of initial learning.
- Match measurement and evaluation with the instruction and the learning outcome desired.

(adapted from Carroll 1971; Guskey 1995)

BOX 13.2 TEACHING COMPETENCE

The teacher uses assessment strategies that take account of the relationship between teaching, learning and assessment

Indicators

The teacher:

- knows and uses a range of assessment strategies to build a holistic picture of individual student learning;
- uses assessment procedures consistent with content and process goals;
- plans an assessment program as part of the teaching and learning program;
- uses assessment to inform future planning;
- encourages student self/peer assessment where appropriate.

Case studies illustrating National Competency Framework for Beginning Teaching, National Project on the Quality of Teaching and Learning, Australian Teaching Council, 1996, Element 4.2, p. 56. Commonwealth of Australia copyright, reproduced by permission.

WHAT WOULD YOU DO?

IT DIDN'T SEEM LIKE A TEST

Dianne had worked very hard to capture the interest of her year 3 charges in a topic on dinosaurs. Although this was one of the lower-ability classes in the school, Dianne was pleased to find that the students became really motivated and extended by related topics such as palaeontology, carnivores and extinction. As the topic drew to a close, Dianne was faced with the task of reporting the progress of the students to parents. She was anxious for the assessment to reflect the involvement of the students and the learning that she felt sure had taken place.

'This was one of the lower-ability classes and they worked so hard. I didn't want to make the test too difficult but really I wanted to show the parents what the children had actually done.'

What would you do? See page 305.

Case studies illustrating National Competency Framework for Beginning Teaching, National Project on the Quality of Teaching and Learning, Australian Teaching Council, 1996, p. 29. Commonwealth of Australia copyright, reproduced by permission.

TRADITIONAL MEASUREMENT STRATEGIES

There is a vast array of measurement strategies, a number of which you will probably be quite familiar with. In selecting a particular approach it is important to consider the relative advantages and disadvantages of each format as well as issues of validity and reliability. Among the common forms of measurement are essays, short-answer questions, projects, objective tests, practicals, simulated tasks and oral presentations.

Essay tests and assignments

Essay tests and assignments have a number of advantages. They are easy to set and they encourage written fluency, the organisation and integration of ideas, and originality. As such, they permit the student to go beyond simple rote memorisation of facts and figures while stimulating a search for information. Unfortunately, marking essay questions can be quite unreliable, the coverage of material might be inadequately sampled by a limited number of questions, and, where the essay is written under test conditions, there might be an undue emphasis on writing speed.

Short-answer questions

Short-answer questions, in which students are required to recall information rather than simply recognise correct responses allow for a broader coverage of the course's content, and for more reliable marking. However, there is little opportunity for students to display argument or originality, and often rote learning is encouraged, particularly when the nature of the questions is indicated in advance of the test. An advantage of many short-answer questions is the ease of marking.

Projects

Projects are commonly used at school to stimulate student interest, motivation and learning by encouraging students to read widely and research information. Because of the originality and individuality characteristic of completed projects, they are difficult to grade objectively. One important aspect of project work to be noted is the potential for it to relate to 'real life', and as the scope can be broad or narrow the approach allows for integration among various curriculum areas.

Objective tests

Objective tests (such as multiple choice, matching, completion and true–false) are frequently used at schools and universities. This form of assessment has significant advantages for the teacher. A wide range of objectives can be assessed within a broad coverage of the syllabus. The marking is objective (i.e. any marker will mark the test in the same way) and precise and rapid feedback is possible (particularly if computer scoring is used). However, there are also significant limitations: objective tests are hard to set; students have to recognise rather than recall information; and there is little scope for divergent responses and higher-order thinking processes.

Practicals, simulated tasks and role plays

Practicals are particularly useful for students to demonstrate psychomotor skills such as playing the recorder, completing an experiment, handling power tools, or typing. However, they can be very time-consuming for the teacher. Associated with practicals are **simulated tasks** or **role plays**. This form of measurement closely approximates what the individual will be required to

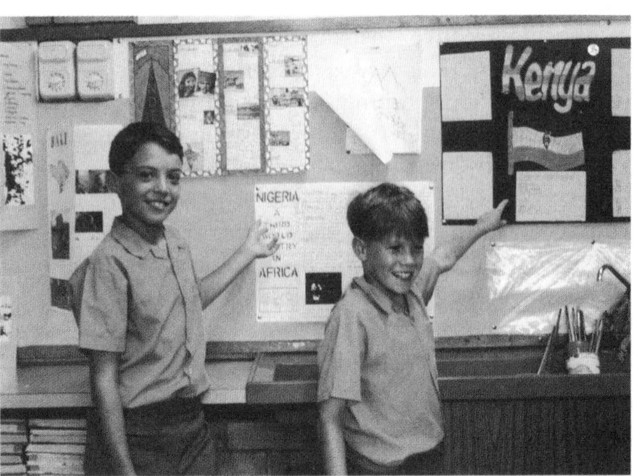

Why is project work a useful alternative for evaluating student achievement? Photo: authors

do 'in the real world' and the coverage of material can be quite broad. Thus it supports the application, rather than regurgitation, of knowledge. When the performance test is a simulation it must resemble the real situation as closely as possible, and clear criteria of performance need to be spelt out in advance. **Work sample assessments** can reflect the highest degree of realism in simulations—for example, student teachers conducting a real lesson in a real classroom, or a jumbo jet flight officer flying his or her first 747 as pilot. In this form of measurement, students perform a representative sample of behaviours under realistic conditions.

Work sample assessments

Oral presentations provide the opportunity for students to tell the examiner what they know. This form of task allows for interpersonal interaction, and for the examiner to elicit information as appropriate. Hence, coverage can be both broad and deep. Oral presentations are particularly useful to confirm other measurements. However, they can be highly subjective and require expert examiner skills. Oral presentations may also be given in front of a class, and as such may induce an audience effect causing anxiety for some students.

Oral presentations

In line with the approach we have taken in this book we advocate that teachers use a variety of the above methods.

Question point: Consider the strengths and weaknesses of the assessment strategies discussed in this chapter. Thinking back to your school days, which assessment strategies seemed most effective at motivating you to greater effort, and which were least effective?

WHAT WOULD YOU DO?

IT DIDN'T SEEM LIKE A TEST (continued)

Rather than use a designated 'test day', Dianne adopted a strategy to integrate the assessment into the actual lesson. Using the words and the terms that she had used in the class and verbal prompts for some of her poorer readers, she asked the students to respond to questions such as 'Why do you think the dinosaurs become extinct?' and 'What does a palaeontologist do?' Dianne was very pleased that the students responded with some high-standard imaginative work.

'I was worried at first about what the parents might think about asking all these difficult questions. But the answers were really terrific. The students drew these pictures of how they thought the dinosaurs became extinct with bits of dust in the air blotting out the sun. I was really impressed.'

Dianne found that her strategy of integrating the test with the classwork and backing her judgment about the students' ability had paid off.

'I found that because I had captured their interest in the first place, when I tested them it didn't seem like a test. They really got involved in the answering of the questions and I got some lovely compliments from the parents.'

What aspects of good measurement and evaluation are demonstrated in this case study? What other assessment strategies could have been used?

Case studies illustrating National Competency Framework for Beginning Teaching, National Project on the Quality of Teaching and Learning, Australian Teaching Council, 1996, p. 29. Commonwealth of Australia copyright, reproduced by permission.

ALTERNATIVES TO TRADITIONAL TESTS AND METHODS OF MEASUREMENT

Authentic measurement strategies

Increasingly today, teachers are employing alternative, 'authentic' strategies to supplement those discussed above (Cambourne & Turbill 1990; Carr & Ritchie 1991; Gullickson 1985; Linn, Baker & Dunbar 1991; Shepard 1991; Swanson, Norman & Linn 1995; Wolf, Bixby, Glenn & Gardner 1991; Woodward 1993).

These strategies include:

- ☐ focused evaluation;
- ☐ pupil profiles;
- ☐ journals and portfolios;
- ☐ work samples;
- ☐ peer and self-evaluations.

Focused evaluation (Edwards & Woodward 1989; Woodward 1993) allows for an intensive evaluation of a student's development over limited periods. Among common methods of assessing children's development are anecdotal records, checklists and observations. Typically, a class is divided up into small groups (five to eight children), each of which becomes the focus of measurement and evaluation for a period of one to two weeks. In this way, all children in the class are focused on once every seven weeks or so. Throughout the year, different learning areas are concentrated on and all children are closely measured and evaluated a number of times in each of these areas. Opportunities are provided for parents and children to have an input. In the early stages of the program, letters are sent home explaining the nature and purpose of focused evaluation. Parents are invited to comment on their child in a particular area (e.g. mathematics or reading) and to provide additional information considered

Intensive evaluation of a student's development

useful for getting a full picture of the child (e.g. the child's hobbies and leisure pursuits). Parental involvement is maintained by asking for written feedback on children's progress and by providing the opportunity for conferences. Both formative and summative evaluations are provided.

Parents find focused evaluation an informative and practical guide to their children's progress (Woodward 1993). Children enjoy being focused on, and usually look forward to taking their reports home because they feel proud of their achievements. Teachers maintain that, although it is a continuous process, the benefits gained from focused evaluation for the children, parents and themselves far exceed any other systems tried.

TABLE 13.6

SOME ADVANTAGES AND REQUIREMENTS OF FOCUSED EVALUATION

Some advantages of focused evaluation

- Teachers are able to get to know the children in the class more quickly and gain a better understanding of how children learn.
- Teachers evaluate their children in normal day-to-day activities rather than in a test situation. This reduces student anxiety.
- All children are evaluated and none of the 'quiet achievers' can slip through unnoticed.
- Parents are provided with a continuous record of specific achievements.
- Any problems can be dealt with as they occur. Children's needs can be identified and future lessons and planning structured to cater to these needs.

Some requirements of focused evaluation

- Reports take $1–1\frac{1}{2}$ hours to complete per focus group.
- Teachers must be well organised. Evaluation sheets, report forms, folders must be accessible and ready for immediate use.
- Teachers need to be flexible as each focus period will have its interruptions—school development days, sports carnivals, book week, education week, and so on.
- Focused evaluation requires teacher commitment.

(adapted from Edwards & Woodward 1989, p. 41)

Pupil profiles

Pupil profiles can be based on anecdotal records as well as on more formal assessment. Evaluation in the early grades of schools (and the reports based on them) are increasingly using the anecdotal format. The following suggestions may be helpful for using anecdotes effectively.

- ☐ *Determine in advance what to observe, but be alert for behaviour that is not typical.* Be wary of recording only behaviour that is out of the ordinary, as this will not give a true picture of the child. To guard against this it is important to have a series of objectives for making observations. The unusual behaviour can then be recorded in this context, and may give valuable insights into the development of the child.
- ☐ *Observe and record enough of the situation to make the behaviour meaningful.* Pupil behaviour can be quite ambiguous. What might be interpreted as aggression by a teacher or parent may, in fact, be perceived by both the actor and other children as good-natured fun. Consequently, it is essential to record enough of the context of the behaviour to ensure that our interpretation is accurate.
- ☐ *Make a record of the incident as soon after the observation as possible.* We have short memories for detail so it is important to make at least brief notes on observations close to the event. These notes can then jog the memory when we come to write fuller comments at a later time.
- ☐ *Limit each anecdote to a brief description of a single incident.* Brief and concise descriptions take less time to write, less time to read, and are more easily summarised. However, make sure that the report is detailed enough for you to make sense of it at a later date when you come to write summative reports.
- ☐ *Keep the factual description of the incident and your interpretation of it separate.* Be factual in your reporting and avoid coloured language. Interpretations that you make on your observation can be subjective but they should be labelled as such and kept separate from the objective reporting of behaviour.
- ☐ *Record both positive and negative behavioural incidents.* We have emphasised repeatedly that teachers should focus on the actual learning that all children are capable of and seek evidence of this learning so that they can support it. Very often teachers focus on the evidence that little learning is taking place, and so anecdotal reports become a depressing record of lack of achievement. Keep a balance. Certainly, it is important to record difficulties and problems, but it is equally important to record successes and achievements.

- ☐ *Collect a number of anecdotes about a pupil before drawing inferences concerning typical behaviour.* We have also emphasised that multiple sources of evidence should be considered before making final judgments about students' typical performance. There are days when all teachers feel 'flat', and their teaching will reflect this. They would hate to have their teaching evaluated on those days. It would be more accurate if evidence was collected over a period of time, in a number of contexts, before judgments were made. It is only after observing a pupil a number of times in a variety of settings that a pattern of behaviour begins to emerge. Until that time we should suspend our judgment.
- ☐ *Obtain practice in writing anecdotal records.* Practice refines a skill. Writing good anecdotal records is a skill that must be worked on. Collaborative work in the school, where a number of teachers help each other write and evaluate anecdotal reports, is a useful means of developing such skill.

(adapted from Gronlund 1985)

Journals and portfolios

Journals and **portfolios** are collections of student work that exhibit the student's efforts, progress and achievements in one or more areas. Paulson, Paulson and Meyer (1991) present the following guidelines for portfolio development:

- ☐ Developing a portfolio offers the student an opportunity to learn about learning. Therefore, the end product must contain information showing that the student has engaged in self-reflection.
- ☐ The portfolio is something that is done *by* the student, not *to* the student.
- ☐ The portfolio is separate and different from the student's cumulative folder.
- ☐ The portfolio must convey explicitly or implicitly the student's activities.
- ☐ The portfolio may serve a different purpose during the year from the purpose it serves at the end.
- ☐ The portfolio should contain information that illustrates growth.
- ☐ Many of the skills and techniques involved in producing effective portfolios do not happen by themselves. Models are needed.

Work samples

Work samples can be assessed in simulated and real environments. A good example of this is work experience where a sample of work, such as class management, can be observed in an actual classroom.

Such performance-based modes of measurement must still demonstrate validity and reliability, although the traditional forms of determining these may not apply. Considerable work is being done by measurement and evaluation experts to develop criteria for ensuring validity of these performance-based modes (Shepard 1991; Swanson, Norman & Linn 1995). There are potential limitations in the use of performance-based tasks:

- ☐ The fact that examinees are tested in realistic performance situations does not make test design and domain sampling simple and straightforward.
- ☐ No matter how realistic a performance-based task is, it is still a simulation, and examinees do not behave the same as they would in real life.
- ☐ Scoring performance-based behaviour can be problematic because of its diversity and complexity.
- ☐ Regardless of the method used, performance in one context does not predict performance in other contexts very well.
- ☐ Correlational studies of the relationship between performance-based test scores and other measurement methods targeting different skills typically produce variable and uninterpretable results.
- ☐ Performance-based methods are often complex to administer.
- ☐ All high-stakes measurement, regardless of the method used, has an impact on teaching and learning. The nature of this impact is not necessarily predictable, and careful studies of (intended and unintended) benefits and side-effects are obviously desirable but rarely done.
- ☐ Neither traditional testing nor performance-based methods of measurement and evaluation is a panacea. Selection of methods should depend on the skills to be measured, and, generally, use of a blend of methods is desirable.

(based on Swanson, Norman & Linn 1995)

ACTION STATION

a

1. (a) State your personal philosophy of how children learn best.
   (b) Take each point raised in your philosophy and show how this will affect teaching methods and 'style'.
   (c) Suggest appropriate assessment strategies to fit your philosophy and teaching methods.
2. Prepare a teaching unit in a given curriculum area, ensuring that:
   (a) assessment strategies are built in as part of the teaching process;
   (b) both formative and summative assessment are included;
   (c) indicators of pupil mastery of key concepts, skills, etc. are stated;

TEACHER'S CASE BOOK

RECORDS OF DEVELOPMENT (RODs)

Records of development are kept as an ongoing folio of children's work samples. They are begun in kindergarten and added to each year until the end of grade 6 when children take them home.

They involve collecting samples of children's work from all areas of the curriculum during the year. At Mr Paynter's school the teachers work on two cycles of collection throughout the year.

Cycle 1
2 maths
1 art
2 writing
1 reading conference
1 other (i.e. science, social studies)

Cycle 2
2 maths
1 art
1 pencil sketch
1 reading conference
1 other
2 writing (narrative)

As each piece of work is collected, teachers write observations and focus on future teaching needs for individual children.

Children in higher grades (i.e. 3–6) contribute to the selection process as they are encouraged to feel ownership of the ROD. It is their personal record and document. In kindergarten, the selection of work is very individual so that teachers can select work which shows a particular breakthrough or discovery.

The comments that teachers include on children's work samples are then incorporated into their planning so the RODs are not separate from the classroom planning. Mr Paynter tries to incorporate them continually into what he is doing in his classroom. RODs are the focus of his parent–teacher interviews which are held after cycle 1. He finds them very useful for focusing parents' attention on particular aspects of their child's development throughout the year and most parents appreciate the depth of comments and the time and effort put into compiling them.

Originals of work samples go home at the end of each year in a profile for each child. Teachers keep a photocopy in the ROD of the last writing, maths, reading conferencing, pencil sketch and report for the future year's teacher. This enables the teachers to see at a glance exactly what stages children are at before they come to their class the following year. In this way, the RODs help provide for a greater sense of continuity of learning throughout children's primary school years.

Case studies illustrating National Competency Framework for Beginning Teaching, National Project on the Quality of Teaching and Learning, Australian Teaching Council, 1996, p. 30. Commonwealth of Australia copyright, reproduced by permission.

Case study activity

Discuss the strengths of this approach to measuring and evaluating student progress. Are there any limitations in this approach?

Teachers can observe and record work habits, attitudes and skills in preparing an accurate, cumulative assessment file for each student, without resorting to formal testing.
Photo: Dianne McPhail

(d) details of methods and time schedules for data collection and recording are organised.

If you design a unit for a senior grade:

(e) design a test as an assessment tool;
(f) ensure that problems are written in clear, positive terms;
(g) include a mixture of test formats.

You may be able to use this unit in teaching practice. If you do, consider the effectiveness of your assessment strategy. How will you ensure that the measurement was valid and reliable?

In Table 13.7 we present some of the essential features of authentic assessment.

TABLE 13.7

ESSENTIALS OF AUTHENTIC ASSESSMENT

For teachers

- Model interest in learning and self-evaluation in real-life contexts.
- Derive assessment tasks from students' everyday learning in school.
- Collect diverse evidence of students' learning from multiple activities over time.
- Design assessment tasks that are varied, functional,

pragmatic and beneficial, to stimulate student learning.
- Design assessment tasks that reflect local values and standards.
- Design activities that encourage student responsibility for self-assessment, peer assessment, and for selecting learning activities and outcomes.

(based on Paris & Ayres 1994)

PEER AND SELF-EVALUATION

Some time ago, when the author was a mere stripling, he studied history for the Leaving Certificate. Our teacher at the time set many essays, but escaped the burden of marking them by exchanging essays between students and getting us to measure and evaluate each other's efforts. We were a bright class and each of us used to rip into the essay written by the other student with great gusto! The author would spend hours looking up obscure references to prove that the causes of the first world war posited by my 'target' student were, in fact, codswallop, and that the real reasons were related to the cost of sugar beet on the world market! At times friendships were strained as we looked in horror at the red lines and comments scrawled over our essays, and waited for the opportunity (in a dark corridor) to get even with the perpetrator. We all seemed to survive the peer evaluation process, however, and in fact did quite well in our history exams.

For peer evaluation to be effective it must share the characteristics of good measurement and evaluation generally. It should be specific, descriptive, predominantly non-judgmental in tone and form, and directed towards the goals of the person receiving it. It must also be well timed. Very importantly, it must be directed at the work and not at the personality of the person who completed the work (often a hard thing to do!). (Comments such as 'You're a fool, writing such rubbish' are not very constructive or helpful.) As students are inexperienced at commenting on the work of others, considerable effort must be expended by the teacher in preparing students for this process. Students, particularly younger ones, should be given guidelines on what is being measured and how to evaluate. Older children can work this out with each other in collaboration with the teacher (Boud 1985).

Characteristics of peer evaluation: specific, descriptive, non-judgmental, goal-directed, well timed

Peer evaluation has particular relevance to **peer tutoring** and **cooperative learning strategies** (see Chapters 6 and 10), and can be used in combination with teacher measurement and evaluation. Sometimes, peer evaluation can be used across the whole class (when, for example, a student makes a classroom presentation and all members of the class complete an evaluation form on the presentation which is given to the presenter). This often happens in peer teaching in teacher education courses. At other times peer evaluation may be one to one—for example, when two students have collaborated in a learning experience (as in **collaborative learning** or peer tutoring). This latter use is probably more valuable. Members of a group can also evaluate each other's mastery of material before a general group presentation to be evaluated by the teacher.

One opportunity we were never given in those Leaving Certificate history classes was that of **self-evaluation**, where we were challenged to set learning goals and to evaluate our achievement of

Self-evaluation

Why are peer and self-evaluation important in constructive learning? Photo: Connie Griebe

these goals in terms of established criteria. We were never given the opportunity, at first hand, to evaluate the quality of our own learning. The evaluation was always filtered through the judgment of our teachers or others. Yet the ability to self-evaluate is fundamental to our effective functioning as adult humans. For several years now there has been growing interest in the educational goals of autonomy and independence in learning, and self-evaluation is an important part of this (Boud 1981, 1985; Falchikov & Boud 1989; Hall 1992; Paris & Ayres 1994; Wolf 1989). Self-evaluation has strong links with the development of metacognitive skills, covered in Chapter 4.

Given the argument that self-evaluation is an essential part of teaching students to be independent learners, the process should be introduced as a component of the regular teaching and learning activities of the classroom rather than as an element only of the formal assessment procedure. As with peer evaluation, children are not naturally inclined or prepared to evaluate their work so the teacher must put considerable effort into preparing them for this task. One way to develop this skill is to introduce a system of co-evaluation.

Co-evaluation and self-evaluation

Measurement and evaluation shared between students and teacher is often termed **co-evaluation** (Hall 1992). This seems an effective and acceptable way of balancing learning strategies—it emphasises autonomy and independence, and teaching responsibilities and accountability. Three questions may be asked as a guide to where the locus of control in individual measurement and evaluation lies. These same three questions can be used to structure various forms of evaluation leading, ultimately, and where appropriate, to full self-evaluation. The questions are:

1. Who is doing the evaluating?
2. Who selects the criteria?
3. For whom is the evaluation carried out?

(adapted from Hall 1992)

Clearly, if the answer to each of these questions is the teacher, then we have teacher-dominated evaluation. However, if we answer 'student' to one or more of the questions, we have a form of co-evaluation. If the answer is the student in each case, we have self-evaluation. Co-evaluation may involve a student evaluating his or her work on the basis of teacher-established criteria, or the teacher evaluating the student on student-established criteria. Both 'doing the evaluating' and the 'selecting of criteria' can be shared so that there is collaboration at each level. The degree to which evaluations are private or public influences the nature of the evaluation in important ways. Forms of co-evaluation commonly used in educational settings are **negotiated evaluation, conferencing**, the **contract system, critiques of performance, journals** and **diaries** (to the extent that the criteria of material to be included and evaluated is decided by the teacher), and **individualised projects** negotiated with the teacher.

Advantages of self-evaluation

Self-evaluation should help motivate student learning. When students evaluate their own achievement they may have new insights into their learning, and may be more able to identify specific problems they are experiencing. As self-evaluation requires honesty of students, there is great potential for a trusting relationship to be developed between students and teacher. Self-evaluation can also help increase students' aspirations and achievements. However, we must be aware that students' perceptions of the quality of their work and the degree of their effort do not always match those of their teachers, so consequently some monitoring of self-evaluation by the teacher is always necessary to ensure evaluations are honest and realistic (Falchikov & Boud 1989; Griffin & Nix 1991).

TEACHER'S CASE BOOK

ASSESSMENT BY THE STUDENTS

At the completion of an English unit with a year 9 class, Mr Blair wanted to provide each student with as much feedback as possible.

Through discussions with students it was decided that each student would present a five minute oral presentation once the English unit was completed. At the completion of the presentation, the student was given a sheet to write a self-evaluation. Two students from the audience were asked to write some constructive comments on the quality of the performance and the work completed by the student. Mr Blair also completed an assessment of the student's work. All this information was photocopied onto an A4 sheet and returned to the presenter.

Such a variety of feedback provides the students with a broad picture of their performance. It also provides the basis of planning for future presentations.

Case studies illustrating National Competency Framework for Beginning Teaching, National Project on the Quality of Teaching and Learning, Australian Teaching Council, 1996, p. 51. Commonwealth of Australia copyright, reproduced by permission.

Case study activity

What are the strengths of peer evaluation? Are there any dangers in this approach that should be guarded against? Is it an approach that can be used across grades and across subjects?

ACTION STATION

Build a resource file of alternative assessment 'tools' for use across the curriculum. Include examples of each where practicable: for example, close passages, pupil-constructed tests, pupil self-assessment.

THE IMPACT OF MEASUREMENT AND EVALUATION ON STUDENTS

For all the complexity of measurement and evaluation in the classroom it cannot be avoided. There is one guiding principle that should be employed whenever we measure and evaluate students: we must do it with the best interests of every child in mind. Unwanted side effects can arise from the nature of the assessment tasks, from the content and skills being tested, and from the methods of reporting. Some measurement and evaluation procedures used by teachers and schools are destructive of children's confidence in learning and motivation to learn (Deutsch 1979). *Evaluations affect children* and they affect children in short-, medium- and long-term ways (Crooks 1988). Crooks enumerates a number of potential positive effects. His list (Table 13.8) is an effective checklist of the qualities of good evaluation.

TABLE 13.8

GOALS OF EVALUATION

Short-term goals

- Reactivating or consolidating prerequisite skills or knowledge prior to introducing new material.
- Focusing attention on important aspects of the subject.
- Encouraging active learning strategies.
- Giving students opportunities to practise skills and consolidate learning.
- Providing knowledge of results and corrective feedback.
- Helping students to monitor their own progress and develop skills of self-evaluation.
- Guiding the choice of further instructional or learning activities to increase mastery.
- Helping students feel a sense of accomplishment.

Medium-term goals

- Checking that students have adequate prerequisite skills and knowledge to be able to learn the material to be covered effectively.
- Influencing students' motivation to study the subject and their perceptions of their capabilities in the subject.
- Communicating and reinforcing the instructor's or the curriculum's broad goals for students, including the desired standards of performance.
- Influencing students' choice of (and development of) learning strategies and study patterns.
- Describing or certifying students' achievement in the course, thus influencing their future activities.

(adapted from Crooks 1988)

Among the long-term goals of measurement and evaluation is to influence students' ability to retain and apply the material learnt in a variety of contexts, to help develop student learning strategies and styles, and to encourage students' continuing motivation, both in particular subjects and more generally (Crooks 1988).

Deep and surface learning

At times, strategies used to measure student performance, such as tests and assignments, simply encourage students to learn, in a relatively superficial way, the material required to pass a test rather than to delve more deeply into the subject matter under study. Indeed, many students become quite adept at picking out what is minimally required by the teacher to pass the test. This approach to learning has been called a **surface approach** and is typically characterised by rote learning (Biggs 1984, 1987a, c). Surface-learning approaches are contrasted with **deep approaches** which are characterised by the individual's active search for meaning, underlying principles and structures in knowledge. If one of our teaching aims is to encourage deep learning, then we should be conscious of the potential effects of various measurement tasks and evaluations based on these measurement tasks. Students are versatile in their choice of learning approaches (Crooks 1988) but, like all of us, will take the line of least resistance, especially when there are competing demands, limited time, and little intrinsic interest in the task. Teachers often labour the need for students to obtain a deep grasp of the importance and relevance of particular learning experiences, while simultaneously communicating what is 'really' important through the more hidden curriculum of the evaluation policy. Students often pay more attention to this covert or hidden curriculum than to the formal curriculum (Crooks 1988).

From time to time, we have both been criticised by students for 'setting too high standards' in work. We believe that higher standards increase student effort and ultimately improve performance. However, if evaluation standards are unrealistically high they are likely to demotivate students (Natriello 1989; Natriello & Dornbusch 1984). Within the classroom context it would appear necessary to set standards that are attainable, which will involve some individualising of standards as needed. We strongly believe that if a teacher accepts sub-standard work, students will be encouraged to work at a minimal level.

Evaluation standards

Evaluation and sense of self

When teachers evaluate students' work they are saying something to them about success or failure. It is important that the manner in which this feedback is given to students encourages further motivation to continue with the task. A failure resulting from poor effort has a different impact to one resulting from lack of ability. As we saw earlier in the chapter on motivation (Chapter 9), our attributions for success and failure in a particular task are important determinants of later motivation for the task. Our own research has shown (McInerney 1991, 1992b; McInerney & Swisher 1995; McInerney, Roche, McInerney & Marsh 1997; see also Covington 1992) that children who believe they are competent, and are told they can achieve by parents and teachers, are more likely to be motivated at school. Children who feel they cannot cope, that it is all beyond them, tend to be poorly motivated and make minimal efforts at learning. Any evaluation we give to children must emphasise their competence and potential for learning growth. This is particularly important for the less able students and requires us to point out clearly where errors are made while designing further learning tasks so that individual success is experienced. Social comparisons with others in the group should be minimised.

It is important to note here that praise as part of the evaluation does not appear to be as important as constructive and positive feedback that emphasises mastery and progress (Crooks 1988).

What is the role of feedback?

Implicit in what has been said above is the notion of feedback to students. There are three characteristics of effective feedback (Crooks 1988). First, feedback is most effective if it focuses students' attention on their progress in mastering educational tasks. Such emphasis on personal progress enhances self-efficacy, encourages effort attributions, and reduces attention to social comparison. Second, feedback should take place when it is still clearly relevant. This usually means that it should be given during the task, or soon after the task is completed, with an opportunity also provided for the student to demonstrate learning from the feedback. How many of us have received feedback so long after task completion that it becomes irrelevant? Furthermore, feedback without the opportunity to practise for improvement would seem to be a waste of time. Finally, feedback should be specific and related to need (see also Hattie 1992 and Kulhavy 1977).

Effective feedback enhances self efficacy, is relevant, is specific, and is related to need

Feedback that brings errors to students' attention in a motivationally favourable way is effective and more advantageous than spending time re-examining work well done (Elawar & Corno 1985). Teachers can ask four useful questions to guide their feedback:

1. What is the key error?
2. What is the probable reason the student made this error?
3. How can I guide the student to avoid the error in the future?
4. What did the student do well that should be noted?

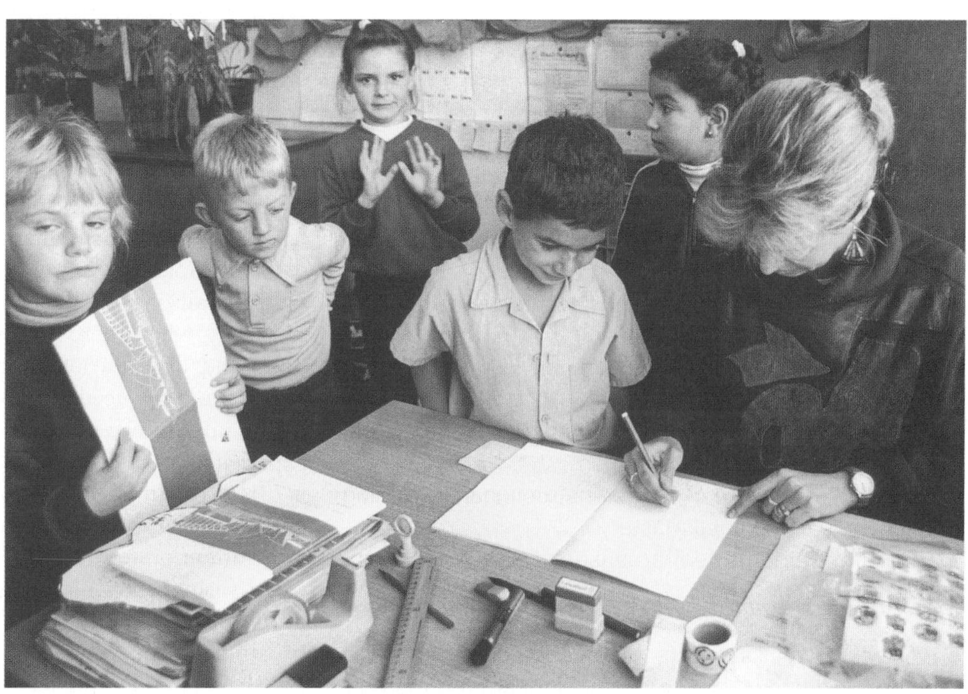

Effective feedback is essential to effective learning. Photo: authors

BOX 13.3 TEACHING COMPETENCE

The teacher monitors student progress and provides feedback on progress

Indicators

The teacher:

- observes and responds to patterns of student learning behaviour;
- draws on a range of information sources in assessing individual student performance;
- provides consistent and timely feedback to students and parents;
- assesses to check progress, identify specific learning difficulties and indicate achievement;
- uses monitoring and assessment activities to enhance the self-esteem of students;
- maintains student achievement records in accordance with school policies.

Case studies illustrating National Competency Framework for Beginning Teaching, National Project on the Quality of Teaching and Learning, Australian Teaching Council, 1996, Element 4.3, p. 57. Commonwealth of Australia copyright, reproduced by permission.

TABLE 13.9

ESSENTIALS OF EFFECTIVE MEASUREMENT AND EVALUATION

For teachers

- Designing a range of assessment tasks that promote meaningful learning.
- Establishing for students the purpose of the measurement and evaluation.
- Establishing for students that the assessment tasks used are valid and fair, and consistent with the regular curriculum and instruction provided in the classroom.
- Designing assessment tasks that elicit students' genuine effort, motivation and commitment to the assessment activity and situation.
- Providing opportunities for all students to demonstrate what they have learned across a variety of assessment tasks.
- Making explicit the criteria for evaluation.
- Providing effective feedback that includes a number of dimensions (such as a mark and a comment).
- Providing periodic and regular assessment rather than irregular and infrequent assessment.
- Ensuring that the assessment tasks are fair and equitable to all students regardless of prior achievement, gender, race, language or cultural background.
- Providing opportunities to measure students' motivation, attitudes and affective reactions to the curriculum as well as their cognitive skills, strategies and knowledge.
- Designing appropriate reporting mechanisms that provide clear and comprehensible information to parents and students.
- Providing opportunities for parents to have an input into the measurement and evaluation process.

(based on Natriello 1989; Paris & Ayres 1994)

REPORTING STUDENT ACHIEVEMENT

Increasingly, considerations of privacy and accountability are being included as essential elements of the data gathering, storing and reporting process. Communicating information to parents on children's achievement is not easy, and no one appears to have developed the perfect system. Verbal descriptions (such as the wonderful one-liners teachers write to sum up students' performance in mathematics or language over a period of twelve months) have an obvious limitation! Simple raw scores (such as 15 marks out of 20) communicate an element of information but fail to indicate whether this shows effective mastery of material or relative performance. Rankings indicate where a child

BOX 13.4 TEACHING COMPETENCE

The teacher maintains records of student progress and reports on student progress to parents and others responsible for the care of students

Indicators

The teacher:

- designs a recording system of appropriate detail and utility;
- records assessment outcomes accurately and consistently;
- adheres to principles of confidentiality;
- provides detailed, accurate and comprehensible reports on progress;
- uses assessment and reporting procedures consistent with school policies;
- prepares information to meet certification requirements.

Case studies illustrating National Competency Framework for Beginning Teaching, National Project on the Quality of Teaching and Learning, Australian Teaching Council, 1996, Elements 4.4 & 4.5, pp. 58–59. Commonwealth of Australia copyright, reproduced by permission.

lies relative to the rest of a group, but fail to indicate what the child's starting point was and how much individual progress characterised the student's performance.

All schools have a policy that guides their reporting on student evaluation. Reports can be **formative** when parents and others are progressively kept up to date on their children's performance. This can be very informal, such as a merit card being sent home reporting a good achievement in a project, or a quick word to a parent in the playground after school. At other times formative reporting might be more formal, such as systematic reports written by the teacher in a homework book or student diary. Cumulative records, kept by teachers and students on students' work, also serve as an effective means of plotting where a student is at any particular time. They are useful for writing up summative reports.

Formative reports: reporting progressively on student progress

Summative reports are usually in the form of written reports and parent–teacher interviews which **summarise**, in a more formal way, a student's achievement. Summative reports usually occur at the end of each term, or bi-annually. Unfortunately, no one has yet invented the perfect report card that effectively communicates to the appropriate audiences what the child has actually achieved. The figure below presents a sample of report cards for you to consider. What do you see as the strengths and weaknesses of each in terms of what has been discussed throughout this chapter?

Summative reports: reporting on student's achievement

This folder gives you a comprehensive report on your child's progress in each of the six key learning areas and on his/her attitude towards school. Please read it carefully and discuss it frankly and sympathetically with your child.

Key: **Effort**	**Achievement/Grade**
O Outstanding	O Outstanding
H High	H High
S Satisfactory	S Satisfactory
L Low	L Low
M Minimal	E Experiencing Difficulty
	I Individual Program

ENGLISH: Reading Writing Listening Speaking

Comments..
....
....
....
....
....
....

☐ Effort ☐ Achievement

	JUNE				NOVEMBER			
PERSONAL DEVELOPMENT	1	2	3	4	1	2	3	4
Completes work on time								
Takes pride in work								
Participates in activities								
Works independently								
Cooperates with others								
Shows initiative								
Accepts responsibility for own actions								
Shows self control								

1 Consistently
2 Usually
3 Sometimes
4 Rarely

November: Position in Grade.

English 0 25 50 75 100

Maths 0 25 50 75 100

• Your child's position indicates X

Teacher comment: (June) ____________

Class Teacher...................... Supervisor ....

Parent comment: ____________

(November) ____________

Class Teacher...................... Supervisor ....

KEY 1 = Consistently 2 = Usually 3 = Rarely

Living Skills			
Cares for own property			
Displays self-confidence			
Mixes well with other children			
Respects property of others			
Displays tolerance			
Displays self control and self discipline			
Is courteous and well-mannered to peers			

Study Skills			
Works independently			
Co-operates in group work			
Responds positively in help and correction			
Listens and carries out instructions			
Begins work promptly			
Completes set tasks			
Takes pride in bookwork			
Is well organised			

GENERAL COMMENTS

DAYS ABSENT ....
INTERVIEW REQUESTED YES/NO
CLASS TEACHER ....
PRINCIPAL ....

English	Level	Effort
Oral Reading		
Comprehension		
Spelling		
Written Communication		
Handwriting		
Talking		
Listening		

Mathematics		
Space		
Measurement		
Number		

Science		
Computers		
Social Studies		
Health & Personal Dev.		
Physical Education		
Music		
Visual Arts		
Craft		
Drama		

Level Attained Code
A - Outstanding **C** - Satisfactory
B - High **D** - Low

English General Comment

Mathematics General Comment

Comment

Assessed Effort Code
A - Outstanding **C** - Satisfactory
B - High **D** - Low

Class _____ **Year** _____ **Days Absent** ________

Social Development		**Work Habits**	
Shows consideration for the rights of others		Listens attentively	
Is polite and courteous		Follows instructions	
Mixes well with other children		Works co-operatively in a group	
Obeys class and school rules		Is reliable	
Accepts constructive criticism		Able to work independently	
Exercises self control		Participates in class activities	
Displays self confidence		Completes set tasks	
Adjusts easily to new situations		Seeks help when required	
Is punctual		Takes pride in work	
Readily accepts responsibility for tasks		Is prepared and organised	
Respects their own and others' property		Completes homework	

Code for Social Development and Work Habits
A - Consistently **B** - Sometimes **C** - Rarely

Teacher's Comment

Teacher ____________________
Supervisor ____________________
Principal ____________________

December 1993

June

ENGLISH	Effort	Achievement
Reading		
Writing		
Speaking		
Listening		
Spelling		
Handwriting		

English general comment

MATHEMATICS		
Number		
Space		
Measurement		

Mathematics general comment

HUMAN SOCIETY AND ITS ENVIRONMENT	Effort
Science and Technology	
Creative and Practical Arts	
P.E. / HEALTH	

Comment

SCALE

EFFORT	**ACHIEVEMENT**
A Outstanding	A Outstanding
B High	B High
C Average	C Average
D Low	D Low
E Minimal	E Minimal

November

ENGLISH	Effort	Achievement
Reading		
Writing		
Speaking		
Listening		
Spelling		
Handwriting		

English general comment

MATHEMATICS		
Number		
Space		
Measurement		

Mathematics general comment

HUMAN SOCIETY AND ITS ENVIRONMENT	Effort
Science and Technology	
Creative and Practical Arts	
P.E. / HEALTH	

Comment

SCALE

EFFORT	**ACHIEVEMENT**
A Outstanding	A Outstanding
B High	B High
C Average	C Average
D Low	D Low
E Minimal	E Minimal

NAME ....

ACHIEVEMENT/GRADE		EFFORT	
O	Outstanding	O	Outstanding
H	High	H	High
S	Satisfactory	S	Satisfactory
L	Low	L	Low
E	Experiencing Difficulty	M	Minimal
F	Follows an Individual Program		

ENGLISH EFFORT ❑

Achievement ❑

MATHEMATICS EFFORT ❑

Achievement ❑

SCIENCE & TECHNOLOGY EFFORT ❑

HUMAN SOCIETY & ITS ENVIRONMENT EFFORT ❑

CREATIVE & PRACTICAL ARTS EFFORT ❑

P.D./HEALTH/P.E. EFFORT ❑

Level Attained Code

A Outstanding Achievement
These students accomplish with ease all of the objectives of the subject that are relevant to their Year. They complete assigned tasks accurately and promptly without need of further assistance from their teacher or peers. Their work frequently shows that they can take the understandings and skills taught in class and develop them further without additional help from the teacher, and it occasionally shows a unique flair or inventiveness.

B High Achievement
These students accomplish nearly all of the objectives of the subject that are relevant to their Year. They complete most assigned tasks accurately and promptly without need of further assistance from their teacher or peers. Their work sometimes shows that they can take the understandings and skills taught in class and develop them further without any additional help from the teacher.

C Satisfactory Achievement
These students accomplish many of the objectives of the subject that are relevant to their Year. They complete many assigned tasks, though not always accurately or promptly, and they sometimes need further assistance from their teacher or peers. Their work occasionally shows that they can take the understandings and skills taught in class and develop them further without additional help from the teacher.

D Low Achievement
These students accomplish a few of the objectives of the subject that are relevant to their Year. They sometimes complete assigned tasks without assistance from their teacher or peers. Their work shows little sign that they can take the understandings and skills taught in class and develop them further without additional help from the teacher.

Effort Code

A Outstanding Application
These student attempt all set tasks and seek assistance when they encounter difficulties. They participate fully and enthusiastically in all whole and small group activities, either as leaders or as supportive followers, and they frequently suggest ideas. They assist other members of the class or school willingly and spontaneously.

B High Application
These students generally attempt the set tasks and either seek assistance, or freely accept it, when they encounter difficulties. They participate fully in all whole and small group activities, either as leaders or as supportive followers, and they often suggest ideas. They willingly assist other members of the class or school if requested.

C Satisfactory Application
These students attempt most of set tasks. They accept assistance when they encounter difficulties, and sometimes seek it. They participate in most whole and small group activities, either as leaders or as supportive followers, and they occasionally suggest ideas. They assist other members of the class or school if requested.

D Low Application
These students attempt some of the assigned tasks but they make reluctant attempts or no attempt to complete others. They rarely seek assistance when they encounter difficulties, and are unenthusiastic about accepting it when it is offered; or they make excessive demands for assistance. They participate in few whole and small group activities. They rarely suggest ideas for classroom activities and are reluctant to help others.

Two types of written report are commonly used—one that relays normative information to parents regarding the relative performance of their child in various learning areas, and one that relates a child's performance to specific criteria of achievement.

When we were in primary school, report cards were considerably different from report cards of today. Listed on the reports were our raw score marks in each of the 'important' subjects, a rank position in that subject (such as 1st out of 40, 15th out of 40), and an overall ranking in class based on some cumulation of the raw scores within a subject and across subjects.

Norm-referenced reports: comparing individual's achievement to other students

While the emphasis on overall place in class has diminished, parents are still very keen to find out how well their children are doing relative to the rest of the class. The most common way of presenting normative reports today is still through raw scores or percentages which are sometimes converted to letter grades. Often grades are awarded according to a pre-determined distribution that loosely reflects the normal curve. In other words, few high and low grades are awarded in comparison to a large number of 'average' grades. The primary purpose of this system of grading is to show how a particular child performs relative to his or her peers. Unfortunately, this system means that there are only a few who can really feel very successful, a large number who may feel adequate, and a number, who by virtue of the system, must feel failures. There is also a problem with cut-offs for the allocation of grades. Is it defensible to award an A to one student and a B or C to another when the difference between their scores may be marginal at the cut-off points? Under such circumstances we are really putting a lot of unwarranted faith in the accuracy of our measurement. No doubt some of you can recall being 'unfairly' graded on the curve.

While written comments such as 'Johnny has worked well this term and is a pleasant boy to teach' may be used to cushion the effect of a low ranking, we all know that parents' eyes home in on the significant information: 33/35. Norm-referenced reporting, in general, does not indicate how much a particular child has learnt relative to his or her starting point, simply where he or she stands relative to the group. If a pretest and post-test format is used for the norm-based assessment, a report can include details on how well an individual has improved over the course of instruction.

'Oh, good. Your mid-year school reports are in. I wonder how well I rated on the Homework and Project items this term?'

The way in which teachers often cumulate raw scores from a diverse set of tasks, without regard to weighting and standardising scores, makes the whole procedure of 'norm-referencing' quite invalid. Few teachers graduate from their training with sufficient skills in measurement to implement such a system (Crooks 1988; Gullickson 1985; Stiggins 1985; Wright & Wiese 1988).

To overcome one limitation in norm-referenced reports, namely, the lack of qualitative information on the student's performance, some reports use a dual system of reporting. On one page teachers report the raw scores, percentages or letter grades for students in key learning areas, and on the opposing page they report a judgment of effort based on a teacher's estimation of the child's ability relative to achievement. There are two problems with this system. First, it is very difficult to measure ability and effort. Second, unless the achievement mark and effort (or attitude) grades coincide reasonably well, the achievement mark would be more influential in most homes (Withers & Cornish 1985).

***Question point:** Teachers often assume that grading cannot be avoided. Is there a practicable alternative to grading?*

Criterion-referenced reporting systems indicate how a child has performed against specific criteria. Reports will typically have a code indicating that the child has met an objective, is on the way to meeting the objective, or has not mastered the objective. There is no attempt to average scores across assignments for the one student, or to average scores across students; indeed, there is essentially no comparison of one student with another. When grades are awarded they are in terms of number of objectives achieved rather than relative performance. Consequently, in contrast to norm-referenced measurement and evaluation, there is no limit to the number of students who can achieve at any particular grade level.

Criterion-referenced reports: comparing individual's achievement to criteria

As we have all experienced, reports are written to parents, and the main person involved, the student, is always referred to in the third person. There is a strong argument that reports should be written primarily to the students themselves (Docking 1984). Table 13.10 lists the advantages of this system. Many schools are adapting this approach with considerable success. What do you think about such a reporting system?

Should reports be written to the student?

TABLE 13.10

A COMPARISON OF STUDENT-ORIENTED AND PARENT-ORIENTED REPORTS

Student-oriented reports

- Student-oriented reports make clear to the students that they are learning for their own sake, not for the benefit or pleasure of their parent(s).
- Student-oriented reports make clear that the learning process is a personal interaction between the learner and the resources (including the teacher), not a public exhibition.
- Student-oriented reports can be more specific and forward-looking as the feedback can relate to particular learning strengths and weaknesses with the prospect of further work to enhance performance.
- Student-oriented reports are easier for teachers to write as they are writing to someone known and in terms that should be more meaningful, precise and with less chance of misunderstanding.
- The child at school is often a different person from the child at home and student-oriented reports give the child the opportunity to break free from family attitudes and constraints.
- The reader of the student-oriented report is an expert who is well informed about the school, needs the feedback the most, and can do most with the information.

Parent-oriented reports

- Parent-oriented reports encourage competitiveness since they are public and very often norm-referenced.
- Parents are powerless to do anything with the information given in a parent-oriented report whereas students can act on the information.
- The parent may have language difficulties that make the report meaningless.
- The information written for parents is often abused by parents who use the material to put their children down, punish or bribe them.
- Teachers sometimes misuse the report form as a threat to 'motivate' their students, warning children that they will get a bad report that will disappoint their parents, or as a bribe to get on the right side of students. Student-oriented reports can be honest and motivating without invoking fear or favouritism.
- The parent-oriented report often takes on much more authority and significance than it deserves

because parents take it at face value as a definitive statement of their child's progress. A student-oriented report is less likely to assume the exaggerated authority traditional reports usually acquire.

- The parents can learn all they need to know from a student-oriented report and probably experience some sense of relief that the school is not laying on their shoulders responsibilities they cannot fulfil, and also a sense of pride that their child is able to be responsible for his/her own development.

(adapted from Docking 1984)

If anything, the complexities of measurement and evaluation, as well as the potential effects on student learning and motivation, should teach us to be humble, flexible and cautious in the way we use measurement results.

ACTION STATION

Review a number of school measurement and evaluation policies. Can the goals of evaluation listed in Table 13.8 be identified in the policies? If particular purposes are not readily identifiable, discuss why.

ACTION STATION

A number of models of report cards are presented on pages 314–16. As a group, design your own report card which reflects what the group believes is the current thinking on appropriate reporting. Justify your report form by referring to principles of measurement and evaluation covered in this chapter.

Recommended reading

Airasian, P. W. (1995) Classroom assessment. In L. W. Anderson (ed.) *International Encyclopedia of Teaching and Teacher Education*, 2nd edn, pp. 290–4. Tarrytown, NY: Pergamon.

Bloom, B. S., Hastings, J. T. & Madaus, G. F. (1971) *Handbook on Formative and Summative Evaluation of Learning*. New York: McGraw-Hill.

Crooks, T. J. (1988) The impact of classroom evaluation practices on students. *Review of Educational Research*, 58, 438-81.

Docking, R. A. (1984) Writing school reports. *Unicorn*, 10, 332–48.

Docking, R. A. (1986) Norm-referenced measurement and criterion-referenced measurement: A descriptive comparison. *Unicorn*, 12, 40–6.

Griffin, P. & Nix, P. (1991) *Educational Assessment and Reporting. A New Approach*. Sydney: Harcourt Brace Jovanovich.

Gronlund, N. E. (1991) *How to Write and Use Instructional Objectives*. New York: Macmillan.

Guskey, T. R. (1995) Mastery learning. In L. W. Anderson (ed.) *International Encyclopedia of Teaching and Teacher Education*, 2nd edn, pp. 161–7. Tarrytown, NY: Pergamon.

Mager, R. F. (1990) *Measuring Educational Results*, 2nd edn. London: Kogan Page.

Mager, R. F. (1990) *Preparing Educational Objectives*, 2nd edn. London: Kogan Page.

Moss, P. A. (1996) Enlarging the dialogue in educational measurement: Voices from interpretive research traditions. *Educational Researcher*, 25, 20–28.

Paris, S. G. & Ayres, L. R. (1994) *Becoming Reflective Students and Teachers with Portfolios and Authentic Assessment*. Washington, DC: American Psychological Association.

Shepard, L. (1993) Evaluating test validity. *Review of Research in Education*, 19, 405–50.

Woodward, H. (1993) *Negotiated Evaluation*. Sydney: Primary English Teachers' Association.

PART 3

Understanding developmental needs of children and effective teaching and learning

Learning and physical/motor development

CHAPTER 14

OVERVIEW

In this chapter we examine issues related to physical and motor development, and, especially, those features that are of most interest to teachers and parents. We consider the importance of physical activity from the broadest perspectives: to support the normal growth of children, to establish good life habits, and to facilitate the development of other systems (such as cognitive, social and personal) which are intrinsically entwined with the physical development of the child.

Topics covered in the first section of the chapter relate to cycles of physical development. In the second section we look specifically at motor development in the light of four key principles: maturation, motivation, experience and practice. Individual and sex differences in both physical growth and motor development are highlighted.

Finally, we consider briefly a range of issues related to general physical health and safety issues with which teachers need to be familiar.

An accurate picture of developmental patterns is fundamental to an understanding of children, and a knowledge of what causes variations in development is essential to an understanding of each individual child.

LEARNER-CENTRED PSYCHOLOGICAL PRINCIPLE 12

As individuals develop, there are different opportunities and constraints for learning. Learning is most effective when differential development within and across physical, intellectual, emotional and social domains is taken into account.

Children learn best when material is appropriate to the developmental level and is presented in an enjoyable and interesting way, while challenging their intellectual, emotional, physical and social development. Unique environmental factors (e.g. the quality of language interactions between adult and child and parental involvement in the child's schooling) can influence development in each area. An overemphasis on developmental readiness, however, may preclude learners from demonstrating that they are more capable intellectually than schools, teachers or parents allow them to show. Awareness and understanding of developmental differences of children with special emotional, physical or intellectual disabilities as well as special abilities can greatly facilitate efforts to create optimal contexts for learning.

Reprinted with permission, APA Task Force on Psychology in Education (1993, January), p. 8.

DEVELOPING PATTERNS OF MOTOR BEHAVIOUR AND THEIR IMPLICATIONS FOR SCHOOLING

Children go through stages of physical and motor growth which bring about new patterns of behaviour. Muscle growth brings about changes in motor capacities and in the number and kinds of activities that children can master and enjoy, especially fine motor activities (such as drawing and writing), games and sport. Changes in the functioning of the endocrine glands, particularly in puberty, also result in new patterns of personal and social behaviour.

Behaviour is influenced by one's general physical condition. Health conditions, physical growth needs, physical defects, and stage and speed of maturity have effects physically, psychologically and emotionally on the school-aged child.

Adjustment difficulties

School-aged children go through periods of rapid growth which can be disturbing. Clearly, there will be some difficulties in adjusting to differences in appearance, clumsiness, pimples, and people's comments and reactions to their growth. Some indications of children experiencing adjustment difficulties may be a finicky appetite, moodiness and unsociability.

Growing pains

Rapid growth in itself is also tiring and can cause children to be moody and irritable. Children may complain of aches and pains (the so-called growing pains), and require sympathetic and caring attention from teachers and parents. Rapid growth may also make children 'frisky' and teachers and parents must ensure that opportunities for children to disperse pent-up energy are provided, along with periods of rest and relaxation.

Diet and nourishment

Children need to be well nourished. As educators we need to be aware that both learning and behavioural difficulties may reflect dietary imbalances, either on a particular occasion or, more generally, through poor eating habits. The type of food and quantity needed will vary according to the age of the child. Without proper nourishment children become listless and irritable. Many schools have introduced breakfast programs for children coming from homes where breakfast may not be adequate, and most schools these days carefully monitor the types of food sold through the school canteen.

Physical growth and self-concept

A counterpart to all physical growth is the development of a concept of self. A healthy concept will depend on successfully mastering the stages of development and having significant others, such as parents, peers and teachers, look favourably upon us. A positive, supportive and happy growing environment is essential for the development of a healthy self-concept.

It is important for parents, teachers and schools to help children develop a respect for their bodies and to understand the roles of adequate rest, exercise and nutrition (Holt 1991; Margolin 1976). Education programs such as those run by the *Family Life Movement* and *Life Be In It* help in this regard, as do educational programs designed to combat substance abuse. One of the most important influences in helping children develop good motor skills and healthy attitudes about their bodies is adult modelling. Parents and teachers who show an enthusiasm for physical activity, whether it be running, swimming or playing ball, and share these activities with children, encourage the children to follow suit.

Perceptual motor development and learning

Giving children the opportunity to develop body skills is very important to their early stages of school learning. **Perceptual motor development** is essential to the effective learning of writing, reading, music, art and mathematics. A good feeling towards one's body skills will predispose a child to feel good about the world in general, which includes 'academic' learning.

In this chapter we look at key aspects of physical and motor development and their implications for educational settings.

GENERAL PRINCIPLES OF PHYSICAL AND MOTOR DEVELOPMENT

Orderly and sequential development

Teachers, parents and other professionals involved in child care and development (such as paediatric doctors and nurses) are interested in the dimensions of growth: growth predictors, growth evaluation and growth assessment. For educators, issues such as the sequence of physical and motor development and its relationship to the development of learning capacities have important implications for the design of academic and non-academic curricula. Such information is used to evaluate the development of individuals and groups of children in order to match educational programs effectively to the specific needs of children. The potential impact on learning of early, late and asynchronous development is of practical concern.

Physical and motor development from conception to adulthood is orderly and sequential. This regularity or continuity in development, impelled by genetic forces, is often referred to as canalisation. There are, however, particular periods of rapid growth and development (Brim & Kagan 1980; Garn 1980; Tanner 1990) as well as dramatic changes in individual growth and maturation caused by the interaction between genetic and environmental forces that influence development (e.g. caloric deprivation can slow growth, delay development and slow the end of adolescence) (Garn 1980; Tanner 1990). **Growth charts** (i.e. graphs representing chronological norms of development for height, weight, skeletal structure, muscles, internal organs, the brain and the sexual system) are very useful for teachers, parents and other professionals involved in child care, for four reasons:

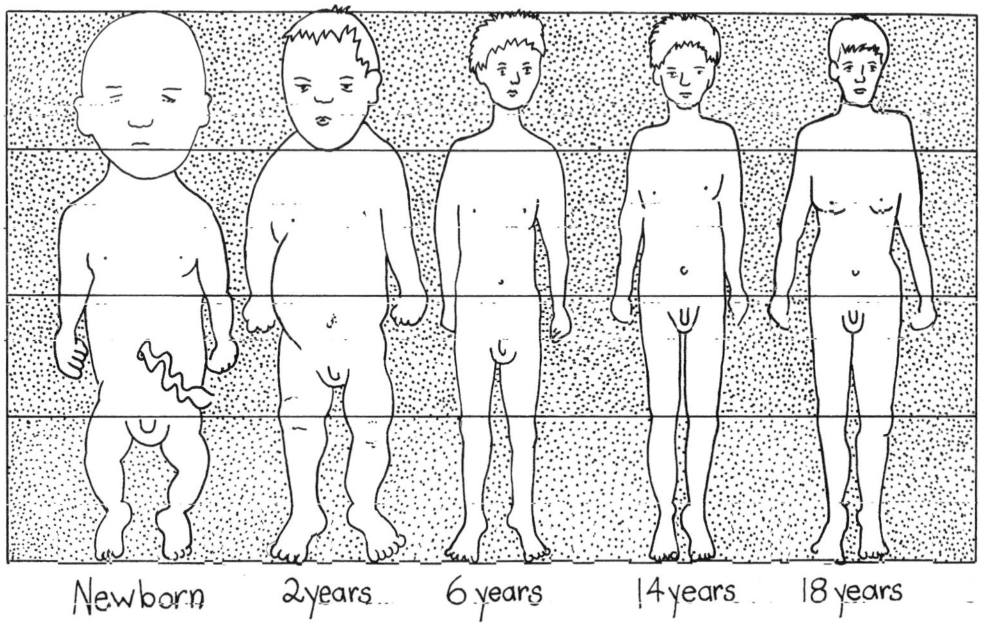

1. Periods of peak human physical development can be seen. This is important in terms of matching diet, rest and exercise to the needs of children at these times. Teachers dealing with children

This diagram illustrates the changing shape and proportions of the human body from birth to maturity.

and adolescents can also be prepared for particular behavioural symptoms of rapid growth.

2. The order in which physical systems become operational can be identified. This is particularly important for scheduling curriculum activities so that they are presented at an optimal time in terms of children's development.
3. Comparisons can be made between the sexes in their growth to physical maturity. This allows questions to be answered about such issues as the appropriateness of particular physical activities to both sexes, the presentation of sex education courses and the need for personal health and dietary information.
4. Children can be evaluated in relation to the general developmental level of children their age and the ability and readiness to learn of the individual child.

(Sinclair 1989; Tanner 1990; Malina & Bouchard 1991)

Head-down and axis-out development

Human growth proceeds in a cephalocaudal and proximodistal direction. **Cephalocaudal growth** refers to the development of physical and motor systems from the head down, while **proximodistal growth** refers to growth from the central axis of the body outward.

Cephalocaudal development and proximodistal development

The human head as a system (brain, sensory receptors) is one of the earliest systems to become functional. The human trunk is next in overall rate of growth, followed by the legs. Motor skills involving the use of the upper body develop before those using the lower body. Infants are capable of lifting their heads before they can lift their trunks, and then sit up and walk. This progression in physical and motor growth continues from conception to young adulthood and is called **cephalocaudal development**. Can you think of other examples?

The internal organs of the body, such as heart and lungs, develop and become operational before the development of the long limbs of the body, then fingers and toes, and the child's capacity to use his or her limbs. This is called **proximodistal development**. Infants, children and adolescents are capable of mastering skills requiring gross motor movements of the body before those requiring the use of fine, or peripheral, motor movement. Typically, we master the movement of shoulders and trunk before we master the use of hands and fingers.

The implications of proximodistal and cephalocaudal growth patterns will be explored later in the chapter.

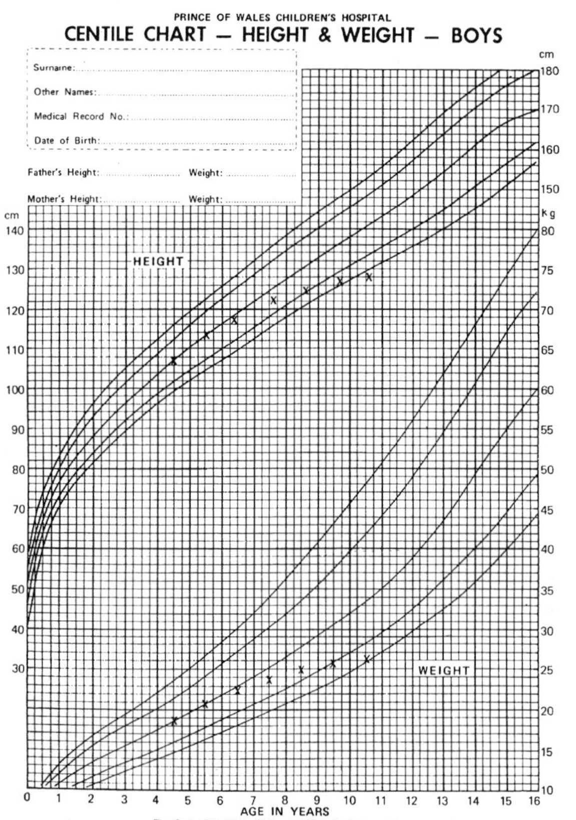

The recorded measurements cross percentile lines and indicate abnormal growth, presumably due to ill health. This is an indication of the need for a full medical investigation.

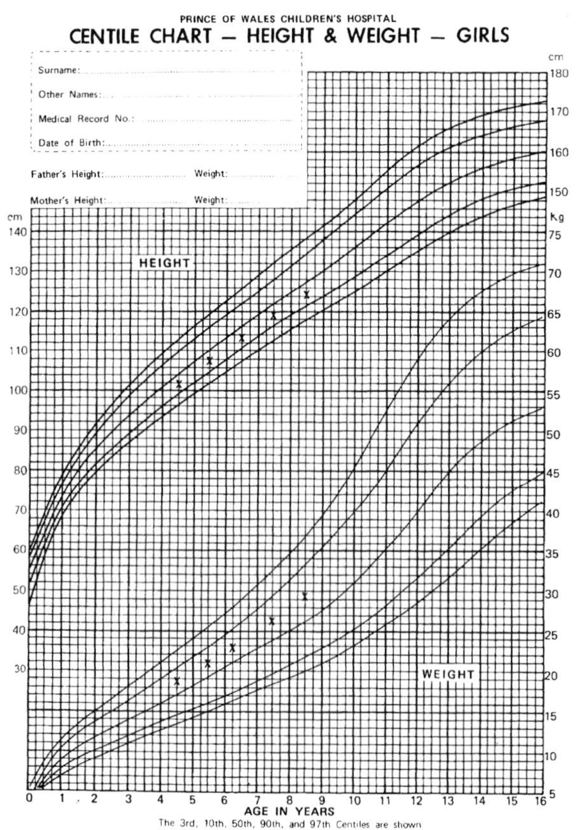

Consecutive annual measurements indicate a normal growth pattern in a developing girl.

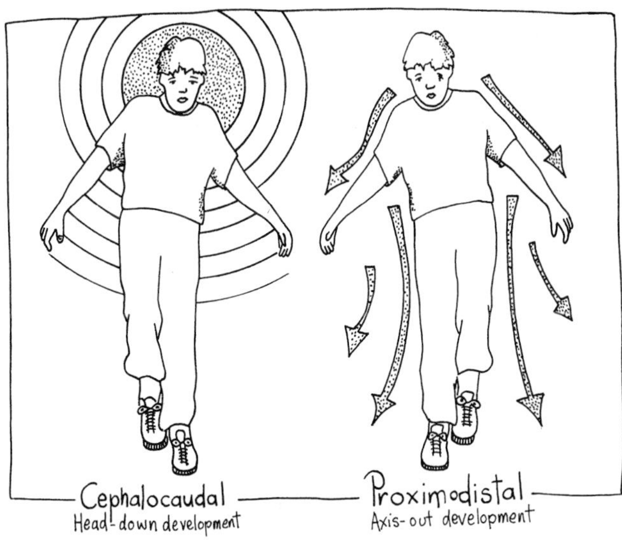

Question point: Recognising that children in educational settings (preschools and schools) are proceeding through physical changes at different rates, how might you, as a sensitive educator, take this into account when programming learning experiences?

KEY CHARACTERISTICS OF GROWTH PATTERNS

Growth patterns are frequently presented in the following cycles:

- ☐ prenatal development and the newborn;
- ☐ infancy: two months to two years;
- ☐ early childhood: two years to six years;
- ☐ middle and later childhood: seven years to puberty;
- ☐ adolescence: puberty to 18 years;
- ☐ adulthood.

These ages are only approximate. We will take brief look at the physical and motor development that characterises each of these periods and draw out the implications for parents and teachers. We should also emphasise that many other developmental systems, such as the cognitive, emotional and personal developmental systems, develop hand in hand with the physical and motor systems. Indeed, they interact to such a degree that a separate examination of each is only useful as a schema around which to organise our ideas. A full picture of the growing child requires us to see the systems acting interactively (Brim & Kagan 1980; Brooks-Gunn & Warren 1989; Holt 1991; Malina 1990).

Ask youself as you read, 'What do I need to keep in mind about this stage of development from my perspective as a caregiver and educator?'

Prenatal development and the newborn

Early physical development

The nine months of pregnancy and the first few months of life are times of rapid growth (Bee 1992; Holt 1991; Turner & Helms 1991). During the 280-day gestation period the child rapidly progresses from a fertilised egg engaged in cell division (often called the ovum or germinal period) to an **embryo** with organ systems developing, and then to a **foetus** which increasingly resembles a human being. The rate of growth may be appreciated when we realise that within four weeks of conception the organism has grown 10 000 times larger than the original fertilised egg, and that internal organs assume nearly adult positions by the fifth week.

The support systems necessary for life—the heart, lungs, brain, nervous system and muscles—are sufficiently developed after 26 weeks (out of 40) for the foetus to survive outside the womb.

Newborn reflexes

At birth, the baby is born with a series of reflexes, such as the sucking and breathing reflexes, that are essential for the child's survival (the newborn attaches to the mother's breast and sucks with great energy only hours after birth). Other reflexes such as the grasping, moro, rooting and stepping reflexes signal the effective operation of the child's nervous system. These reflexes are used by paediatricians at regular times to assess the physiological development of the child (Berk 1996, 1997; Holt 1991).

Birth problems that may affect development

During the prenatal and neonatal period, genetic or environmental influences may cause developmental problems for the individual which become manifest in delaying or limiting physical, motor and intellectual development. In particular, a range of **genetic diseases** (such as cystic fibrosis, phenylketonuria), **chromosomal abnormalities** (such as Down syndrome and Klinefelter syndrome), **birth complications** (such as oxygen deprivation—called *anoxia*), **drugs** taken by the mother during pregnancy (such as alcohol, nicotine, cocaine or heroin), maternal diseases passed on to the infant (such as AIDS) and malnourishment of the foetus and newborn, have been shown to be related to later developmental problems. It is beyond the scope of this text to describe these in detail and you are referred to Berk (1996, 1997) for further details.

Infancy and early childhood

The first month after birth is a period during which the infant, often referred to as a **neonate**, learns to coordinate its body into a more efficiently functioning system. The subsequent period is generally named

infancy and lasts around two years. During infancy there is a lengthening of the lower limbs and, in general, the baby's body proportions become more adult-like. On average, the child gains about 9 kilograms in weight and 40 centimetres in height in the period between two months and two years.

Major **developmental tasks** of infancy relate to their rapidly developing motor skills. In particular, the infant learns to adjust to liquid and solid foods, to control the neck and shoulders, and to sit, reach and walk. There is also a development of fine muscle movement and the ability to grasp and hold with the fingers. Major **social developments** that occur alongside the physical and motor development are learning to talk and to form basic relationships with adults. The increasing mobility of the infant, coupled with language development, is accompanied by an increasing resentment of being babied and a growing desire to be independent. It is very important for parents to give the child frequent and sustained contact during these early years. Adults should also supply a stimulating environment that helps the child develop a feeling of having some control over what happens.

Major developmental tasks of infancy

In these first two years the difference between boys and girls in growth rate and body proportions is of no practical significance. As the child becomes more mobile, is able to communicate effectively and becomes a more social creature, the age of infancy comes to an end.

Early childhood

While the rate of growth during this period is slower than during infancy, the considerable changes that take place are nevertheless significant. Fatty tissue which characterised the bouncing baby is gradually replaced by the developing muscle systems, beginning with the **broader muscle systems**, and then the **finer muscle systems**. The trunk and legs of the child grow rapidly and the skeletal system becomes more developed; new bone is established with the conversion of cartilage into bone and the growth of existing bones. By about three years most children have a complete set of baby teeth. On average, children grow about 6 centimetres in height and weight increases 2–3 kilograms per year.

The development of broad and fine muscle systems

Cranial growth is slow during this period; however, by the age of five the brain has reached 75% of its adult weight and, within another year, 90%. The nervous system also develops during this time and the sheathing of the nerve fibres in the brain is substantially completed by the end of this period (Schmidt 1975, 1982).

Cranial growth

By six years of age, children have substantially assumed the body proportions they will have as adults. Girls, even at this early age, tend to mature faster than boys. As a ready reckoner, by two years of age, females have achieved approximately half their adult height. By two and a half years, males have reached about half their adult height. Parents, particularly grandparents, often mourn the passing of the period of infancy as children lose some of their cuddliness and become more lean and mean action machines! There is a temptation at this time for caregivers to overfeed children to compensate for their apparent loss of weight. However, as children get taller, body shape and levels of fat change naturally.

Changing body proportions

Major **developmental tasks** for children at this time are the coordination of body movements and, in particular, learning gross motor skills such as running, skipping, hopping, catching and balancing, and fine motor skills such as writing and drawing. This is also an important time when healthy children begin to form concepts of social and physical reality and are intensely curious about the world around them.

Major developmental tasks of early childhood

As physical activity and the expenditure of great energy is typical of this age, teachers and parents must be prepared for this in both its constructive and destructive modes. The energy needs to be channelled: children should be given the opportunity to exercise gross motor and fine motor skills in both directed and undirected settings and to be responsible for doing 'important' things—for example, kitchen chores, dressing and undressing. Pride in doing these things is important to foster, as is encouragement to copy and be involved in adult activities. In this context it is important that adults are reasonable in what they expect from children and to avoid making comparisons between them.

There is very little difference between the size of boys and girls during early childhood and they have very much the same body proportions. While girls tend to retain more fat than boys, boys develop more muscle tissue. There is, however, no justification for different physical education, sport or health programs for boys and girls. Their coordination skills are the same. Any apparent differences in performance are likely to be the result of differing social expectations, and the opportunities presented to girls and boys (Berk 1996, 1997; Corbin 1980; Gallahue 1976, 1982; Thomas & French 1985). It is important, therefore, that girls and boys are given opportunities to engage in a wide range of physical activities and are not limited to those that might be considered sex-typed. It is not uncommon for children,

Few sex differences

from an early age, to be encouraged by parents, siblings and peers to engage in different physical activities that are sex stereotyped. For example, fathers might play ball with their sons in the backyard, but less frequently play ball with their daughters. Cricket bats and footballs are purchased for sons, while skipping ropes and jacks are purchased for girls. As children get older, differences in motor skills between girls and boys increase, reflecting the social pressures on boys to be active and physically skilled, and girls to be more passive and skilled at fine motor activities. Increasingly, childcare settings and schools are encouraging young children to participate equally in physical activities such as dancing, skipping and team ball games. These are presented as a means of developing physical fitness and team cooperation that is appropriate to all.

Middle and later childhood to puberty

Refinement of motor skills

This is a period of steady growth which ends with the dramatic arrival of puberty. If well nourished, children grow 4.4 to 6.6 centimetres in height and gain from 2 to 2.75 kilograms per year. Children's bodies gradually approach adult dimensions. By 12 years of age, children have reached approximately 90% of their adult height. Significant advances are made in gross and fine motor skill coordination. Children now have the ability to tie shoelaces, fasten buttons, dress and feed themselves. Many school activities such as playing musical instruments and detailed art and craft activities become possible. Children work to develop and perfect many motor skills, enjoying the sense of achievement when skills are perfected. This is also an important period for developing a healthy self-identity as children test the interactions of their body with the world and also the reactions of others to their growing competencies.

The role of the family is very important at this time as it is an arena for learning appropriate sex roles, developing relationships and achieving personal independence. School is also very significant as it is the first wide social environment of the child that facilitates the development of attitudes towards social groups and institutions, learning to get along with age-mates, and life skills.

Children in the infant grades appear to be in perpetual motion and have a great need for running, chasing and climbing activities. As a result, they are easily susceptible to injury and fatigue. Gross motor skills are more developed than fine motor skills, and hand–eye, foot–eye coordination are being developed. Many of these finer skills do not come to full maturity until adolescence. During this time the first teeth begin to fall out (or are wiggled out by a compulsive tongue) and the tooth fairy becomes very busy. Permanent teeth appear and many smiles are cutely 'marred' by toothless gaps and oversized teeth.

Oral hygiene

As speech, appearance and body image are all affected by the health of teeth, sound oral hygiene and dental care must be encouraged by parents and teachers. Children in the infants grades can also be very individualistic, curious, imaginative, creative and dramatic. They often display a great desire to please and excel, and to assume leadership and responsibility. Nevertheless, they seek to establish this independence in a secure environment.

Each of these children is eight years old. Growth differences reflect a number of factors. What are some of these? Photo: Debbie Blazley

By about fourth grade children are aware of growing up, and feel that they are too big for little ones (first graders) and too little for the big ones (sixth graders). Children at this age tend to display very distinctive individual characteristics, argue over fairness, and may become, at times,

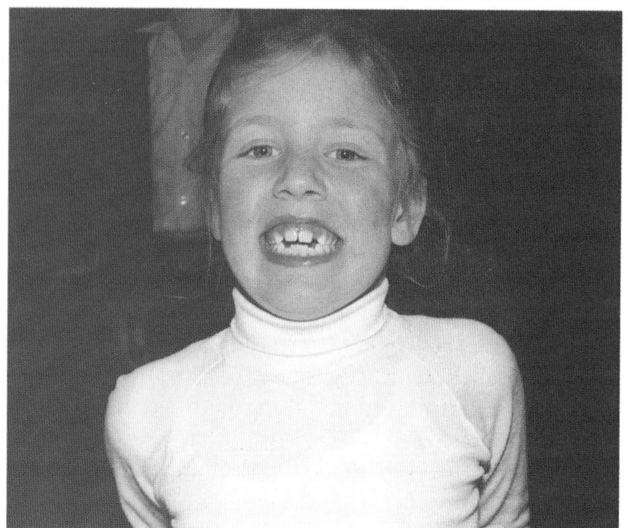

Second teeth—a badge of growing maturity.
Photo: Connie Griebe

aggressive and quarrelsome. They are capable of longer attention spans, and are highly creative and imaginative.

By fifth grade many children are going through another period of rapid physical growth with the development of muscular strength and bone length paralled by the development of motor skills and coordination. Children in upper primary enjoy vigorous physical activities, and are increasingly interested in competitive activities and organised games. During these games they are very concerned with game rules and their correct application. This attitude is generalised to an interest in ethics and values, and the desire to make fair judgments. You can see here the interaction of cognitive, social and moral development.

At this time there will be considerable differences in rates of development and children may show increasing interest in growth patterns, comparing who is the smallest and who is the tallest. As girls tend to mature earlier than boys, the development of sexual characteristics may become noticeable.

Many children at this time begin to display independent behaviour demonstrated in some forms of rebellion against teachers and parents. It is also a period of strong peer allegiance and hero worship.

Among the major **developmental tasks** for this period are the development and refinement of physical skills for games and academic purposes, and acquiring a healthy concept of self. Social skills in dealing with peers, appropriate social and sex roles and aspects of personal independence also develop along with intellectual capacity. Within this context, children learn many moral and social concepts required for daily living, including conscience, morality and values.

Major developmental tasks of middle childhood

Individual and group differences Some body parts grow at different rates relative to others during middle to late childhood and some awkwardness and lankiness may characterise children's appearance and coordination. The growth of the skeleton, for example, is frequently more rapid than the growth of the muscles and ligaments. **Asynchrony** is the term used to describe this differential development.

Asynchrony: differential growth spurts

Because children's bodies are undergoing significant structural changes during the primary years, schools should be careful that children sit in desks and chairs that fit, wear shoes that fit, and don't carry unreasonably heavy loads of books to school.

The end of this period comes with puberty which ushers in another period of rapid and often uneven growth.

ACTION STATION

a

The objective of this activity is to compare the physical features of children in different grades—in particular, height, weight, strength, coordination, teeth distribution and growth, head circumference, finger length, body proportions and any asynchronous features.

Is there any evidence of significant differences in development trends across grades? How might this information assist the teacher with programming? What about the degree of individual variation from these trends? Share your information with a group and, using the pooled information, construct timelines for development, concentrating on three broad bands: grades 1 and 2, grades 3 and 4, and grades 5 and 6.

Question point: *If there is little average difference between males and females in physical capacity pre-puberty, why do we get such different performance from them in physical education classes, and in the playground? Why do some teachers have different attitudes towards males and females regarding their performance levels in such classes?*

Puberty and adolescence

Physiological differences between males and females that are related to average developmental rates, disposition of muscle and fat tissue, rate of skeletal ossification, and overall strength and size are programmed genetically at conception (Brooks-Gunn & Petersen 1983; Corbin 1980; Lockhart 1980a, b; Malina & Bouchard 1991; Tanner 1990). These differences are, for all intents and purposes, minor before puberty, and are less significant than individual

TEACHER'S CASE BOOK

THERE IS MORE TO HIM THAN HIS BODY

Tony, the 'fat boy' in Miss Rodgers' class, suffered much teasing about his size and had very low self-esteem. She ran a session where class members said things about each of the other students in the class and, excluding physical attributes, described what made each person special. The comments about Tony were not size-related, but were 'caring'; a 'good friend'; 'happy and funny'.

Two days later she found out that one of the most popular girls in the class was now his 'steady' girlfriend. When Miss Rodgers spoke to her about this, she said: 'I realised that there is lots more to Tony than his body.'

Miss Rodgers was aware of her power to influence the students' attitudes and planned to use a deliberate approach that would focus on the students' thoughts about the broad range of positive personal attributes their peers possessed.

Case studies illustrating National Competency Framework for Beginning Teaching, National Project on the Quality of Teaching and Learning, Australian Teaching Council, 1996, p. 15. Commonwealth of Australia copyright, reproduced by permission.

Case study activity
How might Miss Rodgers develop a program to focus on the students' thoughts about the broad range of positive personal attributes their peers possessed?

differences within the sexes. In any one classroom we find slight and heavy boys and girls, and quite large differences between the tallest and shortest, heaviest and lightest children. Children's development reflects hereditary influences, nutrition, exercise and developmental stage (some will be prepubertal, some pubertal).

It is strikingly obvious, however, that the quantity and quality of change that marks adolescence is different for the sexes. This is caused by the difference in hormonal activity occurring in the bodies of males and females at this time. When the pituitary gland, situated at the base of the brain, is called into action to stimulate growth, it activates the sex glands to greater activity, producing hormones characteristic of either the male androgens or female oestrogens. Of significance here are the ovaries and testes which produce enough hormones to accelerate the growth of the genitals and the appearance of secondary sex characteristics.

Pubescence: growing hairy

The onset of puberty comes with the physiological development of the sexual system which leads into a longer period of physical development called **adolescence. Pubescence** (derived from the Latin 'to grow hairy'!) refers to changes that result in sexual maturity. In boys, these changes include the enlargement of the testes and penis; growth of pubic, underarm and facial hair; changes in the voice; and the production of and ability to ejaculate semen.

In girls, pubescence is characterised by rapid physical growth, particularly of the uterus, vagina and fallopian tubes. Other changes are the occurrence of the first menstrual cycle (menarche or period); a slight lowering of the voice; an enlargement and development of the breasts; rounding of the pelvic area; and growth of pubic and underarm hair (Brooks-Gunn & Petersen 1983; Daniel 1983; Faust 1983; Malina 1990; Malina & Bouchard 1991; Peterson & Taylor 1980; Tanner 1990; Warren 1983).

Dramatic and rapid physical changes

While the biological system (the ability to procreate) matures relatively early in this period, physical changes of quite large proportions continue for a number of years. One of the most obvious changes is the **growth spurt**, when adolescents always seem to be growing out of their shoes and clothing. Perhaps some of you remember meeting a relative for the first time after a few months and being greeted with the comment: 'Struth, what are they feeding you!' Such unthinking reactions can be quite upsetting for the teenager trying to cope with the countless physical and mental changes that are occurring. One teenager we knew developed the habit of stooping so that he would not attract comments about his height.

Differences in timing of growth spurt for boys and girls

This abrupt increase in stature begins between the ages of $8\frac{1}{2}$ and $10\frac{1}{2}$ for the average girl and reaches its peak around 12, while for boys the growth spurt occurs between the ages of $10\frac{1}{2}$ and $12\frac{1}{2}$ and reaches peak rates of increase at about 14 or 15. So, in general, boys begin the pubertal growth spurt after girls, but it lasts three to four years longer than girls. Because of this, girls are initially taller and heavier than boys in the age range 11 to 14+ but boys surpass them and end up, on average, significantly taller and heavier than girls.

Racial differences in onset of puberty

We should note here that there are racial differences in the age of onset of puberty and the growth spurt (Malina & Bouchard 1991; Tanner 1990). Furthermore, norms for height and weight derived from Western groups may not be representative of many groups in Australia and New Zealand (e.g. children from a number of racial groups are typically lighter and shorter at each level of development, while others are typically heavier) and care should be used, therefore, when applying norms in racially diverse societies.

The increase in muscle growth during adolescence is greater for boys than for girls, and is more marked in the arm than in the calf. Hence the adolescent male is stronger than the adolescent female. The overall average size and strength difference between boys and girls after puberty is due to the longer preadolescent growth period of males prior to the onset of puberty.

Physiological differences between sexes

Males usually develop larger hearts and lungs, together with a greater capacity for absorbing oxygen in the blood and for eliminating the biochemical products of exercise. Males also develop wider shoulders, while females develop a wider pelvis and store more fat in their tissues. Lastly, most men develop deeper voices than females.

At this developmental stage there is some justification for differentiated sporting and health programs for boys and girls. Unfortunately, this has often been interpreted in the past as support for vigorous physical activity for boys and relatively sedentary physical activities for girls. Consequently, beyond the age of 10 to 12 years, there are rather substantial differences between the average male and female *in all areas of physical performance*. We should ensure that all girls and boys receive appropriate fitness and endurance training, including vigorous physical activity for girls (Wilmore 1989). As noted earlier, over the last decade schools have increasingly encouraged girls to participate in a wide range of male sex-stereotyped sports, such as cricket, touch football and golf. However, the number of girls engaged in such vigorous sports is still not great.

Asynchrony during adolescence

We have already mentioned the notion of asynchrony in the context of late childhood development. Asynchrony refers to the differential rate at which different body parts grow. In late childhood, individuals appear to be blissfully unaware of their gawkiness but asynchronous development seems to cause distress for some adolescents. There are two types of asynchrony: **interpersonal**, where development varies from individual to individual, and **intrapersonal**, where there is an uneven progression of development within an individual (Collins & Plahn 1988; Cramer 1980; Wright 1989).

The onset of development can vary quite markedly within any cohort of age peers, so that in any year six grade there might be prepubescent, pubescent and adolescent children. This is a case of interpersonal asynchrony. For example, while most boys acquire pubic hair before the height spurt, and most girls' breasts have nearly finished growing before menarche, some individuals deviate from this sequential pattern. This can be a source of serious worry for them.

Interpersonal asynchrony: development varies from individual to individual

For any individual, **intrapersonal asynchrony** can also cause concern. The nose, for example, develops to full size very early and consequently appears disproportionately large on a youngster's face. Ears, limbs and fingers also give an appearance of gawkiness to this age group. The sebaceous (oil-producing) glands of the skin can develop more quickly than the ducts, causing the blockages and infections known as acne. Shoulders and hips may grow out of sequence for girls, giving them an overly masculine appearance or an exaggerated 'pear' shape.

Intrapersonal asynchrony: uneven development within an individual

'Go on! Make our day!'
Early and late development can cause special problems for some children.

Both intrapersonal and interpersonal asynchrony can have an effect on boys' and girls' self-concept and self-confidence. Teachers, in particular, need to be aware of and alleviate potential problems in sensible and sensitive ways. For example, the custom of children changing clothing publicly for sport can be embarrassing for many children. Alternative opportunities for children to change should be provided.

Early and late maturation

One form of interpersonal asynchrony is the age of onset of pubertal development. Some children develop early, while others develop relatively late. Research has studied the effects of early and late maturation on boys and girls (Faust 1983; Livson & Peskin 1980; Petersen 1987; Tobin-Richards et al. 1983). Among the findings are that early maturing boys appeared more self-assured, more relaxed, more masculine, better groomed, and more poised and handsome than both the late and average group. Late maturers apparently stood out for their restless attention seeking, their tense manner, and their boyish eagerness and social awkwardness. Early maturers appeared more popular with their male peers than the late maturers and they were chosen in preference to both late and average maturers in contests for leadership. The late maturers were judged by adults to be less responsible and less mature than other boys their age in their relationships with girls. Late maturers emerged at a disadvantage to early maturers in virtually all areas of behaviour and adjustment during adolescence. While in later life the physical differences between these groups has been shown to disappear, personality differences may persist (Mussen & Jones 1957, 1958).

Characteristics of early and late maturing boys

What might be the cause of these differences? Early maturing boys are expected by parents and teachers to be more competent than less developed peers and therefore may be given more responsibilities and opportunities to develop personality characteristics such as independence and responsibility. Any difference between early and late maturers could well be artefacts of socialisation. Furthermore, many physically underdeveloped males are sufficiently cognitively, socially and emotionally developed to benefit from these same responsibilities and opportunities, but are often denied them, which may breed resentment and poor adjustment. On the other hand, some physically advanced males may not be cognitively and emotionally prepared for the responsibilities they are expected to assume. As sensitive parents and teachers we must look at all developmental aspects of the child when deciding when it is appropriate increasingly to relinquish our control and give the children greater responsibility.

Most research on early and late maturing girls finds very few differences between the two groups. The explanation might be the relatively shorter pubertal period for girls, and the fact that late maturing girls still have boys of the same age who are less developed physically and sexually than they are. However, early developing girls sometimes experience emotional and social difficulties that may be reflected in lack of popularity, withdrawal and low self-confidence (Berk 1996). This may be because early maturers' psychological preparedness is inadequate to cope with the physical stress of menstruating or the added responsibilities that they might be expected to assume. In some cases, parents of early maturing girls become more restrictive in an attempt to protect them from potential sexual dangers, and consequently frustrate their attempts to become more independent. This stands in marked contrast to the way that early maturing boys are treated. Finally, early maturing girls may feel isolated from their peer group. (See Hill & Lynch, 1983, for a discussion of gender-related role expectations during early adolescence.)

Characteristics of early and late maturing girls

In this regard, parents and teachers must be alert to messages that children give about developmental stress, and be sympathetic, empathetic and loving in their caring for the children. This will not always be easy as developing individuals struggle to understand why they may be different when they want to be the same as others, and may feel that adults could not possibly understand their fears and disappointments about their appearance.

Longitudinal research indicates that several aspects of adolescent adjustment may remain evident into middle adulthood. In one study the social skills of early maturing males were still in evidence at age 38, while the late maturing adolescents remained more impulsive and assertive over the years (Livson & Peskin 1980). It is evident, however, that there can be some interesting reversals. For example, many late maturing boys and early maturing girls, who initially lacked self-assurance, developed into very self-assured and caring adults. In contrast, many confident and self-assured early maturing boys and late maturing girls became somewhat discontented adults (Berk 1996; Peterson 1996). These findings show that earlier social experiences can have differential effects on the long-term development of early and late maturers. Perhaps as a result of the 'deviant' timing of their development, late maturing males and early maturing females encounter more adjustment problems which give them superior skills for dealing with the stresses of adult life (Peterson 1996).

Are there long term consequences of early or late maturing?

Trend towards larger size and earlier maturation
During the past 100 years or so there has been a trend towards accelerated maturation in height and weight among boys and girls. Similar observations have been made with respect to sexual maturation. This tendency has been termed the **secular trend** towards earlier

growth (Frisch 1983; Garn 1980; Tanner 1990; Warren 1983). It has been suggested that the age for the onset of puberty has decreased by about four months per decade in western Europe over the past 120 years. There are a number of suggested explanations for this and you might like to discuss these with friends and parents, particularly older people. One explanation is that improved nutritional standards, together with the conquest of several major childhood illnesses, have led to the secular trend. It is also suggested that inter-marriage among a wider genetic pool, the result of increased world travel and immigration, may be implicated. For example, people from warmer climates appear to mature earlier, and certain races appear to mature earlier. There is also a suggestion that our present Western culture's emphasis on sexuality might be hastening puberty for modern adolescents. In other words, psychological factors could be having an effect on the purely physiological process. Gives us much food for thought, doesn't it? Current research indicates that this trend ceases to have an impact when a nation's (or cultural/social group's) health and nutritional standards reach an optimal level. Just as well—otherwise, like the Japanese, we would all be redesigning our buildings with higher doorways!

The secular trend: Accelerated physical and sexual development

Question point: *What adjustment problems may be generated by differential growth spurts of males and females in a co-ed class? What are the implications of the differential physical development in adolescent males and females for physical education and sport activities?*

ACTION STATION

On pages 331–332 we list some possible reasons for the secular trend in maturation.

1. What do you think about these reasons?
2. Interview a number of older adults of varying ages regarding this issue and discuss in a group the various explanations given. Your interview could start: 'It appears that children today are growing bigger and maturing earlier than children 50 years ago. Have you noticed this? If so, how do you account for the increased growth and earlier maturation?'

Adolescents and 'ideal' body type

Adolescents appear to have a preoccupation with their looks and popularity. Peer and social pressures during adolescence dictate appropriate sexual attitudes and behaviour for each gender. As well as this, the 'ideal' body type for males and females, as presented through the mass media, may lead those who vary from such types to feel negative towards themselves (Faust 1983; Langlois & Stephan 1981; Lerner & Korn 1972; Staffieri 1972; Tobin-Richards et al. 1983). Two factors that are basic to the adolescent's concern with physique are the desire to meet culturally prescribed standards of beauty, and the desire to have the requisite sex-appropriate characteristics. Some children experience considerable anxiety over such issues as weight, strength and attractiveness. When rating photographs of various male body types, males between the ages of ten and twenty clearly preferred strong athletic types on dimensions such as leadership, popularity and ability to endure pain. Stereotypes associated with the other physical types, such as skinny and fat, were generally negative. Adolescents, therefore, who perceive their bodies as fat or skinny probably feel bad about themselves and believe that their peer group dislikes them (Lerner 1969). For both men and women, the degree of positive self-concept is correlated with the degree of satisfaction with one's own bodily characteristics (Cavior & Dokecki 1973; Cavior & Lombardi 1973; Faust 1983; Lerner 1969; Lerner & Korn 1972; Staffieri 1967, 1972; Styczynski & Langlois 1977; see also Marsh & Craven, in press).

Adolescent preoccupation with looks and popularity

These issues, and the general concern generated by such a period of rapid development, can introduce greater personality problems in adolescence than at any other stage of development. Sympathetic and reassuring teachers and parents are comforting to the adolescent at this time.

EATING DISORDERS

Research in the last decade has pointed to a high prevalence of body dissatisfaction among adolescents (especially females) causing many of them to diet unwisely through crash diets and unhealthy eating habits (Paxton et al. 1991). At a time when the mass media (and especially television and magazine advertisements for fashion, diet foods and entertainment) seem to promote the ideal that to be attractive and popular one needs to be slim, adolescents are going through a growth spurt that leads to weight gain! It appears that many adolescent girls confuse obesity with normal weight gain that occurs with the pubertal growth of bones, muscles, breasts and hips (Peterson 1996). As a consequence of this, many adolescent girls wish they were thinner (Berger 1991). Peer and parental influence may also contribute to these unhealthy attitudes and behaviours of adolescents in

The influence of media, peers and family

regard to weight, body shape and eating (Levine, Smolak & Hayden 1994; Paxton, Schutz & Muir 1996; Wertheim, Mee & Paxton 1996). For example, a study by Paxton, Schutz and Muir (1996) showed that if an adolescent girl perceived that her friends were concerned and talked about dieting, and encouraged her to diet, and she had a tendency to compare her body with others, her own attitudes and behaviours towards body image and dieting would be strongly affected. A further study indicated that friendship cliques operate as an important subcultural environment that influences broader sociocultural pressures for thinness in adolescent girls. In other words, girls who belong to friendship cliques that do not emphasise calorie counting and dieting are less likely to be involved in dieting (Paxton Schutz, & Muir 1996).

It appears that body dissatisfaction increases with age, with the onset beginning for many children in late childhood (Davies & Furnham 1986; Levine, Smolak & Hayden 1994). Recent reports indicate that girls as young as eight are dieting, some to the point of starvation, because they wish to grow up to be supermodels (*Sydney Morning Herald* 1996). As a result these children go without morning and afternoon tea, and often refuse to eat dinner in their quest to have the perfect body type. Unfortunately, children who starve themselves become lethargic, unable to concentrate during lessons or take part in sport. Damage can also be long-term.

Body dissatisfaction increases with age

Offer, Ostrov, Howard & Atkinson (1988) conducted a comprehensive cross-cultural study of adolescent self-image, and found body image in Australian girls to be the lowest and in Australian boys the second lowest of the Western industrialised countries examined. These findings are cause for concern as poor body image and weight loss behaviours have been associated with disordered eating among female adolescents (Attie & Brooks-Gunn 1989).

In some cases this preoccupation with dieting leads to a severe eating disorder called **bulimia nervosa**. This disorder means that the sufferer engages in uncontrollable binge eating followed by a combination of purging of the stomach contents through laxatives, diuretics or self-induced vomiting, strict fasting and strenuous exercise (Griffiths & Channon 1996). As you can appreciate, cycles of binge eating, followed by purging and severe dieting, can cause physical and psychological health problems that can be life-threatening (Johnson & Conners 1987). Recent Australian estimates suggest that about 2% of adolescent girls and 1% of adolescent boys are clinically bulimic, and one teenager in 1000 is anorexic. Similar figures are obtained in New Zealand (Bushnell et al. 1990, 1994; Maude et al. 1993).

Bulimia nervosa can lead to the development of the most serious eating disorder—**anorexia nervosa**. Anorexic individuals restrict their eating to such an extent that they become painfully thin, and the malnutrition that accompanies the illness leads to additional side-effects such as brittle, discoloured nails, pale skin, fine dark hairs appearing all over the body and extreme sensitivity to cold. Menstrual periods also cease (Berk 1996). Anorexia is a severe disorder for which proper medical help must be obtained. While adolescent girls seem to be most susceptible to both bulimia nervosa and anorexia nervosa, boys and adults of both sexes are also affected.

As we have suggested, there are many explanations of the causes of dieting and eating disorders such as bulimia nervosa and anorexia nervosa, including cultural, familial and psychological conditions, and a range of treatments exists which are beyond the scope of this book (see Berger 1991; Berk 1996; Fairburn & Beglin 1990; Romeo 1986). As educators you have an important responsibility to advise your students about healthy eating habits, particularly through the personal development program in place at your school. Where possible, stereotypes of ideal body types portrayed in the media should be discussed in the context of 'normal' adolescent development.

Treatment of eating disorders

Where it becomes apparent that a particular student may be bulimic or anorexic, professional help and guidance should be obtained. Early identification of anorexic students is very important in order to permit treatment before the development of irreversible medical complications. Five per cent of anorexic individuals die as a result of the severity of this problem (Romeo 1986).

It is of interest here to consider whether there are cultural differences in the onset of eating disorders. In particular, are there differences between cultures for which food is a more or less central aspect of socialising within the family and community? Do children who come from ethnic backgrounds that emphasise healthy and plentiful eating become socialised into the pursuit of thinness, and defy family and cultural expectations regarding food in their quest for the 'ideal' body shape?

Question point: *We have indicated a number of implications for school programs and facilities derived from our knowledge of the ways in which boys and girls grow. Discuss these in the context of your own school experiences. What changes would you make in the way that your school taught you?*

Question point: *What role should schools play in sex education? Does the cultural mix of the school make a difference?*

Question point: Discuss eating disorders among adolescents and adults. What might the sensitive teacher do to help prevent and alleviate such problems?

PRINCIPLES OF MOTOR DEVELOPMENT

Paralleling the physical growth of the body is the development of the individual's motor coordination. From what appears to be a rather helpless bundle of non-coordination rapidly develops a well-coordinated child, able to walk, run, skip and jump. Motor development continues throughout childhood and adolescence, and into adulthood, following a predictable sequence. Motor development should be seen as part of the holistic development of the individual which includes perception, action and cognition (Thelen 1995).

Sequence of motor development

As children mature, motor capacities develop gradually from a set of reflex actions to a complex set of motor abilities. A lot of research has been done on the sequence of motor development and its relationship to physical development (Bayley 1956; Connolly & Dalgleish 1989; Corbin 1980; Fagard & Jacquet 1989; Gallahue 1976, 1982; Gesell 1925; Matthew & Crook 1990; Thomas 1990). Researchers have also been interested in whether motor development can be accelerated through environmental influences. While it does not appear that motor development can be accelerated, there is considerable evidence that physical and motor development can be retarded under the impact of poor environmental conditions such as sickness, accident or gross physical neglect.

Differentiation and integration

Motor development proceeds by way of the dual processes of differentiation and integration. **Differentiation** is associated with the gradual progression of children from gross overall movement patterns to more refined and functional movements as they mature. **Integration** refers to bringing various opposing muscle and sensory systems into coordinated interaction with one another (Gallahue 1976, 1982).

Key principles of motor development are maturation, motivation, experience and practice (Gallahue 1976, 1982; Malina & Bouchard 1991; Schmidt 1975, 1982; Wickstrom 1983). These elements are not hierarchical but mutually independent (Thelen 1995).

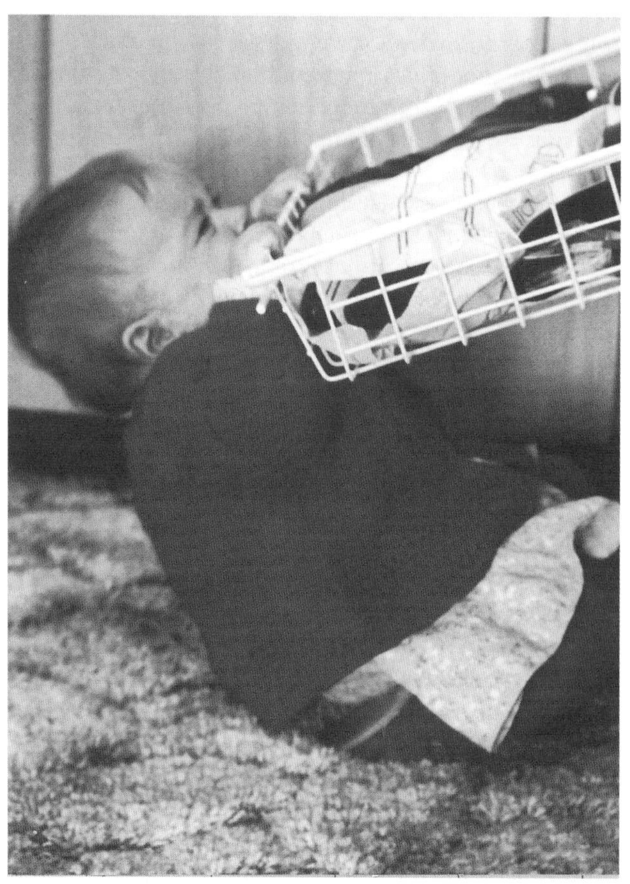

I thought I could manage it! Photo: authors

It's not always this easy when you're little! Photo: authors

Cutting with scissors is a motor skill developed over time with plenty of practice. Photo: authors

Neurological maturation

Neurological maturation is important because not all the centres of the brain are operational at birth—many brain centres that control movement develop over time. By approximately five years of age, however, the brain is capable of stimulating the wide range of activities in which children engage. **Growth in perceptual capacities** is also very important to the development of motor skills (Thelen 1996). Maturation of the physical systems also develops progressively. Larger muscle systems, controlling large body movements such as walking, running and holding, develop before the striated muscle systems which control finer movements such as the manipulation of fingers on a keyboard, or the use of a pair of scissors. These striated muscles are not really fully developed until adolescence, and so there are motor movements beyond children until after puberty. Nevertheless, children are generally capable of a full range of differentiated motor movements that are later integrated into performing complex motor skills by middle childhood. For example, while children of five can hop, skip and jump, they have yet to develop the coordination skills necessary to combine these fluently into one action—hop-skip-jump.

As children's bodies mature, they try out an increasing number of physical activities. Photo: authors

Maturation: point of readiness

It is unwise, therefore, for parents and teachers to attempt to teach children motor skills before they are maturationally ready. Activities such as toilet training, feeding and dressing should be left until children give evidence that they are ready to be taught. This is usually expressed by an imperative 'I can do it!' by the youngster. Our experience is that it is relatively easy for the parent and teacher to know when a child is ready and willing to learn new motor skills—just listen to and watch the child. Children will leave you in no doubt as to what they think you should let them do. (Be prepared to put up with mess and chaos at this time in the knowledge that, under most circumstances, it will be short-lived.)

In recent theories of motor development, **motivation** is considered to be the driving force behind children acquiring motor skills rather than prespecified genetic instructions (Thelen 1996). Children appear to be innately interested in learning a wide range of motor skills in order to achieve goals such as putting a toy in the mouth or crossing the room. Even tasks as ordinary as undoing buttons and tying shoelaces, which signify some independence from adults, can motivate children to acquire important motor skills through practice. At particular times, motor skills become the focus of much voluntary activity and children will spend endless time learning to skip, play with a yo-yo or master elaborate string games in order to demonstrate skills comparable to their peers.

Motivation

At the point of readiness (indicated by the child's maturity and motivational level), parents and teachers must give children **appropriate experiences** to develop motor skills. It is potentially quite harmful if the play equipment is wrongly sized or if the social climate surrounding the practice of the skills is overly competitive, restrictive or demanding. In these cases the enthusiasm of children to acquire the skills can be dampened. Limited competence in fundamental motor skills at an early age can negatively affect future performance in physical and motor activities (Gallahue 1989) with related consequences to self-concept. Past the point of readiness, motivation may dissipate, and later attempts to learn particular skills may be more difficult. Youngsters can learn to roller skate and swim much more easily than older people. Even after the optimal age, however, motor skills may still be learnt, although the earlier a skill is learnt the better, because children are more supple, adventurous, agreeable to repetition, and have more time to practise. Children who fail to develop motor skills appropriate for their age participate less in organised sports and other physical programs. This has significant consequences for their individual well-being.

Experience

Implicated in what we have said above is the **need for practice** to facilitate the development of motor skills. Some systems mature without much practice, such as bowel and bladder control; other skills based on muscle control, such as skipping, need extensive practice. When children show a readiness to learn particular motor skills, they are often also willing to put endless hours into practising the skill. You can probably recall various motor skills that you acquired after many hours of dedicated practice. An interesting aspect of this is that it doesn't appear to bore children. Whether it is learning to click one's fingers, whistle or roller skate, the activity often appears quite compulsive to children until it is mastered. As we get older, such dedication to acquiring new motor skills begins to wane.

Practice

Are there individual differences in motor development?

While motor development follows a predictable pattern, there are many individual differences. Some children never crawl and some learn to walk earlier than others. Some children never develop a skill in balance, while others rival tightrope walkers. Some children are precocious in most skills, while others may be slow.

As well as genetic influences, the child's experiential background affects the growth of motor skills. Some children are encouraged and stimulated in their efforts and exposed to a wide range of models demonstrating diverse motor skills. In other cases, demanding, critical or overprotective parents may inhibit the development of confidence, while limited experiences and a deprived environment may stultify growth. For all of these variations, there exist general age-related norms for the development of motor skills. If a child does not reach a given level of development within these norms then an abnormality may be present. The delayed development may be the result of a poorly maturing physiological system, or the absence of relevant experiences. We live in a house perched on a cliff. The garden is precipitous, full of steps and with no flat areas of grass. Our children, as youngsters, could clamber up and down steps from an early age, but fell over every time they had to walk along a straight path! The early detection of motor problems and the start of appropriate intervention programs is very important to eliminate or hold to a minimum many physical and related emotional problems that may impact on the child's learning (Walkley, Holland, Treloar & Probyn-Smith 1993).

Children also go through stages when they appear awkward, when motor skills are occasionally insufficiently developed for body maturation. Suddenly hands and feet become too big to use. While adolescents become less coordinated in particular tasks from time to time, Malina (1990) found no point in the adolescent growth process at which children become consistently less coordinated or skilful on physical tasks. A pathology should only be suspected when children's control over body movements falls well below age norms (Holt 1991). Children vary in their awkwardness, and at every age more children tend to fall below the norm in **motor coordination** than above it. The one individual may be awkward at some activities but not at others.

Awkwardness

Are there sex differences in motor development?

It is hard to know whether or not there are any inherent differences in the growth of motor skills between the sexes prior to puberty. Physiologically, there seems

Cultural conditioning

Non-sexist educational programs

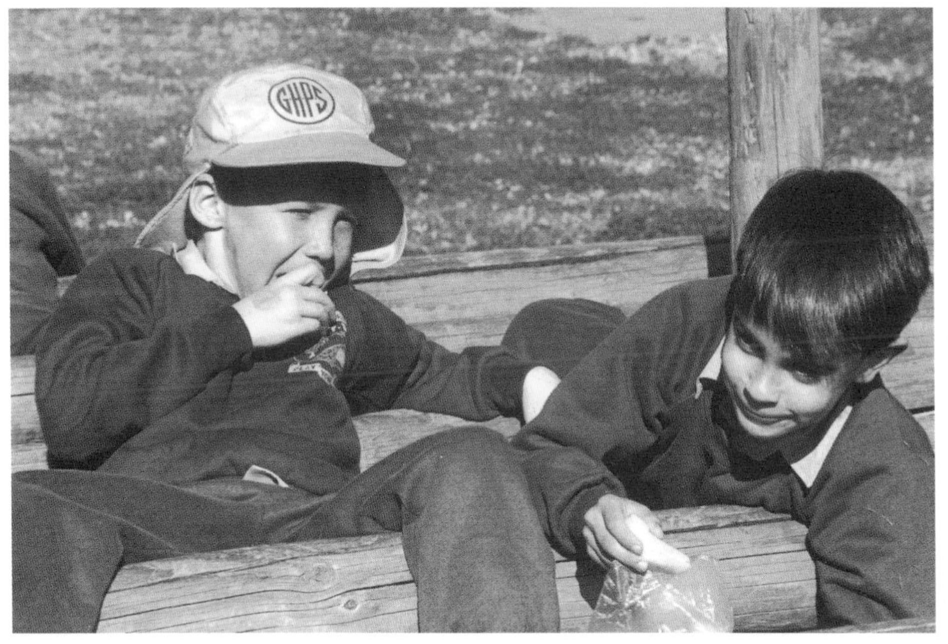

Periods of rest and relaxation alternating with periods of activity are needed for growing bodies.
Photo: Connie Briebe

to be no reason why boys and girls shouldn't develop the same motor skills. Cultural conditioning, however, ensures that boys and girls develop different motor skills that are seen as sex-'appropriate'. Boys are generally expected to learn skills that require daring, strength and endurance, while girls are expected to learn skills that require precision, dexterity and patience, such as sewing and knitting. As a consequence of **non-sexist educational programs** a number of these features of sexist conditioning of motor skills are changing. For example, many schools are

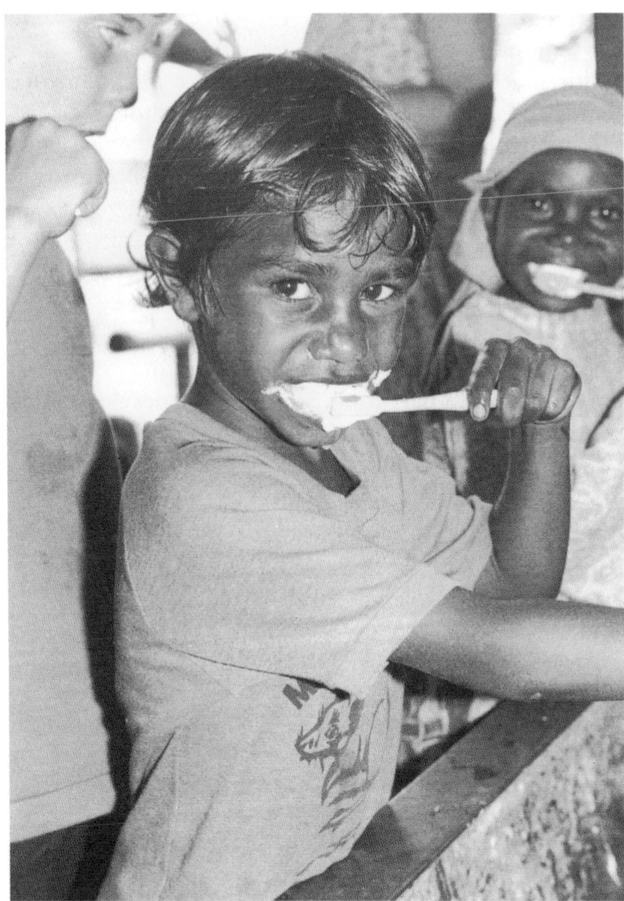
Yandeyarra's tooth cleaning routine—funded by Healthway's grant. Learning to keep healthy is a part of an overall education.
Photo: WA Education News

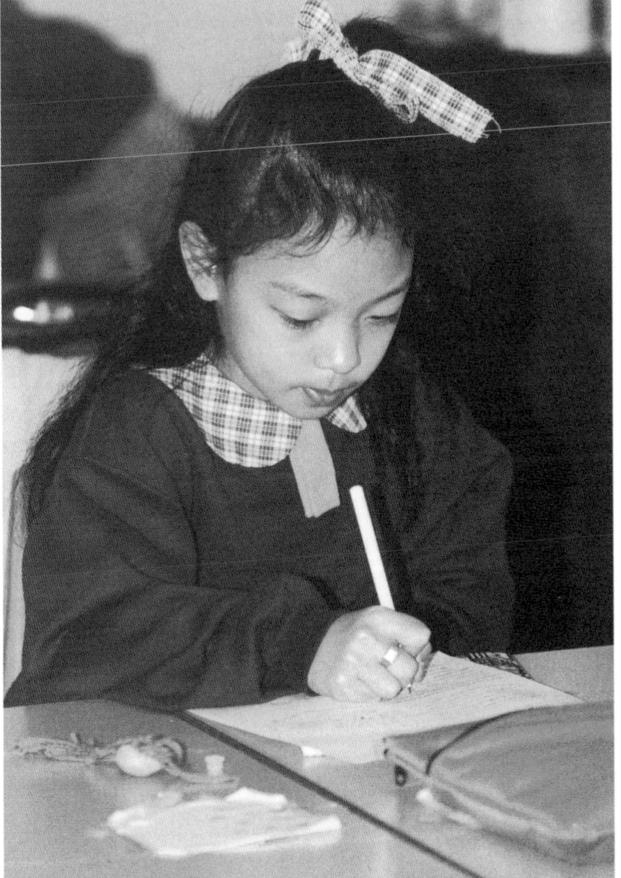
Learning to write is a motor skill that takes enormous concentration and practice.
Photo: authors

Why are young children happy to expend great energy developing motor skills? Photo: authors

introducing cross-sex and mixed-sex sporting and health programs, and craft activities, such as woodwork, sewing and knitting, are being taught to both girls and boys. Many schools resist co-educational classes, however, because of the perceived differences in ability between girls and boys, the desire to allow girls to participate free of the domination of males, and the restrictions imposed by single-sex sporting organisations and competitions.

Question point: *Havighurst (1959) defined a 'developmental task' as a task that arises at or about a certain period in the life of an individual, successful achievement of which leads to happiness and success with later tasks, while failure leads to unhappiness in the individual, disapproval by society and difficulty with later tasks.*

For Havighurst, the 'teachable moment' is an optimal educational time when the body is ready, society approves and the self is prepared.

1. *Discuss the notion of 'developmental task'.*
2. *List what you consider to be major developmental tasks for each of the developmental stages noted in this chapter.*
3. *Discuss the notion of 'teachable moment'. Relate this discussion to the developmental tasks you listed in 2. How would you, as an educator, ensure that these developmental tasks were accomplished successfully by your students?*

ACTION STATION

The objective of this exercise is to observe the physical skill of skipping with a rope for children of ages 5 years, 6 years and 7 years. Select three children, one of each age. They should show average physical development for age in terms of height, weight and general coordination skills.

Ask each of the children to skip using a skipping rope and make observations during the skipping. In particular, observe the position of hands and feet, skill in jumping the rope, skill in hand and foot coordination, and any idiosyncratic mannerisms as the child is skipping.

Compare the skipping behaviour of the three children and relate your findings to the developmental sequence outlined in this chapter. You should discuss the principles of maturation, motivation, experience, practice, optimal age and individual differences in your report.

ACTION STATION

Draw a timeline of your personal biography in terms of physical and motor development. In particular, highlight the developmental tasks of most importance to you, personally. How did you progress through these tasks? You might like to discuss your biography in a small group and evaluate individual differences and similarities.

ACTION STATION

This activity is designed so that you can compare the physical and motor coordination skills of children across grades. Some activities require fine muscle coordination which develops only with time. For example, cutting out paper models may be a very difficult task for young children. What other tasks may be very difficult for young children? What coordination tasks may cause difficulty in late childhood and adolescence? Why?

Select a range of motor activities such as skipping, balancing, running, hopping, swinging, dancing, clapping, cutting paper, building matchstick houses, colouring-in, writing, drawing, throwing, catching, tying laces, doing up buttons. Select a group of children from infants to middle high school and compare their performance on a selection of the tasks. Use the following table to collate your results. Discuss your findings within a small group. What general principles do you see illustrated?

PHYSICAL FORM AND OPPORTUNITIES FOR DEVELOPMENT

According to Sheldon (1940, 1970; Sheldon & Stevens 1942; Sinclair 1989), body type gives a clue to personality characteristics. Sheldon developed two descriptive schema, one dealing with temperament with three major classifications—viscerotonia, somatonia and cerebrotonia—and one dealing with physique—endomorphs, ectomorphs and mesomorphs. His research showed a very high level of relationship between temperament and physique.

Body type and personality

Large, round people, known as **endomorphs**, were more likely to be sociable, jolly, happy, placid and slow-moving (viscerotonia). Skinny, angular people, known as **ectomorphs**, were more likely to be non-sociable, intense, shy and intellectual (cerebrotonia); and muscular, solid people, known as **mesomorphs**, were more likely to be forceful, aggressive, unsympathetic, loud, direct and action-oriented (somatonia).

Nobody belongs exclusively to only one of these types. According to Sheldon each of us has elements of all three in us, and in measuring a person's physique Sheldon assigned a score of 1 to 7 on each of them, which is known as the person's somatotype.

A number of reasons have been suggested for the striking relationship between predominant body type, abilities and personality. For example, an individual's body type may limit the range of activities engaged in or, conversely, present particular opportunities for the individual to develop in specific ways. It is also believed that the relation between physique and temperament may be a

Physique sometimes limits opportunity

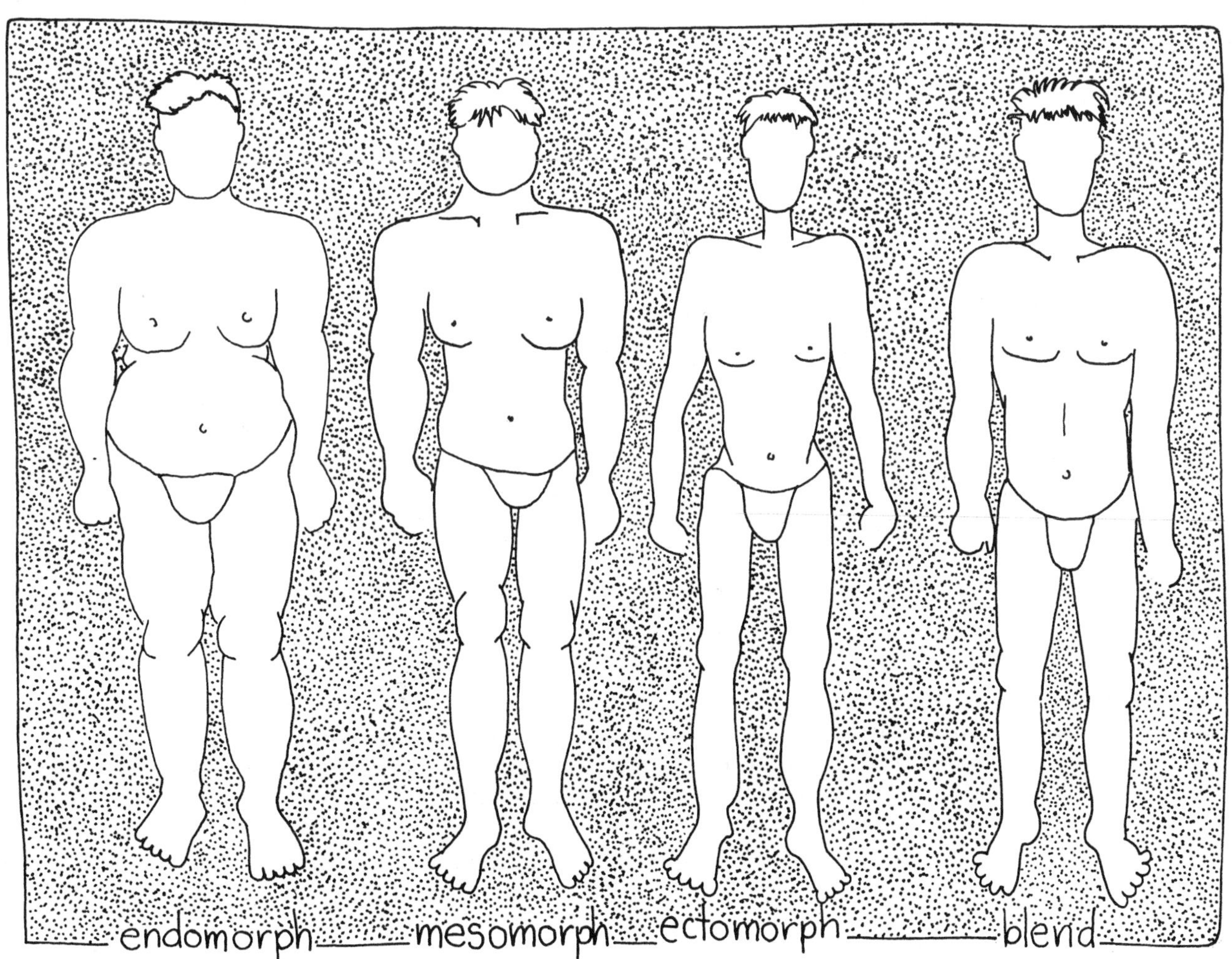

What purpose does sports afternoon serve in the school timetable? *Photo: authors*

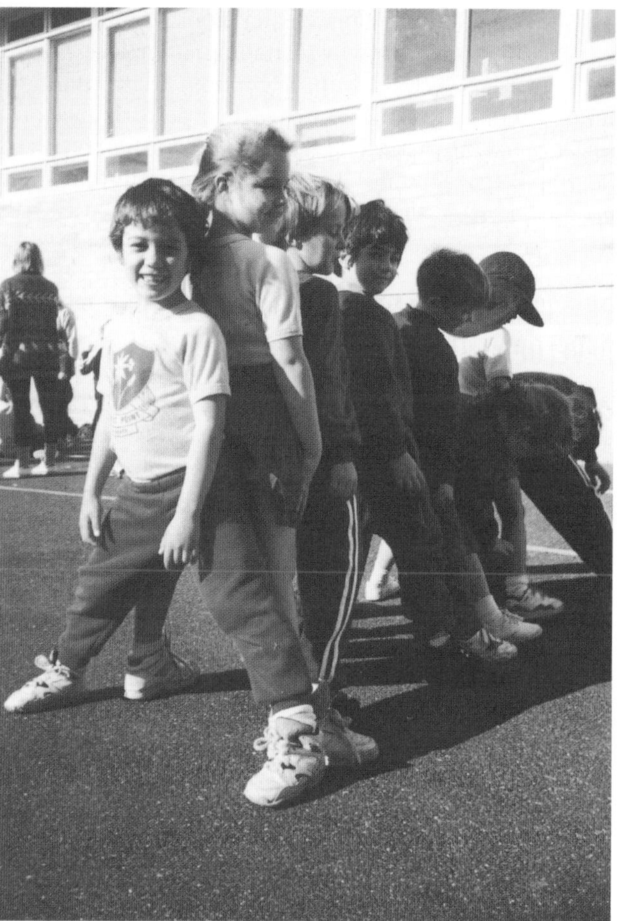

Group games are a fun way of developing physical and motor skills. *Photo: Natalie Thew*

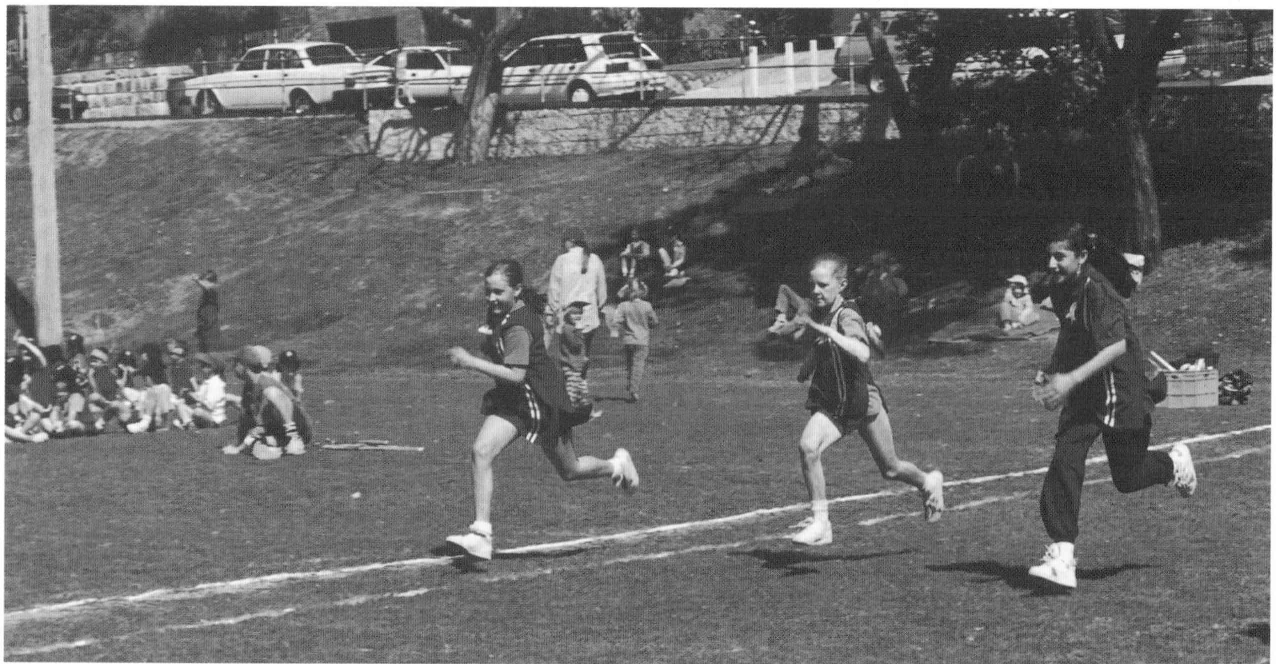

Testing one's physical prowess becomes quite exhausting. *Photo: authors*

product of stereotyping and the social expectations that individuals incorporate into their behaviour. A further explanation may be that the environmental factors that influence the development of physique may be the same ones that influence the development of personality. For example, parents who are determined to make their children great athletes may not only encourage the training and development of the body through exercise and relentless practice, but develop the mind as well to cope with the discipline such training demands. And, finally, it is thought that the genes that lead to the development of body type may also be influential in the development of personality (see Hall & Lindzey 1970; Liebert & Spiegler 1987). In any event, a large number of studies have indicated a substantial relationship between physique and temperament (although not to the level found in Sheldon's work) (Fontana 1986).

Are there educational implications of body type?

Unfortunately, little new research into Sheldon's work has been carried out in recent years, which means we are still unable to draw firm conclusions from it, although it appears to have some well-founded support (Fontana 1986; Wells 1983). Sheldon's theory has made a valuable contribution in alerting us to the fact that our body shape may very much influence our view of self. How we and others view our body shape becomes incorporated into our self-concept. Indeed, most recent self-concept scales include a subscale for physical self-concept (see, for example, Marsh 1993; Marsh & Craven, in press). Research (Lerner 1969; Lerner & Korn 1972; Staffieri 1967) has shown that from early childhood through to adolescence the preferred body shape is mesomorphic. In children's stories the mesomorph is described as brave, attractive, strong and intelligent. Less favourable adjectives are reserved for the ectomorph and endomorph. Furthermore, mesomorphs appear to be more popular in the classroom than either of the other body types (Staffieri 1967).

Children should be exposed to a full range of physical and mental activities

Clearly, educators need to avoid stereotyping children on the basis of their physique. There are several potential dangers in doing so. We might, for example, expect muscular-looking children (mesomorphs) to be mainly, or perhaps exlusively, interested in sport and consequently supply little encouragement for their talents in music or dance. We might expect thin, angular children (ectomorphs) to be only good at, and interested in, intellectual activities, and fail to provide the opportunities and encouragement for them to become involved in physical activities. Finally, fatter children (endomorphs) may be consigned to passive activities, with no great physical or intellectual challenges being made available. Furthermore, educators may inadvertently contribute to children's negative self-images by choosing the more stereotypically attractive for public roles such as presentations and demonstrations.

The fact that attitudes to body types are socially conditioned is very easily demonstrated cross-culturally. In Fiji and a number of other islander communities, body bulk is considered highly desirable, and instead of starving before their wedding (which is often the norm in Western societies) brides-to-be eat up to ensure good rounded proportions!

Physically attractive and unattractive students

Related research into teachers' expectations, impressions and judgments of physically attractive students indicates that these students are usually judged more favourably by teachers in a number of dimensions including intelligence, academic potential, grades and various social skills (Ritts, Patterson & Tubbs 1992). It appears that teachers expect physically attractive students to be more intelligent and to attain a higher level of education than less physically attractive students. Furthermore, physically attractive students are rated by teachers as more friendly, more attentive, more popular and more outgoing (Ritts, Patterson & Tubbs 1992). When judged in terms of committing a serious misconduct, physically less attractive students were considered to be more chronically antisocial than more attractive students, for whom the behaviour was considered an aberration (Dion 1972).

The root of these expectations is not clear. However, it behoves us as teachers to take care not to hold unwarranted assumptions about students because of physical appearance. We develop this notion further in Chapter 9.

Question Point: *Does our body shape influence our view of self? How might teachers overcome the influence on children and adolescents of physical stereotypes that are portrayed so dynamically in the media?*

GENERAL PHYSICAL HEALTH AND THE SCHOOL ENVIRONMENT

Children spend many hours at school and it is our responsibility as teachers to make the school's physical environment as healthy as possible for them. Good lighting, heating and ventilation are essential in every classroom. Children should sit at desks that are the proper height, and in seats that support their backs. Playgrounds should have adequate shelter from the elements, as well as shade and proper seating. This is particularly important as schools introduce student welfare policies that include skin-care provisions. There should be adequate open spaces for children to run around in, and areas should be designated for particular physical activities. It is potentially dangerous when 12-year-old boys and girls mix with younger children when playing. Many children go home with scrapes and bruises received when run into by hurtling missiles (human, or inanimate ones such as tennis balls). Toilets should be well designed, ventilated and clean. There should always be adequate soap and toilet paper. Schools should also supply mirrors so that children can groom themselves.

Potential health problems

From time to time, physical problems that go unnoticed in the home become apparent in school. Difficulties with sight and hearing, for example, can impede the effective learning of the child at school. Routine testing of sight and hearing when children begin school is an important means of minimising difficulties. Vigilant teachers can alert parents to seek medical attention in minor cases. At other times children may require special school facilities (see Chapter 11).

Some children may undergo periods of temporary deafness as a result of ear infections, particularly in the infant grades. Teachers and parents should monitor these events to prevent long-term problems. Apart from hearing difficulties affecting learning and motivation, continued absences, as a result of ineffective treatment of the problem, will cause children to fall further and further behind in their work. This will also have repercussions in terms of self-esteem and self-confidence.

Hearing problems

Most vision problems can easily be corrected by the use of eye glasses. Parents and teachers should be on the lookout for temporary eye disorders such as conjunctivitis, which can be caused by children rubbing their eyes with dirty hands. This is readily treated with antibiotics; however, if left untreated it can lead to serious eye problems such as scarring of the cornea (Harris 1985; Lunde & Lunde 1980; Smart & Smart 1977; Starfield & Pless 1980).

Seeing problems

How might this playground environment be improved? Photo: authors

As discussed earlier, dietary deficiencies are often responsible for abnormal growth patterns. In Western societies such as Australia and New Zealand there should be no excuse for children being **malnourished**. There are children, however, who do arrive in our schools **undernourished**. Sometimes this is a result of poor parenting, and lower socioeconomic status. Obviously, under circumstances where school learning and motivation suffer, the school must assume some responsibility for the adequate nourishment of the child.

Nutrition, malnourishment, undernourishment; obesity

Counterpointing undernourishment is the problem of **obesity**. Many children are obese, which reduces their ability to exercise the physical and motor structures in their body essential for healthy development. Some obesity may be genetically linked, but many overweight children become so through a poor diet that includes too much food and empty calories for their level of activity, and laziness, with too much time spent in front of the television predisposing them to little exercise and endless snacking on the wrong kinds of food. In part, poor eating habits are set up in the home through parental feeding practices, such as rewarding children with high-calorie foods and snacks. At other times, poor eating may be associated with stress reduction or traumatic events such as divorce or death (see Berk 1996). Again, while teachers and schools are not responsible in the first instance for children's

Rough and tumble play is characteristic of middle childhood. Photo: Connie Griebe

obesity, a school's health program should be designed to educate children in good eating and exercise habits.

From time to time, children miss school due to childhood illnesses and bouts of flu and colds. Irregular attendance of children due to ill health needs to be carefully monitored and some form of intervention program developed to assist the child and the family. Some children miss substantial periods at school because of chronic and persistent illnesses such as respiratory problems, asthma and bronchitis, urinary tract infections, migraines and diabetes (Holt 1991; Starfield & Pless 1980). As a result they may also develop behavioural and learning problems, and have restricted opportunities for physical activity. Teachers need to support the child and its family through encouragement and remedial help. The policy of mainstreaming means that increasing numbers of children with chronic illnesses and impairments will be found in the regular classroom. This issue is dealt with in Chapter 11.

Childhood illnesses may lead to behavioural and learning problems

All teachers need to be familiar with the range of common illnesses that affect children during the early years of schooling. Particular infectious diseases must be notified to a doctor, and children excluded from school for the prescribed period. While there has been a decline in infectious diseases such as measles, mumps and polio since mass immunisation for these diseases became common, it is apparent that increasing numbers of parents are not having their children immunised. As a result, more and more children are coming to school having suffered debilitating bouts of these illnesses.

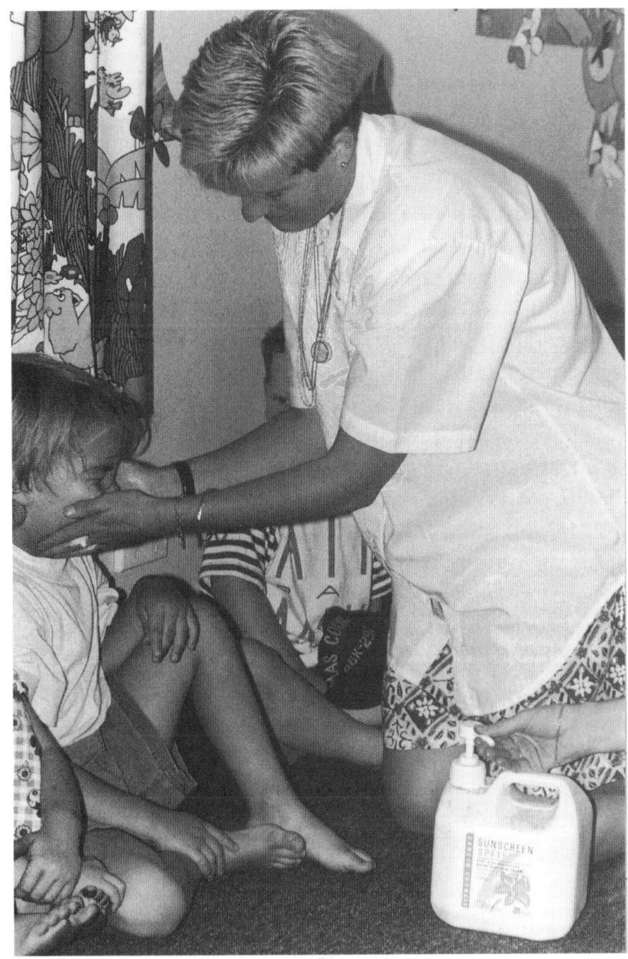

Most educational settings have a student health and safety policy. Here a teacher is applying sun blockout to preschoolers before they go out to play. Photo: authors

'It's called a sandwich!'

Physical safety and legal requirements

As described above, the early childhood and primary years of schooling coincide with periods of rapid physical growth and motor development during which children are particularly energetic and keen to test out their newly developing physical skills. Accidents such as broken arms and legs, concussion, scrapes and bruises increase sharply at this time (Heffey 1985) but such injury can be minimised by appropriate supervision by parents and teachers. The **'duty of care'** that teachers have as part of their role means that they must be aware of dangerous activities, and possess qualifications for sports coaching. For any physical activity there should be proper physical conditioning; proper supervision of the sport; well-fitted protective equipment (such as helmets, knee and elbow pads, groin protectors, mouthguards); careful grouping of children according to weight, height and ability; and opportunity for every child who wishes to participate in some sport in accordance with his or her skills, health and level of physical maturation to do so (Lunde & Lunde 1980).

Duty of care and the legal responsibilities of teachers

There is a significant legal responsibility on teachers to ensure the safety of their students. T. Bransgrove (1990) says that in some contexts (e.g. outdoor excursions such as hiking and camping and other sporting activities) teachers sometimes badly judge the capacity of children to cope with the experiences. Some teachers decide that, regardless of age, it is well within the individual capacity of a child to perform certain tasks, given the child's size and strength. Such decisions may be very hazardous, and overly demanding on children. Their natural excitement, curiosity and adventurousness may place them at risk unless the teacher is aware of this and takes steps to maximise safety. The author vividly recalls taking a group of 35 year 5 boys to the Sydney Harbour Bridge pylon lookout as part of an excursion. It appeared that whatever level of the pylon he was on, most of the boys were on other levels, hanging over edges to get better views! He was beside himself trying to keep all of them safely behind the barriers and sighed with relief at the end of the day that no disaster had befallen the group! Our experience leads us to believe that, whenever children are taken on an excursion, the teacher must plan carefully for every eventuality. Many Departments of Education require teachers supervising excursions to have various first aid certificates.

Recommended reading

Corbin, C. B. (1980) *A Textbook for Motor Development*. Dubuque, Iowa: Wm. C. Brown.

Gallahue, D. L. (1989) *Understanding Motor Development: Infants, children, adolescents*, 2nd edn. Brisbane: John Wiley.

Griffiths, R. A. & Channon-Little, L. (1996) Psychological treatments and buliminia nervosa: An update. *Australian Psychologist*, 31, 79–96.

Holt, K. S. (1991) *Child Development. Diagnosis and Assessment*. London: Butterworth-Heinemann.

Malina, R. M. & Bouchard, C. (1991) *Growth, Maturation, and Physical Activity*. Champaign, Ill: Human Kinetics Books.

Maude, D., Wertheim, E. H., Paxton, S., Gibbons, K. & Szmukler, G. (1993) Body dissatisfaction, weight loss behaviours and bulimic tendencies in Australian adolescents with an estimate of female data representativeness. *Australian Psychologist*, 28(2), 128–32.

Paxton, S., Wertheim, E., Gibbons, K., Szmukler, G. L., Hillier, L. & Petrovich, J. L. (1991) Body image satisfaction, dieting beliefs, and weight loss behaviours in adolescent girls and boys. *Journal of Youth and Adolescence*, 20, 361–97.

Sinclair, D. (1989) *Human Growth after Birth*. Oxford: Oxford University Press.

Tanner, J. M. (1990) *Fetus into Man. Physical Growth from Conception to Maturity* (revised and enlarged). Cambridge, MA: Harvard University Press.

Thelen, E. (1995) Motor development. A new synthesis. *American Psychologist*, 50, 79–95.

CHAPTER 15

Personal development and effective learning

OVERVIEW

Academic learning does not just depend upon things such as intelligence, but also on the whole range of personal qualities that a child brings to bear on the learning task. In this and the following chapter we consider personality development and, in particular, how children develop as people: how they relate to others and to themselves, how they develop personal goals and ambitions in life, how they acquire moral values, and how they react to the many problems and challenges they meet in life. The major focus in this chapter is the work of Erikson, Freud, Rogers and Maslow. Each of these personality theorists has made a valuable contribution to our understanding of how individuals develop a sense of self.

In the description of Erikson's psychosocial theory of personality development we cover the stages of psychosocial development and the process of identity formation. We emphasise, especially, the importance of caregivers, teachers and peers in a child's personality development, and that of parental and grandparental involvement in schools. We briefly describe elements of Freudian theory that are of interest to educators.

We also consider the humanistic theories of Rogers and Maslow. Our major focus here is on the notion that parents, caregivers and teachers act as facilitators of children's personal and intellectual development by supplying appropriate opportunities, resources, support and non-evaluative feedback to them.

LEARNER-CENTRED PSYCHOLOGICAL PRINCIPLE 13

Personal beliefs, thoughts and understandings resulting from prior learning and interpretations become the individual's basis for constructing reality and interpreting life experiences.

Unique cognitive constructions form a basis for beliefs and attitudes about others. Individuals then operate out of these 'separate realities' as if they were true for everyone, often leading to misunderstandings and conflict. Awareness and understanding of these phenomena allow greater choice over the degree to which one's beliefs influence one's actions and enable one to see and take into account others' points of view. The cognitive, emotional and social development of a child and the way that child interprets life experiences are a product of prior schooling, home, culture and community factors.

Reprinted with permission, APA Task Force on Psychology in Education (1993, January), p. 9.

BOX 15.1 TEACHING COMPETENCE

The teacher develops positive relationships with students

Indicators

The teacher:

- regards all students as individuals and treats them with respect;
- acts to establish a learning community in which all students are engaged;
- encourages students to take intellectual risks;
- is sensitive to students' emotional needs and provides support;
- applies skills of negotiation, mediation and conflict resolution.

Case studies illustrating National Competency Framework for Beginning Teaching, National Project on the Quality of Teaching and Learning, Australian Teaching Council, 1996, Element 2.2, p. 38. Commonwealth of Australia copyright, reproduced by permission.

THE DEVELOPING PERSON

The personal self

Personality is stable; that is we do not change into fundamentally different people from day to day. Personality is also organised—that is its attributes are interrelated. Personality is formed as a result of the interaction between innate biological mechanisms and the environment, and it is distinctive, each personality being unique (Fontana 1986). In the following sections we examine a number of theories of personality development. Consider each theory in terms of the points above and, especially, the implications of each for your role as an educator or parent.

ERIKSON'S STAGES OF PERSONAL DEVELOPMENT

A personality theory with great intuitive appeal and usefulness for teachers in understanding and supporting the development of personality in children under their care, is Erik Erikson's personality theory (Erikson 1963, 1968; Elkind 1977). Erikson has built upon many of the basic notions of Freudian theory which we cover briefly later in this chapter. However, while Freud's focus was on psychosexual development, Erikson focuses on **psychosocial** development. Furthermore, while Freud believed that the first five or so years of life set the foundations for lifelong personality characteristics, Erikson sees personality development as a lifelong journey which he has aptly named the **eight ages of man** (perhaps today we should refer to the 'eight ages of people', but it loses something in the adaptation).

Our classrooms are full of different personalities. This variety presents us with one of the great joys of teaching. Photo: Connie Griebe

Side by side with the stages of **psychosexual development** described by Freud are the **psychosocial stages of ego development**, in which the individual has to establish new basic orientations to the social world. At each stage there is the potential for positive and negative experiences. A healthy personality is, by and large, one that has successfully accomplished the tasks appropriate to each stage. Erikson allows for the fact that earlier poorly resolved conflicts may be compensated for, in part, by later fulfilling experiences.

Psychosocial stages of ego development

Table 15.1 lists these eight stages and compares them with Freud's psychosexual stages.

Infancy and early personal development

The infant requires nurturant care. Quality, loving care leads to feelings of well-being and a sense of the world as a safe place to be. Inconsistent or rejecting care fosters within children a basic mistrust, fear and apprehension of the caregivers, which may be generalised to other people and to the world at large. The dichotomy between **trust** and **mistrust** arises at each successive stage of development.

Infancy: trust versus mistrust

With greater mobility and a growing command of language, toddlers test themselves out in the world of experience. Of course, this means that children increasingly run into controls exerted by parents and other caregivers. Depending on the amount of **autonomy** allowed and support given, children develop a sense that they are able to control themselves. On the other hand, if the caregivers are overly restrictive, harshly critical or impatient, and consistently do for children what they could do for themselves, children may develop a sense of shame and **doubt** about their capacities to do things. When our daughter Ali was three she often pushed our hands away with an imperative 'I can do it!' Children at this age need to be given opportunities to pour drinks, feed themselves, flush toilets, dress themselves and so on. Accidents will occur and must be handled sympathetically by the adult. Naturally, a balance must be struck between the need to allow children autonomy to explore and do new and exciting things, and the need to protect them from danger.

Infancy: autonomy versus doubt

TABLE 15.1

ERIKSON'S EIGHT STAGES OF PERSONALITY DEVELOPMENT

Period of development	*Freud's psychosexual stages*	*Erikson's psychosocial stages*
Birth to 1 year	Oral stage	Basic trust vs mistrust
1 to 3 years	Anal stage	Autonomy vs shame & doubt
3 to 6 years	Phallic stage	Initiative vs guilt
6 years to puberty	Latency stage	Industry vs inferiority
Adolescence	Genital stage	Industry vs role confusion
Young adulthood		Intimacy vs isolation
Middle adulthood		Generativity vs self-absorption
Old age		Ego integrity vs despair

Parental love provides a secure start for children.
Photo: authors

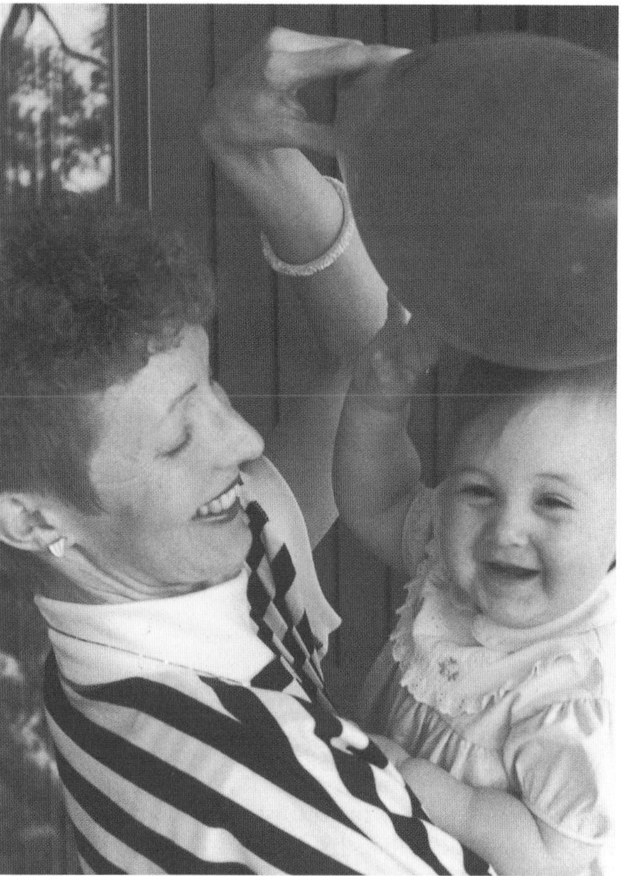

Enjoying fun together builds up a sense of trust in the infant.
Photo: authors

Early to late childhood personal development

Early to middle childhood is a time when children initiate many activities, confident and assured of their own motor and intellectual abilities. However, it is also a time when the energy of children can be exasperating for parents and teachers as they struggle to cope with the five-hundredth question of the day. Children who are given freedom and opportunity to initiate and test their newly acquired powers of communication and physical agility develop initiative and self-assurance. In contrast, if children are overly restricted or made to feel that they are engaging in a 'silly' or 'wrong' activity, making a mess, or taking up too much time, they may develop a sense of **guilt** over self-initiated activities that will persist through later life stages. Often, different expectations are held for girls and boys, such that differential restrictions are applied by parents (and at times by teachers) (Fontana 1986). This can lead to problems when children wish to initiate activity in supposed gender-inappropriate areas. For example, boys who want to dance and girls who want to play football sometimes come in for a hard time and are made to feel uncomfortable and guilty over their choices. Schools are implementing anti-sexism programs to address this problem, although many homes still strongly support children's initiatives in sex-stereotyped areas.

Early childhood: initiative versus guilt

The period of **industry** versus **inferiority** coincides with late childhood and is a time of great productivity. We remember how excited both our daughters were to be involved in producing projects, inventions, craftwork and stories. Children at this time show a great interest in what makes the world tick, how things are done, and why they are done in a certain way. They are capable of increasingly sophisticated thought and argument. Of course, this is also a busy time for parents and teachers as they bat and field questions related to all manner of things, and have to defend their right (as adults) to make the final decision at times, against the protests of children who think they know better! This is a time to encourage children in their productivity and creativity as they make and build things. Children who are restricted, criticised, told not to make a nuisance of themselves or a mess, may develop feelings of

Late childhood: industry versus inferiority

An important sign of growing independence.
Photo: authors

First days at school are always exciting. They indicate developing independence. Photo: authors

inferiority. The child's peer group becomes an increasingly important influence also as it gives feedback to the child about his or her abilities which helps to reinforce feelings of industry or inferiority.

Adolescence, identity formation and personal development

The period of **identity** versus **role confusion** is a particularly important stage for the development of self-identity. This period occurs during adolescence and is a time of increasing social contacts. Children integrate what they have learnt about themselves and begin to test their identity out in the wider world. In particular, children compare their experiences with their peers, and become interested in relationships, religions, politics, and society in general. Becoming members of sporting associations, religious groups and social networks outside the family grows increasingly important, and helps to define for individuals where they belong. Role confusion results when an adolescent feels lost, unattached or confused in social identity. This might be the result of inadequate opportunities to form social networks outside the family, or be residual from poorly resolved conflicts in earlier stages. For example, individuals who already feel inferior and guilty may choose not to test themselves in the wider community of peers and relationships and, therefore, deny themselves further opportunities for personal growth. Conversely, individuals with a poorly developed identity may either go to extremes to become part of a group, or engage in antisocial or antipersonal behaviour, such as delinquency and substance abuse, to reduce their sense of confusion.

Adolescence: identity versus role confusion

TABLE 15.2

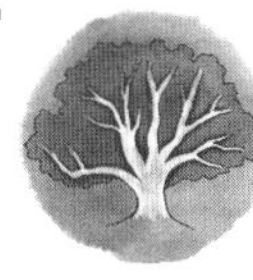

ESSENTIALS OF ADOLESCENT IDENTITY FORMATION

For adolescents

- Developing a philosophy of life that includes moral values and an orientation to religion.
- Integrating enduring temperamental qualities and basic dispositions into a well-rounded adult character.

- Establishing a gender-role identity.
- Developing a sense of self as a sexual being.
- Developing a sense of self in relation to politics and social issues.
- Contemplating future intimate relationships.
- Developing a vocational identity.

(based on Erikson 1968; Peterson 1996)

Some writers suggest that, unless adolescents go through some type of **identity crisis**, where they clarify and become aware of personal values that they commit themselves to, little psychological growth can occur. Research suggests that many adolescents do not undergo such a crisis and therefore fall short of mature identity achievement (Marcia 1980). Instead, **identity foreclosure** results, in which adolescents prematurely identify with the values and goals of their parents without questioning whether they are right for them. James Marcia, basing his work on that of Erikson, proposed four identity statuses that resolve the identity crisis. Each status relates to an individual's commitment to a career, personal value system, sexual attitudes and religious beliefs.

Identity crisis: clarifying and becoming aware of personal values

1. *Identity diffusion*: where there is no crisis and no commitment. This is exemplified in the adolescent or young adult who flits from job to job, commitment to commitment, and relationship to relationship with little personal investment. Identity diffusion may be the product of earlier unresolved conflicts, or may result from perceived blocks in the environment, such as parental disapproval, or cultural barriers. It is often characterised by self-doubt, anxiety, depression and apathy.
2. *Foreclosure*: where there is no crisis, and commitment is based on the will of the parents or other significant people, such as ministers of religion or romantic partners. This is exemplified by the young adult who becomes a teacher or chemist because 'Dad and Mum expect it', or goes into Dad's business, without any personal valuing of the career. It might also occur as a result of an adolescent falling into a career in which he or she already has a perceived interest or talent (e.g. sporting or artistic skills), without leaving scope to develop other areas of interest. Identity foreclosure can lead to discontent in later life.
3. *Moratorium*: where the individual is experiencing crisis and working out roles and commitments. This is exemplified by the young adult who tries out a variety of personal and social options before making a commitment. The delay in making a commitment may be the product of family events, socioeconomic position, educational deprivation and other social barriers. An individual may drop out of university for a period of time to 'sort out' whether this is really the right career path. Choosing to return, or to go in a different direction, facilitates the achievement of identity. Some students delay making a choice until they have temporarily broken the ties of their families and schooling. Again, this process can facilitate the ultimate choice in which there is a personal commitment.
4. *Identity achieved*: having already explored alternatives, identity-achieved individuals are committed to a clearly formulated set of self-chosen values and goals. They feel a sense of psychological well-being, of knowing who they are and where they are going. When asked about career or life changes they might respond that they are pretty sure that what they are doing is right for them.

Identity achievement and moratorium are considered healthy alternatives, whereas adolescents who can't proceed past the identity diffusion or identity foreclosure stage have difficulties in adjustment. These need extra assistance and counselling to answer the important question 'Who am I?'

A relevant question to ask about Marcia's identity statuses, particularly in countries such as Australia and New Zealand which are characterised by ethnic diversity, is whether they occur only in Western countries such as the United States. Cross-cultural research seems to indicate that the same patterns do occur across cultures (Scarr, Weinberg & Levine 1986).

Identity formation and cultural differences

The notion of identity crisis is certainly thrown into strong relief when we consider children within Australia and New Zealand who come from ethnic minority groups. In their case, there may be an even stronger clash of forces orienting the development of their sense of identity. For example, while the Anglo-Australian child or Pakeha is socialised within a world in which society at large, family and peer group share many common values and traditions, children from other groups, such as Lebanese, Chinese, Maori and Aboriginal, may well find that they are influenced by conflicting forces. For example, while Anglo-Australian children are encouraged by society, family and peer group to develop individuality and autonomy, many ethnic children may be encouraged by their families and cultural groups to remain interdependent. These children, therefore, receive conflicting messages from the wider society, school, peers and their cultural

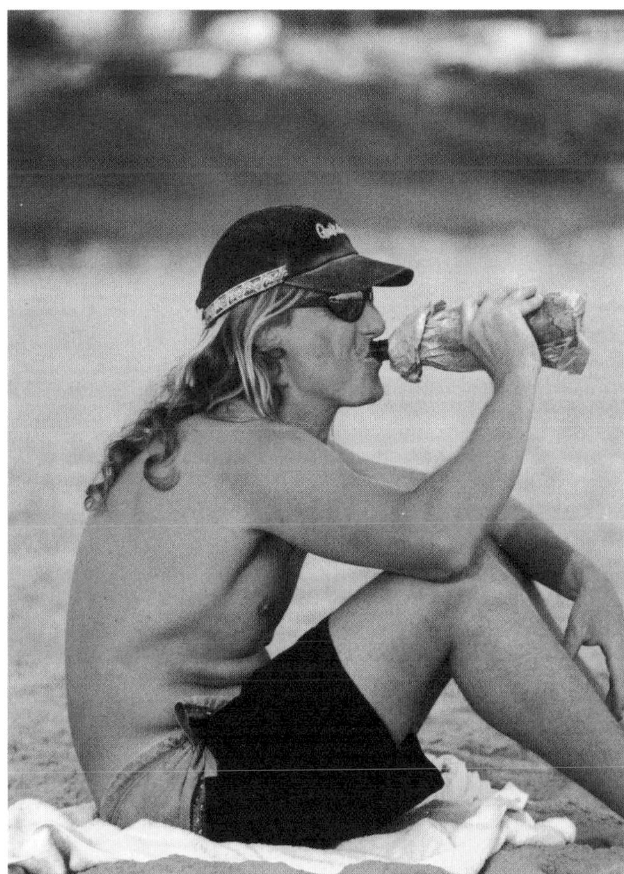

What elements of identity characterise this adolescent? How might these be different for adolescents from other cultural groups? Photo: authors

community. On multiple levels such as moral values, dress, use of spare time, political views, dating, education, career choice and religion there is potential for conflicting messages and identity conflict (Partington & McCudden 1992). This may be further exacerbated for females who traditionally are given even less freedom to make personal decisions (on such matters as dating, education and career choice) than males in particular ethnic communities.

Australian and New Zealand initiatives in multicultural education are aimed (among other goals) at fostering and supporting some important elements of cultural continuity (such as language maintenance) so that children from minority cultural groups are supported in their developing sense of self. Indeed, it seems that some children adjust well to a situation in which they are bicultural and able to function effectively in both worlds with an integrated sense of self (Cahill & Ewen 1987). Inevitably, however, there will be culture clashes, and your primary task as an educator will be to assist the child in resolving the conflict.

'Unfortunately, err ... it's Faith and Sky isn't it ... although these suggestions are splendid, school uniform design is entirely determined by the Department.'

Adolescent identity formation and parental developmental problems

Probably the most critical factor in the development of a sense of identity is the nature of the relationship that children maintain with their parents (Conger 1977; Santrock & Yussen 1992). Establishing a strong **ego identity** will be facilitated if a sufficiently rewarding, interactive relationship exists between the child or adolescent and both parents. It is important that the same-sex parent serves as an adequate model for personally and socially effective and appropriate behaviour. It is also important that the opposite-sex parent is an effective individual, and approves of the model provided by the same-sex parent and the child's own identification with this model.

Having adolescent children can be quite trying for parents. Adolescents challenge cherished values, such as religious beliefs, moral values, political allegiances and parental authority (Montemayor & Flannery 1991; Steinberg 1991). It is also important to note that this can be a period of change and personal stress for parents. With adolescent children, many parents are entering their middle years; as well as having ambivalent attitudes towards the growing independence of their children, and often lack of expertise in handling the developmental problems of this age, parents may also be experiencing their own emotional problems and conflicts that impact on parent–child interactions—problems such as marital dissatisfaction, economic burdens, career re-evaluation, and health and body concerns (Santrock & Yussen 1992; Silverberg & Steinberg 1990). The lack of communication between parents and children and the conflicts that often result can be better understood, and better advice given, if this parental perspective is taken into account. Such problems may be exacerbated for migrant parents who see, as well, cherished cultural values dissipating as their children become increasingly assimilated into the cultural norms of their new country.

At the time that adolescents are moving away from parent dependency, they often substitute peer dependency. Adolescents seek out and listen to the advice of peers on many issues, especially those involving immediate consequences, such as clothes, entertainment, fads and so on. Peers exert a great deal of pressure on each other to conform. They also give each other the opportunity to express the frustrations and problems they have at home. However, adults often exaggerate the power of the peer group, particularly as it relates to sexual behaviour, substance abuse and delinquency. It is important to note that, as well as parents and peers, other forces within society strongly influence the adolescent, including the popular media and other adults such as teachers, coaches and part-time employers.

Adolescent identity formation and peer dependency

Young adulthood and beyond

During the next period, of **intimacy** versus **isolation**, young adults develop the ability to share with others and care about other people selflessly. It is through this selfless caring that we develop a sense of intimacy with others. If a sense of intimacy is not established with friends or a marriage partner, the result, according to Erikson, is a sense of isolation, of being alone without anyone to share with or care for.

Young adulthood: intimacy versus isolation

In the earlier stages of personality development, people are somewhat self-absorbed in the sense that experiences are interpreted in terms of what they mean to the individual. As psychologically healthy individuals progress through the stages they become more other-oriented. In the seventh stage which occurs during middle adulthood and is referred to as **generativity** versus **self-absorption**, individuals become aware of, and more involved with, things and people outside their immediate families. They become concerned for the future of the world and the younger generation. Those who fail to establish a sense of generativity stagnate in a state of self-absorption in which their personal concerns and comforts become of primary concern.

Middle adulthood: generativity versus self-absorption

In the final period, **integrity** versus **despair**, there is still the potential for personal growth. Integrity characterises the older individual who looks upon life's journey as an adventure of self-discovery, in which positive and negative experiences have been melded into a personality with which the individual is content. On the other hand, old age may bring to the individual despair and regret for lost opportunities and direction. The task of sharing wisdom and encouraging others is accepted with enthusiasm by those who develop integrity.

Late adulthood: integrity versus despair

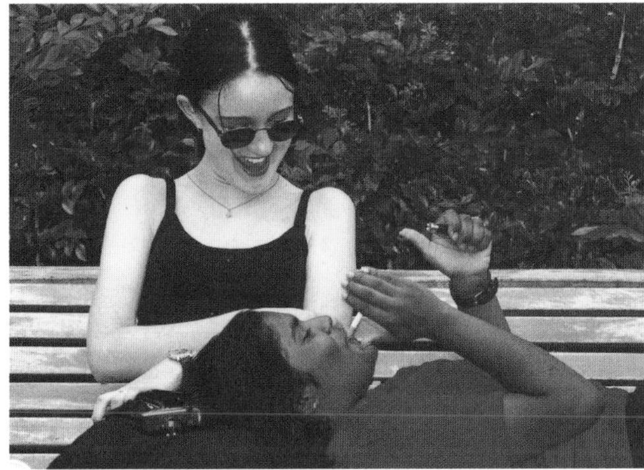

Why are peers so important as adolescents move away from dependence on parents? Photo: authors

As with the earlier stages, society has an important role to play here in fostering within individuals a sense of integrity. Communities and families that respect the elderly and give them opportunities to be productive facilitate the development of a sense of integrity. On the other hand, elderly people who are 'shelved' and left to finish their lives isolated from events of importance, such as sharing in the rearing and teaching of children, may feel very undervalued and despair. We should remember that old age means many different things in different societies. Ours, along with many other Western and rapidly changing societies, tends to undervalue the contributions that older people may make.

The role of society in personal development of the elderly

Question point: *How might Erikson's theory help you, as an educator, to understand the day-to-day behaviour of children and adolescents in an educational setting?*

CLASSROOM APPLICATIONS OF ERICKSON'S THEORY

Importance of teachers and peers

There are several features of Erikson's theory that make it attractive to people in the helping professions such as teaching. Freud's theory suggests that the early years of life and, in particular, parenting practices related to feeding, toilet training and the inculcation of sexual identity and values, have the major role to play in personality development, with other events and interpersonal contacts being of relatively minor importance. Erikson's theory, while agreeing that there is an initial onus on parents to support positive personal growth in children, argues strongly that other people, such as teachers and peers, become increasingly important as children grow older, and that personality development is a continuous process, with growth, development and change occurring whenever children are given positive or negative experiences.

Furthermore, earlier negative experiences such as parental neglect, which leads to a sense of mistrust in children, can be alleviated by later positive experiences such as a caring school and teacher, thereby fostering a sense of trust within the children. Children who have their sense of industry derogated at home can have it revitalised at school through the actions of caring and stimulating teachers. We must add here, however, that action can occur both ways. A child who comes to school with a well-developed sense of trust may have it undermined by an uncaring teacher, or bullying peers, and a child who is always building and inventing at home may lose interest in a classroom dominated by regulation and a lock-step curriculum that demands conformity to the norm.

Positive psychosocial experiences compensate for negative ones

A key to understanding Erikson's theory is the knowledge that, at each period of development, experiences can be positive or negative and the total personality reflects the balance struck between them. If children experience basically negative or confusing experiences, they may be unable to establish a sense of self-identity, a process that Erikson called **role confusion**. This may be reflected in delinquent behaviour, losing one's identity in the group or extreme identification with atypical groups (such as punk gangs), or substance abuse. Younger children may simply withdraw from mainstream experiences, while older children may 'drop out'.

Parental and grandparental involvement in school

Erikson's theory gives a sound rationale for parental and grandparental involvement in schools. Many older people are given little opportunity to contribute to the development of the society, especially to the personal and academic growth of youngsters. As grandparents, many are excluded from any significant participation in the rearing of their grandchildren or of children in general, yet they have an enormous contribution to make. This can be as simple as paying attention to children's play and responding to their questions, listening to children read, acting as a sounding board for ideas (when parents and teachers are too busy), and modelling different attitudes and values for children to incorporate into their growing sense of self. Childcare settings and schools should actively encourage parental and grandparental involvement in their programs, and develop appropriate structures to facilitate this.

Parental involvement in schools contributes greatly to children's learning. Photo: authors

Of course, there are tremendous benefits for the older people as well. In a sense, they are extending their period of generativity, and maximising the positive forces that will lead them to feel a sense of integrity for a life well spent.

Table 15.3 indicates some supportive classroom and school practices suggested by Erikson's approach.

FREUD'S PSYCHOSEXUAL THEORY

Freud (1856–1939) is familiar to everyone in one way or another. Our language is replete with expressions, such as **ego**, **superego**, **repression** and **rationalisation**,

TEACHER'S CASE BOOK

PARENT HELP!

On his first day in year 2, Phillip told Miss Carter: 'I can't read and I can't write.' A literacy assessment revealed that his language skills were at a similar level to those of most children entering Transition. Concerned to provide Phillip with the extra support he needed, Miss Carter tried to set aside 15 minutes each day during the language block to work with him. But she hadn't taken into account Phillip's tenacity: whenever she sat down to write with him he would commence long-winded anecdotes about his family, show her a treasure he had brought to school, anything to avoid focusing on the writing task. Because of the limited time Miss Carter had allowed she found herself becoming frustrated and impatient and then feeling guilty because she knew this would only serve to worsen his already negative attitude to writing.

Miss Carter spoke about her problem to a more experienced staff member, who told her of a parent, Mrs Burke, who had just completed the Parents as Tutors course and was eager to begin working with children in the school. At first Miss Carter was reluctant to contact Mrs Burke, being worried that she would regard Miss Carter's problem as a failure. However, when she finally did enlist Mrs Burke's support she realised how much help parents can be to a classroom teacher. Once a week Mrs Burke spends the whole language block guiding Phillip through reading and writing activities that she and Miss Carter have planned together.

Miss Carter still tries to set aside 15 minutes for Phillip each day but she no longer gets impatient or tries to rush him because she is now confident that he is receiving adequate support with literacy from Mrs Burke.

Case studies illustrating National Competency Framework for Beginning Teaching, National Project on the Quality of Teaching and Learning, Australian Teaching Council, 1996, p. 20. Commonwealth of Australia copyright, reproduced by pemission.

Case study activity
How else might parents be welcomed into the classroom as facilitators of students' learning? What advantages and potential problems might there be?

that have been taken from his theoretical work. Freud's theory is powerful and controversial and the study of personality owes much to the original work of this man. Indeed, many later theories of personality can only be understood in the context of Freud's work (Fontana 1986; Liebert & Spiegler 1987). Fontana (1986, pp. 44–5) suggests that:

For the teacher, Freud's main contribution is that he gave us a new way of looking at childhood in stark contrast to the belief that misbehaviour and other personality problems in children are the invariable result of wilfulness to be corrected by stern and rigid discipline. To Freud, the child is very much more sinned against by the adult world than sinning, very much more a victim of the mistakes of his parents than of mistakes of his own making. But Freud did more than simply focus attention upon childhood experiences. He suggested that the way in which these experiences influence later personality development can only be understood if we explore the unconscious as well as the conscious mind.

TABLE 15.3

ESSENTIALS OF ERICKSON'S THEORY FOR CLASSROOM PRACTICES

For teachers

- *Trust vs mistrust*—support and encourage the child. Alleviate distress and uncertainty promptly. Be responsive and consistent.
- *Autonomy vs doubt*—allow opportunities for self-control, self-care and responsibility. Free choice of activities should be included in the curriculum.
- *Initiative vs guilt*—encourage children to make decisions, choose activities and have a real impact on the work of the classroom. Be tolerant of accidents, mistakes and 'mess' as children 'go it alone'. Avoid labels such as 'good' and 'bad'.
- *Industry vs role confusion*—help children set realistic goals of achievement, and help them to feel a sense of accountability for what they achieve. Set the classroom up so that it is mutually supportive through the operation of group goal structures. Alleviate the negative effects of competition and peer pressure. Reward and acknowledge the achievement of goals.
- *Identity vs role confusion*—encourage the development of trust, autonomy, initiative and industry as these form the basis of the sense of identity the adolescent strives to achieve at this time. Be sensitive to the needs of the adolescent as he or she copes with the ambivalent and confusing messages received from parents, teachers, peers and society in general. Be consistent, warm and understanding. Be prepared to give advice when sought, and be prepared to see the advice not taken.

Components of personal development

Freud (1962a, b, 1973) likened the mind to an iceberg in which the smaller visible part represents the region of the consciousness, while the much larger mass below the water represents the region of the unconscious. In this vast domain of the unconscious is a great underworld of vital, unseen forces that exercise a strong control over the conscious thoughts and deeds of individuals. The life force of personal action is called **Libido** (the creative energy in all individuals), and **Thanatos** (the destructive urge in all individuals). For Freud, healthy personality growth is the product of an individual passing through a series of **psychosexual** experiences with an eventual balance being struck between three forces—the **id**, which may be described as the source of basic biological needs and desires, the **ego**, which might be described as the conscious, rational part of personality, and the **superego**, which might be described as the seat of conscience. While these three systems can be identified as separate hypothetical structures, behaviour for the mature person is nearly always the product of an interaction among the three. Rarely does one system operate to the exclusion of the other two, except in cases where the balance is broken.

Id

Ego

Superego

Stages of psychosexual development

As these three mental systems evolve, children experience five clearly distinguishable developmental stages. Each of these can be defined in terms of individuals satisfying needs through three erogenous zones—the mouth, the anus and the genital organs. Actions by children involving these zones bring children into conflict with their parents. The resulting frustrations and anxieties, as well as satisfying experiences, stimulate the development of a large number of adaptations, defences, compromises and sublimations which are ultimately incorporated into the mature personality (Hall 1964; Hall & Lindzey 1970; Liebert & Spiegler 1987; Pervin 1989).

Healthy personality development and psychosexual stages

During the **oral** stage, breast feeding and supplying the comfort needs of the child are the primary focus of attention. The quality of nurturing that children receive during this time affects their feelings of dependence and trust in the world.

Oral stage

During the **anal** stage, toilet training and controlling the child's impulses are a major focus of attention. If the training and discipline emphasises positive independence and control, feelings of confidence in self are developed. Alternatively, if experiences during this time are overly restrictive or punitive, negative personal characteristics develop, such as destructiveness, messiness, and so on.

Anal stage

During the **phallic** stage, sexual feelings associated with the functioning of the genital organs are the focus of activity. This is the time when the individual identifies with the same-sex parent and sexual identity is developed. Finally, after a period of latency, children enter the **genital** stage when there is the transformation of the individual into a reality-oriented, socialised adult. During adolescence, sexual attraction, socialisation, group activities, vocational planning, and preparations for marrying and raising a family begin to come to the fore in well-stabilised behaviours. Table 15.4 presents each of these stages.

Phallic stage

Genital stage

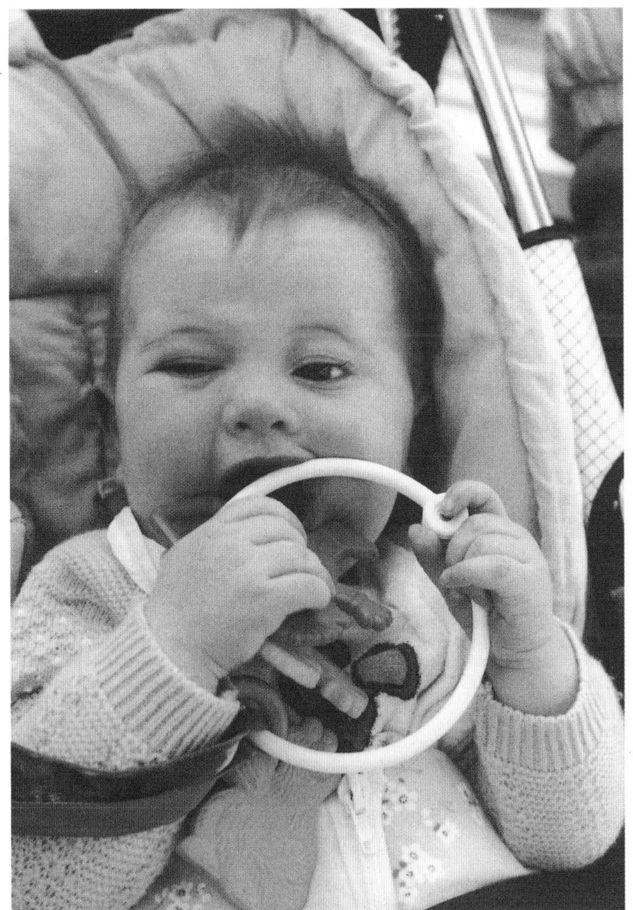

Children learn about the world by a variety of means—including chewing! Photo: authors

TABLE 15.4

FREUD'S STAGES OF PERSONALITY DEVELOPMENT

Oral
(lasts about one year)
The mouth is the principal focus of dynamic activity.

Anal
(2 to 4 years)
The anus is the principal focus of dynamic activity.

Phallic
(4 to 5 years)
The sex organs are the principal focus of dynamic activity.

Latency
(approximately 6 years to pubescence)
Period during which sexual impulses are held in a state of repression.

Genital
(puberty through to adulthood)
The genitals are the principal focus of dynamic activity.

Anxiety, defence mechanisms and personal development

Throughout Freud's personality development stages there is a dynamic interaction between the three elements of personality—id, ego and superego. Depending on the nature of the conflicts experienced and of the modes of resolving them, individuals will develop positive or negative personality characteristics. Freud considered it vital that these three systems remain in balance, with a smooth transfer of energy from id to ego to superego. When the balance is upset, the personality may break down into excessive anxiety. As any one of the three systems can dominate, this means that we can have three distinct forms of anxiety: neurotic, realistic or moral (Fontana 1986).

Forms of anxiety: neurotic realistic moral

Neurotic anxiety occurs when the individual fears that the instinctive forces of the id will control his or her behaviour. **Realistic anxiety** exists when the individual is dominated by the ego to such an extent that id-driven behaviour (such as eating or sexual behaviour) becomes impossible to enjoy, and the individual is unable to devote energy to any superego demands such as the welfare of others. **Moral anxiety** occurs when the superego dominates and the individual becomes trapped in an over-rigid value system taken over from his or her parents. The individual is excessively scrupulous and compulsively on guard against anything that might arouse feelings of guilt. He or she rejects both the pleasure principle of the id and the reality principle of the ego and inhabits, instead, an unreal world of taboos and forbidden things (Fontana 1986).

One of the goals of ego behaviour is to protect and enhance one's sense of self. At times, defence mechanisms activate which protect an individual's sense of self (Liebert & Spiegler 1987). All defence mechanisms have two characteristics in common:

1. They deny, falsify and/or distort reality.
2. They operate unconsciously so that the person is not aware of what is taking place.

Defence mechanisms as normal behaviour

While the use of defence mechanisms is normal (and all of us resort to them unconsciously from time to time), overuse of them impedes the development of a mature personality. The major defences are:

1. repression
2. reaction formation
3. rationalisation
4. regression
5. fixation
6. projection
7. fantasy
8. denial.

Repression: removing from consciousness painful thoughts

Repression is removing from consciousness painful or shameful experiences and thoughts, or the process of preventing unacceptable impulses or desires from reaching consciousness. The purpose is essentially to protect the ego from processes that are incompatible with the individual's high evaluations of self. For example, a soldier may flee the battlefield in a moment of cowardice, and be found wandering dazed some time later, with absolutely no recollection of what has occurred.

Reaction formation: replacing repressed feeling with opposite

Reaction formation occurs when a repressed feeling or emotion is replaced by its opposite; for example, a feeling such as hatred may be hidden from awareness by the substitution of its opposite. A wife with an invalid husband may unconsciously wish to be rid of him, but this negative wish may be expressed as unusual concern for his welfare. At this point, readers sometimes ask: 'But how does one pick out the genuine concern from one that is a reaction formation?' In general, the reaction formation is characterised by excessiveness: it is showy, extravagant and compulsive.

Rationalisation: giving socially acceptable reasons for our conduct

Rationalisation is a defence mechanism we can all understand and relate to. It occurs when we unconsciously give socially acceptable reasons for our conduct in place of real reasons. We may tell ourselves that it is better that we eat the leftover chocolates so that our sister doesn't get pimples or too fat, or that we should go to the movies with our friend instead of studying because the other person really needs our company. Come on, own up—have you used rationalisation to justify your behaviour to yourself? Most people have.

Regression: retreating to an earlier form of coping behaviour

Regression occurs when a child or adult engages in behaviour more characteristic of an earlier stage of development in order to reduce tension and anxiety. An older child may begin to wet the bed again when a new baby arrives in the home. The child fears being displaced and seeks attention, but can't express it consciously because the need arises out of jealousy and is therefore unacceptable. While some forms of regression are indicative of severe problems, such as the adult psychotic who plays with dolls when under stress, most forms of regression are relatively mild. Many adults chew pens during an exam, eat excessively when worried, or masturbate when stressed. In each case the individual retreats to an earlier level of coping with anxiety.

Fixation: using immature defence mechanisms

Fixation occurs when an immature form of defence mechanism is consistently used rather than a more mature defence mechanisms, such as sublimation. In extreme cases, this may lead to the emergence of a personality disorder in which the further growth of character is blocked by an obsessive personality pattern (Peterson, Beck & Rowell 1992).

Projection: ascribing our unconscious motivation to other people

Projection is a defence mechanism that many of us can relate to. It occurs when we ascribe our own unconscious motivation to other people, such as when we accuse others of being angry, hateful or deceitful as a defence against our own anger, hatred or deceit.

Fantasy: imaginary satisfactions in place of real ones

Fantasy protects the ego by seeking imaginary satisfactions in place of real ones. In the past, children were often told that it was wrong to have 'impure thoughts', although the fantasy sexual world that is created alleviated the need for children to engage in inappropriate overt sexual behaviour. Today, there is much debate over video pornography in which violence is portrayed and its supposed effect on reducing or increasing sexual crimes. One argument goes that individuals who may otherwise engage in such activities use these videos to fantasise and sublimate their sexual drives in a relatively harmless way. What do you think?

We also talk about the effect of modelled violence where no punishing consequences follow, and how this can increase the likelihood of the enactment of the behaviour in the real world (see the discussion of social modelling in Chapter 6).

Denial: denying existence of painful experience

When **an individual denies the existence of painful experiences and thoughts** (such as a refusal to accept that a loved one has died), **denial** functions as a defence. Some grossly overweight or underweight people deny that they have a problem and distort their body image accordingly.

Current status of Freud's theory

While few psychologists today accept all Freud's major theoretical concepts (and we have given only the briefest overview of some of these), the theory is still considered very important. It provides a broad insight into the development of personality, especially the importance of our unconscious in motivating behaviour, as well as the influence of early socialisation within families on subsequent personality development. In this sense, Freud's theoretical framework helps us understand the emotional development and problems of children.

On a broader level, Freud's theory has been influential in the development of many other theoretical perspectives on personality development. Educational and psychological literature on personality development very often presumes that the reader has some basic understanding of Freudian psychology (Liebert & Spiegler 1987; Mischel 1986; Pervin 1989).

Criticisms of Freud's theory

Nevertheless, Freud's theory has been criticised for two basic reasons. First, many consider that his theory overemphasises the sexual nature of personality development. In his emphasis on critical events related to the oral, anal and phallic stages, and the successful resolution of problems at these times, he appears to have neglected other important dimensions affecting the development of personality (such as community and intellectual influences). Furthermore, Freud's emphasis that the early years of development leave an indelible mark on the personality for good or ill seems to be contradicted by evidence that the personality is in a state of continual development, and that later life experiences can and do make up for inadequate experiences in early life (Liebert & Spiegler 1987). Other criticisms relate to the lack of clear definitions of some of the components of his system, and the difficulty inherent in empirically testing and measuring these components (Pervin 1989).

Classroom implications of Freud's theory

Elements of Freud's theory are useful for teachers in understanding behaviour in the classroom. Identification, anxiety, displacement and defence mechanisms are very useful concepts.

Identification with teachers

Much personality development results from children incorporating values held by significant others through the process of **identification**, and teachers as well as parents are powerful models in this process.

Anxiety

Earlier we discussed three forms of anxiety: neurotic anxiety, realistic anxiety and moral anxiety. Children can develop **neurotic anxiety** if they are not helped by teachers and parents to recognise and come to terms with their instinctual behaviour. They need to recognise that instinctual drives are normal but that they need to strive to strike a balance between what is an acceptable/unacceptable satisfaction of these drives. A preoccupation with these instinctual drives can develop into neuroticism. Neurotic anxiety sometimes displays itself in **acting-out behaviour**, for example, when an apparently placid and well-controlled child has a violent outburst of rage.

Realistic anxiety may be caused by brutal shocks or frightening experiences, but it may also be caused in children by such things as excessive demands for academic success or standards of behaviour, by a background of domestic strife, or the uncertainties of having to start a new school with a new teacher.

Moral anxiety may be produced by repressive moral training, and may provoke self-punishment in children through feelings of unworthiness or inadequacy. Sometimes ritualistic gestures such as excessive handwashing (called obsessional-compulsive behaviour) develop in an attempt to remove such feelings symbolically (Fontana 1986).

Displacement as school behaviour

Classroom and school behaviour will sometimes reflect **displacement**. For example, children will be 'out of sorts' at times, owing to a range of causes, and will displace their annoyance, aggression and anger on their peers and teachers. Children who are abused at home may act in very antisocial ways at school. It is well to remember that children's behaviour (as well as our own) is the result of a complex interplay of unconscious forces, and we as teachers and parents must take the time to work through the possible reasons for specific behaviour, particularly when the behaviour is different from the typical or is apparently inexplicable.

Pupil use of defence mechanisms

When under stress, children will unconsciously resort to **defence mechanisms** to protect their ego, that component of the personality that suffers the anxiety feelings. One example we remember was hearing a teacher berate a very young child for stealing money from her purse, with the child protesting her innocence. 'But you were seen doing it!' The teacher became more and more exasperated and the child more upset. Under these circumstances Freudian theory would suggest that the teacher desist, for the child's response may very well be what the child believes, with **repression** or **denial** blocking an acceptance of the reality.

Under stress some children may **regress** and resort to thumb sucking or wetting themselves. This is not uncommon when children first start school. Of course, rather than reprimanding the child, a supportive and loving environment must be provided so that the child can feel secure and resolve the conflict in a healthy fashion. Stress such as that caused by **test anxiety** may also lead to **regression**. In some cases this regression may be relatively harmless, such as eating excessively or masturbating at these times; on other occasions it may be more serious, such as an inability to cope with the situation and engaging in withdrawal or bizarre behaviour. For example, graffiti, scatological toilet graffiti, and school vandalism may be examples of both regression and 'acting out' behaviour. Again, when such behaviour is severe, it is important to investigate the reasons for the behaviour and attempt to alleviate the conditions causing it.

Many accusations and counter accusations between children at school are the result of **projection**; for example, John says he doesn't want to play with Bill because Bill doesn't like him, when the truth is that John is afraid that Bill doesn't want to play with him. Some children may project that their teacher is lazy and a poor teacher when the student is in fact the lazy one.

Rationalisation is commonly used by children to excuse sloppy work, cheating and a range of inappropriate behaviour within the school context, while **fantasy** is used to relieve boredom and inability to cope.

Finally, Freudian theory emphasises the important role that significant individuals, such as teachers, play in the early personality formation of children. Excessively restrictive practices (such as extreme discipline) lead to resentment and an attempt by children to resolve the conflict in potentially harmful ways.

Question point: *Discuss the role of defence mechanisms in the personality development of children and adolescents.*

ACTION STATION

Try your hand at classifying defence mechanisms. In the following story a number of alternative endings are given. Suggest which defence mechanism (if any) is operating.

Jack, an accountant, was ambitious and worked very hard at his job to obtain a promotion to chief accountant of his firm. Then his colleague, John, was promoted to the position desired by Jack and became Jack's superior. Jack was very unhappy about this state of affairs and in his reveries thought of all sorts of nasty events that could befall John so that he would then be able to assume his rightful place as chief accountant. After a number of months John suffered a serious heart attack and ended up in hospital. Jack was shocked.

1. Jack became very solicitous of John's welfare, spending long hours with him in hospital. Defence mechanism: ____________

2. While shocked, Jack believed that John had been unsuited to the job and had brought the heart attack on himself by his ambition and overwork. Defence mechanism: ____________________
3. While shocked, Jack believed that he had only the best interests of the company at heart and that ultimately it would be better for the company if he was made chief accountant. Defence mechanism: ____________________
4. When questioned regarding his future intentions for the position, Jack denied ever having wanted the job. Defence mechanism: ____________________
5. Jack began to drink heavily and appeared to lose interest in his job. Defence mechanism: ____________________

HUMANISM AND PERSONAL DEVELOPMENT

Humanistic psychologists stress the individual potential for good in all human beings. They perceive people as free and unique, self-directed, capable of setting goals, making choices and initiating action. Humanist psychologists further believe that, in order to function most effectively and to maximise their potential, individuals must first become aware of their internal thoughts and feelings regarding themselves and the world. By consciously describing such thoughts and feelings, individuals become more aware of how these influence their behaviour and may therefore be better able to control them. The thoughts and feelings that individuals have about themselves focus around three broad areas (Weinstein & Fantini 1970):

Human development and self-knowledge, self-control and productive living

1. *Identity:* Who am I? Where am I going?
2. *Connectedness:* How do I fit or relate with other people? Do people like me?
3. *Power:* What are my limits? What control do I have over my life?

For humanist psychologists, personal development is a process of answering these questions. Humanism further holds that a critical aspect of this learning process is the ability to judge whether or not our thoughts and feelings are personally productive, and then make whatever modifications are necessary. The ultimate goals of this search for self-knowledge are greater self-control and more positive living. This process of self-knowledge depends on people's interactions with one another as it is through this interaction that we become aware of our own identity.

Carl Rogers and 'realness'

Much of the impetus for this approach can be traced to the work of the clinical psychologist Carl Rogers (1961, 1969, 1976, 1977, 1983). Rogers' personality theory is based on two major assumptions:

1. Human behaviour is guided by each person's unique self-actualising tendency.
2. All humans need positive regard (Liebert & Spiegler 1987).

Two terms drawn from Rogers' writings illustrate well the emphasis he places upon the individual's role in the development of personality. First, **client-centred therapy** (as opposed to directive therapy) relates to Rogers' belief that individuals strive to fulfil themselves, and that we all, given a supportive interpersonal environment, have the necessary resources within ourselves to achieve this. In other words, an individual's personal growth towards healthy, competent and creative functioning is largely inner controlled and driven rather than outer directed (as is implied in contrasting behavioural approaches, see Chapter 6).

Client-centred therapy: emphasises the individual's role in development

The second term is phenomenology, which denotes Rogers' belief that an individual's 'real' world is what the individual *perceives*, rather than what may actually be. In other words, reality is personal and subjective. Perceived reality is known as our **phenomenological field**. Simply speaking, if we perceive that we are ugly, untalented and unlikeable, objective evidence to the contrary may make little difference to our sense of self. Instead, our phenomenological field has to be altered so that 'reality' may be perceived in a different light.

Phenomenology: what the individual perceives rather than what actually may be

Humanists, such as Rogers, redefine the role of parents and teachers in childrearing and education. Parents and teachers must stand back and, in a sense, allow room for children to grow in a caring but non-controlling environment. Parents and teachers become **facilitators** of children's development by supplying appropriate opportunities, resources, support and non-evaluative feedback to promote children's growth, development, maturity, and ability to cope with life. Of fundamental importance here is the need for parents and teachers to be *real* to the children in the sense of being caring, trustworthy, dependable and consistent at a deep level. In essence, parents and teachers need to be perceived by the child as part of their phenomenological world, for it is only in this circumstance that they can effectively facilitate children's personal growth. Independence, creativity,

Parents and teachers as facilitators of children's personal development

self-reliance and self-evaluation are all encouraged, and children take responsibility for their own learning and development. There is a strong emphasis in this approach on interpersonal relationships and feelings, where parents and teachers are perceived as joint voyagers with children on the way to self-discovery. Indeed, the approach suggests that, as teachers and parents, we grow as well through this process, and that unless we also develop as 'real' people we cannot hope to be facilitators of others' growth to realness.

Maslow's hierarchy of needs

Another humanist psychologist, Maslow (1968, 1970, 1976), viewed personal development as a process of natural growth in which all individuals would realise their potential provided the environment was supportive. He believed that individuals seek to satisfy particular needs, the ultimate goal being that of **self-actualisation**, and conceived of human needs as arranged in a hierarchy. The lower levels of this hierarchy, basic needs, are termed **deficiency needs** while the higher levels are called **growth needs** or **metaneeds**.

Deficiency needs and growth needs

Physiological needs come first, according to Maslow. Children who are hungry, thirsty or sleepy will be preoccupied with actions to alleviate this need, and there will be little motivation to be involved in other activities. A number of schools in low socioeconomic areas have instigated breakfast programs for children who come from homes where they may not have been adequately fed in the morning. The purpose is, of course, to satisfy this need so that the children can concentrate more effectively on learning, a need higher up in the hierarchy. The physiological needs do not have to be as graphic as illustrated by persistently hungry children.

Physiological needs: hunger, thirst, rest

This teacher is showing a humanistic approach towards her student. What might be the likely outcome?
Photo: Connie Griebe

Just being too cold, or too hot, or too hungry for 'little lunch' is enough to distract children (and teachers) from the task of learning.

The next level is **safety needs**. Children have a need to feel safe and secure. Preoccupation with their physical welfare will distract children from personal development and effective learning. A teacher in a school that served a refugee hostel near an aerodrome in Sydney recalls the experience of children in her class from wartorn Lebanon ducking under their desks whenever a plane flew overhead. Her first weeks of teaching were taken up with restoring the children's sense of safety. Another graphic example of this need for safety are children who come from homes where physical abuse is prevalent. These children often withdraw from involvement in classroom activities as they are preoccupied with the events that dominate their lives at that time.

Safety needs: security and welfare

All schools have introduced pastoral care policies which attempt to identify and alleviate the problems suffered by neglected and battered children. On a less graphic level, children who are being pushed around by other students, or who fear the wrath of the teacher may also be using a lot of mental energy working through these threats and protecting themselves (physically and mentally) instead of attending to their learning. The lives of these children are made miserable to varying extents, and, as a result, they are often insecure and lacking in self-esteem (Smith & Ahmad 1990). Continued insecurity makes it very difficult for them to reacquire confidence in themselves, and, of course, confidence is a prerequisite of effective learning.

Pastoral care programs

The third level of Maslow's hierarchy is the **need to belong**. Initially, this need is fulfilled through the family, but as children widen their social network this need must also be fulfilled through contact with others outside the family. A feeling of being one of the group and having a cohort with whom to identify within the school is important to children. Isolates and outcasts, or children scorned by others, can be distracted from their schoolwork. Children can be cruel to each other and great unhappiness often results when an individual feels isolated from the group. Teachers must be aware of this and facilitate good interpersonal relationships within the classroom which foster good classroom motivation.

Need to belong

The fourth need, **need for self-esteem**, relates to an individual's need to feel worthwhile and important in the eyes of others. Again, the initial way in which this is fulfilled is through the family. However, we are all aware that there are times when children are denigrated within the family

Need for self-esteem

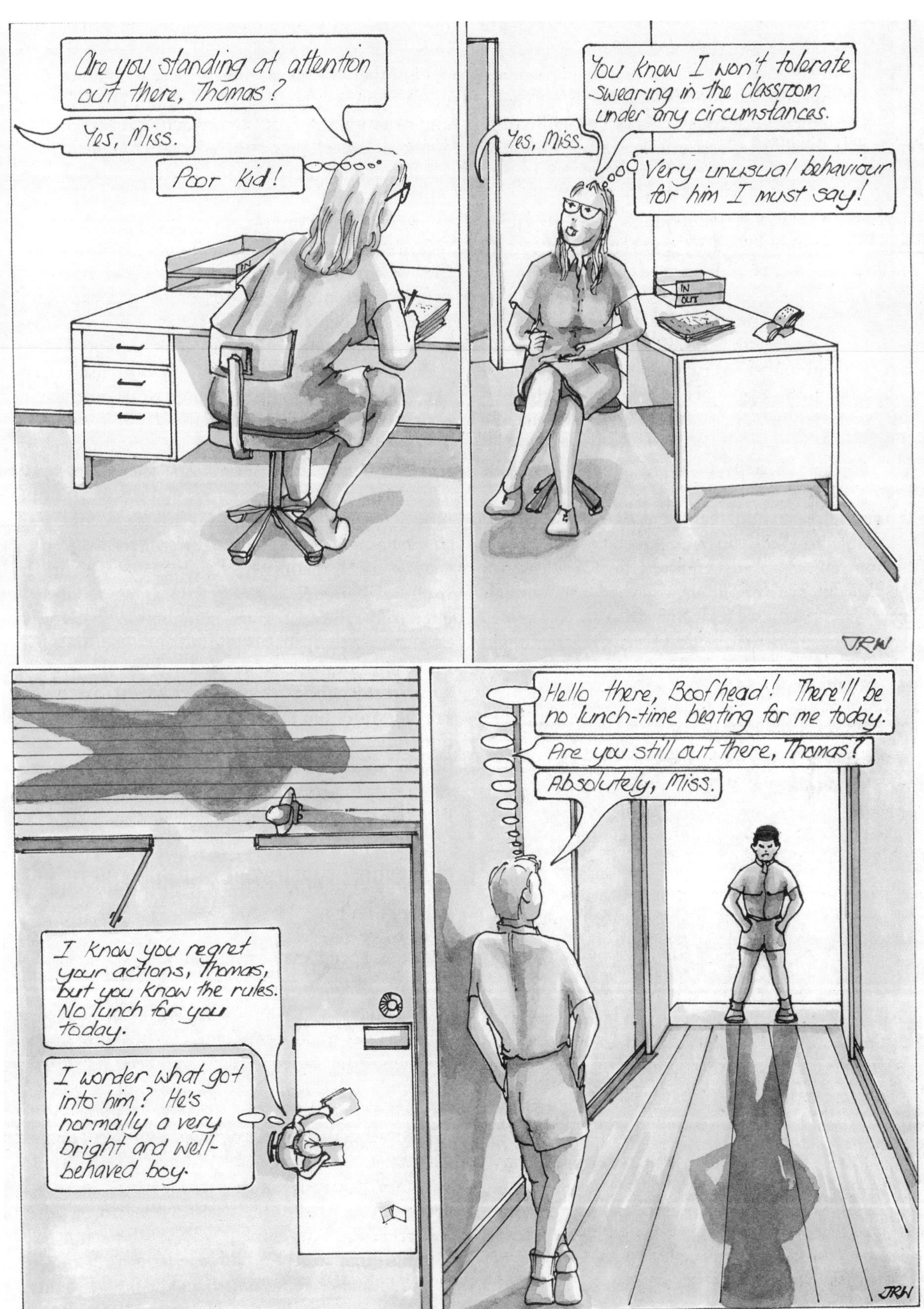
Are you standing at attention out there, Thomas?
Yes, Miss.
Poor kid!
You know I won't tolerate swearing in the classroom under any circumstances.
Yes, Miss.
Very unusual behaviour for him I must say!
JRW
I know you regret your actions, Thomas, but you know the rules. No lunch for you today.
I wonder what got into him? He's normally a very bright and well-behaved boy.
Hello there, Boofhead! There'll be no lunch-time beating for me today.
Are you still out there, Thomas?
Absolutely, Miss.
JRW

and come to school with very negative self-concepts. In these cases the school (and teachers) must do everything in their power to enhance the individual's feelings of self-confidence, worth, strength, capability and adequacy. School programs and procedures, as well as classroom practices, must be designed to maximise students' feelings of self-worth. Last, according to Maslow, is the need for **self-actualisation.** At this level, individuals strive to satisfy their need to grow intellectually and spiritually.

Self-actualisation

Maslow proposes that these needs are hierarchically ordered so that higher-level needs (or motivators) only become operational as lower-order needs are satisfied. We should consider the developmental stages of children in this context. Very young children will be dominated by physiological needs, while older children will be interested in testing themselves out in the environment, especially in relation to their physical abilities and their capacity to avoid danger. In middle childhood, as well as these needs, children will be testing themselves out in the social world, where the need for affection and belonging becomes relatively more important. Last, as children grow older they develop clearer ideas about themselves as individuals with varying capacities which they wish to test. Thus, the need to feel competent, and to receive approval and recognition from others, becomes increasingly important.

While we note that human needs appear to arrange themselves in a hierarchical order, and that success at one level of need usually requires prior satisfaction of another more prepotent need, human motivation is affected by biological, cultural and situational forces, all interacting together. While acknowledging the apparent logic of Maslow's hierarchy, humans are very complex creatures, and there are many situations that contradict his approach. For example, many people will persist at a task long after they become hungry or thirsty because they are intensely interested in their work. At times, people are motivated to perform behaviour that appears to contradict their basic needs for safety and belongingness because of the functioning of a higher need such as self-esteem or self-actualisation. In the activities related to this chapter, you will be asked to consider the whys and wherefores of this issue.

Other influences on personal development

Maslow's hierarchy is generally presented as a triangle with basic needs at the base and self-actualisation at the apex. We have always found the model somewhat static. It does not effectively suggest the dynamic and organic nature of motivation as perceived by humanist psychologists. We prefer our *sunflower model* instead which, we believe, more effectively illustrates the interaction between basic needs, growth needs and fulfilment. The sunflower can burst into flower even while other elements of the structure (such as leaves and stem) are withering. Furthermore, the model represents a more organic and integrated system, and truly captures the spirit of the humanist ideal of self-actualisation. Given a reasonably supportive environment, the seed contains the dynamism for growth of the sunflower.

WHAT WOULD YOU DO?

DANIEL'S PET

In order to better understand the children in my grade 2 class during my final semester of early childhood field experience, I devised some questionnaires asking a variety of questions. One question was 'My pet's name is ...'.

In respect of this question, Daniel had crossed out this question and wrote 'I hate the word pet'. I am ashamed to admit that when I saw this I took it quite personally and was offended. I felt it was a simple question requiring a simple answer. I felt I was a reasonable/agreeable person, and I had never forced any child to answer any question if they didn't wish to. Therefore, he didn't have any right to cross out one of *my* questions and write a silly comment such as the fact that he doesn't like the word 'pet'.

Analyse this case study from a humanist perspective. What might have caused Daniel's reaction? Why did the teacher react in this way? What might the resolution be? ***See page 365 for the resolution.***

Case studies illustrating National Competency Framework for Beginning Teaching, National Project on the Quality of Teaching and Learning, Australian Teaching Council, 1996, p. 32. Commonwealth of Australia copyright, reproduced by pemission.

CLASSROOM IMPLICATIONS OF HUMANISTIC PERSPECTIVES

Realness, acceptance and empathy

Humanists believe that effective teaching and classroom management is largely a function of positive teacher–student and student–student relationships. In this, the teacher's role is central in building positive interpersonal relationships and promoting a positive socioemotional climate (Sokolove, Sadker & Sadker 1986). Rogers (1976) emphasises three qualities *in teachers* that he believes will have maximum effect in facilitating learning in their students: **realness**—that is, being in touch with one's self, willing to disclose one's feelings, and developing along the path to self-actualisation; **acceptance**—that is, prizing the learners as individuals having worth in their own right, being able to suspend judgment and accept the prerogative of

THE McINERNEY SUNFLOWER MODEL OF HUMAN SELF-ACTUALIZATION

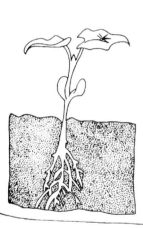

(Based on Maslow, 1954)

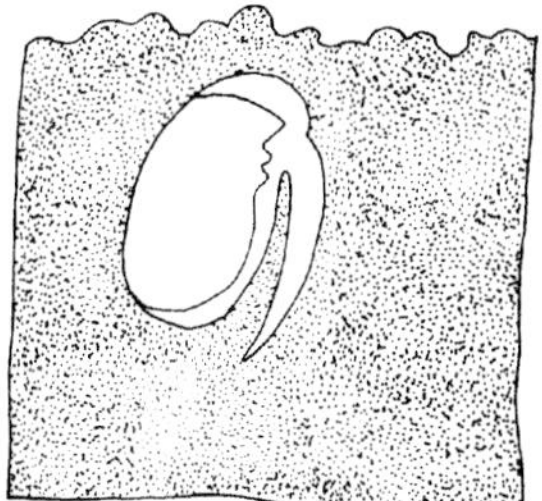

1 The seed has within itself the potential for growth.
The human child has within itself the potential for growth

2 Appropriate warmth and moisture stimulate the seed to growth.
Children need to have their psychological and security needs met in order to grow.

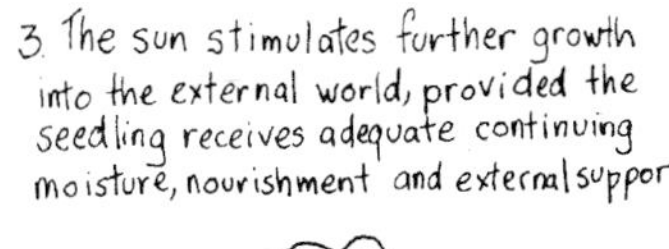

3 The sun stimulates further growth into the external world, provided the seedling receives adequate continuing moisture, nourishment and external support.

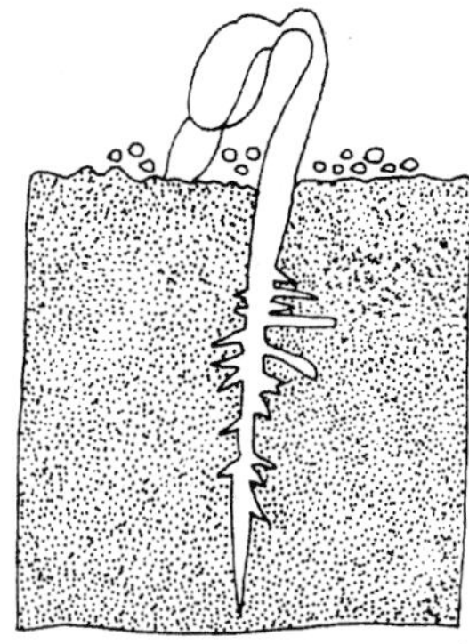

As children grow older they need to feel a sense of belonging and self-esteem in order to develop socially and emotionally.
DEFICIENCY NEEDS
4. At this point the plant's energy is directed towards developing a sunflower. Inadequate moisture, nourishment and warmth will retard the developing flower although the plant itself may survive.
Provided a child's basic needs are met, growth is directed towards intellectual and aesthetic needs. However if these basic needs are not adequately met the child's intellectual growth may be hindered.
GROWTH NEEDS

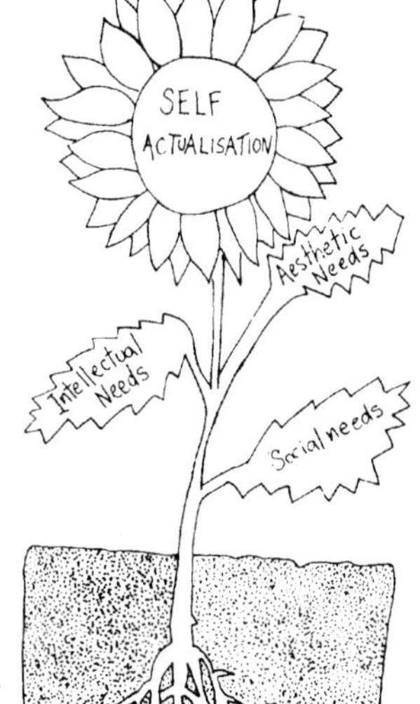

SELF ACTUALISATION
Aesthetic Needs
Intellectual Needs
Social needs
5. The developing sunflower bursts forth in all its glory while the need to maintain continuing nourishment and moisture becomes less important. The mature sunflower provides the seeds for renewed growth – the cycle of growth continues and is ever renewed.

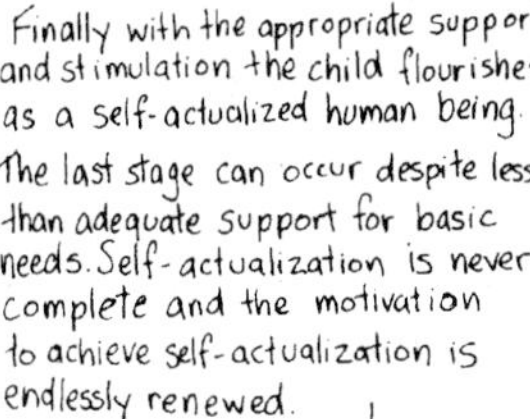

Finally with the appropriate support and stimulation the child flourishes as a self-actualized human being.
The last stage can occur despite less than adequate support for basic needs. Self-actualization is never complete and the motivation to achieve self-actualization is endlessly renewed.

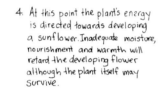

others to hold their own values; and **empathetic understanding**—that is, having the ability to understand the student's reactions from the inside, and a sensitive awareness of the way the process of education and learning appears to the student.

In essence, Rogers considers that the development of a positive self-concept and positive self-regard in an individual is derived from empathetic others helping the child to see and develop inherent potential. This is achieved by interacting with that individual in a positive, accepting way, even if disapproval is felt at outward actions.

Safe classrooms and schools

Schools need to be safe and secure environments in which children can work energetically. According to Maslow, teachers need to work within this needs framework to make learning environments satisfying to children and to maximise their motivation. As basic needs are satisfied, the metaneeds, or the needs related to self-actualisation, become important.

Open classrooms

Clearly, the most important aspect of humanism for teachers is the socioemotional climate established within the classroom. Humanism does not necessitate a particular approach to teaching; indeed, approaches as diverse as behavioural and cognitive (see Chapters 3, 4, 5 and 6) can be effectively suffused with humanism. It is a frame of mind about the centrality of the student in the learning process and the importance of a supportive and non-restrictive learning environment. Nevertheless, humanistic practitioners have attempted to develop a range of teaching approaches that more clearly reflect the humanistic philosophy. These have included open education, open classrooms, open scheduling and many forms of curricula that emphasise affective learning such as **values clarification** (see Thibadeau 1995). Open education is a form of education, the goal of which is to respond to children on the basis of their individual behaviours, needs and charateristics (Thibadeau 1995). Many other practices encouraged by the humanist approach are now part of mainstream educational practice: child-centred programming, individualising instruction, encouraging independent work, pupil choice and responsibility, de-emphasising competition and emphasising cooperation. Alternative forms of assessment such as observation and portfolios, negotiated curricula and negotiated assessment, together with an emphasis on criterion-referenced evaluation rather than norm-referenced evaluation, also fit within a humanist philosophy of child-centred education. Many of these approaches are discussed in this book.

Socioemotional climate and humanistic classroom practices

Research does not support the notion that approaches such as open classrooms are more effective than conventional schools and classroom practices (Jackson & Harve, 1991). Indeed, while there was a strong push for open classrooms and open schools in the 1970s, they have all but disappeared in the 1990s. While research demonstrates that, on average, open classrooms of the 1970s did not lead to achievement gains greater than those in standard classroom programs, most research also finds that students' academic achievement did not suffer in open classrooms; in several areas, such as creativity, self-concept and attitudes towards school, students in open classrooms did better than students in traditional classrooms (Giaconia & Hedges 1982; Rothenberg 1989). Unfortunately, because of the many mistakes made in the design and implementation of open classrooms their potential was never realised (Jackson & Harvey 1991; Rothenber 1989; Thibadeau 1995). One problem, for example, was that teachers were not well prepared to teach effectively in open settings. A number of research studies at the time that claimed to demonstrate the ineffectiveness of this approach also facilitated its demise. Subsequent reanalysis of the data and methodology of several of these studies has shown them to be flawed (see Asher & Hynes 1982; Walberg 1984). Perhaps open education and free schools were more effective than believed at the time.

Other psychologists have adopted views similar to those of Rogers, based largely on his philosophy. Noteworthy among these are Ginott, Glasser, Gordon and Dreikurs who have developed humanistic ideas for the classroom, particularly with regard to forms of communication and discipline. As we have indicated earlier, teachers are an integral part of the interactive process in their classroom. By modelling interpersonal communication skills, teachers may help to initiate and facilitate teacher–student and student–student interaction which in turn will guide students in learning to use these skills.

Ginott (1972) maintains that, in effective communication, the teacher should address the situation (i.e. the actual behaviour) rather than the individual's personality. Consequently, a teacher would say to a student 'Not completing homework prevents effective learning' rather than 'You are a lazy so-and-so for not completing your homework'. Glasser (1969), on the other hand, stresses teacher involvement with the student, in an accepting, non-judgmental manner. He focuses on the development of the student's social responsibility and feelings of self-worth. Dreikurs' (Dreikurs & Pearl 1972) viewpoint emphasises the democratic classroom in which the teacher maintains his or her position as leader, but encourages a sharing of responsibility and mutual trust.

We have described these approaches only briefly, and you are recommended to follow them up in other sources. A number of these approaches are considered in greater detail in the chapter on classroom management (Chapter 10).

HUMANISM AND CONSTRUCTIVISM

We emphasise that a principal application of humanism to education is the establishing of effective classroom communication between both teachers and students, and students and students. This emphasis has survived and is flourishing in all good classrooms. The open classroom philosophy and principles derived from it are also very well suited to the types of educational programs being advocated today. Humanism encourages

WHAT WOULD YOU DO?

DANIEL'S PET (continued)

Daniel was away sick for a few days so I wasn't able to ask him about it until nearly a week later. I reminded him of the question on the sheet and of the comment he had written, then asked why he didn't like the word 'pet'.

At first Daniel didn't want to talk about it. I have to admit that I thought he was just trying to avoid having to confront that he had done something inappropriate. However, Henry was seated next to him and overheard the question. He said he knew what it was all about. Daniel told him not to tell but Henry blurted out that Daniel's cat had recently died.

Daniel then reluctantly told me that it was true. He looked quite upset and said that he still felt sad. He said that when he read the question it made him want to cry. I apologised for the fact that the question on the sheet had upset him and that it had brought back sad memories for him. He seemed to accept my apology and said it was okay.

I then made a mental note never to jump to conclusions about a child's intentions without giving them the benefit of the doubt and asking them about it first.

Case studies illustrating National Competency Framework for Beginning Teaching, National Project on the Quality of Teaching and Learning, Australian Teaching Council, 1996, p. 32. Commonwealth of Australia copyright, reproduced by pemission.

Show how this case study illustrates the elements of Roger's humanism—realness, acceptance and empathetic understanding.

students to construct their own learning, facilitated by effective teachers and an appropriate learning environment that is connected to the students' experiences and concerns (Rothenberg 1989).

TABLE 15.5

ESSENTIALS OF HUMANISM FOR EDUCATION

For teachers

- Be in touch with yourself and willing to disclose your feelings.
- Establish the primacy of the learner.
- Prize the learner as an individual having worth in his or her own right.
- Develop realness, acceptance and empathetic understanding.
- Suspend judgment and accept the prerogative of others to hold their own values.
- Develop the ability to understand students' reactions from the inside.
- Establish a safe and secure classroom and school environment.
- Establish a non-restrictive learning environment.

TEACHER'S CASE BOOK

THE WATER DROP STORY

I see part of my teaching role as being a liaison between parents and children. I have a number of children in my third class whose parents are divorcing, and each child is experiencing his or her own set of problems.

One little girl in particular was having trouble coping with the problems at home and was coming to school engaging in antisocial behaviour. She was fighting, name-calling, teasing and taking other children's things. This had been going on for about eight months, since before the last Christmas holidays. The source of her problems became more evident to me in her writing. While writing a story about a drop of water, she mentioned marriage and a life without divorce. I felt it was my responsibility to make an interview with each of the parents separately to bring the situation to their attention.

Mum took the child's writing with her on a regularly scheduled visit to the child's counsellor. Dad has since remarried. Both parents appreciated the feedback and agreed on how important the contact is between both homes and school to help this little girl try to overcome her problems. One good thing is that this child has developed quite a good friendship with another girl who has had a similar experience in her family.

Case studies illustrating National Competency Framework for Beginning Teaching, National Project on the Quality of Teaching and Learning, Australian Teaching Council, 1996, p. 21. Commonwealth of Australia copyright, reproduced by pemission.

Case study activity
How does this case study illustrate a number of the issues discussed in this chapter?

Question point: *Which theory of personality appeals to you most? Why? Are the theories mutually exclusive?*

Question point: *Consider the implications of each of the theories covered in this chapter for children living in tribal settings (such as Australian Aboriginal and Maori children), rural Westernised settings and urbanised settings. What different factors are likely to affect development in each case?*

Recommended reading

Erikson, E. H. (1963) *Childhood and Society*, 2nd edn. New York: Norton.

Erikson, E. H. (1968) *Identity: Youth and Crisis*. New York: Norton.

Fontana, D. (1986) *Teaching and Personality*. Oxford: Basil Blackwell.

Lerner, R.M., Peterson, A.C. & Brooks-Gunn (eds) (1991) *Encyclopedia of Adolescence*. Vol. 2. N.Y.: Garland.

Rogers, C. R. (1983) *Freedom to Learn: For the 80's*. Columbus, OH: Merrill.

Thibadeau, G. (1995) Open education. In L. W. Anderson (ed.) *International Encyclopedia of Teaching and Teacher Education*, 2nd edn, pp. 167–71. Tarrytown, NY: Pergamon.

Social, emotional and moral development

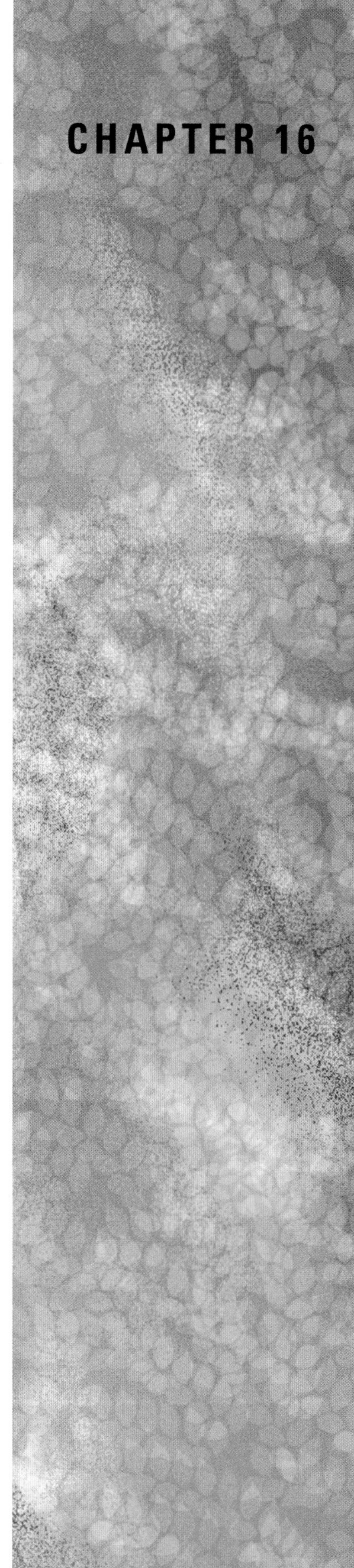

OVERVIEW

In contemporary societies the school is the one major social institution, other than the family, with which virtually all people are deeply involved during the critical developmental years of childhood and adolescence. Many of the functions of traditional socialisation agencies, such as the family, the workplace and the church, have been passed over to the school. No longer is the school simply responsible for developing the cognitive skills of children, but also for developing many skills in a wide range of socially related areas.

In this chapter we consider the influence of the family, school and peer group on the social, emotional and moral development of the child. In particular, we concentrate on three important aspects. The first of these is the continuing process by which our sense of personal identity is established. The second is the nature of family relationships and their effects on the child's self-reliance and independence. The third is the importance of peer group interaction for heterosexual development and group acceptance. In this context we look at the function of groups, gangs, cliques and friendships. We also look at adolescent alienation, and the issue of adolescent suicide in particular.

An important aspect of social, emotional and moral development is the development of a sense of self as a worthwhile human being. We consider the nature and development of the self-concept, how it is structured and formed, whether (and how) it changes over time, whether there are group differences in self-concept, and what effect it has on motivation and behaviour.

Finally, in this chapter we consider moral development in detail and examine closely the work of Piaget, Kohlberg, Gilligan and Turiel. Piaget's stages of moral reasoning are discussed, together with the notions of a morality of constraint and a morality of cooperation. In line with recent thinking about Piagetian stage theory, we provide a critique of his approach to moral development. Kohlberg's stages of moral development—preconventional, conventional and postconventional—are described, and the current status of the theory is explored. In particular, we examine sex differences in moral development, the relationship between moral reasoning and moral behaviour, and cross-cultural implications. Turiel's views on the acquisition of moral values in social contexts are also considered.

Finally, classroom implications of social, emotional and moral development, and the relationship of these to effective learning are considered.

Children who are well adjusted and happy enjoy school. Photo: Connie Griebe

SOCIAL AND EMOTIONAL DEVELOPMENT IN CHILDHOOD

What is the importance of family relationships to social and emotional development? The development of a social identity becomes increasingly important to children as they grow older. Sociability has its roots in the interactions of the baby and its parents or other caregivers, and these early experiences will either encourage or deter the baby's tendency to approach other human beings. In the early years in the home, parents and siblings are the most important elements in the development of a child's social self.

As children grow older, mothers typically spend less time with them while fathers become more important influences in their development, involving themselves more in children's activities such as hobbies, sport and clubs. In our Western society parents begin to give their

LEARNER-CENTRED PSYCHOLOGICAL PRINCIPLE 14

Learning is influenced by social interactions, interpersonal relations and communication with others.

Quality personal relationships give the individual access to higher-order, healthier levels of thinking, feeling and behaving. Teachers' (or other significant adults') states of mind, stability, trust and caring are preconditions for establishing a sense of belonging, self-respect, self-acceptance and positive climate for learning. Healthier levels of thinking are those that are less self-conscious, insecure, irrational and self-deprecating. Self-esteem and learning are mutually reinforcing.

Reprinted with permission, APA Task Force on Psychology in Education (1993, January), p. 8.

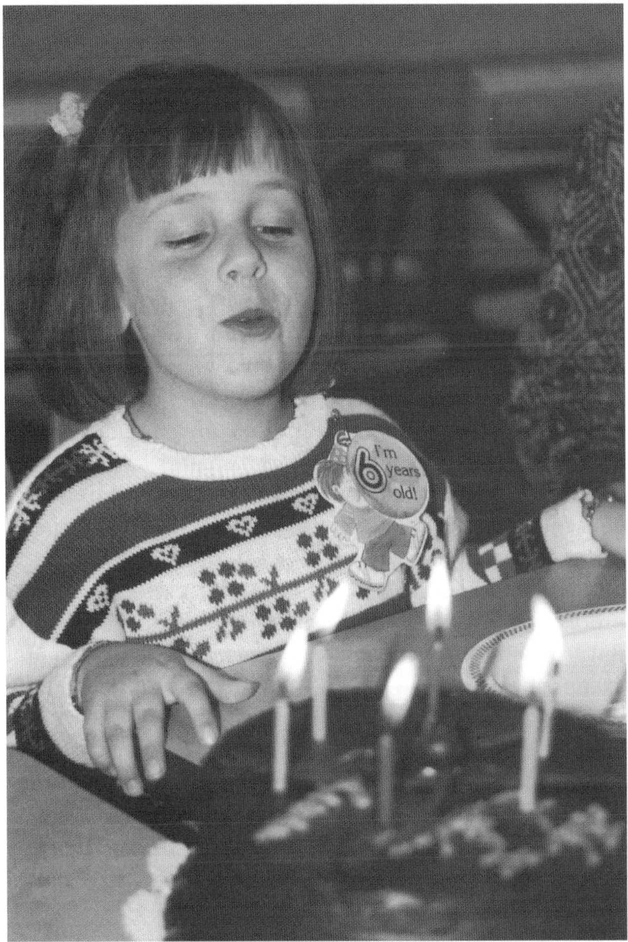

Birthdays are usually a happy social event in families, signifying growth to maturity. Photo: authors

children increasing independence as they grow older (although this is not a universally practised custom). Many parents also encourage their children to take on part-time paid work and to achieve independent goals, thereby fostering a sense of industry (refer to the section on Erikson in Chapter 15).

In many households both parents work, so increasing numbers of children leave for school and arrive home after school without adult supervision. Many children in our classrooms also come from single-parent homes, the result of separation, divorce or parental death. It is increasingly common for the single parent to be the father. Many children suffer trauma as a result of such effects of divorce as custodial arrangements, the nature of the custodial parent–child relationship, and the availability and reliance on support systems (Berk 1996; Santrock & Yussen 1992). Recent research has indicated that the negative effects of divorce are diminished over a period of years if parental conflict is absent. In this, and in other circumstances where children lose parents, the classroom teacher becomes an important element in the child's support structure.

The role of siblings in socialisation

Siblings also act as important socialising influences on each other. The most persuasive characteristics of this relationship are competition and concern about being treated equally by parents. While competitive interaction is a fact of sibling life, there are many positive and neutral interactions that benefit the child's social and emotional development. Someone close in age to the child may be able to communicate more effectively than parents can. In areas such as dealing with peers, coping with difficult teachers, and discussing taboo subjects, siblings are often of more assistance and support than parents. Older siblings may model appropriate behaviour and attitudes to a range of events dealing with identity, physical appearance and sexual behaviour, areas in which the parents may be unwilling or incapable of helping the child. Of course, sometimes the reverse can occur with older siblings modelling inappropriate behaviour and attitudes.

The changing nature of society and family structure has brought new responsibilities to the school and teachers. During middle and late childhood, peers, teachers and other adults become more important (Berk 1991; Peterson 1989; Santrock & Yussen 1992).

The importance of the peer group

Peer group importance

Cliques

Sex cleavages

The significance of the peer group increases as children progress through school. As this occurs, children sometimes organise themselves into more or less exclusively girl or boy **cliques**. Often rituals and rules are established to keep other individuals out of the group, but cliques become less rigid as children

The relationship between siblings is a very important element in social development. Photo: authors

approach puberty. Most schools now implement non-sexist practices that cut across sex-based cliques, although in out-of-school activities most children prefer to get together in single-sex groups.

Non-sexist education practices

Small friendship groups are very important to the identity of the child. Through **peer modelling** and reinforcement children can acquire and test out their growing personal, social and physical skills in a group that is supportive (Williams & Stith 1980). Peer interactions are reciprocal. An important aspect of these friendships is in the area of **emotional development.** In coping with emotional conflict, young friends express considerable emotion, sympathy and support for each other (Peterson 1989). Family and cultural backgrounds play critical roles in the development of both informal and formal peer groups. Children's perception of security in the mother–child relationship, for example, has been shown to be related to the formation of positive peer relationships in middle childhood (Kerns, Plepac & Cole 1996). Therefore, even though children and adolescents often spend greater amounts of time with their peers than with their parents, isolation from parental values does not necessarily ensue (Jarvinen & Nicholls 1996).

Emotional development and small group membership

Often personal, social and emotional problems begin to surface as children enter school, with rates of referral for primary children being considerably higher than for preschool children. Many of these problems are school-related—for instance, oppositional and acting-out behaviour, poor discipline, and personal characteristics such as shyness, unhappiness and withdrawal.

Play

Play is very important to the social and emotional development of children. To understand the role of play it may be helpful to categorise the social elements of children's play in the following way:

- ☐ *Solitary:* the child plays alone, unaware of others.
- ☐ *Onlooker:* the child looks on at the play of others but is not directly involved in it.
- ☐ *Parallel:* children play alongside others doing similar things, but with little or no interaction.
- ☐ *Associative:* children play as a group, using the same materials, but do not appear to share a plan of action or common purpose.
- ☐ *Cooperative:* children play with each other, making up and taking turns in games that have a shared goal.

(Parten 1932)

ACTION STATION

a

Consider the types of play listed above. In what ways would the development of social, emotional and communication skills occur in each?

As children develop, so do the complexity and social nature of their play. While **solitary** and **onlooker** play is characteristic of young children, and **associative** and **cooperative** play more typical of the older child, it is inaccurate to use the categorisation of social play as a marker of social maturity. Just as young children may take part in the interactive games of associative play when they play pretend games and chatter to each other (Howes, Unger & Seidner 1989), so older children may also engage in solitary play in which they play quietly for a period by themselves, showing that they are now able to concentrate on a task (Smith 1978). As for onlooker play, even adolescents may remain to the side until they have worked up the confidence to participate in a group 'game' to which they are newcomers. While intellectual development may be quite advanced, the young person may lack the social skills and self-esteem to engage in cooperative interaction with unfamiliar individuals or those who appear exclusive.

Symbolic re-enactments of real-life and imaginary experiences is referred to as sociodramatic play. Sociodramatic play in childhood provides the greatest opportunity for children to learn social skills and gain an understanding of how they respond to others (and vice versa) in a social group of peers. For instance, the choice of who is allowed to participate in dramatic play or to contribute to the rules of the game sends messages about one's self-worth. Adult and societal roles are also explored or re-enacted in dramatic play when children become television characters or members of their family, not only in manner but in vocalisation. In the following example, Laura was debating with two friends their respective roles in a dramatisation of *The Wizard of Oz.*

Sociodramatic play: symbolic re-enactments of real-life

'You be the Wicked Witch and I'll be the Good Witch coz I've got blonde hair.'

'So you have to sound all cackley and mean, and I have to be beautiful and wear a pretty dress, and talk sweetly.'

'Who's going to be the Wizard? We don't have any boys!'

'We'll have to skip that bit.'

'What about when Dorothy gets back home? Her aunty would be really worried about her—maybe she should cry.'

'I think she would give Dorothy a smack for being gone so long.'

In addition to social skills, many language and interpersonal skills are learned through cooperative and associative play as children have to interact with one another in the business of problem solving, negotiating, resolving disputes, turn-taking and sharing resources. The teacher has an important role to play in providing the language needed to describe the conflicts that erupt in children's play and to assist children in understanding the perspective of others who may often inadvertently thwart them.

Cooperative and associative play

ACTION STATION

Schools are significant influences in the social development of children. The classroom forms a mini world for the child with leaders and followers, responsibilities, rules and roles to be performed. Much can be learnt about the social interaction in a classroom by compiling a **sociogram**.

Procedure

Ask a class of children to select three partners from their class that they would like to work with in a free activity, such as project work or craft. For very young children in infants it may be necessary to ask each child individually rather than expect them to write names down. The children should be picking partners on the basis of friendship rather than expertise and they should not discuss their choices with one another prior to their selection. Assure the children that their choice will be confidential. Collect the data and construct a matrix that illustrates the choices each child has made, using a key that indicates first, second or third choice. From the data you will be able to gather the following insights into your class.

1. The children who are popular with each individual for a particular activity.
2. The number of times each child was chosen (referred to as the child's *sociometric status*).
3. Self-contained groups or mutual choices in the classroom (clusters, triangles, cliques, reciprocal choices).
4. Any cleavages that exist between groups in the classroom based on sex, race, ability, etc.
5. The most popular children in the class (*stars*).
6. The least popular children in the class.
7. Non-chosen children who make choices (*isolates*).

The information can be represented diagrammatically by constructing a target sociogram. On a large sheet of paper draw three concentric circles. Using triangles for males and circles for females, represent each child on the graph, with those with the highest sociometric status (those who were chosen frequently) in the innermost circle, and the least chosen in the outer circle. Draw arrows radiating from each person to the people chosen. A colour key should be used to represent first, second or third choice. Reciprocal choices may be represented by double arrowheads. Patterns of social interaction may be seen at a glance from these diagrams.

It might be necessary to experiment with the format to obtain the clearest diagram. Shifts in social interaction may be noted by drawing sociograms for a range of activities (which may lead to different choices), and by giving sociometric tests over a 12-month period, one each month.

Erikson's stages in relation to play In the context of Erikson's stages of psychosocial development, there are three that are particularly relevant to children's play. Between the ages of about one and three, in the stage of autonomy that has grown out of the trust consolidated in the earlier stage of infancy, children enter a **period of exploration.** In terms of exploratory play, a sense of independence grows as the caring adult demonstrates respect for the child's growing capabilities in his or her beginning language and physical actions on the world, and shows warmth in the relationship with the child. Where doubt is expressed about the child's abilities by significant others, self-doubt may develop.

During the **period of play**, as the years between three and six, before children begin formal schooling, are known (Jones & Reynolds 1992), the exercise of initiative becomes paramount. In the course of play, this may be demonstrated in rough-and-tumble games, investigations into hitherto unknown places and things, and acts of physical and verbal daring. We can think of many occasions when our youngest has disappeared for a surprisingly long period of time (when it is quiet for too long, invariably something is going on), only to discover that she has taken the initiative to explore a box of glitter, fabric paints to paint her legs, or to see how the tape recorder and tapes work. It takes a great deal of parental restraint not to show anger when the paint exploration ends in a stained cream carpet, and the tape recorder will only work at slow speed. The danger of dampening a child's sense of initiative and turning it to guilt is very real in countless experiences of such play. According to Erikson, the ability to choose, plan and accomplish actions without anxiety during this stage is the key to healthy psychosocial development.

When children are in middle childhood and at school, they enter the **period of investigation** where

Onlooker play. Photos: authors

Cooperative play. Photos: authors

Associative play. Photos: authors

Parallel play. Photos: authors

TEACHER'S CASE BOOK

IT'S MY HOLE!

Consider the following episode taken from a scene at a preschool where two three-year-olds (Sarah and Zach) begin to fight because each has accidentally invaded the other's territory, in this case, while they were absorbed in parallel play in a sandpit. The teacher intervenes in the following way:

'Zach, what do you want to tell Sarah?' she asks, squatting down between them. Zach is crying; Sarah has punched him hard.

'I don't like her. She's stupid,' sobs Zach.

'You're really angry at Sarah. Can you tell her what she did to make you mad?'

'Hit me,' says Zach sadly.

'You hit me first,' Sarah retorts indignantly.

'Zach, did you hit Sarah?' He nods.

'Why?'

'My hole!' he wails, the memory of the violation of his play suddenly much more painful than his sore shoulder. 'She messed up my hole!' He tries to hit Sarah again.

'What hole?' frowns Sarah, genuinely puzzled. 'I didn't mess up no hole.'

'Can you show Sarah your hole, Zach?' the teacher asks. He certainly can.

'Here,' he shouts. 'It was right here, and I digged it and digged it...'

'Sarah, Zach is really sad about his hole,' explains the teacher. 'Do you think maybe you could help him fix it?'

Sarah nods vigorously, grabbing her bulldozer.

'No!' says Zach. 'No 'dozer!'

'Do you want to fix the hole yourself, Zach?' the teacher asks. He nods yes. 'Then could you show Sarah where to drive her bulldozer so that she won't muck up your hole again?'

Zach gestures a wide detour with his arm. Sarah bulldozes off in the correct direction. Zach begins to dig again with his shovel, and his very important hole begins to reappear.

(adapted from Jones & Reynolds 1992, p.27)

Case study activity

There are many ways in which different teachers might have reacted to the children in this instance, from a permissive 'Let them work it out for themselves' to a stern reprimand for hurting each other, or even the loss of the 'privilege' to play while they were sent to the naughty corner to 'think about what they had done wrong'. What do you think of the teacher's reaction? Is it what you would have done?

industry leads them to develop a sense of personal control rather than a sense of incompetence and inferiority. Play activities through which this development can be fostered include both physical and social games such as sports or hand clapping, marbles and card or board games, as well as the investigative classroom experiences designed by teachers. Structured cooperative learning activities during this time allow children to learn and practise social skills such as turn-taking, encouraging others and negotiating, as well as language and communication skills such as asking questions, active listening, clarifying and explaining (see Chapter 10 for further discussion of cooperative learning). Once again, support from the child's social environment helps to resolve the developmental conflict at this stage and leads into the period of identity formation during adolescence.

Using play in the social and emotional development of the child We have already described the importance of the teacher in providing an environment in which children can feel challenged and stimulated intellectually, as well as feeling safe to explore and to express themselves. Just as important is the role of the teacher in fostering the social and emotional development of the child. This can be done through a range of activities including role play, semi-structured shared conversations in which children can relate personal experiences and feelings, and the use of puppets to act out social problems for preschoolers and kindergarten children, or drawings and stories for older children.

SOCIAL/EMOTIONAL DEVELOPMENT, SOCIAL IDENTITY AND ADOLESCENCE

Few developmental periods are characterised by so many changes at so many different levels as adolescence (Eccles et al. 1993). We consider a number of these changes in earlier chapters. While it is not uncommon for adolescents to experience some problems during this time, most pass through puberty and adolescence without significant psychological or emotional difficulties, develop a positive sense of personal identity, and manage to form adaptive peer relationships at the same time as maintaining close relationships with their families. A number, nevertheless, experience difficulties that cause deep emotional stress and anxiety which leads them into a downward spiral that ends in academic failure and dropping out of school (Eccles et al. 1993; Petersen et al. 1985, 1995; Simmons & Blyth 1987). Educators must be sensitive to the needs of all adolescents at this time in order to provide the emotional supports needed for healthy social and emotional development (Frydenberg & Lewis 1993, 1991, 1990).

Identity formation and social development

Social development and identity formation during the adolescent years acquires more significance than it had at any previous time. When considering overall **social development** during adolescence, attention should be focused on

Are there sex differences in the games children play? What effect might this have on social development?
Photo: NSW Board of Studies

four important aspects. The first of these is the continuing process by which a sense of personal identity is established (we consider this in some detail in Chapter 15). The second aspect is the nature of the family relationships and its effect on the adolescent's self-reliance and independence. The third, peer group interaction, focuses specifically on the development of heterosexual relationships and group acceptance, while the fourth aspect deals with the opportunities provided by social environments, including the school, for healthy personal and social development of the individual.

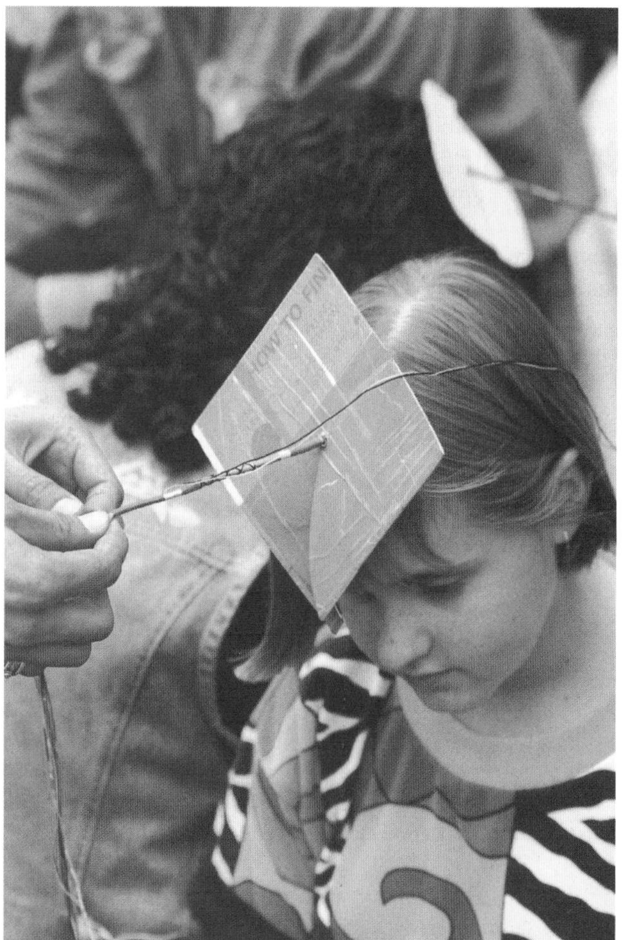

Hair braiding at puberty. Why do adolescents place such importance on hairstyles, clothing and doing 'cool' things?
Photo: authors

Family relationships and social development

As discussed earlier (Chapter 15), probably the most critical factor in the development of ego identity is the nature of the relationship the child continues to have with his or her parents. In the last decade, developmentalists have begun to explore the role of *connectedness to parents* in adolescent development. Findings suggest that attachment to parents may facilitate adolescents' social competence and well-being, as reflected through self-esteem, emotional adjustment and physical health (Kobak & Sceery 1988; Santrock & Yussen 1992). Adolescents who have secure relationships with their parents have higher self-esteem and better emotional well-being. Attachment to parents during adolescence may serve the adaptive function of providing a secure base from which adolescents can explore and master new environments and a widening social world in a psychologically healthy way (Santrock & Yussen 1992). This connectedness to parents also promotes competent peer relations and positive close relationships outside the family (Kerns, Klepac & Cole 1996).

Closely allied with the relationship of the adolescent to his or her parents are the issues of adolescent

autonomy and **independence** (Peterson 1989). There is typically a temporary increase in family conflict during adolescence over autonomy and control while the dimensions of these are renegotiated (Buchanan, Eccles & Becker 1992). The degree of difficulty that the adolescent encounters in establishing independence depends on a number of factors: the consistency, rate and extent, and complexity of independence training that is sanctioned by the society as a whole, and reflected in organisations such as schools, together with the childrearing practices and models of behaviour provided by the parents.

Independence training and the development of autonomy

In optimal situations parents reinforce and stimulate this process of growing autonomy, self-determination and independence. For adolescents to feel a sense of autonomy they should perceive that they have an input into family decision making. It appears that those who feel they have such an input have higher self-esteem and greater school motivation. It appears, also, that such young children also make an easier transition into high school (Eccles et al. 1993). In contrast, excessive parental control is linked to lower intrinsic school motivation, to more negative changes in self-esteem following high school transition, to more school misconduct associated with this transition, and to greater investment in peer social attachments and even delinquency (Eccles et al. 1993; Mak 1994). It is not possible to determine whether the parental control is the cause or result of these aspects of adolescent behaviour. They probably interact. It is also necessary to add that too little parental control also leads to significant negative consequences.

During adolescence children move in wider social circles and are increasingly exposed to the values and modes of behaviour of their peer group, and to belief systems of different families. This circumstance may provide the basis for conflict within the home, particularly when there is a perceived clash between what peers are able to do within their families, and what the individual is able to do in his or her own family.

Independence and conflict within the home

In multiracial countries such as Australia and New Zealand, the norms for autonomy and independence training vary widely from one cultural group to another and from one set of parents to another. This variation can cause considerable difficulty for some children from groups that do not encourage independence in the same way as mainstream groups. There can be a cultural clash when children are expected to behave in contradictory ways depending on social circumstances. We deal with this issue in Chapter 12 (see also Rosenthal, Ranieri & Klimidis 1996).

Question point: *We should be cautious of the common assertion that parental and peer group values are necessarily mutually incompatible and that an inevitable consequence of heightened peer group dependence during adolescence is a sharp decline in parental influence. What evidence have you seen for this assertion? What contrary evidence is there?*

Adolescent grouping

At the time when adolescents are moving away from parent dependency, they often substitute peer dependency. Peers exert a great deal of pressure on each other to conform. Adolescents seek out and listen to the advice of peers on certain issues, especially those involving immediate con-

The peer group

Being part of a group sometimes requires the adoption of some customs. What customs might characterize this group? Photo: authors

sequences, such as clothes, entertainment, fads and so on. Adults, however, often exaggerate the power of the peer group, particularly as it relates to sexual behaviour, drug use and delinquency (Berger 1991). Indeed, research suggests that peers play a vital role in the psychological development of most adolescents. Changes in the structure of Western society, a decline in the extended family, growing numbers of two-career families, increasing institutionalisation of age segregation whereby we enshrine age segregation within our society's structures—for example, though exclusive retirement villages, cheaper insurance for over-50s, fewer employment opportunities for those over 50 and so on, expanded communication networks among the young, and delayed entrance into adult society, have increased the importance of the peer group as a developmental influence (Conger 1977). Other groups, such as adults, teachers, coaches and part-time employers also influence adolescents strongly.

Crowds, cliques and friendships

An adolescent group contains several interrelated levels of organisation. The most inclusive peer group structure is the **crowd**; next is the **clique**; and then there are individual **friendships**. The crowd is the least personal of these groups and the members of a crowd meet because of their mutual interest in particular activities, such as sporting activities, rather than because they are mutually attracted to each other. The clique is smaller in size. Members are attracted to each other on the basis of similar interests and social ideals. Cliques involve greater intimacy among members, and have more group cohesion than crowds. A more intense interaction characterises these groups. Finally, adolescents develop a number of personal friendships vital to their emotional and social development (Dunphy 1969; Hill 1995; Peterson 1989; Santrock & Yussen 1992; Zigler & Stevenson 1993). Research on friendships during adolescence has identified these distinct features:

- loyalty and faithfulness;
- avoidance of intense competition, while aiming for equality through sharing;
- the perception of relationships as emotionally supportive.

(Berndt & Perry 1990)

While popularity and peer acceptance may be stable from childhood to adolescence, sexual maturation and heterosexual behaviour provide new influences that affect an adolescent's behaviour within a group. Among some of these new factors and influences affecting peer group acceptance are dress, entertainment, sport, dating, drugs, dropping-out and politics. The group or clique one belongs to makes a statement about the values held by the individual in a social context. Group identity at this time often overrides individual identity (Santrock & Yussen 1992).

Question point: *Discuss the importance of the peer group to adolescent development.*

Same sex friendships are important in the social and emotional development of adolescents. Photo: authors

Adolescent sexuality

The fact that puberty equips the adolescent for mature sexual enjoyment and for reproduction makes sexuality another special concern during this phase of life. Adolescent sexuality relates to social and personal identity formation in a dramatic way, and it also relates to parental influences and peer group associations. Sexual maturity on one level leads to a growing sense of independence and maturity in the adolescent, while on another it may lead to rebellion against the mores of both parents

TEACHER'S CASE BOOK

HAPPY FAMILIES

Miss Osbourne's grade 10 drama class was one of diverse interests, mixed ability and widely differing social groups. These students had never worked together in four years of high school. Miss Osbourne decided to embark on a children's theatre production in first term in order to establish positive and supportive relationships within the class. She let them know that she had high expectations of all members of the group.

The production was carefully cast to suit the personality and qualities of each individual and each student was able to experience success, not just the more able students. All students were treated equally and each role was valued in the production, no matter how small or large it was. Miss Osbourne worked at building a good rapport and positive relationships with all of the students.

The production was a great success and the children from associated primary schools proved to be enthusiastic audiences. The entire experience was tremendously positive for Miss Osbourne's students and their self-esteem soared.

Miss Osbourne was able to build upon the positive and supportive relationships which had been developed and secured through this successful group enterprise. Students who had never worked together in four years of high school had come together as a cohesive group. They now looked forward to working together and for the remainder of the year referred to themselves as the 'happy family'.

Case studies illustrating National Competency Framework for Beginning Teaching, National Project on the Quality of Teaching and Learning, Australian Teaching Council, 1996, p. 46. Commonwealth of Australia copyright, reproduced by permission

Case study activity
At the beginning of each school year new classes are made up of many students who don't know each other. As teachers, what activities can you devise that might ensure that each new group refers to itself as a 'happy family'? Why is this important?

and society (Brooks-Gunn & Furstenberg 1989). The hormonally induced increase that takes place in sexual drive, and the unfamiliar, frequently unpredictable and mysterious feelings, fantasies and impulses that accompany this phenomenon often create tensions for the adolescent (Brooks-Gunn & Furstenberg 1989; Turner & Helms 1991). Many adolescents find sexual adjustment difficult. Integrating sexuality meaningfully with other aspects of the adolescent's developing sense of self and of relations to others, with as little conflict and disruption as possible, is a major developmental task for both girls and boys (Peterson 1989; Santrock & Yussen 1992).

School environments and the development of adolescents

Mismatch between school and adolescent needs

As suggested above, adolescence is a time of great personal change on a number of levels. The rapidity and depth of these changes often cause considerable problems for adolescents. At the time when hormonal activity is causing changes to body shape, intellectual development and personal development, and when families are reshaping expectations of appropriate roles for the maturing individual, the adolescent is set adrift, in a sense, from the security of primary school. It is an interesting phenomenon that during adolescence, along with all the other changes, profound changes also occur in the individual's educational environment. It is at this stage that many children who were doing well at, and enjoying school, begin to lose interest and develop patterns of behaviour inimical to successful school completion. Many educationalists suggest that this occurs because **there is a mismatch between what the school offers in terms of a supportive social and intellectual environment for adolescents, and what they actually need** (Eccles et al.

Why is socialising with the opposite sex important for adolescents? Photo: authors

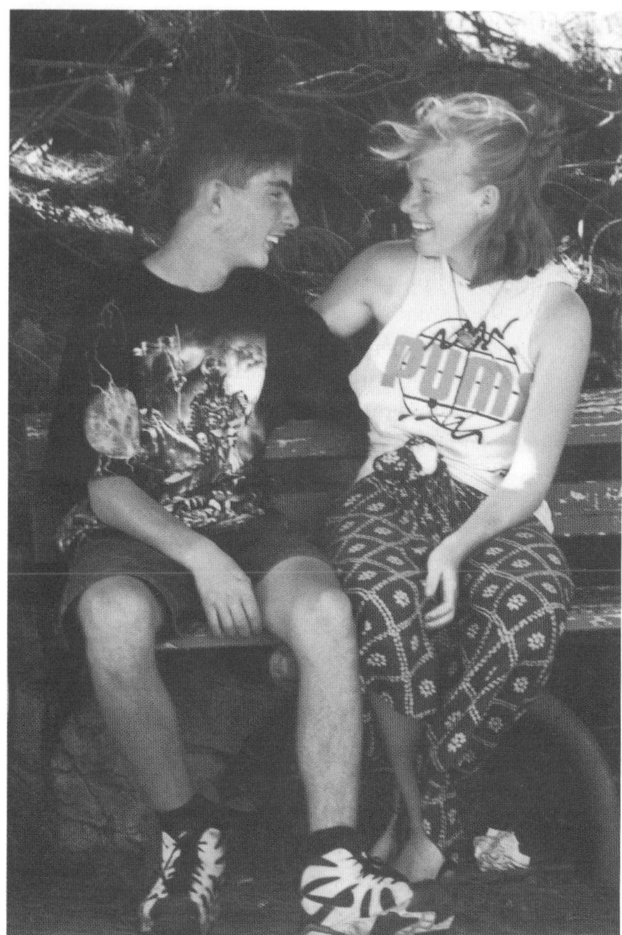

Boyfriends and girlfriends become an increasing interest during puberty. Photo: authors

1993). Eccles et al. (1993, p. 94) believe that:

> ***... the environmental changes often associated with transition to junior high school seem especially harmful in that they emphasize competition, social comparison, and ability self-assessment at a time of heightened self-focus; they decrease decision making and choice at a time when the desire for control is growing; they emphasize lower level cognitive strategies at a time when the ability to use higher level strategies is increasing; and they disrupt social networks at a time when adolescents are especially concerned with peer relationships outside of the home.***

For many adolescents in high school, the best parts of the day are before and after school. How can schools motivate learning during adolescence? Photo: authors

Eccles et al. (1993) demonstrate that a decline in motivation for learning as adolescents enter high school is not an inevitable result of the students' adolescent development, but rather reflects non-adaptive school and classroom practices which lead to these declines. With appropriate school and classroom strategies in place, adolescents can proceed through high school with enhanced motivation for learning.

In Chapter 9 we considered characteristics of school environments that might have a negative impact on students' learning and motivation, such as task structure, grouping practices, evaluation techniques, motivational strategies, locus of responsibility for learning, and the quality of student–teacher interactions. We also suggest alternative strategies that provide for a better student–school match in Chapters 9, 10, 11, 12 and 13.

***Question point:** Discuss and evaluate the role of the school in the development of social identity in adolescents.*

TABLE 16.1

ESSENTIALS OF A HEALTHY SCHOOL ENVIRONMENT FOR ADOLESCENT STUDENTS

For teachers and administrators

- Provide a 'small school' feel for students so that they can identify with the organisation.

- Develop positive student–teacher and student–student relationships within what is perceived as a caring and safe environment.
- Develop a sense of teacher efficacy—feel that as a teacher you can make a change.
- Provide the optimal level of structure for children's current level of maturity while also providing a sufficiently challenging environment to encourage further cognitive and social development.
- Implement assessment strategies that emphasise personal improvement and achievement rather than those based on competition and social comparison. Avoid using normative grading criteria and public forms of evaluation.
- Provide opportunities for students to work in a number of social groupings—teacher/student, peer/peer, small groups and full class.
- Provide opportunities for students to have a choice of learning activities and assignments.
- Provide opportunities for students to have some control over classroom management (such as class rules, seating arrangement, homework) and discipline practices.
- Trust students and provide opportunities for student autonomy, decision making, participation and self-regulation.
- Discuss classroom processes with students so that they perceive and make use of the opportunities made available for autonomy and control.

(based on Eccles et al. 1993; Maehr 1991; Maehr & Anderman 1993; Maehr & Midgley 1991)

SELF-CONCEPT, SELF-ESTEEM AND EFFECTIVE LEARNING

Throughout much of what we have discussed so far are woven the notions of **self-concept** and **self-esteem**. The terms 'self-esteem' and 'self-concept' are often used interchangeably. However, some researchers argue that self-concept is descriptive—that is, it refers to descriptive information about oneself such as height, hair colour, ability in sports and so on, whereas self-esteem is the evaluative component of self-concept that is, it refers to how one feels about these objective qualities of self-description. In this sense, self-esteem reflects the components of self-concept judged to be important by a particular individual. We will use the term 'self-concept' in our discussion to cover both the descriptive and evaluative dimensions.

Self-concept: individual beliefs about self

Broadly, we all have a general idea of what we mean by the term self-concept, and often use it in our everyday speech. We talk about some people having a good self-concept while others are thought to have a poor self-concept. In essence, we are referring to an individual's self-beliefs relating to perceived competence in a variety of areas such as academic schoolwork and sport, and to beliefs about physical attractiveness, sociability, self-worth, and so on. Generally, we also believe that a person's self-concept influences their behaviour. Individuals who have a positive self-concept are expected to be more motivated to perform particular activities than those who have a poor self-concept, and success in performing certain activities is believed to enhance self-concept. The relationship between self-concept and behaviour (particularly in terms of success and failure) is presumed to be reciprocal (see, for example, Marsh & Craven, in press).

The many faces of self-concept

The notion of self-concept has a long history (Wylie 1979), and has been the subject of much research attempting to study its content and structure, its changes over time, group differences in its composition, and its effects on motivation and behaviour (Marsh & Craven, in press; Marsh, 1990a; Wigfield & Karpathian 1991). Initially, self-concept was considered a unidimensional construct. In other words, individuals were thought to have a positive or negative view of themselves in a global sense. Instruments were designed which, in essence, summed up a person's self-concept with one score. Most people now reject the idea that a personality characteristic as rich as self-concept can be summarised so simply. Today, most researchers (such as Harter 1990; Shavelson et al. 1982, 1986; Marsh & Shavelson 1985) consider self-concept as **multidimensional**, that is, comprising many dimensions. Some theorists believe that these dimensions are organised in a hierarchy from differentiated lower levels to more general notions about self, while others believe that the dimensions are relatively distinct, but may also be accompanied by a more general concept of self.

Constructs and self-concept

Marsh (1990a; Marsh & Craven, in press), for example, believes that an individual's multidimensional self-concept is composed of lower-level self-concepts such as those for physical ability, physical appearance, peer relationships, parent relationships, reading ability, general school ability and mathematics ability. These are then clustered into higher-order self-concepts such as non-academic self-concept, academic English self-concept and academic mathematics self-concept. At a higher level still, there is the general self-concept. Relationships

Multidimensional and hierarchical notions of self-concept

exist laterally and vertically among the various dimensions. As you can see, this type of model explores the richness and complexity of the self-concept construct, and makes a nonsense of generalising that a person has a single positive or negative self-concept. Of course, one difficulty with this approach is that one is never sure whether the model actually includes all the possible forms that self-concept might take, or, indeed, whether the most important ones have been included. How would you describe your own self-concept, generally, and in relation to specific dimensions as described in the Marsh model?

How is self-concept formed?

Theorists believe that the self-concept is formed through **social interaction** and **social comparison.** Social **frames of reference** indicate to us what our capacities and qualities are under particular circumstances. For example, on an objective criterion, some individuals may be quite good at mathematics, yet when they use others who are superior at mathematics as a frame of reference, they may develop a relatively negative maths self-concept (e.g. see Marsh & Craven, in press; Marsh, Walker & Debus 1991; Marsh & Johnston 1993). This is sometimes referred to as an **external frame of reference.** Furthermore, according to Marsh, we tend to compare our self-perceived skills in one area (such as mathematics) with our self-perceived skills in another (such as English), and use this internal, relativistic impression as a second basis for arriving at our self-concept in particular areas (Marsh 1991). This is sometimes referred to as an **internal frame of reference.** Hence, individuals who are good at both maths and English may, nevertheless, have a more negative self-concept in maths if they perceive that they are better at English and vice versa. This explains why even slow learners differentiate their self-concepts across subjects and hold high self-concepts in some areas, even though their objective performance may be poor. Marsh (1990b; Marsh & Craven, in press) has called this effect the **internal–external frame of reference effect.** Feedback from significant others such as parents, siblings, peers and teachers is influential in the growth of one's multifaceted self-concept.

External and internal frames of reference

Because of the operation of this internal/external frame of reference effect all children have positive and less positive self-concepts in some areas of their learning. Teachers often make the erroneous assumption that those students who are perceived to have high ability and who are doing well academically must have uniformly high positive self-concepts in all areas, while those who are perceived as low-ability and are doing less well academically must have uniformly low self-concepts across all areas. In fact, as we have indicated, self-concept is much more differentiated than this—we all feel more positive about ourselves in some areas and less positive in other areas.

Does self-concept change as children grow older?

It appears that the foci of self-concept change as children grow older. Young children seem to focus on behavioural and physical characteristics, whereas older children focus on more abstract psychological characteristics (Wigfield & Karpathian 1991). As children's notions of what constitutes effort, ability, achievement, success and failure develop over time, so also do their beliefs about their competencies (and hence self-concept).

Developmental changes in self-concept

It also appears that in infants and early grades children's self-concepts across a range of areas are uniformly high and less differentiated than older children's. As children have more academic and non-academic experiences, their self-concepts become more differentiated and begin to be less positive. Throughout high school, individuals revise aspects of their self-concept, and some aspects become more positive relative to others. After adolescence (beginning in year 9 or year 10), multifaceted self-concept begins to rise once more in a variety of

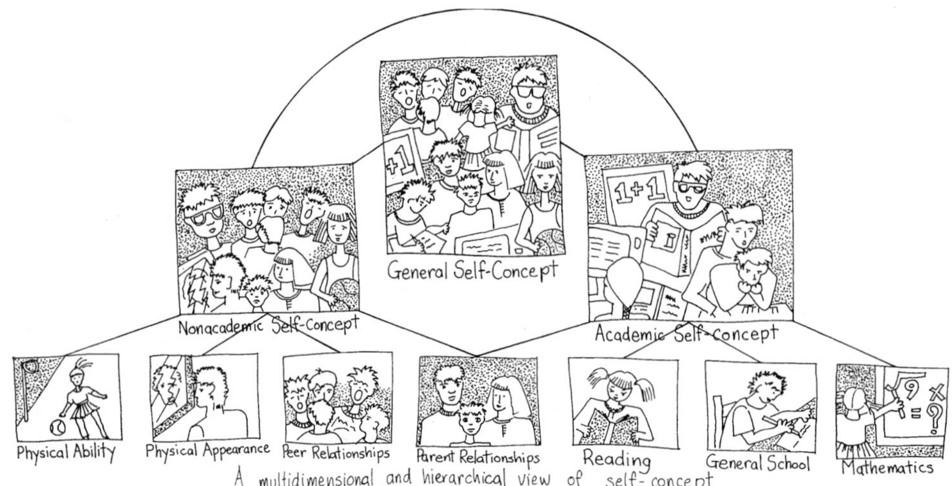

A multidimensional and hierarchical view of self-concept

(adapted from Marsh 1990)

areas and becomes relatively stable (Eccles et al. 1993; Marsh 1990a; Marsh & Craven, in press). Can you speculate on reasons why this might occur?

Is there a relationship between self-concept, average school performance and school achievement?

There is a relationship between a student's self-concept and school performance, but this is content-specific. In other words, maths performance is related to maths self-concept, English performance is related to English self-concept, and so on. As suggested above, our self-concept is formed in interaction with others, hence educational settings influence an individual's self-concept. For this reason it is often better for a bright individual to be a big fish in a little pond—that is, doing well among a mixed ability group—than to be a little fish—that is, performing at an average level in a high-ability group. In the former case it is easier for students to establish and maintain positive feelings about their academic accomplishments, which serve to reinforce further academic pursuits. In selective educational environments, where the average ability of students is high, it is more difficult to establish and maintain these positive feelings. Selective high schools, and gifted and talented classes may, therefore, be disadvantageous to some students because of this **'big fish little pond'** effect (see Marsh & Craven, in press). In these selective settings, high-ability students may choose less demanding coursework and have lower academic self-concepts, lower achievement scores, lower educational aspirations, and lower occupational aspirations than comparison groups in non-selective educational environments. It appears from this that high-ability students are better off in non-streamed schools. This point of view is controversial—what do you think? In Table 16.2 we suggest some strategies to enhance self-concept in educational settings.

Big fish little pond effect

TABLE 16.2

ESSENTIALS OF DEVELOPING POSITIVE SELF-CONCEPT IN EDUCATIONAL SETTINGS

For teachers

- Develop assessment tasks that encourage individual students to pursue their own projects that are of particular interest to them. To the extent that students pursue their own unique projects and feel positive about the results, they should be able to maintain a positive academic self-concept.
- Reduce social comparison and competitive learning environments.
- Provide students with feedback in relation to criterion reference standards and personal improvement over time rather than comparisons based on the performance of other students.
- Emphasise to each student that he or she is a very able student, and value the unique accomplishments of each student so that all students feel good about themselves.
- Enhance students' feelings of being connected to other students in the classroom.

(based on Marsh & Craven, in press)

We have suggested that feeling good about one's abilities in an academic area fosters academic striving behaviours that can maximise and even change academic achievement. Studies indicate that it is possible to enhance self-concept, which in turn may enhance school achievement. We hope that we provide you with many suggestions throughout this text on how to enhance the self-concept of students in your care.

Can self-concept be enhanced?

An alternative view of self-concept formation

An alternative view of self-concept is put forward by Higgins (1987; Roche & Marsh 1993). In contrast to Marsh's rather structured view of the composition of the self-concept, Higgins suggests that self-concept is phenomenologically based. For Higgins, the relationships (or discrepancies) between our perception of our actual self and five potential standards of self (or 'self-guides') influence our beliefs and feelings about self and ultimately motivate behaviour. The discrepancies between the perceived actual self and these other 'self-guides' are also related to an individual's overall

Self-guides and self-concept formation

Effective classrooms can do a great deal to foster a healthy self-concept in children. Photo: authors

feelings of self-esteem. The 'self-guides' are: the ideal person we would like to be; the person we feel obliged to be, given social and personal norms; what we believe other significant people (such as parents and teachers) consider is our actual self; what we believe other significant people consider we should ideally be like; and what we believe other significant people consider we ought to be like, given our realistic limitations. Not all these 'self-guides' are salient to particular individuals. Higgins' contribution is important to our understanding of the self-concept as it highlights important elements of the self-system influencing motivated behaviour and self-esteem.

Our major focus in this text is individual learning and motivation. A crucial question for us to answer, therefore, is how a child's self-concept relates to his or her motivation, behaviour and school achievement. We discuss this question a number of times throughout the text.

Question point: *Consider the notion of a multi-dimensional self-concept. In particular, discuss how frames of reference (internal and social comparison) may influence the development of self-concept at each of the different developmental stages of early primary, middle and upper primary, lower secondary and upper secondary. Are the influences of frames of reference more likely to be significant at one level than another or for different areas of school activity (such as academic, clubs, sporting and so on)?*

ACTION STATION

This activity is designed to sensitise you to some of the sources of information that orient the development of our self-concept. It is best performed in a small group of peers.

1. List five characteristics that would describe you as you are (perceived self).
2. List five characteristics that would describe you as you would like to be (ideal self).
3. List one characteristic of each member of the group (observed self). The observed self-ratings are distributed to the relevant group member.
4. Compare your perceived, ideal and observed self. What differences do you notice? What is the real self? Discuss your findings within the group.

SOCIAL DEVELOPMENT, SELF-ESTEEM AND ALIENATION

In our rapidly changing world many children and adolescents become alienated. At its most severe, alienation can manifest itself in psychophysiological and psychological disturbances such as obesity, anorexia nervosa, migraine, gastrointestinal upsets, anxiety, phobias and depression; and in its most extreme form, suicide (Santrock & Yussen 1992; Zigler & Stevenson 1993). Alienation can also express itself in dropping out of school, truancy, delinquency, and substance use and abuse. Our role as teachers is to identify students at risk of alienation and to implement policies and teaching programs to assist them to develop a positive identity of themselves as individuals and school learners. In much of this book we describe many features of effective teaching that will help reduce the occurrence of **alienation** (at least as far as the school and teachers are able).

Adolescent suicide

There has been growing public concern over the level of adolescent suicide in Australia, New Zealand and the United States (Davis 1992; Garland & Zigler 1993; Kosky 1987; Pritchard 1992). Across these countries there are approximately 11 suicide deaths per 100 000 individuals in the adolescent age range each year. These figures are considered a low estimate as it is difficult to ascertain whether some deaths ascribed to accidents

WHAT WOULD YOU DO?

MORE THAN HISTORY ON HIS MIND

I had occasion to talk to a 16-year-old student in one of our year 11 history classes about his recent irregular attendance. When he came through the door I could not help noticing how tall he was, nor could I miss the very closely cut hair and the rather large earring. I sensed a possible confrontation looming so I spoke quite softly to him. I told him it was my duty to speak to him and I also reminded him that his work output, or lack of it, indicated a likelihood of failing the subject.

He clearly appreciated what I was saying but when I went on to tell him that I should inform his parents, tears began to well up in his eyes. It was immediately clear that history was not really on this young man's mind. I asked David to sit down and we talked. From what I could gather the past three years of David's life had been a living hell. Years of physical abuse had left a residue of guilt and fear, and he had recently become an intravenous drug user.

What would you do to help David? See page 385.

Case studies illustrating National Competency Framework for Beginning Teaching, National Project on the Quality of Teaching and Learning, Australian Teaching Council, 1996, p. 54.

Are there differences between boys and girls in how they spend their leisure time? How might this influence their sense of belonging or alienation? Photo: authors

(such as car accidents or drug overdoses) are actually suicides. There is also a reluctance to report suicides among some groups owing to religious implications, insurance problems, and family concerns.

Suicide is the third most frequent cause of death among adolescents after motor accidents and murder (Garland & Zigler 1993). Of further concern is the fact that the rates for adolescent suicide have increased dramatically over the last 30 years in comparison with the general population increase. Males complete suicide approximately four times as often as females; however, females attempt suicide at least three times as often as do males. This statistical difference in attempted suicide rates might be an artifact of reporting methods and in particular data collected through mental health clinics, which are utilised more by females than males. Not included in the data are attempted suicides by incarcerated males, which is quite common. If these figures were taken into account the gender difference in attempted suicide rates would diminish.

Male and female differences in suicide rates

The difference in completed suicide rates between males and females may also be explained by the different methods used, with males more likely to impulsively use violent methods, such as shooting and hanging, that are successful. In contrast, females more often use less violent methods, such as overdoses of substances, that allow time for treatment. Furthermore, females may benefit from protective factors such as a greater reliance on interpersonal relationships for support and more positive help-seeking attitudes and behaviours (Garland & Zigler 1993).

There are ethnic differences in suicide rates with white Anglo males more likely to commit suicide than males from other ethnic groups. This difference appears to reflect religious and cultural values that establish

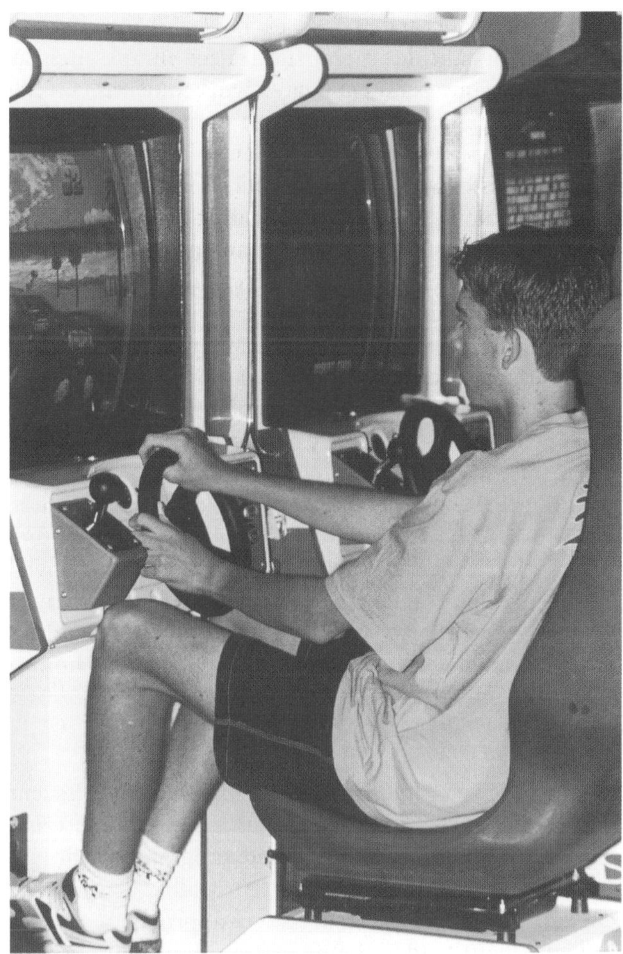

Are there differences between boys and girls in how they spend their leisure time? How might this influence their sense of belonging or alienation? Photo: authors

protective taboos within particular groups, and perhaps the **extended social network** in which adolescents from particular ethnic groups receive more immediate support (Eskin 1992, 1995; Lester & Icli 1990; Wasserman & Stack 1993). Suicide has also been linked to antisocial, aggressive behaviour, and as the incidence of this is greater among males this could partly explain their greater levels of completed suicide. Aboriginal and Maori youth are disproportionately represented in suicide rates and these have increased substantially over recent years from previous very low levels (Hunter 1991). Among the reasons given for this increase in suicide rates among indigenous people is the cumulative effects of changing patterns of family life over the past two decades.

Ethnic differences in suicide rates

Although the number of adolescents who commit suicide is of great concern it is still a relatively infrequent occurrence. It is difficult, therefore, to discover clearly the primary factors that cause adolescents to attempt suicide.

Risk factors for adolescent suicide

Primary risk factors appear to be drug and alcohol abuse, prior suicide attempt, affective illness such as depression, antisocial or aggressive behaviour, family history of suicidal behaviour, and the availability of a firearm (Garland & Zigler 1993). Among other suggested risk factors are stressful life events, such as family turmoil, increased pressure on children to achieve and to be responsible at an early age, and the mass media giving publicity to suicide which encourages social imitation.

However, in many cases of attempted suicide none of these factors appears to play an obvious part, while in many other cases adolescents who have exposure to some or all of these factors do not attempt suicide. In short, it is very difficult to predict suicide behaviour.

What precipitates suicide?

It appears that in cases of completed suicide there has been a preceding shameful or humiliating experience, such as an arrest, a perceived failure at work or school, a rejection by a loved one such as a parent, or difficulties resulting from sexual orientation such as homosexuality (Garland & Zigler 1993).

What can we do to prevent suicide?

Programs have been initiated to help prevent adolescent suicide. Two common approaches are **telephone crisis counselling** and **curriculum-based programs**, although the latter are less common in Australia. Garland & Zigler (1993) believe that these approaches are of limited benefit, and in the case of curriculum programs, may be dangerous because they tend to 'normalise' suicide as a reaction to stress which can affect all adolescents. By de-emphasising the fact that most adolescents who commit suicide are mentally ill, these programs reduce potentially protective taboos against suicide. These programs also tend to overstate the incidence of suicide, therefore making it appear more normal. When this is added to increased media coverage of adolescent suicide it could well be that a number of susceptible individuals become convinced that it is appropriate behaviour in times of stress.

Primary prevention strategies

We suggest above that many of the primary factors associated with youth suicide are common to other alienated behaviours, such as delinquency and substance abuse. As a result, some primary prevention programs have been designed to address negative behaviours such as depression, lack of social support, poor problem-solving skills and hopelessness. In addressing these it is thought that the root source of much adolescent suicide behaviour is also addressed. Many schools, therefore, have personal development, health and physical education programs which address healthy living issues. In particular, it is felt that problem-solving skills training and self-efficacy enhancement for adolescents may be the most effective suicide prevention programs (Cole 1989). We stress the importance of these factors throughout our text as a means of enhancing effective learning and the development of a sense of self within learners.

Family support programs

Family support programs have also been instigated for families undergoing crisis and these appear to alleviate a range of problems including substance abuse and delinquency. As these factors are also associated with adolescent suicide, it is thought that family support programs provide a primary preventative against suicide as well.

It is very important that teachers, counsellors and school personnel are well informed about adolescent suicide, know how to recognise students at risk, and have in place appropriate support procedures to assist individuals and their families. Table 16.3 presents some warning signs of suicide. When an individual's behaviour becomes atypical and includes a number of these features it might be an indication that the adolescent is thinking about suicide. At these times, effective teacher counselling, support and referral are necessary.

TABLE 16.3

SIGNS OF SUICIDE

- Putting personal affairs in order, such as giving away treasured possessions and/or making amends.
- Talking about suicide directly or indirectly ('you won't have to worry about me much longer') and/or saying goodbye to family and friends.
- Protracted periods of sadness, despondency and/or 'not caring' any more.
- Extreme fatigue, lack of energy, boredom.
- Emotional instability—spells of crying, laughing.
- Inability to concentrate, becoming easily frustrated and/or distractible.
- Deviating from usual patterns of behaviour, e.g. decline in grades, absence from school and/or discipline problems.
- Neglect of personal appearance.
- Change in body routines, e.g. loss of sleep or excessive sleep, eating more or less than usual, and/or complaints of headache, stomach ache, backache.

(based on Capuzzi 1989)

WHAT WOULD YOU DO?

MORE THAN HISTORY ON HIS MIND (continued)

After almost an hour of listening, I explained to him that I was not equipped to help him but that there were a number of people in the school who were trained to help him overcome his burdens. I advised him to seek out one of these people. The next day Margaret, a colleague, asked to speak to me. She told me that David had told her that he had been speaking to me and he had told her a lot of his problems. He had agreed to Marg's suggestion that they would sit down with his parents to try and solve them.

David has since left our school and taken a course at a commercial college. Margaret sees David and his family regularly and two months later tells me that things are now going really well for David.

I feel good about this story for a number of reasons. I think I was partly instrumental in helping David begin to solve his personal problems. Secondly, I am proud of the fact that one of my colleagues was willing and able to find the time to work closely with the family in helping David work things out.

What do you think took place at the discussion between David, his parents and Margaret? Why did this appear to work so successfully? What special skills would a teacher need to initiate the action that Margaret took?

Case studies illustrating National Competency Framework for Beginning Teaching, National Project on the Quality of Teaching and Learning, Australian Teaching Council, 1996, p. 54. Commonwealth of Australia copyright, reproduced by permission

THE DEVELOPMENT OF THE MORAL SELF

As caregivers, parents and educators, we are intimately involved in the process of communicating values to children and adolescents. It is helpful to understand, therefore, the ways in which the development of the moral self is believed to occur. Widely differing conceptions exist of how we develop a sense of morality and whether morals are universal or culturally based and acquired through socialisation. In this section we look at the theories put forward by Piaget, Kohlberg, Gilligan and Turiel.

PIAGET AND MORAL DEVELOPMENT

Morality of constraint and morality of cooperation

Developmental theories such as those of Piaget and Kohlberg present the view that increasingly sophisticated moral reasoning develops through an invariant sequence of stages. Piaget contends that all morality consists of a system of rules that is handed from adults to children. Through training, practice and developing intellect, children learn to nurture respect for these standards of conduct (Hoffman 1980; Piaget 1965). In order to collect his data, Piaget used the same clinical interviewing approach used to elicit responses to cognitive tasks, and questioned scores of Swiss children aged between 5 and 13 years about their understanding of rules, and their interpretations of right and wrong. In particular, Piaget examined the relationship between **intention** and notions of **right** and **wrong.** Children were given two stories and asked to judge which of the two boys in the story was naughtier: the boy who was well intentioned but caused more damage, or the boy who was not well intentioned and caused less damage. Children were asked to give reasons for their answers.

Story A: ***A little boy called John is in his room. He is called to dinner. He goes into the dining room. But behind the door there was a chair, and on the chair there was a tray with 15 cups on it. John couldn't have known that there was all this behind the door. He goes in, the door knocks against the tray, bang go the 15 cups, and they all get broken.***

Story B: ***Once there was a little boy whose name was Henry. One day when his mother was out he tried to get some jam out of the cupboard. He climbed up on a chair and stretched out his arm. But the jam was too high up and he couldn't reach it and have any. But while he was trying to get it he knocked over a cup. The cup fell down and broke.***

(Piaget 1965)

Heteronomous morality

In general, Piaget found two different **moral orientations**, one typical of preoperational children and one typical of children in the late concrete substage (10 to 12 years). He found that younger children tend to focus on observed consequences of actions and believe in absolute, unchanging rules handed down by outside authorities. Piaget named this stage one of **heteronomous morality** or **moral realism**, in which children adopt the morality of constraint ('heteronomous' means under the authority of another). Children in this stage tend to view behaviours as totally right or wrong, and think everyone views them in the same way. Children judge whether an act is right or wrong on the basis of the magnitude of the consequences, the extent to which it conforms to established rules, and whether the act is punished.

Autonomous morality

With older children, the focus is on the inferred intentions behind the act with a belief that rules can be constructed and changed by social agreement. This stage is referred to as the stage of **autonomous morality** where children adopt the **morality of cooperation** (Cowan 1978; Hersh,

Paolitto & Reimer 1979; Hoffman 1980). In the context of Piaget's stories, therefore, younger children believe that John is the naughtier because he broke more cups, despite the fact that he didn't break them on purpose. Older children judge that Henry is the naughtier child because they take into account the intention behind the act leading to the damage.

Children in the heteronomous stage show a great concern for rules and believe they can't be changed, whereas children at the autonomous stage no longer view rules as fixed, but rather as flexible, socially agreed upon principles of cooperation that can be changed with the agreement of others affected by the rules. A greater sense of **reciprocity** characterises the moral reasoning of older children; that is, the welfare of others and a concern for fairness is important, because it is only then that one can expect fairness in return. At this stage, the belief in a morality of reciprocity means that duty and obligation are no longer defined in terms of obedience to authority, but as a social contract reflecting the mutual needs of oneself and others, called a **morality of reciprocity**.

Reciprocity in moral reasoning

Young children also believe in **immanent justice** and believe that if they are punished they must have done wrong. Older children can differentiate punishment from wrongdoing; in other words, they can maintain their innocence in the face of punishment. Older children also recognise that others may hold different points of view, and in their judgments of right and wrong stress intentions as well as consequences. Punishment should fit the 'crime' rather than being the capricious act of a powerful 'other'.

Immanent justice

Piaget believes that the narrow perspective of the younger child reflects the strong 'coercive' influence that adults have over children of this age. Younger children have a rigid view of discipline and punishment while older children distinguish between punishment and guilt. The development from stage one to stage two reflects the growing ability of children to decentre, that is, to take the perspective of others. This development is facilitated by peer interaction through which one's individual perspective is challenged by the perspectives, needs and demands of other individuals. The resulting **cognitive disequilibrium** motivates children to resolve the conflict and contradictions by reorganising patterns of moral thought (refer to Chapter 2).

Peer interaction and moral development

a

ACTION STATION

Piaget studied the development of morality by presenting to children of various ages pairs of stories that illustrated different degrees of responsibility for particular actions. For example, in one story a child accidentally knocks over a tray and breaks 15 cups. In its companion story, a boy climbing up to steal jam out of a cupboard, against his mother's orders, knocks over one cup which falls on the floor and breaks. Younger children consider the first child 'naughtier' because he broke more cups. Older children consider the disobedient boy naughtier. There is a shift from objective responsibility to a consideration of subjective intentions. Piaget states that the answers children gave to his stories express two distinct moral attitudes, one that judges actions according to their material consequences, and one that takes only intentions into account. These two attitudes may co-exist at the same age and even in the same child, but broadly speaking they do not synchronise. Objective responsibility diminishes on the average as the child grows older, and subjective responsibility gains correlatively in importance.

In this activity you will evaluate Piaget's belief that these two fundamental levels characterise children's moral thinking. Select three children of differing ages, say six, nine and twelve. Tell the children the following two stories:

Story 1
A little boy called Frank once noticed that his mother's sink was full of dirty dishes. While the mother was in the yard Frank began to wash the dishes so that when his mother came in the washing-up would be done. But while he was washing-up he dropped five dishes and smashed them.

Story 2
Although his mother had told him not to, a little boy called Robert thought it would be fun playing with his mother's dishes. While he was playing one dish dropped and smashed.

After telling the stories, ask the subjects to say which child is naughtier and to give the reasons for their answers. Record verbatim the responses of the children and write a brief report illustrating what the experiment shows about the moral judgments of children. To further complicate the issue you could add to the first story that the mother had told the child not to touch anything in the kitchen! You might also like to hold the consequences the same—that is, that the children break the same number of dishes.

Critique of Piaget's theory

In general, Piaget's view that children pass from a morality of constraint to a morality of cooperation, and that this is facilitated by intellectual growth, peer interaction, and a diminution in adult authority, has been supported by research (Berk 1991). However, as with Piaget's theory of cognitive development, this theory has also been subjected to considerable criticism. In particular, it appears that even quite young children can distinguish between social-conventional and moral rules, with the former far less immutable. We discuss this further in our next section on Kohlberg. Furthermore, it is believed that the stories told by Piaget underestimated children's moral understanding. If you refer back to stories A and B you will see that the good intention was coupled with more damage, while the poor intention was coupled with less damage. It is possible that this confused children in their understanding of intention versus consequences, and they focused their answers on the consequences.

When stories are modified to make the intentions the focus rather than the consequences, by holding the consequences constant while varying the intentions or giving the character's intentions last in the story, or by making story events very meaningful to children by role-playing the behaviour, preschool and primary children are quite able to judge the difference between well-intentioned and ill-intentioned behaviour in terms of naughtiness (Grueneich 1982; Nelson-Le Gall 1985; Yuill & Perner 1988).

Finally, Piaget's conception of a two-stage developmental sequence in moral development appears too simple to explain the complexity of moral development as it occurs across the lifespan. The next section deals with the work of Lawrence Kohlberg who brings a lifespan view to moral development which he relates to the complex life events of developing individuals.

KOHLBERG'S STAGES OF MORAL DEVELOPMENT

Piaget did not work out his theory of moral development in any detailed fashion. However, his initial ideas were built on by Lawrence Kohlberg who developed the most extensive theory of moral development to date. Kohlberg's developmental stage theory (Kohlberg 1976, 1977, 1978, 1981) is based on three assumptions:

1. Each level of moral judgment must be attained before the individual can perform at the next higher level.
2. The attainment of a higher level of moral judgment appears to involve the reworking of earlier thought patterns rather than an additive process of development.
3. Moral development occurs as an invariant sequence no matter what the national or subcultural group happens to be.

WHAT WOULD YOU DO?

MORAL OBLIGATIONS

As part of a year 10 science options unit students examine the bioethical issues which arise in science. One strategy involves students working in groups and role-playing a hospital ethics committee where they must select four patients who will receive a liver transplant. Students are given a list of 15 potential patients to choose from. Students must negotiate until they reach a consensus on the four patients who will receive this life-saving operation. An important part of the activity is a debriefing where as a class they debate why they chose or rejected particular patients.

In this particular class, Jenny, an intelligent forthright student, argued against the selection of Patient F, a 4-year-old refugee who would be adopted after the operation. 'He should not be considered. Our taxes should not be used to give transplants to foreigners who have not contributed to this country,' she stated.

How would you proceed from this point? Consider what the teacher did on page 390.

Case studies illustrating National Competency Framework for Beginning Teaching, National Project on the Quality of Teaching and Learning, Australian Teaching Council, 1996, p. 42. Commonwealth of Australia copyright, reproduced by permission.

Kohlberg's methodology

To assess level of cognitive reasoning, Kohlberg adopted a similar methodology to Piaget, that is, a form of clinical interview. Children were presented with three moral dilemmas on which they had to make a moral judgment. Depending on the justification given for their judgment, children were categorised as belonging to a particular stage of moral development (rather like children being categorised as preoperational, concrete or formal thinkers on the basis of their answers to Piagetian problems, see Chapter 2). To understand the procedure, we ask you to complete the following exercise taken from Kohlberg's work.

Moral dilemma

In Europe, a woman is near death from a special kind of cancer. There is one drug that the doctors think might save her. It is a form of radium that a druggist in the same town has recently discovered. The drug is expensive to make, but the druggist is charging ten times what the drug cost him to make. He paid $200 for the radium and is charging $2000 for a small dose of the drug. The sick woman's husband, Heinz, goes to everyone he knows to borrow the money, but he can get together only about $1000, which is half of what it costs. He tells the druggist that his wife is dying and asks him to sell the drug cheaper or let him pay later.

The druggist says, 'No, I discovered the drug and I'm going to make money from it.' Heinz is desperate and considers breaking into the man's store to steal the drug for his wife.

1. *Should Heinz steal the drug? Why or why not?*
2. *If Heinz doesn't love his wife, should he steal the drug for her? Why or why not?*
3. *Suppose the person dying is not his wife but a stranger. Should Heinz steal the drug for a stranger? Why or why not?*
4. *(If you favour stealing the drug for a stranger): Suppose it's a pet animal he loves. Should Heinz steal to save the pet animal? Why or why not?*
5. *Why should people do everything they can to save another's life, anyhow?*
6. *It is against the law for Heinz to steal. Does that make it morally wrong? Why or why not?*
7. *Why should people generally do everything they can to avoid breaking the law, anyhow?*
8. *How does this relate to Heinz's case?*

(from Hersh, Paolitto & Reimer 1979)

Answers to the dilemma

Typically, answers to the dilemma will range across the following beliefs: that stealing the drug isn't bad because Heinz asked to pay for it first, or will pay for it in the future; that he only wants to save his wife, and after all the druggist is a bit of a crook himself; that stealing in itself is wrong, but can be excused if the reason is good, such as saving the life of one's wife, or because the action of the druggist is bad; and that, despite the obvious need to steal, Heinz must be prepared to accept punishment and pay back the money. Other answers refer either to the need for individuals to maintain the social order reflected through rules and regulations, or to adhere to higher-order principles—for example, while social order is important, the principle of preserving human life is more important still. In this latter case, it is morally right to steal the drug because human life is more important than property rights (see Rest 1973, 1979; Sprinthall & Sprinthall 1990). Kohlberg categorised responses to these dilemmas under three major levels of moral development: **preconventional,** which reflects a concern for avoiding punishment; **conventional**, which reflects a concern with rules and regulations; and **postconventional,** which reflects higher-level ethical principles (Kohlberg 1981). These levels are described more fully in Table 16.4.

We note here that Kohlberg was not so much interested in the actual decision as to whether Heinz should steal the drug or not but rather the reasons given for the decision. In effect, individuals at all levels could say 'steal the drug', but for the preconventional thinker it might be because Heinz probably won't get caught, for the conventional thinker it might be because punishment can be willingly accepted for a good, but not legal act, while for the postconventional thinker it might be because the law is a bad law.

We have often set the above exercise for students ranging from five or six years of age through to adulthood. We and our students have found that it is relatively easy to group the answers into one of three basic categories: a morality that seems to reflect a concern for **avoiding punishment** and **egocentric concerns**; a morality that seems to reflect an understanding of **rules and regulations** and their function in a society; and a morality that seems to be concerned with **ethical principles** which may take precedence over laws. Through these case studies we have found anecdotal evidence for Kohlberg's three major levels of moral development: **preconventional**, **conventional** and **postconventional** levels (Kohlberg 1981). However, when attempting to make finer distinctions within each level in accordance with Kohlberg's theory, we have tended to become confused, and often disagreed over the particular stage of reasoning. Kohlberg divides each level into two stages. Table 16.4 outlines the components of each, based on the work of Kohlberg (1981) in *The Philosophy of Moral Development*.

ACTION STATION

a

Some time ago in Queensland laws were promulgated against public protest marches. On one occasion, just before the Commonwealth Games, a large demonstration was organised to protest against the Government's dilatory approach to granting Aboriginal citizens land rights. It is interesting to consider the various arguments of people interviewed at the time to justify or oppose marching. Some argued that laws were laws and hence, irrespective of the worthiness of the cause, should be respected; otherwise, how could we tell our children to obey laws? Others argued that it wasn't wise to march as there was a risk of fines and possible gaol sentences. Many were concerned about the negative opinion our overseas visitors would have of Australians (and Aboriginal Australians in particular) if the marches disrupted the Commonwealth Games. Some argued that the rights of Aboriginals to land justice was a more important consideration than obeying laws, concern for personal welfare or being seen as doing the right thing by our fellow citizens. Others weren't particularly concerned with the land rights issue, but considered the law against marching an immoral law, in itself, and believed that individuals were obligated to protest against such a law whenever possible.

TABLE 16.4

ASPECTS OF MORAL REASONING

Level and stage	Individual's moral perspective
Level 1 Preconventional *Stage 1: Punishment and obedience*	A person at this stage doesn't consider the interests of others or recognise that they may differ from one's own. Actions are considered in terms of physical consequences such as to avoid punishment and obtain rewards. Those in authority have superior power and should be obeyed. Punishment should be avoided by staying out of trouble.
Stage 2: Individualism, instrumentality and exchange	A person at this stage is aware that everybody has interests to pursue and that these can conflict, so integrates conflicting demands through instrumental exchange of services, letting others meet their own interests and being fair. However, the needs of the individual are paramount, and it's all right to do things (such as cheating, bribing and stealing) if you get away with it and no one else is hurt in the process.
Level 2 Conventional *Stage 3: Mutual interpersonal expectations, relationships and conformity*	A person at this stage is aware of shared feelings, agreements and expectations that take primacy over individual interests. Believes in the Golden Rule, putting oneself in the other person's shoes. Does not yet consider generalised system perspective, and likes to be seen as doing the right thing by other people. Behaviour conforms strictly to the fixed conventions of society in which one lives.
Stage 4: Social system and conscience	A person at this stage takes the viewpoint of the system, which defines roles and rules. The individual 'does one's duty', shows respect for authority, and believes in maintaining social order for its own sake. He or she considers individual relations in terms of place in the system. In other words, the individual is willing to go against social convention and the desire to be one of the crowd and please others in order to uphold laws that are seen as important for the stability of the community.
Level 3 Postconventional or principled *Stage 5: Prior rights and social contract*	The person at this stage is aware of values and rights prior to social attachments and contracts. Norms of right and wrong are defined in terms of laws or institutionalised rules, which are seen to have a rational base such as expressing the will of the majority, maximising social utility or welfare, and are necessary for institutional or social cohesion and functioning. Duty and obligation are defined in terms of contract, not the needs of individuals. At this stage, laws can be challenged as being 'good' or 'bad', and indeed the interpretation of the law itself can be challenged. Lawyers, Supreme and High Court judges spend much of their time arguing at this level. Fundamentally, laws are viewed as human inventions and, as such, are modifiable and not sacrosanct.
Stage 6: Universal ethical principles	In stage six, individuals consider circumstances and the situation, as well as the general principles and the reasons behind the rules. Orientation is not only to existing rules and standards, but to principles of moral choice involving appeal to logical universality and consistency. Although law is important, moral conflict is resolved in terms of broader moral principles. Indeed, at times it may be moral to disobey laws.

(see Damon 1983; Hersh, Paolitto & Reimer 1979; Hoffman 1980)

Each of these arguments may be categorised according to Kohlberg's schema. Why don't you try your hand at it? By the way, the Queensland laws against public marches have been repealed.

Question point: *In their explanations of moral development, both the behavioural theory and the social cognitive theory, with the former's emphasis on the roles of reinforcement and punishment in learning moral values, and the latter's emphasis on learning through observing models, offer significant challenges to the stage concept of moral growth. In fact, the social cognitive theorist, Bandura, maintains that moral judgments are quite situation-specific and that: 'Stage theorists are able to classify people into types only by applying arbitrary rules to co-existing mixtures of judgments spanning several "stages" and by categorising most people as being in transition between stages' (Bandura 1977a, p. 43). Is the stage concept really useful in explaining moral development?*

WHAT WOULD YOU DO?

MORAL OBLIGATIONS (continued)

I waited for comment from the students. It is important that they form their own ethical stance rather than be told what to think. Thus, in general, I deliberately avoid stating my own opinions. In this situation, however, I felt I must speak.

'Jenny, Australia is a wealthy country and as such has a moral obligation to assist other countries, especially in the medical area. In fact, health funding is allocated specifically for compassionate medical assistance.'

Katrina raised her hand. 'Yes, Katrina,' I said.

'I agree,' she said. 'Even though he can't pay for the operation, when he is adopted he will grow up and pay taxes just like our parents.'

At the end of this lesson I reflected on my comment. I decided that, even though each student must develop their own ethical values, they also need to be informed about the values which are generally held by our society.

What do you think? Was the teacher's response appropriate? What did you suggest? How does the case study illustrate the development of moral reasoning as proposed by Piaget and Kohlberg?

Case studies illustrating National Competency Framework for Beginning Teaching, National Project on the Quality of Teaching and Learning, Australian Teaching Council, 1996, p. 42. Commonwealth of Australia copyright, reproduced by permission.

ACTION STATION

The basic teaching procedure for developing moral awareness, according to Kohlberg, is group discussions on hypothetical and real-life moral conflict situations. The aim of Kohlberg's moral dilemma situations is to challenge children to raise their level of moral reasoning by confronting them with points of view that illustrate higher levels of reasoning. Structure a situation where several people discuss the story of Heinz included earlier in the chapter. In this exercise you will attempt to categorise children's level of moral reasoning according to Kohlberg's framework. Observe and record their viewpoints about the story of Heinz. Is there any conflict? Any changing of positions? Naturally, if you have access to a class of children or adolescents you might like to try it out on the class. The following grid will help you classify the responses.

Subject	Response	Level	Reason for categorisation
Age Sex			
Age Sex			
Age Sex			

Current status of Kohlberg's theory

Dynamics of moral growth

From his research Kohlberg believed that the responses of children to moral dilemmas represent underlying forms or structures of moral thought which are universal—that is, not dependent on particular socialisation practices within particular cultural communities. He also felt that moral development is an active process with children generating moral structures through interaction with other persons and through role-taking in social situations. In particular, children are stimulated to move onto a higher stage of moral development when confronted with some genuine moral conflict that calls into question their typical beliefs.

In questioning the belief that young children are incapable of advanced moral reasoning, Shweder, Mahapatra and Miller (1990) make the intriguing point that language (which is used to elicit moral judgments) is very often a quite inadequate means of explaining how individuals reason and think. Shweder et al. state:

Kohlberg's theory of moral development is about the development of moral understandings, yet his moral dilemma interview methodology is a verbal production

task that places a high premium on the ability to generate arguments, verbally represent complex concepts, and talk like a moral philosopher. It is hazardous to rely on such a procedure when studying moral understandings because one of the most important findings of recent developmental research is that knowledge of concepts often precedes their self-reflective representation in speech. Young children know a great deal more about the concept of number, causation, or grammaticality than they can state.

... Those who study moral understandings with Kohlberg's moral dilemma interview have reduced the study of moral concepts to the study of verbal justification of moral ideas. The study of moral understanding has been narrowed ... to the study of what people can propositionalise. That is dangerous because what people can state is but a small part of what they know. (p. 143)

This statement gives a lot of food for thought. Obviously, children and adults may be able to reason at a higher moral level than their feeble attempts at explanation indicate. It might help to explain why so few individuals are classified as operating at the principled level. It appears that those who have been classified as such (e.g. Mahatma Ghandi, Martin Luther King and Mother Teresa) were also skilled communicators of their thoughts! This gap between language skills and moral reasoning is illustrated by a response of our daughter's. We asked Laura, at $3\frac{1}{2}$ (almost 4, as she kept telling us), how she knew what was good and what was bad. 'Because I have a good brain!' she replied with glee.

As with most theories, Kohlberg's is not set in concrete and the passing years have seen a number of changes to the theory, largely as a result of the intensive research that has been conducted. Basically, Kohlberg's framework has stood up well to the scrutiny of these researchers. Evidence has accumulated that individuals do move from very unsophisticated and egocentric forms of moral reasoning to increasingly sophisticated forms, and the stages outlined by Kohlberg, by and large, have received empirical support. The progression appears to be invariant, that is, an individual doesn't regress from a typically higher form of reasoning to a typically lower form, and stages are not skipped (Walker 1982).

Modifications to the theory

If you look back at Table 16.4, you will see that Kohlberg's original theory consisted of six stages. In the light of subsequent research, however, there have been a number of modifications and elaborations to the theory (Kohlberg, Levine & Hewer 1983). It is now clear that principled reasoning does not emerge in any substantial way during the secondary-school years, and that most children up to about year 10 are functioning at stage 2 and stage 3, with stage 2 rapidly declining. In the latter years of high school and early adulthood, stage 1 thinking has virtually disappeared, stage 2 thinking is considerably reduced, and stage 3 begins to decline with the rise of stage 4 thinking. Basically, the ages at which various levels of moral reasoning decline and rise have been revised upwards in the light of new evidence and a re-evaluation of old data (Sprinthall & Sprinthall 1990). Furthermore, because postconventional thinking was so rare among the subjects interviewed, stage 6 has been dropped from the reformulation of the theory, while stage 5 has been modified to include some of the features of stage 6 (Damon 1983; Shweder et al. 1990).

Modal stage of moral reasoning

It has also become quite apparent that individuals do not reason at one stage exclusively, but, rather, while typically reasoning at one stage, called the **modal stage,** they also understand and value reasoning at the next level up on the scale. Part of their reasoning is also at one stage lower (Rest 1973; Turiel 1966, 1983). It is important to note here that the dynamism for moving from one stage to the next higher stage appears to be the cognitive conflict engendered when one is confronted with a level of reasoning higher than one's current level. For educators and parents this gives a rationale for holding moral dilemma discussions among individuals functioning at varying (but close) stages of moral reasoning. However, research tends to indicate that the challenge should not be too great; for example, when there is a mismatch between a stage 2 and a stage 4 or 5 thinker (see Enright et al. 1983; Mosher 1980; Norcini & Snyder 1983; Walker 1983).

TURIEL'S PERSPECTIVE ON THE DEVELOPMENT OF MORALITY IN SOCIAL SETTINGS

Some criticisms of the Piagetian and Kohlbergian approaches relate to the confusion that may exist between **conventional rules** and **moral imperatives.** Writers such as Turiel and Nucci (Nucci 1987; Turiel 1983; Wainryb & Turiel 1993) argue that an understanding of social conventions such as rules of dress, greetings, and appropriate behaviour in social settings progresses through developmental levels reflecting underlying concepts of social organisation, and that this development is different from the stages of moral development relating to issues that are universal and unchangeable such as proscriptions against stealing, injury and slander. Moral transgressions are viewed as wrong, irrespective of the presence of governing rules, while conventional acts are viewed as wrong only if they violate an existing rule or standard. Children's and adults' responses to events in the moral domain focus on features intrinsic to the acts (such as harm or justice), while responses in the context of conventions focus on aspects of the social order (rules, regulations, normative expectations). Moral transgressions are viewed as more serious than violations of convention, and acts performed for a moral reason are considered more positive than ones performed because of convention (Nucci 1982; Turiel 1983; Wainryb & Turiel 1993).

Of course, some rules have both an implied moral and conventional dimension, and conformity to the rule may reflect either moral or conventional reasoning, or a combination of both forms. For example, many drivers don't exceed the prescribed alcohol level while driving because they generally feel that it is immoral to endanger the lives of other drivers on the road. Other drivers obey the law because they are afraid of random breath testing and the consequences if they are over the limit. Most people are probably influenced by both motives.

Three important influences on our moral behaviour are the moral values we have internalised through our socialisation, our exposure to models of moral behaviour, and the informational assumptions that provide the basis for our decision making (Wainryb & Turiel 1993). An individual's informational beliefs and assumptions about relevant aspects of reality have a bearing on the individual's interpretation of an event. For example, the belief that a foetus is (as assumed fact) a person makes abortion comparable to murder. On the other hand, if a foetus is not considered human life then abortion is seen as a personal choice that does not involve a moral transgression. It is for these reasons that people can have so many different moral perspectives on the same act (Wainryb & Turiel 1993).

Influences on the development of moral behaviour

Moral actions and conventional actions

A major difference between this perspective and those of Kohlberg and Piaget is the belief that even very young children can differentiate between actions that are moral and those that are conventional. For example, children believe that they shouldn't break the classroom rule against talking (conventional rule), but that talking would be okay if the rule were removed. On the other hand, children believe it is wrong to hurt another child irrespective of the existence of a rule forbidding it. Because of this differentiation, moral and values education should reflect this distinction.

Young children are also able to distinguish just and unjust authority, and take into account the age and status of authority figures, their formal position in the social hierarchy, their ability to sanction and punish, and the extent of their expertise and knowledge. For example, children accept parental commands regulating activities such as house chores, but reject parental commands to steal or cause harm (Wainryb & Turiel 1993).

Authority

For Turiel and others, it seems that children's moral judgments do not simply and directly reflect adults' values, teaching and commands, nor the attitudes and opinions of significant groups such as religious ones. Rather, it appears that moral and social understandings and decisions result from a developmental process that stems from the child's social interactions and observations, which are then interpreted and modified according to the child's understandings and assumptions.

Research examining the relationship between moral reasoning and moral action has found only a weak relationship. Nevertheless, the relationship is in the expected direction. In other words, people who have been classified as functioning at a higher level of moral reasoning will avoid behaviour such as cheating more often than those who have been classified as functioning at a lower level (Blasi 1980; Damon 1983).

Moral reasoning, moral behaviour and explanations

Various reasons are given for the weak link between moral reasoning and moral behaviour. We are all aware that circumstances can facilitate or inhibit what we believe to be moral behaviour irrespective of our moral beliefs. For example, for a woman with a large family of young children, the possibility of another pregnancy may persuade her to practise contraception, even though this may be proscribed by her church. All of us have had tussles of conscience when competing demands make a simple direct relationship between moral beliefs and behaviour problematic.

GENDER DIFFERENCES IN MORAL DEVELOPMENT: GILLIGAN'S VIEW

Kohlberg's stage theory has been criticised by Carol Gilligan (1977, 1982) who has highlighted the potential for gender bias in the methodology used by Kohlberg, which may lead to men being classified as functioning at higher levels of moral reasoning than females. She argues that, because all Kohlberg's original subjects were male, the 'model' reasons derived for moral decisions used to structure the stage theory reflect a male perspective rather than a universal one. For example, she believes that men speak of rights, while women speak of responsibilities; men highlight rationality, while women highlight caring and concern; men are seen as searching for general principles that can be applied to any moral dilemma and women as concentrating on particular situations, relationships and people. Gilligan maintains that Kohlberg's system of scoring the interviews, therefore, based upon male reasoning, penalises women so that more women are represented at lower levels of moral reasoning relative to men. Furthermore, she believes that, as the stages are based on a male perspective, they present a very limited view of moral reasoning. While Gilligan and her colleagues argue that traditional Kohlbergian measures are biased against females, most research shows that Kohlberg's measurement methods and scoring schemes do not yield reliable gender differences in moral judgment scores (Braebeck 1982; Damon 1983; Sprinthall & Sprinthall 1990; Walker 1984; Walker, De Vries & Trevetham 1987).

Justice and caring

Despite the apparent controversy, Gilligan has nevertheless highlighted some important dimensions of moral reasoning not emphasised in Kohlberg's theory. While Kohlberg emphasises the **justice perspective**—a perspective that focuses on the rights of the individual: individuals stand alone and independently make moral decisions—Gilligan (1982) focuses on a **care perspective** that views people in terms of their connectedness with others, and concern for others.

In studies with girls aged from 6 to 18 years of age, Gilligan (1982) shows that girls consistently reveal a detailed knowledge about and interest in human relationships. Gilligan believes that this causes a dilemma for many girls who perceive that their intense interest in intimacy and relationships is not highly regarded in a male-dominated culture. Although society values women as caring and altruistic, such characteristics may limit females' opportunities in the society at large. Females who choose to adopt achievement-driven values characteristic of the male are considered selfish. If they don't, they are not regarded as the equal of males! Gilligan believes that the conflict experienced can have a serious impact on the development of the female's self-concept and lead to depression and eating disorders among adolescent girls (Santrock & Yussen 1992).

Morality of care

There has been considerable research support for Gilligan's claim that the moral reasoning of females and males is concerned with different issues. Some schools have taken seriously Gilligan's ideas that girls should have greater value placed on their **morality of care**, rather than encouraging them to be independent and self-sufficient. They have done so by emphasising cooperation rather than competition across the curriculum, a theme developed in Chapters 9 and 10. It is also believed that boys benefit from such teaching approaches.

It is important to note that there is not an absolute gender difference and the two perspectives are not incompatible (Santrock & Yussen 1992). Indeed, males can express deep concern for the welfare of others and develop intimacy and altruistic characteristics, while females can be justice-oriented. In many cases neither perspective dominates.

ACTION STATION

Compare and contrast the perspectives of Kohlberg and Gilligan. Organise a debate on the topic 'That women are more care-oriented than men'. Does this hold true today in Western society? What about in other cultures?

Question point: Discuss the belief implicit in Kohlberg's theory that moral values are universal.

MORALITY AND CROSS-CULTURAL CONSIDERATIONS

Cultural relevance

Not everyone agrees with the notion that moral development is contingent upon the natural unfolding of structures as the child matures and with the emphasis placed on the process of self-discovery of social moral rules, independent of social context or culture. Shweder, Mahapatra and Miller (1987) argue that young children acquire their social knowledge through a process of cultural transmission. From this perspective the cultural milieu of the child takes on a greater role in shaping moral responses, leading to a relative rather than a universal stance on questions of right and wrong (see also DiMartino 1989).

Naturally, Kohlberg's comprehensive theory of moral development, with its claims to universalism, has been tested in a wide range of cultural contexts. Two issues are worth noting here. First, the original stories constructed by Kohlberg reflect a Western, middle-class orientation and, as such, may not be suited for use in other cultural contexts. Attempts have been made to rewrite the stories for particular cross-cultural use (DiMartino 1989; Sprinthall & Sprinthall 1990).

Are there universal moral values?

A greater problem than culturally suitable stories really hits at the heart of the theory, and this is the conception that there are universal moral values that characterise postconventional moral thinking, values such as liberty, equality, safety, the elimination of suffering and the preservation of human life. Other writers (DiMartino 1989) suggest that, far from being universal, moral values may be culturally specific, for example—the value of free speech and human individual dignity may very well reflect a democratic perspective, rather than a universal value. Even on contentious issues within the one community, such as Australia or New Zealand, we see a diversity of opinion on laws related to abortion, euthanasia and homosexuality, so that when we move to other cultures the complexity becomes even greater. For example, birth control is considered immoral in many cultures, while polygamy is considered moral. Those holding to the universalistic notion argue that, irrespective of the recognition of wrongness (in behaviour such as polygamy or abortion), certain behaviours are wrong regardless of social mores and man-made laws. In his latest formulation of the theory, Kohlberg paid greater attention to this issue (Kohlberg, Levine & Hewer 1983; Shweder, Mahapatra & Miller 1990). As you can see, this is a very complicated issue, and one that is far from resolution.

MORAL DEVELOPMENT AND CONSTRUCTIVISM

The process of development of moral concepts arises from children's experiences in the social world. It is in making sense of these social experiences that children perceive their salient moral aspects—for example, pain or injustice—and generate ideas on how people should act towards each other. These moral rules are not based on given rules or adult teachings but, rather, children construct their own judgments through abstractions from their experiences. As children grow older they re-evaluate existing concepts and construct new ones that are qualitatively different.

CLASSROOM APPLICATIONS OF MORAL DEVELOPMENT THEORY

Children and moral values

At the very least, our consideration of theories of moral development has highlighted a number of important issues for educators and parents. First among these is the notion that moral reasoning increases in sophistication as children get older, and that there is a relationship between moral reasoning and cognitive development. We cannot therefore expect children to hold the same moral perspective as ourselves, and indeed children may consider it all right to cheat and lie if, for example, it's for a good reason, or can be concealed. Sermonising to children about their 'immoral' behaviour may well be a fruitless exercise if we are using arguments based on stages more than one in advance of the child's modal level.

Testing moral rules

Second, our discussion has drawn attention to the importance for moral growth of the child's own direct social experience and his or her active efforts to draw meaning from its contradictions. Clearly, the school and classroom supplies the first large environment in which children test out their moral rules. Cooperative grouping will provide a good environment for peer interaction that will promote cognitive and moral growth (see Chapters 2 and 10).

Can we teach moral values?

Our discussion calls into question many of the traditional methods of 'teaching' moral values. Indeed, the whole notion that moral values can be taught must be reconsidered. When we went to school it was common practice for social studies texts to present moral stories based on the lives of famous people such as Abraham Lincoln, Lewis Carroll, Helen Keller, Florence Nightingale, Mahatma Ghandi, Albert Schweitzer and the occasional (but very infrequent) Australian. It was anticipated that the reader would learn to be moral by reading about moral behaviour.

At the most elementary level such a didactic approach fails to take heed of the gap between the moral behaviour practised by great people such as Albert Schweitzer or Marie Curie, and children's ability to understand, evaluate and incorporate the values so demonstrated. We can remember vividly as ten-year-olds wondering what 'on earth' we were supposed to get out of the stories. Were we to go to darkest Africa and convert the heathens, or perhaps discover radium, or free slaves (we had only a limited understanding of what slaves were)? Furthermore, the absence of contemporary models made the exercise somewhat unreal for children and the approach predominantly reflected a Christian viewpoint of morality which is increasingly inappropriate in multicultural Australia and New Zealand. Such approaches to teaching, based on behaviourism and social learning theory, are still popular, but the question must be asked whether children are learning meaningful values which they can incorporate into their behaviour, or simply learning to listen and, perhaps, recall what was said.

Another popular approach is to have students accept uncritically values being presented around them in a didactic manner. For example, campaigns such as 'Just say no to drugs' or 'Say yes to old-fashioned values' may be of limited value because they fail to take into account the complexities of moral development and decision making that we discuss above.

Effective moral education should account for the complexities of social and moral reasoning (Wainryb & Turiel 1993). It should, therefore, be geared towards stimulating the development of moral concepts, fostering an understanding of the distinctions, relations and conflicts between moral and social concepts, as well as guiding children's comprehension of the ways access to information modifes social and moral decisions.

Moral dilemmas

Today, the approach to teaching moral values is more likely to be through discussion of problems that are real and meaningful to children at their particular stages of development. One popular approach is **moral dilemma presentations**. The first step in this may be the presentation of a moral problem by a teacher. Children are invited to contribute their views on appropriate solutions, and in particular their reasons for the solution. These solutions and views may be listed on a board, and discussed. Within any group there will be a range of views expressed, and these will usually represent a range of stages. In the discussion, children are challenged to consider their own point of view. For children reasoning at higher levels, lower-level solutions expressed by their peers will be understood but rejected. However, cognitive conflict will be set up for children reasoning at lower stages, and they will be challenged to move upward. Judicious comments by the teacher, together with elaboration of views by children functioning at the higher levels, facilitates this movement (Peak 1971). Research tends to support the belief that children do progressively make more sophisticated judgments as a consequence of being exposed to such programs.

Question point: *Consider the implications of each of the theories covered in this chapter for children living in tribal settings (such as Australian Aboriginal and Maori children), rural Westernised settings and urbanised settings. What different factors are likely to affect development in each case?*

ACTION STATION

In the context of personal development education, and the threat posed by HIV/AIDS, have a group of adolescents debate whether condom-vending machines should be placed in high schools. Attempt to categorise the various responses using Kohlberg's schema. Monitor the expressed views of the students. Is there any shifting of perspective because of the social interaction? Report your findings.

Recommended reading

Anderman, E. M. & Maehr, M. L. (1994) Motivation and schooling in the middle grades. *Review of Educational Research*, 64, 287–309.

Buchanan, C.M., Eccles, J. S. & Becker, J. B. (1992) Are adolescents the victims of raging hormones? Evidence for the activational effects of hormones on moods and behavior at adolescence. *Psychological Bulletin*, 111, 62–107.

Davis, A. (1992) Suicidal behaviour among adolescents: Its nature and prevention (pp. 89–103). In R. Kosky, H.S. Eshkevari & G. Kneebone (eds) *Breaking Out: Challenges in Adolescent Mental Health in Australia*. Canberra: Australian Government Publishing Service.

Eccles, J. S. et al. (1993) Development during adolescence. The impact of stage–environment fit on young adolescents' experiences in schools and in families. *American Psychologist*, 48, 90–101.

Garland, A. & Zigler, E. (1993) Adolescent suicide prevention. Current research and social policy implications. *American Psychologist*, 48, 169–82.

Hill, J. (1995) School culture and peer groups. In L. W. Anderson (ed.) *International Encyclopedia of Teaching and Teacher Education,* 2nd edn, pp. 332–6. Tarrytown, NY: Pergamon.

Jarvinen, D. W. & Nicholls, J. G. (1996) Adolescents' social goals, beliefs about causes of social success, and satisfaction in peer relations. *Developmental Psychology*, 32, 435–41.

Jones, E. & Reynolds, G. (1992) *The Play's the Thing*. New York: Teachers College Press.

Kohlberg, L. (1981) *The Philosophy of Moral Development*. San Francisco: Harper & Row.

Mak, A. (1994) Parental neglect and overprotection as risk factors in delinquency. *Australian Journal of Psychology*, 46, 107–11.

Marsh, H. W. (1990) A multidimensional, hierarchical model of self-concept: Theoretical and empirical justification. *Educational Psychology Review*, 2, 77–172.

Marsh, H. W. & Craven, R. (in press) Academic self-concept: Beyond the dustbowl. In G. Phye (ed.) *Handbook of Classroom Assessment: Learning, Achievement, and Adjustment.* Orlando, Fl: Academic Press.

Moyles, J. R. (ed.) (1995) *The Excellence of Play*. Buckingham, UK: Open University Press.

Pritchard, C. (1992) Youth suicide and gender in Australia and New Zealand compared with countries of the Western world (1973–1987). *Australian and New Zealand Journal of Psychiatry*, 26, 609–17.

Rogers, C. S. & Sawyers, J. K. *Play in the Lives of Young Children.* Washington DC: NAEYC.

Rosenthal, D., Ranieri N. & Klimidis, S. (1996) Vietnamese adolescents in Australia: Relationships between perceptions of self and parental values, intergenerational conflict, and gender dissatisfaction. *International Journal of Psychology*, 31, 81–91.

Simmons, R. G. & Blyth, D. A. (1987) *Moving into Adolescence: The Impact of Pubertal Change and School Context*. Hawthorne, NY: Aldine de Gruyter.

Smilansky, S. (1990) Sociodramatic play: Its relevance to behavior and achievement in school. In E. Klugman & S. Smilansky, *Children's Play and Learning* (pp.18–42). New York: Teachers College Press.

Turiel, E. (1983) *The Development of Social Knowledge: Morality and Convention*. New York: Cambridge University Press.

Wainryb, C. & Turiel, E. (1993) Conceptual and informational features in moral decision making. *Educational Psychologist*, 28, 205–18.

References

Abrami, P. C., Chambers, B., d'Apollonia, S., Farrell, M. & De Simone, C. (1992) Group outcome: The relationship between group learning outcome attributional style, academic achievement, and self-concept. *Contemporary Educational Psychology*, **17**, 201–10.

Abrami, P. C., Chambers, B., Poulsen, C., De Simone, C., d'Apollonia, S. & Howden, J. (1995) *Classroom Connections: Understanding and Using Cooperative Learning*. Ontario, Canada: Harcourt Brace.

Abramson, L. Y., Seligman, M. E. P. & Teasdale, J. D. (1978) Learned helplessness in humans: critique and reformulation. *Journal of Abnormal Psychology*, **87**, 49–74.

Adams, P. (1991) The video vanguard opens fire. *The Weekend Australian*, April 13–14.

Adams, T. (1992) Looking forward by looking backward. In C. Bigum & B. Green (eds), *Understanding the New Information Technologies in Education*. Geelong, Vic. Centre for Studies in Information Technologies and Education, Deakin University.

Adelson, J. (ed.) (1980) *Handbook of Adolescent Psychology*. New York: John Wiley & Sons.

Aiken, L. R. (1979) *Psychological Testing and Assessment*, 3rd edn. Boston: Allyn & Bacon.

Ainley, M. (1986) What is it like if it's too big too grasp? *SET Research Information for Teachers*, number 1, item 7.

Airasian, P. W. (1995) Classroom assessment. In L. W. Anderson (ed.) *International Encyclopedia of Teaching and Teacher Education*, 2nd edn, Tarrytown, NY: Pergamon: 290–4.

Airasian, P. W. (1991) *Classroom Assessment*. New York: McGraw-Hill.

Alberto, P. A. & Troutman, A. C. (1982) *Applied Behavior Analysis for Teachers. Influencing Student Performance*. Columbus, OH: Charles E. Merrill.

Alcorso, C. & Cope, B. (1986) *A Review of Multicultural Education Policy* 1979–1986. NACCME Commissioned Research Paper No. 6. Woden, Australia: National Advisory and Coordinating Committee on Multicultural Education.

Alessi, S. M. & Trollip, S. R. (1991) *Computer-Based Instruction*. Englewood Cliffs, NJ: Prentice Hall.

Alexander, P. A. (1995) Superimposing a situation-specific and domain-specific perspective on an account of self-regulated learning. *Educational Psychologist*, **30**, 189–93.

Alexander, P. A., Kulikowich, J. M. & Jetton, T. L. (1994) The role of subject-matter knowledge and interest in the processing of linear and non-linear texts. *Review of Educational Research*, **64**, 210–52.

Allen, M. (1986) And are they intelligent? *Journal of Christian Education*, Papers 85, 35–43.

Alper, S. & Ryndak, D. L. (1992) Educating students with severe handicaps in regular classes. *Elementary School Journal*, **92**, 374–87.

Ames, C. (1984) Competitive, cooperative, and individualistic goal structures: a cognitive-motivational analysis. In R. Ames & C. Ames (eds) *Research on Motivation in Education: Vol. 1. Student Motivation*. Orlando: Academic Press.

Ames, C. (1990) Motivation: What teachers need to know. *Teachers College Report*, **91**, 409–21.

Ames, C. (1992) Classrooms: Goals, structures, and student motivation. *Journal of Educational Psychology*, **84**, 261–71.

Ames, C. & Ames, R. (eds) (1985) *Research on Motivation in Education*: Vol. 2. *The Classroom Milieu*. Orlando: Academic Press.

Ames, C. & Ames, R. (eds) (1989) *Research on Motivation in Education*: Vol. 3. *Goals and Cognitions*. Orlando: Academic Press.

Ames, R. A. & Ames, C. (eds) (1984) *Research on Motivation in Education*: Vol.1. *Student Motivation*. Orlando: Academic Press.

Ames, R. & Ames, C. (1991) Motivation and effective teaching. In L. Idol & B. F. Jones (eds) *Educational Values and Cognitive Instruction: Implications for Reform*. Hillsdale, NJ: Lawrence Erlbaum.

Anastasi, A. (1990) Ability testing in the 1980s and beyond: Some major trends. *Public Personnel Management*, **18**, 471–85.

Anderman, E. M. & Maehr, M. L. (1994) Motivation and schooling in the middle grades. *Review of Educational Research*, **64**, 287–309.

Anderson, D. & Walker, R. (1990) Approaches to learning of beginning teacher education students. In M. Bezzina & J. Butcher (eds) *The Changing Face of Professional Education. Collected Papers of the AARE Annual Conference, Sydney University, 1990*. Sydney: AARE.

Anderson, J. R. (1982) Acquisition of Cognitive Skill. Psychological Review, **89**, 369–406.

Anderson, J. R. (1983) *The Architecture of Cognition*. Cambridge, MA: Harvard University Press.

Anderson, J. R. (1990) *Cognitive Psychology and its Implications*, 3rd edn. New York: Freeman.

Anderson, J. R., Reder, L. M. & Simon, H. A. (1997) Situative versus cognitive perspectives: From versus substance. *Educational Researcher*, **26**, 18–21.

Anderson, J.R., Reder, L. M. & Simon, H.(1996) Situated learning and education. *Educational Researcher*, **25**, 5–11.

Anderson, L. M. & Prawat, R. S. (1983) Responsibility in the classroom: A synthesis of research on teaching self-control. *Educational Leadership*, **41**, 62–6.

Anderson, L. W. (1985) A retrospective and prospective view of Bloom's 'Learning for Mastery'. In M. C. Wang & H. J. Walberg (eds) *Adapting Instruction to Individual Differences*, Berkeley, CA: McCutchan.

Anderson, L. W. (1986) Research on teaching and educational effectiveness. *Curriculum Report*, **15**, April.

Anderson, L. W. (ed.) (1989) *The Effective Teacher. Study Guide and Readings*. McGraw-Hill: New York.

Anderson, L. W. & Burns, R. B. (1987) Values, evidence, and

mastery learning. *Review of Educational Research*, **57**, 215–22.

Anderson, V. & Hidi, S. (1989) Teaching students to summarize. *Educational Leadership*, **46**, 26–8.

Andre, T. (1986) Problem solving and education. In G. D. Phye & T. Andre (eds) *Cognitive Classroom Learning: Understanding Thinking and Problem Solving*. Orlando: Harcourt Brace Jovanovich.

Andrews, G. R. & Debus, R. L. (1978) Persistence and causal perception of failure: Modifying cognitive attributions. *Journal of Educational Psychology*, **70**, 154–66.

APA Task Force on Psychology in Education. (1993, January) *Learner-centered Psychological Principles: Guidelines for School Redesign and Reform*. Washington, DC: American Psychological Association and Mid-continent Regional Educational Laboratory.

Apple Computer Inc. (1996) Apple press release on Newton available through the Internet at http://www.newton.apple.com *Australian Journal of Psychology*, **48**, 100.

Archee, R. (1993) Virtual reality: Exploring the potential. *Australian Educational Computing*, 8, ACEC '93 Edition, 25–30.

Arlin, M. (1984) Time, equality, and mastery learning. *Review of Educational Research*, **54**, 65–86.

Armstrong, D. & Savage, T. (1983) *Secondary Education: An Introduction. New York: Macmillan.*

Arnheim, R. (1962) *Picasso's Guernica: The Genesis of a Painting*. Berkeley: University of California Press.

Aronson, E., Blaney, N., Stephan, C., Sikes, J. & Snapp, M. (1978) *The Jigsaw Classroom*. Beverly Hills, CA: Sage.

Ashby, M. S. & Wittmaier, B. C. (1978) Attitude changes in children after exposure to stories about women in traditional or nontraditional occupations. *Journal of Educational Psychology*, **70**, 945–49.

Asher, W. & Hynes, K. (1982) Methodological weaknesses in an evaluation of open education. *Journal of Experimental Education*, **51**, 2–7.

Ashman, A. F. & Conway, R. N. (1993) Using Cognitive Methods in the Classroom. New York: Routledge.

Ashman, A. F. & Elkins, J. (1990) *Educating Children with Special Needs*. Sydney: Prentice Hall Australia.

Ashton, P. T. & Webb, R. B. (1986) *Making a Difference: Teachers' Sense of Efficacy and Student Achievement*. White Plains, NY: Longman.

Atkins, W. & Lewis, P. (1982) Partial integration of the severely retarded and the normal child. ASET, 3, 23–7.

Atkinson, J. W. (ed.) (1958) *Motives in Fantasy, Action and Society*. Princeton, NJ: Van Nostrand.

Atkinson, J. W. (1964) *An Introduction to Motivation*. Princeton, NJ: Van Nostrand.

Atkinson, J. W. & Feather, N. T. (eds) (1966) *A Theory of Achievement Motivation*. New York: John Wiley.

Atkinson, J. W. & Raynor, J. O. (1974) *Motivation and Achievement*, Washington, DC: V. H. Winston.

Attie, I. & Brooks-Gunn, J. (1989) Development of eating problems in adolescent girls: A longitudinal study. *Developmental Psychology*, **25**, 70–9.

Au, W. K. & Leung, J. P. (1991) Problem solving, instructional methods and Logo programming. *Journal of Educational Computing Research*, **7**, 455–67.

Australian Education Council (1985) *Education for girls*. Melbourne: Australian Education Council.

Australian Teaching Council. (1996) *Case Studies Illustrating National Competency Framework for Beginning Teaching. National Project on the Quality of Teaching and Learning.* Canberra: AGPS.

Ausubel, D. P. (1963) *The Psychology of Meaningful Verbal Learning*. New York: Grune & Stratton.

Ausubel, D. P. (1966a) Cognitive structure and the facilitation of meaningful verbal learning. In R. C. Anderson (ed.) *Readings in the Psychology of Cognition*. New York: Holt, Rinehart & Winston.

Ausubel, D. P. (1966b) In defense of verbal learning. In R. C. Anderson (ed.) *Readings in the Psychology of Cognition*. New York: Holt, Rinehart & Winston.

Ausubel, D. P. (1968) *Educational Psychology: A Cognitive View*. New York: Holt, Rinehart & Winston.

Ausubel, D. P. (1977) The facilitation of meaningful verbal learning in the classroom. *Educational Psychologist*, **12**, 162–78.

Ausubel, D. P. (1978) In defense of advance organizers. A reply to the critics. *Review of Educational Research*, **48**, 251–7.

Bailey, J. (1992) Australian special education: Issues of the eighties. Directions for the nineties. *Australian Journal of Special Education*, **16**, 16–25.

Bailey, S. M. (1993) The current status of gender equity research in American schools. *Educational Psychologist*, **28**, 321–39.

Bain, A. (1992) Issues in the integration of regular and special education: An Australian Perspective. *Australian Journal of Education*, **36**, 84–99.

Bakopanos, V., & White, R. (1990) Increasing meta-learning. Part 1: Encouraging students to ask questions. *SET Research Information for Teachers*, number 1, item 11.

Ball, S. (1984) Student motivation: some reflections and projections. In R. Ames & C. Ames (eds) *Research on Motivation in Education: Vol. 1. Student Motivation.* Orlando: Academic Press.

Balla, D. & Zigler, E. (1975) Preinstitutional social deprivation, responsiveness to social reinforcement and IQ change in institutionalized retarded individuals. *American Journal of Mental Deficiency*, **80**, 228–30.

Balson, M. (1992) *Understanding Classroom Behaviour*, 3rd edn. Hawthorn, Vic. ACER.

Bandura, A. (1962) Social learning through imitation. In N. R. Jones (ed.) *Nebraska Symposium on Motivation*. Lincoln, NE: University of Nebraska Press.

Bandura, A. (1969) *Principles of Behavior Modification*. New York: Holt, Rinehart & Winston.

Bandura, A. (1976) Self-efficacy: Toward a unifying theory of behavioral change. *Psychological Review*, **84**, 191–215.

Bandura, A. (1977a) *Social Learning Theory*. Morristown, NJ: General Learning Press.

Bandura, A. (1977b) Analysis of modeling processes. In H. F. Clarizio, R. C. Craig & W. A. Mehrens (eds) *Contemporary Issues in Educational Psychology*, 3rd edn. Boston: Allyn & Bacon.

Bandura, A. (1986) *Social Foundations of Thought and Action.* Englewood-Cliffs, NJ: Prentice Hall.

Bandura, A (1986) Social Foundations of *Thought and Action.* Englewood-Cliffs, NJ: Prentice Hall.

Bandura, A. (1991) Self-regulation of motivation through anticipatory and self-regulatory mechanisms. In R. A. Dienstbier (ed.) *Perspectives on Motivation: Nebraska Symposium on Motivation* (Vol. 38, pp. 69–164). Lincoln, NE: University of Nebraska Press.

Bandura, A. (1993) Perceived self-efficacy in cognitive

development and functioning. *Educational Psychologist*, **28**, 117–48.

Bandura, A., Ross, D. & Ross, S. A. (1963) Imitation of film-mediated aggressive models. *Journal of Abnornal and Social Psychology*, **66**, 3–11.

Bandura, A. & Walters, R. (1963) *Social Learning & Personality Development*. New York: Holt, Rinehart & Winston.

Bandura, L. (1974) *The Teaching of Talented Pupils*. Warsaw: NK Warsaw.

Bangert, R. L., Kulik, J. A. & Kulik, C-L. C. (1983) Individualized systems of instruction in secondary schools. *Review of Educational Research*, **53**, 143–58.

Bangert-Drowns, R. L. (1993) The word processor as an instructional tool: A meta-analysis of word processing in writing instruction. *Review of Educational Research*, **63**, 69–93.

Bangert-Drowns, R. L., Kulik, J. A. & Kulik, C-L. C. (1985) Effectiveness of computer-based education in secondary schools. *Journal of Computer-Based Instruction*, **12**, 59–68.

Bangert-Drowns, R. L., Kulik, J. A. & Kulik, C-L. C. (1991) Effects of frequent classroom testing. *Journal of Educational Research*, **85**, 89–99.

Banks, J. A. (1993) Multicultural education: Historical development, dimensions, and practice. *Review of Research in Education*, **19**, 3–49.

Barnes, G. R. & McInerney, D. M. (1996) A motivational model of intention to enrol in senior secondary science courses in New South Wales Schools. *Australian Journal of Psychology*, **48**, 86.

Barron, F. (1969) *Creative Person and Creative Process*. New York: Holt, Rinehart & Winston.

Barry, K. & King, L. (1993) *Beginning Teaching*, 2nd edn. Wentworth Falls: Social Science Press.

Bar-Tal, D. (1978) Attributional analysis of achievement-related behavior. *Review of Educationl Research*, **48**, 259–71.

Bayley, N. (1956) Individual patterns of development. *Child Development*, **27**, 45–74.

Beane, J. A. & Lipka, R. P. (1984) *Self-Concept, Self-Esteem, and the Curriculum*. Boston: Allyn & Bacon.

Bee, H. (1992) *The Developing Child*, 6th edn. New York: HarperCollins.

Beilin, H. (1987) Current trends in cognitive development research: Towards a new synthesis. In B. Inhelder, D. de Caprona & A. Cornu-Wells (eds) *Piaget Today*. London: Lawrence Erlbaum.

Bell, H. (1986) White teacher, black learner: The influence of the cross-cultural context on teaching practice. *Australian Journal of Adult Education*, **26**, 29–33.

Bell, H. (1988) An overview of some Aboriginal teaching and learning strategies in traditionally oriented communities. *Aboriginal Child at School*, **16**, 3–23.

Bellanca, J. & Fogarty, R. (1991) *Blueprints for Thinking in the Cooperative Classroom*, 2nd edn, revised in Australia by J. Dalton. Vic. Hawker Brownlow Education.

Benton, R. (1989) Will it hurt? Teaching in Maori, or Pitjantjatjara. *SET Research Notes for Teachers*, number 1, item 13.

Berger, K. S. (1991) *The Developing Person Through Childhood and Adolescence*, 3rd edn. New York: Worth.

Berk, L. E. (1996) *Infants, Children and Adolescents*, 2nd edn. Boston: Allyn & Bacon.

Berk, L. E. (1997). *Child Development*, 4th edn. Boston: Allyn & Bacon.

Berkowitz, S. J. (1986) Effects of instruction in text organization on sixth-grade students' memory for expository reading. *Reading Research Quarterly*, **21**, 161–78.

Berliner, D. C. (1985) Comments on Part Two. A. How is adaptive education like water in Arizona? In M. C. Wang & H. J. Walberg (eds) *Adapting Instruction to Individual Differences*, Berkeley, CA: McCutchan.

Berliner, D. C. (1986) In pursuit of the expert pedagogue. *Educational Researcher*, **15**, 5–13.

Berliner, D. C. (1988) Simple views of effective teaching and a simple theory of classroom instruction. In D. Berliner & B. Rosenshine (eds) *Talks to Teachers*. New York: Random House.

Berliner, D. C. (1989) Furthering our understanding of motivation and environments. In C. Ames & R. Ames (eds) *Research on Motivation in Education: Vol. 3. Goals and Cognitions*. Orlando: Academic Press.

Berliner, D. C. & Tikunoff, W. (1976) The California Beginning Teacher Evaluation Study: Overview of the ethnographic study. *Journal of Teacher Education*, **27**, 24–30.

Berlyne, D. E. (1960) *Conflict, Arousal and Curiosity*. New York: McGraw-Hill.

Berlyne, D. E. (1977) Notes on intrinsic motivation and intrinsic reward in relation to instruction. In H. F. Clarizio, R. C. Craig & W. A. Mehrens (eds) *Contemporary Issues in Educational Psychology*, 3rd edn. Boston: Allyn & Bacon.

Berndt, T. J. (1992) *Child Development*. Orlando: Harcourt Brace Jovanovich.

Berndt, T. J. & Perry, T. B. (1990) Distinctive features and effects of early adolescent friendships. In R. Montmayor, G. Adams & T. Gullotta (eds) *From Childhood to Adolescence: A Transition Period?* New York: Russell Sage.

Berrell, M. M. (1993) Classrooms as the site of citizenship education. In K. Kennedy, O. Watts & G. McDonald (eds) *Citizenship Education for a New Age*. Toowoomba: The University of Southern Queensland Press.

Berry, J. W. (1979) Research in multicultural societies. Implications of cross-cultural methods. *Journal of Cross-Cultural Psychology*, **9**, 415–34.

Berry, M. (1993) Implementing hypercard in a small school. In S. Wawrzyniak & L. Samootin (eds) *Sharing the Vision: Proceedings of the 11th Annual Computers in Education Conference*. Sydney: NSW Computer Education Group.

Berry, P. (1989) Mental handicap. In P. Langford (ed.) *Educational Psychology. An Australian Perspective*. Sydney: Longman Cheshire.

Berry, P. & Langford, P. (1989) Integration and mainstreaming. In P. Langford (ed.) *Educational Psychology. An Australian Perspective*. Sydney: Longman Cheshire.

Bidell, T. R. & Fischer, K. W. (1992) Beyond the stage debate: Action, structure, and variability in Piagetian theory and research. In R. J. Sternberg & C. A. Berg (eds) Intellectual Development. New York: Cambridge University Press.

Biehler, R. F. & Snowman, J. (1990) Psychology Applied to Teaching, 6th edn. Boston: Houghton Mifflin.

Bigge, J. & Sirvis, B. (1982) Physical and multiple handicaps. In N. Haring (ed.) *Exceptional Children and Youth*. Columbus, OH: Charles E. Merrill.

Bigge, M. L. (1971) *Learning Theories for Teachers*. New York: Harper & Row.

Biggs, J. B. (1978) Individual and group differences in study processes. *British Journal of Educational Psychology*, **48**, 266–79.

Biggs, J. B. (1984) Motivational patterns, learning strategies and subjectively perceived success in secondary and tertiary students. In J. R. Kirby (ed.) *Cognitive Strategies and Educational Performance*. New York: Academic Press.

Biggs, J. (1987a) Reflective thinking and school learning. An introduction to the theory and practice of metacognition. *SET Research Information for Teachers*, number 2, item 10.

Biggs, J. (1987b) *The Learning Process Questionnaire: Manual.* Hawthorn, Vic. ACER.

Biggs, J. (1987c) *Student Approaches to Learning and Studying.* Melbourne: ACER.

Biggs, J. (1988a) Approaches to learning and to essay writing. In R. R. Schmeck (ed.) *Learning Strategies and Learning Styles.* New York: Plenum Press.

Biggs, J. (1988b) The role of metacognition in enhancing learning. *Australian Journal of Education*, **32**, 127–38.

Biggs, J. B. (1991a) Good learning: What is it? In J. B. Biggs (ed.) *Teaching for Learning*. Hawthorn, Vic. ACER.

Biggs, J. B. (ed.) (1991b) *Teaching for Learning. The View from Cognitive Psychology*. Hawthorn, Vic. ACER.

Biggs, J. & Collis, K. (1982) *Evaluating the Quality of Learning: The SOLO Taxonomy*. New York: Academic Press.

Biggs, J. B. & Moore, P. J. (1993) *The Process of Learning*, 3rd edn. Sydney: Prentice Hall Australia.

Biggs, J. B. & Telfer, R. (1981) *The Process of Learning*. Sydney: Prentice Hall Australia.

Biggs, J. B. & Telfer, R. (1987a) *The Process of Learning*, 2nd edn. Sydney: Prentice Hall Australia.

Biggs, J. B. & Telfer, R. (1987b) St*udent Approaches to Learning and Studying*. Hawthorn, Vic. ACER.

Bigum, C. & Green, C. (1992) Understanding the new information technologies. In C. Bigum & B. Green (eds) *Understanding the New Information Technologies in Education*. Geelong, Vic. Centre for Studies in Information Technologies and Education, Deakin University.

Bigum, C., Green, B., Fitzclarence, L. & Kenway, J. (1993) *Multimedia and monstrosities: Reinventing computing in schools again?* Paper presented at the 11th Annual Computers in Education Conference (28 June–1 July), Penrith, NSW.

Biklen, D., Ferguson, D. & Ford, A. (eds) (1989) *Schooling and Disability: (NSSE Year-book Series)*. Chicago: University of Chicago Press.

Birkerts, S. (1994) *The Gutenberg Elegies: The Art of Reading in an Electronic Age*. Boston: Faber & Faber.

Blackburn, J. E. & Powell, W. C. (1976) *One at a Time. All at Once: The Creative Teacher's Guide to Individualized Instruction Without Anarchy*. Glenview, IL: Scott, Foresman.

Blanck, G. (1990) Vygotsky: The man and his cause. In L. C. Moll (ed.) *Vygotsky and Education. New York: Cambridge University Press.*

Blasi, A. (1980) Bridging moral cognition and moral action: A critical review of the literature. *Psychological Bulletin*, **88**, 1–45.

Bleichrodt, N. & Drenth, P. J. D. (1991) *Contemporary Issues in Cross-Cultural Psychology*. Amsterdam/Lisse: Swets & Zeitlinger.

Block, J. H. (ed.) (1971) *Mastery Learning: Theory and Practice*. New York: Holt, Rinehart & Winston.

Bloom, B. S. (ed.) (1956) *Taxonomy of Educational Objectives. Handbook 1: Cognitive Domain*. London: Longman.

Bloom, B. S. (1984) The 2 sigma problem: The search for methods of group instruction as effective as one-to-one tutoring. *Educational Researcher*, **13**, 4–16.

Bloom, B. S. (1987) A response to Slavin's mastery learning reconsidered. *Review of Educational Research*, **57**, 507–8.

Bloom, B. S., Hastings, J. T. & Madaus, G. F. (1971) *Handbook on Formative and Summative Evaluation of Learning*. New York: McGraw-Hill.

Bloom, B. S., Krathwohl, D. R. & Masia, B. B. (1964) *Taxonomy of Educational Objectives. Book 2 Affective Domain.* London: Longman.

Bloom, B. S., Madaus, G. F. & Hastings, J. T. (1981) *Evaluation to Improve Learning*. New York: McGraw-Hill.

Blumenfeld, P. C. (1992) Classroom learning and motivation: Clarifying and expanding goal theory. *Journal of Educational Psychology*, **84**, 272–81.

Boag, C. (1989) What makes a great teacher? *The Bulletin*, 18 July, 46–54.

Boekarts, M. (1995) Self-regulated learning: Bridging the gap between metacognitive and metamotivation theories. *Educational Psychologist*, **30**, 195–200.

Boggiano, A. K. & Barrett, M. (1992) Gender differences in depression in children as a function of motivational orientation. *Sex Roles*, **26**, 11–17.

Bornholt, L. J. & Cooney, G. H. (1993) How good am I at school work and compared with whom? *Australian Journal of Education*, **37**, 69–76.

Boud, D. (1981) Towards student responsibility for learning. In D. Boud (ed.) *Developing Student Autonomy in Learning pages*. London: Kogan Paul.

Boud, D. (1985) *Studies in Self Assessment. Implications for Teachers in Higher Education*. Occasional Publication No. 26. Sydney: Tertiary Education Research Centre, The University of New South Wales.

Bourke, S. (1989) Teaching methods. In P. Langford (ed.) *Educational Psychology. An Australian Perspective*. Sydney: Longman Cheshire.

Bower, G. H., Clark, M., Lesgold, A. M. & Winzenz, D. (1969) Hierarchical retrieval schemes in recall of categorized word lists. *Journal of Verbal Learning and Verbal Behaviour*, **8**, 323–43.

Boyd, R. (1993) Gender differences in gifts and/or talents. *International Journal of Educational Research*, **19**, 51–64.

Boylan, C., Battersby, D., Wallace, A. & Retallick, J. (1991) Understanding exemplary teaching. *SET Research Information for Teachers*, number 1, item 13.

Brady, L. (1985) *Models and Methods of Teaching*. Sydney: Prentice Hall Australia.

Braebeck, M. (1982) Moral judgement: Theory and research on differences between males and females. *Developmental Review*, **3**, 274–91.

Braggett, E. J. (1985) *Education of Gifted and Talented Children. Australian Provision*. Canberra: Commonwealth Schools Commission.

Braggett, E. (1987) Recent developments in provision for the gifted: Across Australia. In J. Relich & J. Ward (eds) *Academically Gifted-Educationally Disadvantaged? Providing for the Intellectually Gifted and Talented*. Sydney: NSWIER.

Brainerd, C. J. (1978) *Piaget's Theory of Intelligence*. Englewood Cliffs, NJ: Prentice Hall.

Brainin, S. S. (1985) Mediating learning: Pedagogic issues in the improvement of cognitive functioning. In E. W. Gordon (ed.) *Review of Research in Education (Vol. 12)*. New York: AERA.

Brandt, R. S. (1986) On creativity and thinking skills: A conversation with David Perkins. *Educational Leadership*, **43**, 12–18.

Brandt, R. (1990) Overview. *Educational Leadership*, **48**, 3.

Bransgrove, T. (1990) Responsibilities of Australian teachers in law: Some implications for teacher training. In M. Bezzina & J. Butcher (eds) *The Changing Face of Professional Education. Collected Papers of the AARE Annual Conference, Sydney University*, 1990. Sydney: AARE.

Brattesani, K. A., Weinstein, R. S. & Marshall, H. H. (1984) Student perceptions of differential teacher treatments as moderators of teacher expectations effects. *Journal of Educational Psychology*, **76**, 238–47.

Braun, C. (1976) Teacher expectations: social psychological dynamics. *Review of Educational Research*, **46**, 185–213.

Brentnall, R. & Hodge, A. (1984) *Policies on Multicultural Education in Australia: An Overview*. Sydney: Sydney CAE.

Brim, O. G. & Kagan, J. (eds) (1980) *Constancy and Change in Human Development*. Cambridge, MA: Harvard University Press.

Broadbent, C. (1989) Personality and learning. In P. Langford (ed.) *Educational Psychology. An Australian Perspective*. Sydney: Longman Cheshire.

Bromley, H. (1992) Culture, power and educational computing. In C. Bigum & B. Green (eds) *Understanding the New Information Technologies in Education*. Geelong, Vic. Centre for Studies in Information Technologies and Education, Deakin University.

Brookhart, S. M. & Freeman, D. J. (1992) Characteristics of entering teacher candidates. *Review of Educational Research*, **62**, 37–60.

Brooks, J. G. (1990, Feb) Teachers and students: Constructivists forging new connections. *Educational Leadership*, **48**, 69–71.

Brooks-Gunn, J. & Furstenberg, F. F. (1989) Adolescent Sexual Behavior. *American Psychologist*, **44**, 249–57.

Brooks-Gunn, J. & Petersen, A. C. (eds) (1983) *Girls at Puberty. Biological and Psychosocial Perspectives*. New York: Plenum Press.

Brooks-Gunn, J. & Warren, M. P. (1989) The psychological significance of secondary sex characteristics in 9- to 11-year old girls. *Child Development*, **59**, 161–69.

Brophy, J. (1981) Teacher praise: A functional analysis. *Review of Educational Research*, **51**, 5–32.

Brophy, J. (1983) Research on the self-fulfilling prophecy and teacher expectations. *Journal of Educational Psychology*, **75**, 631–61.

Brophy, J. (1985a) Teacher–student interactions. In J. Dusek (ed.) *Teacher Expectancies*. Hillsdale, NJ: Erlbaum.

Brophy, J. (1985b) Teachers' expectations, motives, and goals for working with problem students. In C. Ames & R. Ames (eds) *Research on Motivation in Education: Vol. 2. The Classroom Milieu*. Orlando: Academic Press.

Brophy, J. (1986) Teacher influences on student achievement. *American Psychologist*, **41**, 1069–77.

Brophy, J. (1987) Synthesis of research on strategies for motivating students to learn. *Educational Leadership*, **45**, 40–8.

Brophy, J. (1988) Research linking teacher behavior to student achievement: Potential implications for instruction of Chapter 1 students. *Educational Psychologist*, **23**, 235–86.

Brophy, J. & Evertson, C. (1976) *Learning from Teaching: A Developmental Perspective*. Boston: Allyn & Bacon.

Brophy, J. & Good, T. L. (1986) Teacher behavior and student achievement. In M. C. Wittrock (ed.) *Handbook of Research on Teaching*. New York: Macmillan.

Brown, A. L. (1988) Motivation to learn and understand: On taking charge of one's learning. *Cognition and Instruction*, **5**, 311–22.

Brown, A. L. & Campione, J. C. (1986) Psychological theory and the study of learning disabilities. *American Psychologist*, **41**, 1059–68.

Brown, J. S., Collins, A. & Duguid, P. (1989) Situated cognition and the culture of learning. *Educational Researcher*, **18**, 32–42.

Brown, A. L., & Palincsar, A. S. (1989) Guided, coooperative learning and individual knowledge acquisition. In L. B. Resnick (ed.) *Knowing, Learning, and Instruction: Essays in Honor of Robert Glaser*. Hillsdale, NJ: Erlbaum & Associates: 393–451.

Brown, M. J. (1982) The Victorian accelerated secondary programme with particular attention to mathematics. *Unicorn*, **8**, 273–80.

Brown, S. K. (1983) The sex factor in the selection of intellectually talented youth. *Education Research and Perspectives*, **10**, 85–103.

Bruckman, A. & Resnick, M. (1996) The MediaMOO project. In Y. Kafai & M. Resnick (eds) *Constructionism in Practice*. New Jersey: Lawrence Erlbaum.

Bruckman, A. (1996) E-mail address: asb@media-lab.mit.edu.

Bruner, J. S. (1960) *The Process of Education*. Cambridge, Massachusetts: Harvard University Press.

Bruner, J. S. (1961) The act of discovery. *Harvard Educational Review*, **31**, 21–32.

Bruner, J. S. (1966) *Toward a Theory of Instruction*. London: Belnap Press.

Bruner, J. S. (1971) *Relevance of Education*. New York: Norton.

Bruner, J. S. (1974) *Beyond the Information Given*. London: George Allen & Unwin.

Bruner, J. S. (1976) The will to learn. In M. L. Silberman, J. S. Allender & J. M. Yanoff (eds) *Real Learning. A Sourcebook for Teachers*. Boston: Little, Brown & Co.

Bruner, J. S. (1985) Models of the learner. *Educational Researcher*, **14**, 5–8.

Bryk, A. S. & Hermanson, K. L. (1993) Educational indicator systems: Observations on their structure, interpretation, and use. *Review of Research in Education*, **19**, 451–84.

Buck, R. & Green, Y. (1993) *Teacher–researcher collaboration to enhance student motivation and learning*. Paper presented at the annual meeting of the American Educational Research Association in Atlanta, April.

Buchanan, C.M., Eccles, J. S. & Becker, J. B. (1992) Are adolescents the victims of raging hormones? Evidence for the activational effects of hormones on moods and behavior at adolescence. *Psychological Bulletin*, **111**, 62–107.

Bullivant, B. M. (1986) Are Anglo Australian students becoming the new self-deprived in comparison with ethnics? New evidence challenges conventional wisdom. In *'Theory, Structure and Action in Education'*, papers of the Annual Conference of the Australian Association for Research in Education, Ormond College, University of Melbourne, November 1986. Melbourne: Australian Association for Research in Education.

Bullivant, B. M. (1988a) Missing the empirical forest for the ideological trees: A commentary on Kalantzis and Cope. *Journal of Intercultural Studies*, **9**, 59–69.

Bullivant, B. M. (1988b) The ethnic success ethic challenges conventional wisdom about immigrant disadvantages in education. *Australian Journal of Education*, **32**, 223–43.

Bushnell, J. A., Wells, J. E., Hornblow, A. R., Oakley-Brown, M.

A., et al. (1990) Prevalence of three bulimia syndromes in the general population. *Psychological Medicine*, **20**, 671–80.

Bushnell, J. A., Wells, J. E., McKenzie, J. M., Hornblow, A. R., et al. (1994) Bulimia comorbidity in the general population and in the clinic. *Psychological Medicine*, **24**, 605–11.

Business Week (1989) Computers in school a loser? Or a lost opportunity? *Business Week*, 17 July, 108–9.

Butler, D. L. & Winne, P. H. (1995) Feedback and self-regulated learning: A theoretical synthesis. *Review of Educational Research*, **65**, 245–81.

Butler, K. (1986) *Learning and Teaching Style*. Australia: Hawker Brownlow.

Butler, R. (1987) Task-involving and ego-involving properties of evaluation: effects of different feedback conditions on motivational perceptions, interest, and performance. *Journal of Educational Psychology*, **79**, 474–82.

Butler, R. (1988) Enhancing and undermining intrinsic motivation: the effects of task-involving and ego-involving evaluation on interest and performance. *British Journal of Educational Psychology*, **58**, 1–14.

Butler, S. (1990) *The Exceptional Child*. Sydney: Harcourt Brace Jovanovich.

Byrne, D. G., Byrne, A. E. & Reinhart, M. I. (1993) Psychosocial correlates of adolescent cigarette smoking: Personality or environment. *Australian Journal of Psychology*, **45**, 87–95.

Cahill, D. & Ewen, J. (1987) Ethnic Youth: Their Assets and Aspirations. Canberra: AGPS.

Cairns, L. (1995) Analysis and modification of behavior. In L. W. Anderson (ed.) *International Encyclopedia of Teaching and Teacher Education*, 2nd edn. Tarrytown, NY: Pergamon: 227–31.

Cambourne, B. & Turbill, J. (1990) Assessment in whole language classrooms: Theory into practice: *Elementary School Journal*, **90**, 337–49.

Campbell, S. J. et al. (1992) *Unlocking Australia's Language Potential. Profiles of Nine Key Languages in Australia: Vol.1. Arabic*. Deakin: The National Languages and Literacy Institute of Australia.

Campbell, W. J. (1980) What Australian society expects of its schools, teachers and teaching. *Education*, **21**, 156–7.

Cameron, J., & Pierce, W. D. (1994) Reinforcement, reward, and intrinsic motivation: A meta–analysis. *Review of Educational Research*, **64**, 363–423.

Cameron, J. & Pierce, W. D. (1996) The debate about rewards and intrinsic motivation: Protests and accusations do not alter the results. *Review of Educational Research*, **66**, 39–51.

Canfield, R. L. & Ceci, S. J. (1992) Integrating learning into a theory of intellectual development. In R. J. Sternberg & C. A. Berg (eds) *Intellectual Development*. New York: Cambridge University Press.

Canter, L. (1990) Assertive discipline: More than names on a board and marbles in a jar. In *Educational Psychology 90/91 Annual Editions*. Connecticut: Duskin.

Canter, L. & Canter, M. (1976) *Assertive Discipline: A Take Charge Approach for Today's Educator*. Seal Beach, CA: Canter & Associates.

Canter, L. & Canter, M. (1992) *Assertive Discipline: Positive Behaviour Management for Today's Classroom*. Santa Monica, CA: Lee Canter & Associates.

Capuzzi, D. (1989) *Adolescent Suicide Prevention*. Ann Arbor, MI: ERIC Counselling and Personnel Services Clearing House.

Care, E. (1996) *Implications of learning style and interests for educational programs*. Paper presented at the 31st Annual Conference of the Australian Psychological Society, Sydney, 25–29 September.

Carey, S. (1987) Theory change in childhood. In B. Inhelder, D. de Caprona & A. Cornu Wells (eds) *Piaget Today*. London: Lawrence Erlbaum.

Carney, R. N., Levin, J. R. & Morrison, C. R. (1988) Mnemonic learning of artists and their paintings. *American Educational Research Journal*, **25**, 107–25.

Carr, K. & Ritchie, G. (1991) Evaluating learning in mathematics. *SET Research Information for Teachers*, item 15, number 1.

Carrier, C. A. & Jonassen, D. H (1988) Adapting courseware to accommodate individual differences. In D. H. Jonassen (ed.) *Instructional Designs for Instructional Courseware*. Hillsdale, NJ: Lawrence Erlbaum.

Carrier, C. A. & Sales, G. C. (1987) Pair versus individual work on the acquisition of concepts in a computer-based instructional lesson. *Journal of Computer-Based Instruction*, **14**, 11–17.

Carroll, J. B. (1971) Problems of measurement related to the concept of learning for mastery, in J. H. Block (ed), *Mastery Learning: Theory and Practice*. New York: Holt, Rinehart & Winston.

Carver, C. S., Scheier, M. F. & Weintraub, J. K. (1989) Assessing coping strategies: A theoretically based approach. *Journal of Personality and Social Psychology*, **56**, 267–83.

Case, R. (1985a) *Intellectual Development: A Systematic Reinterpretation*. New York: Academic Press.

Case, R. (1985b) *Intellectual Development. Birth to Adulthood*. Orlando: Academic Press.

Case, R. (1992) Neo-Piagetian theories of child development. In R. J. Sternberg & C. A. Berg (eds) *Intellectual Development*. NY: Cambridge University Press.

Casey, W., Jones, D., Kugler, B. & Watkins, B. (1988) Integration of Down's syndrome children in the primary school: a longitudinal study of cognitive development and academic attainments. *British Journal of Educational Psychology*, **587**, 279–86.

Castles, S., Kalantzis, M., Cope, B. & Morrissey, M. (1988) *Mistaken Identity. Multiculturalism and the Demise of Nationalism in Australia*. Sydney: Pluto Press.

Catania, A. C. (1980) Operant Theory: Skinner. In G. M. Gazda & R. J. Corsini (eds) Theories of Learning. Itasca, IL: F. E. Peacock.

Cavior, N. & Dokecki, P. (1973) Physical attractiveness, perceived attitude similarity, and adacemic achievement as contributors to interpersonal attraction among adolescents. *Developmental Psychology*, **9**, 44–54.

Cavior, N. & Lombardi, D. A. (1973) Developmental aspects of judgment of physical attractiveness in children. *Developmental Psychology*, **8**, 67–71.

Cazden, C. B. (1990) Differential treatment in New Zealand: Reflections on research in minority education. *Teaching and Teacher Education*, **6**, 291–303.

Cellerier, G. (1987) Structures and functions. In B. Inhelder, D. de Caprona & A. Cornu-Wells (eds) *Piaget Today*. London: Lawrence Erlbaum.

Center, Y., Ward, J., Ferguson, C., Conway, B. & Linfoot, K. (1989) *The integration of children with disabilities into regular schools: A naturalistic study*. Stage 2 Report. Macquarie University: Special Education Centre.

Chambers, S. M. & Clarke, V. A. (1987). Is inequity cumulative?

The relationship between disadvantaged group membership and students' computing experience, knowledge, attitudes and intentions. *Journal of Education Computing Research*, **3**, 495–518.

Chapman, J. W. (1988) Learning disabled children's self-concepts. *Review of Educational Research*, **58**, 347–71.

Charles, C. M. (1992) *Building Classroom Discipline*, 4th edn. White Plains, NY: Longman.

Chen, M. (1986) Gender and computers: The beneficial effects of experience on attitudes. *Journal of Educational Computing Research*, **2**, 265–82.

Chess, S. & Gordon, S. G. (1984) Psychosocial development and human variance. In E.W. Gordon (ed.) *Review of Research in Education* (Vol. 11). Washington: AERA.

Chi, M. T. H., Glaser, R. & Rees, E. (1982) Expertise in problem solving. In R. Sternberg (ed.) *Advances in the Psychology of Human Intelligence* (Vol. 1). Hillsdale, NJ: Lawrence Erlbaum.

Chinn, C. A. & Brewer, W. F. (1993) The role of anomalous data in knowledge acquisition: A theoretical framework and implications for science instruction. *Review of Educational Research*, **63**, 1–49.

Clarizio, H. F., Craig, R. C. & Mehrens, W. A. (eds) (1977) *Contemporary Issues in Educational Psychology*, 3rd edn. Boston: Allyn & Bacon.

Clarke, A. M. (1984) Early experience and cognitive development. In E. W. Gordon (ed) *Review of Research in Education (Vol. 11)*. Washington: AERA.

Clarke, V. (1987) Why are girls under-represented? A study of primary school children. *Australian Educational Computing*, **2**, 39–48.

Clarke, V. A. (1990) Sex differences in computing participation: Concerns, extent, reasons and strategies. *Australian Journal of Education*, **34**, 52–66.

Clayborne, B. M. (1985) Parents' expectations for their children's computer achievement. In *The Computing Teacher*, February, 47.

Clements, D. H. & Nastasi, B. (1988) Social and cognitive interactions in educational computer environments. *American Educational Research Journal*, **25**, 87–106.

Clyne, M. (1983) Bilingual education as a model for community languages in primary schools. *Journal of Intercultural Studies*, **4**, 23–35.

Clyne, M. (1988) Bilingual education. What we can learn from the past? *Australian Journal of Education*, **32**, 95–114.

Coates, B., Pusser, H. E. & Goodman, I. (1976) The influence of 'Sesame Street' and 'Mister Rogers' Neighborhood' on children's social behavior in the preschool. *Child Development*, **47**, 138–44.

Cobb, J. A. (1972) Relationship of discrete classroom behaviors to fourth-grade academic achievement. *Journal of Educational Psychology*, **63**, 74–80.

Cobb, P. (1994) Where is the mind? Constructivist and sociocultural perspectives on mathematical development. *Educational Researcher*, **23**, 13–20.

Cohen, E. (1994a) *Designing Group Work: Strategies for the Heterogeneous Classroom*, 2nd edn. NY: Teachers College Press.

Cohen, E. G. (1982) Expectation states and interracial interaction in school settings. *Annual Review of Sociology*, **8**, 209–35.

Cohen, E. G. (1986) *Designing Groupwork: Strategies for the Heterogeneous Classroom*. New York: Teacher's College Press.

Cohen, E. G. (1994b) Restructuring the classroom: Conditions for productive small groups. *Review of Educational Research*, **64**, 1–35.

Coladarci, T. (1983) High-school dropout among native Americans. *Journal of American Indian Education*, **23**, 15–22.

Cole, A. (1989) The impact of external information on depressive cognitions of severely disturbed people. *Dissertation Abstracts International*, Vol. 50 (5-B) 2148, November.

Cole, D. A., Vandercook, T. & Rynders, J. (1988) Comparison of two peer interaction programs: Children with and without severe disabilities. *American Educational Research Journal*, **25**, 415–39.

Cole, P. G. & Chan, L. K. S. (1987) *Teaching Principles and Practice*. Sydney: Prentice Hall Australia.

Cole, P. G. & Chan, L. K. S. (1990) *Methods and Strategies for Special Education*. Sydney: Prentice Hall Australia.

Collins, A. (1991) Cognitive apprenticeship and instructional technology. In L. Idol & B. F. Jones (eds) *Educational Values and Cognitive Instruction: Implications for Reform*. Hillsdale, NJ: Lawrence Erlbaum.

Collins. A., Brown, J.S. & Newman, S.E. (1991) Cognitive apprenticeship: Teaching the craft of reading, writing and mathematics. In L. B. Resnick (ed.) *Cognition and Instruction: Issues and Agendas*. Hillsdale, NJ: Lawrence Erlbaum.<+>

Collins, J. K. & Plahn, M. R. (1988) Recognition accuracy, stereotypic preference, aversion, and subjective judgment of body appearance in adolescents and young adults. *Journal of Youth and Adolescence*, **17**, 317–34.

Collis, B. (1987) Research windows. *The Computing Teacher*, **15**, 42.

Collis, K. (1989) Evaluation. In P. Langford (ed.) *Educational Psychology. An Australian Perspective*. Sydney: Longman Cheshire.

Collis, K. & Biggs, J. (1986) Using the SOLO taxonomy. *SET Research Information for Teachers*, number 1, item 3.

Commonwealth Schools Commission (1983). *Participation and Equity in Australian Schools: The Goal of Full Secondary Education*. Canberra: AGPS.

Computer Education Unit (1985) Handle with Care. NSW Department of Education.

Conger, J. J. (1977) *Adolescence and Youth. Psychological Development in a Changing World*, 2nd edn. New York: Harper & Row.

Conklin, K. R. (1976) Wholes and parts in teaching. In M. L. Silberman, J. S. Allender & J. M. Yanoff (eds) *Real Learning. A Sourcebook for Teachers*. Boston: Little, Brown & Co.

Conner, K. et al. (1985) Using formative testing at the classroom, school, and district levels. *Educational Leadership*, **43**, 63–7.

Conners, R., Nettle, E. & Placing, K. (1990) Learning to become a teacher: An analysis of student teachers' perspectives on teaching and their developing craft knowledge. In M. Bezzina & J. Butcher (eds) *The Changing Face of Professional Education. Collected Papers of the AARE Annual Conference, Sydney University, 1990*. Sydney: AARE.

Connolly, K. & Dalgleish, M. (1989) The emergence of a tool-using skill in infancy. *Developmental Psychology*, **25**, 894–912.

Constantini, A. F. & Hoving, K. L. (1973) The effectiveness of reward and punishment contingencies on response inhibition. *Journal of Experimental Child Psychology*, **16**, 484–94.

Cooley, M. (1992) Human-centred education. In C. Bigum & B. Green (eds) *Understanding the New Information Technologies in Education*. Geelong, Vic. Centre for Studies in Information

Technologies and Education; Deakin University.

Cooper, H. & Tom, D. Y. H. (1984) Socioeconomic status and ethnic group differences in achievement motivation. In R. Ames & C. Ames (eds) *Research on Motivation in Education: Vol. 1. Student Motivation.* Orlando: Academic Press.

Cooper, J. M. (ed.) (1986) *Classroom Teaching Skills*, 3rd edn. Lexington, MA: D.C. Heath.

Copeland, A. P. & Weissbrod, C. S. (1980) Effects of modeling on behavior related to hyperactivity. *Journal of Educational Psychology*, **71**, 875–83.

Copeland, W. D. (1987) Classroom management and student teachers' cognitive abilities: A relationship. *American Educational Research Journal*, **24**, 219–36.

Copen, P. (1995) Connecting classrooms through telecommunications. *Educational Leadership*, **53**, 2, 44–7.

Corbin, C. B. (ed.) (1980) *A Textbook of Motor Development.* Dubuque, Iowa: Wm. C. Brown.

Corkill, A. J. (1992) Advance organizers: Facilitators of recall. *Educational Psychology Review*, **4**, 33–67.

Corno, L. (1992) Encouraging students to take responsibility for learning and performance. *The Elementary School Journal*, **93**, 69–83.

Corno, L. & Mandinach, E. B. (1983) The role of cognitive engagement in classroom learning and motivation. *Educational Psychologist*, **18**, 88–108.

Corno, L. & Rohrkemper, M. M. (1985) The intrinsic motivation to learn in classrooms. In C. Ames & R. Ames (eds) *Research on Motivation in Education: Vol. 2. The Classroom Milieu.* Orlando: Academic Press.

Corno, L. & Snow, R. E. (1986) Adapting teaching to individual differences among learners. In M. C. Wittrock (ed.) *Handbook of Research on Teaching*, 3rd edn. New York: Macmillan.

Corson, D. (1993) Restructuring minority schooling. *Australian Journal of Education*, **37**, 46–68.

Costa, A. L. (1984) Mediating the metacognitive. *Educational Leadership*, **42**, 57–62.

Costa, A. L. & Marzano, R. (1987) Teaching the language of thinking. *Educational Leadership*, **45**, 29–33.

Cotton, J. L. & Cook, M. S. (1982) Meta-analysis and the effects of various reward systems: Some different conclusions from Johnson et al. *Psychological Bulletin*, **92**, 176–83.

Covington, M. V. (1984) The motive for self-worth. In R. Ames & C. Ames (eds) *Research on Motivation in Education: Vol. 1. Student Motivation.* Orlando: Academic Press.

Covington, M. V. (1992) *Making the Grade. A Self-Worth Perspective on Motivation and School Reform.* New York: Cambridge University Press.

Covington, M. V. & Omelich, C. L. (1979). Effort: The double-edged sword in school achievement. *Journal of Educational Psychology*, **71**, 169–82.

Covington, M. V. & Omelich, C. L. (1984a) An empirical examination of Weiner's critique of attribution research. *Journal of Educational Psychology*, **76**, 1214–25.

Covington, M. V. & Omelich, C. L. (1984b) Task-oriented versus competitive learning structures: Motivational and performance consequences. *Journal of Educational Psychology*, **76**, 1038–50.

Covington, M. V. & Omelich, C. L. (1987) 'I knew it cold before the exam': A test of the anxiety-blockage hypothesis. *Journal of Educational Psychology*, **79**, 393–400.

Cowan, P. A. (1978) *Piaget: With Feeling. Cognitive, Social and Emotional Dimensions.* New York: Holt, Rinehart & Winston.

Cramer, P. (1980) The development of sexual identity. *Journal of Personality Assessment*, **44**, 601–12.

Cravioto, J. & DeLicardie, E. R. (1975) Environmental and learning deprivation in children with learning disabilities. In W. M. Cruickshank & D. P. Hallahan, *Perceptual and Learning Disabilities in Children (Vol. 2).* New York: Syracuse University Press.

Crawford, J. (1989) Teaching effectiveness in Chapter 1 classrooms. *The Elementary School Journal*, **90**, 33–46.

Crawley, P. (1996) Personal communication with Mr Peter Crawley, Principal, Trinity Grammar, Kew, Melbourne.

Crooks, T. J. (1988) The impact of classroom evaluation practices on students. *Review of Educational Research*, **58**, 438–81.

Crooks, T. J. & Mahalski, P. A. (1986) Relationships among assessment practices, study methods, and grades obtained. In J. Jones & M. Horsburgh (eds) *Research and Development in Higher Education (Vol. 8).* Sydney: Higher Education Research and Development Society of Australasia.

Cropley, A. J. (1993a) Creativity as an element of giftedness. *International Journal of Educational Research*, **19**, 17–30.

Cropley, A. J. (1993b) Giftedness: Recent thinking. *International Journal of Educational Research*, **19**, 89–97.

Cruickshank, W. M., Hallahan, D. & Bice, H. V. (1976) The evaluation of intelligence. In W. M. Cruickshank (ed.) *Cerebral Palsy: A Developmental Disability*, 3rd edn. Syracuse, NY: Syracuse University Press.

Csikszentmihalyi, M. (1975) *Beyond Boredom and Anxiety.* San Francisco: Jossey-Bass.

Csikszentmihalyi, M. & Nakamura, J. (1989) The dynamics of intrinsic motivation: a study of adolescents. In C. Ames & R. Ames (eds) *Research on Motivation in Education: Vol. 3. Goals and Cognitions.* Orlando: Academic Press.

Curry, L. (1990) A critique of the research on learning styles. *Educational Leadership*, **48**, 51–5.

Cuthbert, A. (1988) The use of computers in special school settings in Tasmania. In *Computers and the Realm of Ideas.* Vic. Commonwealth Schools Commission, Ministry of Education.

Cutler, A. B. (1993) *The first year of teaching: Developing a teacher persona.* Paper presented at the Annual Meeting of the American Educational Research Association, Atlanta, Georgia, April.

Cziko, G. A. (1992) The evaluation of bilingual education. From necessity and probability to possibility. *Educational Researcher*, **21**, 10–15.

Dall'Alba, G. (1986) Learning strategies and the learner's approach to a problem solving task. *Research in Science Education*, **16**, 11–20.

Dalton, D. W., Hannafin, M. J. & Hooper, S. (1989) The effects of individual versus cooperative computer-assisted instruction on student performance and attitudes. *Educational Technology Research and Development*, **37**, 15–24.

Dalton, J. (1985) *Adventures in Thinking.* Melbourne: Thomas Nelson.

Dalton, J. (1992) *Adventures in Thinking: Creative Thinking and Cooperative Talk in Small Groups.* South Melbourne, Australia: Thomas Nelson.

Damon, W. (1980) Patterns of change in children's social reasoning: A two-year longitudinal study. *Child Development*, **51**, 1010–17.

Damon, W. (1983) *Social and Personality Development.* New York: W. W. Norton.

Damon, W. (1984) Peer education: The untapped potential.

Journal of Applied Developmental Psychology, **5**, 331–43.

Damon, W. & Phelps, E. (1989) Critical distinctions among three approaches to peer education. *International Journal of Educational Research*, **13**, 9–19.

Daniel, W. A. (1983) Pubertal changes in adolescence. In J. Brooks-Gunn & A. C. Petersen (eds) *Girls at Puberty. Biological and Psychosocial Perspectives*. New York: Plenum.

Dansereau, D. F. (1985) Learning strategy research. In J. W. Segal, S. F. Chipman & R. Glaser (eds) *Thinking and Learning Skills (Vol. 1)*. Hillsdale, NJ: Lawrence Erlbaum: 209–39.

Dansereau, D. F. (1985) Learning strategy research. In J. W. Segal, S. F. Chipman & R. Glaser (eds) *Thinking and Learning Skills*: *Vol. 1. Relating Instruction to Research*, Hillsdale, NJ: Lawrence Erlbaum: 209–39.

Dansereau, D. F. (1988) Cooperative learning strategies. In C. E. Weinstein, E. T. Goetz & P. A. Alexander (eds) *Learning and Study Strategies*. San Diego, CA: Academic Press.

Dansereau, D. F., O'Donnell, A. M. & Lambiotte, J. G. (1988) Concept maps and scripted peer cooperation: interactive tools for improving science and technical education. Paper presented at the Annual Meeting of the American Educational Research Association, New Orleans, LA.

Darley, J. & Fazio, R. (1980) Expectancy confirmation processes arising in the social interaction sequence. *American Psychologist*, **35**, 867–81.

Dart, B. C. & Clarke, J. A. (1990) Modifying the learning environment of students to enhance personal learning. In M. Bezzina & J. Butcher (eds) *The Changing Face of Professional Education. Collected Papers of the AARE Annual Conference, Sydney University*, 1990. Sydney: AARE.

Dasen, P. R. (1972a) The development of conservation in Aboriginal children: A replication study. *International Journal of Psychology*, **7**, 75–85.

Dasen, P. R. (1972b) Cross-cultural Piagetian research: *A summary. Journal of Cross-Cultural Psychology*, **3**, 23–39.

Dasen, P. R. (1974) The influence of ecology, culture and European contact on cognitive development in Australian Aborigines. In J. W. Berry & P. R. Dasen (eds) *Culture and Cognition*. London: Methuen.

Dasen, P. R. (1975) Concrete operational development in three cultures. *Journal of Cross-Cultural Psychology*, **6**, 156–72.

Dasen, P. R. & Heron, A. (1981) Cross-cultural tests of Piaget's theory. In H. C. Triandis & A. Heron (eds) *Handbook of Cross-Cultural Psychology: Vol. 4. Developmental Psychology*. Boston: Allyn & Bacon.

Dator, J. (1989) "What do `You' do when your robot bows, as your clone enters holographic MTV?" *Futures*, **2**, 361–65.

Davey, B. & McBride, S. (1986) Effects of question-generation training on reading comprehension. *Journal of Educational Psychology*, **78**, 256–62.

Davidson, G. R. (1984) Cognitive testing of educational minorities: A search for alternatives. *Australian Educational and Developmental Psychologist*, **1**, 39–53.

Davidson, M. & Firkin, J. (1985) *Who is Using the Computer in Our School?* Victorian Institute of Secondary Education.

Davidson, N. (1991) An overview of research on cooperative learning related to mathematics. *Journal for Research in Mathematics Education*, **22**, 362–5.

Davies, E. & Furnham, A. (1986) The dieting and body shape concerns of adolescent females. *Journal of Child Psychology and Psychiatry*, **27**, 417–28.

Davis, A. (1992) Suicidal behaviour among adolescents: Its nature and prevention (pp. 89–103). In R. Kosky, H.S. Eshkevari & G. Kneebone (eds) *Breaking Out: Challenges in Adolescent Mental Health in Australia*. Canberra: Australian Government Publishing Service.

Davies, E. & McGlade, M. (1982) Cultural values affecting the child at school. In J. Sherwood (ed.) *Aboriginal Education. Issues and Innovations. Perspectives in Multicultural Education (Vol. 2)*. North Perth: Creative Research.

Davis, H. L., & Pratt, C. (1995) The development of children's theory of mind: The working memory explanation. *Australian Journal of Psychology*, **47**, 25–31.

Davydov, V. (1995) The influence of L. S. Vygotsky on education theory, research, and practice (translated by S. T. Kerr). *Educational Researcher*, **24**, 12–21.

de Charms, R. (1968) *Personal Causation*. New York: Academic Press.

de Charms, R. (1972) Personal causation in the schools. *Journal of Applied Social Psychology*, **2**, 95–113.

de Charms, R. (1976) *Enhancing Motivation: Change in the Classroom*. New York: Irvington.

de Charms, R. (1984) Motivation enhancement in educational settings. In R. Ames & C. Ames (eds) *Research on Motivation in Education: Vol. 1. Student Motivation*. Orlando: Academic Press.

Deci, E. L. (1978) Applications of research on the effects of rewards. In M. R. Lepper & D. Greene (eds) *The Hidden Costs of Reward: New Perspectives on the Psychology of Human Motivation*. NJ: Lawrence Erlbaum.

Deci, E. L. & Ryan, R.M (1991) A motivational approach to self: Integration in personality. In R. A. Dienstbier (ed.) *Perspectives on motivation. Nebraska symposium on motivation, 1991* (pp. 237–88). Lincoln, NB: University of Nebraska Press.

Deci, E. L., Vallerand, R. J., Pelletier, L. G. & Ryan, R. M. (1991) Motivation and education: The self-determination perspective. *Educational Psychologist*, **26**, 325–46.

DeCorte, E. (1990) Learning with new information technologies in schools: Perspectives from the psychology of learning and instruction. *Journal of Computer Assisted Learning*, **6**, 69–87.

Dede, C. (1996) Distance learning—distributed learning: Making the transformation. *Learning and Leading with Technology*, **23**, 25–30.

de Lemos, M. M. (1969) The development of conservation in Aboriginal children. *International Journal of Psychology*, **4**, 255–69.

de Lemos, M. M. (1990) School entrance age in Australia: The current debate. In M. Bezzina & J. Butcher (eds) *The Changing Face of Professional Education. Collected Papers of the AARE Annual Conference, Sydney University, 1990*. Sydney: AARE.

Demetriou, A. (ed.) (1987) The neo-Piagetian theories of cognitive development: Toward an integration [Special Issue]. *International Journal of Psychology*, **22** (5/6).

Dempster, F. N. (1988) The spacing effect: A case study in the failure to apply the results of psychological research. *American Psychologist*, **43**, 627–34.

De Mott, R. M. (1982) Visual impairments. In N. Haring (ed.) *Exceptional Children and Youth*. Columbus, OH: Charles E. Merrill.

Dennis, W. (1973) *Children of the Creche*. New York: Appleton-Century-Crofts.

Department of Employment, Education and Training (1992) *Technology for Australian Schools. Interim Statement*. Canberra: AGPS.

Deparment of School Education (1991) *Who's Going to Teach My Child? A Guide for Parents of Children with Special Needs*. Sydney: Author.

Deregowski, J. B. (1980) Perception. In H. C. Triandis & A. Heron (eds) *Handbook of Cross-Cultural Psychology: Vol. 3. Basic Processes*. Boston: Allyn & Bacon.

Derry, S. J. (1989) Putting learning strategies to work. *Educational Leadership*, **46**, 4–10.

Derry, S. J. & Murphy, D. A. (1986) Designing systems that train learning ability: From theory to practice. *Review of Educational Research*, **56**, 1–39.

Deutsch, D. (1979) The improvement of children's oral reading through the use of teacher modeling. *Journal of Learning Disabilities*, **12**, 172–75.

Deutsch, M. (1979) Education and distributive justice: Some reflections on grading systems. *American Psychologist*, **34**, 391–401.

De Vos, G. A. (1968) Achievement and innovation in culture and personality. In E. Norbeck, D. Price-Williams & W. M. McCord (eds) *The Study of Personality. An Interdisciplinary Appraisal*. New York: Holt, Rinehart & Winston.

Diaz, R. M. (1983) Thought and two languages: The impact of bilingualism on cognitive development. In E. W. Gordon (ed.) *Review of Research in Education (Vol. 10)*. Washington: AERA.

Diaz, R. M., Neal, C. J. & Amaya-Williams, M. (1990) The social origins of self-regulation. In L. C. Moll (ed.) *Vygotsky and Education*. Cambridge: Cambridge University Press.

Diener, C. I. & Dweck, C. S. (1978) An analysis of learned helplessness: Continuous changes in performance, strategy, and achievement cognitions following failure. *Journal of Personality and Social Psychology*, **36**, 451–62.

Dillon, J. T. (1984) Research on questioning and discussion. *Educational Leadership*, **42**, 50–6.

DiMartino, E. C. (1989) The growth of moral judgement in young children: The role of culture. *Education*, **109**, 262–7.

Dion, K. (1972) Physical attractiveness and evaluation of children's transgressions. *Journal of Personality and Social Psychology*, **24**, 207–13.

diSessa, A. (1987) The third revolution in computers and education. *Journal of Research in Science Teaching*, **24**, 343–67.

Dockett, S. (1994) Pretend play and the young child's theory of mind. *Journal for Australian Research in Early Childhood Education*, **1**, 51–63.

Dockett, S. (1995a) Young children's play and language as clues to their developing theories of mind. *Journal for Australian Research in Early Childhood Education*, **2**, 61–72.

Dockett, S. (1995b). *'I tend to be dead and you make me alive': Developing Understandings through Sociodramatic Play*. Watson, ACT: Australian Early Childhood Association.

Dockett, S. (1996) Children as theorists. In M. Fleer (ed.) DAPcentrism: *Challenging Developmentally Appropriate Practice*. Watson, ACT: Australian Early Childhood Association.

Dockett, S. & Lambert, P. (1996) *The Importance of Play*. North Sydney: Board of Studies, NSW.

Docking, R. A. (1984) Writing school reports. *Unicorn*, **10**, 332–48.

Docking, R. A. (1986) Norm-referenced measurement and criterion-referenced measurement: A descriptive comparison. *Unicorn*, **12**, 40–6.

Dockterman, D. A. (1991) *Great Teaching in the One Computer Classroom*. Watertown, MA: Tom Snyder Productions, Inc.

Doherty, P. J. (1982) Strategies and initiatives for special education in New South Wales. A report of the Working Party on a Plan for Special Education in NSW.

Downes, T. (1985) Using databases in the classroom. In K. Duncan & D. Harris (eds) *Computers in Education. Amsterdam*: North-Holland, 265–9.

Downes, T. (1993) *Chasing the Rainbow*. Is IT Worth It? Paper presented at the 11th Annual Computers in Education Conference (28 June–1 July), Penrith, NSW.

Dowson, M. & McInerney, D. M. (1996a) Investigating relations between students' multiple achievement goals and key aspects of their cognitive engagement and academic performance. *Australian Journal of Psychology*, **48**, 99–100.

Dowson, M. & McInerney, D. M. (1996b) Psychological parameters of students' social and academic goals: A qualitative investigation. *Australian Journal of Psychology*, **48**, 100.

Doyle, W. (1980) *Classroom Management*. West Lafayette, IN: Kappa Delta Phi.

Doyle, W. (1983) Academic work. *Review of Educational Research*, **52**, 159–99.

Doyle, W. (1986) Classroom organisation and management. In M. C. Wittrock (ed.) *Handbook of Research on Teaching*. New York: Macmillan.

Doyle, W. & Rutherford, B. (1984) Classroom research on matching learning and teaching styles. *Theory into Practice*, **23**, 20–5.

Dowson, M., & McInerney, D. M. (1997) *Psychological parameters of students' social and academic goals: A qualitative investigation*. Paper presented at the Annual Meeting of the American Educational Research Association, Chicago, 24–28 March.

Draguns, J. G. (1979) Culture and personality. In A. J. Marsella, R. G. Tharp & T. J. Ciborowski (eds) *Perspectives on Cross-Cultural Psychology*. New York: Academic Press.

Dreikurs, R. (1968) *Psychology in the Classroom: A Manual for Teachers*, 2nd edn. New York: Harper & Row.

Dreikurs, R., Grunwald, B. & Pepper, F. (1982) *Maintaining Sanity in the Classroom*, 2nd edn. New York: Harper & Row.

Dreikurs, R. & Pearl, C. (1972) *Discipline Without Tears*. New York: Hawthorn Books.

Driver, R., Asoko, H., Leach, J., Mortimer, E. & Scott, P. (1994) Constructing scientific knowledge in the classroom. *Educational Researcher*, **23**, 5–12.

Dubois, P. A. & Schubert, J. G. (1986) Do your school policies provide equal access to computers? Are you sure? *Educational Leadership*, **43**, 41–4.

Duda, J. L. (1980) A Cross-Cultural Analysis of Achievement Motivation in Sport and in the Classroom. Unpublished doctoral dissertation, University of Illinois, Urbana-Champaign.

Dunkin, M. J. (1990a) Willingness to obtain student evaluations as a criterion of academic staff performance. *Higher Education Research and Development*, **9**, 51–60.

Dunkin, M. J. (1990b) The induction of academic staff to a university: Processes and products. *Higher Education Research and Development*, **10**, 47–66.

Dunkin, M. J. (1991) Orientations to teaching, induction experiences and background characteristics of university lecturers. *The Australian Educational Researcher*, **18**, 31–52.

Dunkin, M. J. & Precians, R. P. (1993) Award winning teachers' self-efficacy regarding teaching. *South Pacific Journal of*

Teacher Education, **21**, 5–14.

Dunn, R. (1990) Bias over substance: A critical analysis of Karvale and Forness report on modality-based instruction. *Exceptional Children*, **56**, 352–6.

Dunn, R., Beaudry, J. S. & Klavas, A. (1989) Survey of research on learning styles. *Educational Leadership*, **47**, 50–8.

Dunn, R., Bruno, J., Sklar, I. K., Zenhausen, R. & Beaudry, J. (1990) Effects of matching and mismatching minority developmental college students: Hemispheric preferences on mathematics scores. *Journal of Educational Research*, **83**, 283–8.

Dunn, R. S. & Dunn, K. J. (1972) Practical Approaches to Individualizing Instruction: *Contracts and Other Effective Teaching Strategies*. New York: Parker.

Dunn, R. S. & Dunn, K. J. (1979) Learning styles/teaching styles: Should they, can they, be matched? *Educational Leadership*, **36**, 238–44.

Dunn, R., Dunn, K. & Price, G. E. (1985) *Learning Style Inventory*. Price Systems, Box 1818, Lawrence, KS 66044–0067.

Dunn, R., Dunn, K. & Price, G. E. (1988) Diagnosing learning styles: A prescription for avoiding malpractice suits against school systems. *Phi Delta Kappan*, **58**, 418–20.

Dunphy, D. C. (1969) *Cliques, Crowds and Gangs*. Melbourne: Cheshire.

Durndell, A. et al. (1995) Gender and computing: Persisting differences. *Educational Research*, **37**, 219–27.

Dusek, J. B., & Joseph, G. (1983) The bases of teacher expectancies: a meta-analysis. *Journal of Educational Psychology*, **75**, 327–46.

Dweck, C. S. (1975) The role of expectations and attributions in the alleviation of learned helplessness. *Journal of Personality and Social Psychology*, **31**, 674–85.

Dweck, C. S. (1985) Intrinsic motivation, perceived control, and self-evaluation maintenance: an achievement goal analysis. In C. Ames & R. Ames (eds) *Research on Motivation in Education: Vol. 2. The Classroom Milieu*. Orlando: Academic Press.

Dweck, C. S. (1986) Motivational processes affecting learning. *American Psychologist*, **41**, 1040–8.

Dweck, C. S. & Repucci, N. D. (1973) Learned helplessness and reinforcement responsibility in children. *Journal of Personality and Social Psychology*, **25**, 109–16.

Dyson, A. H. (1989) *Multiple Worlds of Child Writers: Friends Learning to Write*. New York: Teachers College Press.

Ebel, R. L. (1977) Behavioral objectives: A close look. In H. F. Clarizio, R. C. Craig & W. A. Mehrens (eds) *Contemporary Issues in Educational Psychology*, 3rd edn. Boston: Allyn & Bacon.

Eberhard, D. R. (1989) American Indian education: A study of dropouts, 1980–1987. *Journal of American Indian Education*, **29**, 32–40.

Eccles, J. & Midgley, C. (1989) Stage-environment fit: Developmentally appropriate classrooms for young adolescents. In C. Ames & R. Ames (eds) *Research on Motivation in Education: Vol. 3. Goals and Cognitions*. New York: Academic Press.

Eccles, J., Midgley, C. & Adler, T. (1984) Grade-related changes in the school environment. In M. L. Maehr (ed.) *Advances in Motivation and Achievement. Greenwich*, CT: JAI Press.

Eccles, J. S. (1983) Expectancies, values, and academic behaviors. In J. T. Spence (ed.) *Achievement and Achievement Motivation* (pp.75–146). San Francisco: Freeman.

Eccles, J. S. et al. (1993) Development during adolescence. The impact of stage–environment fit on young adolescents' experiences in schools and in families. *American Psychologist*, **48**, 90–101.

Eccles, J., Wigfield, A., Harold, R. D. & Blumenfeld, P. (1993) Age and gender differences in children's self and task perceptions during elementary school. *Child Development*, **64**, 830–47.

Edwards, R. & Edwards, J. (1987) Corporal punishment. In A Thomas & J. Grimes (eds) *Children's Needs: Psychological Perspectives*. Washington, DC: National Association of School Psychologists: 127–31.

Edwards, S. & Woodward, H. (1989) Negotiating evaluation. In R. Parker (ed.) *Evaluation and Planning for Literacy and Learning: Proceedings of the Tenth Macarthur Reading/Language Symposium*. Sydney: University of Western Sydney, Macarthur.

Eggen, P. D. & Kauchak, D. P. (1988) *Strategies for Teachers: Information Processing Models in the Classroom*, 2nd edn. Englewood Cliffs, NJ: Prentice Hall.

Elawar, M. C. & Corno, L. (1985) A factorial experiment in teachers' written feedback on student homework: Changing teacher behavior a little rather than a lot. *Journal of Educational Psychology*, **77**, 162–73.

Elkind, D. (1974) *A Sympathetic Understanding of the Child: Birth to Sixteen*. New York: McGraw-Hill.

Elkind, D. (1977) One man in his time plays many psychosocial parts. Erik Erikson's Eight Ages of Man. In D. Elkind & D. C. Hetzel (eds) *Readings in Human Development: Contemporary Perspectives*. New York: Harper & Row.

Elkind, D. & Hetzel, D. C. (eds) (1977) *Readings in Human Development: Contemporary Perspectives*. New York: Harper & Row.

Elkins, J. (1987) Education without failure? Education for all? *The Exceptional Child*, **34**, 5–19.

Elkins, J. (1992) The Des English memorial lecture: Journeying. *Australasian Journal of Special Education*, **16**, 5–15.

Elliott, A. (1993) Enhancing thinking skills in computer supported contexts. *Australian Educational Computing*, **8**, ACEC '93 Edition, 81–4.

Elliott, E. S. & Dweck, C. S. (1988) Goals: An approach to motivation and achievement. *Journal of Personality and Social Psychology*, **54**, 5–12.

Emmer, E. T., Evertson, C. M., Sanford, J. P., Clements, B. S. & Worsham, M. E. (1989) *Classroom Management for Secondary Teachers*, 2nd edn. Englewood Cliffs, NJ: Prentice Hall.

Enright, R. Lapsley, D., Harris, D. & Shawyer, D. (1983) Moral development interventions in early adolescence. *Theory into Practice*, **22**, 134–44.

Entwisle, D. R., Alexander, K. L., Cadigan, D. & Pallas, A. (1986) The schooling process in first grade: Two samples a decade apart. *American Educational Research Journal*, **23**, 587–613.

Entwistle, N. J. (1991) Cognitive style and learning. In K. Marjoribanks (ed.) *The Foundations of Students' Learning*. Oxford: Pergamon.

Epstein, J. L. (1985) Home and school connections in schools for the future: Implications of research on parental involvement. *Peabody Journal of Education*, **78**, 373–80.

Epstein, J. L. (1989) Family structures and student motivation: A developmental perspective. In C. Ames & R. Ames (eds) *Research in Motivation in Education: Vol.3. Goals and*

Cognitions. New York: Academic.

Ericson, D. P. & Ellett, F. S. Jr (1990) Taking student responsibility seriously. *Educational Researcher*, **19**, 3–10.

Erikson, E. H. (1963) *Childhood and Society*, 2nd edn, New York: Norton.

Erikson, E. H. (1968) *Identity: Youth and Crisis*. New York: W. W. Norton.

Eskin, M. (1992) Opinions about and reactions to suicide, and the social acceptance of a suicidal classmate among Turkish high school students. *The International Journal of Social Psychiatry*, **38**, 280–6.

Eskin, M. (1995) Adolescents' attitudes toward suicide and a suicidal peer: A comparison between Swedish and Turkish high school students. *Scandinavian Journal of Psychology*, **36**, 201–7.

Esveldt-Dawson, K. & Kazdin, A. E. (1982) How to use Self-control. Lawrence, KS: H & H Enterprises.

Evans, E. D. (1970) *Adolescents. Readings in Behavior and Development*. Hillsdale, IL: Dryden.

Evans, G. T. & Poole, M. E. (1987) Adolescent concerns: A classification for life skills access. *Australian Journal of Education*, **31**, 55–72.

Evertson, C. M. & Emmer, E. T. (1982) Effective management at the beginning of the school year in junior high classes. *Journal of Educational Psychology*, **74**, 485–98.

Evertson, C. M., Emmer, E. T., Clements, B. S., Sanford, J. P. & Worsham, M. E. (1989) *Classroom Management for Elementary Teachers*, 2nd edn. Englewood Cliffs, NJ: Prentice Hall.

Evertson, C. M. (1995) Classroom rules and routines. In L. W. Anderson (ed.) *International Encyclopedia of Teaching and Teacher Education,* 2nd edn. Cambridge, UK: Pergamon.

Fairburn, C. G. & Beglin, S. J. (1990) Studies of the epidemiology of bulimia nervosa. *American Journal of Psychiatry*, **147**, 401–8.

Fagard, J. & Jacquet, A. (1989) Onset of bimanual coordination and symmetry versus asymmetry of movement. *Infant Behavior and Development*, **12**, 229–35.

Falchikov, N. & Boud, D. (1989) Student self-assessment in higher education: A meta-analysis. *Review of Educational Research*, **59**, 395–430.

Fanshawe, J. (1984) Possible characteristics of an effective teacher of adolescent Aboriginals? *Wikaru*, **12**, 72–98.

Farivar, S. & Webb, N. (1993) Helping—an essential skill for learning to solve problems in cooperative groups. *Cooperative Learning*, **13**, 20–3.

Farver, J. M. & Wimbarti, S. (1995) Indonesian toddlers' social play with their mothers and older siblings. *Child Development*, **66**, 1493–1503.

Faust, M. S. (1983) Alternative constructions of adolescent growth. In J. Brooks-Gunn & A. C. Petersen (eds) *Girls at Puberty. Biological and Psychosocial Perspectives*. New York: Plenum.

Feldhusen, J. F. (1989) Synthesis of research on gifted youth. *Educational Leadership*, **46**, 6–11.

Feldhusen, J. F (1995) Creativity: Teaching and assessing. In L. W. Anderson (ed.) *International Encyclopedia of Teaching and Teacher Education*, 2nd edn. Tarrytown, NY: Pergamon: 476–81.

Fennema, E. & Peterson, P. (1987) Effective teaching for boys and girls. The same or different? In D. C. Berliner & B. V. Rosenshine (eds) *Talks to Teachers*. New York: Random House.

Fennessy, D. (1982) *Primary teachers' assessment practices: Some implications for teacher training*. Paper presented at the 12th annual conference of the South Pacific Association for Teacher Education, Frankston, Victoria, Australia, July.

Ferguson, G. A. & Takane, Y. (1989) *Statistical Analysis in Psychology and Education*, 6th edn. New York: McGraw-Hill.

Fergusson, D. M., Horwood, L. J. & Shannon, F. T. (1982) Family ethnic composition, socio-economic factors and childhood disadvantage. *New Zealand Journal of Educational Studies*, **17**, 171–9.

Fergusson, D. M., Lloyd, M. & Horwood, L. J. (1991) Family ethnicity, social background and scholastic achievement—an eleven year longitudinal study. *New Zealand Journal of Educational Studies*, **26**, 49–63.

Feshbach, N. D. & Feshbach, S. (1987) Affective processes and academic achievement. *Child Development*, **58**, 1335–47.

Feshbach, S. & Singer, R. D. (1971) Television and Aggression. San Francisco: Jossey-Bass.

Fetterman, D. M. (1996) Videoconferencing on-line: Enhancing communication over the Internet. *Educational Researcher*, **25**, 4, 23–7.

Feuerstein, R. (1978) *Just a Minute . . . Let Me Think*. Baltimore, MD: University Park Press.

Feuerstein, R. (1980) *Instructional Enrichment*. Baltimore, Maryland: University Park Press.

Feuerstein, R. (1991). Cultural difference and cultural deprivation: Differential patterns of adaptability. In N. Bleichrodt & P. J. D. Drenth (eds) *Contemporary Issues in Cross-Cultural Psychology*. Amsterdam/Lisse: Swets & Zeitlinger.

Field, D. (1981) Can preschool children really learn to conserve? *Child Development*, **52**, 326–34.

Fields, B. A. (1990) The efficacy of the remedial/resource teacher model of service delivery. In M. Bezzina & J. Butcher (eds) The Changing Face of Professional Education. *Collected Papers of the AARE Annual Conference, Sydney University, 1990*. Sydney: AARE.

Finger, G. & Grimmett, G. (1993) Twelve issues to consider for managing and supporting future technology initiatives in schools. *Australian Educational Computing*, 8, ACEC '93 Edition, 85–92.

Fisher, A., Monsen, J., Moore, D. W. & Twiss, D. (1989) Increasing the social integration of hearing-impaired children in a mainstream school setting. *New Zealand Journal of Educational Studies*, **24**, 189–204.

Flavell, J. H. (1976) Metacognitive aspects of problem solving. In L. B. Resnick (ed.) *The Nature of Intelligence*. Hillsdale, NJ: Erlbaum.

Flavell, J. H. (1979) Metacognition and cognitive monitoring: A new era of cognitive developmental inquiry. *American Psychologist*, **34**, 906–11.

Flavell, J. H. (1985) Cognitive Development, 2nd edn. Englewood Cliffs, NJ: Prentice Hall.

Flavell, J. H., Miller, P. H. & Miller, S. A. (1993) *Cognitive Development*, 3rd edn. Englewood Cliffs, NJ: Prentice-Hall.

Floden, R. E. & Klinzing, H. G. (1990) What can research on teacher thinking contribute to teacher preparation? A second opinion. *Educational Researcher*, **19**, 15–20.

Flynn, J. R. (1996) What environmental factors affect intelligence: The relevance of IQ gains over time. In D. K. Detterman (ed.) *The Environment. Current Topics in Human Intelligence*, Vol. 5. Norwood, NJ: Ablex: 17–29.

Folds, R. (1987) *Whitefella School*. Sydney: Allen & Unwin.

Foltz, P. W. (1996) Comprehension, coherence, and strategies in hypertext. In J. Rouet, J. Levonen, A. Dillon & R. J. Spiro (eds), *Hypertext and Cognition*. New Jersey: Lawrence Erlbaum.

Fontana, D. (1977) *Personality and Education*. London: Open Books.

Fontana, D. (1986) *Teaching and Personality*. Oxford: Basil Blackwell.

Forman, G. E. (1980) Constructivism: Piaget. In G. M. Gazda & R. J. Corsini (eds) *Theories of Learning*. Itasca, IL: F. E. Peacock.

Forman, G. & Pufall, P. B. (1988) *Constructivism in the Computer Age*. Hillsdale, NJ: Lawrence Erlbaum.

Forsterling, F. (1985) Attributional retraining. *Psychological Bulletin*, **98**, 495–512.

Forsterling, F. (1986) Attributional conceptions in clinical psychology. *American Psychologist*, **41**, 275–85.

Fosnot, C. (1992) Constructing constructivism. In T.M. Duffy & D. H. Jonassen (eds) *Constructivism and the Technology of Instruction*. Hillsdale, NJ: Lawrence Erlbaum: 167–76.

Foster, L. E. (1988) *Diversity and Multicultural Education. A Sociological Perspective*. Sydney: Allen & Unwin.

Fraser, N. (1993) Hypermedia technology as a cross curriculum teacher tool. *Australian Educational Computing*, **8**, ACEC '93 Edition, 95–101.

Frasier, M. M. (1989) Poor and minority students can be gifted too. *Educational Leadership*, **46**, 16–18.

Frederiksen, N. (1984) Implications of cognitive theory for instruction in problem solving. *Review of Educational Research*, **54**, 363–407.

Freiberg, K. L. (ed.) (1992) *Educating Exceptional Children. Annual Editions*, 6th edn. Guilford, Connecticut: Duskin.

Freud, S. (1962a) *Two Short Accounts of Psychoanalysis*. Harmondsworth, Middlesex: Penguin Books.

Freud, S. (1962b) *A General Introduction to Psychoanalysis*. New York: Washington Square Press.

Freud, S. (1973) *An Outline of Psychoanalysis*. London: The Hogarth Press.

Friedrich, L. K. & Stein, A. H. (1975) Prosocial television and young children: The effects of verbal labeling and role playing on learning and behavior. *Child Development*. **46**, 27–38.

Friedrich-Cofer, L. K., Huston-Stein, A., Kipnis, D. M., Susman, E. J. & Clewett, A. S. (1979) Environmental enhancement of prosocial television content: Effects on interpersonal behavior, imaginative play, and self-regulation in a natural setting. *Developmental Psychology*, **15**, 637–46.

Frieze, I. H. & Snyder, H. N. (1980) Children's beliefs about the causes of success and failure in school settings. *Journal of Educational Psychology*, **72**, 186–96.

Frisch, R. E. (1983) Fatness, puberty, and fertility: The effects of nutrition and physical training on menarche and ovulation. In J. Brooks-Gunn & A. C. Petersen (eds) *Girls at Puberty. Biological and Psychosocial Perspectives*. New York: Plenum.

Frydenberg, E., & Lewis, R. (1990) How adolescents cope with different concerns: The development of the Adolescent Coping Checklist (ACC). *Psychological Test Bulletin*, **3**, 63–73.

Frydenberg, E., & Lewis, R. (1991). Adolescent coping: The different ways in which boys and girls cope. *Journal of Adolescence*, **14**, 119–33.

Frydenberg, E., & Lewis, R. (1993) Boys play sport and girls turn to others: Age, gender and ethnicity as determinants of coping. *Journal of Adolescence*, **16**, 253–66.

Fryer, M. (1987) Computers and Aboriginal Students. *Unicorn*, **13**, 1, 54–5.

Fuchs, D., Fuchs, L. S. & Fernstrom, P. (1993) A conservative approach to special education reform: Mainstreaming through transenvironmental programming and curriculum-based measurement. *American Educational Research Journal*, **30**, 149–77.

Fuller, F. G. (1969) Concerns of teachers: A developmental conceptualization. *American Educational Research Journal*, **6**, 207–26.

Fuller, F. & Brown, O. H. (1975) Becoming a teacher. In K. Ryan (ed.) *Teacher Education: The Seventy-fourth Yearbook of the National Society for the Study of Education (Part II)*. Chicago: University of Chicago Press.

Fyans, L. G., Maehr, M. L., Salili, F. & Desai, K. A. (1983) A cross-cultural exploration into the meaning of achievement. *Journal of Personality and Social Psychology*, **44**, 1000–13.

Gagne, E. D. (1985) *The Cognitive Psychology of School Learning*. Boston: Little, Brown & Co.

Gagne, R. M. (1966) The acquisition of knowledge. In R. C. Anderson & D. P. Ausubel (eds) *Readings in the Psychology of Cognition*. New York: Holt, Rinehart & Winston.

Gagne, R. M. (1970) *The Conditions of Learning*, 2nd edn. London: Holt, Rinehart & Winston.

Gagne, R. M. (1977) Learning hierarchies. In H. F. Clarizio, R. C. Craig & W. A. Mehrens (eds) *Contemporary Issues in Educational Psychology*, 3rd edn. Boston: Allyn & Bacon.

Gagne, R. M. & White, R. T. (1978) Memory structures and learning outcomes. *Review of Educational Research*, **48**, 187–222.

Gale, F., Jordan, D., McGill, G., McNamara, N. & Scott, C. (1987) Aboriginal education. In J. P. Keeves (ed.) *Australian Education. Review of Recent Research*. Sydney: Allen & Unwin.

Gall, M. D. (1984) Synthesis of research on teachers' questioning. *Educational Leadership*, **41**, 40–7.

Gall, M. D. & Artero-Boname, M. T. (1995) Questioning. In L. W. Anderson (ed.) *International Encyclopedia of Teaching and Teacher Education*, 2nd edn, NY: Pergamon: 242–8.

Gallagher, J. J. (1989) The impact of policies for handicapped children on future early education policy. *Phi Delta Kappan*, 121–3.

Gallagher, J. J. (1990) New patterns in special education. *Educational Researcher*, **19**, 34–6.

Gallagher, J. M. & Easley, J. A. Jr (eds) (1978) *Knowledge and Development: Vol. 2. Piaget and Education*. New York: Plenum.

Gallahue, D. L. (1976) *Motor Development and Movement Experiences for Young Children*. New York: John Wiley.

Gallahue, D. L. (1982) *Understanding Motor Development in Children*. New York: John Wiley.

Gallahue, D. L. (1989) *Understanding Motor Development: Infants, Children, Adolescents,* 2nd edn. Brisbane: John Wiley.

Gallimore, R. & Tharp, R. (1990) Teaching mind in society: Teaching, schooling and literate discourse. In L. C. Moll (ed.) *Vygotsky and Education*. New York: Cambridge University Press.

Galst, J. P. & White, M. A. (1976) The unhealthy persuader: The reinforcing value of television and children's purchase-influencing attempts at the supermarket. *Child Development*, **47**, 1089–96.

Gamoran, A. (1992) Is ability grouping equitable? *Educational Leadership*, **50**, 11–17.

Garcia, E. E. (1993) Language, culture, and education. *Review of Research in Education*, **19**, 51–98.

Gardner, H. (1983) Frames of Mind: *The Theory of Multiple Intelligences*. New York: Basic Books.

Gardner, H. (1993) *Multiple Intelligences: The Theory in Practice. A Reader*. New York: Basic Books.

Gardner, H. & Hatch, T. (1989) Multiple intelligences go to school. Educational implications. *Educational Leadership*, **18**, 4–10.

Gardner, M. K. (1985) Cognitive psychological approaches to instructional task analysis. In E. W. Gordon (ed.) *Review of Research in Education (Vol 12)*. New York: AERA.

Gardner, M. K. & Clark, E. (1992) The psychometric perspective on intellectual development in childhood and adolescence. In R. J. Sternberg & C. A. Berg (eds) *Intellectual Development*. New York: Cambridge University Press.

Garland, A. & Zigler, E. (1993) Adolescent suicide prevention. Current research and social policy implications. *American Psychologist*, **48**, 169–82.

Garn, S. M. (1980) Continuities and change in maturational timing. In O. G. Brim & J. Kagan (eds) *Constancy and Change in Human Development*. Cambridge, MA: Harvard University Press.

Garner, R. (1990) When children and adults do not use learning strategies: Toward a theory of settings. *Review of Educational Research*, **60**, 517–29.

Garner, R. & Alexander, P. A. (1989) Metacognition: Answered and unanswered questions. *Educational Psychologist*, **24**, 143–58.

Gay, G. (1986) Interaction of learner control and prior understanding in computer-assisted video instruction. *Journal of Educational Psychology*, 78, 225–7.

Gazda, G. M. & Corsini, R. J. (eds) (1980) *Theories of Learning*. Itasca, IL: F. E. Peacock.

Geisert, G. & Dunn, R. (1991) Effective use of computers: Assignments based on individual learning style. *The Clearing House*, March/April, 219–24.

Gelman, R. & Baillargeon, R. (1983) A review of some Piagetian concepts. In P. Mussen (series ed.), J. H. Flavell & E. M. Markman (vol. eds) *Handbook of Child Psychology: Vol.3. Cognitive Development*. New York: Wiley.

Gesell, A. L. (1925) *The Mental Growth of the Preschool Child*. New York: Macmillan.

Getzels, J. & Csikszentmihalyi, M. (1976) *The Creative Vision: A Longitudinal Study of Problem Finding in Art*. New York: John Wiley.

Getzels, J. & Jackson, P. (1962) *Creativity and Intelligence: Explorations with Gifted Students*. New York: Wiley.

Giaconia, R. M. & Hedges, L. V. (1982) Identifying features of effective open education. *Review of Educational Research*, **52**, 579–602.

Gibbons, M. (1971) *Individualized Instruction. A Descriptive Analysis*. New York: Teachers College Press.

Gibbs, G. (1991) Eight myths about assessment. *The New Academic*, **1**, 2–4.

Gibson, S. & Dembo, M. H. (1984) Teacher efficacy: A construct validation. *Journal of Educational Psychology*, **76**, 569–82.

Gillam, B. (1992) The status of perceptual grouping 70 years after Wertheimer. *Australian Journal of Psychology*, **44**, 157–62.

Gilligan, C. (1977) In a different voice: Women's conceptions of self and morality. *Harvard Educational Review*, **47**, 481–517.

Gilligan, C. (1982) *In a Different Voice*. Cambridge, MA: Harvard University Press.

Gilligan, C. (1990) Teaching Shakespeare's sister. In C. Gilligan, N. Lyons & T. Hanmer (eds) *Making Connections: The Relational Worlds of Adolescent Girls at Emma Willard School*. Cambridge, MA: Harvard University Press.

Gilstrap, R. L. & Martin, W. R. (1975) *Current Strategies for Teachers*. Pacific Palisades, CA: Goodyear.

Ginott, H. G. (1972) *Teacher and Child: A Book for Parents and Teachers*. New York: Macmillan.

Ginsburg, H. & Opper, S. (1988) *Piaget's Theory of Intellectual Development*, 3rd edn. Englewood Cliffs, NJ: Prentice Hall.

Glaser, R. (1985) Cognition and adaptive education. In M. C. Wang & H. J. Walberg (eds) *Adapting Instruction to Individual Differences*, Berkeley, CA: McCutchan.

Glasser, W. (1969) *Schools Without Failure*. New York: Harper & Row.

Glasser, W. (1992) *The Quality School*. New York: HarperCollins.

Gloet, M. B. (1992) Cooperation, competition and individualism in the clever country. Proceedings of the 10th Annual Computers in Education Conference, July, 210–16.

Goldenberg, C. (1992) The limits of expectations: A case for case knowledge about teacher expectancy effects. *American Educational Research Journal*, **29**, 517–44.

Goldschmid, M. L., Bentler, P. M., Debus, R. L., Rawlinson, R., Kohnstamm, D., Modgil, S., Nichols, J. G., Reykowski, J., Strupczewska, B. & Warren, N. (1973) A cross-cultural investigation of conservation. *Journal of Cross-Cultural Psychology*, **4**, 75–88.

Good, T. L. (1987) Two decades of research on teacher expectations: findings and future directions. *Journal of Teacher Education*, **38**, 32–47.

Good, T. L. (1995) Teacher expectations. In L. W. Anderson (ed.) *International Encyclopedia of Teaching and Teacher Education*, 2nd edn. Tarrytown, NY: Pergamon: 29–35.

Good, T. L. & Brophy, J. (1977) Teachers' expectations as self-fulfilling prophecies. In H. F. Clarizio, R. C. Craig & W. A. Mehrens (eds) *Contemporary Issues in Educational Psychology*, 3rd edn. Boston: Allyn & Bacon.

Good, T. L. & Brophy, J. E. (1990) *Educational Psychology. A Realistic Approach*, 4th edn. White Plains, NY: Longman.

Good, T. L. & Brophy, J. E. (1991) *Looking in Classrooms*, 5th edn. New York: HarperCollins.

Good, T. L. & Stipek, D. J. (1983) Individual differences in the classroom: A psychological perspective. In G. D. Fenstermacher (ed.) *Individual Differences and the Common Curriculum. Eighty-second Yearbook of the National Society for the Study of Education, Part 1*. Chicago: Chicago University Press.

Good, T. L. & Tom, D. Y. H. (1985) Self-regulation, efficacy, expectations, and social orientation: teacher and classroom perspectives. In C. Ames & R. Ames (eds) *Research on Motivation in Education: Vol. 2. The Classroom Milieu*. Orlando: Academic Press.

Goodman, D., O'Hearn, D. J. & Wallace-Crabbe, C. (eds) (1991) *Multicultural Australia. The Challenges of Change*. Newham, Vic. Scribe.

Goodnow, J. J. (1976) The nature of intelligent behavior: Questions raised by cross-cultural studies. In L. B. Resnick (ed.) *The Nature of Intelligence*. New York: Erlbaum.

Goodnow, J. J. (1988) Issues and changes in the assessment of people from minority groups. In G. Davidson (ed.) *Ethnicity and Cognitive Assessment: Australian Perspectives*. Darwin: Darwin Institute of Technology.

Goodnow, J. J. (1990) The socialization of cognition: what's involved? In J. W. Stigler, R. Shweder & G. Herdt (eds) *Cultural Psychology. Essays on Comparative Human Development*. Cambridge: Cambridge University Press.

Gordon, E. W., DeStefano, L. & Shipman, S. (1985) Characteristics of learning persons and the adaptation of learning environments. In M. C. Wang & H. J. Walberg (eds) *Adapting Instruction to Individual Differences*. Berkeley, CA: McCutchan.

Gordon, I. E. & Earle, D. C. (1992) Visual illusions: A short review. *Australian Journal of Psychology*, **44**, 153–6.

Gordon, T. (1974) *Teacher Effectiveness Training*. New York: Peter H. Wyden.

Gordon, T. (1975) *Parent Effectiveness Training*. New York: New American Library.

Gordon, W. J. J. (1961) *Synectics: The Development of Creative Capacity*. New York: Harper & Row.

Gow, L. (1989) *Review of Integration in Australia: Summary Report*. Canberra: Department of Employment, Education and Training.

Gow, L. (ed.) (1992) *Review of Literature on Service Provision for Students with Disabilities*. Paper submitted to the Committee Reviewing SSPs in the Metropolitan South West Region NSW Department of School Education, July.

Gow, L., McClellan, K., Balla, J. & Taylor, D. (1988) The teaching-learning staircase: a model of instruction to demystify special education. *Australian Journal of Remedial Education*, **20**, 26–31.

Gow, L., Snow, D., Balla, J. & Hall, J. (1987) *Report to the Commonwealth School Commission on Integration in Australia*, **1–5**, Canberra: CSC.

Graham, S. (1988) Can attribution theory tell us something about motivation in blacks? *Educational Psychologist*, **23**, 3–21.

Graham, S. & Golan, S. (1991) Motivational influences on cognition: Task involvement, ego involvement, and depth of processing. *Journal of Educational Psychology*, **83**, 187–94.

Graves, N. & Graves, T. (1990) *A Part to Play*. Melbourne: Latitude Publications.

Grbich, C. & Sykes, S. (1992) Access to curricula in three school settings for students with severe intellectual disability. *Australian Journal of Education*, **36**, 318–27.

Green, B. & Bigum, C. (1993) Aliens in the classroom. *Australian Journal of Education*, **37**, 2, 119–41.

Green, K. D., Forehand, R., Beck, S. J. & Vosk, B. (1980) An assessment of the relationships among measures of children's social competence and children's academic achievement. *Child Development*, **51**, 1149–56.

Greene, R. L. (1986) Sources of recency effects in free recall. *Psychological Bulletin*, **99**, 221–28.

Greeno, J. G. (1997) On claims that answer the wrong questions. *Educational Researcher*, **26**, 5–17.

Greenwood, C. R. et al. (1992) The classwide peer tutoring program: Implementation factors moderating students' achievement. *Journal of Applied Behavior Analysis*, **25**, 101–16.

Greenwood, C. R., Delquadri, J. C. & Hall, R. V. (1989) Longitudinal effects of classwide peer tutoring. *Journal of Educational Psychology*, **81**, 371–83.

Gregory, J. B. & Wicks, J. M. (n.d.) *New Effective Social Studies*. Sydney: Horwitz-Martin.

Gresham, F. M. (1981) Social skills training with handicapped children: A review. *Review of Educational Research*, **51**, 139–76.

Griffin, P. & Nix, P. (1991) *Educational Assessment and Reporting. A New Approach*. Sydney: Harcourt Brace Jovanovich.

Griffiths, R. A. & Channon-Little, L. (1996) Psychological treatments and bulimia nervosa: An update. *Australian Psychologist*, **31**, 79–96.

Groisser, P. (1964) *How to Use the Fine Art of Questioning*. New York: Teacher's Practical Press.

Grolnick, W. S. & Ryan, R. (1989) Parent style and children's self-regulation. *Journal of Educational Psychology*, **81**, 143–54.

Gronlund, N. E. (ed.) (1968) *Readings in Measurement and Evaluation*. London: Macmillan.

Gronlund, N. E. (1985) *Measurement and Evaluation in Teaching*, 5th edn. New York: Macmillan.

Gronlund, N. E. (1991) *How to Write and Use Instructional Objectives*. New York: Macmillan.

Grossman, P. L. (1990) *The Making of a Teacher: Teacher Knowledge and Teacher Education*. New York: Teachers College Press.

Grossman, P. L. (1992) Why models matter: An alternative view on professional growth in teaching. *Review of Educational Research*, **62**, 171–9.

Grueneich, R. (1982) Issues in the developmental study of how children use intention and consequence information to make moral evaluations. *Child Development*, **53**, 29–43.

Guilford, J. P. (1959) Three faces of intellect. *American Psychologist*, **14**, 469–79.

Guilford, J. P. (1967) *The Nature of Human Intelligence*. New York: McGraw-Hill.

Guilford, J. P. (1985) The structure-of-intellect model. In B. B. Wolman (ed.) *Handbook of Intelligence*. New York: Wiley.

Gullickson, A. R. (1984) Teacher perspectives of the instructional use of tests. *Journal of Educational Research*, **77**, 244–8.

Gullickson, A. R. (1985) Student evaluation techniques and their relationship to grade and curriculum. *Journal of Educational Research*, **79**, 96–100.

Gurin, P., Gurin, G., Lao, R. & Beattie, M. (1969) Internal-external control in the motivational dynamics of Negro Youth. *Journal of Social Issues*, **25**, 29–53.

Guskey, T. R. (1987) Rethinking mastery learning reconsidered. *Review of Educational Research*, **57**, 225–9.

Guskey, T. R. & Gates, S. L. (1986) Synthesis of research on the effects of mastery learning in elementary and secondary classrooms. *Educational Leadership*, **43**, 73–80.

Guskey, T. R. (1995) Mastery learning. In L. W. Anderson (ed.) *International Encyclopedia of Teaching and Teacher Education*, 2nd edn, Tarrytown, NY: Pergamon: 161–7.

Guthrie, L. F. & Hall, W. S. (1983) Continuity/discontinuity in the function and use of language. In E. W. Gordon (ed.) *Review of Research in Education (Vol. 10)*. Washington: AERA.

Haertel, E. (1985) Construct validity and criterion-referenced testing. *Review of Educational Research*, **55**, 23–46.

Hager, P. & Kaye, M. (1990) Critical thinking ability and teacher effectiveness. In M. Bezzina & J. Butcher (eds) *The Changing Face of Professional Education. Collected Papers of the AARE Annual Conference, Sydney University, 1990*. Sydney: AARE.

Haight, W. L. & Miller, P. J (1993) *Pretending at Home: Early Development in a Sociocultural Context*. Albany, New York: SUNY Press.

Hales, L. W. & Tokar, E. (1975) The effects of quality of preceding responses on the grades assigned to subsequent responses to an essay question. *Journal of Educational Measurement*, **12**, 115–17.

Halford, G. S. (1982) *The Development of Thought*. Hillsdale, NJ: Erlbaum.

Halford, G. S. (1989) Reflections on 25 years of Piagetian cognitive developmental psychology, 1963–1988. *Human Development*, **32**, 325–57.

Halford, G. S. (1993) *Children's understanding: The development of mental models*. London: Lawrence Erlbaum.

Hall, C. S. (1964) *A Primer of Freudian Psychology*. New York: Mentor Books.

Hall, C. S. & Lindzey, G. (1970) *Theories of Personality*, 2nd edn. New York: John Wiley & Sons.

Hall, J., Gow, L. & Konza, D. (1987) Are we integrating or maindumping students with special needs? *The NSW Journal of Education*, 7, 20–4.

Hall, K. (1992) Co-assessment: *The bridge between student self-assessment and teacher-assessment*. A paper presented at the 12th Annual International Seminar for Teacher Education, The University of New England, Armidale, NSW, April 24–30.

Hallahan, D. & Kauffman, J. (1988) Exceptional Children: Introduction to Special Education, 4th edn. Englewood, Cliffs, NJ: Prentice Hall.

Hancock, D. R. (1995) What teachers may do to influence student motivation: An application of expectancy theory. JGE: *The Journal of General Education*, **44**, 171–9.

Hannan, B. (1985) *Assessment and Evaluation in Schooling*. Victoria: Deakin University.

Hanson, S. L. & Ginsburg, A. L. (1988) Gaining ground: Values and high school success. *American Educational Research Journal*, **25**, 334–65.

Harari, O. & Covington, M. V. (1981) Reactions to achievement behavior from a teacher and student perspective: A developmental analysis. *American Educational Research Journal*, **18**, 15–28.

Haraway, D. J. (1991) *Simians, Cyborgs, and Women. The Reinvention of Nature*. New York: Routledge.

Harel, I. (1991) *Children Designers: Interdisciplinary Constructions for Learning and Knowing Mathematics in a Computer-rich School*. Norwood, NJ: Ablex.

Harris, M. (1985) *Textbook of Child Care and Health*. Sydney: Science Press.

Harter, S. (1990) Issues in the assessment of the self-concept of children and adolescents. In A. LaGreca (ed.) *Through the Eyes of a Child*. Boston: Allyn & Bacon.

Hartshorne, H. & May, M. A. (1928) *Studies in the Nature of Character (Vol. 1). Studies in Deceit*. New York: Macmillan.

Hartshorne, H. & May, M. A. (1929) *Studies in the Nature of Character (Vol.2). Studies in Service and Control*. New York: Macmillan.

Harvey, D. & Green, C. (1984) Attitudes of New Zealand teachers, teachers in training and non-teachers toward mainstreaming. *New Zealand Journal of Educational Studies*, **19**, 34–44.

Hattie, J. (1990) Performance indicators in education. *Australian Journal of Education*, **34**, 249–76.

Hattie, J. (1992) Measuring the effects of schooling. *Australian Journal of Education*, **36**, 5–13.

Hattie, J. & Fitzgerald, D. (1987) Sex differences in attitudes, achievement and use of computers. *Australian Journal of Education*, **31**, 3–26.

Havighurst, R. J. (1959) *Human Development and Education*. New York: Longmans, Green.

Haviland, J. M., (1979) Teachers' and students' beliefs about punishment. *Journal of Educational Psychology*, **71**, 563–70.

Hawkins, J. (1985) Computers and girls: rethinking the issues. *Sex Roles*, **13**, 165–80.

Hayes, A. (1990) Developmental psychology, education and the need to move beyond typological thinking. *Australian Journal of Education*, **34**, 235–41.

Hayes, S. C., Rosenfarb, I., Wuhfert, E., Munt, E. D., Korn, Z. & Zettle, R. D. (1985) Self-reinforcement effects: An artifact of social standard setting? *Journal of Applied Behavior Analysis*, **18**, 201–14.

Hayles, N. K. (1990) *Chaos Bound. Orderly Disorder in Contemporary Literature and Science*. Ithaca: Cornell University Press.

Healy, C. C. & Welchert, A. J. (1990) Mentoring relations: A definition to advance research and practice. *Educational Researcher*, **19**, 17–21.

Heckhausen, H. (1991) *Motivation and Action*. Berlin: Springer-Verlag (trans. by Peter K. Leppmann).

Hedberg, J. & McNamara, S. (1990) Information technology: Basic skills for today's teachers. In M. Bezzina & J. Butcher (eds) *The Changing Face of Professional Education. Collected Papers of the AARE Annual Conference, Sydney University, 1990*. Sydney: AARE.

Hedmore, G. A. (1969) *Piaget. A Practical Consideration*. Oxford: Pergamon.

Heffey, P. G. (1985) The duty of schools and teachers to protect pupils from injury. *Monash Law Review*, **11**, 12.

Heller, R. S. & Martin, C. D. (1987) Measuring the level of teacher concerns over microcomputers in instruction. *Education and Computing*, **3**, 133–9.

Helson, R. (1971) Women mathematicians and the creative personality. *Journal of Consulting and Clinical Psychology*, **36**, 210–20.

Henderson. J. G. (1992) *Reflective Teaching. Becoming an Inquiring Educator*. New York: Macmillan.

Hendry, G.D. (1996) Constructivism and educational practice. *Australian Journal of Education*, **40**, 19–45.

Hennigan, K. M. et al. (1982) Impact of the introduction of television on crime in the United States: Empirical findings and theoretical implications. *Journal of Personality and Social Psychology*, **42**, 461–77.

Heron, A. & Dowel, W. (1973) Weight conservation and matrix-solving ability in Papuan children. *Journal of Cross-Cultural Psychology*, **4**, 207–19.

Hersh, R. H., Paolitto, D. P. & Reimer, J. (1979) *Promoting Moral Growth: From Piaget to Kohlberg*. New York: Longman.

Hertz-Lazarowitz, R. (1985) Internal dynamics of cooperative learning. In R. Slavin et al. (eds) *Learning to Cooperate, Cooperating to Learn*. New York: Plenum Press.

Hess, R. D. & Miura, I. T. (1985) Gender differences in enrollment in computer camps and classes. *Sex Roles*, **13**, 193–203.

Hewitt, J. & Scardamalia, M. (1996) Design principles for the support of distributed processes. Paper presented at the annual meeting of the American Educational Research Association, New York, April 8–12.

Higgins, E. T. (1987) Self-discrepancy: A theory relating self and affect. *Psychological Review*, **94**, 319–40.

Hiley, M. (1993) *Writing for Multimedia*. The Electronic Author, 2.

Hill, J. P. & Lynch, M. E. (1983) The intensification of gender-related role expectations during early adolescence. In J. Brooks-Gunn & A. C. Petersen (eds) *Girls at Puberty. Biological and Psychosocial Perspectives*. New York: Plenum.

Hill, J. (1995) School culture and peer groups. In L. W. Anderson (ed.) *International Encyclopedia of Teaching and Teacher Education*, 2nd edn, Tarrytown, NY: Pergamon: 332–6.

Hill, S. & Hill, T. (1990) *The Collaborative Classroom*. South Yarra: Eleanor Curtin Publishing.

Ho, R., & McMurtrie, J. (1991) Attibutional feedback and underachieving children. Differential effects on causal attributions, success expectations, and learning processes. *Australian Journal of Psychology*, **43**, 93–100.

Ho, R. (1994) Cigarette advertising and cigarette health warnings: What role do adolescents' motives for smoking play in their assessment? *Australian Psychologist*, **29**, 49–56.

Hocking, H. (1990) School-based evaluation: professional discourse or public accountability? In M. Bezzina & J. Butcher (eds) *The Changing Face of Professional Education. Collected Papers of the AARE Annual Conference, Sydney University, 1990*. Sydney: AARE.

Hodge, A. (1987) *Communicating across Cultures*. Willoughby, NSW: Janus.

Hoffman, M. L. (1980) Moral development in adolescence. In J. Adelson (ed.) *Handbook of Adolescent Psychology*. New York: John Wiley.

Hoge, R. D. (1988) Issues in the definition and measurement of the giftedness construct. *Educational Researcher*, **17**, 12–16.

Hoge, R. D. & Coladarci, T. (1989) Teacher-based judgments of academic achievement: A review of literature. *Review of Educational Research*, **59**, 297–313.

Hoge, R. D., & Renzulli, J. S. (1993) Exploring the link between giftedness and self-concept. *Review of Educational Research*, **63**, 449–65.

Hohepa, M., Jenkins, K. & McNaughton, S. (1992) Maori pedagogies, the role of the individual and language development. Paper presented at the AARE/NZARE conference 'Educational research: Discipline and diversity'. Geelong, Vic.

Holland, C. J. & Kobasigawa, A. (1980) Observational Learning: Bandura. In G. M. Gazda & R. J. Corsini (eds) *Theories of Learning*. Itasca, IL: F. E. Peacock.

Hollins, E. R. (1996) *Culture in School Learning. Revealing the Deep Meaning*. Mahway, NJ: Lawrence Erlbaum.

Holt, K. S. (1991) *Child Development. Diagnosis and Assessment*. London: Butterworth-Heinemann.

Hooper, S. (1992a) Cooperative learning and computer-based instruction. *Educational Technology Research and Development*, **40**, 21–38.

Hooper, S. (1992b) The effects of peer interaction on learning during computer-based mathematics instruction. *Journal of Educational Research*, **85**, 108–89.

Hoowe, A. & Johnson, J. (1975) Intellectual development and elementary science. *Science and Children*, **13**, 30–1.

Horn, J. M. (1983) The Texas adoption project: Adopted children and their intellectual resemblance to biological and adoptive parents. *Child Development*, **54**, 268–75.

Hornett, D. (1989) The role of faculty in cultural awareness and retention of American Indian college students. *Journal of American Indian Education*, **29**, 12–18.

Horowitz, F. D. & O'Brien, M. (1986) Gifted and talented children. State of knowledge and directions for research. *American Psychologist*, **41**, 1147–52.

Howes, C., Unger, O. & Seidner, L. B. (1989) Social pretend play in toddlers: Parallels with social play and social pretend. *Child Development*, **60**, 77–84.

Hoy, W. K. & Woolfolk, A. E. (1990) Socialization of student teachers. *American Educational Research Journal*, **27**, 279–300.

Huck, S. W. & Bounds, W. G. (1972) Essay grades: An interaction between graders, handwriting clarity and the neatness of examination papers, *American Journal of Educational Research*, **9**, 279–83.

Hughes, B., Sullivan, H. J. & Mosley, M. L. (1985) External evaluation, task difficulty, and continuing motivation. *Journal of Educational Research*, **78**, 210–15.

Hughes, P. (1984) A call for an Aboriginal pedagogy. *The Australian Teacher*, **9**, 20–2.

Hunter, E. M. (1991) An examination of recent suicides in remote Australia. Further information from the Kimberley. *Australia and New Zealand Journal of Psychiatry*, **25**, 197–202.

Hunter, M. (1982) *Mastery Teaching*. El Segundo, CA: TIP Publications.

Hunter, M. (1991) Hunter design helps achieve the goals of science instruction. *Educational Leadership*, **48**, 79–81.

Hunter, M. & Barker, G. (1987) 'If at first . . . ': Attribution theory in the classroom. *Educational Leadership*, **45**, 51–3.

Huston, A. C. & Carpenter, C. J. (1985) Gender differences in preschool classrooms: the effects of sex-typed activity choices. In L. C. Wilkinson & C. B. Marrett (eds) *Gender Influences in Classroom Interaction*. Orlando: Academic Press.

Idol, L. & Jones, B. F. (1991) *Educational Values and Cognitive Instruction: Implications for Reform*. Hillsdale, NJ: Lawrence Erlbaum.

Idol, L., Jones, B. F. & Mayer, R. E. (1991) Classroom instruction: The teaching of thinking. In L. Idol & B. F. Jones (eds) *Educational Values and Cognitive Instruction: Implications for Reform*. Hillsdale, NJ: Lawrence Erlbaum.

Idol, L. & West, J. F. (1993) *Effective Instruction of Difficult to Teach Students. Instructors' Manual*. Austin, TX: Pro-Ed.

Ingvarson, L. & Greenway, P. (1984) Portrayals of teacher development. *The Australian Journal of Education*, **28**, 45–65.

Inhelder, B. & de Caprona, D. (1987) Introduction. In B. Inhelder, D. de Caprona & A. Cornu-Wells (eds) *Piaget Today*. London: Lawrence Erlbaum.

Inhelder, B., de Caprona, D. & Cornu-Wells, A. (1987) *Piaget Today*. London: Lawrence Erlbaum.

Iran-Nejad, A. (1990) Active and dynamic self-regulation of learning processes. *Review of Educational Research*, **60**, 573–602.

Irvine, S. H. & Berry, J. W. (1988) The abilities of mankind: A reevaluation. In S. H. Irvine & J. W. Berry (eds) *Human Abilities in Cultural Context*. Cambridge: Cambridge University Press.

Irvine, S. H. & Berry, J. W. (eds) (1988) *Human Abilities in Cultural Context*. Cambridge: Cambridge University Press.

Irwin, K. (1989) Multicultural Education. The New Zealand Response. *New Zealand Journal of Educational Studies*, **24**, 3–18.

Irwin, K. (1991) Maori education 1991: A review and discussion. In H. Manson (ed.) New Zealand Annual Review of Education. Wellington: Education Department, Victoria University.

Irwin, K. (1992) Maori education in 1991: A review and discussion. In Department of Education, *New Zealand Annual Review of Education*. Wellington, NZ: Education

Department, Victoria University.

Irwin, K. (1993) Maori education in 1992: A review and discussion. In H. Manson (ed.) *New Zealand Annual Review of Education*. Wellington, NZ: Education Department, Victoria University.

Irwin, K. & Davies, L. (1992) *A regional study of the school based factors affecting achievement for Maori girls in bilingual immersion and mainstream classes, units and schools at primary level.* Paper presented at the AARE/NZARE conference 'Educational research: Discipline and diversity'. Geelong, Vic.

Iversen, I. H. (1992) Skinner's early research: From reflexology to operant conditioning. *American Psychologist*, **47**, 1318–29.

Jackson, K. & Harvey, D. (1991) Open schools or conventional: Which does the job better? *New Zealand Journal of Educational Studies*, **26**, 145–53.

Jackson, P. W. (1985) Private lessons in public schools: Remarks on the limits of adaptive instruction. In M. C. Wang & H. J. Walberg (eds) *Adapting Instruction to Individual Differences.* Berkeley, CA: McCutchan.

Jackson, P., Reid, N. & Croft, C. (1980) SHEIK: Study Habits Evaluation and Instruction Kit. Hawthorn, Vic. ACER.

Jacobi, M. (1991) Mentoring and undergraduate success: A literature review. *Review of Educational Research*, **61**, 505–32.

Jarvinen, D. W. & Nicholls, J. G. (1996) Adolescents' social goals, beliefs about causes of social success, and satisfaction in peer relations. *Developmental Psychology*, **32**, 435–41.

Jenkins, J. & Heinen, A. (1989) Students' preferences for service delivery: pull-out, in-class, or integrated models. *Exceptional Children*, **55**, 516–23.

Jenkins, J. R., Odom, S. L. & Speltz, M. L. (1989) Effects of social integration on preschool children with handicaps. *Exceptional Children*, **55**, 420–8.

Jenkins, J., Spelz, M., Odom, L. & Samuel, L. (1985) Integrating normal handicapped pre-schoolers: effects on child development and social interaction. *Exceptional Children*, **52**, 7–17.

Jenkinson, J. & Gow, L. (1989) Integration in Australia: a research perspective. *The Australian Journal of Education*, **33**, 267–84.

Johnson, C. & Conners, M. E. (1987) *The Etiology and Treatment of Bulimia Nervosa: A Biopsychosocial perspective.* New York: Basic Books.

Johnson, D. S. (1981) Naturally acquired learned helplessness: The relationship of school failure to achievement behavior, attributions, and self-concept. *Journal of Educational Psychology*, **73**, 174–80.

Johnson, D. W. & Johnson, R. T. (1975) *Learning Together and Alone: Cooperation, Competition, and Individualization.* Englewood Cliffs, NJ: Prentice Hall.

Johnson, D. W. & Johnson, R. T. (1985a) Cooperative learning and adaptive education. In M. C. Wang & H. J. Walberg (eds) *Adapting Instruction to Individual Differences*. Berkeley, CA: McCutchan.

Johnson, D. W. & Johnson, R. T. (1985b) Motivational processes in cooperative, competitive, and individualistic learning situations. In C. Ames & R. Ames (eds) *Research on Motivation in Education: Vol. 2. The Classroom Milieu.* Orlando: Academic Press.

Johnson, D. & Johnson, R. (1987) Computer-assisted cooperative learning. *Educational Technology*, **26**, 12–18.

Johnson, D. W. & Johnson, R. T. (1989a) Toward a cooperative effort: A response to Slavin. *Educational Leadership*, **46**, 80–1.

Johnson, D. & Johnson, R. T. (1989b) *Cooperation in the Classroom*. Edina, MN: Interaction Book Company.

Johnson, D. W. & Johnson, R. T. (1989c) Cooperative Learning. In L. W. Anderson (ed.) *The Effective Teacher*. New York: McGraw-Hill.

Johnson, D. W. & Johnson, R. T. (1989–1990) Social skills for successful group work. *Educational Leadership*, **47**, 30.

Johnson, D. W., Maruyama, G., Johnson, R. T., Nelson, D. & Skon, L. (1981) Effects of cooperative, competitive, and individualistic goal structures on achievement: A meta-analysis. *Psychological Bulletin*, **89**, 47–62.

Johnson, D. W. & Johnson, R. T. (1992) Encouraging thinking through constructive controversy. In N. Davidson & T. Worsham (eds) *Enhancing Thinking through Cooperative Learning*. New York: Teachers College Press.

Johnson, D. W. & Johnson, R. T. (1994) *Learning Together and Alone: Cooperative, Competitive, and Individualistic Learning*, 4th edn. Boston, MA: Allyn & Bacon.

Johnson, G. O. (1950) A study of the social position of the mentally retarded child in the regular grades. *American Journal of Mental Deficiency*, **55**, 60–89.

Johnson, L. V. & Bany, M. A. (1970) Classroom Management: *Theory and Skill Training*. New York: Macmillan.

Johnson, R. T., Johnson, D. W. & Stanne, M. B. (1986) Comparison of computer-assisted cooperative, competitive, and individualistic learning. *American Educational Research Journal*, **23**, 382–92.

Johnston, S. (1990) 'I only teach girls—how can gender be an issue?' A study of teachers' responses to conflicting curriculum pressures. In M. Bezzina & J. Butcher (eds) *The Changing Face of Professional Education. Collected Papers of the AARE Annual Conference, Sydney University, 1990.* Sydney: AARE.

Jones, E. & Reynolds, G. (1992) *The Play's the Thing*. New York: Teachers College Press.

Jones, F. (1987a) *Positive Classroom Discipline*. New York: McGraw-Hill.

Jones, F. (1987b) *Positive Classroom Instruction*. New York: McGraw-Hill.

Jones, J. (1981) Study skills: panacea, placebo or promise? *SET Research Information for Teachers*, number 2, item 13.

Jones, M. B. (1988) Autism: The child within. In K. L. Frieberg (ed.) *Educating Exceptional Children*, 6th edn. Guilford, CT: Duskin.

Jones, V. F. & Jones, L. S. (1995) *Comprehensive Classroom Management: Creating Positive Learning Environments*, 4th ed. Boston: Allyn & Bacon.

Jordan, D. F. (1984) The social construction of identity: The Aboriginal problem. *The Australian Journal of Education*, **28**, 274–90.

Jordan, D.W. (1997) Social skilling through cooperative learning. *Educational Research*, **39**, 3–21.

Joyce, B., Showers, B. & Rolheiser-Bennett, C. (1987) Staff development and student learning: a synthesis of research on models of teaching. *Educational Leadership*, **45**, 11–22.

Joyce, B. & Weil, M. (1972) *Models of Teaching*. Englewood Cliffs, NY: Prentice Hall.

Judge, C. (1987) *Civilization and Mental Retardation*. Mulgrave: Magnetic Press.

Kagan, D. M. (1988) Teaching as clinical problem solving: A critical examination of the analogy and its implications. *Review of Educational Research*, **58**, 428–505.

Kagan, D. M. (1992) Professional growth among preservice and beginning teachers. *Review of Educational Research*, **62**, 129–69.

Kagan, J. (1965) Reflection-impulsivity and reading ability in primary grade children. *Child Development*, **36**, 609–28.

Kagan, J. (1966) Reflection and impulsivity: The generality and dynamics of conceptual tempo. *Journal of Abnormal and Social Psychology*, **71**, 17–24.

Kagan, J. & Kogan, N. (1970) Individual variations in cognitive processes. In P. Mussen (ed.) *Carmichael's Manual of Child Psychology*. New York: Wiley.

Kagan, S. (1985) Learning to cooperate. In R. Slavin et al. (eds) *Learning to Cooperate, Cooperating to Learn*. New York: Plenum Press.

Kagan, S. (1992) *Cooperative Learning*. San Juan Capistrano, CA: Kagan Cooperative Learnings.

Kagan, S. (1994) *Cooperative Learning*. San Juan Capistrano, CA: Kagan Cooperative Learning.

Kahle, J. B., Parker, L. H., Rennie, L. J. & Riley, D. (1993) Gender differences in science education: Building a model. *Educational Psychologist*, **28**, 379–404.

Kail, R. & Bisanz, J. (1992) The information-processing perspective on cognitive development in childhood and adolescence. In R. J. Sternberg and C. A. Berg (eds) *Intellectual Development*. New York: Cambridge University Press.

Kalantzis, M. & Cope, B. (1987) Multicultural education in crisis? The needs of non English speaking background students. *Migration Action*, **9**, 23–9.

Kalantzis, M. & Cope, B. (1988) Why we need multicultural education: A review of the `ethnic disadvantage' debate. *Journal of Intercultural Studies*, **9**, 39–57.

Kalantzis, M., Cope, B., Noble, G. & Poynting, S. (1990). Cultures of Schooling: *Pedagogies for Cultural Difference and Social Access*. London: Falmer.

Kantowitz, B. H. & Roediger, H. L. (1980) Memory and information processing. In G. M. Gazda & R. J. Corsini (eds) *Theories of Learning*. Itasca, IL: F. E. Peacock.

Kaplan, R. M. & Pascoe, G. C. (1977) Humorous lectures and humorous examples: Some effects upon comprehension and retention. *Journal of Educational Psychology*, **69**, 61–5.

Karvale, K. A. & Forness, S. R. (1987) Substance over style: Assessing the efficacy of modality testing and teaching. *Exceptional Children*, **54**, 228–39.

Karvale, K. A. & Forness, S. R. (1990) Substance over style: A rejoinder to Dunn's animadversions. *Exceptional Children*, **56**, 357–61.

Karweit, N. (1985) Time spent, time needed, and adaptive instruction. In M. C. Wang & H. J. Walberg (eds) *Adapting Instruction to Individual Differences*. Berkeley, CA: McCutchan.

Kauchak, D. P. & Eggen, P. D. (1993) *Learning and Teaching. Research Based Methods*, 2nd edn. Needham Heights, MA: Allyn & Bacon.

Kazdin, A. E. (1973) The effect of vicarious reinforcement on attentive behavior in the classroom. *Journal of Applied Behavior Analysis*, **6**, 71–8.

Kearins, J. (1988) Cultural elements in testing: The test, the tester and the tested. In G. Davidson (ed.) *Ethnicity and Cognitive Assessment: Australian Perspectives*. Darwin: Institute of Technology.

Kearney, G. E., de Lacey, P. R. & Davidson, G. R. (eds) (1973) *The Psychology of Aboriginal Australians*. Sydney: Wiley.

Kearney, G. E. & McElwain, D. W. (eds) (1976). *Aboriginal Cognition*. Canberra: Australian Institute of Aboriginal Studies.

Keats, D. (1994) Cultural contributions to schooling in multicultural environments. In E. Thomas (ed.) *International Perspectives on Culture and Schooling: A Symposium of Proceedings*. London: Institute of Education: 278–305

Keats, D. M., Munro, D. & Mann, L. (eds) (1989). *Heterogeneity in Cross-Cultural Psychology*. Lisse: Zwets & Zeitlinger.

Keats, D. M. & Keats, J. A. (1988) Human assessment in Australia. In S. H. Irvine & J. W. Berry (eds) *Human Abilities in Cultural Context*. Cambridge: Cambridge University Press.

Keefe, J. W. & Ferrell, B. G. (1990) Developing a defensible learning style paradigm. *Educational Leadership*, **48**, 57–61.

Keeves, J. P. (ed.) (1987) *Australian Education. Review of Recent Research*. Sydney: Allen & Unwin.

Keeves, J. P. (1987) New perspectives in teaching and learning. In J. P. Keeves (ed.) *Australian Education. Review of Recent Research*. Sydney: Allen & Unwin.

Keith, T. Z., Reimers, T. M., Fehrmann, P. G., Pottebaum, S. M. & Aubrey, L. W. (1986) Parental involvement, homework, and TV time: Direct and indirect effects on high school achievement. *Journal of Educational Psychology*, **78**, 373–80.

Kelly, E. B. (1988) Learning disabilities: A new horizon of perception. In K. L. Frieberg (ed.) *Educating Exceptional Children*, 6th edn. Guilford, CT: Duskin.

Kelly, I. & Duckett, G. E. (1993) Current pre-service teacher education: Handicapping the computer, the teacher and the student! *Australian Educational Computing*, **8**, ACEC '93 Edition, 133–8.

Kelly, K. & Rheingold, H. (1993) The dragon ate my homework. *Wired*, July–August, 70–3.

Kennedy, N. (1971) Culture, Personality and Adjustment Implications for Aboriginal School Children. Unpublished BA (Hons) thesis. Flinders University, Adelaide, South Australia.

Kernan, A. (1990) *The Death of Literature*. Yale University Press.

Kerns, A., Klepac, L. & Cole, AK. (1996) Peer relationships and preadolescents' perceptions of security in the child–mother relationship. *Developmental Psychology*, **32**, 457–66.

Kidd, G. J. (1996) *Links between tertiary students' interests, learning styles, and academic achievement*. Paper presented at the 31st Annual Conference of the Australian Psychological Society, Sydney, 25–29 September.

King, A. (1990) Enhancing peer interaction and learning in the classroom through reciprocal questioning. *American Educational Research Journal*, **27**, 664–87.

King, A. (1991) Effects of training in strategic questioning on children's problem-solving performance. *Journal of Educational Psychology*, **83**, 307–17.

King, A. (1992a) Comparison of self-questioning, summarizing, and notetaking-review as strategies for learning from lectures. *American Educational Research Journal*, **29**, 303–23.

King, A. (1992b) Facilitating elaborative learning through guided student-generated questioning. *Educational Psychologist*, **27**, 111–26.

King, A. (1993) From sage on the stage to guide on the side. *College Teaching*, **41**, 30–5.

King, A. (1994) Questioning and knowledge generation. *American Educational Research Journal*, **31**, 338–68.

King, L., Barry, K., Maloney, K. & Tayler, C. (1993) *A study of the teacher's role in small-group cooperative learning during elementary mathematics lessons*. Paper presented at the American Educational Research Association in Atlanta, Georgia, 12–16 April.

King, N. J., Ollendick, T. H. & Gullone, E. (1990) School-related fears of children and adolescents. *Australian Journal of Education*, **34**, 99–112.

Kingsley, H. L. & Garry, R. (1957) *The Nature and Conditions of Learning*, 2nd edn. Englewood Cliffs, NJ: Prentice Hall.

Kirk, M. (1991a) Interview on assessment issues with Lorrie Shepard. *Educational Researcher*, **20**, 21–3.

Kirk, M. (1991b) Interview on assessment issues with James Popham. *Educational Researcher*, **20**, 24–6.

Kirk, S. & Gallagher, J. (1983) The exceptional child in modern society; individual differences and special education; children with visual impairments; children with multiple, severe and physical handicaps. In S. Kirk & J. Gallagher (eds) *Educating Exceptional Children*, 4th edn. Boston: Houghton Mifflin.

Klahr, D. & Wallace, J. G. (1976) Cognitive Development: *An Information Processing View*. Hillsdale, NJ: Erlbaum.

Kleinbaum, D. G., Kupper, L. L. & Muller, K. E. (1988) *Applied Regression Analysis and Other Multivariate Methods*, 2nd edn. Boston: PWS-Kent.

Kleinfeld, J. (1975) Effective teachers of Indian and Eskimo students. *School Review*, **83**, 301–44.

Klich, L. Z. (1988) Aboriginal cognition and psychological nescience. In S. H. Irvine & J. W. Berry (eds) *Human Abilities in Cultural Context*. Cambridge: Cambridge University Press.

Kobak, R. R. & Sceery, A. (1988) Attachment in adolescence: Working models, affect regulation, and representations of self and others. *Child Development*, **59**, 135–46.

Koffka, K. (1935) *Principles of Gestalt Psychology*. New York: Harcourt, Brace.

Kogan, N. (1971) Educational implications of cognitive styles. In G. S. Lesser (ed.) *Psychological and Educational Practice*. Glenview, IL: Scott, Foresman & Co.

Kohlberg, L. (1969) *Global Rating Scale: Preliminary Moral Judgment Scoring Manual*. Cambridge, MA: Center for Moral Education.

Kohlberg, L. (1976) Moral stages and moralization: The cognitive-developmental approach to socialization. In D. A. Goslin (ed.) *Handbook of Socialization Theory and Research*. Chicago: Rand McNally.

Kohlberg, L. (1977) The cognitive-developmental approach to moral education. In H. F. Clarizio, R. C. Craig & W. A. Mehrens (eds) *Contemporary Issues in Educational Psychology*, 3rd edn. Boston: Allyn & Bacon.

Kohlberg, L. (1978) Revisions in the theory and practice of moral development. In W. Damon (ed.) *Moral Development*: New Directions for Child Development (No. 2). San Francisco: Jossey-Bass.

Kohlberg, L. (1981) *The Philosophy of Moral Development*. San Francisco: Harper & Row.

Kohlberg, L., Levine, C. & Hewer, A. (1983) *Moral Stages. A Current Formulation and Response to Critics*. Basel, Switzerland: Karger.

Kohler, W. (1925) *The Mentality of Apes* (E. Winter, trans.). New York: Harcourt, Brace.

Kohn, A. (1991) Group grade grubbing versus cooperative learning. *Educational Leadership*, **48**, 83–7.

Kohn, A. (1996) By all available means: Cameron's and Pierce's defense of extrinsic motivators. *Review of Educational Research*, **66**, 1–4.

Kolb, D. (1976) *Learning-style Inventory. Technical Manual*. Boston: McBer.

Koop, T. & Koop, G. (1990) Reflective teaching as professional empowerment. In M. Bezzina & J. Butcher (eds) *The Changing Face of Professional Education. Collected Papers of the AARE Annual Conference, Sydney University, 1990*. Sydney: AARE.

Kornadt, H-J., Eckensberger L. H. & Emminghaus, W. B. (1980) Cross-cultural research on motivation and its contribution to a general theory of motivation. In H. C. Triandis & W. Lonner (eds) *Handbook of Cross-Cultural Psychology: Vol. 3. Basic Processes*. Boston: Allyn & Bacon.

Kosky, R. (1987) Is suicidal behaviour increasing among Australian youth? *Medical Journal of Australia*, **147**, 164–6.

Kounin, J. S. (1970) *Discipline and Group Management in Classrooms*. New York: Holt, Rinehart & Winston.

Kounin, J. S. (1977) *Discipline and Group Management in Classrooms*. New York: Holt, Rinehart & Winston.

Kozulin, A. & Presseisen, B. Z. (1995) Mediated learning experience and psychological tools: Vygotsky's and Feuerstein's perspectives in a study of student learning. *Educational Psychologist*, **30**, 67–75.

Krathwohl, D. R., Bloom, B. S. & Masia, B. B. (1956) *Taxonomy of Educational Objectives. The Classification of Educational Goals. Handbook 11: Affective Domain*. London: Longman.

Krueger, M. S. (1991) *Artificial Reality II*. Reading, MA: Addison-Wesley.

Kukla, A. (1972) Attributional determinants of achievement-related behavior. *Journal of Personality and Social Psychology*, **21**, 166–74.

Kulhavy, R. W. (1977) Feedback in written instruction. *Review of Educational Research*, **47**, 211–32.

Kulik, C-L. C., Kulik, J. A. & Schwalb, B. J. (1983) College programs for high-risk and disadvantaged students: A meta-analysis of findings. *Review of Educational Research*, **53**, 397–414.

Kulik, J. A. & Kulik, C-L. C. (1984) Effects of accelerated instruction on students. *Review of Educational Research*, **54**, 409–25.

Kulik, J. A. & Kulik, C-L. C. (1988) Timing of feedback and verbal learning. *Review of Educational Research*, **58**, 79–97.

Kumar, V. K. (1971) The structure of human memory and some educational implications. *Review of Educational Research*, **41**, 379–417.

Kutnick, P. & Jules, V. (1993) Pupils' perceptions of a good teacher: A developmental perspective from Trinidad and Tobago. *British Journal of Educational Psychology*, **63**, 400–13.

Kyriacou, C. (1986) *Effective Teaching in Schools*. Oxford: Basil Blackwell.

Kyriacou, C. (1991) *Essential Teaching Skills*. Oxford: Basil Blackwell.

Laboratory of Comparative Human Cognition (1986) Contributions of cross-cultural research to educational practice. *American Psychologist*, **41**, 1049–58.

Lam, T. C. M. (1992) Review of practices and problems in the evaluation of bilingual education. *Review of Educational Research*, **62**, 181–203.

Lambiotte, J. G., Dansereau, D. F., Cross, D. R. & Reynolds, S.B. (1989) Multirelational semantic maps. *Educational Psychology Review*, **1**, 331–67.

Lampert, M. & Clark, C. M. (1990) Expert knowledge and expert thinking in teaching: A response to Floden and Klinzing. *Educational Researcher*, **19**, 21–3.

Lange, D. (1988) *Tomorrow's Schools: The Reform of Education Administration in New Zealand*. Wellington, NZ: Department of Education.

Langford, P. (ed.) (1989) *Educational Psychology. An Australian Perspective*. Sydney: Longman Cheshire.

Langlois, J. H. & Stephan, C. W. (1981) Beauty and the Beast: The role of physical attractiveness in the development of peer relations and social behaviour. In S. S. Brehm, S. M. Kassin & F. X. Gibbons (eds) *Developmental Social Psychology*. New York: Oxford University Press.

Larkins, A. G., McKinney, C. W., Oldham-Buss, S. & Gilmore, A. C. (1985) Teacher enthusiasm: A critical review. In H. S. Williams (ed.) *Educational and Psychological Research Monographs. Hattiesburg*, MS: University of Southern Mississippi.

Laskey, L. & Hallinan, P. (1990) Reflection and reality: The prospects for teacher candidates 11. In M. Bezzina & J. Butcher (eds) *The Changing Face of Professional Education. Collected Papers of the AARE Annual Conference, Sydney University, 1990*. Sydney: AARE.

Layman, J. & Hall, W. (1991) Applications of hypermedia in education. *Computers in Education*, **16**, 113–29.

Lave, J. & Wenger, E. (1991) *Situated Learning: Legitimate Peripheral Participation*. New York: Cambridge University Press.

Leder, G. C. (1988) Teacher-student interactions: the mathematics classroom. *Unicorn*, **14**, 107–11.

Lee, V. E., Bryk, A. & Smith, J. B. (1993) The organization of effective secondary schools. *Review of Research in Education*, **19**, 171–267.

Lepper, M. R. & Greene, D. (eds) (1978) *The Hidden Cost of Reward: New Perspectives on the Psychology of Human Motivation*. Hillsdale, NJ: Lawrence Erlbaum.

Lepper, M. R., & Hodell, M. (1989) Intrinsic motivation in the classroom. In C. Ames & R. Ames (eds) *Research on Motivation in Education, Vol.3, Goals and Cognitions*. San Diego: Academic Press: 73–105.

Lepper, M. R., Keavney, M. & Drake, M. (1996) Intrinsic motivation and extrinsic rewards: A commentary on Cameron and Pierce's meta-analysis. *Review of Educational Research*, **66**, 5–32.

Lerner, R. M. (1969) The development of stereotyped expectancies of body-build-behavior relations. *Child Development*, **40**, 137–41.

Lerner, R. & Korn, S. (1972) The development of body build stereotypes in males. *Child Development*, **43**, 908–20.

Lester, D. & Icli, T. (1990) Beliefs about suicide in American and Turkish students. *The Journal of Social Psychology*, **130**, 825–7.

Lett, W. R. (1971) Achievement behaviour, vocational aspirations, and action research with high school Aboriginal students. *Australian Journal of Social Issues*, **6**, 217–27.

Lett, W. R. (1972) The New England Diploma in Education student: 1968–70. *Australian Journal of Education*, **16**, 246–53.

Lett, W. (1989) Creativity and giftedness. In P. Langford (ed.) *Educational Psychology. An Australian Perspective*. Sydney: Longman Cheshire.

Levin, B. (1985) Equal educational opportunity for children with special needs: The federal role in Australia. *Law and Contemporary Problems*, **48**, 213–73.

Levin, J. R. (1985) Educational applications of mnemonic pictures: Possibilities beyond your wildest imagination. In A. A. Sheikk (ed.) *Imagery in Education: Imagery in the Educational Process*. Farmingdale, NY: Baywood.

Levin, J. R., Shriberg, L. K. & Berry, J. K. (1983) A concrete strategy for remembering abstract prose. *American Educational Research Journal*, **20**, 277–90.

Levine, M. P., Smolak, L. & Hayden, H. (1994) The relation of sociocultural factors to eating attitudes and behaviours among middle school girls. *Journal of Early Adolescence*, **14**, 471–90.

Lewandoski, L. J. & Cruickshank, W. M. (1980) Psychological development of crippled children and youth. In W. M. Cruickshank (ed.) *Psychology of Exceptional Children and Youth*, 4th edn. Englewood Cliffs, NJ: Prentice Hall.

Lewis, R. (1991) *The Discipline Dilemma*. Hawthorn, Vic. ACER.

Lewis, R. (1992) Keynote address, Annual Queensland Guidance Counsellors' Association.

Lewis, R. & Lovegrove, M. N. (1984) Teachers' classroom control procedures: Are students' preferences being met? *Journal of Education for Teaching*, **10**, 97–105.

Lewis, R. & Lovegrove, M. N. (1987) Teacher as disciplinarian. *Australian Journal of Education*, **31**, 187–204.

Lewis, R., Lovegrove, M. N. & Burman, E. (1991) Teachers' perceptions of ideal classroom disciplinary practices. In M. N. Lovegrove & R. Lewis (eds) *Classroom Discipline*. Sydney: Longman Cheshire.

Lewis, R. (1994) Classroom discipline: Preparing our students for democratic citizenship. Paper presented at the Annual Conference of the Australian Association for Research in Education, Newcastle, November.

Liebert, R. M. & Spiegler, M. D. (1987) *Personality. Strategies and Issues*, 5th edn. Chicago: The Dorsey Press.

Linn, M. C. & Petersen, A. C. (1985) Emergence and characterization of sex-differences in spatial ability: A meta-analysis. *Child Development*, **56**, 1479–98.

Linn, R. L., Baker, E. L. & Dunbar, S. B. (1991) Complex, performance-based assessment: Expectations and validation criteria. *Educational Researcher*, **20**, 15–21.

Lipsky, D. & Gartner, A. (eds) (1989) *Beyond Separate Education: Quality Education for All*. Baltimore, MD: Paul H. Brookes.

Lipson, M. Y. (1983) The influence of religious affiliation on children's memory for text information. *Reading Research Quarterly*, **18**, 448–57.

Livson, N. & Peskin, H. (1980) Perspectives on adolescence from longitudinal research. In J. Adelson (ed.) *Handbook of Adolescent Psychology*. New York: John Wiley.

Loader, D. (1997) *The Inner Principal*. London: Falmer Press.

Loader, D. (1993) Reconstructing an Australian School. In I. Grasso & M. Fallshaw (eds) *Reflections of a Learning Community: Views on the Introduction of Laptops at MLC*. Kew: Methodist Ladies' College.

Loader, D. & Nevile, L. (1993) Educational computing: Resourcing the future. In I. Grasso & M. Fallshaw (eds) *Reflections of a Learning Community: Views on the Introduction of Laptops at MLC*. Kew: Methodist Ladies' College.

Lo Bianco, J. (1987) *National Policy on Languages*. Canberra: AGPS.

Lo Bianco, J. (1988) Multiculturalism and the national policy on languages. *Journal of Intercultural Studies*, **9**, 25–38.

Lo Bianco, J. (1990) A hard-nosed multiculturalism: revitalising multicultural education? *Vox*, **4**, 80–94.

Lockhart, A. S. (1980a) Motor learning and motor development during infancy and childhood. In C. B. Corbin (ed.) A Textbook of Motor Development, 2nd edn. Dubuque, Iowa: Wm. C. Brown.

Lockhart, A. S. (1980b) Practices and principles governing motor learning of children. In C. B. Corbin (ed.) *A Textbook of Motor Development*, 2nd edn. Dubuque, Iowa: Wm. C. Brown.

Lockley, T. H. (1981) The extension teaching programme: An attempt to assist children of above average ability. *Unicorn*, **7**, 249–53.

Logan, L. M. & Logan, V. G. (1971) *Design for Creative Teaching*. Toronto: McGraw-Hill.

Lohman, D. F. (1989) Human intelligence: An introduction to advances in theory and research. *Review of Educational Research*, **59**, 333–73.

Lorayne, H. & Lucas, J. (1974) *The Memory Book*. New York: Stein & Day.

Louden, D. M. (1978) Internal versus external control in Asian and West Indian adolescents in Britain. *Journal of Adolescence*, **1**, 283–96.

Louie, S. (1985) Locus of control among computer-using school children. *The Computing Teacher*, October, 10.

Lovat, T. J. & Davies, M. (1990) The centrality of research skills development in the modern teacher education programme. In M. Bezzina & J. Butcher (eds) *The Changing Face of Professional Education. Collected Papers of the AARE Annual Conference, Sydney University, 1990*. Sydney: AARE.

Lovegrove, M. N. & Lewis, R. (1991) *Classroom Discipline*. Sydney: Longman.

Lovegrove, M. N., Lewis, R. & Burman, E. (1989) Pupils prefer: Democratic participation in the classroom. *The Best of Set*: Discipline. Item 7.

Lovegrove, M. N., Lewis, R. & Burman, E. (1991) *You Can't Make Me*. Bundoora, Vic. La Trobe University Press.

Lovegrove, T. (1985) *C.A.P.S. Computers and the Duke: Three Mini Studies*. Flinders University, Adelaide (Aboriginal Post Primary Education Project).

Loveland, K. K. & Olley, J. G. (1979) The effect of external reward on interest and quality of task performance in children of high and low intrinsic motivation. *Child Development*, **50**, 1207–10.

Lowe, S. (1996) On-line in Oz. Sydney: Addison-Wesley.

Lunde, D. T. & Lunde, M. K. (1980) *The Next Generation. A Book of Parenting*. New York: Holt, Rinehart & Winston.

McCaleb, J. & White, J. (1980) Critical dimensions in evaluating teacher clarity. *Journal of Classroom Interaction*, **15**, 27–30.

MacCallum, J. A. (1990) Does the moral judgement level of teachers really matter? In M. Bezzina & J. Butcher (eds) *The Changing Face of Professional Education. Collected Papers of the AARE Annual Conference, Sydney University, 1990*. Sydney: AARE.

McCann, T. E. & Sheehan, P. W. (1985) Violent content in Australian television. *Australian Psychologist*, **20**, 33–42.

McClellan, V. (1989) Young smokers: Rebellion, conformity and imitation. *SET Research Notes For Teachers*, number 1, item 5.

McClelland, D. C. (1953) *The Achievement Motive*. New York: Appleton-Century-Crofts.

McClelland, D. C. (1961) *The Achieving Society*. Princeton, NJ: Van Nostrand.

McClelland, D. C. (1987) *Human Motivation*. Cambridge: Cambridge University Press.

McClelland, D. C., Atkinson, J. W., Clark, R. A. & Lowell, E. L. (1953) *The Achievement Motive*. New York: Appleton-Century-Crofts.

McClelland, D. C., Baldwin, A. L., Bronfenbrenner, U. & Strodbeck, F. L. (1958) *Talent and Society. New Perspectives in the Identification of Talent*. Princeton, NJ: Van Nostrand.

McClurg, P. A. & Chaille, C. (1987) Computer games: environments for developing spatial cognition? *Journal of Educational Computing Research*, **3**, 95–111.

McCombs, B. L. & Marzano, R. J. (1990) Putting the self in self-regulated learning: The self as agent in integrating will and skill. *Educational Psychologist*, **25**, 51–69.

McCombs, B. L. & Pope, J. E. (1994) *Motivating Hard to Reach Students*. Washington, DC: American Psychological Association.

McCormack, S. (1989) Response to Render, Padilla, and Krank: But practitioners say it works! *Educational Leadership*, **46**, 77–9.

McCroarty, M. (1992) The societal context of bilingual education. *Educational Researcher*, **21**, 7–9.

McDaniel, T. (1983) `Well begun is half-done': A school-wide project for better discipline. *SET Research Information for Teachers*, number 1, item 9.

McDougall, A. (1990) Children, recursion and logo programming: an investigation of Papert's conjecture about the variability of Piagetian stages in computer-rich environment. In A. McDougal & C. Dowling (eds) *Computers in Education. WCCE 90 Sydney, Australia, July 9–13*, 1990. Amsterdam: North Holland.

McElwain, D. W. & Kearney, G. (1970) *The Queensland Test*. Melbourne: ACER.

McGaw, B., Banks, D. & Piper, K. (1991) *Effective Schools. Schools that make a Difference*. Hawthorn, Vic. ACER.

McInerney, D. M. (1979). Education for a Multicultural Society Report. Sydney: Milperra College of Advanced Education.

McInerney, D. M. (1984) *Inquiries into Creativity*. Sydney: Macarthur Institute of Higher Education.

McInerney, D. M. (1986) The determinants of motivation of Aboriginal students in school settings. In L. Lippman (Chair), Aboriginal & Islander Issues. Paper presented at the inaugural research conference of the Australian Institute of Multicultural Affairs entitled *Ethnicity and Multiculturalism 1986 National Research Conference*, Melbourne, May 14–16.

McInerney, D. M. (1987a) Teacher attitudes towards multicultural curriculum development. *Australian Journal of Education*, **31**, 129–44.

McInerney, D. M. (1987b) The need for the continuing education of teachers: a multicultural perspective. *Journal of Intercultural Studies*, **8**, 45–54.

McInerney, D. M. (1987c) The need for the continuing education of teachers in non-racist education-an Australian perspective. *Multicultural Teaching. Special Issue: Continuing Education*, **6**, 31–5.

McInerney, D. M. (1988a) A cross-cultural analysis of student motivation in school settings: An Australian perspective. In E. Thomas (Chair), Educational issues and cross-cultural psychology. Symposium conducted at the 9th International IACCP Congress, Newcastle, Australia.

McInerney, D. M. (1988b) *Psychological determinants of motivation of urban and rural non-traditional Aboriginal students in school settings: Summary of findings, conclusion and recommendations*. Paper presented at the Annual National Conference on Aboriginal Issues, Nepean CAE.

McInerney, D. M. (1988c) The psychological determinants of motivation of urban and rural non-traditional Aboriginal students in school settings: A cross-cultural study. Unpublished doctoral dissertation presented to the University of Sydney, Australia.

McInerney, D. M. (1989a) A cross-cultural analysis of student motivation. In D. M. Keats, D. Munro & L. Mann (eds) *Heterogeneity in Cross-Cultural Psychology*. Lisse: Zwets & Zeitlinger.

McInerney, D. M. (1989b) Urban Aboriginal parents' views on education: a comparative analysis. *Journal of Intercultural Studies*, **10**, 43–65.

McInerney, D. M. (1989c) Psychological determinants of motivation of urban and rural non-traditional Aboriginal students in school settings. In P. Moir and M. Durham (eds) *Contemporary Issues in Aboriginal Studies*: Sydney: Firebird Press.

McInerney, D. M. (1990a) The determinants of motivation for urban Aboriginal students: a cross-cultural analysis. *Journal of Cross-Cultural Psychology*, **21**, 474–95.

McInerney, D. M. (1990b) Sex differences in motivation for Aboriginal students in school settings. In M. Bezzina & J. Butcher (eds) *The Changing Face of Professional Education. Collected Papers of the AARE Annual Conference, Sydney University, 1990*. Sydney: AARE.

McInerney, D. M. (1991a) The behavioural intentions questionnaire. An examination of construct and etic validity in an educational setting. *Journal of Cross-Cultural Psychology*, **22**, 293–306.

McInerney, D. M. (1991b) Key determinants of motivation of urban and rural non-traditional Aboriginal students in school settings: Recommendations for educational change. *Australian Journal of Education*, **35**, 154–74.

McInerney, D. M. (1992a) *Indigenous Educational Research: Can it be Psychometric?* Paper presented at the AARE/NZARE conference 'Educational research: Discipline and diversity', Geelong, Vic.

McInerney, D. M. (1992b) Cross-cultural insights into school motivation and decision making. *Journal of Intercultural Studies*, **13**, 53–74.

McInerney, D. M. (1992c) Contemporary issues in cross-cultural studies. *Journal of Intercultural Studies*. **13**, 74–6.

McInerney, D. M. (1993) *Psychometric perspectives on school motivation and culture*. Paper presented at the symposium: International Perspectives on Culture and Schooling. Department of International and Comparative Education. Institute of Education, London University, 11–13 May.

McInerney, D. M. & McInerney, V. (1990) Causes and correlates of dropping out: A cross-cultural comparison. In R. A. Peddie (ed.) *Nationhood, Internationalism and Education*. Proceedings of the Eighteenth Annual Conference of the Australian and New Zealand Comparative and International Education Society. University of Auckland, 3–5 December. Auckland: ANZCIEA.

McInerney, D. M. & Sinclair, K. E. (1991) Cross-cultural model testing: Inventory of school motivation. *Educational and Psychological Measurement*, **51**, 123–33.

McInerney, D. M. & Sinclair, K. E. (1992) Dimensions of school motivation. A cross-cultural validation study. *Journal of Cross-Cultural Psychology*, **23**, 389–406.

McInerney, D. M (1994) Psychometric perspectives on school motivation and culture. In E. Thomas (ed.) *International Perspectives on Culture and Schooling: A Symposium of Proceedings*. London: Institute of Education: 327–53.

McInerney, D. M. & Swisher, K. (1995). Exploring Navajo motivation in school settings. *Journal of American Indian Education*, **34**, 28–51.

McInerney, D. M. & McInerney, V. (1996) School socialization and the goals of schooling: What counts in classrooms and schools characterized by cultural diversity. Paper presented at the annual meeting of the American Educational Research Association, New York, April 8–12.

McInerney, D. M., Dowson, M. & Hinkley, J. (1996) Relations between students' academic performance and teachers' perceptions of their conduct. *Australian Journal of Psychology*, **48**, 121.

McInerney, D. M., Hinkley, J. & Dowson, M. (1996) Children's beliefs about success in the classroom: Are there cultural differences? *Australian Journal of Psychology*, **48**, 121.

McInerney, D. M., McInerney, V. & Roche, L. (1994a) Universal goals of school motivation? An application of LISREL to cross-cultural research. Paper presented at the Australian Association for Research in Education Conference, Newcastle, 27 November to 1 December, 1994.

McInerney, D. M., McInerney, V. & Roche, L. (1994b) Achievement goal theory and indigenous minority school motivation: The importance of a multiple goal perspective. Paper presented at the Australian Association for Research in Education Conference, Newcastle, 27 November to 1 December, 1994.

McInerney, D. M., Roche, L., McInerney, V. & Marsh, H. W. (1997) Cultural perspectives on school motivation: The relevance and application of goal theory. *American Educational Research Journal*, **34**, 207–36.

McInerney, V., McInerney, D. M. & Sinclair, K. E. (1990) *Student teacher attitudes to computer usage: Interrelations between computer anxiety, age, gender and ethnicity*. Paper presented at the AARE annual conference, The Changing Face of Professional Education, University of Sydney, 27 November–2 December.

McInerney, V., McInerney, D. M. & Sinclair, K. E. (1994). Student teachers, computer anxiety and computer experience. *Journal of Educational Computing Research*, **11**, 27–50.

McInerney, V. & McInerney, D. M. (1996) Cooperative, self-regulated learning or teacher-directed instruction? Efficacy and effect on computer anxiety and achievement. An aptitude-treatment-interaction study. *Australian Journal of Psychology*, **48**, 122.

McInerney, V., McInerney, D. M. & Marsh, H. W. (in press). Effects of metacognitive strategy training within a cooperative group learning context on computer achievement and anxiety. *Journal of Educational Psychology*.

Macintosh, T. (1993) Education taps into info high-tech style. *The Australian*, June 15.

MacKay, G. (1990) Writing and computer skills of first year teacher trainees. In M. Bezzina & J. Butcher (eds) *The Changing Face of Professional Education. Collected Papers of the AARE Annual Conference, Sydney University, 1990*. Sydney: AARE.

McKeachie, W. J. (1977) The decline and fall of the laws of learning. In H. F. Clarizio, R. C. Craig & W. A. Mehrens (eds) *Contemporary Issues in Educational Psychology*, 3rd edn. Boston: Allyn & Bacon.

McKeachie, W. J., Pintrich, P. R. & Lin, Y-G. (1985) Teaching learning strategies. *Educational Psychologist*, **20**, 153–60.

McKeith, W. T. & Daniel, J. (1990) Extension for gifted and talented children-P.L.C. Sydney, Australia. *Unicorn*, **16**, 177–83.

McKinney, C. W., Larkins, A. G., Kazelskis, R., Ford, M. J., Allen, J. A. & Davis, J. C. (1983) Some effects of teacher enthusiasm on student achievement in fourth-grade social studies. *Journal of Educational Research*, **76**, 249–53.

MacKinnon, D. (1962) The nature and nurture of creative talent. *American Psychologist*, **17**, 484–95.

McKinnon, D., Owens, L. & Nolan, P. (1992) *The learning mode preferences of primary, intermediate and secondary students in New Zealand*. Paper presented at the AARE/NZARE conference 'Educational research: Discipline and diversity', Geelong, Vic.

McLoyd, V. C. (1979) The effects of extrinsic rewards of differential value on high and low intrinsic interest. *Child Development*, **50**, 1010–19.

McMeniman, M. (1989) Motivation to learn. In P. Langford (ed.) *Educational Psychology. An Australian Perspective*. Sydney: Longman Cheshire.

McMillan, J. H. (1992) *Educational Research. Fundamentals for the Consumer*. New York: HarperCollins.

McMillan, J. H. & Schumacher, S. (1989) *Research in Education. A Conceptual Introduction*, 2nd edn. New York: HarperCollins.

McNally, D. W. (1977) *Piaget, Education and Teaching*. Sussex: Harvester Press.

Madden, N. A. & Slavin, R. E. (1983) Mainstreaming students with mild handicaps: Academic and social outcomes. *Review of Educational Research*, **53**, 519–69.

Maehr, M. L. (1974a) Culture and achievement motivation. *American Psychologist*, **29**, 887–96.

Maehr, M. L. (1974b) *Sociocultural Origins of Achievement*. Monterey, CA: Brooks/Cole.

Maehr, M. L. (1978) Sociological origins of achievement motivation. In D. Bar-Tal & L. Saxe (eds) *Social Psychology of Education: Theory and Research: Vol 1*. New York: Hemisphere.

Maehr, M. L. (1984) Meaning and motivation: Toward a theory of personal investment. In R. Ames & C. Ames (eds) *Research on Motivation in Education: Vol. 1*. Student Motivation. Orlando: Academic Press.

Maehr, M. L. (1989) Thoughts about motivation. In C. Ames & R. Ames (eds) *Research on Motivation in Education: Vol. 3. Goals and Cognitions*. Orlando: Academic Press.

Maehr, M. L. (1991) The 'psychological environment' of the school: A focus for school leadership. In P. Thurston & P. Zodhiates (eds) *Advances in Educational Administration*. Greenwich, CT: JAI Press.

Maehr, M. L. & Anderman, E. M. (1993) Reinventing schools for early adolescents: Emphasizing task goals. *The Elementary School Journal*, **93**, 593–610.

Maehr, M. L. & Braskamp, L. A. (1986) *The Motivation Factor: A Theory of Personal Investment*. Lexington, Mass: Lexington.

Maehr, M.L & Buck, R.M. (1993) Transforming school culture. in M. Sashkin & H. Walberg (eds) *Educational Leadership and Culture: Current Research and Practice*. Berkeley, California, McCutchan.

Maehr, M. L. & Fyans, L. J. (1989) School culture, motivation, and achievement. In M. L. Maehr & C. Ames (eds) *Advances in Motivation and Achievement: Vol. 6. Motivation Enhancing Environments*. Greenwich, CT: JAI Press.

Maehr, M. L. & Lysy, A. (1979) A comparison of achieving orientations of preschool and school-age children. *International Journal of Intercultural Relations*, **2**, 38–69.

Maehr, M. L. & Midgley, C. (1991) Enhancing student motivation: a school-wide approach. *Educational Psychologist*, **26** (3 & 4), 399–427.

Maehr, M. L., Midgley, C. & Urdan, T. (1992) Student investment in learning: a focus for school leaders. *Educational Administration Quarterly*, **18**, 412–31.

Maehr, M. L. & Nicholls, J. C. (1980) Culture and achievement motivation. A second look. In N. Warren (ed.) *Studies in Cross-Cultural Psychology (Vol. 2)*. London: Academic Press.

Mageean, B. (1991) Self-report: A note on psychology and instruction. *Australian Journal of Education*, **35**, 41–59.

Mager, R. F. (1973) *Measuring Instructional Intent or Got a Match*. Belmont, CA: Fearon.

Mager, R. F. (1990a) *Preparing Instructional Objectives*, 2nd edn. London: Kogan Page.

Mager, R. F. (1990b) *Measuring Instructional Results*, 2nd edn. London: Kogan Page.

Maggs, A., Argent, I., Clarke, R., Falls, J. & Smart, G. (1980) Australian direct instruction research across classrooms. *The A.S.E.T. Journal*, **12**, 13–23.

Magolda, M. B. & Rogers, J. L. (1987) Peer tutoring: Collaborating to enhance intellectual development. *The College Student Journal*, **21**, 288–96.

Mahmood, M. A. & Medewitz, J. N. (1989) Assessing the effect of computer literacy on subject's attitudes, values, and opinions toward information technology: An exploratory longitudinal investigation using the linear structural relations (LISREL) model. *Journal of Computer Based Instruction*, **16**, 20–8.

Mak, A. (1994) Parental neglect and overprotection as risk factors in delinquency. *Australian Journal of Psychology*, **46**, 107–11.

Maker, J. (1987) Teaching the gifted and talented. In V. R. Koehler (ed.) *Handbook for Educators*. White Plains, NY: Longman.

Malin, M. (1990) The visibility and invisibility of Aboriginal students in an urban classroom. *Australian Journal of Education*, **34**, 312–29.

Malina, R. M. (1990) Physical growth and performance during the transitional years (9–16). In R. Montemayor, G. R. Adams & T. P. Gullotta (eds) *From Childhood to Adolescence. A Transitional Period?* Newbury Park: Sage.

Malina, R. M. & Bouchard, C. (1991) *Growth, Maturation, and Physical Activity*. Champaign, IL: Human Kinetics Books.

Management Review: NSW Education Portfolio. (1989) *Schools Renewal. A Strategy to Revitalize Schools Within the New South Wales Education System*. Milson's Point: NSW Education Portfolio.

Maples, M. F. & Webster, J. M. (1980) Thorndike's Connectionism. In G. M. Gazda & R. J. Corsini (eds) *Theories of Learning*. Itasca, IL: F. E. Peacock.

Marchant, G. J. (1985) An information processing model: Structures and implications. Unpublished manuscript, Northwestern University, Evanston, IL.

Marcia, J. E. (1966) Development and validation of ego identity status. *Journal of Personality and Social Psychology*, **3**, 551–8.

Marcia, J. E. (1967) Ego identity status: Relationship to change in self-esteem, 'general adjustment,' and authoritarianism. *Journal of Personality*, **35**, 119–33.

Marcia, J. E. (1980) Identity in adolescence. In J. Adelson (ed.) *Handbook of Adolescent Psychology*. New York: Wiley

Margolin, E. (1976) *Young Children. Their Curriculum and Learning Processes*. New York: Macmillan.

Marjoribanks, K. (1980) *Ethnic Families and Children's Achievements*. Sydney: George, Allen & Unwin.

Marjoribanks, K. (1987) Gender/social class, family environments and adolescents' aspirations. *Australian Journal of Education*, **31**, 43–54.

Marjoribanks, K. (ed.) (1991) *The Foundations of Students' Learning*. Oxford: Pergamon Press.

Marks, G. (1992a) *Integration of students with disabilities: Confusing social justice and economic imperatives*. Paper presented at the AARE/NZARE conference 'Educational research: Discipline and diversity', Geelong, Vic.

Marks, G. (1992b) *The politicisation of the language of integration*. Paper presented at the AARE/NZARE conference 'Educational research: Discipline and diversity', Geelong, Vic.

Markus, H. & Kunda, Z. (1986) Stability and malleability of the self-concept. *Journal of Personality and Social Psychology*, **51**, 858–66.

Marsella, A. J., Tharp, R. G. & Ciborowski, T. J. (1979) *Perspectives on Cross-Cultural Psychology*. New York: Academic Press.

Marsh, H. W. (1984) Self-concept, social comparison, and ability grouping: A reply to Kulik and Kulik. *American Educational Research Journal*, **21**, 799–806.

Marsh, H. W. (1990a) A multidimensional, hierarchical model of self-concept: Theoretical and empirical justification. *Educational Psychology Review*, **2**, 77–172.

Marsh, H. W. (1990b) Influences of internal and external frames of reference on the formation of math and English self-concepts. *Journal of Educational Psychology*, **82**, 107–16.

Marsh, H. W. (1991) Failure of high-ability high schools to deliver academic benefits commensurate with their students' ability levels. *American Educational Research Journal*, **28**, 445–80.

Marsh, H. W. (1993) Physical fitness self-concept: Relations of physical fitness to field and technical indicators for boys and girls aged 9–15. *Journal of Sport and Exercise Psychology*, **15**, 184–206.

Marsh, H. W. (1990) A multidimensional, hierarchical model of self-concept: Theoretical and empirical justification. *Educational Psychology Review*, **2**, 77–172.

Marsh, H. W. & Craven, R. (in press) Academic self-concept: Beyond the dustbowl. In G. Phye (ed.) *Handbook of Classroom Assessment: Learning, Achievement, and Adjustment*. Orlando, FL: Academic Press.

Marsh, H. W. & Johnston, C. F. (1993) Multidimensional self-concepts and frames of reference: Relevance to the exceptional learner. In F. E. Obiakor & S. W. Stile (eds) *Self-Concept of Exceptional Learners: Current Perspective for Educators*. Dubuque, Iowa: Kendall/Hunt.

Marsh, H. W. & Shavelson, R. (1985) Self-concept: Its multifaceted, hierarchical structure. *Educational Psychologist*, **20**, 107–23.

Marsh, H. W., Walker, R. & Debus, R. (1991) Subject specific components of academic self-concept and self-efficacy. *Contemporary Educational Psychology*, **16**, 331–45.

Marshall, H. H. (1987) Motivational strategies of three fifth-grade teachers. *Elementary School Journal*, **88**, 135–50.

Marshall, H. H. & Weinstein, R. S. (1984) Classroom factors affecting students' self-evaluation: An interactional model. *Review of Educational Research*, **54**, 301–25.

Martin, J. C. (1978) Locus of control and self-esteem in Indian and white students. *Indian Education*, **18**, 23–9.

Marzano, R. J. & Arredondo, D. E. (1986a) *Tactics for Thinking*. Aurora, CO: Mid-continent Regional Educational Laboratory.

Marzano, R. J. & Arredondo, D. E. (1986b) Restructuring schools through the teaching of thinking skills. *Educational Leadership*, **43**, 20–6.

Marzano, R. J. & Costa, A. L. (1988) Question: Do standardized tests measure general cognitive skills? Answer: No. *Educational Leadership*, **45**, 66–71.

Maslow, A. H. (1968) *Toward a Psychology of Being*, 2nd edn. Princeton, NJ: Van Nostrand.

Maslow, A. H. (1970) *Motivation and Personality*, 2nd edn. New York: Harper & Row.

Maslow, A. H. (1976) Defense and growth. In M. L. Silberman, J. S. Allender & J. M. Yanoff (eds) *Real Learning. A Sourcebook for Teachers*. Boston: Little, Brown & Co.

Mason, J. & Levi, N. (1992) *The Identification of Effective Teaching Practices. A Study of Teachers in Years K-12 in the Liverpool Cluster of the Metropolitan South-West Region*. Sydney: Faculty of Education, University of Western Sydney, Macarthur.

Masselos, G. & Hinley, C. (1981) The child with special needs from a migrant family. *Australian Journal of Early Childhood*, **6**, 35–8.

Matiasz, S. (1989) Aboriginal children and early childhood education. *Early Childhood Development and Care*, **52**, 81–91.

Matthew, A. & Crook, M. (1990) The control of reaching movements by young infants. *Child Development*, **61**, 1238–57.

Maude, D., Wertheim, E. H., Paxton, S., Gibbons, K. & Szmukler, G. (1993) Body dissatisfaction, weight loss behaviours and bulimic tendencies in Australian adolescents with an estimate of female data representativeness. *Australian Psychologist*, **28(2)**, 128–32.

Maurer, A. (1974) Corporal punishment. *American Psychologist*, **29**, 614–26.

Maxwell, T. W., Marshall, A. R. A., Walton, J. & Baker, I. (1989) Secondary school alternative structures: semester courses and vertical grouping in non-state schools in New South Wales. *Curriculum Perspectives*, **9**, 1–15.

Mayer, R. E. (1989) Models for understanding. *Review of Educational Research*, **59**, 43–64.

Meeker, M., Meeker, R. & Roid, G. (1985) *Structure-of-Intellect Learning Abilities Test (SOI-LA)*. Los Angeles, CA: Western Psychological Services.

Messick, S. (1995) Cognitive style and learning. In L. W. Anderson (ed.) *International Encyclopedia of Teaching and Teacher Education*, 2nd edn. Tarrytown, NY: Pergamon: 387–90.

Meier, S. (1985) Computer Aversion. *Computers in Human Behavior*, **12**, 327–34.

Merrett, F. & Tang, W. M. (1994) The attitudes of British primary school pupils to praise, rewards, punishments and reprimands. *British Journal of Educational Psychology*, **64**, 91–103.

Merrett, F. & Wheldall, K. (1990) *Positive Teaching in the Primary School*. London: Paul Chapman.

Messer, S. B. (1976) Reflection-impulsivity: A review. *Psychological Bulletin*, **83**, 1026–52.

Messick, S. (1976) *Individuality in Learning: Implications of Cognitive Styles and Creativity for Human Development*. San Francisco: Jossey-Bass.

Messick, S. (1984) The nature of cognitive styles. Problems and promise in educational practice. *Educational Psychologist*, **19**, 59–74.

Messick, S. (1989) Meaning and values in test validation: The science and ethics of assessment. *Educational Researcher*, **18**, 5–11.

Metherell, T. (1989) NSW Department of Education press release 'Technology High Schools: Meeting the Challenge'.

Miles, D. T. & Robinson, R. E. (1977) Behavioral objectives: An even closer look. In H. F. Clarizio, R. C. Craig & W. A. Mehrens (eds) *Contemporary Issues in Educational Psychology*, 3rd edn. Boston: Allyn & Bacon.

Miller, G. A. (1956) The magical number seven, plus or minus two: Some limits on our capacity for processing information. *Psychological Review*, **63**, 81–97.

Miller, L. & Olson, J. (1995) How computers live in schools. *Educational Leadership*, **53**, 2, 74–7.

Mingione, A. D. (1965) Need for achievement in Negro and white children. *Journal of Consulting Psychology*, **29**, 108–11.

Mingione, A. D. (1968) Need for achievement in Negro, white and Puerto Rican children. *Journal of Consulting and Clinical Psychology*, **10**, 157–72.

Ministry of Education (1987a) *Better Schools in Western Australia: A Programme for Improvement*. Perth: Author.

Ministry of Education (1987b) *Switch it on Miss*. A joint publication by the State Computer Education Centre and the Ministerial Advisory Committee on Multicultural and Migrant Education, Victoria.

Ministry of Education (1993) *First Steps*. Perth, WA: Author.

Mischel, W. (1986) *Introduction to Personality. A New Look*, 4th edn. New York: Holt, Rinehart & Winston.

Miura, I. T. (1986, April) *Computer self-efficacy: a factor in understanding gender differences in computer course enrolment*. Paper presented at the annual meeting of the American Educational Research Association, San Francisco, CA.

Modgil, S. & Modgil, C. (eds) (1976) *Piagetian Research*, Windsor: NFER.

Modgil, S. & Modgil, C. (eds) (1982) *Jean Piaget: Concensus and Controversy*. New York: Praeger.

Moll, L. C. (ed.) (1990) *Vygotsky and Education*. Cambridge: Cambridge University Press.

Mollick, L. B. & Etra, K. S. (1981) Poor learning ability or poor hearing? In K. L. Frieberg (ed.) *Educating Exceptional Children*, 6th edn. Guilford, CT: Duskin.

Montemayor, R., Adams, G. R. & Gullotta, T. P. (eds) (1990) *From Childhood to Adolescence. A Transitional Period?* Newbury Park: Sage.

Montemayor, R. & Flannery, D. J. (1991) Parent-adolescent relations in middle and late adolescence. In R. M. Lerner, A. C. Petersen & J. Brooks-Gunn (eds) *Encyclopedia of Adolescence (Vol. 2)*. New York: Garland.

Moore, B. (1986) Equity in education: gender issues in the use of computers. A review and bibliography. *Review and Evaluation Bulletins*, **6**, 1–59.

Moore, P. (1991) Reciprocal teaching of study skills. In J. B. Biggs (ed.) *Teaching for Learning. Hawthorn*, Vic. ACER.

Morgan, M. (1984) Reward-induced decrements and increments in intrinsic motivation. *Review of Educational Research*, **54**, 5–30.

Morton, A. (1993) Computer simulations: Do they have merit? *Australian Educational Computing*, **8**, ACEC '93 edition. 161–5.

Mosher, R. (ed.) (1980) *Moral Education: A First Generation of Research and Development*. New York: Praeger.

Moshman, D. (1982) Exogenous, endogenous, and dialectical constructivism. *Developmental Review*, **2**, 371–84.

Moss, P. A. (1992) Shifting conceptions of validity in educational measurement: Implications for performance assessment. *Review of Educational Research*, **62**, 229–58.

Moss, P. A. (1996) Enlarging the dialogue in educational measurement: Voices from interpretive research traditions. *Educational Researcher*, **25**, 20–8.

Moyles, J. R. (ed.) (1995) *The Excellence of Play*. Buckingham, UK: Open University Press.

Mulryan, C. M. (1996) Cooperative small groups in mathematics: The perceptions and involvement of intermediate students. *Set Research Information for Teachers*, One, **12**, 1–4.

Munnings, A. (1980) A cross cultural investigation of strategies used in concept learning by Australian and Malaysian adolescents. Unpublished honours thesis, Department of Psychology, University of Newcastle, Australia.

Munns, G. (1996) Teaching resistant Koori students. Towards non-reproductive education. Unpublished doctoral dissertation presented to the University of New England, Armidale, Australia.

Munter, S. (1993). Learning for tomorrow. *The Gen*, June, 2.

Munter, S. (1996) Cyber-learning. *The Gen*, January/February. Commonwealth Department of Employment Education and Training, Australia. http:/www.deet/gov.au/pubs/the_gen

Murray, F. B. (1988) The child-computer dyad and cognitive development. In G. Forman & P. B. Pufall (eds) *Constructivism in the Computer Age*. Hillsdale, NJ: Lawrence Erlbaum.

Murray, J. P. (1973) Television and violence: Implications of the Surgeon General's Research Program. *American Psychologist*, 472–8.

Musgrave, P. (1989) Personal and career development of teachers. In P. Langford (ed.) *Educational Psychology. An Australian Perspective*. Sydney: Longman Cheshire.

Mussen, P. H. & Jones, M. C. (1957) Self-conceptions, motivations and interpersonal attitudes of late- and early-maturing boys. *Child Development*, **28**, 243–56.

Mussen, P. H. & Jones, M. C. (1958) The behavior-inferred motivations of late- and early-maturing boys. *Child Development*, **29**, 61–7.

Nanlohy, P. & Howe, A. (1996) Not so much a superhighway as a virtual village. p.nanlohy@uws.edu.au.

National Board of Employment Education and Training (1990) *Teacher Education in Australia*. Canberra: AGPS.

Natriello, G. (1987) The impact of evaluation processes on students. *Educational Psychologist*, **22**, 155–75.

Natriello, G. (1989) The impact of evaluation processes on students. In R. E. Slavin (ed.) *School and Classroom Organization*. Hillsdale, NJ: Erlbaum.

Natriello, G. & Dornbusch, S. M. (1984) *Teacher Evaluative Standards and Student Effort*. New York: Longman.

Naveh-Benjamin, M. (1991) A comparison of training programs intended for different types of test-anxious students: Further support for an information-processing model. *Journal of Educational Psychology*, **83**, 134–9.

Neate, G. (1975) *Difficulties Encountered in Teaching Australian Aborigines in School Systems, and Attempts to Overcome These Difficulties*. Conference Paper, AIAS.

Nedd, D. M. & Gruenfeld, L. W. (1976) Field dependence-independence and social traditionalism. A comparison of ethnic subcultures of Trinidad. *International Journal of Psychology*, **11**, 23–41.

Neisser, U. et al. (1996) Intelligence: Knowns and unknowns. *American Psychologist*, **51**, 77–101.

Nelson, R. B., Cummings, J. A. & Boltman, H. (1991) Teaching concepts to students who are educable mentally retarded. In K. L. Frieberg (ed.) *Educating Exceptional Children*, 6th edn. Guilford, CT: Duskin.

Nelson-Le Gall, S. A. (1985) Motive-outcome matching and outcome foreseeability: effects on attribution of intentionality and moral judgments. *Developmental Psychology*, **21**, 332–7.

Newby, T. J. (1991) Classroom motivation: Strategies of first-year teachers. *Journal of Educational Psychology*, **83**, 195–200.

New South Wales Department of School Education (1990) *Multicultural Activities for Schools*. Sydney: Author.

New South Wales Department of School Education (1991) *Policy for the Education of Gifted and Talented Students*. Sydney: Author.

New South Wales Department of School Education (1991) *NSW Government Strategy for the Education of Gifted and Talented Students*. Sydney: Author.

New South Wales Department of School Education (1991) *Implementation Strategies for the Education of Gifted and Talented Students*. Sydney: Author.

Nicholls, J. G. (1976) Effort is virtuous, but it's better to have ability: Evaluative responses to perceptions of effort and ability. *Journal of Research in Personality*, **10**, 306–15.

Nicholls, J. G. (1984) Conceptions of ability and achievement motivation. In R. Ames & C. Ames (eds) *Research on Motivation in Education: Vol. 1. Student Motivation*. Orlando: Academic Press.

Nicholls, J. G. (1989) *The Competitive Ethos and Democratic Education*. Cambridge: Harvard University Press.

Nickerson, R., Perkins, D. N. & Smith, E. (1985) *The Teaching of Thinking Skills*. Hillsdale, NJ: Lawrence Erlbaum.

Nixon, P. (1991) Alison has the right concepts. *Western Australian Education News*, Ministry of Education, October, 9.

Nixon, P. (1992) Telematics: High-tech communications. *Western Australian Education News*, Ministry of Education, April, 28.

Nolan, P., McKinnon, D. & Owens, L. (1992) *The learning mode preferences of students in the Freyberg Integrated Studies Project in New Zealand*. Paper presented at the AARE/NZARE conference 'Educational research: Discipline and diversity', Geelong, Vic.

Nolen, S. B. (1988) Reasons for studying: Motivational orientations and study strategies. *Cognition and Instruction*, **5**, 269–87.

Nolen, S. B. & Nicholls, J. G. (1993) Elementary school pupils' beliefs about practices for motivating pupils in mathematics. *British Journal of Educational Psychology*, **63**, 414–30.

Nolen, S. B. & Nicholls, J. G. (1994) A place to begin (again) in research on student motivation: Teachers' beliefs. *Teaching and Teacher Education*, **10**, 57–69.

Norcini, J. & Snyder, S. (1983) The effects of modeling and cognitive induction on the moral reasoning of adolescents. *Journal of Youth and Adolescence*, **12**, 101–15.

Nordland, F. H. (1986) Teaching for higher cognitive levels: a Piagetian perspective. In *Proceedings of the Twelfth Annual Conference of Science Education Association of Western Australia, the University of Western Australia, Perth*. Perth: Science Education Association of Western Australia.

Novak, J. D. (1981) Effective science instruction: The achievement of shared meaning. *The Australian Science Teachers Journal*, **27**, 5–13.

Nucci, L. (1982) Conceptual development in the moral and conventional domains. Implications for values education. *Review of Educational Research*, **49**, 93–122.

Nucci, L. (1987) Synthesis of research on moral development. Educational Leadership, 44, 86–92.

Nuthall, G. & Alton-Lee, A. (1990) Research on teaching and learning: Thirty years of change. *The Elementary School Journal*, **90**, 547–70.

Oblinger, D. G. & Maruyama, M. K. (1996) *Distributed Learning. Higher Education*, IBM North America.

Offer, D., Ostrov, E., Howard, K. L. & Atkinson, R. (1988) *The Teenage World: Adolescents' Self-image in Ten Countries*. New York: Plenum Medical.

Office of Multicultural Affairs (1990) *Multicultural Policies and Programs: An Overview*. Canberra: AGPS.

Ogbu, J. G. (1983) Minority status and schooling in plural societies. *Comparative Education Review*, **27**, 168–90.

Ogbu, J. G. (1992) Understanding cultural diversity and learning. *Educational Researcher*, **21**, 5–14.

Ogbu, J. G. & Matute-Bianchi, M. E. (1986) Understanding sociocultural factors in education: Knowledge, identity, and adjustment in schooling, in California State Department, Bilingual Education Office, *Beyond Language: Social and Cultural Factors in Schooling Language Minority Students. Sacramento*, CA: California State University, Los Angeles, Evaluation, Dissemination and Assessment Center.

O'Leary, K. D. & O'Leary, S. G. (1977) *Classroom Management. The Successful Use of Behavior Modification*, 2nd edn. NY: Pergamon.

O'Neil, J. (1990) Making sense of style. *Educational Leadership*, **48**, 4–9.

O'Neil, J. (1995) A conversation with Chris Dede. *Educational Leadership*, **53**, 2, 6–12.

Open University (1981) *Measuring Learning Outcomes*. Milton Keynes: Open University Press.

Orr, E. (1989) 'Engineers don't carry handbags?!' *SET Research Information for Teachers*, number 1, item 7.

Osborn, A. (1957) *Applied Imagination*. New York: Charles Scribner's.

Osborne, B. (1982) Field dependence/independence of Torres Strait Islander and Aboriginal pupils. *Journal of Intercultural Studies*, **3**, 5–18.

Osborne, R. (1980) *Force: LISP Working Paper Number 16*. Hamilton, NZ: SERU, University of Waikato.

Osborne, R. J. & Gilbert, J. K. (1980) A technique for exploring students' views of the world. *Physics Education*, **15**, 376–9.

O'Shea, T. & Self, J. (1983) *Learning and Teaching with Computers: Artificial Intelligence in Education*. Brighton, UK: Harvester.

Owens, L., Nolan, P. & McKinnon, D. (1992) *A comparison of the learning mode preferences of students in four countries-Australia, New Zealand, England, USA*. Paper presented at the AARE/NZARE conference 'Educational research: Discipline and diversity', Geelong, Vic.

Paikoff, R. L. & Brooks-Gunn, J. (1990) Physiological processes: What role do they play during the transition to adolescence? In R. Montemayor, G. R. Adams & T. P. Gullotta (eds) *From Childhood to Adolescence. A Transitional Period?* Newbury Park: Sage.

Palincsar, A. S. & Brown, A. L. (1984) The reciprocal teaching of comprehension-fostering and comprehensions-monitoring activities. *Cognition and Instruction*, **1**, 117–75.

Papalia, D. E. & Olds, S. W. (1989) *Life Span Development. First Australian Edition*. (Australian eds Lindsay Gething & Desmond Hatchard). Sydney: McGraw-Hill.

Papert, S. (1980) *Mindstorms: Children, Computers and Powerful Ideas*. Brighton, UK: Harvester.

Papert, S. (1987) Computer Criticism versus Technocentric Thinking. *Educational Researcher*, January–February, 22–30.

Papert, S. (1988) The Conservation of Piaget: The computer as grist to the constructivist mill. In G. Forman & P. B. Pufall (eds) *Constructivism in the Computer Age*. Hillsdale, NJ: Lawrence Erlbaum.

Papert, S. (1993) *The Children's Machine. Rethinking School in the Age of the Computer*. New York: Basic Books.

Paris, S. G. & Ayres, L. R. (1994) *Becoming Reflective Students and Teachers with Portfolios and Authentic Assessment*. Washington, DC: American Psychological Association.

Paris, S. G., Lipson, M. Y. & Wixson, K. K. (1983) Becoming a strategic reader. *Contemporary Educational Psychology*, **8**, 293–316.

Paris, S. G. & Oka, E. R. (1986) Self-regulated learning among exceptional children. *Exceptional Children*, **53**, 103–8.

Parten, M. B. (1932) Social participation among preschool children. *Journal of Abnormal and Social Psychology*, **27**, 243–69.

Partington, G. & McCudden, V. J. (1990) Classroom interaction: Some qualitative and quantitative differences in a mixed-ethnicity classroom. *Australian Journal of Teacher Education*, **15**, 43–9.

Partington, G. & McCudden, V. (1992) *Ethnicity and Education*. Wentworth Falls: Social Science Press.

Pascuale-Leone, J. (1969) Cognitive development and cognitive style. Unpublished doctoral dissertation, University of Geneva.

Paterson, J. F. (1992) *Attitudes towards the integration of students with disabilities*. Paper presented at the AARE/NZARE conference 'Educational research: Discipline and diversity', Geelong, Vic.

Paulson, F. L., Paulson, P. R. & Meyer, C. A. (1991) What makes a portfolio a portfolio? *Educational Leadership*, **48**, 60–3.

Pavan, B. N. (1992) The benefits of nongraded schools. *Educational Leadership*, **50**, 22–5.

Paxton, S. J., Schutz, H. K. & Muir, S. (1996) Friend and peer-related variables predict body image dissatisfaction, dieting, binge eating and extreme weight loss behaviours in adolescent girls. Paper presented at the 31st Annual Conference of the Australian Psychological Society, 25–29 September, Sydney.

Paxton, S., Wertheim, E., Gibbons, K., Szmukler, G. L., Hillier, L. & Petrovich, J. L. (1991) Body image satisfaction, dieting beliefs, and weight loss behaviours in adolescent girls and boys. *Journal of Youth and Adolescence*, **20**, 361–97.

Pea, R. D. (1985) Beyond amplification: Using the computer to reorganise mental functioning. *Educational Psychologist*, **20**, 167–82.

Peacock, D. & Yaxley, B. (1990) Teacher as reflective practitioner: an evolving research agenda. In M. Bezzina & J. Butcher (eds) *The Changing Face of Professional Education. Collected Papers of the AARE Annual Conference, Sydney University, 1990*. Sydney: AARE.

Peak, G. J. (1971) The cognitive-developmental approach to moral education: An American Viewpoint. *Inside Education*, August, 779–83.

Pease-Alvarez, L. & Hakuta, K. (1992) Enriching our views of bilingualism and bilingual education. *Educational Researcher*, **21**, 4–6.

Pederson, P. (1979) Non-western psychology: the search for alternatives. In A. J. Marsella, R. G. Tharp & T. J. Ciborowski (eds) *Perspectives on Cross-Cultural Psychology*. New York: Academic Press.

Pelham, W. E. & Murphy, H. A. (1986) Attention deficit and conduct disorders. In M. Hersen (ed.) *Pharmacological and Behavioral Treatment: An Integrative Approach*. New York: Wiley.

Pellegrini, A. D. & Horvat, M. (1995) A developmental contextualist critique of attention deficit hyperactivity disorder. *Educational Researcher*, **24**, 13–19.

Penney, R. K. (1967) Effect of reward and punishment on children's orientation and discrimination learning. In R. H. Walters et al. (eds) *Punishment*. Harmonsworth, Middlesex: Penguin Books.

Pennypacker, H. S. (1992) Is behavior analysis undergoing selection by consequences? *American Psychologist*, **47**, 1491–8.

Perkins, D. G. (1980) Classical Conditioning: Pavlov. In G. M. Gazda & R. J. Corsini (eds) *Theories of Learning*. Itasca, IL: F. E. Peacock.

Perkins, D. N. (1981) *The Mind's Best Work*. Cambridge, MA: Harvard University Press.

Perkins, D. N. (1988) Creativity and quest for mechanism. In R. J. Sternberg & E. E. Smith (eds) *The Psychology of Human Thought*. Cambridge: Cambridge University Press.

Perkins, D. N. (1992) What constructivism demands of the learner. In T.M. Duffy & D. H. Jonassen (eds) *Constructivism and the Technology of Instruction*. Hillsdale, NJ: Lawrence Erlbaum: 161–5.

Perret-Clermont, A. N. & Schubauer-Leoni, M. L. (1989) Social factors in learning and teaching: Towards an integrative perspective. *International Journal of Educational Research*, **13**, 573–684.

Perry, C. (1996) Learning styles and learning outcomes based on Kolb's learning style inventory. *SET Research Information for Teachers*, **10** (1), 1–4.

Pervin, L. A. (1989) Personality. *Theory and Practice*. New York: John Wiley.

Petersen, A. C. (1987) Those gangly years. *Psychology Today*. June, 28–34.

Peterson, A. C. & Taylor, B. (1980) The biological approach to adolescence. In J. Adelson (ed.) *Handbook of Adolescent Psychology*. New York: John Wiley.

Petersen, A. (1985) Pubertal development as a cause of disturbance: Myths, realities, and unanswered questions. *Genetic, Social, and General Psychology Monographs*, **111**, 205–32.

Petersen, A. C. et al. (1995) Adolescent development and the emergence of sexuality. *Suicide and Life-Threatening Behavior*, **25**, 4–17.

Peterson, C. (1989) *Looking Forward Through the Lifespan: Developmental Psychology*, 2nd edn. Sydney: Prentice Hall Australia.

Peterson, C. (1996) *Looking Forward Through the Lifespan: Developmental Psychology*, 3rd edn. Sydney: Prentice Hall Australia.

Peterson, C., Beck, K. & Rowell, G. (1992). *Psychology. An Introduction for Nurses and Allied Health Professionals*. Sydney: Prentice Hall Australia.

Peterson, P. L. (1988) Teachers' and students' cognitional knowledge for classroom teaching and learning. *Educational Researcher*, **17**, 5–14.

Peterson, P. L. & Fennema, E. (1985) Effective teaching, student engagement in classroom activities, and sex-related differences in learning mathematics. *American Educational Research Journal*, **22**, 309–35.

Phillips, D. C (1995) The good, the bad, and the ugly: The many faces of constructivism. *Educational Researcher*, **24**, 5–12.

Phillip Institute of Technology (1984) *Review of the Commonwealth Multicultural Education Program: Volume 1*

(Report to the Commonwealth Schools Commission). Canberra: The Commission.

Phye, G. D. & Andre, T. (1986) *Cognitive Classroom Learning. Understanding Thinking and Problem Solving*. Orlando: Harcourt Brace Jovanovich.

Piaget, J. (1954) *The Construction of Reality in the Child* (trans. by M. Cook). New York: Basic Books.

Piaget, J. (1963) *Origins of Intelligence in Children* (trans. by M. Cook). New York: Norton.

Piaget, J. (1965) *The Moral Judgment of the Child*. New York: Free Press.

Piaget, J. (1970) *The Science of Education and the Psychology of the Child*. New York: Orion Press.

Piaget, J. (1970) Piaget's Theory. In P. H. Mussen (ed.) *Carmichael's Manual for Child Psychology*. New York: Wiley.

Piaget, J. (1971) *The Children's Conception of the World* (trans. by J. Tomlinson & A. Tomlinson). London: Routledge & Kegan Paul.

Piaget, J. (1974) *Understanding Causality* (trans. by D. Miles & M. Miles). New York: Norton.

Pick, A. D. (1980) Cognition: Psychological perspectives. In H. C. Triandis & W. Lonner (eds) *Handbook of Cross-Cultural Psychology: Vol. 3. Basic Processes*. Boston: Allyn & Bacon.

Pines, A. L. & Leith, S. (1981) What is concept learning in science? Theory, recent research and some teaching suggestions. *The Australian Science Teachers Journal*, **27**, 15–20.

Pintrich, P. (1988) A process-oriented view of student motivation and cognition. In J. S. Stark & L. A. Mets (eds) *Improving Teaching and Learning Through Research. New Directions for Instructional Research*, **57**. San Francisco: Jossey-Bass.

Pintrich, P. R. & De Groot, E. V. (1990) Motivational and self-regulated learning components of classroom academic performance. *Journal of Educational Psychology*, **82**, 33–40.

Pintrich, P. R., & Garcia, T. (1991) Student goal orientation and self-regulation in the college classroom. In M. L. Maehr & P. R. Pintrich, (eds.) *Advances in Motivation and Achievement: Goals and Self–regulatory Processes*, Vol. 7 Greenwich, CT: JAI Press: 371–402.

Pintrich, P. R. & Schrauben, B. (1992) Students' motivational beliefs and their cognitive engagement in classroom academic tasks. In D. Schunk & J. Meece (eds) *Student Perceptions in the Classroom*. Hillsdale, NJ: Lawrence Erlbaum.

Pintrich, P. R., Marx, R. W. & Boyle, R. (1993) Beyond 'cold' conceptual change: The role of motivational beliefs and classroom contextual factors in the process of conceptual change. *Review of Educational Research*, **63**, 167–99.

Poe, E. A. (1945) The philosophy of composition. In P. van Doren (ed.) *The Portable Edgar Allan Poe*. New York: Viking Press.

Pokay, D. & Blumenfeld, P. C. (1990) Predicting achievement early and late in the semester: The role of motivation and use of learning strategies. *Journal of Educational Psychology*, **82**, 41–50.

Polesel, J. (1990) ESL, ideology and multiculturalism. *Journal of Intercultural Studies*, **11**, 64–72.

Pollin, L. (1989) Research windows. *The Computing Teacher*, **17**, 7–8.

Poole, M. E. (1987) Multiculturalism, participation and equity: discussions on educational processes, policies and outcomes. *Australian Educational Researcher*, **15**, 21–36.

Poplin, M. S. (1988) Holistic/constructivist principles of the teaching/learning process: Implications for the field of learning disabilities. *Journal of Learning Disabilities*, **21**, 401–16.

Porter, A. C. & Brophy, J. (1988) Synthesis of research on good teaching: Insights from the work of the Institute for Research on Teaching. *Educational Leadership*, **45**, 74–85.

Porter, R. P. (1990) *Forked Tongue: The Politics of Bilingual Education*. New York: Basic Books.

Powell, J. P. & Anderson, L. W. (1985). Humour and teaching in higher education. *Studies in Higher Education*, **10**, 79–90.

Prawat, R. S. (1989) Promoting access to knowledge, strategy, and disposition in students: A research synthesis. *Review of Educational Research*, **59**, 1–41.

Pressley, M. (1995) More about the development of self-regulation. Complex, long-term, and thoroughly social. *Educational Psychologist*, **30**, 207–12.

Pressley, M., Harris, K. R. & Marks, M. B. (1992) But good strategy instructors are constructivists. *Educational Psychology Review*, **4**, 3–31.

Pressley, M., Johnson, C. J., Symons, S., McGoldrick, J. A. & Kurita, J. A. (1989) Strategies that improve children's memory and comprehension of text. *The Elementary School Journal*, **90**, 3–32.

Pressley, M., & Woloshyn, V. (1995) *Cognitive Strategy Instruction that Really Improves Children's Academic Performance*. Cambridge, MA:Brookline.

Print, M. (1981) The curriculum enrichment project for primary schools. *Unicorn*, **7**, 265–71.

Pritchard, C. (1992) Youth suicide and gender in Australia and New Zealand compared with countries of the western World (1973–1987). *Australian and New Zealand Journal of Psychiatry*, **26**, 609–17.

Pufall, P. B. (1988) Function in Piaget's System: Some notes for constructors of microworlds. In G. Forman & P. B. Pufall (eds) *Constructivism in the Computer Age*. Hillsdale, NJ: Lawrence Erlbaum.

Pulaski, M. A. S. (1971) *Understanding Piaget*. New York: Harper & Row.

Qin, Z., Johnson, D. W. & Johnson, R. T. (1995) Cooperative versus competitive efforts and problem solving. *Review of Educational Research*, **2**, 129–43.

Quine, S. (1973) Achievement Orientation of Aboriginal and White Adolescents. Unpublished doctoral dissertation, Australian National University, Canberra.

Ramirez, M., Castaneda, A. & Herold, P. L. (1974) The relationship of acculturation to cognitive style among Mexican Americans. *Journal of Cross-Cultural Psychology*, **5**, 424–33.

Raths, J. (1987) Enhancing understanding though debriefing. *Educational Leadership*, **45**, 24–7.

Raths, J., Wojtaszek-Healy, M. & Della-Piana, C. K. (1987) Grading problems: A matter of communication. *Journal of Educational Research*, **80**, 133–7.

Reimann, J. (1985) *Education for Girls. Girls and Computing Project*. South Australia: Angle Park Computing Centre.

Reimann, J. & Filsell, J. (1987) Bridging the technology gap. *Information Transfer*, **7**, 12–19.

Reis, S. M. (1989) Reflections on policy affecting the education of gifted and talented students. Past and future perspectives. *American Psychologist*, **44**, 399–408.

Relich, J. & Ward, J. (eds)(1987) *Academically Gifted-Educationally Disadvantaged? Providing for the Intellectually Gifted and Talented*. Sydney: NSWIER.

Render, G. F., Padilla, J. N. & Krank, H. M. (1989) What research really shows about assertive discipline. *Educational Leadership*, **46**, 72–5.

Renner, J., Stafford, A., Lawson, J., McKinnson, J., Friot, F. & Kellogg, D. (1976) *Research, Teaching, and Learning with the Piaget Model*. Normal: University of Oklahoma Press.

Renzulli, J. S. (1986) The three-ring conception of giftedness: A developmental model for creative productivity. In R. J. Sternberg & J. E. Davidson (eds) *Conceptions of Giftedness*. New York: Cambridge University Press.

Resnick, L. B. (1987) Learning in school and out. *Educational Researcher*, **16**, 13–20.

Rest, J. R. (1973) The hierarchical nature of moral judgment: A study of patterns of comprehension and preference with moral stages. *Journal of Personality*, **41**, 92–3.

Rest, J. R. (1979) *Development in Judging Moral Issues*. Minneapolis: University of Minnesota Press.

Reynolds, A. (1992) What is competent beginning teaching? A review of the literature. *Review of Educational Research*, **62**, 1–35.

Reynolds, M. C. (1984) Classification of students with handicaps. In E. W. Gordon (ed.) *Review of Research in Education (Vol 11)*. Washington: AERA.

Reynolds, S. B., Patterson, M. E., Skaggs, L. P. & Dansereau, D. F. (1991) Knowledge hypermaps and cooperative learning. *Computers in Education*. **16**, 167–73.

Rhode, G., Morgan, D. P. & Young, K. R. (1983) Generalization and maintenance of treatment gains of behaviorally handicapped students from resource rooms to regular classrooms using self-evaluation procedures. *Journal of Applied Behavior Analysis*, **16**, 171–88.

Rickard, A. G. (1981) The planning of a district-based innovation for gifted children. *Unicorn*, **7**, 254–74.

Ridberg, E. H., Parke, R. D. & Hetherington, E. M. (1971) Modification of impulsive and reflective cognitive styles through observation of film-mediated models. *Child Development*, **5**, 369–77.

Rietveld, C. (1988) Adjusting to school. Eight children with Down's syndrome. *SET Research Information for Teachers*, number 1, item 2.

Ringbom, H. (1987) *The Role of the First Language in Foreign Language Learning*. Avon, UK: Multilingual Matters.

Ritchie, J. (1983) Corporal punishment and attitudes to violence of secondary school students. *New Zealand Journal of Educational Studies*, **18**, 84–7.

Ritts, V., Patterson, M. L & Tubbs, M. E. (1992) Expectations, impressions, and judgements of physically attractive students: A review. *Review of Educational Research*, **62**, 413–26.

Roche, L. A. & Marsh, H. W. (1993) The comparison of nomothetic (highly structured) and idiographic (open-ended) measures of multifaceted self-concepts. Paper presented at the AARE Annual Conference, Fremantle, WA.

Robinson, F. P. (1961) *Effective Study*. New York: Harper & Row.

Roe, A. (1963) Psychological approaches to creativity in science. In M. A. Coler & H. K. Hughes (eds) *Essays on Creativity in the Sciences*. New York: New York University Press.

Rogers, B. (1990) *You Know the Fair Rule*. Hawthorn, Vic. ACER.

Rogers, B. (1994) *The Language of Discipline: A Practical Approach to Effective Classroom Management*. Plymouth, UK: Northcote House.

Rogers, B. (1995) *Behaviour Management: A Whole-school Approach*. Gosford, NSW: Ashton Scholastic.

Rogers, C. R. (1951) *Client-centered Therapy: Its Current Practice, Implications and Theory*. Boston: Houghton Mifflin.

Rogers, C. R. (1961) *On Becoming a Person*. Boston: Houghton Mifflin.

Rogers, C. R. (1969) *Freedom to Learn*. Columbus, Ohio: Charles E. Merrill.

Rogers, C. R. (1976) The interpersonal relationship in the facilitation of learning. In M. L. Silberman, J. S. Allender & J. M. Yanoff (eds) *Real Learning. A Sourcebook for Teachers*. Boston: Little, Brown & Co.

Rogers, C. R. (1977) Learning to be free. In H. F. Clarizio, R. C. Craig & W. A. Mehrens (eds) *Contemporary Issues in Educational Psychology*, 3rd edn. Boston: Allyn & Bacon.

Rogers, C. R. (1980) *A Way of Being*. Boston: Houghton Mifflin.

Rogers, C. R. (1983) *Freedom to Learn: For the 80s*. Columbus, Ohio: Charles E. Merrill.

Rogers, C. S. & Sawyers, J. K.(1988) *Play in the Lives of Young Children*. Washington DC: NAEYC.

Rogers, K. B. & Kimpston, R. D. (1992) Acceleration: What we do vs what we know. *Educational Leadership*, **50**, 58–61.

Rogers, W. A. (1989) *Making a Discipline Plan. Developing Classroom Management Skills*. South Melbourne, Vic. Nelson.

Rogoff, B. (1990) *Apprenticeship in Thinking. Cognitive Development in Social Context*. New York: Oxford University Press.

Rogoff, B. (1995) Observing sociocultural activities on three planes: participatory appropriation, guided appropriation and apprenticeship. In J. V. Wertsch, P. Del Rio & A. Alverez (eds) *Sociocultural Studies of the Mind*. Cambridge: Cambridge University Press: 139–64.

Rogoff, B. & Chavajay, P. (1995) What's become of research on the cultural basis of cognitive development? *American Psychologist*, **50**, 859–77.

Rohwer, W. D., Rohwer, C. P. & B-Howe, J. R. (1980) *Educational Psychology. Teaching for Student Diversity*. New York: Holt, Rinehart & Winston.

Romeo, F. F. (1986) *Understanding anorexia nervosa*. Springfield, IL: Thomas.

Rosen, B. C. (1959) Race, ethnicity and the achievement syndrome. *American Sociological Review*, **24**, 47–60.

Rosen, B. C. (1962) Socialization and achievement motivation in Brazil. *American Sociological Review*, **27**, 612–24.

Rosen. L. D., Sears, D. C. & Weil, M. M. (1987) Computerphobia. *Behavior Research Methods, Instruments, and Computers*, **19**, 167–79.

Rosenberg, M. (1979) *Conceiving the Self*. New York: Basic Books.

Rosenshine, B. & Meister, C. (1995) Direct instruction. In L. W. Anderson (ed.) *International Encyclopedia of Teaching and Teacher Education*, 2nd edn. Tarrytown, NY: Pergamon: 143–9.

Rosenshine, B., Meister, C. & Chapman, S. (1996) Teaching students to generate questions: A review of the intervention studies. *Review of Educational Research*, **66**, 181–221.

Rosenshine, B. V. (1971) *Teaching Behaviours and Student Achievement*. London: National Foundation for Educational Research.

Rosenshine, B. V. (1979) Content, time and direct instruction. In P. L. Peterson and H. J. Walberg (eds) *Research on Teaching: Concepts, Findings, and Implications*. Berkeley: McCutchan.

Rosenshine, B. V. (1986) Synthesis of research on explicit teaching. *Educational Leadership*, **43**, 60–9.

Rosenshine, B. & Stevens, R. (1986) Teaching functions. In M. C. Wittrock (ed.) *Handbook of Research on Teaching*, 3rd edn. New York: Macmillan.

Rosenthal, D., Ranieri, N. & Klimidis, S. (1996) Vietnamese adolescents in Australia: Relationships between perceptions of self and parental values, intergenerational conflict, and gender dissatisfaction. *International Journal of Psychology*, **31**, 81–91.

Rosenthal, R. (1973) The Pygmalion effect lives. *Psychology Today, September*, 56–63.

Rosenthal, R. & Jacobson, L. (1968) *Pygmalion in the Classroom: Teacher Expectations and Pupils' Intellectual Development*. New York: Holt, Rinehart & Winston.

Rosenthal, R. & Jacobson, L. (1971) Pygmalion in the classroom. An excerpt. In M. L. Silberman (ed.) *The Experience of Schooling*. New York: Holt, Rinehart & Winston.

Rothenberg, S. (1989) The open classroom reconsidered. *The Elementary School Journal*, **90**, 69–86.

Rothman, S. L. (1990) A critical analysis of education for children identified as gifted and talented and implications for teacher education. In M. Bezzina & J. Butcher (eds) *The Changing Face of Professional Education. Collected Papers of the AARE Annual Conference, Sydney University, 1990*. Sydney: AARE.

Rouet, J. F. (1990) Interactive text processing by inexperienced (hyper-)readers. In A. Rizk, N. Streitz & J. Andre (eds.) *Hypertexts: Concepts, Systems, and Applications*. Cambridge, England: Cambridge University Press: 250–60.

Rouet, J. & Levonen, J. J. (1996) Studying and learning with hypertext: Empirical studies and their implications. In J. Rouet, J. Levonen, A. Dillon & R. J. Spiro (eds) *Hypertext and Cognition*. New Jersey: Lawrence Erlbaum.

Rowe, H. (1984) Problem solving strategies. *SET Research Information for Teachers*, number 2, item 13.

Rowe, H. A. H. (1984) *Problem Solving and Intelligence*. Hillsdale, NJ: Lawrence Erlbaum.

Rowe, H. A. H. (1987) Learning to learn: The development of independent and transferable cognitive abilities. *Curriculum Exchange*, **5**, 48–61.

Rowe, H. A. H. (1988a) Metacognitive skills: Promises and problems. *Australian Journal of Reading*, **2**, 227–37.

Rowe, H. A. H. (1988b) Teaching thinking and learning skills. *Curriculum Issues*, **15**. Sydney: Catholic College of Education.

Rowe, H. A. H. (1988c) *The Teaching of Critical Thinking: Assumptions, Aims, Processes and Implications*. Hawthorn, Vic. ACER.

Rowe, H. (1989a) Teach Learning Strategies. *SET Research Information for Teachers*, number 1, item 14.

Rowe, H. (1989b) Individual differences in learning. In P. Langford (ed.) *Educational Psychology. An Australian Perspective*. Sydney: Longman Cheshire.

Royer, J. M. (1986) Designing instruction to produce understanding: An approach based on cognitive theory. In G. D. Phye & T. Andre (eds) *Cognitive Classroom Learning. Understanding Thinking and Problem Solving*. Orlando: Harcourt Brace Jovanovich.

Ruffels, M. J. (1986) A study of critical thinking skills in grade 10 students in a Tasmanian high school. Unpublished Masters thesis submitted to the Tasmanian State Institute of Technology.

Rumberger, R. W. (1983) Dropping out of high school: The influence of race, sex, and family background. *American Educational Research Journal*, **20**, 199–220.

Rumberger, R. W. (1987) High school dropouts: A review of issues and evidence. *Review of Educational Research*, **57**, 101–21.

Rundus, D. & Atkinson, R. C. (1970) Rehearsal processes in free recall: A procedure for direct observation. *Journal of Verbal Learning and Verbal Behaviour*, **9**, 99–105.

Ryan, R. M., Connell, J. P. & Deci, E. L. (1985) A motivational analysis of self-determination and self-regulation in education. In C. Ames & R. Ames (eds) *Research on Motivation in Education: Vol. 2. The Classroom Milieu*. Orlando: Academic Press.

Ryan, R. M. & Deci, E. L. (1996) When paradigms clash: Comment on Cameron and Pierce's claim that rewards do not undermine intrinsic motivation. *Review of Educational Research*, **66**, 33–8.

Ryder, S. (1988) Computers and Aboriginal students. In N. Hooley (ed.) *Computers and the Realm of Ideas*. Commonwealth Schools Commission, Ministry of Education, Victoria.

Rysavy, S. D. M. & Sales, G. C. (1991) Cooperative learning in computer-based instruction. *Educational Technology Research and Development*, **39**, 70–9.

Sachs, J. (1989) Match or mismatch: Teachers' conceptions of culture and multicultural education policy. *Australian Journal of Education*, **33**, 19–33.

Sachs, J. (1990) Towards a critical pedagogy of technology and education. In M. Bezzina & J. Butcher (eds) *The Changing Face of Professional Education. Collected Papers of the AARE Annual Conference, Sydney University, 1990*. Sydney: AARE.

Sachs, J., Chant, D. & Smith, R. (1989) Adolescents' use of Information Technology: Some implications for teacher education. Paper presented at the AARE Conference, University of Adelaide, November.

Sadker, D. & Sadker, N. (1985) Is the o.k. classroom o.k.? *Phi Delta Kappan*, **66**, 350–61.

Salomon, G., Globerson, T. & Guterman, E. (1989) The computer as a zone of proximal development: Internalizing reading-related metacognitions from a Reading Partner. *Journal of Educational Psychology*, **81**, 620–7.

Salomon, G. (1993) No distribution without individuals' cognition: A dynamic interactional view. In G. Salomon (ed.) *Distributed Cognitions* New York: Cambridge University Press: 111–38

Salomon, G. (1996) Technology's promises and dangers in a psychological context: Implications for teaching and teacher education. Unpublished paper, School of Education, Haifa University, Israel.

Salomon, G., Perkins, D. N. & Globerson, T. (1991) Partners in cognition: Extending human intelligence with intelligent technologies. *Educational Researcher*, **20**, 2–9.

Sanders, J. S. & Stone, A. (1986) *The Neuter Computer: Computers for Girls and Boys*. New York: Neal-Schuman.

Sanson, A. & Di Muccio, C. (1993) The influence of aggressive and neutral cartoons and toys on the behaviour of preschool children. *Australian Psychologist*, **28**, 93–9.

Sanson, A., Prior, M., Smart, D. & Oberkaid, F. (1993) Gender differences in aggression in childhood: Implications for a peaceful world. *Australian Psychologist*, **28**, 86–92.

Santrock, J, W. & Yussen, S. R. (1992) *Child Development. An Introduction*, 5th edn. Dubuque, IA: Wm. C. Brown.

Sarason, I. G. (1972) Experimental approaches to test anxiety: Attention and the uses of information. In C. D. Spielberger (ed.) *Anxiety: Current Trends in Theory and Research (Vol. II)*. New York: Academic Press.

Sarason, I. G. (1975) Test anxiety and the self-disclosing coping model. *Journal of Consulting and Clinical Psychology*, **43**, 143–53.

Scardamalia, M. & Bereiter, C. (1995) CSILE and progressive discourse: Evolving designs. Paper presented at the annual meeting of the American Educational Research Association, San Francisco, April 18–22.

Scardamalia, M., Bereiter, C., McLean, R. S., Swallow, J. & Woodruff, E. (1989) Computer-supported intentional learning environments. *Journal of Educational Computing Research*, **5**, 51–68.

Scarr, S. & Weinberg, R. A. (1983) The Minnesota adoption studies: Genetic difference and malleability. *Child Development*, **54**, 260–7.

Scarr, S., Weinberg, R. A. & Levine, A. (1986) *Understanding Development*. San Diego, CA: Harcourt Brace Jovanovich.

Schraw, G. M & Moshman, D. (1995) Metacognitive theories. *Educational Psychology Review*, **7**, 351–71.

Schloss, P. J. (1992) Mainstreaming revisited. *Elementary School Journal*, **92**, 233–44.

Schmeck, R. R. (ed.) (1988) *Learning Strategies and Learning Styles*. New York: Plenum.

Schmidt, R. (1975) *Motor Skills*. New York: Harper & Row.

Schmidt, R. (1982) *Motor Control and Learning: A Behavioral Emphasis*. Champaign, IL: Human Kinetics.

Schneider, E. (1953) *Coleridge, Opium and Kubla Khan*. Chicago: University of Chicago Press.

Scholl, G. T. (1987) Appropriate education for visually handicapped students. In K. L. Frieberg (ed.) *Educating Exceptional Children, 6th edn*. Guilford, CT: Duskin.

Schubert, J. G. et al. (1984) *Ideas for Equitable Computer Learning*. Palo Alto: American Institutes for Research.

Schunk, D. H. (1982) Effects of effort attributional feedback on children's perceived self-efficacy and achievement. *Journal of Educational Psychology*, **74**, 548–56.

Schunk, D. H. (1983) Ability versus effort attributional feedback. Differential effects on self-efficacy and achievement. *Journal of Educational Psychology*, **75**, 848–56.

Schunk, D. (1985) Self-efficacy and school learning. *Psychology in the Schools*, **22**, 208–23.

Schunk, D. H. (1987) Peer models and children's behavioral change. *Review of Educational Research*, **57**, 149–74.

Schunk, D. H. (1989) Self-efficacy and cognitive skill learning. In C. Ames & R. Ames (eds) *Research on Motivation in Education (Vol. 3). Goals and Cognitions*. Orlando: Academic Press.

Schunk, D. H. (1990) Goal setting and self-efficacy during self-regulated learning. *Educational Psychologist*, **25**, 71–86.

Schunk, D. (1991a) Goal setting and self-evaluation: A social cognitive perspective on self-regulation. In M. L. Maehr & P. R. Pintrich (eds) *Advances in Motivation and Achievement. A Research Annual (Vol. 7)*. Greenwich, CT: JAI.

Schunk, D. H. (1991b) Self-efficacy and academic motivation. *Educational Psychologist*, **26**, 207–31.

Schunk, D. H. (1991c) *Learning Theories: An Educational Perspective*. New York: Merrill.

Schunk, D. H. (1996) Motivation in education: Current emphases and future trends. *Mid-Western Educational Researcher*, **9**, 5–11.

Schutz, H. K., Paxton, S. J. & Muir, S. (1996) Friendship clique similarity on body image attitudes and dieting-related behaviours in adolescent girls. Paper presented at the 31st Annual Conference of the Australian Psychological Society, 25–29 September, Sydney.

Scriven, M. (1967) The methodology of evaluation. In R. Tyler, R. Gagne & M. Scriven (eds) *Perspectives of Curriculum Evaluation*. Chicago, IL: Rand McNally.

Scriven, M. (1989) The state of art in teacher evaluation. In J. Lokan & P. McKenzie (eds) *Teacher Appraisal: Issues and Approaches*. Melbourne: ACER.

Seagoe, M. V. (1972) *The Learning Process and School Practice*. Scranton, Pennsylvania: Chandler.

Semb, G. B. & Ellis, J. A. (1994) Knowledge taught in school: What is remembered? *Review of Educational Research*, **64**, 253–86.

Sewell, D. F. (1990) *New Tools for New Minds. A Cognitive Perspective on the Use of Computers with Young Children*. London: Harvester Wheatsheaf.

Sharan, Y. & Sharan, S. (1992) *Expanding Cooperative Learning Through Group Investigation*. New York: Teacher's College Press.

Shaughnessy, M. F. (1993) The concept of giftedness. *International Journal of Educational Research*, **19**, 5–15.

Shavelson, R. J. & Bolus, R. (1982) Self-concept: The interplay of theory and methods. *Journal of Educational Psychology*, **73**, 3–17.

Shavelson, R. J. & Marsh, H. W. (1986) On the structure of self-concept. In R. Schwarzer (ed.) *Anxiety and Cognitions*. Hillsdale, NJ: Lawrence Erlbaum.

Sheldon, W. H. (1940) *The Varieties of Human Physique: An Introduction to Constitutional Psychology*. New York: Harper.

Sheldon, W. H. (1970) Atlas of Men. *A Guide for Somatotyping the Adult Male at all Ages*. Darien, CT: Hafner.

Sheldon, W. H. & Stevens, S. H. (1942) *The Varieties of Temperament*. New York: Harper & Row.

Shepard, L. A. (1989) Why we need better assessments. *Educational Leadership*, **46**, 4–9.

Shepard, L. A. (1991) Psychometricians' beliefs about learning. *Educational Researcher*, **20**, 2–16.

Shepard, L. A. (1993) Evaluating test validity. *Review of Research in Education*, **19**, 405–50.

Sherman, J. G. (ed.) (1974) *PSI. Personalized System of Instruction. 41 Germinal Papers. A Selection of Readings on the Keller Plan*. Menlo Park, CA: W. A. Benjamin.

Sherman, B. & Judkins, P. (1992) *Glimpses of Heaven and Hell: Virtual Reality and its Implications*. Kent: Hodder & Stoughton.

Shipman, S. & Shipman, V. C. (1985) Cognitive styles: Some conceptual, methodological, and applied issues. In E. W. Gordon (ed.) *Review of Research in Education (Vol. 12)*. New York: AERA.

Shlechter, T. M. (1990) The relative instructional efficiency of small group computer-based training. *Journal of Educational Computing Research*, **6**, 329–41.

Shulman, L. S. (1982) Educational psychology returns to school. In A.G. Kraut (ed.) *The G. Stanley Hall Lecture Series* (Vol.2, pp.77–117). Washington, DC: American Psychological Society.

Shuell, T. J. (1986) Cognitive conceptions of learning. *Review of Educational Research*, **56**, 411–36.

Shuell, T. J. (1988) The role of the student in learning from instruction. *Contemporary Educational Psychology*, **13**, 276–95.

Shuell, T. J. (1990) Phases of meaningful learning. *Review of Educational Research*, **60**, 531–47.

Shuker, R. (1989) 'I Want My MTV'. *SET Research Information for Teachers*, number 1, item 4.

Shulman, L. S. (1976) Psychological controversies in teaching. In

M. L. Silberman, J. S. Allender & J. M. Yanoff (eds) *Real Learning. A Sourcebook for Teachers*. Boston: Little, Brown & Co.

Shweder, R. A., Mahapatra, M. & Miller, J. C. (1987) Cultural and moral development. In J. Kagan & S. Lamb (eds) *The Emergence of Morality in Young Children*. Chicago: University of Chicago Press.

Shweder, R. A., Mahapatra, M. & Miller, J. C. (1990) Culture and moral development. In J. W. Stigler, R. A. Shweder & G. Herdt (eds) *Cultural Psychology. Essays on Comparative Human Development*. Cambridge: Cambridge University Press.

Siegal, M. (1991) *Knowing Children. Experiments in Conversation and Cognition*. Hillsdale: Lawrence Erlbaum.

Siegler, R. S. (1991) *Children's Thinking*, 2nd edn. Englewood Cliffs, NJ: Prentice Hall.

Siegler, R. S. & Richards, D. D. (1982) The development of intelligence. In R. J. Sternberg (ed.) *Handbook of Human Intelligence*. Cambridge: Cambridge University Press.

Sigel, I. E. & Cocking, R. R. (1977) *Cognitive Development from Childhood to Adolescence: A Constructivist Perspective*. New York: Holt, Rinehart & Winston.

Silberman, M. L. (ed.) (1971) *The Experience of Schooling*. New York: Holt, Rinehart & Winston.

Silberman, M. L. (ed.) (1973) *The Open Classroom Reader*. New York: Random House.

Silberman, M. L., Allender, J. S. & Yanoff, J. M. (eds) (1976) *Real Learning. A Sourcebook for Teachers*. Boston: Little, Brown & Company.

Silverberg, S. B. & Steinberg, L. (1990) Psychological well-being of parents with early adolescent children. *Developmental Psychology*, **26**, 658–66.

Simkin, K. (1991) Classroom management and ethnic diversity. In M. N. Lovegrove & R. Lewis (eds) *Classroom Discipline*. Melbourne: Longman.

Simmons, R. G. & Blyth, D. A. (1987) *Moving into Adolescence: The Impact of Pubertal Change and School Context*. Hawthorne, NY: Aldine de Gruyter.

Simpson, E. J. (1972) The classification of educational objectives in the psychomotor domain. *The Psychomotor Domain (Vol. 3)*. Washington: Gryphon House.

Sinclair, D. (1989) *Human Growth after Birth*. Oxford: Oxford University Press.

Sinclair, K. E. & McKinnon, D. H. (1987) Using computers in the high school curriculum: Teacher concerns. *Australian Educational Researcher*, **15**, 12–26.

Sinclair, K. E. & Nicoll, V. (1981) Sources and experience of anxiety in practice teaching. *South Pacific Journal of Teacher Education*, **9**, 1–18.

Skelton, K. (1993) Who'd be a teacher? *EQ Australia*, **1**, 24–6.

Skinner, B. F. (1948) *Walden Two*. New York: Macmillan.

Skinner, B. F. (1951) How to teach animals. *Scientific American*, **185**, 26–9.

Skinner, B. F. (1954) The science of learning and the art of teaching. *Harvard Educational Review*, **24**, 86–97.

Skinner, B. F. (1965) *Why teachers fail. Saturday Review*, 80–1, 98–102 (October 16).

Skinner, B. F. (1968) *The Technology of Teaching*. New York: Appleton-Century-Crofts.

Skinner, B. F. (1971) *Beyond Freedom and Dignity*. New York: Alfred A. Knopf.

Skinner, B. F. (1977) The free and happy student. In H. F. Clarizio, R. C. Craig & W. A. Mehrens (eds) *Contemporary Issues in Educational Psychology*, 3rd edn. Boston: Allyn & Bacon.

Skinner, B. F. (1984) The shame of American education. *American Psychologist*, **39**, 103–10.

Skinner, B. F. (1986) Programmed instruction revisited. *Phi Delta Kappan*, **68**, 103–10.

Sladeczek, I. E. & Kratochwill, T. R. (1995) Reinforcement. In L. W. Anderson (ed.) *International Encyclopedia of Teaching and Teacher Education*, 2nd edn. Tarrytown, NY: Pergamon: 224–7.

Slavin, R. E. (1980) Cooperative learning. *Review of Educational Research*, **50**, 315–42.

Slavin, R. E. (1983) When does cooperative learning increase student achievement? *Psychological Bulletin*, **94**, 429–45.

Slavin, R. E. (1985) Team-assisted individualization: A cooperative learning solution for adaptive instruction in mathematics. In M. C. Wang & H. J. Walberg (eds) *Adapting Instruction to Individual Differences*, Berkeley, CA: McCutchan.

Slavin, R. E. (1985) An introduction to cooperative learning research. In R. Slavin, S. Sharan, S. Kagan, R. Hertz-Lazarowitz, C. Webb & R. Schmuck (eds) *Learning to Cooperate, Cooperating to Learn*. New York: Plenum Press.

Slavin, R. E. (1987a) Ability grouping and student achievement in elementary schools: A best-evidence synthesis. *Review of Educational Research*, **57**, 293–336.

Slavin, R. E. (1987b) Mastery learning reconsidered. *Review of Educational Research*, **57**, 175–214.

Slavin, R. E. (1987c) Developmental and motivational perspectives on cooperative learning: A reconciliation. *Child Development*, **58**, 1161–7.

Slavin, R. E. (ed.) (1989a) *School and Classroom Organization*. Hillsdale, NJ: Lawrence Erlbaum.

Slavin, R. E. (1989) On mastery learning and mastery teaching. *Educational Leadership*, **46**, 77–9.

Slavin, R. E. (1990) *Cooperative Learning. Theory, Research, and Practice*. Massachussets: Allyn & Bacon.

Slavin, R. E. (1991) Group rewards make groupwork work. *Educational Leadership*, **48**, 71–82.

Slavin, R. E. (1991) *Educational Psychology. Theory into Practice*, 3rd edn. Englewood Cliffs, NJ: Prentice Hall.

Slavin, R. et al. (eds) (1985) *Learning to Cooperate, Cooperating to Learn*. New York: Plenum Press.

Slavin, R. E. (1992) When and why does cooperative learning increase achievement? Theoretical and empirical perspectives. In R. Hertz-Lazarowitz & N. Miller (eds) *Interaction in Cooperative Groups: The Theoretical Anatomy of Group Learning*. Cambridge: Cambridge University Press: 145–73.

Slavin, R. E. (1995) *Cooperative Learning*. In L. W. Anderson (ed.) *International Encyclopedia of Teaching and Teacher Education*, 2nd edn. Tarrytown, NY: Permagon: 139–43.

Smagorinsky, P. (1995) The social construction of data: Methodological problems of investigating learning in the zone of proximal development. *Review of Educational Research*, **65**, 191–212.

Smail, B. (1983) Spatial visualization skills and technical crafts education. *Educational Research*, **25**, 230–1.

Smart, M. S. & Smart, R. C. (1977) *Children. Development and Relationships*, 3rd edn. New York: Macmillan.

Smilansky, S. (1990) Sociodramatic play. Its relevance to behavior and achievement in school. In E. Klugman & S. Smilansky (eds) *Children's Play and Learning*. New York: Teachers College Press: 18–42.

Smith, I. (1987) Gifted and talented children. Are they educationally disadvantaged? *Current Affairs Bulletin*, **63**, 28–32.

Smith, J. (1979) Violence and Television. New Research Findings. *The Primary Journal*, **4**, 2–6.

Smith, L. & Land, M. (1981) Low-inference verbal behaviors related to teacher clarity. *Journal of Classroom Interaction*, **17**, 37–42.

Smith, N. & Smith, H. (1991) *Physical Disability and Handicap*. Melbourne: Longman Cheshire.

Smith, P. K. (1978) A longitudinal study of social participation in preschool children: Solitary and parallel play re-examined. *Developmental Psychology*, **12**, 517–23.

Smith, P. K. & Ahmad, Y. (1990) The playground jungle: Bullies, victims and intervention strategies. *SET Research Information for Teachers*, number 1, item 6.

Smolicz, J. J. (1986) National policy on languages: A community language perspective. *Australian Journal of Education*, **30**, 45–65.

Smolicz, J. J. (1987) Education for a multicultural society. In J. P. Keeves (ed.) *Australian Education. Review of Recent Research*. Sydney: Allen & Unwin.

Smolicz, J. J. (1991) Language, culture and the school in a plural society: An Australian perspective for the 1990s. *Migration Monitor*, **23–24**, 3–15.

Smolucha, F. (1992) Social origins of private speech in pretend play. In R. M. Diaz & L. E. Berk (eds), *Private Speech: From Social Interaction to Self-regulation*. Hillsdale, N. J: Erlbaum: 123–141.

Snider, V. E. (1990) What we know about learning styles from research in special education. *Educational Leadership*, **48**, 53.

Snodgrass, D. M. (1991) *The parent connection. Adolescence*, **26**, 83–7.

Snow, C. E. (1992) Perspectives on second-language development: Implications for bilingual education. *Educational Researcher*, **21**, 16–19.

Snow, R. E. (1986) Individual differences and the design of educational programs. *American Psychologist*, **41**, 1029–39.

Snowman, J. (1986) Learning tactics and strategies. In G. D. Phye & T. Andre (eds) *Cognitive Classroom Learning. Understanding Thinking and Problem Solving*. Orlando: Harcourt Brace Jovanovich.

Snyder, I. (1993) The impact of computers on students' writing: A comparative study of the effects of pens and word processors on writing context, process and product. *Australian Journal of Education*, **37**, 5–25.

Snyder, I. (1996) Taking the hype out of hypertext. Paper presented at the American Educational Research Association Annual Meeting, New York, April 8–12.

Soar, R. (1966) *An Integrative Approach to Classroom Learning*. ERIC Document Reproduction Service No. ED 033 749.

Soar, R. & Soar, R. (1979) Emotional climate and management. In P. Peterson & H. Walberg (eds) *Research on Teaching: Concepts, Findings, and Implications*. Berkeley, CA: McCutchan.

Sofo, F. (1988) Critical thinking skills and self-esteem. In Educational research in Australia: Indigenous or exotic? Unpublished papers presented at the annual conference of the Australian Association of Research in Education held at the University of New England, Armidale, New South Wales, 30 November–4 December. Armidale, NSW: Australian Association for Research in Education.

Sokolove, S., Garrett, J., Sadker, D. & Sadker, M (1986) Interpersonal communications skills. In J. Cooper (ed.) *Classroom Teaching Skills: A Handbook*. Lexington, MA: DC Heath.

Solas, J. (1992) Investigating teacher and student thinking about the process of teaching and learning using autobiography and repertory grid. *Review of Educational Research*, **62**, 205–25.

Solomon, D., Watson, M., Schaps, E., Battistich, V. & Solomon, J. (1990) Cooperative learning as part of a comprehensive classroom program designed to promote prosocial development. In S. Sharan (ed.) *Recent Research on Cooperative Learning*. New York: Praeger.

Sommerlad, E. A. & Bellingham, W. P. (1972) Cooperation-competition: A comparison of Australian European and Aboriginal school children. *Journal of Cross-Cultural Psychology*, **3**, 149–57.

Spearman, C. E. (1927) *The Abilites of Man*. London: Macmillan.

Spender, D. (1995) *Nattering on the Net: Women, Power and Cyberspace*. North Melbourne: Spinifex Press.

Splitter, L. (1988) On teaching children to be better thinkers. *Unicorn*, **14**, 40–7.

Springer, C. (1991) The pleasure of the interface. *Screen*, **32**, 303–23.

Sprinthall, R. C., Schmutte, G. T. & Sirois, L. (1991) *Understanding Educational Research*. Englewood Cliffs, NJ: Prentice Hall.

Sprinthall, N. A. & Sprinthall, R. C. (1990) *Educational Psychology. A Developmental Approach*, 5th edn. New York: McGraw-Hill.

Staffieri, J. R. (1967) A study of social stereotype of body image in children. *Journal of Personality & Social Psychology*, **7**, 101–4.

Staffieri, J. R. (1972) Body build and behavioral expectancies in young females. *Developmental Psychology*, **6**, 125–7.

Stager, G. (1993) Computers for kids . . . not schools. In I. Grasso & M. Fallshaw (eds) *Reflections of a Learning Community: Views on the Introduction of Laptops at MLC*. Kew: Methodist Ladies' College.

Stallings, J. A. & Kaskowitz, D. H. (1975) *A study of follow-through implementation*. Paper presented at the meeting of the American Educational Research Association, Washington, DC.

Stanley, J. (1978) Radical acceleration: Recent educational innovations at Johns Hopkins University. *Gifted Child Quarterly*, **20**, 66–75.

Stanley, J. (1980) On educating the gifted. *Educational Researcher*, **9**, 8–12.

Starfield, B. & Pless, I. B. (1980) Physical health. In O. G. Brim & J. Kagan (eds) *Constancy and Change in Human Development*. Cambridge, MA: Harvard University Press.

State Services Commission (1989) *Employment for Education. A Guide for School Trustees and Principals*. Wellington: Author.

Stead, R. (1990) Problems with learning from computer-based simulations: A case study in economics. *British Journal of Educational Technology*, **21**, 106–17.

Steinberg, L. (1991) Parent–adolescent relations. In R. M. Lerner, A. C. Petersen & J. Brooks-Gunn (eds) *Encyclopedia of Adolescence*. New York: Garland.

Stephens, R. & Stephens, G. (1986) Integration at the chalk face. *SET Research Information for Teachers*, number 1, item 6.

Stern, N. (1992) Editable selves: Thought-experiments with information technology. In C. Bigum & B. Green (eds) *Understanding the New Information Technologies in*

Education. Geelong, Vic. Centre for Studies in Information Technologies and Education, Deakin University.

Sternberg, R. (1986) *Intelligence Applied: Understanding and Increasing Your Own Intellectual Skills*. New York: Harcourt Brace Jovanovich.

Sternberg, R. J. (1985) *Beyond IQ: A Triarchic Theory of Human Intelligence*. New York: Freeman.

Sternberg, R. J. & Davidson, J. E. (1985) Cognitive development in the gifted and talented. In F. D. Horowitz & M. O'Brien (eds) *The Gifted and Talented: Developmental Perspectives*. Washington, DC: American Psychological Association.

Sternberg, R. J. & Powell, J. S. (1983) The development of intelligence. In J. H. Flavell & E. M. Markham (vol. eds) *Handbook of Child Psychology: Vol.111. Cognitive Development*, 4th edn. New York: Wiley.

Stiggins, R. J. (1985) Improving assessment where it means the most: In the classroom. *Educational Leadership*, **43**, 69–74.

Stigler, J. W., Shweder, R. A. & Herdt, G. (eds) (1990) *Cultural Psychology*. Cambridge: Cambridge University Press.

Stigler, S. M. (1978) Some forgotten work on memory. *Journal of Experimental Psychology: Human Learning and Memory*, **4**, 1–4.

Stipek, D. J. (1984) The development of achievement motivation. In R. Ames & C. Ames (eds) *Research on Motivation in Education: Vol. 1. Student Motivation*. Orlando: Academic Press.

Stoll, C. (1995) *Silicon Snake Oil*. New York: Doubleday.

Stoneman, Z. & Brody, G. H. (1981) Peers as mediators of television food advertisements aimed at children. *Developmental Psychology*, **17**, 853–8.

Styczynski, L. & Langlois, J. H. (1977) The effects of familiarity on behavioral stereotypes associated with physical attractiveness in young children. *Child Development*, **48**, 1137–41.

Sultana, R. (1989) What's keeping them back?! Life choices and life chances. *SET Research Notes for Teachers*, number 1, item 12.

Sulzer-Azaroff, B. (1995) Behavioristic theories of teaching. In L. W. Anderson (ed.) *International Encyclopedia of Teaching and Teacher Education*, 2nd edn. Tarrytown, NY: Pergamon: 96–101.

Sulzer-Azaroff, B. & Mayer, G. R. (1986) Achieving educational excellence using behavioural strategies. New York: Holt, Rinehart & Winston.

Sund, R. B. (1976) *Piaget for Educators: A Multimedia Program*. Columbus, OH: Charles E. Merrill.

Swan, K. (1991) Programming objects to think with: LOGO and the teaching and learning of problem-solving. *Journal of Educational Computing Research*, **7**, 89–112.

Swan, S. & White, R. (1990) Increasing meta-learning. Part 2 Thinking books. *SET Research Information for Teachers*, number 2, item 11.

Swanson, D. B., Norman, G. R. & Linn, R. L. (1995) Performance-based assessment. Lessons from the health professions. *Educational Researcher*, **24**, 5–11.

Swanson, H. L., O'Connor, J. E. & Cooney, J. B. (1990) An information processing analysis of expert and novice teachers' problem solving. *American Educational Research Journal*, **27**, 533–56.

Sweller, J. (1990) Cognitive processes and instructional procedures. *Australian Journal of Education*, **34**, 125–30.

Sweller, J. (1993) Some cognitive processes and their consequences for the organisation and presentation of information. *Australian Journal of Psychology*, **45**, 1–8.

Swift, J. N. & Gooding, C. T. (1983). Interaction of wait time feedback and questioning instruction on middle science teaching. *Journal of Research in Science Teaching*, **20**, 721–30.

Switch it on Miss! (1987) A joint publication by State Computer Education Centre (SCEC) and the Ministerial Advisory Committee on Multicultural and Migrant Education (MACMME), Ministry of Education, Vic.

Symonds, P. M. & Chase, D. H. (1992) Practice vs motivation. *Journal of Educational Psychology*, **84**, 282–9.

Talbert, E. G. & Frase, L. E. (eds) (1972) *Individualized Instruction. A Book of Readings*. Columbus, OH: Charles E. Merrill.

Talkington, L. W. & Altman, R. (1973) Effects of film-mediated aggressive behavior and affectual models on behavior. *American Journal of Mental Deficiency*, **77**, 420–5.

Tamir, P. (1995) Discovery learning and teaching. In L. W. Anderson (ed.) *International Encyclopedia of Teaching and Teacher Education,* 2nd edn, Tarrytown, NY: Pergamon: 149–55.

Tannenbaum, A. J. (1986) Giftedness: A psychosocial approach. In R. J. Sternberg & J. E. Davidson (eds) *Conceptions of Giftedness*. New York: Cambridge University Press.

Tanner, J. M. (1961) *Education and Physical Growth. Implications of the Study of Children's Growth for Educational Theory and Practice*. London: University of London Press.

Tanner, J. M. (1990) *Fetus into Man. Physical Growth from Conception to Maturity*. Revised and enlarged. Cambridge, MA: Harvard University Press.

Tasker, R. (1981) Children's views and classroom experiences. *The Australian Science Teachers Journal*, **27**, 33–7.

Taylor, R. P. (ed.) (1980) *The Computer in the School: Tutor, Tool, Tutee*. New York: New York Teachers College Press.

Teasdale, B. & Teasdale, J. (1993) *Culture and Schooling in Aboriginal Australia*. Paper presented at the symposium International Perspectives on Culture and Schooling, at the Department of International and Comparative Education, Institute of Education, London University, May.

Teasdale, R. & Teasdale, J. (1994) Culture and schooling in Aboriginal Australia. In E. Thomas (ed.) *International Perspectives on Culture and Schooling: A Symposium of Proceedings*. London: Institute of Education: 174–96.

Tharp, R. G. & Gallimore, R. (1988) *Rousing Minds to Life*. New York: Cambridge University Press.

The National Languages and Literacy Institute of Australia (1993) *Languages at the Crossroads. The Report of the National Enquiry into the Employment and Supply of Teachers of Languages other than English*. East Melbourne, Vic.: Author.

Thelen, E. (1995) Motor development. A new synthesis. *American Psychologist*, **50**, 79–95.

Thibadeau, G. (1995) Open education. In L. W. Anderson (ed.) *International Encyclopedia of Teaching and Teacher Education,* 2nd edn. Tarrytown, NY: Pergamon: 167–71.

Thies, A. P. (1985) Neuropsychological approaches to learning disorders. In E. W. Gordon (ed.) *Review of Research in Education (Vol. 12)*. New York: AERA.

Thomas, A. (1979) Learned helplessness and expectancy factors: Implications for research in learning disabilities. *Review of Education Research*, **49**, 208–21.

Thomas, E. (1994) (ed.) *International Perspectives on Culture and Schooling: A Symposium Proceedings*. University of London Institute of Education: Department of International and Comparative Education.

Thomas, E. L. & Robinson, H. A. (1972) *Improving Reading in every Class: A Sourcebook for Teachers*. Boston: Allyn & Bacon.

Thomas, G. (1988) Room management in mainstreamed/integrated classrooms. *SET Research Information for Teachers*, number 1, item 5.

Thomas, J. R. & French, K. E. (1985) Gender differences across age in motor performance: A meta-analysis. *Psychological Bulletin*, **98**, 260–82.

Thomas, J. W. (1988) Proficiency at academic studying. *Contemporary Educational Psychology*, **13**, 265–75.

Thomas, J. W. & Rohwer, W. D. (1986) Academic studying: The role of learning strategies. *Educational Psychologist*, **21**, 19–41.

Thomas, R. M. (ed.) (1990) *The Encyclopedia of Human Development and Education. Theory, Research and Studies*. Oxford: Pergamon Press.

Thompson, T. (1993) Characteristics of self-worth protection in achievement behaviour. *British Journal of Educational Psychology*, **63**, 469–88.

Thorndike, E. L. (1913) *The Psychology of Learning*. New York: Macmillan.

Thorndike, E. L. (1931) *Human Learning*. New York: Appleton-Century-Crofts.

Thorndike, R., Hagen, E. & Sattler, J. (1986) The *Stanford-Binet Intelligence Scale*, 4th edn. Chicago: Riverside.

Thurstone, L. (1938) *Primary Mental Abilities*. Chicago: University of Chicago Press.

Tiedemann, J. (1989) Measures of cognitive styles. A critical review. *Educational Psychologist*, **24**, 261–75.

Tiggemann, M. & Crowley, J. R. (1993) Attributions for academic failure and subsequent performance. *Australian Journal of Psychology*, **45**, 35–9.

Tobias, J. (1993) Trends in Educational Software. Paper presented at the 11th Annual Computers in Education Conference, 28 June–1 July, Penrith, NSW.

Tobias, S. (1985a) Test anxiety: Interference, defective skills, and cognitive capacity. *Educational Psychologist*, **20**, 135–42.

Tobias, S. (1985b) Computer-assisted instruction. In M. C. Wang & H. J. Walberg (eds) *Adapting Instruction to Individual Differences*, Berkeley, CA: McCutchan.

Tobias, S. (1994) Interest, prior knowledge, and learning. *Review of Educational Research*, **64**, 37–54.

Tobin, K. (1987) The role of wait time in higher cognitive level learning. *Review of Educational Research*, **57**, 69–95.

Tobin-Richards, M. H., Boxer, A. M. & Petersen, A. C. (1983) The psychological significance of pubertal change: Sex differences in perceptions of self during early adolescence. In J. Brooks-Gunn & A. C. Petersen (eds) *Girls at Puberty. Biological and Psychosocial Perspectives*. New York: Plenum.

Tolhurst, D. (1993) Hypertext and learner acceptance of control: learning outcomes of hypertext use. *Australian Educational Computing*, **8**, ACEC '93 Edition, 245–53.

Torrance, E. P. (1962) *Guiding Creative Talent*. Englewood Cliffs, NJ: Prentice Hall.

Torrance, E. P. (1966) *Torrance Tests of Creative Thinking: Norms-technical manual*. Princeton, NJ: Personnel Press.

Torrance, E. P. (1973) Non-test indicators of creative talent among disadvantaged children. *Gifted Child Quarterly*, **17**, 3–9.

Torrance, E. P. (1986) Teaching creative and gifted learners. In M. Wittrock (ed.) *Handbook of Research on Teaching*, 3rd edn. New York: Macmillan.

Townsend, M. A. R., Manley, M. & Tuck, B. F. (1991) Academic helpseeking in intermediate-school classrooms: Effects of achievement, ethnic group, sex and classroom organization. *New Zealand Journal of Educational Studies*, **26**, 35–47.

Treffinger, D. (1982) Gifted students, regular classrooms: Sixty ingredients for a better blend. *Elementary School Journal*, **82**, 267–83.

Triandis, H. C. (1972) *The Analysis of Subjective Culture*. New York: Wiley.

Triandis, H. C. (1980) Introduction. In H. C. Triandis & W. W. Lambert (eds.) *Handbook on Cross-Cultural Psychology: Vol. 1. Perspectives*. Boston: Allyn & Bacon.

Triandis, H. C. & Heron, A. (eds) (1981) *Handbook of Cross-Cultural Psychology. Vol. 4. Developmental Psychology*. Boston: Allyn & Bacon.

Tuckman, B. W. (1988) Conducting Educational Research, 3rd edn. San Diego: Harcourt Brace Jovanovich.

Tudge, J. (1990) Vygotsky, the zone of proximal development and peer collaboration: Implications for classroom practice. In L. C. Moll (ed.) *Vygotsky and Education*. New York: Cambridge University Press.

Turiel, E. (1966) An experimental test of the sequentiality of developmental stages in the child's moral judgment. *Journal of Personality and Social Psychology*, **3**, 611–18.

Turiel, E. (1983) *The Development of Social Knowledge: Morality and Convention*. New York: Cambridge University Press.

Turiel, E. (1983) *The Development of Social Knowledge: Morality and Convention*. New York: Cambridge University Press.

Turkle, S. (1995) *Life on the Screen: Identity in the Age of the Internet*. New York: Simon & Schuster.

Turkington, C. (1987) Special talents. In K. L. Frieberg (ed.) *Educating Exceptional Children*, 6th edn. Guilford, CT: Duskin.

Turner, J. S. & Helms, D. B. (1991) *Lifespan Development*, 4th edn. Fort Worth: Holt, Rinehart & Winston.

Turney, C., Clift, J. C., Dunkin, M. J. & Traill, R. D. (1973) *Microteaching: Research, Theory and Practice*. Sydney: Sydney University Press.

Turney, C. et al. (1978) *Inner City Schools*. Sydney: University of Sydney Press.

Turney, C. et al. (1985a) *Sydney Micro Skills Redeveloped, Series 1 Handbook*, Sydney: University of Sydney Press.

Turney, C. et al. (1985b) *Sydney Micro Skills Redeveloped, Series 2 Handbook*, Sydney: University of Sydney Press.

Turney, C. & Wright, R. (1990) Where the Buck Stops. *The Teacher Educators*. Sydney: Sydmac Academic Press.

Twiss, D. (1986) Signing. Learning a language through a sign system. *SET Research Information for Teachers*, number 1, item 5.

Ulich, R. (1950) *History of Educational Thought*. New York: American Book Company.

Urban, K. K. (1993) Fostering giftedness. *International Journal of Educational Research*, **19**, 31–49.

Urdan, T. C., & Maehr, M. L. (1995) Beyond a two goal theory of motivation and achievement: A case for social goals. *Review of Educational Research*, **65**, 213–43.

US Congress (1975) *The Education for all Handicapped Children Act of 1975*. Washington, DC: US Government Printing Office.

Vallance, R. & Vallance, D. (1988) Punmu wangka: A 'right way' desert school curriculum 1984–1987. *Curriculum Perspectives*, **8**, 71–6.

Van Patten, J., Chao, C-I. & Reigeluth, C. M. (1986) A review of strategies for sequencing and synthesizing instruction. *Review of Educational Research*, **56**, 437–71.

Van Tassel-Baska, J. (1989) Appropriate curriculum for gifted learners. *Educational Leadership*, **46**, 13–15.

Veenman, S. (1984) Perceived problems of beginning teachers. *Review of Educational Research*, **54**, 143–78.

Vetta, A. (1972) Conservation in Aboriginal children and 'genetic hypothesis'. *International Journal of Psychology*, **7**, 247–56.

Vialle, W. (1991) Tuesday's Children: A study of five children using multiple intelligences theory as a framework. Unpublished doctoral dissertation, University of South Florida.

Vialle, W. (1993) Identifying children's diverse strengths: a broader framework for cognitive assessment. Paper presented at the 17th national AASE conference.

Vialle, W. (1994) Profiles of intelligence. *Australian Journal of Early Childhood,* **19**, *30–34.*

Virilio, P. (1987) The overexposed city. *Zone*, **1**, **2**, 15–31.

Virilio, P (1991) *The Aesthetics of Disappearance.* New York: Semiotext(e).

Vockell, E. L. & Schwartz, E. M. (1992) *The Computer in the Classroom.* Watsonville, CA: Mitchell McGraw-Hill.

Volet, S. E. & Renshaw, P. D. (1990) The significance of metacognitive assessment for university students' learning. In M. Bezzina & J. Butcher (eds) *The Changing Face of Professional Education. Collected Papers of the AARE Annual Conference, Sydney University, 1990.* Sydney: AARE.

von Glaserfeld, E. (1995) *Radical Constructivism: A Way of Knowing and Learning.* London: Falmer Press.

Vygotsky, L. S. (1962) *Thought and Language* (ed. and trans. by E. Hanfmann & G. Vakar). Cambridge, MA: MIT Press.

Vygotsky, L. S. (1978) *Mind in Society. The Development of Higher Psychological Processes* (ed. by M. Cole, V. John-Steiner, S. Scribner & E. Souberman). Cambridge, MA: Harvard University Press.

Vygotsky, L. S. (1987) *Thinking and Speech* (edited and translated by N. Minick). New York: Plenum.

Wadsworth, B. J. (1989) *Piaget's Theory of Cognitive Development*, 4th edn. New York: Longman.

Wainryb, C. & Turiel, E. (1993) Conceptual and informational features in moral decision making. *Educational Psychologist*, **28**, 205–18.

Wagner, D. A. & Stevenson, H. W. (1982) *Cultural Perspectives on Child Development.* San Francisco: W. H. Freeman.

Wagner, R. K. & Sternberg, R. J. (1984) Alternative conceptions of intelligence and their implications for education. *Review of Educational Research*, **54**, 179–223.

Walberg, H. J. (1984) Improving the productivity of America's schools. *Educational Leadership*, **41**, 19–27.

Walberg, H. J. (1985) Instructional theories and research evidence. In M. C. Wang & H. J. Walberg (eds) *Adapting Instruction to Individual Differences.* Berkeley, CA: McCutchan.

Walden, E. L. & Thompson, S. A. (1981) A review of some alternative approaches to drug management of hyperactive children. *Journal of Learning Disabilities*, **14**, 213–17.

Walden, R. & Walkerdine, V. (1986) Characteristics, views and relationships in the classroom. In L. Burton (ed.) Girls into Maths Can Go. London: Holt, Rinehart & Winston.

Walker, D. F. (1987) Logo Needs Research: A Response to Papert's Paper. *Educational Researcher*, **16**, 9–11.

Walker, L. J. (1982) The sequentiality of Kohlberg's stages of moral development. *Child Development*, **53**, 1330–6.

Walker, L. J. (1983) Sources of cognitive conflict for stage transition in moral development. *Developmental Psychology*, **19**, 103–10.

Walker, L. J. (1984). Sex differences in the development of moral reasoning: A critical review. *Child Development*, **55**, 677–91.

Walker, L., De Vries, B. & Trevetham, S. (1987) Moral stages and moral orientations in real-life and hypothetical dilemmas. *Child Development*, **58**, 842–58.

Walker, R. A. & Barlow, K. (1990) The provision of education for gifted and talented children in private primary schools: A critical examination. In M. Bezzina & J. Butcher (eds) *The Changing Face of Professional Education. Collected Papers of the AARE Annual Conference, Sydney University, 1990.* Sydney: AARE.

Walkley, J., Holland, B., Treloar, R. & Probyn-Smith, H. (1993) Fundamental motor skill proficiency of children. *The ACHPER National Journal,* Spring, 11–14.

Wallace, A., Boylan, C., Sharman, J. & Kay, R. (1990) The all girls science class: A longitudinal study. In M. Bezzina & J. Butcher (eds) *The Changing Face of Professional Education. Collected Papers of the AARE Annual Conference, Sydney University, 1990.* Sydney: AARE.

Wallace, R. C (1985) Adaptive education: Policy and administrative perspectives. In M. C. Wang & H. J. Walberg (eds) *Adapting Instruction to Individual Differences.* Berkeley, CA: McCutchan.

Wallach, M. & Kogan, N. (1965) *Modes of Thinking in Young Children.* New York: Holt, Rinehart & Winston.

Wallas, G. (1926) *The Art of Thought.* New York: Harcourt, Brace.

Walters, J. (1993) Computer education beacon schools. *Australian Educational Computing*, **8**, ACEC '93 Edition, 81–4.

Walters, R. H., Cheyne, J. A. & Banks, R. K. (eds) (1972) *Punishment.* Harmondsworth, Middlesex: Penguin Books.

Walters, G. C. & Grusec, J. E. (1977) *Punishment.* San Francisco: W. H. Freeman.

Wang, M. C., Gennari, P. & Waxman, H. C. (1985) The adaptive learning environments model: Design, implementation and effects. In M. C. Wang & H. J. Walberg (eds) *Adapting Instruction to Individual Differences.* Berkeley, CA: McCutchan.

Wang, M. C. & Lindvall, C. M. (1984) Individual differences and school learning environments. In E. W. Gordon (ed.) *Review of Research in Education*, **11**, Washington: AERA.

Wang, M. C. & Walberg, H. J. (eds) (1985) *Adapting Instruction to Individual Differences*. Berkeley, CA: McCutchan.

Wang, M. C., Reynolds, M. C. & Walberg, H. J. (eds) (1988) *Handbook of Special Education: Research and Practice.* Oxford, England: Pergamon.

Wang, M. C., Walberg, H. & Reynolds, M. C. (1992) A scenario for better-not separate -special education. *Educational Leadership*, **50**, 35–7.

Ware, M. C. & Stuck, M. F. (1985) Sex-role messages vis-a-vis microcomputer use: a look at the pictures. *Sex Roles*, **13**, 205–14.

Warren, J. (1996) Personal communication. John Warren is Manager of the School of the Future, Technology Park, South Australia.

Warren, M. P. (1983) Physical and biological aspects of puberty. In J. Brooks-Gunn & A. C. Petersen (eds) *Girls at Puberty. Biological and Psychosocial Perspectives*. New York: Plenum.

Wasserman, I. & Stack, S. (1993) The effect of religion on suicide. An analysis of cultural context. *Omega - Journal of Death and Dying*, **27**, 295–306.

Watkins, D. & Hattie, J. (1981) The learning process of Australian university students: Investigations of contextual and personological factors. *British Journal of Educational Psychology*, **51**, 384–93.

Watson, A. (ed.) (1988) *Intelligence: Controversy and Change*. Hawthorn, Vic. Thomas, J. W. & Rohwer, W. D. (1986) Academic studying: The role of learning strategies. *Educational Psychologist*, **21**, 19–41.

ACER.

Watson, J. B. (1913) Psychology as the behaviorists view it. *Psychological Review*, **20**, 157–8.

Watson, J. B. (1916) The place of a conditioned reflex in psychology. *Psychological Review*, **23**, 89–116.

Watson, J. B. (1930) *Behaviorism*, 2nd edn. Chicago: University of Chicago Press.

Watson, L. S. (1975) *Child Behavior Modification: A Manual for Teachers, Nurses, and Parents*. New York: Pergamon.

Watts, B. H. (1971) Some determinants of the academic progress of Australian Aboriginal adolescent girls. Unpublished doctoral dissertation, University of Queensland.

Watts, B. H. (1973) Personality factors in the academic success of adolescent girls. In G. E. Kearney, P. R. de Lacey & J. R. Davidson (eds) *The Psychology of Aboriginal Australians*. Sydney: John Wiley.

Watts, B. H. (1976) *Access to Education. An Evaluation of the Aboriginal Secondary Grants Scheme*. Canberra: AGPS.

Watts, B. H. (1981a) Objectives in the education of Aborigines. Some parental views. *The Aboriginal Child at School*, **8**, 43–54.

Watts, B. H. (1981b) *Aboriginal Futures. Review of Research and Development and Related Policies in the Education of Aborigines*. Brisbane: Schonell Educational Research Centre.

Watts, B. H. (1982) *Aboriginal Futures. A Review of Research and Development and Related Policies in the Education of Aborigines*. A Summary, (Report No. 33). Canberra: ERDC.

Webb, N. (1980) A process-outcome analysis of learners in group and individual settings. *Educational Psychology*, **15**, 69–83.

Webb, N. (1982) Peer interaction and learning in cooperative small groups. *Journal of Educational Psychology*, **74**, 642–55.

Webb, N. (1985a) Verbal interaction and learning in peer-directed groups. *Theory into Practice*, **24**, 32–8.

Webb, N. M. (1985b) Student interaction and learning in small groups: A research summary. In R. Slavin, S. Sharan, S. Kagan, R. Hertz-Lazarowitz, C. Webb & R. Schmuck (eds) *Learning to Cooperate, Cooperating to Learn*. New York: Plenum Press.

Webb, N. (1987) *Helping behavior to maximize learning*. Paper presented at the annual meeting of the American Educational Research Association, Washington, DC, April.

Webb, N. (1989) Peer interaction and learning in small groups. *International Journal of Educational Research*, **13**, 21–39.

Webb, N. N. & Kenderski, C. N. (1985) Gender differences in small-group interaction and achievement in high-and-low achieving classes. In L. C. Wilkinson & C. B. Marrett (eds) *Gender Influences in Classroom Interaction*. Orlando: Academic Press.

Webb, N. M. & Lewis, S. (1988) The social context of learning computer programming. In R. E. Moyer (ed.) *Teaching and Learning Computer Programming: Multiple Research Perspectives*. Hillsdale, NJ: Lawrence Erlbaum.

Webb, N. M. (1989) Peer interaction and learning in small groups. *International Journal of Educational Research*, **13**, 21–40.

Webb, N. M. & Farivar, S. (1994) Promoting helping behaviour in cooperative small groups in middle school mathematics. *American Educational Research Journal*, **32**, 369–95.

Webb, P. K. (1980) Piaget: Implications for teaching. *Theory into Practice*, **19**, 93–7.

Weil, M., Rosen, L. & Sears, D. (1987) The Computerphobia Reduction Program: Year 1. Program Development and Preliminary Results. *Behavior Research Methods. Instruments and Computers*, **19**, 180–4.

Weill, M. P. (1987) Gifted/Learning disabled students. Their potential may be buried treasure. *The Clearing House*, **60**, 341–3.

Weiner, B. (1972) Attribution theory, achievement motivation, and the educational process. *Review of Educational Research*, **42**, 203–15.

Weiner, B. (1979) A theory of motivation for some classsroom experiences. *Journal of Educational Psychology*, **71**, 3–25.

Weiner, B. (1984) Principles for a theory of student motivation and their application within an attributional framework. In R. Ames & C. Ames (eds) *Research on Motivation in Education. Vol. 1. Student Motivation*. Orlando: Academic Press.

Weiner, B. (1990) History of motivational research in education. *Journal of Educational Psychology*, **82**, 616–22.

Weiner, B. (1994) Integrating social and personal theories of achievement striving. *Review of Educational Research*, **64**, 557–73.

Weiner, B. & Kukla, A. (1970) An attributional analysis of achievement motivation. *Journal of Personality and Social Psychology*, **15**, 1–20.

Weinert, F. E. & Helmke, A. (1995) Interclassroom differences in instructional quality and interindividual differences in cognitive development. *Educational Psychologist*, **30**, 15–20.

Weinstein, C. E. & Mayer, R. E. (1986). The teaching of learning strategies. In M. C. Wittrock (ed.) *Handbook of Research on Teaching*, 3rd edn. New York: Macmillan.

Weinstein, C. E. & Ridley, D. S., Dahl, T. & Weber, S. (1989) Helping students develop strategies for effective learning. *Educational Leadership*, **46**, 17–19.

Weinstein, C. E. & Underwood, V. L. (1985) Learning strategies: The how of learning. In J. W. Segal, S. F. Chipman & R. Glaser (eds) *Thinking and Learning Skills: Relating Instruction to Research (Vol. 1)*. Hillsdale. NJ: Lawrence Erlbaum.

Weinstein, C. S. & Mignano, A. J. (1993) *Elementary Classroom Management*. New York: McGraw-Hill.

Weinstein, C. S., Woolfolk, A. E., Dittmeier, L. & Shanker, U. (1993) *Exploring student teachers' thinking about classroom management*. Paper presented at the Annual Meeting of the American Educational Research Association, Atlanta, Georgia, April 1993.

Weinstein, J. A. & Fantini, M. F. (1970) *Toward Humanistic Education: A Curriculum of Effect*. New York: Praeger.

Weinstein, R. S. (1989) Perceptions of classroom processes and student motivation: Children's views of self-fulfilling prophecies. In C. Ames & R. Ames (eds) *Research on Motivation in Education: Vol. 3. Goals and Cognitions*. Orlando: Academic Press.

Weinstein, R. S., Marshall, H. H., Sharp, L. & Botkin, M. (1987)

Pygmalion and the student: Age and classroom differences in children's awareness of teacher expectations. *Child Development*, **58**, 1079–93.

Weiser, M. (1991) The computer for the 21st century. *Scientific American*, **265**, 66–75.

Wellman, H. M. & Gelman, S. A. (1992) Cognitive development: Foundation theories of core domains. *Annual Review of Psychology*, **43**, 337–75.

Wells, B. W. P. (1983) *Body and Personality*. London: Longman.

Wenderoth, P. (1992) Perceptual illusions. *Australian Journal of Psychology*, **44**, 147–51.

Wentzel, K. R. (1991a) Social competence at school: Relation between social responsibility and academic achievement. *Review of Educational Research*, **61**, 1–24.

Wentzel, K. R. (1991b) Social and academic goals at school: Motivation and achievement in context. In M. L. Maehr & P. R. Pintrich (eds) *Advances in Motivation and Achievement. A research Annual*, Vol. 7. Greenwich, CT: JAI Press: 185–212.

Wertheim, E. H., Mee, V. & Paxton, S. J. (1996) Body image and weight loss behaviours among adolescent girls and their parents. Paper presented at the 31st Annual Conference of the Australian Psychological Society, 25–29 September, Sydney.

Wertheimer, M. (1980) Gestalt Theory of Learning. In G. M. Gazda & R. J. Corsini (eds) *Theories of Learning*. Itasca, IL: F. E. Peacock.

Wessells, H. G. (1982) *Cognitive Psychology*. New York: Harper & Row.

Westwood, P. (1995) Effective teaching. Paper presented at the North West Region inaugural special education conference Priorities, Partnerships (and plum puddings). Armidale 25–27, June.

Wheldall, K. (ed.) (1987) *The Behaviourist in the Classroom*. London: Allen & Unwin.

Wheldall, K. & Merrett, F. (1990) What is the behavioural approach to teaching? In V. Lee (ed.) *Children's Learning in School*. London: Hodder & Stoughton.

White, R. & Baird, J. (1991) Learning to think and thinking to learn. In J. B. Biggs (ed.) *Teaching for Learning. The View from Cognitive Psychology*. Hawthorn, Vic. ACER.

White, R. T. & Gunstone, R. F. (1989) Metalearning and conceptual change. *International Journal of Science Education*, **11**, 577–86.

Wickstrom, R. L. (1983). *Fundamental Motor Patterns*, 3rd edn. Philadelphia: Lea & Febiger.

Wigfield, A. & Karpathian, M. (1991) Who am I and what can I do? Childrens' self-concepts and motivation in achievement situations. *Educational Psychologist*, **26 (3 & 4)**, 233–61.

Wigfield, A. (1994) Expectancy-value theory of achievement motivation: A developmental perspective. *Educational Psychology Review*, **6**, 49–78.

Wigfield, A. & Eccles, J. S. (1989) Test anxiety in elementary and secondary school students. *Educational Psychologist*, **24**, 159–83.

Wilkins, R. (1987) A school discipline strategy. *SET Research Information for Teachers*, number 1, item 14.

Wilkinson, L. C. (1988–1989) Grouping children for learning. Implications for kindergarten education. *Review of Research in Education*, **15**, 203–50.

Williams, J. & Stith, M. (1980) *Middle Childhood. Behavior and Development*, 2nd edn. New York: Macmillan.

Williamson, A. (1991) Learning 'white way': Curriculum, context, and custom in schooling Torres Strait Islanders before World War II. *Australian Journal of Education*, **35**, 314–31.

Willig, A. C., Harnisch, D. L., Hill, K. T. & Maehr, M. L. (1980) *Sociocultural and Motivational Correlates of Success-Failure Attributions in the School Setting*. Paper presented at the Annual Meeting of the American Educational Research Association, Boston, Massachusetts, April.

Willis, S. (1987) Computers in Education: The dilemmas of equity and access. *Australian Educational Researcher*, **15**, 27–52.

Willis, S. (1988) Access to the program by girls and disadvantaged groups. In N. Hooley (ed.) *Computers and Disadvantage*. Commonwealth Schools Commission, Ministry of Education, Vic.

Wills, T. A. (1986) Stress and coping in early adolescence: Relationships to substance use in urban high schools. *Health Psychology*, **5**, 503–29.

Wilmore, J. H. (1989) The female athlete. *SET Research Information for Teachers*, number 2, item 5.

Wine, J. D. (1971) Test anxiety and study habits. *Journal of Educational Research*, **65**, 852–4.

Winefield, H. R. et al. (1988) Psychological and demographic predictors of entry to tertiary education in young Australian females and males. *British Journal of Developmental Psychology*, **6**, 183–90.

Winitsky, N. E.(1991) Classroom organisation for social studies. In J. P. Shaver (ed.) *Handbook of Research on Social Studies Teaching and Learning*. New York: Macmillan.

Winkler, R. C. (1985) Behaviour modification and clinical psychology in Australia. In N. T. Feather (ed.) *Australian Psychology. Review of Research*. Sydney: Allen & Unwin.

Winn, W. & Bricken, W. (1992) Designing virtual worlds for use in mathematics education: The example of algebra. *Educational Technology*, **32**, 12–19.

Winne, P. H. & Marx, R. W. (1989) A cognitive-processing analysis of motivation within classroom tasks. In C. Ames & R. Ames (eds) *Research on Motivation in Education: Vol. 3. Goals and Cognitions*. Orlando: Academic Press.

Winne, P. H. (1995a) Information processing theories of learning. In L. W. Anderson (ed.) *International Encyclopedia of Teaching and Teacher Education*, 2nd edn. Tarrytown, NY: Pergamon: 107–12.

Winne, P. H. (1995b) Inherent details in self-regulated learning. *Educational Psychologist*, **30**, 173–87.

Withers, G. & Cornish, G. (1985) Assessment in practice: Competitive or non-competitive. In B. Hannan (ed.) *Assessment and Evaluation in Schooling*. Victoria: Deakin University.

Witkin, H. A., Moore, C. A., Goodenough, D. R. & Cox, P. W. (1977) Field-dependent and field-independent cognitive styles and their educational implications. *Review of Educational Research*, **47**, 1–64.

Witte, K. L. & Grossman, E. E. (1971) The effects of reward and punishment upon children's attention, motivation, and discrimination learning. *Child Development*, **42**, 537–42.

Wittrock, M. C. (1986) *Handbook of Research on Teaching*, 3rd edn. New York: Macmillan.

Wittrock, M. C. (1986) Student's thought processes. In M. C. Wittrock (ed.) *Handbook of Research on Teaching*, 3rd edn. New York: Macmillan.

Wittrock, M. C. (1992) Generative learning processes of the brain. Educational Psychologist, **27**, 531–42.

Wittrock, M. C. & Alesandrini, K. (1990) Generation of summaries and analogies and analytic and holistic abilities. *American Educational Research Journal*, **27**, 489–502.

Wolf, D. P. (1989) Portfolio assessment: Sampling student work. *Educational Leadership*, **46**, 35–9.
Wolf, D., Bixby, J. Glenn, J. III & Gardner, H. (1991) To use their minds well: Investigating new forms of student assessment. *Review of Research in Education*, **17**, 31–74.
Wolfgang, C. H. & Glickman, C. D. (1986) *Solving Discipline Problems. Strategies for Classroom Teachers*, 2nd edn. Boston: Allyn & Bacon.
Wollen, K. A., Weber, A. & Lowry, D. (1972) Bizarreness versus interaction of mental images as determinants of learning. *Cognitive Psychology*, **3**, 518–23.
Wolman, B. B. (1989) *Dictionary of Behavioral Science*, 2nd edn. New York: Academic Press.
Woodward, H. (1993) *Negotiated Evaluation*. Sydney: Primary English Teachers Association.
Woolfolk, A. E. (1993) *Educational Psychology*, 5th edn. Needham Heights, MA: Allyn & Bacon.
Workman, E. A. (1982) *Teaching Behavioral Self-Control to Students*. Austin, TX: Pro-Ed.
Wortman, C. B. & Loftus, E. F. (1992) *Psychology*. New York: McGraw-Hill.
Wragg, E. C. (1995) Lesson structure. In L. W. Anderson (ed.) *International Encyclopedia of Teaching and Teacher Education*, 2nd edn. Tarrytown, NY: Pergamon: 207–11
Wright, D. & Wiese, M. J. (1988) Teacher judgment in student evaluation: A comparison of grading methods. *Journal of Educational Research*, **82**, 10–14.
Wright, M.R. (1989) Body image satisfaction in adolescent girla and boys. *Journalof Youth and Adolescence*, **18**, 71–84.
Wright, M. M. & Parker, J. L. (1978) The relationship of intelligence, self-concept and locus of control of school achievement for Aboriginal and non-Aboriginal children. *The Exceptional Child*, **25**, 167–79.
Wylie, R. (1979) The self-concept: Theory and research on selected topics. Lincoln, NE: University of Nebraska Press.
Yanoff, J. M. (1976) The functions of the mind in the learning process. In M. L. Silberman, J. S. Allender & J. M. Yanoff (eds) *Real Learning. A Sourcebook for Teachers*. Boston: Little, Brown & Co.
Yates, F. A. (1966) *The Art of Memory*. Chicago: University of Chicago Press.
Yates, G. C. R. & Yates, S. M. (1978) The implications of social modelling research for education. *The Australian Journal of Education*, **22**, 161–78.
Yee, A. H. (1992) Asians as stereotypes and students: Misperceptions that persist. *Educational Psychology Review*, **4**, 95–132.
Yelland, N. (1995) Young children's attitudes to computers and computing. *Australian Journal of Early Childhood*, **20**, 20–5.
Yelon, S. L. & Weinstein, G. W. (1977) *A Teacher's World. Psychology in the Classroom*. New York: McGraw-Hill.
Yewchuk, C. R. (1993) The handicapped gifted. *International Journal of Educational Research*, **19**, 65–75.
Yuill, N. & Perner, J. (1988) Intentionality and knowledge in children's judgements of actors' responsibility and recipients' emotional reaction. *Developmental Psychology*, **24**, 358–65.
Zeidner, M. (1995) Adaptive coping with test situations: A review of the literature. *Educational Psychologist*, **30**, 123–33.
Zellermayer, M., Salomon, G., Globerson, T. & Givon, H. (1991) Enhancing writing-related metacognitions through a computerised writing partner. *American Educational Research Journal*, **28**, 373–91.
Zellner, D. A., Harner, D. E. & Adler, R. L. (1989) Effects of eating abnormalities and gender perceptions of desirable body shape. *Journal of Abnormal Psychology*, **98**, 93–6.
Zelniker, T. & Jeffrey, W. (1976) Reflective and impulsive children: Strategies of information processing underlying differences in problem solving. *Monographs of the Society for Research in Child Development*, **41**, (5, Serial No. 168).
Zigler, E. F. & Stevenson, M. F. (1993) *Children in a Changing World. Development and Social Issues*, 2nd edn. Pacific Grove, CA: Brooks/Cole.
Zimmerman (eds), *Self-regulation of learning and performance: Issues and educational applications.* Hillsdale, NJ: Lawrence Erlbaum: 3–21.
Zimmerman, B. J. (1990) Self-regulated learning and academic achievement: An overview. *Educational Psychologist*, **25**, 3–17.
Zimmerman, B. J. (1994) Dimensions of academic self-regulation: A conceptual framework for education. In D. H. Schunk & B. J. Zimmerman *(eds), Self-regulation of learning and performance: Issues and educational applications* (pp. 3–21). Hillsdale, NJ: Lawrence Erlbaum.
Zimmerman, B. J. (1995) Self-regulation involves more than metacognition: A social cognitive perspective. *Educational Psychologist*, **30**, 217–21.
Zimmerman, B. J., Bandura, A. & Martinez-Pons, M. (1992) Self-motivation for academic attainment: The role of self-efficacy beliefs and personal goal setting. *American Educational Research Journal*, **29**, 663–7.
Zimmerman, B. J. & Blotner, R. (1979) Effects of model persistence and success on children's problem solving. *Journal of Educational Psychology*, **71**, 508–13.
Zimmerman, B. J. & Schunk, D. H. (eds) (1989) Self-regulated Learning and Academic Achievement: Theory, Research and Practice. New York: Springer: Verlag.
Zuroff, D. C. (1980) Learned helplessness in humans: An analysis of learning processes and the roles of individual and situational differences. *Journal of Personality and Social Psychology*, **39**, 130–46.

Index

M